Jews and Intermarriage

A study in personality and culture

Jews and Intermarriage

A study in personality and culture

By Louis A. Berman

Associate Professor of Psychology
University of Illinois at Chicago Circle

Thomas Yoseloff
New York - South Brunswick - London

Thomas Yoseloff, Publisher
Cranbury, New Jersey 08512

Thomas Yoseloff, Ltd.
18 Charing Cross Road
London W.C. 2, England

*To the memory
of my parents*

6758

Printed in the United States of America

Preface

If the topic of Jews and intermarriage is reasonably familiar to you, this book won't tell you much that you don't already know. In all likelihood, however, some of the things you know about Jews and intermarriage are *not* altogether true, and this—I believe—is what obscures your appreciation for the things you know that *are* true. The task of this book is to help you identify and label all the things you know on this topic, so that you can discard those that don't fit the facts. Here is a list of false assumptions, ambiguities, opinions that parade as facts, and one-sided viewpoints that pose as common knowledge:

The Jews are a religious minority. *(Only half true!)*

In a democratic society the eventual disappearance of minority groups is inevitable and even desirable. *(False!)*

In order to successfully participate in the mainstream of American life, a Jew must break away from his past. *(False!)*

The Jewish bias against mixed marriage is a purely theological issue and cannot be logically defended in a secular age. *(False!)*

American Jews have a dilemma to solve, a hard choice to make: whether to segregate themselves in a ghetto-like enclave, or accept the practices of an open democratic society which looks with favor upon intermarriage. *(False!)*

Jewish group life has nothing worthwhile to offer that one cannot find in the mainstream of American society. *(False!)*

Endogamy was possible when Jews were walled off from the Gentile world. In a society where Jews and Gentiles are free to mingle, a continual rise in intermarriage is inevitable because (a) opposites attract, and (b) it is human nature for young people to fall in love. *(Half true, but which half?)*

The Jewish bias against intermarriage is a form of racism. *(False!)*

Jewish family life is a thing of the past because people move around too much nowadays. *(False!)*

People who cling to Jewish values do so out of neurotic fear of change or a fixation on the past. *(False!)*

Jews are no different from anybody else. *(Perfectly true or absolutely false, depending on what you mean!)*

Unfortunately, the assumptions and opinions I have listed above becloud the thinking not only of ordinary people, but of psychologists, sociologists, textbook writers, teachers, researchers, and clinicians—Jewish and Gentile. The purpose of this book is to set the facts straight by matching these opinions and assumptions against the observations of clinicians and counselors (such as this author), against the evidence gathered through behavioral science research, against the insights offered by contemporary novelists and social commentators, and against the writings of Kurt Lewin, Sigmund Freud, Theodor Reik, Milton Steinberg, Richard L. Rubenstein, and Albert Memmi.

This book grew out of my work as a counseling psychologist at an urban university, where for eleven years I have been listening to the thoughts, feelings, and perplexities of young people trying to find a place for themselves in an ambiguous and changing world. Over the years I have listened to both Jews and Gentiles reflect on their feelings and experiences in cross-ethnic dating and courtship. When I was granted a sabbatical leave, I decided to see what the scholarly literature had to say on the topic of intermarriage. I was captivated by an unexpected richness, diversity, and utter disarray of published materials on this topic, and I felt challenged to arrange it in some kind of order into which I could fit some of my own case materials. (Each case report has been so altered as to conceal the client's identity without, I hope, either overdramatizing or obscuring the significance of that person's experience.)

Out of this plan has come a report that I hope will be of interest to my colleagues in the behavioral sciences—psychologists, psychiatrists, sociologists, anthropologists—to marriage counselors, rabbis, students of Jewish life, and educated laymen. In reading a book addressed to a mixed audience, you must expect to find an occasional section that seems esoteric or cryptic, and others that belabor (what is for you) the obvious. I hope you will find this a small price to pay for what the book has to offer, a psychologist's approach to the question of what it means to be Jewish, and an empirically guided statement on how this "state of being" shapes Jewish attitudes toward marriage and intermarriage.

This is a controversial book, but writing it has been by no means a lonely battle. At every stage of the manuscript I have had the encouragement and help of friends and colleagues who somehow found it possible to help me at just the time when their contribution was needed. Roger Brown, James Creaser, I. E. Farber, Benjamin Feyn, Lawrence Fuchs, E. Lowell Kelly, Harold Klehr, U. Harold Males, David Polish, Carl Rogers, and Walter Zenner read and commented usefully on large or small portions of the manuscript, though I must of course accept responsibility for what the book became. From the inception of this project, Wilbert J. McKeachie demonstrated a degree of interest and moral support that deserves special mention. My colleague Theta Wolf has been extraordinarily helpful as a critical reader and editor. For assistance in translating French source materials, thanks are due to Marie Johnson and Rose Katzel; and for help in German translations, Traute Page. Thanks are likewise due to student help at Chicago Circle's Student Counseling Service, who pounded the typewriter and chased down library references willingly and well: Stewart Brekke, Helen Trzeciak, Gabriele Valatkaitis, and Dorothy Zieff. For help in proofreading, thanks are due to my wife, my son Daniel, and to Traute Page, Patricia Runkle Kelly, and Ethel Hilkevitch. This project would have been impossible without the cooperation of the Deering Library at Northwestern University, and the Leaf Library at the Chicago College of Jewish Studies.

My wife Irene learned from direct experience why an author pays tribute to his wife for enduring the countless inconveniences that befall a household in which an author is at work. Looking over my bibliography, it unexpectedly occurred to me that some of the key background books for this study came into my possession as birthday gifts from my wife, which gives her a special kind of partnership in the development of this book.

Because this book disagrees with famous and important people, I have tried to make this presentation complete, and thoroughly documented. (For the average reader, the book is too meticulously documented, but this feature is intended to help students and scholars go back to the original sources, and forward to new studies and findings.) My disagreement with various writers on the topic of minority group membership and intermarriage is not intended to cast doubt on their work outside these areas. It has been my privilege to examine with the perspective of the 1960's what others wrote in the 1940's and 50's. The meaning of Jewishness has undergone significant changes over the past decade, and this study is an attempt to keep up with these changes.

Louis A. Berman
Chicago Circle
April 16, 1968

Acknowledgments

Grateful acknowledgement is made to the following copyright holders for permission to reprint selections from the following published materials:

AMERICAN ACADEMY OF ARTS AND SCIENCES—"Assimilation in America: Theory and Reality," by Milton M. Gordon, *Daedalus,* Spring, 1961.

AMERICAN IMAGO—"Neurotic Downward Identification," by George Devereaux, *American Imago,* Vol. 22, No. 1-2, 1965.

AMERICAN JEWISH YEAR BOOK—"Studies of Jewish Intermarriage in the United States," by Erich Rosenthal, 1963.

AMERICAN SOCIOLOGICAL ASSOCIATION—"Ethnicity and Extended Familism in an Upper-Middle-Class Suburb," by Robert Winch, Scott Greer, and Rae Lesser Blumberg, American Sociological Review, April, 1967.

APPLETON-CENTURY-CROFTS—*Hilgard and Marquis' Conditioning and Learning,* by Gregory Kimble, 1961, by Appleton-Century-Crofts.

BASIC BOOKS—*Jews in the Mind of America,* by Charles Herbert Stember, 1966.

BEACON PRESS—*Intermarriage,* by Albert I. Gordon, reprinted by permission of the Beacon Press, copyright 1964 by Albert I. Gordon.

BLOCH PUBLISHING COMPANY—*Mixed Marriage and the Jewish Future,* by David Kirschenbaum, 1958.

B'NAI B'RITH VOCATIONAL SERVICE BUREAU—*Small Town Jewry Tell Their Story*, by Robert Shosteck, 1953.

DOUBLEDAY & COMPANY, INC.—*Proverbs, Ecclesiastes* (The Anchor Bible) translated and with an introduction and notes by R. B. Y. Scott. Copyright 1965 by Doubleday & Company, Inc. *The Religious Factor* by Gerhard Lenski. Copyright 1961 by Gerhard Lenski. *A Treasury of Jewish Humor* edited by Nathan Ausubel. Copyright 1951 by Nathan Ausubel. Reprinted by permission of Doubleday & Company, Inc.

DAVID MAX EICHORN—*Conversion to Judaism*, by David Max Eichorn, D. D., Ktav, 1965, reprinted by permission of the author.

FARRAR, STRAUS & GIROUX, INC.—*Pagan Rites in Judaism* by Theodor Reik, reprinted by permission of Farrar, Straus & Giroux, Inc., Copyright 1964 by Theodor Reik.

GAMUT PRESS, INC.—*Jewish Wit*, by Theodor Reik, 1962.

HARPER & ROW, PUBLISHERS, INC.—*Motivation and Personality*, by A. H. Maslow, 1954. *Old World Traits Transplanted*, by Robert E. Park and Herbert A. Miller, 1921.

THE HERZL PRESS—*Intermarriage and Jewish Life, a Symposium* by Werner J. Cahnman, ed., 1963, The Herzl Press and the Jewish Reconstructionist Press, publishers.

JEWISH SOCIAL STUDIES—"Patterns of Socialization and Association between Jews and Non-Jews," by John P. Dean, *Jewish Social Studies*, Vol. 17, 1955. "Conversion to Judaism by Reform and Conservative Rabbis," by David Eichhorn, *Jewish Social Studies*, Vol. 16, 1954. "Intermarriage Among Jews in Germany, USSR, and Switzerland," by Uriah Z. Engelman, *Jewish Social Studies*, Vol. 2, 1940.

J. B. LIPPINCOTT COMPANY—*Remember Me to God*, by Myron S. Kaufmann. Copyright 1957 by Myron S. Kaufmann.

McGRAW-HILL BOOK COMPANY—*Mental Health in the Metropolis*, by Leo Srole, Thomas Langner, Stanley T. Michael, Marvin K. Opler, and Thomas A. C. Rennie. Copyright 1962 by McGraw-Hill. *Today's American Jew*, by Morris Kertzer. Copyright 1967 by McGraw-Hill.

NATIONAL WOMEN'S LEAGUE OF THE UNITED SYNAGOGUE OF AMERICA—"Not Only Converted—Convinced," by Frances Price, *Outlook*, September, 1957.

ORION PRESS—*Liberation of the Jew,* by Albert Memmi, 1960.

THE PHYLON QUARTERLY—"Comparison of Religious Beliefs and Practices of Jewish, Catholic and Protestant Students," by Joseph Maier and William Spinrad, *The Phylon Quarterly,* Fourth Quarter, 1957.

THE RONALD PRESS COMPANY—*Clinical Studies in Culture Conflict,* edited by Georgene Seward, Copyright 1958 The Ronald Press Company, New York.

W. B. SAUNDERS COMPANY—*Sexual Behavior of the Human Male,* by Alfred C. Kinsey, W. B. Pomeroy, and C. E. Martin, 1948. *Sexual Behavior of the Human Female,* by Alfred C. Kinsey, W. B. Pomeroy, C. E. Martin, and P. H. Gebhard, 1953.

CHARLES SCRIBNER'S SONS—*Human Nature and the Social Order,* by Charles Horton Cooley, Revised Edition, 1922.

SOCIAL FORCES—"Toward a Refinement of the 'Marginal Man' Concept," by Aaron Antonovsky, *Social Forces,* 1956, published by the University of North Carolina.

SOCIOLOGY AND SOCIAL RESEARCH—"Social Factors in Amalgamation," by J. S. Slotkin, *Sociology and Social Research,* March, 1942.

EVERETT V. STONEQUIST—*The Marginal Man,* by Everett V. Stonequist, Charles Scribner's Sons, 1937, reprinted by permission of the author.

JOSEPH WORTIS, M.D.—*Fragments of an Analysis with Freud,* by Joseph Wortis, Simon and Schuster, Inc., 1954, reprinted by permission of the author.

The author acknowledges with thanks, permission granted by the following authors for the use of selections from their unpublished manuscripts:

SAMUEL R. LEHRMAN, M.D.—"Psychopathology in Mixed Marriages." Paper presented at the June 1, 1965, meeting of the Long Island Psychoanalytic Society.

PHILIP M. ROSTEN—"The mischling; child of the Jewish- Gentile marriage." Honors paper submitted to the Department of Social Relations, Harvard University, 1960.

SAMUEL TEITELBAUM—"Patterns of adjustment among Jewish students." Unpublished Ph.D. dissertation, Northwestern University, 1953.

Contents

Preface Acknowledgments Introduction

Introduction

The choice of one's marriage partner is probably the most important single choice in the life of most persons. In making this decision, the individual determines not only the nature of his closest and most enduring interpersonal relationship, but he also determines—to a considerable degree—the number of children he will have and what sort of a person each will become. Whether one believes in the dominance of genetic determinants ("blood will tell"), or of environmental effects ("as the twig is bent"), the selection of a specific person to be the mother or father of one's children has far-reaching consequences for the composition and character of each family. This decision, in spite of its critical importance, is often made with surprisingly little awareness of the bases for the decision.

Although the potential field of eligible marriage partners is theoretically very large, one's choice is in fact limited by several factors. One's circle of acquaintances is but a tiny fraction of the unmarried persons of the opposite sex and appropriate age. It is limited chiefly by geographical propinquity—people we know are those who live in our own neighborhood, attend the same school or church, belong to the same clubs, or work in the same business or industry. Among all of one's acquaintances there will be a much smaller number of persons with whom one may develop a friendship. This reciprocated choice is usually based on shared activities, skills, hobbies, or interests. Any unmarried friend of the opposite sex is of course, a likely dating partner and a potential lover and spouse. The change of a relationship from that of friends to lovers—sometimes slow and almost imperceptible, sometimes sudden and dramatic—is little understood. Clearly, it has a biological basis and hormonal overtones, but no one can predict with much certainty which friendships will lead to love and which will not. However, we can predict with considerable confidence that when friends fall in love, they are very likely to consider marriage.

Because of the universal taboo against marrying a close blood relative, every marriage is in effect an intermarriage, i.e., the union of two persons not only of different sexes but from different families. It involves not only a merger of distinctive genetic strains but a union between two persons, each of whom has learned a different set of habits, attitudes, traditions, customs and values in the family of his own parents. To the degree that homogamy—i.e., similarity in the choice of friendship pairs and marriage partners—is the rule, problems resulting from non-shared or conflicting practices and values are minimized.

Since most of us are reasonably confident in the essential correctness of the beliefs, habits, attitudes and values which we acquire as children, we are likely to regard persons who differ from us in these respects as not suitable for friendship—much less for marriage. A large majority of individuals do not become friends with and thus never consider the possibility of marriage to persons who are very different from themselves. The selection of friends and dating partners is usually guided by fairly rigid—though not consciously maintained—criteria of religion, race, political orientation, income level, ethnic origin, and even habits of dress and speech. Thus it is hardly surprising that most people marry someone of the same race, near their own age, of the same religion, of the same political persuasion, and with a similar level of education and income. And because these characteristics tend to be those passed on from parents to children, most parents are likely to approve their child's choice of marriage partner.

Increasingly, however, young people are choosing their marriage partners with less regard to the importance of certain of these criteria formerly regarded as essential, especially by their parents. Although interracial marriages are still relatively rare, intermarriages of persons of different nationalities, different ethnic stocks, and different religions are certainly on the increase. This change appears to be a function of many factors, including greater geographical mobility, more extensive education in secular schools, the assimilation of historically and ethnically separate groups into society, and a decreasing role of religion in the lives of so many persons. Some observers welcome this increase in the incidence of intermarriage as heralding a decrease in intergroup tensions; others view it as a threat to the preservation of cherished values and traditions, as a disturbance of family solidarity and group identity.

In this unique book, Dr. Berman focuses on the problem of intermarriage and its implication for Jews. For this particular group, a minority in all countries except Israel, the problems of intermarriage are both complex and poignant. Throughout their long and tragic history of oppression in many different countries, Jews have managed to survive as an ethnic group largely by embedding their religious beliefs into an elaborate sub-culture of traditions and practices associated not only with worship but with almost every aspect of family life. Probably no other national or ethnic group in history has been as much concerned with the role of parents in teaching their children to become good members of the immediate and extended family, and of the sub-culture with which the family is identified. Understandably, therefore, most Jewish parents hope to see their children develop into good Jews, marry Jews, and give them Jewish grandchildren.

But Jewish parents want more of their children than that they become good Jews. They place a very high value on education and are willing to make great sacrifices in order to provide good educational opportunities for children. Their children are urged to compete with non-Jews for good grades in school and later for prestigeful positions in society. But the opportunities for good education and good positions in the larger society require that their children attend public schools and universities, where they will invariably interact with Gentiles. While most

Jewish children eventually marry other Jews, this is not always the case. Some first make friends with, then date, and later decide to marry a Gentile.

The decision to marry a person of Gentile origin—an option which an increasing minority of young Jews are taking—raises a host of questions that are both perplexing and fascinating. How should the parents and synagogue react? Should they seek to prevent the marriage? If not—what kind of a ceremony is called for, and where should it occur? What kinds of Jews decide to marry a Gentile? What are their motivations? What kinds of Gentiles decide to marry a Jew? What are the prospects for such a marriage? What kinds of problems does it present, and what solutions are most promising? Shall one member of the couple convert to the religion of the other? What are the problems facing the children of such intermarriages? Does the increasing incidence of intermarriage between Jew and Gentile promise to reduce the marginality of the Jewish people, or does it threaten to assimilate them out of existence as an ethnic group?

These and similar questions are extremely important for the individuals involved in a prospective or actual intermarriage of a Jew and Gentile, and for their parents. They are also important for counselors, members of the clergy, and other professional persons who may be consulted by individuals contemplating or involved in a Jewish-Gentile marriage.

As a psychologist-counselor in a large urban university, Dr. Louis Berman, one of my former students, found himself more and more intrigued with the complex questions posed by Jewish-Gentile marriages. Although he knew that there were no neat categorical answers to any of them, he decided to undertake an exhaustive study of the problem. In doing so, he found it necessary to approach the subject from many angles and to seek the opinions of experts representing many different disciplines: history, theology, anthropology, sociology, psychology, and psychoanalysis. In addition, he has effectively utilized the ideas and insights provided by novelists, biographers and clinicians. The result is this scholarly volume of several hundred pages and more than 1500 footnotes!

Dr. Berman does not pretend that his efforts have provided any

clear-cut answers to the thorny problems posed by Jewish intermarriage. His book, however, makes a number of important contributions:

a. He has identified a wide array of issues and clearly posed
the critical questions.

b. For those questions that permit empirical answers, he has
assembled and evaluated the available evidence; when the
evidence is inadequate, as is often the case, he suggests the
kinds of additional studies required to provide better answers.

c. For those questions whose answers involve value judge-
ments, he has effectively summarized the positions and very
often conflicting views of writers representing different
theories and disciplines.

d. He has done an admirable job of emphasizing the inter-
relatedness of the issues involved in intermarriage and, in
turn, their relation to broader theoretical issues of personality development and culture.

e. Finally, although the book is in no sense a "How to do it"
manual, this comprehensive discussion of the issues of intermarriage cannot but be valuable to anyone engaged in
marital counseling.

Because Judaism is both a religion *and* an ethnic culture, and
because for many Jews the cultural aspects of Judaism are far
more important than the religious ones, Dr. Berman found it
essential to devote nearly half of his book to the history of
Jewish culture, to the factors promoting segregation or assimilation, and to a discussion of the implications for intermarriage
of Jewish sex roles, norms and practices. One entire chapter is
devoted to a topic usually avoided by psychologists, that of
whether there are traits peculiarly characteristic of Jewish
people.

As a psychologist whose major research has been a longitudinal
study of psychological factors in assortative mating and marital
compatibility, I regard his treatment of the problems of Jews
and intermarriage as comprehensive, analytical and well-bal-
anced. As a non-Jew, I found his discussion of Jewish culture,
customs and family life most enlightening. He makes very effec-

tive use of a series of well-chosen case histories drawn from many sources, including his own counseling experience. Dr. Berman has undertaken the difficult task of addressing a mixed audience, and has produced a book which will appeal to a wide array of readers, laymen as well as scholars and professionals. Few persons will read such a large volume in its entirety at one time, but it is difficult to image anyone who will not find certain parts fascinating and others highly provocative. Thanks to a full table of contents and an excellent index, it is easy for the reader to locate those topics in which he is most interested. But regardless of where the reader begins, I suspect that sooner or later he is likely to finish the entire volume.

E. Lowell Kelly
Professor of Psychology
University of Michigan

Jews and
Intermarriage

A study in personality and culture

For a man stamps many coins in one mold and they are all alike, but . . . the Holy One, blessed be he, stamped every man in the mold of the first man, yet not one of them resembles his fellow.

Hence it is said: How great are thy works, O Lord.

—The Midrash

1

Jewish-Gentile Intermarriage: Introduction to the Problem and a Survey of Prevailing Viewpoints

PARADOX OR DILEMMA?

From *Abie's Irish Rose*,[1] Broadway hit of the 1920's, to *The Rabbi*[2] on the best seller lists of 1966, the topic of intermarriage has been a recurrent theme in the American Jewish novel,[3] the Broadway drama, and the musical comedy.[4] The topic of intermarriage is a subject of lively interest to Jews of all persuasions, from Orthodox to secular; it is a topic of sermons, editorials, letters to the editor, books, jokes and everyday conversation. It would be easy to say that the topic of intermarriage is a Jewish obsession; perhaps it would be more accurate to say that intermarriage is a significant paradox, if not a dilemma, of Jewish life.

The Jew's paradoxical attitude toward intermarriage is well portrayed in a letter published in "Bintel Brief," advice column of the Yiddish language newspaper, the *Jewish Daily Forward*. Although it appeared in print in 1921, the letter still has a contemporary ring:

"My daughter is married to an Italian who is a very good man. . . . My tragedy is even greater because I am a free thinker. Theoretically, I consider a *goy* just as much a man as a Jew. . . . Indeed I ask myself these questions: What would happen if my daughter married a Jewish fellow who was a good-for-nothing? . . . And what do I care if he is an Italian? But I cannot seem to answer these delicate questions. The fact is that I would prefer a refined man; but I would sooner have a common Jew than an educated *goy*. Why this is so I do not know, but that is how it is, of that there is no doubt. And this shows what a terrible chasm exists between theory and practice."[5]

The correspondent may be disturbed by the logical incongruity between her secularism and her distress over her daughter's intermarriage, but the priority of values she expresses is quite consistent with Jewish norms. "A generation or two ago," said Hertzler in 1942, ". . . intermarriage was an unforgivable sin, more sinister and dangerous than religious apostasy. . . ."[6]

Although the ethos of the present-day Jewish community unites it against intermarriage, there is much private embarrassment and public soul-searching over whether this attitude is consistent with the values that Jews proudly and explicitly avow as Jews. In 1963 *Commentary* Editor Norman Podhoretz shocked his readership by announcing his conviction "that the wholesale merging of the two races" would be the most desirable outcome of the Negro problem. He confessed that he would not *like* the idea of his daughter marrying a Negro, but he would hope to curb his anger and agony, and act on the basis of moral courage and duty. The article created an even greater sensation than Podhoretz anticipated; it drew over 300 letters (*twenty times* as many as a controversial article usually provoked), and "dozens of articles and editorials commenting on the piece were printed in other magazines and newspapers." In his 1967 autobiography, Podhoretz rendered a curiously ambiguous judgment on his interracial marriage pronouncement: "I was probably wrong, though not, I think, morally."[7]

The Southern white racist and Jewish liberal make strange bedfellows indeed, but it is a fact that Jews look with special disfavor upon Negro-Jewish intermarriage and are generally unwilling to adopt the offspring of unmarried Jewish mothers and

Negro fathers.[8] Controversy between the rabbis and the Jewish community revolves around the reluctance of Jews to accept the faithful convert as a member of the community. Rabbis register indigation over being pressed into emergency service by distraught parents to avert the impending marriage of their offspring to an outsider.[9] Rabbis likewise oppose Jewish parents who *demand* that a prospective in-law convert, so that the family can make a Jewish wedding.[10] Controversy within the rabbinate revolves around the question of whether engagement to a Jew does not in itself cast doubt on the sincerity of a Gentile's motives for conversion.[11] While Orthodox and Conservative rabbis hold to the rule against officiating at mixed marriages, among Reform rabbis this is likewise a topic of controversy.[12]

A reader unacquainted with the traditional Jewish attitude toward intermarriage might well be shocked by the polemical tone of the entry on *Intermarriage* in Dagobert Runes' 1966 *Concise Dictionary of Judaism,* quoted below in full:

Intermarriage
Opposed by Judaism as leading to deterioration of both faiths, since in at least one of the pair faith is sacrificed to eroticism, and not because of reason or religious doubt. Offspring will prove basically alien to one or both. Intermarriage does not improve, but confuses human relations.[13]

Jews who fight against real estate covenants, school quotas, and job discrimination, says Rabbi Bernard J. Bamberger, are "busily engaged in creating conditions that favor intermarriage . . .

We encourage participation in community affairs. We engage eagerly in interfaith activity, and try to break down barriers to understanding. . . . Most American Jews, far from advocating segregation, desire the exact opposite. If our children attend the same schools, join the same civic and recreational and political organizations, work in the same stores and offices as non-Jews, how can they escape the social contacts that sometimes lead to love and marriage?[14]

Jewish youth are being "led to waters but forbidden to drink," warns a contributor to *Commentary*.[15] "The psychological toll which this problem exacts from the minds and hearts of these young people should not be underestimated."[16] In his survey of research on intermarriage, Milton M. Barron appeals to his fellow social scientists "to bring to the attention of laymen the inconsistency of their conservative attitudes toward intermarriage, on the one hand, with their activities on the other hand, in creating social and cultural conditions favoring intermarriage. . . . The recognition of this dilemma is a fundamental beginning to any intelligent approach to the problem," Barron concludes.[17] In his sociological study of *American Judaism,* Nathan Glazer likewise views the contradiction between the Jews' "strong desire for integration into American society" and their negative attitude toward intermarriage as "one of the major dilemmas of Judaism in America."[18]

Although writers may use the terms *problem, paradox, dilemma,* and *contradiction* interchangeably, it goes beyond hairsplitting to insist that these terms are not synonymous. If we talk about a dilemma, then we mean the situation demands a sacrifice, a choice between equally unsatisfactory alternatives. Perhaps there is room for some sort of compromise between the alternatives—but the concept of a *dilemma* implies that some decision must be taken, a choice must be made.

A paradox is something else. A paradox is more like a puzzle; it *seems* like a contradiction because of how the facts are presented, or because certain essential facts are hidden. To solve a paradox, one looks below the surface, one tries to find the missing pieces. As we look upon the contradiction between the Jew's drive for full participation in a democratic society and his strong bias against intermarriage, are we confronted by a dilemma or by a paradox?

Complex life problems probably contain dilemmas as well as paradoxes. This study addresses itself in particular to the paradoxical aspects of the intermarriage problem. We propose to examine various ways of arranging the available facts, and to search for the missing facts which may help dispel the paradox. Our goal is *not* to solve the puzzle so that it will no longer trouble the minds of Jewish youth, their counselors, elders, and observers, but rather to define the intermarriage problem more completely and more clearly so that discussion of this topic becomes more intelligent, research more productive, soul-searching more enlightened, and counseling less encumbered by ignorance or bias.

Why—except for ethnocentric reasons—should a scholarly study focus specifically on *Jewish-Gentile* intermarriage? Would it not be more scientific to search for universal laws covering every kind of intermarriage? On the contrary, the uncritical adoption of common-sense, everyday categories can prove worse than useless for purposes of scientific analysis. In everyday discourse, *intermarriage* covers marriage between Catholic and Protestant, Methodist and Lutheran, Italian and German, white and Negro, Jew and Gentile, German Jew and Russian Jew, European Jew and North African Jew. A complex social phenomenon often becomes accessible to scientific study only when analysis is limited to something approximating a "pure case." For this reason, limiting our study to Jewish-Gentile intermarriage makes scientific as well as practical sense.

We shall therefore make no attempt to bring together the entire literature on intermarriage,[19] but neither shall we ignore what has been written about intermarriage outside of the Jewish-Gentile area. We shall, instead, introduce theory and observations on other varieties of intermarriage either by way of contrast or as a source of hypotheses about Jewish-Gentile intermarriage where data on this specific topic are scanty.

A psychologist's approach. This study emerged from the experience of a counseling psychologist whose work at a state university calls upon him to help young people deal with personal as well as academic and career problems. Over a period of eleven years, a number of cases seemed to illuminate one aspect or another of the intermarriage paradox. The author has supplemented his direct experience by reading the clinical and research literature on intermarriage, and by rereading some of the classic psychoanalytic writings which bear on this topic. Historical, sociological, and anthropological materials—as well as the Judaic literature—have provided a cultural context within which the lives of patients and the statistical findings of investigators fall into place.

A counseling psychologist is a scholar as well as a practitioner, and must be forgiven for looking in unlikely places for clues concerning a practical problem. We shall therefore search for clues concerning motivations for intermarriage wherever behavior is studied: in the experimental laboratory, in preliterate societies, in the findings of Gallup polls, as well as in the office of a counseling psychologist, or psychiatrist. We shall draw upon the work of novelists not for evidence, but to help define the issues.

The therapist working at a college counseling center often encounters motivations toward intermarriage in their earliest manifestations: as a latent wish, as a nascent thought, as a disturbing yet fascinating idea, or as a not yet worked out design for living. In this respect he has an advantage over most psychiatrists or case workers, who work with an older age group and are more likely, therefore, to encounter Jewish-Gentile intermarriage as a *fait accompli,* an aspect of the patient's past experience which may be studied as an item of personal history, but has relatively little relevance to his *present* needs and strivings.

In the college setting, the counselor participates in his client's life at a time when he is relatively uncommitted, when his future is indeed more open to change. The counselor's responsibility is therefore all the greater in dealing with a young person, than in helping a middle-aged client who has already chosen (perhaps not too wisely) an occupation and a mate, and now needs some help in making a better adjustment to his established position as spouse, parent, and worker.

The campus environment affords the student new opportunities for cross-ethnic dating, which may in turn stimulate him to re-examine his old attitudes toward intermarriage. College brings young people together during the marrying years, removes them from their homes and neighborhoods, and provides them with an opportunity for close association with age mates from diverse geographical, class, religious, and ethnic backgrounds. A. I. Gordon, like other writers on the topic of intermarriage, identifies the campus as a significant place for making cross-ethnic acquaintanceships that may lead to marriage.[20]

Where counselors agree—and disagree. When a college student comes to a counselor with whatever problem in personal or social adjustment, the counselor is likely to encourage the student to make friends, to affiliate with student groups, to learn to enjoy the company of the opposite sex. Psychological theory leaves little room for doubt about the value of friendship, mutual loyalty, belongingness, and the exchange of affection. The enjoyment of positive interpersonal relations is both an expression of normal personality development and the vehicle by which it is attained. Whatever techniques the counselor may employ, whatever his theoretical orientation, the counselor is committed to help his client become a more socialized person.

Counselors, therefore, share the general viewpoint of society that friendship is good, dating is good, and preparation for marriage is good. But counselors are undoubtedly divided on questions of cross-ethnic dating and intermarriage, because theorists in the behavioral sciences, from whose writings counselors draw their professional orientations, are sharply divided on the meaning and value of cross-ethnic marriage—and so is society in general. What are the disagreements and differences on this topic within the behavioral science community? Before plunging into the research and clinical findings on intermarriage, let us first survey some divergent behavioral science viewpoints on topics which bear directly on the problem of intermarriage.

A SURVEY OF
BEHAVIORAL SCIENCE VIEWPOINTS

The doctrine of adjustment. The scientific view of man in society emphasizes man's adjustment or adaptation to changing conditions. "Absolute standards" and "eternal values" have no place in this realm of thought. A classic problem revolves around the concepts of "cultural lag," "survivals," "atavisms," "petrified remnants" of an older era. Why do customs sometimes linger after they appear to have outworn their usefulness? How can social change be facilitated? What can be done to make society more responsive to change; to unburden the individual of customs that have outworn their usefulness?[21]

In his classic 1936 study on *The Psychology of Social Norms*, Sherif set the stage for his presentation with the statement that "of course there is no finality about customs, traditions, laws and social standards. They are not absolute. Different societies have different customs, and customs may change in different periods—sometimes gradually, at other times abruptly."[22]

Social norms follow a natural life cycle; they are born out of some social necessity; they flourish and take root, spreading their influence long after they have lost their vitality and function, persisting as *survivals* "which are abnormal for the existing conditions . . . [causing] harm and friction among individuals and classes of people. . . ."[23]

> As long as life with its many aspects is well settled and runs more or less smoothly from day to day, very few doubt the validity of existing norms; very few challenge their authority . . .

> But when social life becomes difficult and there are stresses and tensions in the lives of many people in the community, the equilibrium of life ceases to be stable, and the air is pregnant with possibilities . . . The rigidity of norms that have come down as survivals from past generations . . . [may] no longer satisfy the requirements for life. . . . Under these delicate conditions the strength of the norms incorporated in the individuals becomes uncertain and liable to break down. Such a delicate, unstable situation is the fertile soil for the rise of doubts concerning the existing norms, and challenge to their authority. . . . These are times of transition from one state to another, from one norm or set of norms to another.[24]

Sherif gives social scientists the serious task of identifying these *survivals*, the outworn and maladaptive social norms, and thereby specifying "what is to be preserved and what is to be abandoned in society. If once a norm and the social practice connected with it are shown to be survivals, the sound course to take is to eliminate their effectiveness by whatever measures may be necessary."[25]

> . . . Norms must change with the change of actual conditions. If it lags behind, terrific friction occurs between groups of people because of the existence of such norms. Those who are at present enjoying vested interests will, of course, do their best to perpetuate norms that 'sanctify' their interests . . .
> People cannot eat and drink norms. The norms cannot give life, if nothing else is left in life. But friction may increase to such a pitch that the whole superstructure of norms collapses; the individual, with countless others like himself, frees himself from his prescribed role, crushes the role of the privileged one,

and with this the oppressor himself . . . The end result is not chaos, but the formation of a new superstructure of norms.[26]

Sherif confesses that it is difficult to make clear-cut comparisons between "the respectable norms in other social structures" and the norms of Western culture "because everything seems to be in a fluid state now."[27] To be sure, Sherif wrote this not only as a social psychologist but as a leftist intellectual of the 1930's; nor was he referring directly to the norms of courtship and marriage. Yet he expresses a viewpoint toward social customs which is well represented in the behavioral science community, and which has both a theoretical and practical bearing on the topic of inter-marriage.

In his 1957 sociological study *American Judaism*, Nathan Glazer appraises the values of American Jews from the standpoint of how well they fit into "the kind of society America wants to become." Glazer argues that if the majority of Jews were "fearful of assimilation . . . [they would] limit themselves to a narrow range of occupations . . . not send their children to public schools [and], live close together in a small area." Since the great majority of Jews on the contrary fight for the kind of social participation which may lead to assimilation—free access to jobs, schools, and neighborhoods—Glazer concludes that "the kind of society America wants to become" is also "the kind of society most Jews want it to be. . . ."[28]

Glazer sees the Jewish prohibition against intermarriage as rooted in a network of "purely theological doctrines" which assert that Jews are "a people apart, and insists that they consider themselves in exile until God restores them to the Land of Israel." American Jews show little involvement in these "purely theological doctrines," Glazer implies, yet they "do not, on the whole, intermarry and they do maintain themselves apart." Significantly, Glazer interprets this state of affairs *not* as a paradoxical phenomenon which calls for more penetrating sociological understanding, but as *a contradiction for American Jews to resolve!*[29]

"The theory of cultural pluralism, which assumed there would be some kind of minority rights, is obviously dead," says Glazer flatly.[30] He endorses the thesis of C. B. Sherman that *"given the constitution of American society,* there is no reason why" ethnic groups should survive. The only future for Jewish survival in America, therefore, is "in the form of a religion. *For America does recognize religions.*"[31] (Italics added.) Accordingly, the final chapter of Glazer's study is entitled "The Religion of American Jews," in which he attempts to analyze "the real structure of American Jewish religious belief,"[32] deplores the absence of "personal religious experience"[33] in the life of American Jews, and entertains the possibility that for at least some small part of the Jewish population the religious life might become "more alive and meaningful"[34] so as to direct a "return to religion" for Jews who do seek a personal religious experience.[35]

Glazer confronts his reader once more with "the embarrassing dilemma" of the modern Jew—"the question whether the Jewish religion is a religion or a means of preserving the Jewish nation." Glazer proposes that a reawakening of spiritual interest and personal commitment to the Jewish *religion* would solve the dilemma, "for then one's membership in the Jewish people is an expression of religious, not group, feeling. And when the Jews feel themselves to be in reality a holy nation, the fact that they are a nation is of no consequence," he adds hopefully.[36] Although Glazer admits that "those moments in Jewish history when the Jews were truly a people of priests and a holy nation required circumstances that can never be repeated,"[37] he closes his study on the hope that Jews in America will somehow find a new significance in their religious heritage so that, at least by comparison, their sense of national loyalty will become less important.

Although Glazer sees the origins of Jewish opposition to intermarriage in a theological doctrine, the power of this prohibition in contemporary Jewish society seems to betoken "some kind of primal attachment to the Jewish people . . . a simple unreflecting attachment to the Jewish people, a subconscious insistence that the Jews be maintained as a people."[38] Glazer seems to be saying that if Jews could learn to care more about their *religious* identity they would then care less about their national survival. Jews would then take their place alongside Catholics and Protestants as another religious denomination, and intermarriage would be of no more importance to Jews than it is to their fellow citizens of other religious persuasions.

Sociologist Werner J. Cahnman, who wrote specifically to the topic of Jewish-Gentile intermarriage in 1964, shows a continuity with the attitudes of Sherif and Glazer when he expresses the view that "in the market-place of democracy, the principle of competition rules supreme. . . . In a mobile, competitive society, there are no fenced-off places, except those harboring petrified remnants somewhere in a forgotten corner. . . . Parents cannot prevent their children from leaving old associations for new, if this is what their children want." Cahnman continues:

> If the world which Jewish parents represent does not appear attractive to the younger generations, parents have no right to say 'Stay with us, be old with us!' Ancient thought and ancient rites retain their value to which we like to return, if the call is compelling enough, but adaptations change. In other words, Jewish youth must not be expected to chain themselves to patterns of adaptations which have outlived their usefulness; rather Judaism must be rejuvenated.[39]

When Cahnman says that "Judaism must be rejuvenated" to meet the conditions of "a mobile, competitive society," he leaves the reader with the impression that Judaism must be redefined to fit the American ethos.[40] If, for example, the Jewish community suffers losses through intermarriage, let these losses be offset by seeking recruits to Judaism. (This may not be the Jewish way of maintaining and augmenting the community, one might object, though it may represent the prevailing way of adjusting to a prevailing situation.) Like his fellow sociologist Glazer, Cahnman finds the Jewish emphasis on kinship bonds out of place in America, and therefore in need of re-examination. ". . . The concept of 'peoplehood' in a democracy [must] be kept free of racist implications. A people is not . . . an inbred clan. . ." He asks that Judaism be defined as "a common heritage, common interests, common hopes . . . open to all comers who can learn about heritage, identify themselves with its interests, and share its hopes."[41] A Judaism "open to all comers" and lacking strong kinship bonds would perhaps be well adapted to the present-day social environment, but would it be Jewish? Apparently part of the "reality" to which Judaism must adjust, according to Cahnman, is the judgment of the Gentile majority.

As one reflects upon the viewpoint of Sherif, Glazer, and Cahn-man—and the many behavioral scientists who share their view—one senses a fascination with the process of social change, which sweeps away the old and ushers in the new. One senses an eager-ness to meet the challenge of change, to participate in the pat-terning of new norms more in harmony with prevailing con-ditions.

The doctrine of cultural relativity. Can one really take an intermarriage taboo seriously if, as a student of cultures, he truly appreciates the endless diversity of social norms? As Doobs observes:

> What is good or holy in one group appears bad or sacrilegious in another. This anthropological finding can raise severe doubts concerning the compelling nature of values within any society.

> Most precious beliefs and practices can be viewed as arbitrary and fortuitous—somewhere there are people who reject them and yet lead sensible, satisfactory lives. Do we, can we, should we wish to rescue ourselves from the implication that follows from this doctrine of cultural relativity? The question is as revolutionary in an ethical sense as the facts which compel its formulation. The reader, the gentle reader, must evolve his own answer before he can find intellectual and spiritual peace.[42]

Sherif advises that the behavioral scientist must gain a certain "distance" from his own social norms so that he can render more objective judgments about man in society:

> The habit of making our little world the center of the universe had to be overcome before there could be a science of astronomy; the habit of making man the center of the animate world had to be overcome before there could be a science of biology. A like principle holds in psychology and the social sciences. Unless we gain "distance" from our own norms, we shall make judgments which are nothing more than a collection of normative verdicts.[43]

Viewed from the standpoint of cultural relativity, a conflict over the intermarriage taboo raises the straightforward question:

After all, this is "wrong" only according to one particular norm; of all the available norms, is this the one which you as as an individual choose to follow?

Intermarriage and social change. Not only does the evolutionary and relativistic viewpoint label all norms as temporary and local, observations on the rate and direction of social change point to a predictable increase in the rate of intermarriage.

> The rate of movement of Americans from place to place . . . has tended to dissolve fixed communities, extended family structures and fabrics of mutual friendship. Migration brings about innumerable circumstances for which conventions are no guide. Physical distance between generations helps to widen the distance between them in belief and practice. Social mobility further widens these separations, which are only slightly counteracted by common exposure to mass media. Cosmopolitan choice of mates—heteronomy and intermarriage—is spurred by this restless moving about.[44]

Rabbi Gordon sympathizes with young people who find themselves hurtled by the currents of social change into a cross-ethnic marriage partnership: "Intermarriage is not always an act of rebellion against parents or their values. It is often reluctantly entered into because circumstances brought together two young people whose love for each other developed before either was fully aware of what was happening. Such intermarriages are not the result of defiance, revolt, rebellion or hostility. They are rather the product of urbanization, mobility, propinquity and other such factors that play so significant a role in our society."[45]

Social changes leading toward intermarriage reveal both positive and negative aspects. On the positive side, Gordon recognizes increased "opportunity to communicate with persons of other faiths . . . opportunities for travel, for recreation . . . for making friends, not of one's own group. . . . Higher education for more young people . . . serves, too, to increase intermarriages. . . . The number of Americans who 'move up' on the economic scale, and as a consequence, on the social scale as well, is increasing. . . . The gap between classes is less marked than it once was. . . . Hence the opportunity for social intercourse afforded by mobility itself is increased as well. . . . Religious, national and even racial barriers are considerably reduced. . . . Groups tend to be less suspicious of or hostile to one another than they were only a generation ago."[46]

Intermarriage, Gordon continues, naturally increases as racial, religious, and economic discrimination is reduced. "As ghetto walls continue to weaken and fall, as segregation in housing is reduced, as the job opportunities for persons of different religion and races are equalized, we may expect further intercommunication and intermingling between different religious and racial groups."[47] From this point of view the intermarriage rate is regarded as a barometer of intergroup harmony, and as a mark of victory against the social evils of prejudice, segregation, and discrimination.

The emergence of new opportunities and new freedoms implies a weakening of an older way of life; here we encounter the negative side of social changes leading to intermarriage:

"Matters once generally regarded as settled and fixed by custom and tradition are today, in ever-increasing degree, openly questioned and traditional attitudes are often disregarded . . . Opinions and decisions with regard to major issues involving the individuals within the family are seldom, if ever, made by the parents alone."[48]

Mixed marriages are viewed as part of a vicious cycle. They are the result of family disorganization and they lead to further social disorganization, since—according to evidence summarized by A. I. Gordon—mixed marriages yield a higher rate of divorce and desertion, fewer offspring, a higher incidence of delinquent children, and a lower percentage of children completing high school.

Intermarriage and the rise of secularism. The decline in the authority of the family is paralleled by the deterioration of the authority of the church. Gordon refers to the widespread indifference to religion in contemporary society. He sees America as a secular society utilizing its churches and synagogues for the pursuit of secular goals: "fellowship and 'fun' [and] an opportunity for making friends through activities and meetings." Gordon cites a number of opinion surveys (mainly of college students) to document the impressive percentages of persons who seldom or never attend church, never read the Bible, rarely or never pray, do not consider loyalty to God as the greatest of all loyalties, answer "Yes" to the question: "Can culture exist without positive religion?" and answer "No" to the question of whether they believe in a "one-person God."[49]

Gordon also cites survey data which links indifference to religion with willingness to marry outside one's faith.[50] He further notes that in about one out of four marriages in the United States the clergy does not officiate; the marriages are performed by civil ceremony exclusively.[51] Religious sanctions against intermarriage are presumably of no consequence to a person who is indifferent to religion, and it matters little whether he chooses a mate who shares his own religious ties. Once again a reciprocal relationship (or "vicious cycle") is evident: secularism reduces the barriers to intermarriage, and intermarriage tends to draw marriage partners away from their religious ties. (At least this generalization seems to hold for a comparison of Catholic marriages with Catholic-Protestant marriages.) "What such marriages may do to the religious beliefs of the children of these mixed marriages," Gordon surmises, "must be even more startling."[52]

From this standpoint, intermarriage is both an indication and an instrument of secularization. Intermarriage represents the influence of science and secular education upon marriage practices. "The reduction of distinctions between men and their religions," Gordon speculates, "makes universalism as a way of thinking, and as a way of life, all the more likely within a generation or two."[53]

The clinical findings of Franzblau agree with the research findings of the Levinsons, to indicate that intermarriage is less likely to be neurotically motivated for partners who share a secular point of view. "There are people who have, to all intents, left their faith long before they contemplate a mixed marriage. The marriage then becomes an incidental and not the crucial factor in the separation" from their religious background. Marriage between a Unitarian and a Reform Jew, says Franzblau, involves less "religious distance" than marriage between a Catholic and an Orthodox Jew, for example. "One might say that the shorter the religious distance in a mixed marriage, the less likelihood of finding neurotic factors operating," and presumably the more likely it is to succeed.[54] Gordon similarly observes that in a successful intermarriage at least "one partner is only a nominal member of a religious group."[55]

Intermarriage and the reduction of racial prejudice. "It has often been remarked," says Tumin, "that intermarriage is the final and only real test of the presence of genuine equality. The infrequency of Jewish-Gentile intermarriage," he adds, "is testimony to the existence of very deep-lying [negative] feelings on *both* sides of the ethnic line."[56] Rabbi Danglow, reporting from Australia, tells of Jews who argue that opposition to mixed marriages "is entirely out of date, and that intermarriage is really desirable as a means of breaking down 'superfluous' social and religious barriers and of cultivating harmonious relations with our Christian fellows."[57]

Rabbi Gordon quotes a colleague who praises converts as "more devout than the average [Jewish] child," and further asserts that they "build a bridge of good will to Christian families in the community."[58] Persons who have intermarried, or favor intermarriage, sometimes describe intermarriage as an instrument of social harmony:

> . . . I, for one, intend to marry 'outside' my own religious group in order to prove once and for all that this is or ought to be one world.[59]

> I felt that it was wrong for people to regard themselves as superior to others. I saw no real difference between people just because their skin color was different.[60]

Tumin's view of intermarriage as a test of social equality was expressed by Hertzler in 1942 when he wrote: "It would seem that wherever Jews have security and are tolerantly treated they lose their clannishness and exclusiveness, and intermarry and intermingle otherwise. Intermarriage is a test of their sense of security as individuals. It implies both an absence of anti-Semitism and the parallel presence of assimilation carried to the point of amalgamation. But the group consciousness, with its ancient memories, militates against it. . . ."[61]

Survey findings on the decline of anti-Semitism. The potential

Table 1:1. How Gentiles Say They Feel About Marrying a Jew
(1950, 1962)*

"How would you feel about marrying a Jew? Which one of these statements (on card) comes closest to your own feelings?"

	Per cent	
	1950 (N=1,272)**	1962 (N=1,483)
"I definitely would not marry a Jew."	57	37
"I would rather not marry a Jew but it wouldn't matter too much."	16	25
"It would make no difference to me."	22	30
No opinion	5	8

* Adapted from Stember, Table 40, page 106.
** Throughout this book, "N" stands for the number of persons included in the population or sample described.

frequency of intermarriage depends upon the willingness of Gentiles to marry a Jew, as well as the willingness of Jews to marry a Gentile. In a 1964 *Commentary* article, Sklare correctly asserts that analysis of the Jewish-Gentile intermarriage problem has focused too exclusively on factors which predispose a Jew to take a Gentile mate, overlooking important changes which are taking place in the willingness of Gentiles to marry a Jew. Survey evidence along this line appears in Stember's 1966 book, *Jews in the Mind of America.*

Stember reports a survey conducted in 1950 and repeated in 1962, in which Gentile samples of 1,272 and 1,483 were asked to express their attitude toward marrying a Jew. In 1950, 57 per cent chose the alternative "I definitely would not marry a Jew." Twelve years later, 37 per cent chose this response—and the majority shifted to a more favorable statement. (*See* Table 1:1.) Stember regards this drop of 20 percentage points in the "definitely not" response as a notable decrease in opposition to Jews as marriage partners over the years 1950–1962. This is not an isolated phenomenon, Stember argues, but matches a similar decline in Gentile hostility toward Jews as neighbors, colleagues, and employees.

Stember brings together the results of ten other surveys conducted between 1938 and 1962, gauging the attitudes of Gentile Americans toward Jews as neighbors, college students, and employees. Results show a consistent decline over the years, in Gentile hostility toward Jews as neighbors, fellow students and employees—following the same trend as the 1950 and 1962 surveys on attitude toward intermarriage. (*See* Figure 1:2.)

Stember concludes that these trends in the key areas of work, residence, education, and marrige "are so nearly parallel as to suggest that attitudes toward social relations with Jews are a unitary phenomenon. Once society admits the Jewish minority to full participation in some of the crucial areas of organized social interaction, growing readiness for intimacy—*up to and including more frequent intermarriage*—is apparently bound to follow."[62] (Italics added.)

An increasingly favorable attitude of Gentiles toward Jewish group affiliation is likewise indicated in the 1966 findings of Goldstein and Goldscheider, whose survey of Providence (Rhode Island) intermarrieds show *a rising rate of conversion to Judaism* among intermarrying Gentiles. In those intermarriages where the husband was 60 or more, none of the non-Jewish spouses had converted; among those aged 40 to 59, four out of every ten intermarriages resulted in conversion to Judaism; and in the under-40 age group, the non-Jewish spouse converted to Judaism in *seven cases out of ten*.[63]

It would oversimplify the facts to ascribe the above change entirely to the rise of Reform Judaism and its lowering of the barrier to conversion. The Jewish group of today is quite different from what it was 40 years ago; it has risen dramatically both in acculturation and in socio-economic level. Today a Jewish father-in-law is more likely to be a well-educated professional and member of a Reform temple, than an immigrant peddler who *davens* in the Anotevker *shul*. The intermarrying Gentile wife is likely to find the Jewish community a congenial home whether she converts to Judaism or not. A. I. Gordon's Minneapolis study led him to conclude that "practically all those who intermarry remain within the Jewish fold. . . . Even when the wife has not been formally converted to Judaism, she is permitted to join the women's organizations of several of the synagogues and occasionally even plays a role of prominence in its affairs."[64]

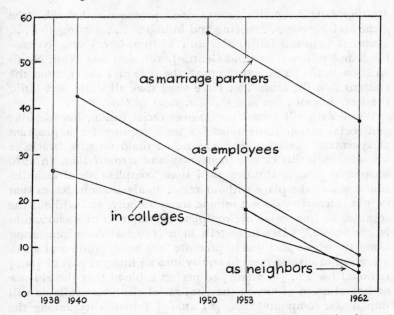

Figure 1:2. The Declining Trend (1938–1962) of Rejection of Jews as Employees, College Students, Neighbors, and Marriage Partners (From Stember, Figure 41, page 107)

This assemblage of findings offers strong empirical support to the impressions voiced by observers of the American scene, on the weakening of traditional prejudices, the reduction of ethnic barriers, and on the psychological effects of increased social interaction between Jews and Gentiles. The acculturation of the Jew and his rise in socio-economic status is one aspect of the situation; perhaps there have also occurred certain changes in the American ethos which makes the Jew "a culture hero"—a conjecture which will be explored in a later section of this chapter.

Racial fusion, pro and con. At the turn of the century, assimilation *versus* Zionism was a topic of open debate among acculturated Jews. In 1908, when the emigration of Russian and Polish Jews to the United States was at its peak, Israel Zangwill rhapsodized over the glory of racial fusion. In his four act play, *The*

Melting Pot, Zangwill's intermarried protagonist beholds "the great Melting-pot . . . roaring and bubbling . . . stirring and . . . seething! Celt and Latin, Slav and Teuton, Greek and Syrian— black and yellow—[Jew and Gentile]. Yes, East and West, North and South, the palm and the pine, the pole and the equator, the crescent and the cross. . . . Here shall they all unite and build the Republic of Man and the Kingdom of God."[65]

While Zangwill waxed poetic over racial fusion, his scientific and social action contemporaries were arguing for a program of systematic "racial amalgamation," a dialogue that Drachsler summarizes in his classic *Democracy and Assimilation.* In 1910 sociologist Jerome Dowd argued that "complete social assimilation cannot take place without racial amalgamation. Races that do not intermarry do not mingle freely socially, and without the stimulus of free social life complete assimilation or socialization is impossible."[66] Drachsler tells of a National Americanization Comittee whose goal was to promote "the assimilation and amalgamation of diverse races in equity into an integral part of [our] national life . . . [to attain] so perfect a blend that the absence or imperfection of any of the vital racial elements available will impair the compound . . . [to attain] impartiality among the races accepted for the blend, with no imputations of inferiority and no bestowal of favors . . . [Thus would America give the world something] of lasting value for its racial problems. . . ."[67]

The "amalgamists" were opposed by "some leading sociologists and biologists," Drachsler notes, who deplored "the over-population of the land by . . . undesirable newcomers."[68] Paul Popenoe and R. H. Johnson declared that "a large part of the immigration is on the average inferior to the older population of the United States, [and are therefore] eugenically a detriment to the future progress of the race. The direct biological result to be expected from the assimilation of the newcomers is the swamping of the best characteristics of the old American stock, and a diminution of the average intelligence of the whole country."[69]

In 1913 sociologist Edward A. Ross deplored the "sub-common blood now being injected into the veins of our people." He describes the new immigrants as bearers of "crooked faces, coarse mouths, bad noses, heavy jaws, low foreheads," small stature, poor physique, low vitality, lax morality and lesser ability than the old pioneering breed. In 1917 Edward G. Conklin warned that "a hybridized people is a badly put together people and a dissatisfied, restless, ineffective people."[70]

Writing in 1920, Drachsler judged that the popular concept of "Americanization" implied a rather "one-sided process. It assumes too often that the immigrant is to take rather than to give, to shed his own personality rather than adapt the finer qualities of American life to himself and thus grow in the direction of his true self. It encourages imitation rather than originality . . . [puts] a premium upon self-effacement . . . [as it directs the immigrant] into already existing well-marked channels. It thus opposes the free interaction and cross fertilization of many cultures. In doing this, it sets itself against the most hopeful currents of contemporary American life."[71]

Four years earlier, John Dewey had observed tartly "that many who talked the loudest about the need of a supreme and unified Americanism of spirit really mean some special code or tradition to which they happen to be attached. . . . In thus measuring the scope of Americanism by some single element . . . they are themselves false to the spirit of America."[72]

The behavioral science consensus, however, tended toward the view that social harmony and individual security was best served when minority group peoples gave up their distinctive characteristics and "sought full membership in the dominant group." In 1942 Hertzler argued that the Jew invites persecution because he is "different" and therefore becomes a "social irritant." The Jew becomes identified with radicals and other obnoxious members of his group because his feelings of group solidarity unwisely lead him to defend *all* Jews against the Gentile community![73] Hertzler argued further that "to cease to be a cultural irritant the Jew must be completely assimilated. Any sense of allegiance to his 'chosen people' idea will have to disappear; he must consciously remove characteristics of behavior which are recognizably Jewish; he must deliberately mold himself and his life on Gentile patterns. . . . He will have to be completely absorbed ethnically. . . . He will have to marry with non-Jews, generation after generation, until he has no grandparents who were considered as Jews and no children who by chance might have any distinguishing 'Jewish' characteristics.

"He will have to give up all pride in his group and his people's history and denationalize himself as a Jew . . . and become 100 per cent conformist so far as the nation of his sojourn is concened. . . . He will have to disappear entirely as a Jew, be dissolved in the life and being of the larger world."[74]

On the literary scene of the mid-1930's, Lewisohn identified Mencken, Dreiser, and Ernest Boyd as "a small group of writers [who] have recently raised the cry that American Jewry must assimilate." Lewisohn added that this was a popularly held view of his own Gentile friends.[75] In a 1933 *Atlantic Monthly* article, Milton Steinberg described in detail the desperate and absurd excesses which at least some Jews practiced to emulate the American majority. "The Jew who once refused to imitate the virtues of the non-Jew now sedulously copies even his vices," Steinberg commented wryly. "The very ritual of the synagogue is often appraised by the alien standards of the outer world."[76]

The assimlationist viewpoint today. The ethnic problem that commands the attention of contemporary scholars and intellectuals revolves around the future of the Negro in America. A number of contemporary scholars explicitly advocate a "genetic solution" to the problem of racial discrimination.[77] Widespread cross-mating, panmixia, the inundation of the Negro genetic pool by a white sea of Caucasian genes, they advise, will wash away the blight of racial prejudice.[78] The assimilation of the Jews into the Gentile majority seems, by comparison, a much less problematical issue—and is explicitly advocated by prominent scholars in contemporary social psychology and neighboring disciplines.

Championed in several important textbooks in social psychology (e.g., Krech and Crutchfield's *Theory and Problems of Social Psychology,* and Newcomb's *Social Psychology*) the assimilationist viewpoint deserves a close analysis from the standpoint of the authors' assumptions and the facts by which they support their conclusions.

The Krech and Crutchfield textbook shows an interesting difference between the authors' original 1948 publication and their 1962 revision. In the original presentation the authors quite openly and explicitly reiterate the Hertzler prescription: assimilation by all available means. Consistent with their "cognitive viewpoint," they argue that racial prejudice can be reduced by eliminating "the physical cues that set people apart into discriminable groups." They acknowledge the "obvious difficulty" that an anti-Semite will not take a Jew as a mate,[79] and acknowledge the fact that "children resulting from some mixed marriages in our society find themselves . . . faced with many difficulties of adjustment."[80] In view of these complications, the authors proposed that the minority group member eliminate his distinctive surname, food habits, recreational patterns and other "sociological cues that identify him as a 'different' person."[81]

Krech and Crutchfield wasted few words over the loss of the old culture. "Not all members of a minority group have strong feelings of belongingness"[82] to their ethnic group anyway, they argued. "Many people will therefore gain more emotional security by conforming to the dominant group . . . than they will by endeavoring to live out their lives within the confines of their own minority sociological class . . . In so far as acculturation is possible, it can be extremely helpful in removing some supports for beliefs and attitudes of racial prejudice," the authors argued.[83]

In their 1965 college textbook on *Racial and Cultural Minorities,* Simpson and Yinger echo Krech and Crutchfield's 1948 optimism, assuring their readers that "race mixture is not biologically inadvisable," and predicting that "intermarriage on a large scale would produce a relatively homogenous population, physically and culturally. The elimination of intergroup conflicts based on race and culture would have societal advantages," the authors promise, "although some would lament the passing of cultural pluralism."[84]

In their 1962 revision Krech and Crutchfield drastically alter their presentation on the problem of minority group membership. Gone is their direct argument in favor of assimilation. Instead the authors ruefully acknowledge (through a lengthy quotation from Milton M. Gordon)[85] the rebuff of the second generation Jew by the white Protestant elite, and the Jew's forced retreat to "the realm of the sociologically possible." Somewhere between 1948 and 1962 Krech and Crutchfield somehow had come to acknowledge what Kurt Lewin had observed in 1940: that the Gentile group "does not want a full assimilation," and that even Jews who fastidiously match the Gentile norms may incur the rebuff of the privileged group.[86]

What Milton Gordon reported in 1961, Stonequist had observed in 1937: "To many young Jews it comes as a distinct shock to discover that they are not fully accepted as Americans."[87] Bloom's 1939 study of Jewish life in Akron, Ohio, yielded the case history of a woman whom we shall call . . .

Eva

". . . A member of one of Akron's well-to-do Jewish families . . . after returning from school in the East, [Eva] married a promising young employee in her father's business . . . [Since] Akron's Jewish society had little challenge to her, she enlarged her sphere of activity and set about cultivating those who, by her own admission, were the best people in town. By virtue of her aggressiveness, not inconsiderable charm, and faculty for giving pleasant parties, she was shortly recognized as a desirable person, and gathered about her a group of friends of semi-intellectual interest, who found her a stimulating and suitable companion, for [Eva] was undeniably a person of culture.

"This group, however, did not include the wealthiest and very best people in Akron, whose parents were able to recall that [Eva's father] began his business career in Akron fifty years before with his establishment on his back. But [Eva] was a persistent person and proceeded to induce amnesia in the minds of these persons by contributing extravagantly, but with good judgment, to the cultural life of the city. [Eva] was responsible for musicales and clever parties which the elite saw fit not to avoid and, having failed to avoid, found necessary to reciprocate. This process lasted over a period of four or five years, in which time [Eva] and her husband, who remained loyal though embarrassed, came to be recognized as necessary adjuncts if not charter members, of Akron's smartest set.

"With the depression, one of the finest homes in the exclusive Green Acres section, which was expressly closed to Jews, was put up for sale. [Eva], who wished to be near her new friends, purchased the property and prepared to move from her pleasant home in the Long Hill district. She redecorated her new home, furnished it carefully and well, and in due time took up her residence there. Much to her surprise, however, the friends who had welcomed her as a guest and who were frequent visitors at her old home failed to make the necessary formal calls. When she herself dispensed with the formality they either were not at home or received her with embarrassed coldness, and it soon became clear to [Eva] that although she had been welcomed as a companion she was not welcomed as a neighbor.

"Disheartened and confused, she escaped to Europe for a year and when she returned to Akron moved into her old home on Long Hill. The fine house in Green Acres stood unlived in, the object of casual comment about Jews who did not know their place. . . . Once more [Eva] gathers about herself the semi-intellectual division of Akron's smart set; and thus insulated against the stares and verbal attacks of her neighbors, she returns to Green Acres. Some of the neighbors have relented, but Green Acres' wives who are too friendly to [Eva and her husband] may encounter criticism themselves. It is incongruous that in Green Acres more than anywhere else, Akron should remind [Eva] of the Jewishness she wishes to forget. But she clings to her home even though it does not lend her the status it should. Her adjustment to the situation is apparently a permanent one."[88]

The role of a minority group member. In 1940 Kurt Lewin suggested that "one might classify Jews into three groups: those who over-emphasize their Jewishness, those who behave normally, and those who try to hide or to under-emphasize their Jewishness. The individual in the middle group who knows in what situation and to what degree to emphasize his Jewishness probably fares best of all. As for the others, the Gentile is more likely to react without hostility to those who over-emphasize than to those who hide their Jewishness. So long as the Gentile does not want a full assimilation, it is evident that he will become easily suspicious against the third type, but feel rather safe in relation to the first. For the uncertain behavior of individuals in the third group would seem to make it more hazardous to give equal privileges to them than to individuals whose position and probable actions are quite clear; the latter are less likely to use equal status in professional life, business or politics, for the purpose of trying to cross the line in a field where such crossing is not wanted."[89]

In their original presentation, Krech and Crutchfield disagreed

with Lewin over the basic question of whether racial prejudice
is an irrational response evoked by certain perceptual cues or—
as Lewin (and later Milton M. Gordon) argued—prejudice is an
attitude by which members of a dominant group defend their
position of privilege and authority against encroachment. In any
case, since Krech and Crutchfield advised minority group members to eliminate the distinctive customs of their group, they were
by clear implication advocating a disregard for the custom of
endogamy in the interest of reducing racial prejudice and fostering the "emotional security" of the individual.[90]

In their 1962 presentation, Krech and Crutchfield let the problems of minority group membership be described through two
extended quotations. In addition to Milton Gordon on the rebuff
and retreat of the acculturated Jew, the authors quote at length
from I. L. Child's 1943 study of second generation Italian Americans (a study which is *not* mentioned in their 1948 edition) .

In 1937-1938 Child interviewed about 30 New Haven Italian-
Americans on their attitudes of belongingness to the culture of
their immigrant parents, and to the American culture. Krech and
Crutchfield report Child's conclusion that three modes of adjustment are available to the minority group member: an *in-group*
reaction of hostility to American culture and loyalty to their old
group; an *apathetic* withdrawal from the conflict of cultural
values; and a *rebellious* assertion of one's wish to identify with
the American culture and divest himself from old world loyalties.

Supporting this analysis, Krech and Crutchfield describe the
offspring of immigrants as "marginal men [occupying] an ambiguous position between two culture groups with contrasting
ways. They are motivated to affiliate with both groups; they are
fully accepted by neither. Severe conflict often develops because
the role behavior appropriate in the two groups is antagonistic."[91] So far as the authors indicate, the marginal man's choice
consists of withdrawal into the old group, active rebellion against
the old group, or apathetic vacillation.

Intermarriage and emotional security, Newcomb vs. Lewin. In
their original text, Krech and Crutchfield implied a two-fold benefit from "eliminating" minority group identifications: (a) reduction of racial prejudice, and (b) increase in the "emotional security" of the individual. In his *Social Psychology,* T. M. New-

comb emphasizes the reciprocal relationship between total identification with the dominant culture and emotional health: "The
poignant and often tragic conflicts" of cultural marginality can
be resolved, Newcomb implies, by abandoning the old group in
order "to achieve full membership in the new group"[92] and
thereby gain access to the tangible rewards of membership in the
dominant culture: "power, prestige and money."[93] The person
who cannot give up his position in his old primary group, says
Newcomb, probably suffers from an unfavorable "early personality development" which has left him "insecure and predisposed
to see threats in any new role which he might take. Such a person is more likely to take the in-group role or the apathetic one
than the rebel role," Newcomb argues. "The one he tends to
take, however, will further influence his personality development
. . . This reciprocal relationship between role taking and personality is particularly conspicuous in marginal people."[94]

Since Newcomb argues that the choice of the *rebel* role indicates both a more favorable early personality development and a
more favorable condition for further personality growth,[95] it
would be instructive to examine in some detail the data from
which Newcomb has drawn his conclusions. Like Krech and
Crutchfield, Newcomb's references to the in-group, the apathetic,
and the rebel roles are drawn from I. L. Child's 1937-1938 interview study. What do Child's rebels (ten in number) say about
themselves that might tell us what kind of people they are?

Child documented the rebels' verbal "aggression toward the
Italian group and its leaders and symbols. Such aggression may
be seen in many references by the rebel informants to other
Italians as ignorant, or deserving of the name 'wop,' as possessing
various traits that Americans regard as reprehensible, etc."[96] One
of these young men, raised by Italian-speaking, Italian-born parents (probably in an Italian neighborhood) , on an Italian diet,
exercised the ultimate in thought control when he denied "that
he ever under any circumstances thinks of himself as Italian or
Italian-American."[97]

It should not be surprising that Child's Italian American rebels
are strongly inclined toward intermarriage. Says Child: "One
easy way for the rebel against the Italian group to express his
general reaction is by paying little attention to girls of Italian

descent. *Two informants have carried this reaction out very thoroughly. Although they lived in neighborhoods where there were many Italian families and have gone out with a number of girls, they report that they have never gone out with a girl of Italian descent.* Others do not carry this reaction so far but still go out more with non-Italian girls than with Italian girls, or . . . make the effort to go out with many [girls] who are not of Italian descent . . ."[98] (Italics added.)

"Most, though not all" of Child's ten rebels expressed negative feelings toward Italian girls. As one rebel put it, "I wouldn't marry an Italian girl because they want everything their own way, and most of them are ignorant."[99]

Like the rebels he admires, Newcomb sees no room for integration of an old identity with participation in the dominant culture. "Membership in both [groups] is incompatible" according to the norms of both the old group and the new, Newcomb insists. The marginal man is somewhat uncharitably described by Newcomb as "neither fish nor fowl," but this unhappy state of affairs need not persist beyond one or two generations "when there is strong motivation to achieve full membership in the new group and abandon the old."[100] (Newcomb gives fair warning that "the more favored group may deny full membership to the marginal person even if he is willing to abandon his incompatible memberships.")[101] It is clear that to Newcomb the mark of emotional health is to abandon the old culture and strive for full membership in the new.[102]

The heritage of Child's study is the widely held theme that the children of immigrants must struggle between loyalty to a mutually antagonistic old group and new group.[103] Invariably the conclusion is reached that the only realistic solution to this "poignant conflict" is "to 'join' American society,"[104] to repudiate the old culture and achieve "assimilation with the dominant culture,[105] "to achieve full membership in the new group and abandon the old,"[106] to eliminate the old group characteristics "by conforming to the dominant group . . . in so far as acculturation is possible . . ."[107]

Eleven years before publication of Newcomb's text, Lewin offered the following analysis of the assimilationist tactic: "Every individual likes to gain in social status. Therefore the member of un underprivileged group will try to leave it for the more privileged majority . . . It would be an easy solution of the minority problem if it could be done away with through individual assimilation. Actually, however, such a solution is impossible for any underprivileged group. Equal rights for women could not be attained by one after another being granted the right to vote. . . . A few Jews might be fully accepted by non-Jews. . . . [But] certainly it is absurd to believe that fifteen million Jews can sneak over the boundary one by one."[108]

Newcomb and Lewin disagree categorically in their analysis of the social-psychological forces which have perpetuated the Jewish community. Newcomb asserts that Jews somehow have lacked "strong motivation to achieve full membership in the new group and to abandon the old," and concludes that "the absence of such motivation seems largely responsible for the continued marginality of many Jewish groups for centuries."[109] Lewin, on the other hand, stresses the point that "every underprivileged minority group is kept together not only by cohesive forces among its members but also by the boundary which the majority erects against the crossing of an individual from the minority to the majority group. It is in the interest of the majority to keep the minority in its underprivileged status. There are minorities which are kept together almost entirely by such a wall around them."[110]

Newcomb's analysis hinges upon his supposition that "Italian-Americans are in many ways typical of many marginal people."[111] (Strodbeck has described in detail significant differences between the Italian immigrant culture and the culture of that classic marginal group, the Jews.)

The negative incubus. The foregoing consensus implies that the more capable and adaptive members of the Jewish minority group tend to shed their ethnic identity, merge with the dominant group, and participate in the good life of the comfortable majority. How could it be otherwise? one might ask, since the Jew is not only attracted by the advantages of the dominant group; he must also be repelled by the stigma of identifying with what David Riesman in 1942 described as a cynical, acquisitive, rootless group whose behavior often gives a certain plausibility to anti-Semitic prejudices.

Riesman described the American Jews as lacking a foothold in the social hierarchy, stigmatized by a "repelled and repellant" lower middle class, and confronted by the presence of a native anti-Semitism more extensive than the anti-Semitic feelings harbored by the people of Nazi Germany.

Is there a future in American society for Jews *as Jews?* Riesman argued that success in business does not augment the Jews' position in the social power hierarchy, which is dominated by the big industrialists, the military and diplomatic services, the Church, the landed gentry and the "old families." (He brushed aside the question of social advancement through the professions.) "American Jews, moreover, are not only weak in the absence of a positive foothold in the social hierarchy. They are saddled, at the bottom of the scale, with the negative incubus of the lower middle-class Jew, a socially repelled and repellant being with hardly a European counterpart . . . [afflicted by] the social malaise and uprootedness of the second-generation Americans. . . . Torn from the religious and cultural ties which supported them in Europe; they are freed from Europe's quasi-feudal restraints on acquisitiveness and acquire a superficial self-assurance based on their money and their legal rights; they are made cheaply cynical by the conflict between American ideals and their own shrewd urban observation of the American prejudice, corruption and greed which they see. . . ."[112] From Riesman's analysis of the situation in 1942, one would conclude that the future of the Jewish group in America was very bleak indeed.

The assimilation timetable. Warner and Srole conclude a 300-page report on their 1930-1935 study of ethnic groups in Yankee City (a New England community) with a "timetable" predicting "the approximate period necessary for the assimilation of each racial and ethnic group," by which they mean the number of generations required "for an entire group to disappear." (The timetable ranks the various ethnic groups according to how well they match—or diverge from—the old Yankee group in physical characteristics, language, religion, occupational practices, and marriage customs.) For European Jews, the authors predict a "short to moderate" time for assimilation, predicting that "five or six generations may see most of the group disappearing." The authors point out that "German, English, and other less racially visible Jews disappeared into the total population more rapidly," but that five or six generations may be necessary for the Eastern European Jews because they are somewhat more "racially variant" from the Old Yankees.

In a concluding paragraph of their study the authors advise their reader that "the future of American ethnic groups seems to be limited; it is likely that they will be quickly absorbed. When this happens one of the great epochs of American history will have ended. . . ."[113]

Uniqueness of the Jewish minority group. In their comfortable unanimity, the behavioral science advocates and forecasters of full cultural absorption overlook two significant facts: First, old world cultures are by no stretch of the imagination uniformly antagonistic to the dominant American culture. As Glazer points out, "the Jewish immigrants who came from Eastern Europe to the United States during 1881-1924 numbered as many . . . impoverished workers as any other ethnic group. But they carried with them the values conducive to [the dominant group value of] middle class success . . . . . . They were not, like the other workers, the sons of workers and peasants, with the traditionally limited horizons of those classes . . . . Jewish workers could almost immediately turn their minds to ways and means of improving themselves that were quite beyond the imagination of their fellow workers . . . . . . The pattern of foresight and sobriety so essential for middle class success was . . . well established in Jewish life . . . . The Jews did not drink; the Jewish students were docile, accepting—as lower class children rarely do today—today's restraints for tomorrow's rewards."[114]

The phenomenal rise in the social and economic position of the Jews in the United States—even "surpassing, for the same period, changes in the socio-economic position of long-settled groups"[115]—makes it difficult to defend the thesis that the Jewish cultural tradition was broadly antagonistic to the dominant group. Indeed, to Graeber's anonymous *Critic*[116] "one of the most startling traits of Jewish culture is the speed with which it takes over the folkways of its hosts. In the United States, for example, the absorption of American folkways is almost complete in one generation."[117]

Secondly, to say that the child of the immigrant has a choice between the old culture and the new is true enough, but to imply that he has no choice *except* the old culture or the new is patently false! There are available to the Jew, for example, several overlapping hybrid or marginal cultures which afford both continuity and adaptation.

Milton M. Goldberg conceptualizes the American Jewish community as a "nongeographic equivalent of the anthropological concept of 'marginal area' . . . a region where two cultures overlap and where the occupying group partakes of the traits of both cultures." He quotes Goldweiser's statement that "psychologically, the marginal area is but a type of culture area, for its cultural content is as much of a unit and has the same value to its human carriers as the content of a full-fledged culture area."

There is a vast difference, as Goldberg argues, between a marginal individual adrift between two antagonistic cultures, and a participant member of a marginal culture who "shares this existence and conditioning process with a large number of individuals in his primary group . . . [participates] in institutional activities manned largely by other 'marginal' individuals like himself, and . . . [experiences] no major blockages or frustrations of his learned expectations and desires . . . . His culture [is] every bit as real and complete to him as is the nonmarginal culture to the nonmarginal man."[118]

The right to be different. In Marden's 1952 analysis of *Minorities in American Society,* he observes that while Jews have adjusted very readily to the non-Jewish milieu in America they have yet remained segregated from the general group. "Of all minority group problems, [he concludes], Gentile-Jewish are most puzzling to explain and are not promising of easy solution."[119] What Marden seems to be saying is that since the behavior of Jews cannot be described by the familiar concepts of total assimilation or total segregation, since Jews are neither undifferentiated Americans nor obviously foreigners, their behavior is something uncanny and mysterious.

This impatience with a phenomenon that does not fit neatly into the traditional compartments of Western thought is well expressed by an intermarried wife whom we have named Gertrude:

When a Swede or Chinese settles down in a foreign land, such as the United States, the Swede makes haste to become a thorough American—at any rate he lets his children become thorough Americans; the Chinese, realizing that this is impossible, lives aloofly in Chinatown, minds his own business, and keeps out of American political affairs. The Jew, however, wants to have his cake and eat it, too. Like the Chinese, he clings to his own race, culture and tradition; he trains his children to cling to these just as tenaciously. Then, like the Swede, he sets out to annex all the privileges of Americanism. He wants to rise to the top of the Gentile social structure, to wield power in Gentile politics of the community, state, and nation. He wants to be left alone, but he also wants the country in which he lives to take good care of him. He wants to have full citizenship in that country, yet retain his citizenship in the Jewish nation.[120]

In his astringent 1941 analysis of "The Jewish Problem," Albert Jay Nock likewise felt impelled to decide first of all whether Jews are Occidentals or Orientals. It is almost as if he reasoned that since Jews are not Occidentals in the full and familiar sense of the term, they must be Orientals, and therefore it is only proper that Jews should adapt to life in America like Chinese or Armenians. But since Jews in America do not live like Chinese or Armenians, they necessarily run the risk of persecution by the American mob. As Gertrude had asserted, "Human nature resents the ascendency of the alien. So long as the Jew wears the cloak of alien colors, so long will his predominance in any tier of the Gentile structure be resented."[121]

Marden, Gertrude, and Nock seem to be expressing the widely held view that in order to be understood in the Western world, the Jew must adopt a role that matches some familiar Western concept—either the concept of citizenship as full and thorough assimilation, or the concept of an aloof and tradition-bound alien who lives out his life inside a foreign enclave. Sartre has suggested the analogy between the rights of Jews to citizenship, and the rights of women. When society faced the question of whether women should be given the right to vote, some argued that if women were to become full citizens they would have to think like men, act like men, and perhaps even dress like men. Others argued that perhaps women as voting citizens could contribute something uniquely their own to political life in America (e.g., intuition, compassion, or humanity). Must citizenship require conformity to the dominent group in outward appearance and manners—asks Sartre—or should it be based on useful participation in the life of the community?

Must the Jews' social behavior be changed to fit Western society's most familiar and long-established concept of citizenship, or can the concept of citizenship be broadened to better fit the facts of social life in America? Glazer and Moynihan have recently advanced the thesis that "the ethnic group in American society [has become] not a survival from the age of mass immigration but a new social form."[122] This statement seems to call for a more factual understanding of group life in America, and the place of the Jews in it.

Assimilation and social adjustment; research findings. The literature yields little research on the effects of various modes of adjustment to Jewish identity. In 1956 Antonovsky reported that he had interviewed a representative sample of 58 second-generation Jewish men in New Haven, and found that only a small minority (14 per cent) fit the classical definition of the "marginal man": unstable, uncertain, and in perpetual conflict over his position. The classic "assimilationist" attitude—just short of hiding one's Jewish identity—fit an even smaller minority (about three per cent) of his sample. The "in-group" mode of adjustment—if one includes both moderately and strongly in-group respondents—characterized just over half (53 per cent) of his sample. In addition to the marginals, assimilationists, and in-group Jews, Antonovsky identified a group similar to I. L. Child's "apathetic" Italian-Americans, and a group holding a moderate and unproblematical attitude toward participation in the larger society—a group which seems to anticipate Peter I. Rose's "bicultural" Jews. The moderate or non-conflicted attitudes of a majority of Antonovsky's respondents conform to the theoretical viewpoint of Milton M. Goldberg, and to the larger empirical study of Kramer and Leventman.

Antonovsky offers an intriguing conjecture as to why college professors give so much emphasis to the marginal Jew, an adjustment pattern that describes less than 10 per cent of Antonovsky's adult Jewish sample. It is quite possibly an outcome of the professors' intimate knowledge of college undergraduate Jews, and

Table 1:3. Adjustment Patterns of 58 Married Second-Generation Jewish Males [Representative Sample of New Haven (Conn.) Population][1,2,3]

Ethnic orientation	Per cent (N)	Intensity of attitudes on matters Jewish	Attitude toward Jewish group survival	Attitude toward assimilation
STRONGLY IN-GROUP	36% (21)	Great	Strongly in favor	Opposed
"You say hello and goodbye to the goyim, but don't mix." "All Jews feel alike; there's no need to go around studying them." "I feel I'm Jewish all the time."				
MODERATELY IN-GROUP	17% (10)	Moderate	Mildly in favor	——
"I see little point to being Jewish, but that's what I am, and there's little point to trying to be something else."				
BI-CULTURAL	14% (8)	Moderate	Favor gradual loosening of in-group cohesion	It's not a good thing
"The Jew has before him the problem of living with both Jews and Gentiles. It's easier done on a 50-50 basis than at either extreme."				
MARGINAL	14% (8)	Great	As a religious group only	It doesn't work
"The greatest anti-Semite is the Jew himself. A Yid begrudges other Jews." "I would put myself in this category [of a 'white Jew'] though it sometimes involves humiliation."				
APATHETIC	16% (9)	Low	Indifferent	Indifferent
"Being Jewish is the least of my worries. I never grew up with guidance about Jewish things, so I've gotten away from it." "We're living in a melting pot country . . . Wherever you are, you should try to be with the rest."				
ASSIMILATIONIST (cf. I.L. Child's rebels)	3% (2)	Minimal	Opposed	Favorable
"I wouldn't hesitate to escape prejudice by avoiding recognition as a Jew." "I see no reason why I should be so high-minded about being Jewish because of some trouble three thousand years ago, or even recently."				

relative ignorance of adult Jews outside the academic profession. During the college years, unstable, conflicted attitudes toward Jewishness seem to be a relatively common occurrence. As young people mature and settle down, their identity crisis is somehow resolved and all but a handful leave the no-man's land of marginality. Antonovsky suggests that the professors confuse a life cycle phenomenon with a pervasive and stable characteristic of the American Jew.

Since Krech and Crutchfield specifically advised the minority group member to eliminate his distinctive surname and other "sociological cues that identify him as a 'different' person,"[124] it is interesting to note the findings of Kugelmass, who interviewed 25 persons listed in court files for having changed their names from a distinctly Jewish one to a distinctly Gentile name. All respondents had lived under their new name for one year or more.

Kugelmass reports that "without exception, all twenty-five said they had been fools. . . . The phrase used in nineteen of the twenty-five conversations was: 'I was a damned fool.' The other six said: 'I am sorry I did it.' " Respondents seemed eager "to prove they were 'still Jews'; in no case could I sense even the remotest inkling of a wish to abandon their Jewishness," Kugelmass reports. Eleven took the trouble to point out that "they were not only members in good standing of congregations, but occupied active posts on their congregations' committees devoted to cultural or similar subsidiary activities."[125]

Kugelmass supposes that the name-changers hoped to avoid the presumed disadvantages of a Jewish name in business or professional life, but they generally found that "life had not changed"; they saw no upsurge of Gentile clientele, no sudden recognition or acceptance in the Gentile world. Some admitted that they had been wrong in attributing their business or professional difficulties to anti-Semitism; *this was the single positive gain which the name-change seemed to have delivered.* On the negative side, name-changers felt that Gentile acquaintances registered disapproval, Jewish friends displayed indignation ("I used to wonder what a sneer was. Now I know."), and the children complained that the name-change inspired more than a little teasing from their peers.

The sharp difference of opinion among Jews regarding the

wisdom of name-changing is conveyed in the following *Our Crowd* anecdote:

> William Seligman, the most snobbish, probably, of the Seligman brothers, journeyed to New York from Paris for a conference with Joseph. William said, "Joe, now that we're getting to be men of substance, I suggest that we change our name."
>
> Joseph looked at him for a moment with hooded, sleepy eyes, smiling his famous semismile. Then he nodded soberly. "I agree that you should change your name, William," he replied. "I suggest you change it to Shlemiel."[126]

When social psychologists advise that the minority group member "eliminate" his ethnic habits, they are asking the Jew to somehow underplay, suppress, or conceal his Jewish identity. How well does this tactic work in the life of the individual? Teitelbaum questioned the popular view "that the so-called assimilated Jew . . . the Jewish student who is least identifiable as a Jew is the best adjusted." On the basis of his experience with Jewish college students, he believed that those "who most openly and directly identify themselves as Jews and integrate themselves with their people are less in conflict with their milieu in the greater society as well as with themselves than are their opposites."[127] Teitelbaum tested this Lewinian hypothesis by means of a questionnaire survey addressed to undergraduate Jewish students at Northwestern University in 1950.

Assured of anonymity, Northwestern's Jewish students were asked to state whether they identify themselves as Jews "openly and unreservedly," or are in some way reserved about their Jewish identification (i.e., are "self-conscious or uncertain about it, prefer not to mention it or to conceal it").[128] He then compared "open" and "reserved" respondents on their adjustment as students.

The entire undergraduate Jewish student body was canvassed, and about one-third co-operated with the survey. Respondents were about equally divided between "open" and "reserved" Jewish identification; women were significantly more "open" than men. Teitelbaum compared "open" and "reserved" students on a number of factors—including attitude toward Gentile

Table 1:4. Comparison between Openly and Reservedly Jewish
Students, by Sex[129]

	N	Openly Identify N	per cent	Reservedly Identify N	per cent
Males	125	(60)	48	(65)	52
Females	85	(56)	66	(29)	34

students, participation in extra-curricular activities, and father's
occupation.

Perhaps the most critical item on Teitelbaum's questionnaire
asked, "Do you feel any sense of strangeness, strain or tension
when you are among Gentile students?"[130] Results indicated that
to a statistically significant degree *"the self-acknowledged Jew is
more at ease and experiences less strain and tension"* in Gentile
company.

Table 1:5. Tension Felt When Among Gentile Students,
by Openly and Reservedly Jewish Students[131]

	Openly Identify (N)	per cent	Reservedly Identify (N)	per cent
Yes (Do feel tension . . .)	(9)	7.8	(20)	21.3
No (Do not feel tension . . .)	(107)	92.2	(72)	76.6
No data			(2)	2.1

"Open" identifiers were not only more active in Hillel activities
but also participated more actively in other extra-curricular activities,[132] although this latter difference did not attain statistical
significance. An interesting footnote to this study is the finding
that the "open" identifiers enjoyed a socio-economic advantage
over the "reservedly" identifiers: "opens" were significantly more
likely to designate father as a professional person or business
owner. "Reserved" identifiers were more likely to describe father's occupation as sales, other, or offer no data on father's occupation.

It appears that at this fashionable and expensive private university, Jewish students who openly identify themselves as Jews
tend to be favored by a more secure socio-economic background,
feel more at ease in Gentile company, and participate more freely

Table 1:6. Comparison of Openly and Reservedly Jewish Students by Father's Occupation[133]

	Openly Identify (N=116)		Reservedly Identify (N=94)	
	(N)	per cent	(N)	per cent
Proprietary	(65)	56.0	(46)	48.9
Professional	(35)	30.2	(21)	22.3
Sales	(8)	6.9	(13)	13.8
Others	(6)	5.2	(6)	6.4
No data	(2)	1.7	(8)	8.5

in campus activities than those who tend to conceal their Jewish identity. Commenting on Teitelbaum's findings, Hsu says they "correspond amazingly" to his personal observations, which lead him to conclude that "Jewish youngsters who are raised as non-Jews have a much harder time to adjust to their peers in college than those who have been raised consciously and militantly to cultivate their identity in Judaic tradition and church life. In other words," says Hsu, "their *complete* identity and assimilation as Americans is always subject to rejection." (Italics added.) Hsu concedes that Teitelbaum's findings do not warrant any "final conclusion on the subject," but that further research is called for.[134]

Richard's Private Dilemma

In *Remember Me to God,* novelist Myron Kaufmann describes the strain and tension of a Jewish Harvard man who has committed himself to total absorption into the Yankee elite:

"Lying awake, he would consider that some of the habits he had marked down to be acquired and mastered did indeed have merit, although others were plainly arbitrary and imitative . . . . . . It was confusing. In a way it was undemocratic to want to learn the mannerisms of the [aristocrats], and purely social aristocracies were certainly the most stupid of all aristocracies; but the challenge to learn all their mannerisms was that if he could not—even though their mannerisms be intrinsically no better—then his inability might indeed give the well-born some sort of argument in their own minds as to their superiority over him.

"He did not want anyone, even a relatively small society of people, to feel in any way a superior order of being to him; even the fact of knowing that people who thought themselves superior were fools was not enough—he did not want the fools to think it was Richard who was a fool. But he was troubled, because he could not explain this to himself without thinking it sounded illiberal and small-minded.

"He felt that such matters were nothing, or should be nothing, and that he shouldn't give them a thought. But he was not sure what quite all [his Yankee acquaintances] really thought of him . . . so that at times he felt an uneasiness with some of these boys, without even being certain who had started the uneasiness, he or they. And then he reasoned that this uneasiness was itself a Jewish neurosis or mannerism that he ought to try to cure."[135]

Intermarriage as a symptom of negative chauvinism. Child's investigation does shed light on psychological factors related to intermarriage, showing that a person who sees his group membership as an obstacle to attaining an important goal tends to seek affiliation through marriage with a group having more direct access to the wanted goal. This shift in group loyalty is accompanied by an idealization of the characteristics of the new group, and a depreciation of the characteristics of the old group. As Lewin pointed out, for a Jew to step across the boundary and identify himself with the majority group he must bring something more than an eagerness to adopt the standards and share the privilege of the majority. Like Child's ten rebels, he must also be predisposed to renounce and conceal "the ideas of the group to which he once belonged" if he wishes to be judged by the ideals and standards of the proud majority. He must be predisposed to *disfavor* Jewish attitudes, appearances, and habits, as Child's rebels deprecated Italian traits, Italian physique and Italian girls. This is what Lewin (1941) describes as "negative chauvinism."[136]

"The feeling of inferiority of the Jew is but an indication of the fact that he sees things Jewish with the eyes of the unfriendly majority," said Lewin. In discussing motives for intermarriage, Rabbi Danglow expresses regret for Jews whose inferiority complex leads them "to regard it as an honor that they are accepted as the husband or wife of a non-Jew."[138]

The concept of "identification with the aggressor" was introduced into the literature of psychology by Anna Freud,[139] but the phenomenon itself is by no means unique to modern times. Hershel Meyer notes from the medieval Jewish literature that "after every pogrom or exile, there usually appeared various . . . admonitions to regard the visitations as punishments for some grave sin." Orlansky adds: "Self castigation can be seen in the frequent assertion by Jews—especially the more assimilated—that the behavior of Jews is partly responsible for anti-Semitism."[140]

The Jew's vulnerability to negative chauvinism, says Lewin, increases as his life increasingly overlaps with the life of the dominant group. In any case, there are all degrees of negative chauvinism, Lewin adds. "After all, we do have a great many Jews who can hardly be classified as anti-Semitic."[141] Ordinarily the minority group member's negative feelings about things Jewish are counterbalanced by feelings of loyalty, pride, belongingness, and responsibility for his fellow Jews. The Jew who lacks these positive feelings about his Jewish identity, who can react only with distaste or embarrassment to anything Jewish, will seek "to cut himself loose from things Jewish. The more typically Jewish people are, or the more typically Jewish a cultural symbol or a behavior pattern is, the more distasteful they will appear to this person."[142]

Lewin refers briefly to the manifestations of self-hatred in Jews who enter into mixed marriages.[143] It would indeed seem likely that an attitude of "negative chauvinism" would make a Jewish mate appear distasteful, and a Gentile mate attractice. To a Jew who dislikes anything Jewish, marriage into the "correct" and privileged majority would seem like a highly attractive goal. Slotkin quotes a Jewish woman's candid expression of this motive for intermarriage:

Alicia

"Not until I got to high school was I really conscious of the difference between Jews and Gentiles . . . . I became resentful and ashamed, and . . . envious that I wasn't a Gentile. I was told to be proud that I was a Jew, but I never felt that way. I

felt . . . that it was an unfortunate circumstance." She admits
that for her intermarriage was an "escape from the stigma of
being identified with Jews."

". . . I would have a non-Jewish name and would be a part of
a non-Jewish group. I felt it would be a distinct advantage. I was
also glad for the children's sake that they wouldn't be Jews."[144]

Describing the attitude toward Jewish identity and intermarriage shared by the second generation of a German Jewish community in Wisconsin, Jessie Bernard says that "if they did not
actually practice [intermarriage] as often as they might, it was
only because they could not hurt their parents to that extent.
But many of them, sensing the strange hold which their unwanted Judaism had upon them, hoped that their children would
marry outside the fold, and thus escape the onus of Israel. They
openly proclaimed the doctrine and espoused the policy of assimilation as a solution to the problem of Jews. (It was only when
Hitler proclaimed that even one-fourth Jewish ancestry made one
a Jew that misgivings showed themselves.) "[145]

Richard L. Rubenstein observes the irony of Jewish men who
protest that "religion makes no difference" in their choice of
dates, and date Gentile girls exclusively![146] These persons "simply
want to get out of Judaism."[147] As Rubenstein sees it, "the principal mode of exit from the Jewish community today remains
intermarriage."[148] Franzblau likewise describes the person who,
"safely married to a person of a different faith . . . feels he has
removed the stigma of his own faith. It may be but a symptom
of a carefully planned, total strategy of escape from oneself and
one's forebears."[149]

Reik points to relationships between conflict with parents, rejection of Jewishness, and feelings of insecurity, in the inner life
of a patient "who for many hours described the shame he felt of
his family."

He said that since boyhood [he] had felt embarrassment that
they, immigrants from Russia, could not speak correct English
and remained orthodox Jews observing all religious holidays.
Later on he had changed his name because it sounded Jewish.
The same patient complained that he had bad luck in his profession, that his marriage had been a failure and that his friends

had deserted him in a critical situation. As I listened to him, apparently from nowhere the following lines occurred to me:

Ver zich sheymt fun zeiner mishpocho
Oif dem ist kein brocho.

. . . Whoever is ashamed of his family, has no luck . . . . There is good psychological sense in this saying: One can choose one's friends or one's mate, but one cannot choose one's parents or ancestors. One must accept them with their good qualities and weaknesses and cannot escape from them. A permanent feeling of being ashamed of them must lead to some unfavorable characterological consequences: the person will not accept himself, since our parents continue to live in us, are introjected in us, and are part of our personality. Thus a kind of flight from oneself begins. Connected with it is the resulting unconscious guilt feeling which leads the person to spoil his own chances in life, to sabotage himself, and unconsciously to stage manage his own bad luck.[150]

Turning from clinical to survey findings, Sarnoff's doctoral dissertation on personality correlates of Jewish anti-Semitism demonstrated a positive correlation between anti-Semitism (as measured by an original A-S scale) and agreement with six statements representing the assimilationist viewpoint.[151] Those who indicated negative attitudes toward Jews also tended to show a preference for underplaying their Jewish identity. Through various projective tests of personality, Sarnoff investigated personality differences between those who scored high on his anti-Semitism scale and those who scored low. Sarnoff's data led him to conclude that Jews who scored high on his A-S scale felt significantly more insecure, anxious, and felt rejected by their parents. He interpreted his findings to mean that the Jewish anti-Semite displaces onto the Jewish community some of the hostility he feels toward his family and toward himself.

In 1940 Engelman pointed out that the years of growth of the Nazi movement in Germany were marked by a steady and marked *increase* in the rate of Jewish-Gentile intermarriage. (The trend was checked only when intermarriage became a crime punishable by law and concentration camp, Engelman notes.) [152] It seemed obvious to Engelman that intermarriage had a special appeal for those who "found their ambitions and careers thwarted by prevailing anti-Semitic pressure. In order to escape it, Jewish men of Germany had recourse to intermarriage, which in many cases was but a prelude to baptism, if not of the intermarried person, most certainly of their offspring."[153]

Some twenty years after Engelman had commented on the motivations of intermarrying German Jews during the 1920's and 30's, John Mayer interviewed a number of intermarrying American Jews, and likewise concluded that the feeling that one lives in an anti-Semitic environment leads to intermarriage. "Stresses engendered by the anti-Semitic social structure," Mayer theorizes, are felt as insecurity, discontent and unrest, and the choice of a Gentile spouse somehow allays this feeling of insecurity.[154] (At the level of private fantasy, the Jewish husband may feel that through intermarriage he has conquered the threatening Majority; at the level of social interaction, the Jew may find that intermarriage gives him direct access to intimate social participation—and a feeling of belongingness—in the Gentile world.)

Mayer quotes from his interview with an intermarried Jewish husband who expressed the relationship between his feeling of insecurity as a Jew and his preference for a Gentile wife, with an unusual candor:

> [Did you have any thought about mixed marriages before you met your wife?] Yes, I had a kind of theoretical idea that the way to break through the Jewish problem was that there should be more mingling, that inter-religious marriages were a constructive thing, that it was a progressive thing to do.
>
> [Did you anticipate that you might marry out of your religious group?] I think so. I think to be frank, I felt an insecurity in being Jewish. I was quite aware of anti-Semitism. I felt a lot of insecurity from adolescence to the middle twenties. I blamed part of this on my being Jewish. To some degree I consciously sought out Gentile girls to go with.[155]

Mayer reiterates Engelman's hypothesis that "the greater the anti-Semitism, the greater will be the ratio of Jewish men and women to Christian men and women who are *motivated* to marry out of their group . . ." ("The kinds of marriages *actually contracted*" will depend, he adds, on other factors. For example, the social role of the male gives him the initiative to select a woman who appeals to him and actively pursue the relationship even in the face of rebuff or discouragement.) [156]

One risk to which the negative chauvinist is vulnerable is that he cannot selectively reject only those aspects of Jewishness which he finds undesirable, or uncongenial to his personal tastes. As Ackerman and Jahoda point out, the Jewish anti-Semite uncritically disavows *all* Jewish traits; as he rejects the bad traits, he also feels impelled to deny desirable qualities usually attributed to Jews. Jewish qualities which are neither bad nor good may be rejected because they are Jewish. The anonymous autobiography of a Jew who passed into Gentile society offers a glimpse of this process, which bears the psychoanalytic label of reaction-formation.

Ted

Ted was obviously dissatisfied with being a Jew. "To escape from the smothering bonds of Jewry" he changed his name, gave up his credits at several universities, moved to another part of the country "and invented . . . a false history, claiming to be descended from non-Jewish Adrianople Turks."[157]

"Was this elaborate lying necessary?" he asks. "Yes, for otherwise, you, my Jewish brethren, would have pulled me back into your community or else punished me for my desertion; while the Gentile world would have accepted me on suffrance, as a 'renegade' Jew." The interesting point is that Ted "had no kin in America nearer than cousins and uncles and aunts." Apparently he attributes this punishment and coercion to the "smothering" Jewish community itself! He gave up his youthful ambition to become a teacher because, like law and medicine, he regarded teaching as an occupation favored by the Jews. He tried a variety of callings: "In succession, I was a garage mechanic, stake man on a survey gang, farmhand, crop-share farmer, laborer, and later foreman on a riprap gang along the Mississippi. . . . I have not despised the work of my hands; I have sweated and grunted and conquered at hard labor; I have built up something that could be seen at the end of a season and existed not merely in a bank book. And I have everywhere been accepted as an equal, despite my slight accent and rather dark complexion and the Balkan ancestry I claimed."[158]

Ted castigates the Jews for following their "painful and arrogant course" of uniqueness, which is an "affront" to the Gentile community, "sure to lead to hatreds and reprisals . . . . Why blame the Gentiles for their scorn," Ted asks, "when the Jews also, even in their choice of the title, God's Chosen, by implication cast all others into inferiority." Everything that is different about the Jews is, in Ted's eyes, undesirable and a justification for Gentile scorn:

> You persist in being unlike other Americans. Your folkways are different from the national ways; your religious days are not the same; your attitude to women and the family, while commendable, is patriarchal; even your food is different—and *you glory in your differences* . . . . You cling to a thousand little things that differentiate you from the people around you —and then you have the temerity to complain when they also treat you as different—and not (since every nation and culture thinks its own ways best) as superior.[159]

Ted appeals to the Jews to cast off their ghetto heritage of "grasping . . . desperate coin collectors . . . [and] become again brave, upstanding farmers and shepherds and builders, soldiers and statesmen and engineers, as were our remote forebears." Here we see a reaction-formation in close-up. Law is bad, engineering is good. Teaching is bad, farming is good. Operating a business is bad, herding sheep is good. Making money is bad, grunting and sweating at hard labor is good. Jewish customs, even those which in themselves might be commendable, are out of place in America because they are different. One cannot blame the Gentiles for their scorn, Ted concludes; Jews who maintain their "unique and lofty" attitude must know that it is "sure to lead to hatreds and reprisals." Anti-Semitism, Ted implies, is the Gentile's normal and natural reaction to Jewish behavior.[160]

Ted completed college under his adopted identity, married, and was "raising children who need never learn to endure snubs, who will never be tempted to retaliate against cruel discrimination . . . . Life is good," he testifies. "I never regret my step."[161] It is interesting to note that Jessie Bernard cites Ted's story as "one case of *successful* assimilation."[162] (Italics added.)

Erik H. Erikson testifies that his clinical experience verifies "the sad truth that [members of an exploited and excluded minority] . . . unconsciously *believe* in the evil image which they are made to represent by those who are dominant." He cites the case of a prominent Western ranch owner whose Jewish identity was known only to his wife. The patient's discomfort was tied up with his inner feelings of anti-Semitism. He believed in Streicher's image of the evil Jew, and apparently couldn't quite convince himself that he himself was a decent person deserving of decent treatment by his neighbors.

His life, while outwardly successful, was made uncomfortable by a network of compulsions and phobias which, in analysis, proved to reproduce and superimpose on his free movements in Western valleys the outline of [the Jewish] neighborhood in which he grew up. His friends and adversaries, his elders and his inferiors, all unknowingly played the roles of the German boys or the Irish gangs who made the little Jewish boy miserable on his daily walk to school . . .[163]

Even among Gentiles anti-Semitism is a symptom of frustration and repressed hostility. It is doubtful that a Jew who harbors deep feelings of anti-Semitism can live a healthy inner life. Georgene Seward describes at length the case of an overtly "fascist" Jewish college student who entered psychotherapy as a patient of Dr. Judd Marmor. One sign of improvement reported by his therapist was the disappearance of his anti-Semitism as he became "able to face directly his own anxieties concerning his Jewish origin . . ." He broke away from his old pattern of seeking promiscuous sexual exploits, and established a relationship with "a Jewish girl from Vienna with similar bohemian and philosophical interests as his own . . . . [He] began a liaison with her, which gradually ripened into a genuine object attachment."[164]

The Jew as a culture hero. What the behavioral scientists have pretty much overlooked has become increasingly clear to literary critics, autobiographers, journalists, rabbis, and a few clinicians —that certain aspects of Jewishness have a considerable appeal to Gentile Americans, and that this appeal is strong enough to lead certain young Gentiles to mingle with Jews, prefer Jewish friends, and choose a Jewish spouse. Leslie Fiedler observes that it is "chic in certain middlebrow, middle-class, middle-liberal quarters to be pro-Jewish. Philo-Semitism is required—or perhaps, by now, only assumed—in the reigning literary and intellectual circles of America, just as anti-Semitism used to be required—and after a while only assumed—in the Twenties."[165]

What does the Jewish writer have to say that is of such compelling interest to the American reading public? "Certainly," says Fiedler, "we live at a moment when, everywhere in the realm of prose, Jewish writers have discovered their Jewishness to be an eminently marketable commodity,[166] their much vaunted alienation to be their passport into the heart of Gentile American culture . . . . The autobiography of the urban Jew . . . has come to seem part of the mystical life history of a nation."[167]

Tumin (1957) points to three ways in which the values of a "mass society" conflict with traditional Western standards: (1) a de-emphasis on inherited criteria of prestige "such as membership in exclusive kinship groups"; (2) the ideal "that all men are ultimately equal [although some may be] temporarily more equal than others. . . ."; and (3) the viewpoint that "it is theoretically permissible and even well-mannered to compete with everyone, no matter what his rank."[168] Faced with these requirements for participating in a "mass society" (which means a society undergoing massive enlargement of the middle class), the Jew does not suffer from deeply internalized conflicts over deference, humility, self-effacement, self-abnegation, self-sacrifice. He comes from a tradition which explicitly sanctions and encourages *yichas atsmo,* status earned through one's own efforts. He comes from a tradition in which differences in social rank are quite limited; a tradition with no landed gentry, no ruling class, no bishops or priests. He comes from a tradition in which a nice distinction is made between audacity and arrogance, and audacity is held in higher esteem than self-effacement. If the new abundance created by modern technology conflicts with the Puritan tradition of self-denial, if the new opportunity for middle-class status conflicts with a Western tradition of self-effacement, the Gentile must view the Jew as having some special gift or charisma that allows him to be both a child of tradition and a participant in a "mass society."

As America emerges from its puritanical small-town and rural past, says Fiedler, it looks to the Jewish-American writer to spell out what it means to live and think and feel like a city-dweller. The historical experience of the Jew uniquely equips him to transform the classic "themes of isolation and terror in the wilderness . . . into themes of urban American loneliness and urban American terror,"[169] says Fiedler. As America's culture heroes become urbanized they also become Judaized: "Huckleberry Finn becomes Augie March; Daisy Miller turns, via Natalie Wood, into Marjorie Morningstar. . . ."[170] Science fiction replaces the Western and detective story, and the Jewish scientist-intellectual (modelled after Oppenheimer or Einstein) replaces the Gentile cowboy and private eye as the dominant hero of popular escapist literature.[171] (Perhaps Mort Sahl, Woody Allen or Alan King replace Will Rogers—as Jules Feiffer replaces James Thurber.)

". . . The Judaization of American culture goes on at levels far beneath the literary and intellectual," Fiedler observes. The Main Street supermarket displays Mogen David wine and Jewish delicacies of all sorts; the small-town gift shop stocks Nebbishes, "sick" notes and "hate" greeting cards, which Fiedler describes as "Jewish humor at its most desperate."[172] "Eddie Fisher is drafted as the symbol of clean American love, while Danny Kaye continues to play the blue-eyed jester. . . ." Elizabeth Taylor and Marilyn Monroe choose Jewish husbands. In his uniquely evocative prose style, Fiedler describes how "Eros himself turns . . . Jewish, as the mythical erotic [shiksa] dream-girls of us all yearn for Jewish intellectuals and learn to make matzo-balls."[173]

The imaginary Jew. Fiedler observes that just as the white American passes his childhood as an imaginary Indian, and his adolescence as an imaginary Negro,[174] in the last couple of decades it has become increasingly probable that "in late youth or early middle age [the white Anglo-Saxon Protestant becomes] an imaginary Jew—modeling himself, in accordance with his politics and taste, on Herman Wouk or Leon Uris, Irwin Shaw, Saul Bellow or Bernard Malamud."[175]

It would be a mistake to suppose that the appeal of the Jewish group to the Gentile American is a phenomenon of the last two decades. Jessie Bernard offers this rare description of the place of the Philo-Semite in a Midwestern Jewish community of the nineteen-thirties: "By no means a unified group, these non-Jews —intellectuals, social workers, radicals and revolutionaries, bohemians—have in common a rejection of the Christian ethos, particularly the implication and necessary consequences of the doctrine of Original Sin. They admire and sometimes even envy the Jew's freedom from any sense of sin or guilt. It is therapeutic to them to associate with Jews and thus escape their own deeply ingrained sense of sin. To drink wine with people who have never been taught to regard alcohol as an evil, to smoke with people who have never dreamed it could be considered immoral, to tell risqué stories with people who do not have to overcome a feeling of shame at the thought of sex—these are exhilarating experiences to the rebel against puritanical restrictions. A great freedom pervades the companionship of non-Jews of this class with Jews. The Jew, assured of sympathy, is at his best; so is the non-Jew, basking in the warmth of a sinless culture. The Jew rarely knows how atypical is the non-Jew with whom he has such close ties. He is often himself deceived as to the relative importance, numerically speaking, of Gentiles of this type. He thinks that at least he personally has solved the millenial problem of Jew-Gentile relationships. It is not he, however, but the non-Jew, who has made the adjustment. The non-Jew has surrendered the core of his Christian background. He has, in a certain very restricted sense, become a Jew."[176]

Rabbi Bamberger tells of his encounters with women who became converts to Judaism through their natural affinity for Jewishness. "One of the most devout Jewesses I know, who is literally venerated in the Jewish community where she lives, is such a person. She had always associated with Jews before she met her husband, just as she continues to do, though he and all his family are long dead."[177]

Bamberger tells of "a young women who had suffered from social contempt in the small town where she was born because she admitted to liking serious books and good music. She fled to a larger city nearby, and found congenial companionship among the young Jews in that city. That she should eventually marry a Jew and adopt Judaism was a normal development."[178]

"Not infrequently," Bamberger reflects, "the quest is more

specifically a spiritual one. There are individuals who feel alien to the Christian outlook, and seek another haven. Occasionally they discover Judaism, but they have almost to storm the walls . . ."[179] (The rabbi appeals to Jews to adopt a more benign attitude toward converts to Judaism.) [180]

Rabbi Eichorn conducted a survey on intermarriage trends throughout America, and learned of a Gentile couple "who fully identified themselves with [a certain reform] Temple, although they are not converts. They are listed as honorary members. They participate in all Jewish activities."

The Gentile as a minority. While Jews constitute a small minority of the general population of the United States, they are "spuriously conspicuous," as Dean has shown,[181] and in some avant-gard or intellectual circles, the Jews may be a prominent if not the dominant group. (In some graduate schools, half the students may be Jews. In professional schools which maintain restrictive practices, the few who are accepted may stand out as an elite group.) Rabbi Rubenstein estimated that one-third of the women he counseled for conversion had already received their Ph.D.'s.[182] Chandler Brossard avers that in New York City intellectual circles the minority group is the Gentile group; the Gentile intellectual is the new "Alienated Man."[183]

The Jewish intellectual's capability for handling his alienation from the majority sometimes "arouses envy among non-Jewish intellectuals. . . . A number of them have on occasion complained to me," comments Rabbi Rubenstein, "that they did not really feel 'in the swing' because they were not Jewish. One former Unitarian minister who had married a Jewish girl was emphatic in expressing this feeling. He said that something inside of him had always wanted to become Jewish but that he had at least settled for marrying a Jewish girl. In this instance, there was no conversion."[184]

The Gentile looks at Jewishness. Several writers have pointed to the special appeal that the Jewish culture holds for Gentiles, and for Gentile women in particular—since a matricentric[185] tradition gives women a privileged status in Jewish life, and trains its sons to be "wonderful husbands," i.e., to recognize and abide by the matricentric tradition. Rabbi Rubenstein sees even more in the appeal of a Jewish husband to the "emancipated" Gentile college woman. In her contact with Jews she discovers that she need not limit herself to the painful choice of an unimaginative Babbitt or an irresponsible Bohemian. The Jewish cultural style seems to combine the best of both worlds: political liberalism, intellectual and aesthetic avant-gardism, a middle-class sobriety without asceticism, and feeling of family solidarity. Marriage to a Jew offers a special resolution of the conflict over whether to get out of middle-class society or stay in it. In a sense the position of the Jew is both in and out, and "it is precisely this delicate balance between acceptance and marginality"[186] which appeals to certain "emancipated" women.

To men and women alike, if they have become disenchanted with their Gentile milieu, the non-dogmatic, worldly quality of the Jewish religion, the non-puritanical attitude toward the pleasures of life, the creative use of alienation, the strong and intimate bonds of kinship, the adherence to middle-class values of education and social advancement, augment the appeal of Jewish group membership—and intermarriage has become the natural mode of entry into the Jewish group.

Mary Ruth

"[Like Ruth] I chose to come as a stranger to the people of Israel. Here I have found a home, a people and a way of life which I cherish. Being a Jew by choice . . . I have no secret doubts about my heritage . . . no regrets about what I am or must be; what I have I sought, I examined, I accepted; I took it to myself as mine, my faith.

"My childhood religion had been an every-Sunday-morning Sunday School kind of experience, with hours spent in choir practice, youth groups, roller skating, potluck suppers and all the other frostings of a highly organized congregation. . . .[But] there was no real religious significance to my Christian affilia- tion. I could not honestly say 'I believe,' 'I have faith,' as one is supposed to do.

"My search for an acceptable answer led me to a university course in comparative religions, where I was greatly impressed by

Judaism, the universality of its concepts, its rich roots which nourished so many later religions, its incomparable ethical standards. I felt drawn to it.

". . . Love for a man played its part in my final decision. I was in love with a wonderful Jew. His fine qualities, the result of a goodly Jewish heritage, exemplified in reality what the university course had revealed in theory.

"I spent a summer vacation in the mountains with my parents, reading and studying about Judaism, wondering, marvelling, rejoicing. My parents were great admirers of my husband-to-be, read and learned about Judaism with me. When I had made up my mind to convert, my father and mother said to me, 'If these are the principles and mores which you accept . . . take them openly and with pride. If there is genuine conviction, you cannot fail to be a credit both to us and to the faith of Israel.' . . .

"I came to Israel because of

the simplicity of its affirmations concerning God and man . . .

. . . Judaism's concern for social justice, communal improvement, the desire to help others in time of need;

. . . the meaningful family rituals and prayers, the inner security of being a people as well as a religion;

. . . the intellectual atmosphere of the Synagogue . . . the freedom of thought, the latitude with regard to creed . . .

the spirit of optimism, that life right here and now is blessed and good and that . . . one's rewards are in and of this life, attitudes particularly significant to one who has been reared in a creed which negates the goodness and blessedness of the here-and-now.

"Through my study and interest in Temple affairs, my husband found his own Judaism more meaningful than ever before. This dedication reached the point where [he] decided to devote himself professionally to the cause of Reform Judaism. . . .

"I am teaching in a public school on Long Island where they have hired Jewish teachers only within the past few years. I take pride in being recognized and respected as a representative of our faith and in the opportunity I have to help develop better understanding between Jew and non-Jew."[187]

Warren

An unusual feature in the case of Warren is the unexpected advice of his prospective in-laws that he *not* convert to Judaism. This should serve to remind us of the diversity of human nature, against which the formulators of principles must always contend. In other ways, however, Warren's experience describes motivations toward intermarriage which will be discussed in the next few chapters of this book.

Warren is an army veteran, age twenty-seven, and married four years. He is the middle child in a family of five children. The atmosphere of his upbringing was shaped by his mother's Protestant Fundamentalism and his father's physical punitiveness. The family was raised in an atmosphere of poverty although Father held a supervisory job at a large manufacturing plant.

Through his religious indoctrination, Warren was taught to abhor the "worldly pleasures." Dancing, going to the movies, or playing baseball on Sunday were labelled "the devil's work." Mother was the active promoter of this Fundamentalist creed, and Father quietly supported her rules and regulations, but each of the children in turn rebelled.

As Warren grew into adolescence, his parents' marriage relationship became openly hostile. For two years they occupied separate bedrooms and mother talked of divorce. Since divorce on grounds other than adultery was forbidden by his mother's church, Warren took his mother's failure to abide by her own principles as an opportunity to rebel openly against the harsh creed he had been brought up by—and against the smugness, arrogance, and hypocricy he saw in its practitioners. Warren felt particularly embarrassed over the racial prejudice fostered by the church—which described the Negro as the son of Ham, forever cursed by God. He likewise felt uncomfortable over his father's open hatred for Catholics and Jews, and his proclivity for blaming all the world's woes on "those damn Jews."

Warren's parents divorced at a time when he was ready for college. He took a room with a friend and attended a city college where he was a serious student majoring in mathematics. For the first time in his life, he made Jewish friends. He liked their outlook on life: they enjoyed learning, they enjoyed the good things of life in moderation, and they made no effort to force their beliefs on him. Invited into Jewish homes, it seemed to Warren that these people knew how to live. Warren was curious to learn more about Judaism. Having alienated himself from radical Protestantism, he had promised himself that he would learn something about a variety of other religious creeds.

During his sophomore year he met Carol, the daughter of a Jewish insurance man, and they felt strongly attracted to each other. Carol was an only child, and seemed to have a strongly competitive and somewhat hostile relationship with her mother. Carol felt that her mother overburdened Carol with housework, and when they quarreled, Mother threatened to tell Father "and that would be bad for his heart." Carol confided to Warren that she had always dreamed of marrying a man who was tall, thin and blond—like Warren. (Carol's father is short, stocky, and dark.)

Warren reflected to his counselor that he had gotten serious with girls before, and always changed his mind before it was too late. Carol was the first girl who was so frankly eager to get married, though she was only eighteen. Perhaps it was to give Carol a chance to grow up that Warren decided to interrupt his studies and "get his military obligation over with." While he was still in basic training, Carol thought they ought to get married right away, so that they could be together during his military enlistment. Warren really liked her, got along well with her parents, and so getting married now seemed like a good idea.

He took the initiative to visit the Jewish chaplain on his base, to learn something about the Jewish religion and prepare himself for marrying into a Jewish family. When Carol's parents learned of this move, they—surprisingly to Warren—advised him to stay away from the chaplain. Her parents were particularly unhappy about the fact that the chaplain was Orthodox, and they apparently feared that he would indoctrinate Warren into practices that Carol's family had long abandoned. Except for High Holy Day services, her parents were quite unobservant, and neither did they maintain close ties with their extended families. They therefore planned no wedding, encouraged Warren and Carol to be married by a judge and thereby bypass the question of conversion to Judaism.

Warren's contact with a counselor was occasioned by marriage difficulties which erupted in the fourth year of their marriage when he was back in college. But he assured the counselor that he gets along fine with his in-laws.

2

Characteristics of Persons
Who Intermarry;
Empirical Findings and Hypotheses

Because most of what counselors know about intermarriage
is based on the observation of persons who seek clinical help,
it is all too easy to regard intermarriage *per se* as a psychological
problem, as the symptom of emotional disturbance[1] or as a
manifestation of social disorganization. As an antidote to this
clinical bias, several investigators [A. I. Gordon (1964), Heiss,
Levinson and Levinson, J. E. Mayer] have surveyed, interviewed,
and tested non-clinical cases of intermarriage; i.e., couples who
had not sought, nor presumably felt a need for, counseling help.
What are these people like, compared with persons who enter
into endogamous marriage? Where do they come from? How
were they brought up? In what ways does their marriage choice
relate to the regularities of their social environment, or to the
accidents of their individual experience? How is intermarriage
related to their values and life goals?

Community size and structure. Mayer offers documentation to
support the principle that "the smaller an ethnic, religious, or
racial group, relative to the surrounding population, the greater

will be the proportion of the subgroup members who contract marriages with outsiders. . . . A relationship of this type has been observed to hold for different racial groups in Hawaii, for Protestants and Catholics who live in Switzerland—and whose relative numbers vary from one canton to the next—and for Jews whose proportionate numbers vary within the provinces of Canada and within the republics of the Soviet Union."[2]

Rossman observed at first hand the qualitative changes that occur in the life of a Jewish minority group as its numbers increase. Reporting on the evolution of social life in a New England suburb, she recalls that "at first, the Jews all felt a community spirit with common participation, but as more Jews came, they tended to divide among themselves, geographically and economically. Jewish life has developed parallel to the rest of the community and not as an integral part of it."[3] As a group becomes large enough to evolve its own community life, endogamous marriages would seem to be encouraged by both the increase in numbers and the cohesiveness of group life.

In Iowa, Jews living in rural areas are twice as likely to intermarry[4] as Jews living in cities of 10,000 and over, as Table 2:1 illustrates.

Table 2:1. Jewish marriages by size of place of marriage, Iowa, 1953–59[5]

	(Total N)	Inmarriages		Intermarriages	
		(N)	per cent	(N)	per cent
Rural Areas	100	(33)	33.0	(67)	67.0
Towns 2,500 to 9,999	53	(14)	35.9	(39)	64.1
Cities 10,000 and over	523	(344)	65.8	(179)	34.2

In the various geographical regions of the United States, the incidence of Catholic versus non-Catholic marriages likewise varies inversely with the relative size of the Catholic community. (Table 2:2 is taken from a study by Locke et al.)

As Cahnman points out, "Canada is the only country in the English-speaking world where detailed and reliable statistical information about the Jewish population and its demographic characteristics is available."[8] A close study of intermarriage rates in Canada shows a consistent patterning, with differences attributable to known characteristics of the various provinces.

Table 2:2. Regional Density of Catholic Population, and Frequency of Interfaith Marriages[6]

Region of U.S.	Percentage of Catholics to total population	Percentage of Interfaith Marriages
New England	47	22
Middle Atlantic	33	24
North East Central	25	26
Mountain	21	29
Pacific	20	34
West South Central	18	23[7]
West North Central	18	30
South Atlantic	5	50
East South Central	4	47

The perennial low intermarriage rate in Quebec has been attributed to several factors: (1) the concentration of Jews in metropolitan Montreal, which contains 40.4 percent of the total Jewish population in Canada, and 98.1 percent of all Jews in the province of Quebec; (2) the language barrier between Jews and Gentiles (French is the language of the overwhelming majority of non-Jewish Quebec; the vast majority of Jews in Quebec speak English or Yiddish) ; (3) a Catholic majority, less amenable to intermarriage than Protestants; (4) segregation of Catholics from Protestants and Jews in the Quebec school system; in some districts the majority of children attending "Protestant" schools are Jewish![9]

In Ontario and Manitoba the Jewish population is likewise concentrated in the capital cities (Winnipeg counting 96.9 percent, and Toronto 81.1 percent of the total Jewish population in the respective provinces) , but children attend non-denominational public schools, and the provinces have a larger Protestant population. The intermarriage rate is about twice the prevailing rate in Quebec.

In the prairie provinces of Saskatchewan and Alberta, more than 40 percent of the total Jewish population live in towns and villages of less than 100 persons, a dispersal which limits Jewish comunity life and is reflected in a significantly higher intermarriage rate.

In the Atlantic provinces of Nova Scotia, New Brunswick, and

Newfoundland dispersion of the Jewish population is greater and so is the intermarriage rate. Halifax, the largest Jewish settlement in this area, comprises only 32 percent of Jews in the Atlantic provinces.

British Columbia's Jews are heavily concentrated in Vancouver (7,374 in 1960, 93.4 percent of all Jews in that province); nonetheless it has the highest intermarriage rate in all Canada. Its social ties are closer to Seattle, Portland, and San Francisco than to the distant Jewish communities of Winnipeg, Toronto, and Montreal. More significantly, perhaps, is the relatively recent origin of the Vancouver Jewish community, which grew from 205 persons in 1901 to 1,370 in 1921 to 7,374 in 1960. This rapid and recent growth suggests a relative absence of traditional Jewish institutions, including the extended family.

Orthodox Jews are less mobile than Reform or secular Jews; hence a relatively *new* Jewish community is likely to be dominated by those who are most amenable to intermarriage: the Reform and secular.[11]

Although Jews from rural areas and small towns will tend to intermarry more frequently than Jews who live in cities, the relationship is by no means direct and linear. The mobility and anonymity of urban life favor intermarriage, while the conservatism and lack of privacy in a small town can strongly inhibit deviation from the community norm. Small towns differ considerably both in their norms and in their cohesiveness. Rabbi Isaac Trainin recalls the observation of a friend on a highly cohesive small town community:

> I come from a small community. If a Jewish boy dates a Gentile, most Jewish families will have nothing to do with him. So some of us boys have to be very careful. In other words, there seems to be a great deal of social control in small communities where people know each other. In a big city . . . you can live on the same block for 30 years and not know the people on your block at all. You can live in the same apartment [building] for a very long time and have a nodding acquaintance with your next-door neighbor, but this is as far as you go. This, of course, prevents strong social ties from arising and makes social control difficult.[12]

Table 2:3. Number and Percentage of Intermarriages Among Jewish Men in Canada and its Provinces in Each of the Five-Year Periods from 1926 to 1960[10]

PROVINCES

Period	Quebec		Ontario		Manitoba		Saskatchewan and Alberta		Atlantic Provinces		British Columbia		TOTAL All Canada	
	(N)	%	(N)	%	(N)	%	(N)	%	(N)	%	(N)	%	(N)	%
1926-30	(63)	2.4	(102)	3.5	(26)	3.6	(22)	8.2	(18)	17.1	(19)	19.4	(250)	3.7
1931-35	(59)	1.9	(97)	3.0	(32)	3.9	(29)	13.6	(06)	7.1	(14)	14.9	(237)	3.2
1936-40	(84)	2.3	(159)	4.5	(48)	4.4	(37)	11.4	(12)	8.2	(46)	28.2	(386)	4.3
1941-45	(112)	2.9	(265)	6.5	(66)	6.9	(65)	21.1	(52)	27.2	(64)	25.3	(624)	6.6
1946-50	(166)	3.7	(290)	6.5	(84)	7.7	(63)	17.3	(16)	12.3	(92)	28.8	(711)	6.6
1951-55	(147)	3.9	(392)	10.0	(78)	9.0	(59)	20.2	(24)	20.7	(83)	28.3	(783)	8.5
1956-60	(192)	5.6	(405)	11.7	(58)	9.1	(66)	34.8	(25)	25.8	(82)	32.2	(828)	10.0

A small town which maintains a rather different norm is described by Sidney I. Goldstein. In this 60-family Jewish community, located in the Deep South, about one-fourth of the families (or 16 in number) are headed by a Jewish father and a Protestant mother who retains her Gentile identity. In four of these families, children attend the town's Jewish religious school, operated by a Reform congregation. In ten of these 16 families, children go to some Protestant Sunday School, Father holds membership in the Reform congregation, and Mother participates in Temple activities on occasion.[13]

Rabbi Levinger documents a similar pattern of adaptation in a group of Jewish cousins who had settled in various small towns in the West:

> About twenty years ago I attended a family reunion with a group of my father's cousins in a little town in the Middle West where I had lived as a child. The sons of a large family had come back from their widely scattered homes: Sam from his farm in Nebraska, Ludwig from the Black Hills, William from his clothing store in a small Iowa city. Even Frank had turned up, all the way from Texas, wearing a ten-gallon hat and wielding a cigarette-holder almost a foot long.
>
> In the whole *mishpocho,* the only Jewish wife, besides my own, was Emil's—he kept a delicatessen store in St. Louis. The children of these mixed marriages were Lutherans, Methodists, Christian Scientists [or Catholics], according to the churches of their mothers.[14]

Kramer and Leventman conclude their study of North City's Jewish community by observing that it is large enough to maintain a well-organized Jewish group, but—unlike the leading cities of the United States—North City is *"not* large enough to allow many to escape the network of institutional affiliation"; not large enough to tolerate the intellectual, the innovator, the skeptic. It is therefore not a *Jewish* community in the fullest sense of the term. Big city Jews "can afford to take their identity for granted. These Jews do not have to hedge their commitment around a battery of clubs and organizations; their number alone safeguards their survival against the threat of the recalcitrant Jew."[15]

Slotkin cites a case (whom we shall call *Ezra*) in which intermarriage is attributed to geographic isolation. The respondent was the son of a *Hasid,* grew up in a Jewish village in Russia where he attended a *yeshiva.*

Ezra

I came to this country alone and went to a town in Indiana. There were very few Jews there and I had to mix with the outside, with all sorts of people. I felt lost, and went through a severe psychological crisis. My old ideas were turned topsy-turvy and I couldn't find myself. I was a studious boy, so the only thing I did was spend a lot of time in the library. It was in this way that I made my friends, including my wife, who was a librarian there. The people in the library were friendly and became interested in me; they invited me to their homes and introduced me to people.[16]

College attendance and intermarriage. Gordon regards it as inevitable that college life favors intermarriage, and Rubenstein expresses the same point of view:

There will always be a correlation between intermarriage and college life. People of varying faiths are thrown together in greater intimacy and with greater persistence at the college level than at most other periods of their lives. One need only contrast the relative social isolation of religious groups which characterizes adult American social life with the more open social possibilities of university life to realize this.[17]

Rubenstein notes further that the graduate school situation especially predisposes to intermarriage. "The proportion of Jews in the better graduate schools . . . reaches as high as 50 per cent of the total enrollment. . . . This means that a Gentile who reaches graduate school is far more likely to meet Jews sharing his vocational and intellectual interests than at college or high school level." The woman graduate student who wants to get married is likely to consider a difference in religious background a smaller risk than to marry a man of lesser educational achievement or intellectual ability. "A lonely graduate student from a small town in her mid or late twenties is rarely going to be stopped from marrying an available and willing man because he is Jewish. . . . The concentration of Jews in intellectual and professional fields thus very frequently throws them together with non-Jewish women [e.g., Jewish doctors and Gentile nurses] for whom their availability and attainments more than compensate for their lack of in-group social status."[18]

College students from smaller towns are apparently more amenable to cross-ethnic dating than New Yorkers. Shanks studied the dating practices of 536 Jewish students attending Columbia University and Barnard College, dividing the group between those who came from "small towns" (population under 500,000) and those who came from "large towns." (The latter group consisted mainly of native New Yorkers.) At the freshman level, 62 per cent of "small towners" had dated a Gentile within the past six months, compared with 32 per cent of the large towners. Twenty-one percent of small towners had gone steady with non-Jews, compared with only four per cent of large towners.

With each additional year of college attendance, however, the difference in rate of cross-ethnic dating decreases, small town Jews and large towners tending to converge upon a common norm. Although Shanks makes the generalization that small towners increasingly conform to the customs of the large towners, his figures (see Table 2:4) show that more seniors hold a favorable attitude toward intermarriage, fewer seniors say they are opposed to intermarriage, and more seniors have dated a Gentile girl within the last six months, compared with freshmen:

Table 2:4. Attitudes Toward Intermarriage and Cross-Ethnic Dating Practices; A Comparison of Jewish Freshmen and Seniors at Columbia and Barnard[19]

| | Per cent | |
	Freshmen	Seniors
Favor intermarriage	29	46
Opposed to intermarriage	26	12
Have dated a Gentile within last six months*	34	56

*Males only

Shanks' respondents seem to be guided by the rule "dating yes, marriage no." Eighty-four per cent claim to have at least one close Gentile friend, yet only nine per cent "have entered a serious relationship with a non-Jew."[20] If marriage rate varies with rate of cross-ethnic dating and "going steady," Shanks' findings would indicate that the intermarriage rate is even smaller in large communities than the known rates in smaller communities in the United States, a phenomenon which runs counter to "all sociologists' generalizations concerning the close relationship between acculturation . . . and intermarriage," says Shanks.[21]

Arthur A. Cohen has suggested that the Jewish college student's identity is challenged not only by the Gentile social groups he finds access to on campus, but by a sometimes overwhelming realization "that Western culture is a Christian culture, that Western values are rooted in the Greek and Christian tradition. [The college student] may hear such phrases as 'Judaeo-Christian tradition' or 'the Hebraic element in Western culture,' but he cannot be deluded into thinking that this is more than a casual compliment."[22]

Marginality of membership to church, family and ethnic group. Probably the largest sample of intermarried persons ever studied is the "Midtown Manhattan" group, which included 1,167 persons of Catholic, Protestant, and Jewish background (and a control group of endogamous respondents) selected by area-probability sampling methods. Heiss addressed himself to the question: What are the characteristics of family and religious experience which reduce the normal barriers to intermarriage? Interview data support a general conclusion that persons who intermarry report loose and less consistent ties to family and church, but a close inspection of his results show that inter-married Catholics and intermarried Jews made systematically *different* contributions to this general conclusion!

Intermarried Catholics, compared with the Catholic control group, grew up with loose or inconsistent *church* affiliations (e.g., religion not at all important to both parents, argued with parents over religion, did not attend parochial school). Intermarried Jews, on the other hand, grew up with tenuous *family* ties (e.g., "did not live with real parents up until age of 16," "grandparents did not live with them," "saw none of their relatives"). Inter-married Catholics recalled "strifeful family interactions" when young (e.g., parents quarrelled often, argued with parents over religion).[23]

While Jews are popularly defined as a religious group, comparable to Catholics and Protestants, Heiss' findings offer a corrective to this misconception—showing that while loyalty to church is critical to the maintenance of a Catholic identity, it is loyalty to an *extended family* which is critical to the maintenance of a Jewish identity.

Corroborating the above evidence are the findings of Maier and Spinrad, who surveyed 156 students at a large urban state university on their religious beliefs and practices. On the question, "To whom do you owe your greatest loyalty?" results were reported as shown in Table 2:5.

Table 2:5. Group Differences in Response to Question: "To whom do you owe your greatest loyalty?"[24]

	Catholics	Protestants	Jews
To God	74%	49%	11%
To family	24	39	74
To people	0	2	8
To government	0	5	5
No answer	2	5	2

The findings of Maier and Spinrad tell us that Jewishness is experienced as a feeling of family loyalty, and illuminate Heiss' finding that intermarriage is most characteristic of Jews whose conditions of upbringing did not favor strong emotional attachments to their extended family; i.e., they never acquired a feeling of *mishpocho*.

Is it possible to conceive of a Jewish upbringing without an extended family? Jessie Bernard quotes from an anonymous autobiography, to describe the significant role of the grandmother in a three-generation Jewish family:

> My grandmother, a cheerful, industrious, pious soul who had a blessing or a prayer for every event in the day, was the real mistress of our household, and we children recognized her as such. It was to her we applied for permission to do this or that; it was to her we came for moral guidance: was this a sin? or that a blessing? And it was she who disciplined us. She helped with the housework and did the cooking. It was

she who set the Jewish stamp upon our home. She said a prayer as she washed her face and hands in the morning. She said a prayer before and after every meal. She sent us off to school with a blessing. There was a blessing when we wore new clothes for the first time. She had a prayer or a blessing for almost everything in fact. We children took it as a matter of course that she would be muttering prayers and blessings over us all the time. She was a much more important person than our mother.[25]

Levinson and Levinson conducted an in-depth interview study of 16 Jews who were married to Protestants, obtaining their sample through informal inquiry of rabbis and other members of the community. They were impressed to discover that most of their cases (12 out of 16) had been " 'marginal' members of the Jewish community long before intermarriage." Interview and projective test material describe the majority of these marginal Jews as "relatively mature and able to function effectively in various life tasks. . . . The decision to marry was not an occasion of great anxiety or stress." Their marriage partners "were similar or complementary in values, life goals and personality." Intermarriage seems not to have occurred by chance, but as an attempt to achieve "a broader, more pluralistic [social] identity," perhaps to replace a weakened Jewish religio-ethnic identity.[26]

The Levinsons encountered acculturated Jewish families in which intermarriage had become a family tradition. Four members of their sample of five intermarrying Jewish women had older brothers, and in three cases these older brothers had intermarried prior to their sisters' marriage.

An earlier study by Slotkin reporting survey data on 183 cases of Jewish-Gentile intermarriage in Chicago (1937–38) estimates that about one-half of the Jewish members of his sample could be described as "emancipated" (a term the Levinsons also employ to describe their marginal majority), having "lost those traits which tend to prevent intermarriage."

Whether one chooses to call Jews without Jewishness "emancipated," "acculturated," "assimilated," separated or estranged from their tradition, this characteristic also shows up in Rosenthal's study of third generation Jews of Washington, D.C. Of those who claimed some religious education, 16.4 percent were intermarried; among those who claimed *no* religious education 30.3 percent were intermarried.[27]

The intermarriage sex-bias. Much of the data on Jewish-Gentile intermarriage deal with Jewish husbands and Gentile wives. In the Levinsons' sample of 16 Jewish-Gentile couples, the husband was Jewish in 11 cases. In Mayer's sample of 45 intermarried couples, the husband was Jewish in 33 cases. According to Mayer, "statistics from different parts of the world consistently reveal that intermarriages of [this] type are more common."[28]

The preponderance of Jewish husband, Gentile wife intermarriages parallels the observed sex-bias of Negro-white intermarriages, and marriages between German Jews and Eastern European Jews;[29] in each case the husband is a member of the underprivileged group. His culturally defined sex-role permits him to offset his ethnic disadvantage with the musculine advantage of taking the initiative in choosing and pursuing the mate of his liking, accepting obstacles and rebuffs as a test of his ardor. (Merton has developed a "trading hypothesis" to account for the sex-bias of Negro-white marriages. We shall make use of his formulations later in this chapter.)

A popular notion that Jewish men are "forced" to intermarry because of local shortages of Jewish women is not supported by the facts, where demographic figures are available. Rosenberg points out that "the intermarriage rate was higher among Jewish men in Manitoba, with a sex ratio in 1951 of 993 males per 1,000 females, than in Quebec and Ontario with a sex ratio of 1,023 males per 1,000 females."[30]

In a society in which exogamy is strongly discouraged, the taboo is more likely to be violated by males, whose sex role designates a greater degree of independence and aggressiveness. The Jewish daughter, on the other hand, would seem to be more vulnerable to threats of ostracism.

Age and intermarriage. According to Heiss, Jews who intermarry do so at a later age than Jews who marry within their group. (This difference did *not* obtain for intermarried Protestants and Catholics compared with endogamous control groups.) In Mayer's total sample the median age of husbands at the time of marriage was twenty-six, the median age of wives was twenty-three.[31] This statistic underscores the Jew's reluctance to intermarry. After a certain number of marriageable years have passed and a Jew has been unable to find a Jewish mate, the intermarriage taboo apparently loses some of its force.

Mayer describes a Jewish woman who was in her middle thirties when she met her husband, referring to this women as one of several in his sample of intermarrieds who were probably not dating other men at the time they met their husband. In Mayer's judgment they "would not be rated very desirable as dates and [their] chances of getting married at all were probably rather limited."[32] Similarly, Mayer refers to several cases in which Jewish men had reached an age at which intermarriage seemed more permissible either in their own eyes or in the judgment of their parents:

"[Jewish son:] I felt who I was going out with was none of my mother's business. I was twenty-six years old at the time."[33]

"[Jewish son:] When I was going with a Gentile before the service, my mother had a fit. She was glad I ceased and desisted. When I got out of the service, she wanted me to get married. She was very anxious about it. Slowly but surely all my friends were getting married, and it annoyed her no end. First I told her I was going with a girl, and then I told her she was non-Jewish. Surprisingly, she wasn't shocked or upset. I think there were two reasons for this. First of all, she was confined to the hospital and was very ill. She was unhappy about this situation both for herself and for me. Aside from this, she was anxious for me to get married, anxious for someone to take care of me."[34]

Previous marriage experience. According to Heiss, persons of Catholic background who intermarry are more likely to have been previously married than are endogamously married Catholics. Presuming that most of these persons were divorced rather than widowed, it would be fair to say that these intermarrieds are likely to turn to intermarriage after they have been through an unsuccessful Catholic marriage and are barred from taking another Catholic mate. Here again we see intermarriage defined by practice as a *faute de mieux* partnership.

Birth order and intermarriage. Heiss reports that "in all of the religious groups those persons who were the youngest in their family have the highest intermarriage rates." Only children are the next highest, and eldest children have the lowest rate of intermarriage.[35] The writings of Alfred Adler and his followers offer some interesting observations on personality characteristics of eldest and youngest children, and how they emerge from their respective positions in the family.

The eldest child begins life as an only child, the unchallenged object of mother's affection and attention. With the birth of a younger sibling this chapter of life experience is closed, and the first-born's fight to regain the center of the stage usually evokes from mother reactions of annoyance, impatience, and further withdrawal of love. This leads the first-born to turn to his father for affection and attention. Whether he does this as a reproach against mother, as Adler suggests,[36] or simply to reach out to a more available source of emotional support, this seems to build the foundation for the conservative, responsible, adult-oriented personality that characterizes the eldest child.

A longitudinal multidiscipline study of 209 Harvard students agrees with Adler on the personality traits of the eldest child, *least* likely (according to Heiss) to intermarry. About a dozen years after the Harvard study was begun, Margaret Lantis interviewed the subjects in their homes, and offered the following composite sketch:

"The eldest child is adult-oriented. He is more likely to be serious, sensitive (that is, his feelings are hurt easily and he doesn't need much punishment), conscientious, 'good,' fond of books, or fond of doing things with adults.

"He may be either a mama's child and shy, even fearful, or he may be self-reliant, independent, and undemonstrative. These may be alternative expressions of the adult orientation. In one case the child has to keep close to an adult and be directed by him or her. In the other case, he imitates the adult and becomes a small facsimile of one."[37]

On the theoretical side, Adler supposes that the eldest child's conservatism is the expression of nostalgia for "the bygone time when he was the center of attention."[38] Perhaps it develops as the older child finds that he can win back a portion of mother's love by serving as a good example, by siding with adult authority.[39] Perhaps his conservatism is based more directly on his identification with Father, to whom he was drawn as a reaction to Mother's rebuff. Either of these three motivational tendencies would seem to predispose the eldest child to a conservative, conventional marriage choice.

A laboratory study by Schachter demonstrated that under experimentally induced conditions of threat, first-born children are more likely to group together rather than suffer alone. This expression of "social feeling" fits Adler's description of the first-born child.

Why is the youngest child most likely to intermarry? The youngest, Adler emphasizes, occupies an "exceptional" position in the family; pampered, doted upon by parents and siblings, this treatment leads to two contradictory personality tendencies. Being the center of attention fosters a certain bravado, ambition, and egocentrism. On the other hand, because he grows up in an environment where everyone is older, stronger, and more experienced, the youngest child suffers from feelings of inferiority. "He loses his courage to succeed by his own effort. Youngest children," says Adler, "are always ambitious. . . ." Even those who are lazy are ambitious, says Adler—for laziness is "a sign of ambition joined with discouragement."[40]

The exceptions. It is commonly supposed that actors, musicians, writers, and other artists take special pleasure in being mildly unconventional, indulging in minor law-breaking, and otherwise behaving as if they were "exceptions" to the ordinary run of mankind. It is commonly supposed that artists and celebrities also intermarry more often than the general population, and Lehrman observes that in this regard also they are playing the role of "exceptions."

"The exception" is a psychoanalytic character type who uses the memory of some traumatic early experience to justify his refusal to accept ordinary social responsibilities, or the social role to which he would normally be assigned.[41] Lehrman claims that *all* of 30 patients he has seen, who were or had been intermarried, showed a marked resemblance to this character type.[42] Lehrman describes a patient (whom we shall call Gwen) whose physical attractiveness and family history marked her as an "exception":

Gwen

Growing up in a family of many older brothers figures prominently in the life story of Gwen, and in her preference for cross-ethnic love objects. Gwen was the youngest member of a large Protestant family; she was also the prettier of two girls, and her father's favorite. "Sometime prior to puberty she and a two-years older brother had engaged in sex play leading to [intercourse] and attended with enormous feelings of guilt. When her father died she wondered if her sexual crimes had killed him. During adolescence she fought against temptation to masturbate, by working hard at cultural and intellectual pursuits." (Perhaps masturbation reactivated her feelings of guilt over transgression of the incest taboo.)

Her older brothers' concern over preserving their pretty, young sister's chastity expressed itself in a harsh, forbidding attitude. For dating, Gwen said, "she felt more comfortable with Jewish boys. They were warm and kind like her father, not harsh and forbidding like her brothers and her mother." Gwen had a sexual adventure with "a Catholic man whom she didn't love, [then] fell in love with a Jewish man who later became her husband."

She came for treatment at age thirty-three because of "unhappiness," frigidity, and obsessions with suicide, which analytic experience related to her disappointment that both her children were girls. (She had apparently invested much hope in resolving her penis envy by giving birth to a male child.) Gwen developed an intensely erotic attachment to her Jewish psychiatrist, as she had with a previous psychiatrist who was also a Jew. Analysis of the transference enabled her to gain understanding and relief. "Her frigidity was relieved, her relations with her husband and children improved and treatment was discontinued."

Gwen returned to her analyst about a year and a half later because her old symptoms had recurred, and she vaguely recognized that there was something neurotic about her having engaged in an affair with a Negro.[43]

Cross-sex siblings. Does growing up with many brothers, as Gwen did, predispose a girl to seek an "outsider" for a husband? The Levinsons unexpectedly discovered " a marked tendency for [intermarried] women to have adjacent brothers, and for the men to have adjacent sisters. Four of the five women in their study have brothers only. . . . Of their 11 male subjects, four have sisters only, and three others have a sister as an adjacent sibling." The Levinsons conclude that "some of the men who had solely female siblings developed the feeling of being surrounded and smothered by women. . . . It contributed to a generalized image of 'the Jewish woman' as nagging, controlling and devaluating."[44] It is also possible that growing up with an adjacent sibling of the opposite sex leads to a somewhat more severely inculcated incest taboo, for an adjacent sibling is ordinarily more available for sex play than the cross-parent.

SOCIAL MOBILITY AND INTERMARRIAGE

Upward mobility. Gordon alludes to the use of intermarriage as an instrument for upward mobility, portraying in hypothetical terms the person "moved by ambition more than by love," who may perhaps unconsciously seek out a mate of aristocratic New England lineage. Mayer records his interview with an intermarried Jew who candidly reflects that his marriage into a socially prominent Protestant family had its origins in his admiration for the aristocratic way of life, acquired during his year as an exchange student in Spain. (We shall name the respondent Milton. He was raised in a Jewish neighborhood by Orthodox Jewish immigrant parents.)

Milton

In Spain I lived with a noble family. . . . I admired their way of life and loved it. [*What appealed to you about their way of life?*] It was an accumulation of small things, although it might be subsumed under a few general headings. There was the proper way that people invite you to their home; there was the attitude toward guests when they were in the home; there was the respect that parents and children showed for each other. These were just instances of some of the things that appealed to me. Their whole way of life was different— everything from sending you a thank-you note for a present to knowing when to rise when a lady came into the room. All this may seem terribly superficial to you and give you an awful

sense of my values—but I do feel that proper form is important
and it does make life more pleasant. . . . In view of my liking
for this type of life and the setting of my life at Princeton
[where he felt "all the time" that "being born Jewish was a
burden"]—it was perfectly logical that I should marry my
wife. My wife is at the top of the social ladder; her parents
are among the elite.

Before I met my wife, I never thought much about mixed
marriages, but I guess I had the feelings in my bones that I
would not marry a Jewish girl. . . . Looking back, I may have
been trying to avoid Jewish girls. There was just something
about them that I did not like—it was probably a kind of
subconscious feeling I had. [*What didn't you like about them?*]
It's hard to say. The ones I met were not brought up with a
proper sense of values—they were overmaterialistic, I just didn't
think they behaved properly, they didn't have any manners.
Frankly, I was embarrassed when I was in their company.[45]

Sherman considers it an "established fact that in a mixed marriage the Jew does not gain social status and the non-Jew loses it
. . ."[46] It is difficult to imagine that a serious observer of Jewish life
would so casually dismiss such a rich and complex aspect of intermarriage motivation. Of the Levinsons' five intermarrying
Jewish women, *all* "married professional men and four of the five
gained slightly in status."[47] All five of the professional men in
their sample of intermarried Jews chose wives who had "either
the same or often somewhat higher class status."[48]

Franzblau refers to the status-achieving intermarriage, for
which "a difference in religion is considered a small price to pay
for the status advantages gained."[49] Likewise Cahnman describes
those who "climb the ladder of professional success and move out
of their social class. They are torn between allegiance to childhood memories and alienation from them. If they meet others
who have traveled a similar distance, no matter where these
companions come from, they will be attracted by them . . ."[50]

The measure of success. How well a person has succeeded in
climbing the status ladder is measured, from a psychological
standpoint, not by how far he has moved through his own talents
and efforts, but by how firmly he is anchored in his new position.
As Sherif has emphasized, without social anchoring, the person

is confused, tossed "in a strange and hostile sea with uncertainty and distress. . . . It is true that man is not satisfied with every kind of status. But satisfaction does not come merely from breaking all ties. The striving is toward new status, i.e., to be anchored at a different level."[51]

The boys

Since wives are "the principal bearers of status in middle-class American life," it seems likely that a Jew who addresses himself to an elite Gentile status audience would feel strongly attracted to a girl who knew those "subtleties of the status game" that invite the approval of the Gentile elite.[52] Seidler and Ravitz describe a remarkably cohesive peer group which was formed by ten Jewish adolescent boys and had thrived for seventeen years at the time of the authors' report. Largely the children of Eastern European immigrants, "the boys" displayed a phenomenal status drive in high school—"holding virtually all the important class offices"[53]—and later distinguished themselves by their social, emotional, romantic, and marital involvement with Gentile girls. Of the ten members, eight had "at least one intense emotional relationship with a non-Jewish girl, in which marriage was a real possibility."[54] At the time the history of "the boys" was documented, six were inmarried, three were married to Gentile girls, and of the one remaining bachelor it seemed "a reasonable likelihood" that he would also marry a Gentile, bringing the group's likely intermarriage rate to 40 percent.

In junior high school "the boys" had shared a "very deep and live interest . . . in public affairs. . . . Social and economic issues interested them profoundly."[55] Their interest in political power was not altogether academic, for during their high school years they established themselves as the "ruling student group of the school. . . . Membership in [the clique] was highly prized and jealously guarded."[56] Gentile girls held a unique place in their dating behavior:

During their high school days "the boys" dated Jewish girls (they were the great majority at the school) almost exclusively. After graduation, however, they made almost as many social ar-

rangements with non-Jewish girls, which is unusual behavior in young Jewish Americans. Not that other Jewish boys
did not date non-Jewish girls; they did, but, as other in-group
males with out-group females, it was to exploit them sexually.
What was unusual was that the non-Jewish girls they dated
were treated as they treated their Jewish girls. These were not
clandestine relationships; non-Jewish girls were openly escorted
to group parties and were received with cordiality and warmth.
They were even introduced to parents.[57]

Although none of "the boys" belonged to the elite Jewish families of their town,[58] all ten of them gained membership in the
professions: six became physicians (of whom four were psychiatrists), one became a serious writer, one a lawyer, two were university professors (one of whom subsequently won elective office).
Although we have no data on the social status of the Gentile
girls they courted and married, we would conjecture that the
Gentile girls who appealed to them tended to be of high social
status. The boys' dating and marriage practices seem to fit the
pattern of social mobility described by their school activities and
vocational goals.

The New Haven Psychoanalysts

A more thoroughly investigated Jewish group which likewise
shows both a high degree of social mobility and a high rate of
intermarriage was brought to light by Hollingshead and Redlich
in their study of *Mental Health and Social Class*. In the course of
inventorying the mental health resources of the city of New
Haven, the investigators' survey yielded the unexpected finding
that 64 percent of the city's psychoanalysts were intermarried.
The status characteristics of the analysts and their wives tell an
interesting story in mobility and intermarriage.

Of New Haven's 30 psychiatrists in private practice, 83 per cent
of the psychoanalysts[59] were Jewish, compared with 19 per cent
of the more conventional and less specialized "directive-organic"
practitioners. Both groups maintained about the same level of
earnings, but by many standards the analysts comprised an elite
group: analysts held medical school faculty appointments, their
directive-organic colleagues were mainly affiliated with public

hospitals (State or Veterans Administration). The analysts worked regular hours, made no house calls or emergency calls, saw only one patient per hour (instead of two to four per hour), and maintained a more highly specialized and intellectual professional practice.

The psychoanalysts were a more strongly mobile group than their directive-organic colleagues. "The analysts . . . outdistanced 83 percent of their brothers and 79 percent of their brothers-in-law in their ascent of the class status ladder," according to the investigators. "The directive-organic group [had] not achieved as much comparatively; 26 percent have moved farther than their brothers, and 31 percent have moved farther up the class scale than their brothers-in-law."[60] The interesting thing about the "phenomenally upward mobile" psychoanalysts is that *a solid majority of them* (64 percent) had married outside their religious group. (The intermarriage rate in the directive-organic group was 38 percent, comprised mainly of Protestant husbands and Catholic wives.) Characteristically, "the wife comes from a family that is one class above the class of [her husband's family], but at the time of the marriage the husband has achieved a higher position than the wife's family of orientation." According to Hollingshead and Redlich, *"this pattern reveals that in mixed marriages, both the husbands and the wives are motivated by strong feelings for upward mobility."*[61] (Italics added.)

Some interesting by-products of mobility and intermarriage are described by the following observations: Of the analysts raised as Jews, "practically all . . . say that their fathers and mothers were active in the religious life of their community." A majority of this group (58 percent) maintained *no* contact with organized religion, and expressed *"doubt and confusion . . .* in their response to questions on how they would like to have their children trained religiously. *The greatest amount of conflict on these questions is shown by psychiatrists who either do not practice their ancestral religion or who have changed to another religion."*[62] (Italics added.)

Psychiatrists who marry within their own ethnic group choose a wife whose family status either approximates their own, "or the wife comes from a higher status family than her husband." This "interesting pattern" tends to prevail "in the marriages of both analytical and directive-organic groups and in each religious group," according to the investigators.[63]

Merton's trading hypothesis. In the Gentile world, the fact and folklore of status-raising marriages draws together a beautiful though lowly heroine and an aristocratic or wealthy suitor. In his analysis of mixed marriages involving Lutherans, Bossard observed that it was indeed the woman who was most likely to gain in status (where a status-difference between the partners could be assumed):

> When the social prestige of the Lutheran and the other church involved is equal, the number of men and women making mixed marriages is about equal; but when the social prestige of the other church is higher than the Lutheran, then the number of Lutheran women who make mixed marriages is much greater than the number of Lutheran men.[64]

A similar pattern manifests itself in Negro-white marriages in the United States; characteristically the partners have been a high-status Negro husband and a low-status white wife.[65] Merton analyzes this partnership to show that a "reciprocal compensatory" exchange has been effected: the wife accepts a loss of ethnic status in exchange for a gain in economic status. Merton "does not at all imply that the 'exchange' is necessarily the result of an explicit utilitarian calculus in which the contractants deliberately weigh the economic and social returns to be gained from the marriage. The event may be experienced by them as simply an affectional relationship, but this psychic reaction," according to Merton, "is manifestly structured by the social organization."[66] A psychoanalytic description of the above phenomenon would probably use the terms "overdetermination" and "unconscious motivation."

Does Merton's "trading hypothesis" fit the observable facts about Jewish-Gentile intermarriage? Is the Gentile wife likely to have a socio-economic status inferior to her husband's? This tended to be so for Slotkin's sample of intermarrieds,[67] and for Gordon's Minneapolis population of intermarrieds,[68] but as we have observed, it was apparently *not* so for the Levinsons' respondents, nor for the New Haven psychoanalysts.

A bridging hypothesis. If a hypothesis about intermarriage is to apply to the Jews, it must make a statement about *mobility* as well as about status. Perhaps the intermarrying Gentile woman accepts a loss in socio-economic status defined by the position of the marriage partner's *parents,* but takes a gain in socio-economic status (to compensate for her loss in ethnic status) as defined by the husband's *attained* position. Now we have evolved what is not only a "trading" hypothesis but is also a "bridging" hypothesis.

Social mobility involves a series of social and psychological transformations; the person must acquire a repertory of habits, practices and attitudes which conforms to the unwritten—and perhaps unspoken—code of the status audience he chooses to address himself to. Ambition, talent, and hard work may qualify a person for phenomenal mobility; whether it is attained, however, may depend upon his acquisition of the subtle and peculiar habits of the social group to which he seeks access. Correct behavior is not simply a matter of "good manners"; to be polite and sober in a particular situation may be as conspicuously inappropriate as to be rude and drunk. Perhaps a man can learn from his wife those subtleties of the status game upon which his success may depend; perhaps the choice of a wife is particularly critical for bridging the gap between the status of one's upbringing and the potential status of one's attainment.

According to this "bridging" hypothesis, a highly mobile man is predisposed to choose a wife whose parental status is intermediate between his parental status and his attained (or aspired) status. Such a mating would have a "reciprocal compensatory" quality since the wife would gain socio-economic status (in exchange for her loss in ethnic status). (Marriage to a woman of the aspired status—as in the case of Milton—would lack reciprocity so far as the receiving and giving of status is concerned.)

Observers seem to agree that intermarriage is most likely to occur at the upper socio-economic levels. In the Greater Washington, D.C. study it was found that Jewish-Gentile marriages "occur most frequently where the persons involved are born in the United States, have received more than a high school education, and have professional status." John L. Thomas reports that "Catholics out-marry more frequently in upper social classes than in lower, as measured by rental areas in one city:"

Among 51,671 families in one large city the percentage of families living in different areas that were based on mixed marriages increased regularly from 8.5 percent in the lowest rental area to 17.9 percent in the highest, with 19.3 percent among suburban families.[69]

High socio-economic status indicates high education level and upward mobility, the loosening of ethnic ties and attraction to the status gains possible through intermarriage. In America the Jews have demonstrated a remarkable rate of upward mobility. Glazer (1955) has amply documented the unparalleled rise of the Jews from an impoverished alien slum-dweller to a highly educated and economically well-established suburbanite.[70] (Terman's follow-up study of gifted children in California included data on the socio-economic status of the children and their parents. Jewish members of the sample ranked below non-Jews in economic status of parents. When Terman's gifted children reached adulthood, the Jewish group had not merely caught up with the non-Jews, but surpassed them in socio-economic rank.)[71] Sherman asserts that because the Jewish group is so upward mobile, an ambitious person has little "need" to intermarry since he can advance himself *within* his ethnic group.[72] For those whose status orientation is toward the Gentile world, however, socio-economic advancement within the Jewish community may hold little appeal.

Intermarriage and downward mobility. A college counselor occasionally encounters a Jewish student whose preference for dating Gentile girls seems closely related to deep feelings of inferiority manifested in his choice of career and other areas of his life. It seems as if he is reluctant to compete with other Jewish boys for dates. He fears that he cannot satisfy the expensive dating standards which he ascribes to Jewish girls; Gentile girls—he is convinced—are grateful for so much less. In a group so strongly oriented toward upward mobility, the relatively few for whom this orientation is psychologically uncongenial may feel badly out of step. Cross-ethnic dating and intermarriage would appear to be a likely resolution of such a conflict, where other factors favor this solution.

Do the facts point in this direction? The Greater Washington

D.C. study showed that the incidence of intermarriage was 18 times greater at the "upper socio-economic levels" than among "manual workers!"[73] Washington D.C., however, is an atypical urban community, whose special characteristics are discussed in a later section of this chapter. Intermarriage *does* seem to be characteristic of the downward-mobile or low-status Jew, at least in small towns. Shosteck's data on intermarriage rate among married children of 260 small-town Jews shows a rate of eight percent for persons whose father's income was *over* $7,500 in 1950, compared with an intermarriage rate of 13 percent for those whose father's income was *under* $7,500 in 1950.[74] (For further evidence on the relationship between intermarriage and *low* socio-economic status, see Table 3:4.)

The Jewish community accords more status to those who command new wealth—according to Kramer and Leventman—than does the Gentile community, with its emphasis on "old money" and long-established local residence. It is quite possible that just as a wealthy Jew might lose status by transferring from the Jewish to the Gentile community, a lower middle-class Jew might *gain* status by transferring into the Gentile community. A Gentile community which has a large working class might well accord a Jewish shop foreman more status than he would find in a uniformly upward-mobile and middle-class Jewish community. In the Gentile community he might be regarded as a more desirable husband and son-in-law, and this might influence him to marry into a Gentile family.

Intermarriage may have high instrumental value for a Jew who is strongly oriented toward *either* upward or downward mobility. Whoever feels "out of step" with the Jewish group may seek affiliation through dating and marriage with a more congenial group.

Ken

An engineering student who is in chronic academic trouble, Ken complains that he has always tended to "lose interest" in whatever he undertakes: school work, a hobby, a girl friend. As Ken cites examples from his life experience, it becomes clear that his "loss of interest" is his way of experiencing loss of self-confidence and loss of hope. This tendency to give up too easily may look, paradoxically, like a fear of success, but it is more likely a fear that he will come agonizingly close to success before he fails, or that if he seems to succeed he will discover that he has failed to choose the goal he really wanted. In any case, Ken seems to live in the shadow of failure.

Ken is the youngest of three boys; his parents are Jewish. Father has always been severely hard of hearing. Ken sees him as a man who does not take much interest in his family or the world around him. It is not unusual for Father to sit at the dinner table with his hearing aid switched off, while Mother talks about him as if he were not present. Ken resents his father's psychological withdrawal from family life. He sees in his father's behavior Ken's own tendency to "lose interest," to lack of self-confidence, and to lack "masculine traits."

Mother does the talking in this family: nagging, complaining, worrying about her husband's limited earnings as a cabinet maker. When she hears Ken talk on the phone about getting tickets for a concert, Mother will use the occasion to complain about how little money she has, and express disappointment that Ken does not pay for his room and board. Mother can also pamper Ken, and she does this best when Father is away. Ken feels he was "too much in the hands of his mother" when he was young. She worried over him and catered to him excessively because he was a puny child. Mother takes Ken into her confidence, telling him of the many grievances she holds against Father. She has told Ken that she wanted to get a divorce shortly after they were married, but she became pregnant during the first year of marriage and had to set aside this wish. She tells Ken that she still intends to divorce Father after Ken leaves home.

Ken's two older brothers show a lack of confidence similar to Ken's. Both hold rather limited jobs. One is now married, the other has been twice married and is now divorced. In each case the wife has been a Gentile. Ken likewise shows a preference for Gentile girls, although he expresses some dissatisfaction about "going outside of my religion" for a girl friend. On the other hand, he feels out of place in a Jewish crowd, and says he finds Jewish girls ostentatious and obnoxious. Their hair styles are pretentious, they use too much makeup, they are arrogant, and they wear the Mogen David necklace as if to flaunt their exclusiveness. He does recall a Jewish girl who was quiet and modest, but she was also unattractive, and her mother was loud and arrogant. He would like to find a girl who will "give him confidence in himself," but Jewish girls seem to bring out his feelings of inferiority, and his ambivalence toward women. Ken quarrels with his mother over the question of paying room and board, over how much he spends on dates, and the fact that he dates Gentile girls. Once Ken threw into such a quarrel the statement that Jewish girls disgust him.

After he had been seeing a counselor for a period of a few months, Ken did find a Jewish girl who was *not* tainted by the traits he associated with that group. Anne was a modest, quiet, pleasant girl who dressed simply and, like Ken, had been brought up in a Gentile neighborhood. Still he worried that he could not give her "what she needs." Ken felt that Anne was really in love with him, and when she once said that "in principle" a girl should be willing to quit school and take a job to help her husband finish his education, Ken felt sure she was ready to do that for him.

Ken elaborated with Anne on his worries about whether he was doing well enough to stay in school. He confessed to her his lack of self-confidence, and his tendency to lose interest in whatever he tries. Anne began to express concern that maybe she and Ken were spending too much time together for their own good. Ken reacted with hurt feelings, and disappointment that Anne was ready to break off their friendship "just when they were getting to know each other."

Ken seemed to have served notice to Anne that he doesn't really expect to accomplish much in life, and is disappointed (and at the same time perhaps relieved) that Anne takes this to mean that Ken would not make a good husband. Ken's feeling that he "doesn't belong" in Jewish society is of course related to his atypical upbringing: he was raised in a non-Jewish neighborhood in a house his father's parents built when the location was "out in the country." His father is a low-paid artisan, and his parents have at times discouraged Ken from going to college. Like his father and two brothers, Ken seems to be out of step with an achievement-oriented Jewish group. Like his two brothers, he may find some comfort in the choice of a marriage partner whom he can perceive as a bland and undemanding Gentile.

Religious disaffection. Rabbi Rubenstein holds that in our culture, intermarriage provides "the principal means of departure from Jewish life," just as during the Middle Ages religious conversion was the "principal mode of exit from Judaism."[75] A person who feels strongly dissatisfied with Judaism may "see no reason" why he should marry a Jew; he may see compelling reasons why he should not. Analogously, a Protestant-born respondent interviewed by Gordon expresses his satisfaction over his departure from his church through intermarriage:

> Maybe it's just as well that I marry a Catholic girl and have my children reared as Catholics. They, at least, will have the Church make their religious decisions for them. I have always been a confused kind of Protestant anyhow. There are just too many different varieties of Protestantism—all of which proves that not one of them really knows the answers to certain basic and fundamental questions. Well, the Catholic Church says it does and that is good enough for me.[76]

Religious disaffection figures in the story of Carlotta, Brazilian wife of a Jewish medical professor. Although she was a devout Catholic until her marriage to Abram, Carlotta recalled to Gordon her family's conflict with their village priest, who had publicly and bitterly denounced her mother for enrolling Carlotta and her sister in a boys' school (the only first-rate school in the area). The humiliation and grief which her mother suffered apparently left Carlotta with a deep ambivalence toward the Church for in her interview with Gordon she recalls, "I gave up Catholicism because of Abram. But as I think about it, I was ready to give up Catholicism because I really no longer believed in it. I wanted to find a life, a theology, in which I could believe and that proved to be Judaism."[77]

To an acculturated and secular Jew who yearns to join The Establishment, who cannot understand his own mixed feelings over intermarriage nor the violent opposition of his family and in-group, the Jewish religion may become the object of his frustration and anger. No longer indifferent to the ancient faith, he now feels impelled to denounce it as "an unpopular minority sect . . . a small cult that really doesn't attract him."[78] For the introspections that may accompany this emotional crisis, we quote from the fictional hero of Myron Kaufmann's *Remember Me to God:*

Richard

He considered that it was natural, normal and healthy to want to conform, to succeed according to the standards of his own country, to be a Protestant in a Protestant land, to be in the center of the community in which one lived and grew, and to rise as high in it as one could . . .

To be fully a part of things did not mean to shut himself up in a minority, to be two people, to split his personality. If he wanted the Yankees to accept him fully into their way of life, he should accept their way of life fully.

. . . Would he be a traitor [to his relatives if he converted?] Would his conversion do any harm or cost anything to any other Jew? Was it anybody's business but his own? Was anybody going to be slaughtered or persecuted because Richard Amsterdam changed his faith? Nonsense.

There is not one rational reason, he said to himself, why I or anyone like me should continue to be a Jew. No matter what men say about spiritual values, deep down they all want a beautiful wife and ten-thousand-a-year [circa 1940]. And why should a modern, educated agnostic force himself to adhere to an unpopular minority sect? If a man really likes that crabbed life, or believes in it as some do, let him adhere. But if he doesn't like it, or if his energies cry to expand into the main-stream of human activity, and he yet restrains himself, out of supposed conscience or sentiment, if he thinks he must closet himself in a small cult that doesn't really attract him—sacri-fice of that kind isn't noble, it's neurotic. Prejudice was going out, and this compulsive need to cling to a religion you don't like should go out with it . . .

There was a good feeling that he was indeed making his own life, and that he was unbound, like primal man born anew. He felt vigorous. There seemed nothing he could not do.[79]

Rebels and angry ones. Marriage is an occasion for separation as well as union. (A Yiddish proverb states, "When a young man gets married he divorces his mother.") A young person who harbors a need to inflict pain upon his parents—or retaliate against parental authority—may find himself moving irresistibly toward a marriage that can both affirm his capacity to love, and express his need to retaliate against parental authority. A rage against the proud majority may likewise bestir a minority group member to take a bride from the dominant group, as a "hostage" and as a gesture of defiance. Here we are supposing *not* that the expression of hostility is a primary motive for marriage, but that it can be an appealing by-product for one who is not firmly committed to the rule of endogamy. Lehrman hypothesizes that Jewish parents who feel hostile toward their group may unconsciously or deliberately encourage their children to contract mixed marriages. This would provide but one more example of how parents find ways of fulfilling their own thwarted motives through the lives of their children.

The hostile parent-child relationship. Slotkin cites the recollection of an intermarried Jew: "As I grew older I had the feeling somewhat of a rebel, and trying to break away from the conventional Jewish thing. And so I felt a feeling of contempt against anything Jewish—I looked on myself as above all this."[80] Likewise, one of Mayer's intermarried Jews is quoted to say: "Yes, I had some thoughts about mixed marriages before meeting my wife. I thought it was a good thing. . . . I was very preoccupied with this whole issue and had many debates with myself about it. I would say to myself that it would be nice to marry a Gentile girl—it would be an indication that I had put certain phoney values behind me. It would be an indication that I was more mature. . . . On the other hand I felt I would be more at home with a Jewish girl. . . . There was a kind of schism in my thinking, I was pulled in opposite directions."[81]

In the case of *Florence,* Lehrman describes an attractive young Jewish woman whose choice of cross-ethnic boys seemed to express her hostility toward her family, whom she felt had rejected her. Her mother favored Florence's older brother; her father favored her younger sister, and treated Florence harshly.

Annette

In the case of *Annette,* Lehrman describes a Protestant woman whose repeated cross-ethnic choices follow an upbringing marred by traumatic and degrading experiences with men of her own milieu. Annette had lost her mother when the patient was a baby. She was indulgently raised by her father, who was killed in an accident when Annette was nine. Annette was brought up by a succession of Protestant foster parents. Prior to puberty, a middle-aged man of her own milieu seduced her into cunnilingus. During adolescence, several of her foster fathers attempted to seduce her; in each case she resisted.

A woman of great beauty, talent, and intelligence, Annette became a professional model and "cover girl." She attempted three marriages: the first to a Catholic, the next two to Jews.

A Jewish husband confessed to Mayer that "in contemplating his marriage [to a Gentile], he had experienced a 'subtle and enjoyable feeling of irking his mother.' "[82] An attitude of rebellion is likewise reflected in the following unidentified quotation from Gordon:

"How is this world going to become 'one world' if we persist in maintaining our differences? I'm tired of that. Religion divides us. It doesn't unite us despite all this talk about the Fatherhood of God and the Brotherhood of Man. There have to be some souls in this world who are sufficiently brave and strong to break down these barriers men have erected and I, for one, intend to marry 'outside' my own religious group in order to prove once and for all that this is or ought to be one world."[83]

Margaret

Gordon cites a case (whom we shall call *Margaret*) in which a Catholic girl's marriage to a Jew climaxed her open rebellion against her mother's attempts to control her. As she struggled to free herself from her mother's domination, she also rebelled against her mother's religious ties:

"I was a very withdrawn child. . . . I never caused [my parents] any trouble . . . until I was about sixteen years old and then I really caused a lot of trouble.

"I sort of rebelled against any kind of pressure from them. . . . My mother was and still is very prejudiced about anybody who isn't Irish Catholic. . . . I rebelled by dating the very type of person she didn't want me to date. I did it quite deliberately . . .

". . . It was at this time too that I started doubting my Catholic religion . . . [and involving mother] in constant arguments. She would cause such ridiculous scenes if I said that I wasn't going to church that it was easier to go. . . . She would get upset. She would cry. . . . Sometimes she said . . . that my behavior was going to kill her. I was getting more and more angry myself all this while. I think that my strong will began to manifest itself and I continued to do the very things . . . that I know she didn't like . . .

". . . It was at the time of all those quarrels that I left home and moved into the city . . . I phoned and all that. But I simply couldn't live with the family any more."[84]

Penny

An attractive eighteen-year old girl, Penny came into counseling because she felt vaguely dissatisfied with her college studies. She finds it difficult to tolerate continual nagging from both her mother and step-father. Penny seems to arouse strongly competitive feelings in her mother, who is just 18 years Penny's senior and who voices regret over the fact that she never had a chance to go to college. Penny's step-father's life is warped by alcoholism and compulsive gambling, problems which add to her mother's chronic irritability. Penny's real father was twice her mother's age when they married. He was physically abusive and Mother left him when Penny was three. For two and one-half years Penny was boarded with a woman whose method of punishment was to lock Penny in a closet. Her mother remarried, took Penny back to live with her and the new father. A year later a baby sister was born, toward whom Penny has always felt quite jealous.

Mother involves herself considerably in Penny's social life, and is both directive and prohibiting. Penny recalls with some guilt that when she was fifteen, Mother encouraged her to date a college boy and "take him for a sucker" by accepting expensive gifts from him though she had no serious interest in him. Currently, Mother seems to set what to Penny seem like unreasonable curfew hours. When Penny continues to date the same boy for a period of time, Mother advises Penny that at her age she should be "playing the field." When Penny tries to follow this advice, Mother criticizes her for being "promiscuous." Mother also expresses an unusual curiosity about what exactly Penny does on her dates, makes provocative comments about her boy friends' intentions, and has on occasion appropriated gifts which Penny has gotten from a boy friend.

Mother also interferes with Penny's studies, offering her the confusing "advice" that Penny is not bright enough to stay at the university, and that the junior college is a waste of time. Mother recently arranged to have Penny's room redecorated the week before final examinations, when Penny could least afford to be distracted from her studies.

There are three boys in Penny's recent dating life. Mother has been encouraging Penny to date Kirk, a college man who is a member of their Protestant church. To Penny he is a boor and she finds him physically unattractive. He takes her to nice places but they have nothing to talk about. Mike is a Protestant engineering student whom she finds boyish and fun-loving but does not show affection. Don is a Jewish boy friend whom she finds congenial, affectionate, and given to serious, intimate conversation.

Penny feels rather insecure about how to deal with the fact that Don is "getting serious." Her step-father expresses contempt over Penny's apparent willingness to "raise a bunch of little Hebes." Her mother voluptuates over Don's masculinity, an example of her inappropriate sexual joking. Penny's strife-ridden, unstable home environment, her mother's repeated failure to find a suitable husband from her own Protestant milieu, undoubtedly predisposes Penny to think of herself as the wife of a gentle and sober Jewish husband. Don has already taken Penny to social functions together with his married siblings and cousins, and Penny has enjoyed this foretaste of family solidarity. Don's ability to talk seriously and straightforwardly about his affection for her likewise seems to give Penny a sense of security which she cannot get from Mike.

Vivian

A vivacious, attractive college sophomore, Vivian entered personal counseling with a vaguely defined unhappiness over her "loss of ideals and values," a feeling of disillusionment and a "loss of faith." She attends a commuter's college, living in a prestige suburb (unlike the typical city college student) with her parents and two younger brothers. She has an older sister who is married. Her parents are American-born Jews; her father is an optometrist, her mother works full-time as an office manager.

At the outset she told of her recent attempt to seek counseling from a rabbi at the synagogue at which her younger brother was bar mitzvah. She described her "loss of faith" to the rabbi in terms of her thoughts of marrying a Catholic and raising her children as Catholics. As Vivian retold the episode, the rabbi responded angrily, saying that her trouble was that she wasn't really a Jew, that she had no roots, no background, that she was a "phoney" like her parents (whose affiliation with his synagogue was quite tenuous). Vivian cried and left the rabbi's office.

Vivian described her conflict with her parents over her dating practices. She prefers the company of Gentile boys, whom she regards as gentlemanly and pleasant. Her parents want her to be more encouraging to Ben, a Jewish medical student whom Vivian considers dull, and whose friends she describes as loud and vulgar. She further complains that her mother, because of her full-time job, overburdens Vivian with housework and intrudes upon her time for dating and study. As Vivian describes her daily routine, when she comes home from school she washes the dishes left over from breakfast, prepares dinner and serves her two younger brothers, then drives over to mother's place of work to pick her up. One afternoon her mother phoned, as usual, and asked Vivian "How are my two children?" Vivian understood mother's slip of the tongue and sharply reminded her mother that she had three children at home, not two, and that Vivian did not like being treated like a maid.

Mother places the blame for Vivian's burden of housework

upon Father, because his limited earnings leave her no choice but to hold a full-time job. In the first few sessions Vivian described her father as a somewhat impractical person, but as very intelligent, artistic, idealistic, and eager to engage Vivian in long philosophical discussions. For a period of time he would take Vivian out for cocktails and dinner several times each week, this gesture serving the dual purpose of showing his fondness for Vivian and expressing resentment toward his wife for being at work instead of at home.

A significant shift in interview content occurred as the sessions continued, marked by Vivian's progressively more open expression of disappointment and deep resentment toward her father for neglecting his responsibility toward her, her older sister and her mother. Father drives a big new car and takes Wednesdays off to affect the manner of a "successful doctor." He holds on to an unprofitable practice in a declining neighborhood, refusing to move his office to a better neighborhood because he doesn't want to deal with Jewish women. As far back as Vivian can remember she has depended upon her own earnings and her mother's for clothing, dental bills, and pocket money. Father neglects routine repair work around the house but finds time to indulge his hobby of watercolor painting.

At breakfast one day mother complained of an abcessed tooth. Father replied, "I can't afford any dentist bills right now." Vivian recalled that her older sister went through adolescence with a broken front tooth. It was repaired only after she married.

Vivian's disappointment with her father was paralleled by a disillusioning romance with a handsome, egotistical Catholic boy. As she recalled the details of her aborted romance with Jim, it became clear that she was an active participant in the sequence of events that led to her disillusionment, and not quite the "victim" she had at first pictured herself.

As counseling continued, Vivian began to see that she could take better control of her future if she was willing to accept responsibility for doing so. Even though father could not afford to send her away to college, she could work out a way to attend college away from home, through part-time work and student loans. This would remove her from a strife-torn home atmosphere and lessen the resentment she had felt toward father for denying

her the experience of going away to school. Meanwhile she began
to recognize her right to put her schoolwork ahead of the housework; that running the house was not her job. Passover was
coming, and if Vivian submitted to all her mother's demands to
help prepare the house for the Seder guests, she would seriously
neglect her schoolwork and threaten her eligibility for a student
loan. She needed the counselor's help in attending to her primary responsibilities while coping with mother's demands and
complaints.

In the eighth week of counseling she reported that she had
found a new boyfriend. She described Dan as tall, blond, idealistic and slightly unconventional. "You'd never know he's Jewish." Dan was a pre-law student and his father was an architect
who apparently took a special liking to Vivian. She recalled with
interest how Dan's father had tried to explain to her the Jewish
concept of joy (perhaps *nachas?*) as the fulfillment of work and
plans.

Toward the closing interview, Vivian's resentment was tempered by a degree of compassion for her father's shortcomings and
ambivalences.

Aside from the money problem and all of the irritations it
spawned, her parents had been good to her in many ways, she
reflected. Although her experience with Jim was disillusioning
she did not have to feel "ruined," and she still had the freedom
to become the kind of person she wanted to be. At the close of
the semester her parents attended the convocation at which Vivian was among those students honored for good scholarship. She
felt vindicated for having set limits to her share of the housework, and was pleased that she had done something which at the
same time advanced her own development and was a source of
pride to her parents.

Interracial marriage and the feeling of rejection. Linton Freeman interviewed a group of 22 University of Hawaii students of
whom eight were interethnically married, and the remainder
"engaged exclusively in interethnic dating."[85] One Caucasian
student changed his name to one with an Oriental sound. "Others
adopted the mannerisms and dress of the group with which they
identified. It was not unusual to see individuals go to extremes
to emulate the behavior of members of the new groups. Often

their orientation was 'more Japanese than the Japanese' or 'more Caucasian than the Caucasians.' "[86]

What led these young people to become converts to a new ethnic group? All 22 of Freeman's subjects "describe early feelings of rejection stemming from their social relationships with their own ethnic groups. Reportedly, such feelings frequently dated back to parent-child relationships and were, without exception, expressed in poor social adjustments in grade and high school. Since most social groups in school were built up around ethnic identity, these individuals tended to generalize their feelings of rejection to all members of their own ethnic groups."[87]

Poor social relations with family and peers led to feelings of rejection and frustration, and hostility toward the ethnic group identified as the source of the frustration. Thus "it became important to escape identity with the group. Often there was a desire to get away from the group and from the things which symbolized it. . . . Most often individuals simply withdrew and refused to participate in group pursuits or work toward group goals. Of course, such activity only tended to increase the rejection of the group and this in turn to reinforce the hostility of the deviants. Thus, a self-perpetuating cycle was built up in which deviation intensified rejection and rejection enhanced deviation."[88]

Rejectees identified readily with another ethnic group, particularly with a group which is "rejected and negatively sanctioned by their own group. . . . Adopting [the cross ethnic group's] values as their own could provide a ready-made system for explaining their rejection as due to their superiority rather than their inadequacies. By this process these individuals were provided with an alternative way of life which rationalized their previous rejection and rewarded their deviation. Their interest soon developed into a full-fledged internalization of the attitudes and values of the new group," an idealization of its norms, and a romantically idealized image of their future mate as a member of the new group.[89] Although the philo-Oriental might fantasy marrying a "typical Japanese woman," such a person is by definition unlikely to want a Caucasian husband. The course and resolution of this "misunderstanding" is discussed at the end of Chapter 4.

Heiss devised an index for rating a person's dissatisfaction with his family, and compared intermarried and inmarried persons on this "dissatisfaction score." This index *did* differentiate between intermarried and inmarried Catholics (significant at the .05 level of confidence), but did *not* distinguish between intermarried and inmarried Jews (or Protestants). Open conflict between generations is apparently more typical of the intermarrying Catholic than the intermarrying Protestant or Jew.[90]

The counterphobic marriage. A person who stands at the margin of minority group membership (as distinct from the full member of a "marginal group") and feels the powerful attraction of the dominant group experiences a strange mixture of love and hate. He stands in awe at the power and authority of the dominant group and fears their power to reject his overtures toward claiming full membership. He needs the security of the old group toward which he might safely retreat, but resents the threat of ostracism that his old group wields. As he interiorizes the values of the new group, he discovers that he has also taken on their prejudices. He must at moments feel uncomfortable about his negative chauvinism, or that—as Cooley might have phrased it— his old and new social selves hate each other, reflecting the conflict between the cultures they represent.

Lewin describes the chronic discomfort of "those who are not fully decided about their belongingness to the Jews. Those marginal men and women are in somewhat the same position as an adolescent who is no longer a child and certainly does not want to be a child any longer, but who knows at the same time that he is not really accepted as a grown-up. This uncertainty about the ground on which he stands and the group to which he belongs often makes the adolescent loud, restless, at once timid and aggressive, over-sensitive and tending to go to extremes, over-critical of others and himself."[91]

For the Jew who takes pride in his courage, intelligence, and adaptiveness, it may be quite painful to admit that he stands in fear of intimidation by his old group and in fear of rejection by an unfriendly majority. In *The Enemy Camp,* Weidman's protagonist is confronted by this harsh state of affairs:

What you're afraid of, George, is the world of the Gentiles.

Somewhere . . . probably at your mother's knee, you've picked
up and believe the same notion about Gentiles that so many
Gentiles have picked up and believe about Jews. That they're
creatures from another world or another planet, with cloven
feet and spiked tails and a passion for drinking human blood.
That they're your natural and implacable enemy. That con-
sorting with them is an act of treachery to your faith and your
people . . .

You're so terrified of the Gentile world that you'll do anything under the sun to make a nice safe nest for yourself in the
part of the Jewish world that you think is completely safe from
attack by the Gentile enemy because it's so effectively camou-
flaged with money . . . the world of the rich Jews.[92]

In this context the choice of a Gentile wife takes on the character of a counterphobic act; this is how one seeks to prove to
himself and to the world that he is indeed *not* afraid of the Gentiles, and that he is *not* afraid of the disapproval of the Jewish
group either. At the same time a Gentile marriage partner represents a step toward fuller affiliation with the dominant group, a
merger of one's identity, and a mingling of one's germ plasm with
the proud majority.

In Lewisohn's 1928 novel *The Island Within,* the protagonist
describes a Jewish acquaintance who is "always in love with some
blond Gentile girl in order to transcend vicariously in conquest
of her his Jewish feeling of inferiority."[93]

As a counterphobic move, a mixed marriage is not an easy victory to consolidate if there is a measure of validity to the testimony of Weideman's protagonist who, after eight years of marriage, avers that no matter how much a Jewish husband and his
Gentile wife love each other, "all his life, deep down inside, that
boy will feel like Joe Louis at a white dinner."[94] Some Jews may
achieve through intermarriage what the Levinsons refer to as
"a more pluralistic identity," but detailed knowledge of this
area of human experience is scant, and the limited facts available
(e.g., the Rosten study) are not encouraging.

The hypomanic personality. Our survey of characteristics of
persons who intermarry has touched upon "the exceptions," the
artists, the socially ambitious, the rebellious, the hostile, the re-

jected, the defiant. These descriptions seem to converge upon what psychologists call the hypomanic personality: excitable, vivacious, overactive, unconventional, buoyant, self-confident, energetic. The hypomanic concept is borrowed from psychopathology but does *not* designate emotional disturbance as such. As Hilgard puts it, "it is easier to characterize illness than health, [and] one way of describing the normal person is to say that he differs from others in the direction of one or another mental illness. . . . [Thus, a hypomanic] resembles the manic but doesn't go that far."[95]

In psychoanalytic theory, the manic re-experiences the feeling of infantile omnipotence "in which everything is received, every wish is granted, with temporary freedom from guilt."[96] Clinical observation of manic patients describe a person who seems immune to embarrassment, "childishly proud and quite intolerant of criticism. . . . The patient courts the limelight, is boastful, flippant, argumentative . . . is full of ambitious schemes . . . is bored with routine. . . . Open hostility to members of the family is common. . . . The hypomanic is often erotic and, if a man, may indulge in [sexual] excesses, while a previously chaste and modest young woman may become sexually promiscuous or marry a man far below her social level."[97]

According to Gilberstadt and Duker, one of the "cardinal features" of the manic type is that they are "frequently married to wives of different religion."[98] At best, the energetic, ambitious, defiant hypomanic may point to *one* type of intermarriage-prone person. Lehrman's observation that *all thirty* intermarrieds whom he had observed clinically, fit the syndrome of "the exceptions" suggests that this may be an important intermarriage-prone type.

The concept of an intermarrying type as defiant and somewhat reckless sheds light on a statistical curiosity cited by Engelman. During World War I there was a spectacular increase in the *ratio* of intermarriage in Germany. Inspection of the data, however, shows that the increased percentage was *not* occasioned by a rise in the actual number of Jewish-Gentile marriages, but to a sharp decline in the number of homogeneous Jewish marriages.

If preference for a homogeneous partner is a mark of conservatism, we would expect the frequency of *in*marriages during a period of social instability to decline, while the marriage rate for the more reckless or defiant types would go unchecked.

Table 2:6. Frequency of homogeneous and mixed marriages in Germany for five-year periods before and after World War I[99]

Period	Total number of Jewish homogeneous marriages	Total number of mixed Jewish-Gentile marriages	Ratio of mixed marriages per 100 homogeneous marriages
1901–05	19,540	3,522	18
1906–10	19,729	4,699	24
1911–15	14,983	5,827	38
1916–20	18,675	7,226	39
1921–25	21,687	8,896	42
1926–29	11,243	6,087	54

3

Man and Wife:
The Intermarried Couple

A search for characteristics of the person who intermarries does not yield a single "pure type." To some observers, Jews who intermarry are not at all distinguishable from the inmarrying majority.[1] Intermarrieds are to be found among leaders of the Jewish community, among the loyal rank-and-file, and among the marginal members. Among both intermarried as well as inmarried groups one finds some who are leading productive and full lives, others who are leading thwarted and neurotic lives, and the many whose degree of success in life is not so easily appraised. A list of distinguished Jews whose wives were not of Jewish birth would include Max Nordau, Martin Buber, Horace M. Kallen, Louis Wirth, Ludwig Lewisohn, Herman Wouk, and Harry Golden. At the 1965 National Conference of Hillel Directors, Yale Hillel Director, Rabbi Robert J. Israel said to his colleagues, "I am sure there is not one of us who doesn't know of a dozen happy, non-neurotic faculty intermarriages on our local college campuses."[2]

Gordon found intermarried Jews among the leaders of several suburban congregations. (In several cases the president or vice president was married to a non-Jew.) [2] Rabbi Isaac N. Trainin tells of a rabbi in a nearby New York City community "who lost his position after only six months in office [presumably] because he delivered a strong sermon against intermarriage. . . . How was he to know that several members of his Board of Directors had Christian wives? Let me emphasize," Trainin adds, "that I am referring to couples who had maintained their different faiths in marriage."[3]

Koenig's study of the Stamford (Connecticut) Jewish community led him to conclude that the majority of Jews who intermarried "continued to be regarded as members of the Jewish community, some of them keeping up their affiliation with it and taking an active part in its affairs. . . ."[4] In their interviews with 69 married third-generation Jewish men in North City, Kramer and Leventman could find no appreciable differences between the five who had intermarried, and the inmarrying majority.

In contrast to the foregoing aspect of intermarriage is the area of clinical observation in which intermarriage is sometimes seen as intimately related to a neurotic problem. The man who is inhibited or impotent with a woman of his own class but can express his sexual impulses toward a woman who is "different"; the man who has a need to fight, abuse, or humiliate his mate and is therefore attracted to a "natural enemy"; the woman who fulfills her unconscious fantasy to have a child by a forbidden person and, according to Franzblau, takes no interest in her husband once she has acted out her wish.[6]

> Rabbi Rubenstein documents the case of a college woman of upper class Protestant background who within a two or three year period of time had twice given birth to a child whose father was Jewish. (In the first case the child was given up for adoption; in the second case, pregnancy was followed by conversion to Judaism and marriage.) [7]

Franzblau includes in his catalog of neurotic intermarriage patterns, that of the woman who seeks an inadequate and dependent man with whom she can establish a mother-infant relationship;[8] perhaps an alcoholic who alternates between irresponsible "temper tantrums" and periods of sweet, kind, adoring repentance and self-abnegation. Franzblau implies that a cross-ethnic partner would somehow better suit the needs of such a wife.

Suffice it to say again what the Levinsons have emphasized: that an intermarriage need not be neurotically motivated. (Perhaps it should also be added that clinicians have identified a profusion of neurotic marriage patterns which have nothing to do with intermarriage. Lehrman has noted that there is no index reference to mixed marriage in Eisenstein's 1954 compilation, *Neurotic Interaction in Marriage*.) With this qualification made explicit beforehand, we shall proceed to discuss what is known and what may be hypothesized about the psychological characteristics of four types of intermarriage partners: Jewish husband, Gentile wife, Gentile husband, and Jewish wife.

THE JEWISH HUSBAND

Intelligence and seriousness. Mayer's interviews with intermarried Gentile wives lead to a description of the Jewish husband as an intellectually gifted, serious-minded, cultured, successful person.

Mayer tells of "a Catholic woman who met her future husband in a company cafeteria, assumed he was a Christian, and was very favorably impressed. "I thought now there's a man with brains. He didn't go on with the usual silly office chatter."[9]

Mayer quotes an intermarried Protestant woman (whom we shall call *Lucy*) : "What I liked most about my husband, compared with these other men I was going with, was his interests. He was interested in better things than they were. I mean, there's nothing wrong with ball games, but that was *all* they ever talked about. My husband was interested in philosophy and lots of other things. Most of these others were in a trade, like being a machinist or something. I knew if I married them I'd be a housewife, have children, and that would be all there'd be in my life. We would never grow or do anything different. I thought that with Stephen my life would be changing and growing all the time. For example, one boy I went steady with—his attitude toward my piano playing was, 'Well,' he said, 'after we're married you're not going to do that anymore!' He thought it was kind of silly."[10]

The socially elite wife of *Milton* described her initial attraction to the son of Eastern European Jewish immigrants:

"I was getting fed up with the man I was going with. There was a lot of heavy drinking in the crowd, and if there was no cocktail party to go to, they were at a complete loss as to what to do. . . . My husband differed from these other men because he had no sophistication. . . . All the things which had been part of my life, like sailing and tennis and the rest of it, [Milton] had never had. He knew no sports and had worked his way through college. Money meant something to him. I had simply thrown it away, and I couldn't understand at first why he didn't want to spend money going to night clubs every night. . . ."[11]

A wife describes her Catholic parents' attitude toward her Jewish husband: ". . . They thought he was agreeable, likeable, friendly, considerate, and it was apparent that he was fond of me. They thought that he would make me happy. He was a physician, and this meant security, and they liked that."[12]

"Of particular interest [says Mayer] are the following remarks by a Catholic girl of Polish descent, who came from an extremely anti-Semitic background: 'Earlier, when I had been hesitant about going out with Jews, I had been in . . . a parochial school. I had never known any Jews and had led a sheltered life. When I went into nurses' training, I was away from home and living at the hospital most of the time. . . . At the hospital there were only a few Jewish doctors, but they were the outstanding ones, and everyone admired them. It was easy to have romantic fantasies about these people. . . . After I was through with nurses' training, I wouldn't have refused to go out with anyone because he was Jewish. . . ."[13]

More than twenty years before Mayer published these convergent comments on the Jewish husband, an intermarried Gentile wife (already referred to as Gertrude) wrote anonymously in *Atlantic Monthly*: "When one of my husband-hunting girl friends asks me, 'Do the Jews make good husbands?' I think of Ben, respecter of women, generous to a fault, kind to every creature, open-minded, witty, sober of habit but gay in manner, imaginative and ambitious, and say with all my heart, 'The best in the world!' "[14]

Conflict and inhibition. Apparently all of the Levinsons' four "reluctant" intermarried Jews were men. Compared with the majority of seven Jewish males in their study, the "reluctants" were described as persons who were strongly Jewish in their emotional investment, tended to regard Gentiles with suspicion, openly disapproved of intermarriage in principle, and placed great emphasis on giving their children "a clear sense of their own Jewishness."[15] Intermarriage for them either occurred as an act of impetuosity (e.g., occurring while home on furlough), or followed a period of great anxiety and inner conflict.[16] In the light of interview and projective test material, it appears to the Levinsons that intermarriage for this one-fourth of their sample represents "an attempt to solve a long-standing neurotic conflict."[17]

Mayer found his male subjects especially reticent to discuss "things about their partners that had especially appealed to them."[18] Questions bearing on the husband's motivations were unexpectedly troublesome. The husbands' discomfort seemed unusual since they had agreed to cooperate in a study on inter-marriage. Interviews were conducted in privacy and in the sub-ject's own home. (Wives were interviewed by the wife of the investigator, in a separate part of the home of the respondents.)

One Jewish fiance in Mayer's group "was [so] extremely sensitive with regard to anything having to do with his courtship (he told us he only agreed to be interviewed out of deference to the rabbi who had given us his name), we could ask him only the most innocuous questions. When we ventured to ask why he had become attracted to his wife, he became so touchy and defensive that this line of questioning had to be abandoned."[19]

". . . As a group, the husbands [in Mayer's study] seemed to be more ill-at-ease during the interview, and their responses were more apt to be abrupt or evasive. The wives, on the other hand, were more apt to express themselves freely and fully and ap-parently felt less constrained."[20] By illustration, we quote from one of Mayer's male subjects: "I don't know even now why there was such a congeniality or comfortableness between myself and Ruth. I can't put it in specific words even now."[21]

This degree of embarrassment and verbal inhibition on the part of Mayer's male subjects may point to the neurotic aspect of their marriage choice. Karl Abraham probably introduced the concept of "neurotic exogamy" in a 1913 clinical paper, defining it as a phenomenon where "a man experiences an insuperable aversion to any close relationship with a woman of his own people or nation. Or to put it more correctly, of his mother's people. This is an indication," Abraham continued, "of special measures taken to avoid the possibility of incest. . . . This flight is a result of his exaggerated phobia of incest."

Abraham observed that with some patients "the underlying reason for this sexual diffidence remains completely unconscious, whilst with others it is fully conscious. . . . One patient told me that being himself a Jew, he could never marry a Jewess, for he could not help seeing his sister in every Jewish girl. In fact this patient had an unusually strong incestuous fixation to his mother and sister. . . . During puberty there had been some degree of sexual intimacy between him and his sister."[22] (The relationship of intermarriage and the incest taboo is discussed in some detail in Chapter 12.)

Philip

Lehrman describes a thirty-one-year-old divorced Jew who could not bring himself to marry his sweetheart, a young and eligible Jewish divorcee. He had demonstrated his potency with her, but "the thought of marriage brought on a fear of impotence." Several years earlier he had married, and subsequently divorced, a Gentile girl "of easy virtue."

To Philip, "every Jewish girl represented his mother and older sister." Since adolescence, his masturbation fantasies involved women with large breasts, and referred mainly to his sister. "He had seen her petting like a 'dirty' girl with her boy friend. He had also felt her breasts while she slept. . . . Sex could be enjoyed only in secret and in fantasy or with degraded women."

Feelings of inferiority and aggression toward his father were apparently at the source of Philip's symptomatic impotence and sexual inhibition. At the termination of his analysis, "his feelings of inferiority lessened, impotence disappeared . . . [and] he felt he was a man in his own right who did not need his father's permission. He began to court a Jewish girl," and about a year after termination of his analysis he married her.[23]

The search for a contrast choice. In the Levinsons' interview group "neurotic exogamy" was most readily inferred from the protocols of those Jewish husbands who intermarried despite great personal reluctance. But even the more mature and emancipated men appeared to have been seeking a wife who differed in certain significant respects from their mothers, whom they regarded as nervous, possessive, overprotective and controlling.[24] Through intermarriage they hoped to find a contrast choice: a mate who would be "emotionally calmer and gentler, less quarrelsome and disparaging. Explicitly or implicitly Gentile women are seen as more likely to fit this pattern."[25] The use of a "contrast choice," as the Levinsons call it, to resolve inner conflicts about marriage, "is not in itself neurotic," they insist, "and it has useful adjustive functions."[26]

Describing the four "reluctants," for whom "emotional difficulties contributed significantly to their cross-ethnic marital choices,"[27] the Levinsons point to conflicted attitudes toward both father and mother. "In their early years the men had close attachments to their mothers . . . and particularly to her critical view of the father. During adolescence or early adulthood . . . they became more sensitive to [her] controlling qualities. . . . They experienced the closeness to her as oppressive and restricting. At the same time they 'discovered' the father; came to like him more . . . and to see 'his side' of the family struggle. These changes are quite conscious and often vividly described."[28] Although they had Jewish friends who were eligible marital partners, they were inhibited in their heterosexual relations, especially with Jews.[29] Their conscious sexual fantasies were diverted to "the image of the *shiksa:* the Gentile girl who is devalued and taboo as a marriage partner, but who is sexually attractive, sensual and more accessible . . . [and is consciously recognized as] the antithesis of mother. . . ." Thus to the sexually inhibited Jewish male the *shiksa* may become "a relatively legitimate and anxiety-free sexual object."[30]

Premarital adventures with a non-Jewish girl lead to the "development of affection and esteem for the partner; guilt over the sexual relationship which could be assuaged by marriage; and perhaps a recognition that intermarriage was the only solution to a conflict about getting married which had prevented [him] from marrying a Jewish woman."[31]

The Hamilton study. In his classic four-year research on marital adjustment, G. V. Hamilton attempted to demonstrate how the affectionate bond between a boy and his mother influences his choice of a wife and the success of his marriage. Hamilton classified 100 married men and 100 married women (including 55 couples) as to whether they were "happily married," married successfully but with qualifications, or unhappily married. (Classification was based on responses to 13 questions; e.g., "What things in your marriage annoy and dissatisfy you most?" The total interview covered 400 questions on marriage adjustment. Male respondents were predominantly college graduates holding positions in a wide range of professions, in business and the arts. A majority of women respondents had attended college.)

Hamilton asked his 100 male respondents: "Is your wife like or unlike your mother in physical appearance—not as your mother is now, but as she was when you were a child?" Of 100 respondents only 17 gave a clear-cut "Like" response. (Sixty said "Unlike," and the remaining 23 gave ambiguous or vague replies.) Those who described their wife as "like" their mother in physical appearance belonged almost entirely to the "happily married" group, while only one-third of the "unlike" group belonged to the "happily married" category.[32]

The question as to whether the respondent's wife resembled

Table 3:1. Husband's comparison of wife with mother, and marital adjustment[33]

Response to question: "Is your wife like or unlike your mother in physical appearance . . .?"	A Total frequency of response	B Frequency of response by husbands rated "happily married"	C Per cent of A/B
Wife described as physically "like" or "very like" mother	17	16	94
Wife described as physically "unlike" mother	60	20	33
Answer ambiguous or vague	23	15	65

his mother in *disposition* gave similar results, but not so clear cut as the question regarding physical resemblance.

"Were you and your mother always on affectionate terms?" Hamilton asked his male respondents. About half of them expressed "moderate and positive" replies, and these men strongly tended to belong to the "happily married" category. A lower incidence of "happily married" rankings characterized those who declared extreme affection, lukewarm or negative feelings toward their mother.

Since the survey group included 55 married couples, it was possible to see how consistently husbands and wives were independently rated as "happily married" when grouped according to the affectionate relationship between husband and mother. Results show that for wives as well as for husbands, marriage happiness is favored by a *positive but moderate* affectional bond between husband and his mother. "Too much or too little mother-love," Hamilton and McGowan conclude, "produced husbands who were less happy in their marriages than the average of the research, and their wives were still less happy. A [moderate and positive] amount of mother-love produced husbands who were happier than the average, and their wives were . . . happier."[34]

Table 3:2. Husband's response to question, "Were you and your mother always on affectionate terms?" and rating for marriage happiness of husbands and their wives[35]

	Total number of respondents		Percentage of respondents rated "happily married"	
Husband's response	Husbands	Wives	Husbands	Wives
Always on *very* affectionate terms	(12)	(8)	42	25
Answer moderate and positive	(54)	(28)	59	64
Lukewarm, "fairly friendly," to frank dislike	(34)	(19)	41	37
	(100)	(55)		

Hamilton's data suggest that a man who is predisposed to find happiness in marriage has enjoyed a positive but moderate bond of affection with his mother, and tends to seek a mate whom he would describe as resembling his mother in physique and to a lesser extent in disposition. *Too much* mother-love, Hamilton and McGowan argued, renders the son incapable of loving another woman "in a natural, grown-up way. . . . At adolescence, the normal time for asserting his own will and seeking love from someone not his mother, this man was a captive to a relationship that should have passed away. . . ."[36] Hamilton and McGowan hypothesized that over-mothering is more likely to occur in smaller families, and where there is a lack of affection between mother and father.[37]

Hamilton and McGowan describe the seductive mother who "not only develops too great a love for her in her son [but] goes on cultivating this abnormal fervor, and dominating his life right through adolescence. She clings to her grown-up little boy so jealously and tenaciously that often he cannot look on any other woman with longing—or at any rate with enough longing to make him break his chains. If he does marry . . . then mother and son are sure to find some excuse for extreme dissatisfaction with the woman who has come between them."[38] In the foregoing statement the authors suggest that the burden of a "mother-complex" might lead a young man to seek a bride who is just deviant enough ("blemished," as Flanzblau has put it) to somehow justify mother's ready-made dissatisfaction, as well as his own mixed feelings toward marriage.

Hamilton and McGowan anticipated the "contrast choice" concept when they hypothesized that the dominating, seductive mother "may make the inevitable struggle to cut the apron strings so difficult for [her son] that he has to focus on girls who don't look like mother at all, if he is to achieve emotional independence."[39]

Occupational status and intermarriage. It should not be too surprising that a Jew who chooses a "Gentile" occupation should also tend to choose a Gentile wife. Even if the two choices do not express a wish to shift one's group affiliations, induction into the world of the salaried professions exerts an important influence on the person's social life.

The salaried professions usher the Jew into a Gentile world unknown to the majority of Jewish businessmen, unknown to

many Jewish doctors, lawyers, and other independent professionals. Until recently few Jews entered college teaching, engineering, architecture or journalism. The world of the salaried
experts is a Gentile world in its geographic mobility; a willingness to relocate is taken for granted. Ties with *mishpocho* and
the Jewish community are weakened or severed, and replaced to
an extent with feelings of loyalty toward a professional community. "Wherever he goes, the organization man has a built-in
social life within his occupational circles. He has no need for
the social resources of any local community."[40] The friendship
of both Jews and Gentiles, a goal which the third generation
Jew aspires to, is ordinarily available only to members of the
salaried professions.[41]

To a young Jewish intellectual, the unimaginative world of
middle class conventionality, against which he is struggling, may
be seen as the Jewish world. His rebellion against social conformity is experienced as a rebellion against the family's plea
that he find a proper profession (e.g., medicine, law, dentistry,
or accounting) and marry a nice Jewish girl. He experiences his
emancipation from middle class conventionality as a revolt
against Judaism or Jewishness. He feels that Judaism has no
special value for him; "that the barriers which exist between
[him] and non-Jews are meaningless. . . . Should his enthusiasm
for his intellectual world be shared by a young woman of another faith, there is little that could hold him to Jewish life," as
Rabbi Rubenstein observes.[42]

What determines whether a third-generation Jew goes into
business or prepares for a profession? In North City "almost all
of the members of the third generation who are in business are
in their father's business."[43] Fewer than five percent aspire to
start a business of their own.[44] A managerial job in a family
business gives a young man status in the Jewish community and
gives him residential roots in the community. A role of leadership in the community, support of its charities and philan-
thropies, naturally falls on his shoulders. The young man who
does not have this ready-made status advantage must make a
career choice. If he wants to affiliate himself with the local ethnic
group and its needs and values, he might be expected to give
priority to the independent professions: medicine, dentistry, law,

accounting. If, on the other hand, he wishes to address himself to a Gentile status audience, if he wants to emancipate or separate himself from the ethnic community, the salaried professions can usher him into the Gentile world. (We are examining here only one aspect of an exceedingly complicated phenomenon, and would not suggest that a person's choice between engineering and law, for example, is established entirely or mainly by whether he has chosen to identify with Gentiles or with Jews.)

Do members of the salaried professions show a higher intermarriage rate than members of more traditionally Jewish occupational groups? According to Rabbi Henry Cohen "approximately 20 percent of the Jewish faculty members at the University of Illinois [at Urbana]—well over twice the national average—are married to Gentile women."[45] Campaign-Urbana's Jewish population is about equally divided between factulty and townsfolk. The 20 percent intermarriage ratio in the faculty community compares with a 6.5 percent ratio for Jewish townsfolk. This difference is especially interesting in view of the fact that most of the faculty are "sons of Eastern European immigrants and grew up in predominantly Jewish neighborhoods. . . . The townspeople, on the other hand—chiefly manufacturers, wholesalers, retailers, and professionals—include a group descended from 'old' German-Jewish families who are firmly rooted in the community and whose predoinant background is Reform."[46]

An even more dramatic difference emerges from the 1956 Washington D.C. survey, when one compares the intermarriage rate of self-employed and government-employed third generation Jewish husbands. Of 705 men in the self-employed group, not a single one was intermarried! Of 994 men in the government service, 235 (24 percent) were intermarried. The same trend obtains (though not so strikingly) for the first and second generation, as shown on Table 3:3.

Blue-collar worker *vs.* white-collar worker represents another distinction between "Gentile" and "Jewish" fields of employment. Are Jews who choose "Gentile" careers below the professional level also more likely to intermarry than Jews who follow the more traditional ways of earning a living? Marriage statistics from the state of Iowa (1953-59) confirm this expectation. The intermarriage rate for all white-collar workers is reported as 27.2

Table 3:3. Jewish husband's employment status and intermarriage rate, Washington, D.C., 1965[47]

	Self-employed			Government-employed		
	Number In-Married	Number Inter-Married	Percent Inter-Married	Number In-Married	Number Inter-Married	Percent Inter-Married
Foreign Born	(1988)	(8)	0.4	(816)	(56)	6.9
Second generation	(2980)	(218)	7.3	(4738)	(468)	8.9
Third generation	(705)	(0)	0	(759)	(235)	23.6

percent. The rate for all blue-collar workers was given as 46.8 percent, as shown on Table 3:4.

The distinction between business owners, independent professionals, and salaried professionals was not maintained in the tabulation of the Iowa statistics (as reported by Rosenthal). The listed category which would be most heavily weighed with business

Table 3:4. Jewish husbands' employment status and intermarriage rate, all applicants for first marriage, Iowa, 1953–59[48]

		Incidence of Intermarriage	
Occupation	(N)	(N)	per cent
Managers, officials and proprietors	(58)	(6)	10.3
Sales workers	(72)	(17)	23.6
Professional, technical and kindred workers	(202)	(65)	32.2
Clerical and kindred workers	(10)	(5)	50.0
Total White-Collar Group	(342)	(93)	27.2
Laborers (except farm and mine)	(6)	(5)	83.3
Service workers, including private household	(2)	(1)	50.0
Craftsmen, foremen and kindred workers	(21)	(9)	42.9
Operatives and kindred workers	(17)	(7)	41.2
Farmers and farm managers	(1)	(0)	0
Farm laborers	(0)	(0)	0
Total Blue-Collar Workers	(47)	(22)	46.8

owners (managers, officials, and proprietors) shows an intermarriage rate of 10.3 percent, while the category most heavily weighed with salaried professionals (professional, technical, and kindred workers) shows an intermarriage rate of 32.2 percent.

Discussions on social status and intermarriage invariably deal with intermarriage as a vehicle for *upward* mobility, as a tactic for reaching above and beyond the ethnic community. The Iowa data shown in Table 3:4 demonstrate that intermarriage also fits into the life pattern of the Jew who falls *below* the norm of the highly mobile Jewish community. Those whose aptitudes or attitudes do not equip them for establishing themselves in business or in a profession may move into a traditionally Gentile occupation and are more likely to choose a Gentile wife. This pattern may hold only for smaller Jewish communities (like those of Iowa) where the character of the community is distinctly upper middle class, and blue-collar workers may be too few to find any real social life inside the Jewish community.

Abram

Gordon describes the case of a man with a strong sense of Jewish identity who, as he approached middle age, accepted intermarriage, with considerable reluctance. In Gordon's interview protocol Abram describes himself as a medical professor whose bachelorhood was unsettled by the enrollment of a postgraduate woman student—a Brazilian Catholic—in his class. Such a person seemed to him "unimaginable" as a marriage partner. He describes his upbringing as the older of two boys and recalls his mother's overwhelming devotion to him, her fervent wish that he become a medical doctor, and her complete faith that he could overcome the financial obstacles to this goal, in contrast with his father's discouraging "realism" about his inability to support this goal from his limited earnings as a civil service worker. The intensity of devotion between mother and son is reflected in the following interview excerpts:

"My folks . . . lived for us boys. There was absolutely nothing we could possibly have needed or wanted that my mother and father wouldn't get for us. No sacrifice was too great.

". . . It was my mother even more than my father who had the

great ambition for her boys. She was anxious for us to become
doctors. . . . Everything was for 'education' . . .

"During my years in medical school, I was doing very well. I
devoted every single waking hour to my work. I was soon recognized as a good doctor. . . . You can't imagine how important
it was for me to do well in my chosen field. My whole life was
tied up with it. I became a good enough doctor for an important
medical school to offer me an assistant professorship shortly after
I was graduated. Of course I was thrilled. . . . But if you think
it was a great moment for me, you should have seen my folks
at that time. It was the greatest thing that had ever happened
to them. I couldn't have done anything greater, if I had become
President of the United States. Both my father and mother were
so thrilled, so happy . . . I had attained such a position in their
eyes I couldn't possibly do anything wrong. Whatever I wanted
was good. Whatever I said was right . . .

"I guess they believed that I was going to remain a bachelor.
. . . They were content to see me to the top of the medical teaching profession. That was all they wanted.

"When Carlotta came to our medical school as a postgraduate
student and we were attracted to each other, it was as much a
surprise to me as to anyone . . . I am older than she is. We had
such utterly different backgrounds, and our religions were different . . .

"My mother had heard that I was going out with a Brazilian
Catholic girl . . . but her letters to me never mentioned it . . . I
guess her love for me was really very great and I know that she
was concerned about my happiness. Yet she was a proud Jewess
and it must have hurt her very much.

"You won't believe this . . . but it hurt me, too. I could never
imagine that I would marry a non-Jewess, and, of all people, a
Catholic. I was essentially a religious person, a religious Jew. I
knew I was a Jew and I wanted to be a Jew. Even though I was
single, I had become a member of a Synagogue and I was rather
active in its program. I used to go to services on Friday nights
very often.

". . . I was an active Jew, a positive Jew. I was active in the
Jewish Federation. I was the Chairman of a B'nai B'rith Lodge.
I was active in the Brotherhood of my Synagogue. I was always

identified with Judaism and the Jewish people. All the students at the medical school knew me as a Jew. I actively helped Jewish students who came to me because I was Jewish. Here we were— two people of different religions, more and more in love all the time. . . . After all the inner conflict I had with myself, I decided that the only real answer was for Carlotta to convert to Judaism. . . . When, after many months of discussion, we both agreed on this, Carlotta went to the rabbi with me and told him how we felt. The rabbi was understanding . . .

"Carlotta and I have been very happy together. I think that she is a good Jewess. We have two lovely children. They are being reared as Jews, of course. Carlotta lights the Sabbath candles and I make the *Kiddush* each Sabbath eve. We go to synagogue services regularly. . . . I think that our marriage has succeeded very well . . ."[49]

THE GENTILE WIFE

Sex appeal and sexual acquiescence. What does the Jewish husband recall about his Gentile wife that especially appealed to him when they first met, and made her seem different from other girls he had dated? This question evoked a good deal of embarrassment in some of Mayer's respondents; perhaps they recalled that in their first encounter with their wife they regarded her as a lighthearted *shiksa* who stirred their fantasies of sexual adventure. Mayer's respondents were not entirely reticent on this issue:

> During this period I wasn't interested in getting married . . . just in having a good time. I really didn't care what the girl's religion happened to be. [He went on to explain that Gentile girls were, in fact, more preferable for his purposes:] Jewish girls are more moral, and it's harder to have a good time with them.[50]

Mayer recalls "a Jewish doctor—who was primarily interested in sex—who felt that Christian girls were 'easier to have a good time with'. . . . [The respondent] succinctly, but meaningfully, conveyed his first impression [of his wife]: 'A nice girl, good looking, well stacked.' "[51] Another intermarried Jew recalled to Mayer that he sought out Gentile sex partners "not only because he believed they were more accessible sexually, but for fear of being trapped into marriage. . . . There was a certain safety in knowing she was of a different religion."[52]

Factors which contribute to a man's judgment that an outgroup woman is more sexually desirable or acquiescent are studied in depth in Chapter 12. Kinsey's survey findings support this stereotype, to the extent that Gentile women recall having their first coital experience at an earlier age than their Jewish counterparts.[53] (See Figure 9:3.) How might one interpret this finding? Are Gentile girls emancipated from parental control at an earlier age? Is it possible that the Jewish girl's culturally patterned aggressiveness better equips her to defend herself against a male's attempts to dominate or exploit her? Restating the same question from another standpoint, does the Gentile norm of self-sacrifice and altruism, "doing everything in one's power to please the other person," predispose a girl to submit, to acquiesce, to surrender herself to her partner's imperious demands?[54] Ehrmann's survey of college students' dating behavior (summarized in detail in Chapter 8) indicated that Jewish males show more self-control toward their dates; Jewish males are less likely than their Gentile peers to leave it up to the girl to decide at what point their petting should stop. Ehrmann's Jewish college men also indicate that they take an especially protective attitude toward their Jewish dates.

Dating, courtship, and marriage involve extremely complex, diverse, and subtle interactions. The transformations of fascination to tenderness, of curiosity to compassion, of lust to love, of physical intimacy to spiritual identity, make the topic of "boy meets girl" a phenomenon of unending interest to artist, behavioral scientist, and clinician alike. While we cannot integrate this diversity with the artistry of a novelist or playwright, we can be attentive to the many levels at which the romantic encounter operates.

Marriage and conversion: the cause-and-effect paradox. Since the candidate for conversion to Judaism—in nine cases out of ten—is engaged to marry a Jew, it is easy to assume that he accepts conversion as a gesture of good will, a compromise or sacrifice for the sake of family harmony. Some rabbis express the attitude that it is therefore foolish to pretend that the Gentile fiance is seriously interested in Judaism as a religion; that it is shameful to conduct a "conversion factory" where classrooms of Gentiles attend the formalities of Jewish instruction as a preliminary to a Jewish marriage.[55]

Rabbi Rubenstein does not agree with this common-sense view of the Gentile fiance's motives for conversion. In some cases the cause-and-effect relationship appears to be reversed: the Gentile wants to join the Jewish group and therefore seeks a Jewish mate. Engagement to a Jew provides a socially accepted motive for conversion to the Jewish faith. "This does not mean," Rubenstein adds, that the Gentile had made "a conscious and deliberate decision to marry a Jew. . . . Nevertheless, the behavioral patterns suggest that an unconscious decision had preceded the actual decision."[56] Rabbi Eichorn agrees that many fiance-converts prove "emotionally, intellectually and spiritually attuned to the teachings of Judaism," to an extent that indicates that their choice of a Jewish mate did not seem accidental.[57]

The literature of intermarriage yields a number of cases of Gentile women who regarded conversion to Judaism as a natural expression of their religious attitudes. One of Mayer's Catholic respondents said, "I was willing and anxious to convert. I had never been a great Catholic, and there were many things about Catholicism I could never accept. I found in Judaism many things I had believed in all along, and it seemed silly not to become a Jew. . . . I felt absolutely no regrets about giving up Catholicism. There were so many questions it couldn't answer to my satisfaction, and there had been for many years."[58] In a case cited by Gordon, a Protestant-born wife had grown up with poorly defined and unsatisfying religious ties, and made it clear to her fiance that "she intended to convert to Judaism whether or not" they could overcome her prospective in-laws' objections.[59] Another case cited by Gordon: Catholic-born Carlotta recalled, "I was ready to give up Catholicism because I really no longer believed in it. I wanted to find a way of life, a theology in which I could believe and that proved to be Judaism."[60]

Rubenstein cites the case of an upper class Protestant girl "of high cultural attainments" as an example of an intermarriage motive which is deeply rooted in the person's life history.

Pamela

". . . Very bright and very attractive, [Pamela made] the Jewish boy she planned to marry [seem] dull by comparison. His basic inclinations were to enter his father's business and to create a world of petty security for himself. He wanted [Pamela] to become Jewish mainly to placate his family and have a Jewish wedding. I suspected almost from the start a basic incompatibility.

"About midway in her studies [for conversion], the young lady told me that she had broken off her engagement, but that she still wanted to become Jewish. At one level it was apparent that, though she was prepared to terminate her relationship with her fiance, she was not prepared to terminate her relationship with the rabbi.

"My reaction to her plea was an insistent refusal. She persisted. She claimed that on the basis of her studies she believed in Judaism and she wanted to be Jewish. From the traditional point of view, it would seem that this would be the best kind of conversion, one unmotivated by any consideration of marriage or anything other than pure respect for Judaism. From my point of view, this was the worst reason for becoming Jewish. If all that was involved was an intellectual or religious assent to Jewish principles, it would seem that she ought rather to become a liberal Protestant. Conversion seemed less and less a religious decision and more and more adhesion to [i.e., striving for affiliation with] a religio-ethnic community.

"I expressed myself to her rather emphatically: [Rabbi Rubenstein continues] 'Look, you can continue to see me and study Judaism as frequently as you like, but I refuse to authorize your conversion until you get yourself another Jewish boy.'

"This seemed very strange to her and she asked me to explain myself. 'Well, the way you are now, you are obviously very Protestant and Anglo-Saxon in appearance. If you tell people that you are Jewish, both Jews and Gentiles alike are going to regard you as odd. Gentiles won't want you because you've turned Jewish; Jews will suspect you because they'll think you are strange. I am more interested in your finding a proper husband than in whether you ultimately become Jewish or Christian. If you really want to become Jewish, find yourself another Jewish boy, become engaged, and then I'll be delighted to authorize the conversion. However, I see certainly no necessity for you to marry someone outside of your own background.'

"She continued to see me weekly for about two months. Then one afternoon she brought a young Jewish professor into the office and introduced me to her new fiancé! Several months later she was converted and married. I always have been convinced that this young woman's unconscious decision to marry a Jew received its first impetus during her childhood treatment by her Jewish analyst [whom she saw nearly every day for several years, beginning at age ten]. In her mind, she had two fathers, a good Jewish father who had lovingly accepted her, and a 'bad' Gentile father who had 'rejected' her. It made very little difference that the real father's decision to send her to the clinic was undoubtedly a loving decision made with much heartache. From her childlike perspective, he had rejected her . . . [The rabbi's efforts to help her become aware of these unconscious origins of her Jewish identification could not alter her present attitude.] . . . Her total life-situation had become somewhat 'Jewish.' She experienced both the alienation and the inner insight which frequently accompanies being a partial stranger to what one knows best. She was no longer like the girls in her peer-group and could never again take seriously the things which concerned them."[61]

Rabbi Rubenstein defends his "bargain" with Pamela; that she find a Jewish husband before the rabbi would authorize her conversion: "Marriage is the best rather than the worst reason for conversion today. Young people create the first nucleus of community life by forming a family. They share each other's fate and destiny. It is best that this be shared within a common religio-ethnic community."[62]

Charlotte

When Charlotte, a non-practicing Presbyterian, married Joel, a Jewish enlistee in the navy, she "felt no need to make a hurried resolution about our religious future," she recalls in an autobiographical essay she wrote some ten years later.[63] Each had a pre-

school child from a previous marriage. ". . . The getting acquainted, the new love, the learning to live together, was
enough." When Charlotte's daughter reached school age and expressed an interest in matters of religious identity, Charlotte responded by visiting various Protestant churches. "The people
were friendly. The sermons were good. . . . Yet each lacked something. I couldn't put my finger on it, but I knew none of them
was for me," Charlotte concluded. After visiting with several
ministers, she still felt "no closer to solving my problem than
when I had started."

Charlotte asked Joel to take her to a synagogue. He was less
than enthusiastic: "I'd rather you didn't consider Judaism. . . .
It's entirely different from anything you've ever known. If you
were to convert, it might prove too much of a change for you.
And later you might regret your decision." Charlotte thereupon
took the initiative to meet and talk with rabbis in the various
towns where Joel was stationed. She attended Sabbath services,
she did considerable reading on Judaism, "and began to ask questions of Jewish wives I met along the way . . ."

Suddenly one day I wanted to light the Sabbath candles. And
I did. What a warm, serene glow pervaded the kitchen from two
such tiny flames! . . . The children were entranced. . . . Joel was
at sea at the time and I wrote him of our experience. When he
came home, he told me how my enthusiasm had rekindled his
own spark of faith he'd almost allowed to die." When a navy
chaplain suggested that it was time that she and her children
started their religious education, "the decision wasn't hard to
make," Charlotte recalls. "In fact, I think it had been made
months before and was only waiting to be recognized."

Charlotte describes her participation in the Sabbath and holidays, of seeing her daughter chosen to play Queen Esther for a
Sunday school Purim party, of witnessing her son's bar mitzvah,
and of the feeling of believing and belonging, which had become
part of her Jewish identity. That she made her first approach to
Judaism in the face of her husband's reluctance ("I'd rather you
didn't consider Judaism") may give a special significance to the
opening sentence of Charlotte's autobiographical essay: "I suppose the idea of conversion from a non-practicing Presbyterian
to Jew occurred to me long before my name changed from Mac-
Donald to Schwartz."

Alienation and belongingness. During the period of time he worked at Harvard University, Rabbi Rubenstein counseled for conversion a total of twenty Gentiles who had chosen Jewish mates. In almost every case it appeared as if the convert was seeking membership in the Jewish community rather than religious conversion *per se*.[64] Seen through Gentile eyes, the Jews comprise "a community of the alienated," a group which has learned to live with the fact that they "do not belong." The feeling of estrangement is not, of course, a uniquely Jewish experience. To a Gentile who feels somehow alienated from her own comfortable majority, who can no longer accept its social rituals and ethos as part of her own identity, "Jewish life may frequently seem attractive because it presupposes with great explicitness the fact of estrangement."[65]

Rabbi Rubenstein describes one of his converts, descendant of a long line of New England ministers and teachers, born into the best society and a member of all the proper Protestant organizations. "As she matured and as her intellectual interests developed, she became more and more convinced that she did not belong. She knew that this was an element in her choice of a Jewish partner. . . . On one occasion, her comments on her interest in marrying a Jew elaborated on this theme. "I don't belong and the Jews don't belong, but at least they have each other," she said.[66] The rabbi tells of asking another of his converts "whether she was prepared to leave the relative security of the Protestant in-group and bring up her children with the relative insecurities of the Jewish out-group . . . [She replied] that the Jews were by no means the only people who did not belong."[67]

To join the fellowship of the alienated makes a two-fold attack on the problem of estrangement: one acquires access to culturally patterned ways of dealing with alienation, and perhaps more importantly one may share an intimate bond of fellowship with those who call themselves "We Jews."

Frances

"Born and raised in a Gentile world, living in a Christian atmosphere, having had the usual schooling in Christianity, I lived a pleasant and satisfying life. I traveled with a wide circle of friends, enjoying social contacts with both Jews and Gentiles.

Christian creeds did not interest me very much, as I found too many unfathomables in their teachings. As I grew older, I arrived at a philosophy satisfactory to me, but hardly in keeping with my earlier Christian training.

"My entrance into Judaism dates from the beginning of my small son's religious education. I had married a Jew and had been living happily with him for many years, experiencing no need of affiliating with Judaism, or for that matter, with any religion. . . . My husband's family and all our Jewish friends were very pleasant people, exhibiting no prejudice at all where I was concerned. No pressure was put upon me to convert to Judaism.

"When our son was five and had reached religious school age, I sent him to a synagogue near our home. My mind began to turn toward Judaism, not only for him but also for myself. . . . What makes a Jew a Jew? How does a Jew think? What are his traditions? These and many other questions nagged at me and, for the sake of my child's religious training, I wanted to know the answers . . .

"Becoming affirmatively Jewish was a gradual process with me. From a growing interest in the festivals and rituals, I went on to study something of the history, philosophy, culture, and other phases of Judaism. Little by little, I could feel a cold analytical study turn into a warm interest and finally to a sincere love for what is now my way of life."

[The author goes on to describe her attachment to the rituals and traditions of Judaism, and describes the maintenance of a kosher home as "one of the highlights of my Jewish life."][68]

Chanele

Daughter of a Norwegian Lutheran father and a Scotch-Irish Methodist mother, Chanele—as she was to call herself after her conversion to Judaism—was born in Fayetteville, Arkansas. She studied art at the University of New Mexico, where she met her husband, an Albequerque stockbroker. Her *cultural* conversion, which is the emphasis of her autobiographical essay, has become the dominant theme of her work as an artist—expressed through paintings and sketches of scenes and people inspired by characters in Sholom Aleichem's stories and other characters of Yiddish literature. Chanele and her husband hope to establish a boy's camp and adult cultural center featuring Yiddish theatre, lectures, and concerts.

"My conversion to Judaism was the beginning of a truly meaningful way of life for me. I refer not only to my religious conversion, but also to a cultural conversion that has enriched my life immeasurably . . .   . . .

"I received the basic religious indoctrination of the Lutheran faith. . . . My parents and I attended church regularly and I went to Sunday School classes. I knew the liturgy by heart and attended my first communion with pride . . .   . . .

"The questions I asked through high school and college were never answered satisfactorily . . .   . . . The whole feeling conveyed by the rituals and prayers of [many Christian] denominations is one of the crushing weight of human guilt. I found this a degrading and incredible view of man's relation to his Creator.

"After reaching intellectual maturity, I knew that I did not and could not honestly believe in the teachings or the rituals of the faith in which I had been reared.

"Through my readings and observations I became interested in Judaism . . .   . . . [but] I did not formally convert to Judaism until after I married my husband, Moishe. [Only one Reform rabbi in our city] would marry us unless I converted first. This I refused to do. I wanted my conversion to Judaism to be completely wholehearted and sincere and not in any sense a forced conversion."

Chanele recalls how her study of Judaism gave her "a love for everything Jewish," how she "became a daughter of Israel proudly and joyfully." Following her conversion she found a textbook in college Yiddish, and "began studying it because I mistakenly thought that all pious Jewish women speak Yiddish." When her misconception was corrected, "it no longer mattered. I had become excited over a language that other Jews take for granted or never bother to learn. I found that through Yiddish I could gain a greater knowledge of Jewish culture and folklore. The language has a feeling of warmth and tenderness. . . . It radiates a feeling of love for the family and happy family gatherings.

"From reading Sholom Aleichem and Peretz in Yiddish, I learned about the Jewish way of life in the 'old country,' of the traditions, joys and sorrows of the *shtetl* Jew. From my readings in the Yiddish classics I gained an understanding of and an appreciation for Jewish humor, the 'laughter with tears' in the stories of the Jew who, frustrated by his problems, finds relief by laughing at himself."

Chanele brings her autobiographical essay to a close with an appreciation of the "precious heirloom" of Yiddish culture.[69]

Cora

Cora was referred for psychiatric treatment because of a post-partum depression. Raised as a Protestant, "she had married a Jew against her mother's advice and had developed a markedly dependent attitude toward her [Jewish] mother-in-law." Analytic interviews unfolded an unusual upbringing which led to considerable hostility toward her mother, and a fantasied Jewish identification.

Cora was toilet-trained early and "abandoned to a housekeeper" so that her mother could resume her position as teacher at an exclusive private school. Cora later attended this school, where she was her mother's pupil. Forced to compete for her mother's attention and approval with a classrom of wealthy children, Cora came to overvalue money and intellect. "To be wealthy meant that mother would love her," Cora's analyst reflected, "since mother paid more attention to the wealthy children in the private school." Sibling rivalry thus became a prominent theme in Cora's emotional life, though she was in fact an only child.

Cora's father, a moderately successful engineer, had been extremely affectionate to Cora. His death, which occurred when Cora was only four, reduced the family's economic security and sharpened the discrepancy between her classmates and herself. In her fantasy world she identified her father with the Jewish Jesus ("Our Father Who art in Heaven"). Her feelings of victimization and castration also supported her identification with the Jews.

Shortly before Cora attained puberty, her mother remarried.

Cora liked her Protestant step-father, and her parents' "explicit speech and free behavior stimulated her sexual fantasies." Since the normal incest-barrier between Cora and her new father was absent, these "misguided attempts at sex education" made it necessary for Cora to erect "an exaggerated taboo against him." Her parents' seductive behavior "aroused her anger, and called forth even stronger defenses. Her selection of a well-to-do Jewish mate," Cora's analyst concludes, "satisfied the unconscious pregenital and Oedipal needs of her childhood and the incest taboos of adolescence," in addition to serving the needs which are normally fulfilled through marriage.

Interestingly, Cora's wish to affiliate with Judaism ran counter to her husband's rejection of Judaism. (Analytic treatment, which her husband, Barney, obtained from a colleague of Cora's analyst, indicated that Barney's "rejection of Judaism represented . . . [a] defense against castration anxiety.") "The analysis of both partners enabled them to become more accepting of each other. [Barney] was able to effect a lukewarm acceptance of Judaism, and [Cora] was able to accept a nonfanatical conversion."[70]

The rabbi-convert relationship. When a Gentile fiancee is prepared for conversion through counseling and instruction by a rabbi, over that period of months the candidate may not only learn much more about Judaism than her future husband or his protesting family claims to know, there may also emerge a special bond of compassion and understanding between rabbi and convert. The rabbi appreciates her intelligence and sensitivity, enjoys her fresh and honest interest in Judaism. The rabbi may feel quite embarrassed and irritated toward the discourtesy of those who question her sincerity or honesty, and outraged at the "surly stand-offishness" which born-Jews may direct toward the convert.[71] The rabbi may find himself playing the role of counselor, protector, advocate and champion of the convert.

Thus Rabbi Bamberger asserts that converts "are as a rule no less observant than the Jewish-born spouses, frequently more so. They often have a much healthier attitude toward their Jewish identity than the complex-ridden Jews among whom they live."[72]

One of Gordon's rabbinical respondents praises converts as "more devout than the average [Jewish] child," and further asserts that they "build a bridge of good will to Christian families in the community."[73] Rabbi Eichorn praises converts to Judaism as "a precious spiritual asset. They challenge the Jewish-born to be more worthy of the priceless spiritual possession which has been given to them by their fathers. They are a constant reminder of the Jew's neglected obligation to share this possession more unselfishly with those non-Jews who are dissatisfied with the faiths of their fathers and yearning for a more meaningful explanation of human existence and a more satisfying way of life."[74]

Eichorn's 1954 survey yielded responses from 785 Conservative and Reform rabbis on the question of how converts compare with Jewish-born members of their congregation, in their "Jewish loyalties and interests." A majority of rabbis ranked both groups "about the same," but rabbis tended to describe converts as "more loyal" more frequently than they accorded this designation to the Jewish-born.

Table 3:5. Loyalty of Jewish-born and Converts, as Rated by 785 Rabbis[75]

	Jewish-born are more loyal	Both groups about the same	Converts are more loyal
Reform rabbis' judgments	10%	56%	34%
Conservative rabbis' judgments	18%	56%	26%

The 1954 survey also revealed that converts had occupied 14 sisterhood presidencies, and 14 other synagogue offices throughout the country.

Table 3:6. Synagogue Offices Occupied by Converts, as Reported by 785 Rabbis[76]

Office	Reform	Conservative
President of sisterhood	10	4
Member of synagogue board of directors	8	1
President of local B'nai B'rith Women	2	1
President of local Hadassah	1	1

Psychoanalysis and Jewish identity. Returning to the experience of Rabbi Rubenstein at Harvard University, he further observes that "at least half of the [20] girls whom I have converted have either been in psychoanalysis or psychoanalytic therapy. In general, these girls were among the most sensitive and the most competent young women I have counseled." Their therapeutic experience made them feel "Jewish" in a certain sense; they recognized "the Jewish intellectual as sharing their alienation, their insights, and their commitments."[77] Is the significant factor in this pattern of experience a bond of loyalty toward a Jewish therapist (as in the case of Pamela), or is it the acquisition through therapy of a "Jewish" mode of adjustment to that attitude of estrangement which led the person into therapy in the first place (and subsequently leads her into conversion and intermarriage)? Rabbi Rubenstein chooses to hypothesize that the therapeutic experience leads to a "Jewish" mode of adjustment:

> In the analytic process, much of what the [patient] deeply believes is called radically into question. . . . In the new integration one does not entirely identify with the roles and affiliations now accepted but previously rejected. One accepts their necessity and their inevitability. One makes the most of them, though something of the estrangement is never lost. One ends estrangement only by ceasing to be a stranger to oneself. Alienation is overcome; one belongs and does not belong at the same time, but one realizes that there is absolutely no other viable choice. One returns to one's first commitments, but with a difference.

> It is not surprising that sensitive Gentiles who have gone through this experience should so frequently choose intellectually and artistically competent Jews as their marital partners.[78]

Whatever the special meaning that Judaism holds for them, intermarried wives may participate in the practices of the Jewish culture with much zest and involvement:

You wouldn't think a little Scotch woman like that would

prepare gefilte fish for him. She makes potato latkes like no-body's business. . . . She makes all sorts of Jewish delicacies better than a lot of Jewish women I know.[79]

[Mayer refers to a Protestant wife who attempted to over-come her parents' opposition to their daughter's marriage to a Jew] . . . by introducing them to Jewish foods and they liked it. I cooked some of the dishes for them I had learned from my husband's mother.[80]

[One of Eichorn's rabbi respondents told of a German-born convert, the wife of a psychiatrist, who showed] . . . genuine depth of Jewish feelings. . . . She makes her own challah every Friday and does not ride on the High Holy Days.[81]

The burden of marginality. The reluctance of Jewish kin and acquaintances to accept the convert as a full member of the Jewish community can burden the convert with a deep sense of disappointment. Thus Carlotta laments that though she has tried to live a good Jewish life, and observes the rituals of Judaism and participates in the organizational life of the Jewish community, Jewish women still regard her as a Catholic, an outsider, someone who doesn't really belong:

Carlotta

I studied and prepared myself [for conversion] very faith-fully. I did everything the rabbi asked me to do and I did it wholeheartedly. . . . I have tried to live a good Jewish life [e.g., light the Sabbath candles and attend the synagogue every Sabbath]. I have broken off every connection with Cathol-icism. . . . My only problem is that after all these years, when I have tried so very hard to live a good Jewish life—and, I think, live it better than many Jews I know—some women who do not observe much, if anything . . . still regard me as a Catholic. How long is this going to continue? . . . Why do they persist in making me feel that I am an outsider? That I don't really belong?

. . . I remember that when I was at home in Brazil that whenever our family got together we would never talk about

Catholicism. But whenever Jewish people get together they talk about Judaism. I can understand that because being part of a people is so important. The Jews are really strange. They are a people and a religion all in one.

. . . I was ready to give up Catholicism because I really no longer believed in it. I wanted to find a way of life, a theology in which I could believe and that proved to be Judaism. This is what is so disturbing. When are these Jewish women, who know far less about Judaism than I, going to stop looking down on me and accept me as a Jewess? That is what I am and that is what I hope to be all the rest of my days. Yet, when I did a really good job for Hadassah, what do you think the women said: 'Isn't it wonderful? Carlotta is not a Jew and she did such a big job.' To them, I'm still not a Jew.[82]

The insecurity of her role in the Jewish community may lead the convert to conceal or deny her Gentile origin. (See "The ethnic convert." Chapter 13.)

THE JEWISH WIFE

Attitudes toward Jewishness. When a Jewish woman marries a Gentile, and thereby acquires a Gentile name, is she inevitably drawn into the dominant group? We have already referred to Slotkin's Alicia, "resentful and ashamed, and envious that she wasn't a Gentile," who sought through intermarriage an "escape from the stigma of being identified with Jews." Mayer quotes a female Jewish respondent on her own receptivity to inter-marrying:

Betty

"I was in favor of mixed marriage. I always felt more comfortable with people who were not Jewish. I don't know why . . . it just happened that way. . . . I guess I anticipated I might marry someone of a different religion, because after my first marriage was annulled I went out with anyone, regardless of their religion. It made no difference to me what their religion

was. I had thought about it, and it still made no difference. . . .
No, I didn't feel hesitant about becoming involved with my
husband because he was non-Jewish. This was because my
upbringing was completely irreligious. My family had never
stressed any of the Jewish traditions or clannishness."[83]

Re-examining Betty's statement one sees the underlying emotional conflict as it manifests itself in these sutble yet puzzling
contradictions: "I was in favor of mixed marriages" *but* "it
made no difference to me." "I anticipated I might marry someone of a different religion" *but* "I had thought about it, and it
still made no difference." "I don't know why I [always felt more
comfortable with people who were not Jewish]—it just happened that way" *but* "this was because my upbringing was completely irreligious."

Certainly marriage to a Gentile would have strong instrumental value to a Jewish woman who felt motivated to "acquire
full membership in the dominant group" for herself and her
children. A Gentile family name and a Gentile husband would
seem to make it relatively safe for such a woman to raise her
children as Gentiles. Rosten's study (though his sample was small)
indicated that the risk of being regarded as a "half-Jew" was
less for the offspring of a mixed marriage whose *father* was
Gentile.[84] Rosenthal's report on intermarriage in Washington,
D.C., notes that in that highly assimilationist community 86.4
per cent of intermarried families where the wife was Jewish were
raising their children as non-Jews (as were 81.4 per cent of
intermarrieds where the husband was Jewish).[85]

A Jewish woman may fall in love with and marry a man who
happens to be a Gentile, and insist upon her right and privilege
of raising her children as Jews. A number of Mayer's intermarried
Jewish wives voice a strong and positive feeling of Jewish
identity for themselves and for their children:

Mildred

"Our children will be brought up Jewish. I feel children
should always be the mother's religion, because the mother is
with them all day. . . . I just think the children should be the
mother's religion regardless of what she is."[86]

Frances A.

"The reasons for deciding to raise the children Jewish were the mother has more influence over the child in religious matters and teaches the child more, and I wouldn't know what else to teach them."[87]

Vera

"We always talked about what the children would be—we each wanted our own religion for them. Then he agreed to them being brought up Jewish, and shortly after that we got engaged. . . . We would have gotten married sooner except that it took [Carlo] such a long time to decide to bring the children up Jewish, which is what I wanted. . . ."[88]

Mayer quotes from his interview with Vera's Catholic husband:

Carlo

"(*How did you happen to decide to raise the children as Jews?*) My wife was going to have the pain and bear the children. I saw it that way. Also, I love her very much. (*Did you ever talk of bringing the children up as Catholics?*) I might have mentioned it in the beginning. But she wanted her own way, and I agreed to it. (*Did you find this an easy or difficult decision to reach?*) Not too easy—you like your way in these things. It was not too difficult to decide. I wanted her bad. I went along with it. You know, you just kind of go along."[89]

Jewish-Negro marriages. Gordon's sixteen intermarried couples cover a wide variety of exogamous pairings (e.g., Catholic-Protestant, white-Negro, Jewish-Gentile, Russian Jewish-German Jewish). Only two Jewish-born wives are represented in his data (which seems unusual since Gordon is a rabbi and presumably has special access to Jewish-Gentile couples), and both were married to uneducated Negroes. Both girls were raised by Eastern European immigrant parents. Both girls reveal distinctly tension-ridden family relations, especially with their fathers. Both girls describe their attraction to their husband in the context of affiliating themselves with a special interest group (in one case political radicalism, in the other jazz music). The following summaries further describe these common features as well as the distinctive characteristics of each case:

Doris

Doris describes her parents as "very good people," but adds that her father has always been preoccupied with business worries, "worked very hard all his life," and not only spent long hours in his store but also required the help of his wife in the business. Doris "didn't see much" of her older brother either ". . . so I was alone a good deal." Her loneliness was compounded by separation from her childhood environment when her family moved from the town in which she was born and raised, into the Jewish neighborhood of a city, close-by her father's new store. "I always thought of that move as being uprooted. Somehow, that made me very unhappy. . . . I gradually lost contact [what little contact she had!] with the family. Dad worked seven days a week. Mother was in the store most of the time, so I really didn't see them. We simply had no home life at all."

Doris relates her friendly attitude toward Negroes to her "special interest in the Negro music and the bands I used to hear on the radio. This was exciting music. I loved it." She describes her affiliation with Paul, her Negro husband, in the context of attending movies and jazz concerts together. Her family violently opposed her interest in Paul. Aside from her mother's tearfully pleading with Doris, her parents prevailed upon Paul's parents to send their boy to live with out-of-town relatives, and Doris' father took her first to a psychiatrist and then to a social worker. Doris' emotional distance from her parents is well expressed by her comment: "Everybody was working on me, but none of it really seemed to matter to me very much. . . . I still cannot understand why my mother and my father got so upset because Paul was a Negro or that he was not a Jew."

Doris promised not to see Paul again but could not tolerate the separation. "I stayed home and stopped eating and became very much upset." "Quite frantic" over Paul's disappearance, Doris located him and they decided to get married. "Had I told my parents about that they would have put me away in a hospital, I'm reasonably certain."

The coldness of Doris' father is revealed by his reaction to his daughter's intermarriage. "My father would have nothing to do with me from that time on to this very day seventeen years later. It's as if I don't exist . . . my father will not talk to me. When my grandmother died and I went to the funeral and tried to talk to him, he told me to move away from him. That's how he is. But I still send him cards on Father's Day, on his birthday or on anniversaries. Nothing will move him. It's as if I didn't exist any longer."

Although she had been raised without Jewish ritual or Hebrew education, Doris became devoutly Jewish and was raising her two sons as observant Jews. Doris speculates that perhaps she has done this "because I really wanted my parents, especially my father who has turned away from me, to know that I was very much of a Jewess. . . ."[90]

Doris' father emerges from her testimony as a somewhat strange and distant person. His choice of a business which occupied his time (days, evenings, and weekends), his thoughts and his energies, raising a family with virtually no home life, his reaction to his daughter's marriage—complete separation for seventeen years—suggests that he had never established strongly positive emotional ties with his daughter. How badly she hungered for his affection is suggested by her persistence, over seventeen years, in sending him Father's Day cards and birthday greetings. Gordon suggests that Doris' exogamous marriage was an act of rebellion. Analysis of her testimony suggests the hypothesis that the emptiness of her childhood home environment led to an unconscious conviction that she would have to go "a long way from home" to assuage her loneliness and satisfy her need for excitement, affection, and security.

Ruth

Ruth was raised by American-born Jewish parents in a thoroughly secular atmosphere, "If you were to judge our Jewishness by the way we kept the Sabbath or the Holy Days, you would never know that there was any association between us

and the Jewish people." Parents were recalled as "fighting all of
the time." Mother felt neglected and jealous of the attentions
her father was giving to other women.

"My father was a real character. He was a most unusual man.
He had a warm personality and was one of the most interesting
people I ever knew in my life. . . . He had little formal education, but he was a naturally smart man and he really made quite
a success of his life in the business world. . . . A flashy dresser
. . . he always looked as if he had just stepped out of the barber
shop. . . . He was a really passionate man. He loved women and
I'm sure that he stepped out a great deal. Of course my mother
was jealous and angry and very much hurt.

". . . It will be hard for you to believe what I am going to
say, but, in the interest of truth, I'm going to tell you what
has to be told.

"My father always seemed to have had a violent 'crush' on
me. I can remember, from the time I was a very little girl, that
he loved me very dearly, and showed his affection for me with
gifts and many kindnesses all through the years I was growing
up. . . . I really think that I was very much in love with my
father. As I look back at it all now, I realize that he really had
no moral sense at all. He just made my mother angry and he
caused me to daydream about father as a lover. . . . I was just
a mixed-up kid. I just didn't know what to do about it. What
with the violent quarrels I used to hear going on between my
mother and my father, I was a very much upset person."

". . . Some people used to say that I was shy. I think I was
more scared of people than anything else. I belonged to a club
or two and I had a boyfriend too. Between my mother and
father, I was anxious to get away from them, to get married and
live my own life. I was getting more and more afraid to be
with either of my parents. . . .

"When I was about seventeen years old, I belonged to a group
that used to talk a good deal against communism and against
fascism. Those were the days of Franco and the Spanish Loyalists.
We were all so much against Franco that we were ready to fight
him and fascism wherever possible. Once, I was invited to attend
a rally against fascism at someone's home. I remember it was
at this rally that I first met Tom, the Negro boy whom I later

married. He was a very nice boy. He had no special training
or learning. He had been a day laborer and apparently we
agreed that fascism should be fought. Before you know it, I was
going with him regularly.

"... As I look back at it now it seemed that by marrying
this Negro boy I could do two important things at the same
time: first, prove that I believed that all people are equal and
that I was not a hypocrite; and second, get away from both my
father and my mother." Ruth's parents were bitterly opposed
to her wishes to marry Tom. "The boy's parents were good,
simple, kind people. They accepted me and tried their best to
make me feel completely at home with them. And I really felt
at home with them."

As the daughter of an enterprising and successful businessman, Ruth could not tolerate the economic hardships of marriage to a Negro laborer. She resented her husband's unconcern
over his limitations as a "provider," and his willingness to accept
months on relief. She began to feel guilty about the burden of
Negro identity that would be borne by her fair-skinned daughter.
Ruth divorced Tom after less than two years of marriage, and
returned to the home of her parents. "My father was still a
'chaser' and my mother was still angry with him. The same
quarrels and fights were still going on. But I no longer minded
it." After a period of time during which she "sat in a rocker
. . . in a kind of a stupor" while mother cared for Ruth's child,
Ruth went back to work. Her mother brought up the child, and
years later Ruth married "a fine Jewish man who is very much
a Jew."[91]

As Ruth's story indicates, she responded to her father's seductive behavior ("father always seemed to have had a violent 'crush'
on me") as something *uncanny* ("It will be hard for you to
believe what I am going to say"), *immoral* ("he really had no
moral sense at all"), *dangerous* ("I was more scared of people
than anything else." "I was anxious to get away from them. . . .
I was getting more and more afraid to be with either of my
parents"), and *confusing* ("I was just a mixed-up kid." "I just
didn't know what to do about it. . . . I was a very much upset
person"). Like Doris, Ruth must have felt that she would have
to travel "a long way from home" to find a place of emotional

safety. With Tom's parents, "good, simple, kind people" she felt accepted, at home, and safe.

Gordon's two cases of intermarried Jewish women differ in a number of ways: Ruth's father was a successful business man; Doris' father was continually burdened by overwork and worry. Ruth's father was charming, seductive, outgoing, quarreling; Doris' father seemed aloof, cold, remote, silent. Ruth's marriage ended in divorce after less than two years; Doris' marriage, after 17 years, seems successful by many standards. The common factors in these women's experience are also striking: Both were raised without Jewish education or participation in Jewish family life and customs. Both had conflict-ridden relations with their father, from which they apparently felt impelled to escape by running "a long way from home." Doris was seventeen when she married Paul, Ruth was eighteen when she married Tom; both their husbands were Negro.

What is the frequency of Negro husband, Jewish wife marriages? What are the tendencies which lead to such marriages? In a study of Negro-white intermarrieds conducted in Philadelphia during the 1940's, Joseph Golden interviewed 50 Negro-white couples, and learned that almost half (19 out of 44) of the white wives were Jewish. (Of the six white husbands, none was Jewish.) Of these 44 white wives, 11 were war brides who had met their Negro husbands in Europe or the Near East, and who were presumably not fully acquainted with the American norms on racially mixed marriage. If we suppose that all of the 19 Jewish wives were native born, they account for 19 out of 33, or 58 per cent of Golden's sample of native-born white wives of Negroes.[92] In the course of his five-year interview study of Negro-white sex relations, Hernton found that "one out of every three white women I interviewed in New York City who were married to Negroes or were intimate with Negroes . . . was a Jew."[93] Cahnman mentions the recurring problem in New York City of finding adoptive homes for illegitimate offspring of Jewish mothers and Negro fathers.[94]

Problems of the Negro's Jewish wife. A Jewish woman pays a particularly heavy price for marriage to a Negro. In the pages of *Judaism,* Mrs. Inge Gibel cries out in anguish and in outrage over the hostility that Jews have directed at her and her brown-skinned children. She concedes that unfortunately a person in her role is stigmatized as "mentally inferior or unstable . . . by large segments of the Negro community" as well as by whites.[95]

The Negro-white couple's problem in obtaining decent housing is complicated by the disbelief of rental agents and neighbors "that the couple is legally wedded and law abiding."[96] The white wife "must forever keep her guard up lest she be insulted by jealous Negro women or by black men who look upon any white woman with a Negro as fair game for all Negroes."[97] According to Hernton, it is commonly supposed by men of both races that a white woman who lives with a Negro is a disreputable person, and this burden "weighs heavily upon any white woman who marries a Negro."[98]

". . . A white woman who marries a black man [will often] assume, on one level or another," says Hernton, "some of the . . . preoccupations of the Negro world." She usually becomes "intensely race-conscious" and adopts "a 'Negro outlook' toward the world."[99] As a Jew she may suffer additionally from the hostility of the Jewish community, because of its taboo against intermarriage, and interpret this treatment as a violation of the Jew's moral obligation to support Negro rights.[100]

Attitudes of the white wife. What are the attitudes that predispose a white woman to become the wife or mistress of a Negro? A "sincere identification with the Negro as an underdog [may require that she make no] deliberate effort to exclude Negroes from the possibility of sexual intimacy," says Hernton. "Such women usually come from radical or liberal family backgrounds and they themselves are often dedicated to 'liberal causes' . . ."[101] To some leftist white women, according to one of Hernton's informants, "having sex with a Negro seemed to be viewed as the only way of 'proving' oneself" to be free from racial prejudice.[102]

"With some white girls from wealthy liberal backgrounds . . . becoming intimate with a Negro frequently represents defiance of parental control, usually of a domineering, successful father,"[103] says Hernton. "Guilt, or a sense of self-loathing, is often among the ingredients that cause white women to seek refuge in the arms of black men. . . . [A] sense of personal failure eventually creates in the woman a desire for atonement, an unconscious yearning to be punished."[104] A relationship with a Negro may bring two forms of punishment: (1) social ostracism, and (2) "a more direct, carnal form of punishment from the very hands of her black lover. . . . She may deliberately or unconsciously cultivate sadistic tendencies in him. . . . Such women as these often marry or become intimate with, if not the most uncouth, definitely the most bitter and racially paranoid Negroes they can find. . . . Some white women suffering from (among other things) racial guilt offer themselves to black men as a living symbol of atonement for the entire system of race prejudice in America. . . ."[105]

Devereaux documents a case which closely matches Hernton's formulation—that of a self-destructive Jewish girl whose choice of a lover was an embittered pseudo-intellectual Negro.

Barbara

An extremely intelligent Jewish girl, born into a socially and intellectually prominent Jewish family . . . already as a high school senior . . . led an extremely dissolute life, associating in preference with the Negro prostitutes to whom one of her lovers had introduced her. Later on, she had a resounding affair with a greatly embittered, pseudo-intellectual American Negro. This man delighted in beating and humiliating her, and, in the midst of love-making, would often call attention, in extremely brutal words, to the fact that he, a Negro, was having sexual relations with—and thereby degrading—a white girl. This painful and debasing relationship terminated only when, because of the man's extreme physical brutality, she no longer felt safe from harm. . . . Her next affair—[also] an abnormal one—involved a [professional person belonging to a low status] . . . ethnic group. . . .[106]

Hernton draws a pathetic (and quite possibly exaggerated) picture of avant garde middle-class white women who choose a Negro husband or lover:

They are social outcasts. They have deserted their families, dropped out of college, run away from home, turned into beatniks, adopted the affectations of the "persecuted minority". . . . Not all of them, but most of them are phonies, psychological disorients, without true convictions or even the maturity to know what they really want. . . . The Negro they discover is merely another stereotype,[107] with his hair uncut and uncombed, usually "broke," talkative as hell but terribly illiterate, humming and shaking his head to the toot-toot of jazz music, mumbling ceaselessly about *his* "oppression," walking half-bent in an apelike gait or gyrating his hips to the "dog."[108]

Apart from those *social* attitudes which predispose a white woman to seek intimacy with a Negro (e.g., guilt over racial prejudice, identification with the underdog, defiance of parental control, resentment over social ostracism), Hernton describes the more specifically *sexual* motives for seeking a Negro partner. He refers to women "who constantly seek out black men to the exclusion of white ones because their psychological make-up, through repeated disappointing experiences with white men, has become so deranged that they can experience sexual satisfaction only with Negro men. Many of these women recognize their condition and sadly resign themselves to it."[109] Devereaux describes "a middle-class woman, in her late thirties, well-educated and well-bred, [who] openly told a lawyer who became interested in her, that she refused to have affairs with whites, especially if they were educated men, since she was exclusively interested in Negro bohemians. In fact, at that particular time she was living with a completely uneducated and rather coarse young Negro, fifteen years her junior."[110]

It appeared to Hernton, on the basis of his interview study, that some white women seek a Negro male as a sex partner in an effort to overcome homosexual feelings, or to break off from a homosexual past. He describes "an active female homosexual from New Orleans [who] came to New York, married a Negro, and has been 'going straight' ever since. . . . It takes blackness to bring out the 'femininity' in otherwise frigid or near-frigid white women," Hernton concludes.[111] Devereaux supports Hernton's observation, stating that women who seek a social inferior as a husband or lover "are usually somewhat masculine, and often either bisexual, or else primarily homosexual."[112]

To what extent do Gordon's two Jewish wives of Negroes fit the generalizations of Hernton and Devereaux? Both had seriously disturbed relations with their fathers, which undoubtedly burdened them with much sexual guilt and anxiety. (Doris' father was strange, distant, punitive. Ruth's father showed "no moral sense at all" by acting out a "violent 'crush'" on his daughter to the point of stimulating incestuous daydreams.) Ruth was attracted to radical causes and wanted to prove that she was "not a hypocrite." Doris became a devotee of Negro jazz before she met her husband.

When Gordon published the cases of Doris and Ruth as an article in *Judaism,* Mrs. Gibel responded by casting grave doubt about the representativeness of Gordon's cases. Herself a partner in a Negro-Jewish marriage, she insisted that none of the nine or ten Negro-Jewish couples who are her close friends shows any resemblance to Gordon's cases. In voicing her objections to Gordon's two cases, Mrs. Gibel casts doubt upon the entire length and breadth of interview research, claiming that normal intermarrieds "usually do not consent to being interviewed," leaving to investigators "the exhibitionists, the fanatics, the would-be martyrs, and those who would, at best, be somewhat confused individuals no matter which road they were traveling."[113]

The "normal intermarried" is of course either a statistical artifact or an idealized portrait. For better or for worse, intermarriage represents a deviation from the social norm. (Mrs. Gibel and her husband are, for example, a German refugee and a Jamaican Negro; is this a "normal intermarried" American couple?) The diversity of adjustments covered by the concept of intermarriage is well illustrated by a comparison of Gordon's and the Levinsons' intermarried Jewish wives. Compare Ruth and Doris, whom we have dealt with in some detail, with the Levinsons' five intermarried Jewish wives, all of whom came from relatively high status families and married into even higher status Gentile society.

Distance from father. Charlotte Buhler describes the case of an intermarried Jewish woman who shares two characteristics of Gordon's cases of Ruth and Doris: (1) a lack of rapport with father, and (2) a home background lacking in Jewishness. (This patient's only "nice" recollection of father involves the celebration of Christmas.) Unlike the cases of Ruth and Doris, this is the case of a woman who, conforming to Heiss' finding on the intermarried Jew, was unable to find a husband during the normal marrying years.

Ilona

A Hungarian Jewish woman well established in Vienna as a sculptor, Ilona was thirty-five years old when the Nazi *Anschluss* forced her to flee the country. She found her way to Washington, D.C., with good letters of introduction, but it seemed impossible for her to re-establish herself professionally, and she "felt lost and lonely in the big city in the company of people whose ideas and interests were completely foreign to her."[114]

Suddenly "a member of an outcast group, in a strange land among strangers . . . she attempted to meet the crisis by throwing herself into a hasty marriage with a man alien to her in cultural background, language, and religion." Her husband was a witty, companionable American businessman "who instantly fell in love with [Ilona's] strange beauty and her fascinating personality."[115] By her precipitate marriage to this charming and breezy Westerner, son of a Protestant minister, Ilona *"hoped to acquire the protective coloration of the new group."*[116] (Italics added.)

". . . She was lost in the mobile, breezy ways of her American-Western husband. . . . She longed for the intimate, closely knit circle of relatives and friends so characteristic of the European-Jewish life in which she had grown up and so utterly unfamiliar to her Gentile husband with his casual acquaintances."[117] Her loneliness was aggravated by frequent moving and her husband's drinking problem which frightened and revolted her "since heavy drinking was rare in her cultural background, [and] she had never encountered it before."[118] After fourteen years of marriage, Ilona entered therapy following "a severe depressive reaction which had climaxed in an acute breakdown. She had been suffering from sleeplessness, headaches, and crying spells."[119]

In the course of therapy it became evident that in fifteen years of her adulthood prior to the political upheaval that disrupted her life, Ilona had been unable to develop a good relationship with men. As a young woman in Vienna she had belonged to a bohemian clique and while in her twenties "had one affair without love" in an attempt to overcome her sexual inhibitions. After a disillusioning relationship with a man with whom she did fall in love, she subsequently had "one or two affairs with men who appealed to her physically but whom she did not care to marry."[120]

Ilona's emotional aloofness from men seemed to have its roots in a "lack of closeness with her father, with his early death, and [with] the entirely female environment in which she grew up. . . ."[121] "There was very little social life in Ilona's childhood home." Her life was peopled by a hypochondriacal mother, a strict governess, and a younger sister. As a child, she had no intimate friends.[122] It seemed clear to Buhler that the choice of a "foreign" husband "was a good excuse for her not to have to come close."[123] "Culture provides a most convenient scapegoat," Buhler comments, and seemed to give Ilona "an excuse for avoiding intimacy in personal relationships."[124]

Ilona's father was a highly respected Jewish banker in Budapest. He died during her elementary school years. Trying to recall her impressions of him, Ilona admitted, "I hardly remember him. He had never time for us children—was quite detached. He never talked with us children about anything. I remember only one nice scene with him, how he took us on a walk on Christmas eve, before we got our presents which Mother laid out under the tree while we were gone. That was a happy excitement. I also can see him at the dinner table. He asked often why I did not say something; I was a very quiet child—quite timid."[125]

Ilona later recalled that there seemed indeed to be certain similarities between her mother's marriage partner and her own: "We both married without love; we married men with whom one could not talk at all—to whom one never could get close, although for different reasons. Father was a distant neurotic, while my husband is a distant American."[126]

Through their husband's eyes. We return now to Mayer's interview material for statements by Gentile husbands in response to Mayer's question on what were the qualities of their Jewish wife which particularly appealed to them. One finds only *one* direct quotation (out of 45 couples!) on this subject:

Carlo

"She was no spender, and she wasn't just looking for a good time. She treated me nice. She wasn't a loud girl. I had respect for her and she had respect for me. . . . She could converse with me, she could keep up a conversation . . . better than the other I knew. I really admired her for that."[127]

Interestingly, Carlo was an Italian-born Catholic who "had only dated a few times before he met his wife who repeatedly described him as having been "terribly shy."[128] Apparently Mayer's American-born Gentile males were even shyer about discussing what they found appealing about their future wife. (As we shall see, Jewish wives tend to describe their cross-ethnic husbands as shy and retiring.) Mayer offers two quotations from Gentile husbands in which they express their initial disbelief that their relations with a Jewish girl could ever get "serious."

"For the first six or eight months I enjoyed going out with her, but had no serious intentions of getting seriously involved. . . . I was really kind of a snob. When I was first dating her, I felt I couldn't get interested in a girl without a college education or a Jew."[129]

"About a month after we met, we went steady and we liked each other a lot. . . . But I didn't think it would become serious. At the time, I didn't know this would happen. At the time, I was just going out and enjoying myself."[130]

THE GENTILE HUSBAND

The polite and acquiescent stranger. We have already noted Mayer's observation that intermarried husbands in general "seemed to be more ill-at-ease during the interview, and their responses were more apt to be abrupt or evasive." They were particularly reticent over discussing "things about their partners that had especially appealed to them." We have already hypothesized that this manifest embarrassment and inhibition might point to a neurotic aspect of the marriage choice.[131]

Does the Gentile male who intermarries show a history of

inhibition with girls of his own group? We have no direct observations on this question, but from the recollections of Jewish wives on their first impressions of their husband, the intermarrying Gentile male takes on the appearance of a shy, correct, retiring person:

"When he came to see me that night after our first meeting, I was living by myself in a four-room apartment. . . . I dressed very unladylike so I wouldn't have any trouble with fellows who came to call. When he left he shook hands with me. It almost knocked me over he was *so polite* . . . and never tried to start anything."[132]

"He made a favorable impression upon me, but I felt it was no use because we were worlds apart. [He came from South Dakota.] . . . He was different from other boys I knew because he had a refreshing personality which was not the brash smart-aleckness of others I knew. There was no suggestiveness in the way he acted. . . . He was corny in a charming sort of way."[133]

". . . The outstanding thing about Larry was he always looked *clean.* . . . He was very much the gentleman while the other seventeen-year-old boys I knew weren't—they were loud and boisterous. . . . When my mother didn't know we were serious about each other or that we were going out together. she said, 'If that boy were Jewish I'd love to have him for a son-in-law.' "[134]

Polly

"In the first class [we attended together] there was a lot of discussion. . . . I was very talkative and he was very quiet and never said a word. My first impression was that he was quiet and confused . . . mixed up personally. I felt he was preoccupied with his own worries and not paying much attention to what was going on around him. Then, about six months later, we were in this counseling class together, and we got to know each other very well. This was a seminar that met once a week for the entire day. We would interview clients and then discuss the interviews amongst ourselves. I began to feel that Harry was the only one I could share my impressions of other people and my work with. But I never thought of going out with him, as I had decided I would never marry a non-Jew. But we happened to live nearby and we always went home together on the subway and talked. . . . After a few months of this I decided his not being Jewish was really no barrier, and I would just accept what came of the relationship. . . .

". . . Having the class together certainly brought us closer together. . . . We found out that we could discuss so many things with each other. . . . He acted very retiring when he first met people, and [if we hadn't been in class together] I wouldn't have been interested. Being in the class together, I got to know him and found that he had very original ideas and was very interesting and not at all retiring when he got to know people."

Comparing Harry with other men she had known at the time, she describes her Jewish boy friends as "awful": One was "super-conventional," the other "tied to his mother's apron strings. Harry was more of an individual—the others were such stereotypes. Harry was much more interested in growing up and becoming more mature. He was more able to see reality. He was more ready to face life and not have so many illusions."[135]

Vera

"My first impression was that I thought him nice, but I didn't particularly care for him. It was not love at first sight. He was terribly shy. . . . When he finally asked me for a date, I saw him for two weeks regularly. Then I decided I wouldn't see him anymore. Why? Because I didn't care for him. But I felt sorry for him—he was so shy—and when he asked me for another date, I couldn't say no. . . ."[136]

Diane

"A Jewish woman who was in her middle thirties when she met her husband at a public dance and lecture" was impressed by her suitor's attentiveness and devotion. "You should have seen what he did for my birthday before we were married. I was at my sister's and he sent candy and flowers [with sighs and exclamations over the cost] and I knew he couldn't afford it!"[137]

The five foregoing impressions bear a striking family resemblance: the Gentile suitor is well-behaved ("never tried to

start anything" . . . not a brash smart-aleck; "no suggestiveness
in the way he acted") , *polite, gentlemanly* (unlike his "loud and
boisterous" Jewish counterparts) , *clean, quiet, shy, retiring,
deferential.* Their future wives were sometimes confused, ambivalent, or puzzled by this behavior; they were presumably
unacquainted with the norm to which this behavior conformed.
("It almost knocked me over he was *so polite.*" "He was corny
in a charming sort of way." "I was talkative and he was very
quiet and never said a word. My first impression was that he
was . . . confused . . . mixed up personally . . . preoccupied with
his own worries and not paying much attention. . . ." "I felt
sorry for him—he was so shy. . . .")

What a Jewish girl admires in her Gentile suitor often seems
quite different from what a Gentile girl admires in her Jewish
suitor (intellectual, cultured, serious-minded, successful.) It seems
consistent with the shy, deferential personality of the intermarrying Gentile husband that he tends to yield to his wife's preference
for raising the children as Jews. (". . . If they're your children,
you love them anyway; it's the same thing. . . . I went along with
it. You know, you just kind of go along.") A remarkable willingness of a majority-group husband to "go along" with the
preferences and standards of his minority-group wife is also
revealed in Anselm Strauss' report on 45 American-Japanese war-
bride marriages:

> Most of the American husbands are professional soldiers; many
> have never done anything else for a living. If faced with an
> overseas assignment, however, they quit the army in order to
> accomodate their wife's need for 'steadiness,' though they
> feel 'insecure in the civilian world and incompetent at non-
> army work.' 'Some of the husbands are small-town boys who
> have moved to Chicago mainly because the wife needed Jap-
> anese companionship.' The husbands seem willing 'to find
> their friends almost solely among other mixed couples.'[138]

Although Strauss' study is based entirely on interviews with the
war-bride wives, they consistently describe their husbands as
acquiescent, withdrawn, and downward-mobile.[139]

Attitudes toward Jewishness. Unlike the Gentile wife, who frequently expresses positive feelings about the Jewish religion and

cultural tradition, the Gentile *husband* rarely expresses positive attitudes toward his affiliation by marriage with the Jewish group. A notable exception in the published literature is a quotation located by Slotkin (1942a) from an essay published in 1920.

Wayne

The writer was raised as a Protestant in a small Arkansas town. While attending a university "a Jewish schoolmate took me to some Jewish parties where they sang Russian and Jewish songs which had a vitality I'd never known before. And the strangeness and newness of it had an exotic effect. . . . They were leading me in a direction that I had vaguely felt—it burst upon me that here are people that had a rounded cosmopolitan as opposed to a provincial outlook, and against which I had rebelled without finding an outlet. I admired them and what they stood for, and I wanted to rise to their stature. They interested me in things I had never dreamed of . . ."[140] and he goes on to add that it was in this group that he met his Jewish wife.

Experience as a college counselor leads this writer to believe that the appeal of Jewish group affiliation to Gentile males is by no means so rare as the published literature would indicate. A college population includes Gentiles of both sexes who seem to be seeking Jewish affiliations, prefer to date Jews, and go steady with one Jewish partner after another, or prefer to affiliate with Jews of both sexes. Judging from those who apply for personal counseling—broken homes or disturbed home environments are often evident, strongly suggesting that the person is reaching out for membership in a stable and supportive family and regards the Jewish family as fitting this model. (No doubt it is easier for a woman to acknowledge a need for security than it is for a member of both the dominant sex and the privileged majority!)

Francis

To Francis, his widowed mother was a chronically irritated, screaming, overcontrolling person, and he felt he had to fight against her efforts to make a sissy out of him. His father had died when Francis was only five and his older brother was eight, and the burden of raising two boys while working full time did not fall easily on his mother's shoulders. Underlying Francis' tendency to resist his mother's efforts to make him behave was his knowledge that Mother had very much wanted her second child to be a girl, and during her pregnancy had hopefully chosen the name Frances. He reacted to his mother's demand for good behavior as if she were asking him to act like a girl.

In his struggle against his mother, Francis found allies in a gang of neighborhood toughs who acted out their contempt for teachers, for schooling, and for middle class decorum. But Francis' background did not make him a natural member of that gang, and when he reached high school age he began to feel a certain admiration for the gifted and serious students in his classes. It seemed to Francis that the tough gang was predominantly Gentile, as he was, and the serious crowd was predominantly Jewish. Becoming a good student meant affiliating himself with Jews.

After graduation from high school, he attended a junior college, but—rebel that he was—abandoned it because it seemed dull and stupid. Working in a department store he struck up an acquaintance with an attractive Jewish college woman who was a part-time saleswoman. She recognized Francis' intellectual gifts, convinced him that he was wasting his life in a department store, and that he really belonged in a university. On the basis of her urgings, he applied for admission at a state university and made a successful beginning. The circumstances of Francis' school and social experience have effected a strong bond between the intellectual, achieving style of life and Jewishness. His broken home background might additionally make affiliation with a close-knit, supportive Jewish family especially attractive to him. In sum, Francis seems like a good candidate for serious cross-ethnic dating.

Paul

It is difficult, of course, for either the marriage partner or an outside observer to separate the satisfactions which a person anticipates from those he actually encounters as the Gentile husband of a Jewish wife. Gordon reports an interview with Paul, Doris' husband and Negro partner in the more successful of the two interracial couples he documents. Although Paul would not endorse intermarriage "for an ordinary guy" he candidly acknowledges the advantages he has enjoyed as husband of a Jewish wife: "I decided to be a truck driver if I could land a job because I figured that it was the best-paying of all the jobs that didn't require an education. *But I wanted nice things in life and I was determined*. Well, I found plenty of actual prejudice in the union. I have had all kinds of trouble upon trouble. I still wouldn't have gotten anywhere with this job if it hadn't been for a few Jewish men in this town who heard that my wife is Jewish. When they heard about my older son and heard that we wanted to give him a good Jewish education, these men really opened up a job for me and *the union wasn't able to stop me*. Negroes just don't find jobs through this union. I tell you, it's very hard; very hard, indeed."[141] (Italics added.)

Let us note that Paul's middle-class orientation and values (prudently choosing the best-paying work for which he was qualified, willingness to deal with considerable opposition to his goal, acknowledging his attraction to the "nicer things in life") show up early and contrast sharply with what we know about the attitudes of Tom, the Negro husband whose Jewish wife left him after less than two years of marriage. An unskilled laborer, Tom accepted months on relief as a matter of course. While Tom's wife was panicked by his indifference toward fulfilling the role of a "provider," Paul's wife must have considered her husband's attitudes quite "normal" by her middle-class standards. This difference may be an important clue as to why Tom and Ruth's marriage ran a brief and unhappy course, while Paul and Doris were able to establish a durable marriage partnership.

Toward the conclusion of the interview, Paul adds, "I have to tell you something else that is important. The way the Jewish people in this neighborhood, in the synagogue, and in the several Hebrew schools have responded to Roy [his eldest son] and to us is just wonderful. They are all excited about Roy who is a devout and studious boy. They have given him scholarships in order to make it possible for him to continue with his Hebrew education. I have actually benefited very much from my marriage to Doris. Because of her being Jewish, I got the job that the union would not have given me. One of my bosses was so excited and pleased at the time of Roy's *bar mitzvah* that he wanted to take charge of everything and make it an especially nice occasion, but I wouldn't permit him to. I was even called 'the black Jew' by some of them. Of course, I'm not a Jew. I have no intention of converting to Judaism." Earlier in the interview he described himself as an agnostic. "I'm just proud of my boys and my wife and I'm glad to see such good Jews in my family. Maybe they all think of me as a freak; but, however they think of me, I'll be grateful to all of them."[142]

Fred

Fred is an energetic but somewhat undisciplined young man who enrolled as a pre-medical student at a residential college but was dropped for poor scholarship. He admits that he spent too much time "fooling around" with his sports car. He gained admission at a city college and sought personal counseling to help himself from wasting his second chance to settle down to college work.

Fred is the only child of a successful insurance broker and his wife who adopted him at infancy. They are Protestants. Father is an indulgent but violent tempered person who in moments of anger would shout to Fred, "We should have left you in the gutter where we found you." Mother apparently feels quite nervous about how badly her husband and son get along. She is constantly trying to intercede and disengage them to the extent that she sometimes interrupts a "hypothetical argument" they are both enjoying, mistaking it for a serious dispute. Tension between parents is apparent to Fred mainly from father's chronic complaints about mother's overspending.

At the city college Fred started going steady with Ethel, a Jewish girl who avoided introducing Fred to her father for fear of his opposition. Ethel's mother liked Fred and apparently helped Ethel keep father unaware of the romance. Fred enrolled himself in a class in Jewish instruction to prepare himself for conversion, and bought an engagement ring. He also insisted on meeting Ethel's father and telling him of their plans because the way Ethel and her mother were handling the situation seemed altogether "too sneaky."

Ethel's father responded to Fred's announcement with a hysterical display of anguish, utttered thoughts about suicide and heart attack, and absolutely forbade that Ethel have anything further to do with Fred. Fred came home shaking with confusion and rage. The family doctor put him to bed with sedatives to "calm his nerves."

As Fred began to reflect over what had happened, he felt bitter toward Ethel for her total capitulation to her father. He felt angry toward her mother for encouraging the romance while keeping it hidden from her husband. Fred felt particularly contemptuous toward Ethel's father for his hysterical and "unmanly" behavior, for his unwarranted hostility toward Fred, and for what to Fred looked like an altogether unreasonable attitude toward his prospective son-in-law. Ethel's father was an uneducated man, went to the synagogue twice a year, and "carried ham sandwiches to work in his lunch pail." What right did he have, asked Fred, to oppose his daughter's marriage to a college student, member of a well-to-do family, who was conscientiously preparing himself for conversion to Judaism? After describing his disillusionment over his romance with Ethel, Fred added that he was going ahead with his religious instruction anyway. When he started something, Fred said, he didn't like to quit.

Within a few months Fred was going steady again. "As it happened" his new girlfriend, Freda, was also Jewish. Her parents, it seemed, were more enlightened and liberal than Ethel's. They were already treating Fred like a member of the family and had established good relations with Fred's parents. When Fred's parents were injured in an automobile accident, Fred was unexpectedly impressed with the strong feelings of "family loyalty" Freda's parents manifested. They travelled a considerable distance to be near Fred's injured parents right away. People who had been friendly with his parents for years and lived in the same neighborhood, Fred observed by contrast, just didn't go out of their way to show an interest or to be helpful.

4

Problems of the Intermarried

Are the problems of the intermarried more severe, more frequent, or in any way different from the difficulties that all families must learn to cope with? A survey of the literature reveals a very considerable range of judgment on this question, ranging from reassurance to alarm. The Levinsons assert matter-of-factly that "the religio-ethnic dilemmas of most intermarried families are not markedly different from those of inmarried Jewish families having similar educational and social values."[1] Likewise, Foote and Cottrell ask their reader to believe that "heterogamy now seems less likely than was formerly thought to interfere with marital harmony."[2] On the other hand, the literature suffers from no shortage of examples of the bitterness, regrets, recriminations, and anguish suffered by intermarried couples, their parents and their offspring. (Kirshenbaum, Chapters 9 and 11, and Baber's 1939 textbook, pages 171-172, contribute richly to the literature of "horrible examples.")

To what extent do the "horrible examples" that appear in the literature of intermarriage represent (or do violence to) Mr. and Mrs. Average Intermarried? In 1950 the president of the Rabbinical Council of America contended that 90 per cent of intermarriages are unsuccessful and only "undermine the stability of the home . . . and bring children into the world with a rift in their souls that can never be healed."[3] Danglow asserts that in forty-one years as a rabbi, he has found that mixed marriages are rarely happy. He recalls cases in which the partner of an apparently mixed marriage "confided to me that his marriage had been a sad mistake . . . [and] urged me to do all I could to dissuade young Jewish people from committing the same irreparable blunder."[4]

Every marriage is an intermarriage to the extent that each partner has a unique family background; and the partners may differ in geographical and social class background as well. Does the *degree* of difference in cultural background predict the amount of strife that the marriage partners are likely to encounter? The research findings of Rokeach deal with one aspect of this question. Limiting his investigation to couples of whom at least one partner was a Methodist, Rokeach demonstrated that couples from more divergent denominational backgrounds (e.g., Methodist and Presbyterian) report more conflict both before and after marriage than couples from similar denominations (e.g., Methodist and Baptist). Rokeach compared these interfaith couples with a number of all Methodist couples, and arrived at the general conclusion that "the greater the dissimilarity, the greater likelihood of conflict both before and after marriage."[5] Franzblau's concept of "religious distance" as a predictor of compatibility clearly anticipated Rokeach's findings.[6]

The pragmatic argument: "It doesn't work." The argument that intermarriage "lowers the chances of success" has always had a straightforward, pragmatic appeal. Gordon summarizes the statistical evidence that intermarried families encounter more difficulties and failures (e.g., divorce, desertion, delinquency) than the inmarried. Bamberger airs the popular Jewish argument that every marriage faces "many problems and difficulties. Why complicate it more? Why enter on a union with a reduced chance of success?"[7]

In opposition to the "blind pragmatists" are those who argue that if differences in cultural background are the real source of marital strife, why worry about mixed marriages in which there are "only nominal differences" between the cultural backgrounds of the partners? If the clergy were primarily concerned with raising the statistical likelihood of success in marriage, Barron asks, would they not also preach caution over *other* cultural differences (e.g., socio-economic class, nationality) which interfere with marriage harmony?[8] Similarly, Rabbi Bamberger asks his colleagues, Why single out intermarriage as the cause of marital strife? "If one is an only child or comes from a broken home, or has never received a religious education, he is (statistically) a poorer marital risk. . . . But no one would offer violent opposition to such an otherwise suitable match because the bride is an only child . . ."[9] In defense of the pragmatic viewpoint it might be noted that one's status as an only child (like a broken home background or lack of religious education) is an unalterable part of the individual's past history, and cannot be changed. But the choice of a marriage partner presumably *is* open to change, and *for those who seek advice* the pragmatic argument, as stated, seems altogether valid. Barron and Bamberger's disagreement with the pragmatists, we conjecture, is that they seize upon the pragmatic argument to conceal an unreasonable prejudice against intermarriage and against converts to Judaism. But the motives of the pragmatists, whatever they may be, do not negate the validity of their argument.

Intermarriage-proneness and divorce-proneness. There is a kernel of truth to the pragmatic argument that an intermarriage is more likely to end in divorce, but we must not suppose that divorce rate is a direct and reliable measure of marital unhappiness. There is more than one basis for conjecturing that if two couples suffer the same amount of marital unhappiness, the intermarried couple would more readily take recourse to divorce. Why should this be so?

Intermarriage is classically viewed as an act of rebellion against social authority. Intermarrieds include more than their share of the headstrong, the rebels, those who think of themselves as "exceptions" to the ordinary rules cf society. Perhaps their unwillingness to yield to society's disfavor of intermarriage reappears as an unwillingness to yield to each other's conflicting interests in the day-by-day drama of married life. Furthermore, attitudes which predispose a person to flout society's opposition to intermarriage should also help him flout society's opposition to divorce. How could it be otherwise? In each case the individual is guided by the dictum that his marital state is a private affair.

Intermarrieds are more likely to remain childless. A couple without children are not "tied to each other" by shared parental responsibility; their marriage lacks an important deterrent to divorce. Something more can be conjectured about a married person who *chooses* to remain childless: there is something in his life which is more important to him than parenthood—whether it be his profession, his leisure interests, or his personal comfort. A person who attaches less importance to parenthood than most people do is also likely to attach less importance to marriage itself. In sum, we conjecture that a readiness to intermarry, a reluctance to raise children, and a willingness to divorce—all these tendencies may stem from a basic lack of commitment to the norms of marriage and parenthood.

Status insecurity. An additional tension in the lives of intermarrieds may be a feeling of insecurity over one's social or job status. In some cases this feeling may be "imaginary," in other cases it is induced by unequivocal social experience. Bossard and Boll describe a Gentile corporation executive who was offered a promotion which hinged upon transfer to a more "conservative" community, on the painful condition that his wife conceal her Jewish identity.[10] Gordon cites the case of a Jew whose place in the family business was threatened by his choice of a Gentile wife.[11] Slotkin (1942a) interviewed an intermarried husband who had converted to Judaism, but explained that "the place where I work is anti-Semitic, and I haven't told them of my marriage or my change of religion." An intermarried Jewish wife likewise explained to Slotkin that "when my husband taught in Arkansas I didn't tell anyone that I was a Jew. We were thought of as a Gentile family."[12]

A Gentile observer described to Bloom how the status of an apartment neighbor changed after her parents were relieved of the suspicion that the couple was Jewish:

"In getting acquainted with other families in the apartment, my mother was disturbed by the fact that she thought that two of the families were Jewish. I can remember conversations between her and my father in which they discussed the undesirability of the apartment building because of the presence of these families. Another impression that I gained from these conversations was the fact that the wife of Mr. S., who was supposedly Jewish, 'did not look at all Jewish.' She did not fit the stereotype of Jews which was to us dark complexion, dark hair, dark eyes, hook nose, loud, showy, and forward 'nature.' I realized that the status of the wife was raised considerably in the eyes of my parents when they discovered that her husband was not Jewish. The status of the man himself, of course, was also raised. Later when these people became quite well acquainted with my family, the misunderstanding of their assuming that Mr. S. was Jewish was a source of amusement to Mr. S., his wife, and my parents. He was 'kidded' about his name and his appearance, both of which fitted the Jewish stereotype."[13]

In-law troubles. Nothing is so universally and perennially the unwelcome by-product of marriage as in-law troubles, and intermarrieds are not exempt from this common lot of mankind. (Anselm Strauss was pleased to note that Japanese war-brides and their soldier—or ex-soldier—husbands were not often involved in in-law troubles, but that was because they were geographically separated from their in-laws.) Landis conjectures that mixed marriages are probably especially vulnerable to in-law troubles.[14] Certainly the interview and clinical literature offers no dearth of examples of such conflicts. Gordon describes a Protestant-Catholic couple whose parents, though liberal and kindly, experienced unexpected anguish over their children's need to make a choice of religious affiliation. The wife's father, a college professor and nominal Protestant, reflected:

> I cannot understand why my wife and I should have been so unhappy when we felt that Mary might convert to Catholicism. After all, we are liberals! But I can understand how unhappy John's parents are because John, Mary and the children are not Roman Catholics and that makes us, too, unhappy for them . . .

> Even in intermarriages such as this where all the persons involved are good people, I'm afraid that someone must get hurt. In this case the direct victims are John's parents. Indirectly, John and the children may suffer.[15]

Just as conflict between husband and wife may elicit racial epithets, in-law trouble may begin as domestic bickering and escalate into racial warfare, as an ethnic slur tossed out like a stone unexpectedly falls on its victim like a rock. Rabbi Kirshenbaum tells of a young wife who sought his counsel because her husband—a convert to Judaism—seemed to be "in a constant state of depression." The rabbi spoke to the husband, who expressed his disillusionment over the fact that his wife had become cold to him. "He felt that she was unfaithful," and had rejected him because of his non-Jewish origin. A discussion with the couple traced the breaking-point of their relationship to an exchange of racial epithets:

Unwittingly the husband let slip a phrase about her mother's 'Jewish interference.' This distressed the wife greatly. 'It's the Gentile in you,' she retorted. . . . There burst forth all the long-suppressed tensions based on their differences of origin. . . . By now reconciliation was out of the question. . . . The husband returned to his family and their religious faith, and the wife to her parents.[16]

Where rebellion against parental control has figured significantly in the decision to intermarry, in-law trouble may simply perpetuate a long history of hostile feelings between parent and offspring. Grandchildren sometimes become pawns in the conflict, but often enough the birth of a baby is "too much for the grandparents to hold out against," and the vicious cycle is reversed. Rabbi Rubenstein consoles intermarried couples with the prospect that when their parents become grandparents their injured feelings "can at least be mollified."[17] Baber tells of a Jew who was raised as an only son, and much pampered by his parents and sisters. When he married a Catholic girl, "his family dropped him suddenly and completely . . ." The drama that followed the birth of his son unexpectedly led to a lasting reunion:

. . . The young father was extremely anxious to have [his new son] brought up as a Jew, which involved early circumcision. But he was fearful lest his wife, still in the hospital, would object, for they had never talked over the matter. He became almost frantic in his anxiety and finally appealed to one of his estranged sisters to go to the hospital and talk to his wife about it, which she finally agreed to do. When she told the young wife of her husband's anxiety, the latter was genuinely angry to think that he had doubted her devotion and submission to his wishes. She said there had never been any question in her mind but that her children should be brought up as Jews. This so delighted the husband's sisters and parents that their animosities were forgotten, and from that day the family relations have been of the happiest.[18]

The value of good relations with in-laws goes beyond sentiment. According to a New Haven survey by Sussman, it is not at all uncommon for parents to give financial aid to young married couples, especially when they are faced with the need to make special outlays because of illness, childbirth, or the purchase of a home or car. The hostility of in-laws at a time when their help is needed may burden a young couple with bitterness toward their parents, jealousy toward their favored siblings, and cynicism toward their ethnic group.

The classic denouement of a Jewish-Gentile intermarriage—total rejection and ceremonial mourning (*shiva*) for the misguided Jewish spouse—is rarely encountered in the recent interview literature of intermarrieds. The Levinsons note that although the family crises precipitated by the decision to intermarry were often severe, "the difficulty was usually short-lived, and . . . often the non-Jewish wife has become the favorite daughter-in-law and has strengthened the relationship between parents and son."[19] Recalling the duration of such a crisis, an intermarried Protestant-born wife reflected, "When I overheard my mother-in-law speak of *me* to a friend as 'my Ruth' then I knew that I was *really* accepted."[20]

Other observers confirm the Levinsons' impression that Jewish parents usually overcome the distress or shock of their child's intermarriage, and eventually establish friendly relations with the young couple. Says Lehrer: "It begins with serious distress and ends quickly in complete reconciliation and warm family relations. The 'stain on the family' is wiped out."[21] Rabbi Kirshenbaum tells of parents who express a special pride in their convert daughter-in-law, and seem to become defenders of intermarriage in principle!

When before have Jews taken pride in non-Jewish ancestry or family relationship—even when the convert in truth followed Judaism? Among certain Jewish parents [says Kirshenbaum ruefully], a proselyte daughter-in-law who can make tasty *gefillte fish* for the Sabbath and *kreplach* for the festivals is more highly regarded than their own daughters and certainly more than their Jewish daughters-in-law. In the presence of these parents not a word must be spoken against mixed marriages.[22]

Rabbi Danglow likewise tells of Jewish parents who try to conceal their disappointment "by dilating . . . upon the splendid qualities of their new son-in-law or daughter-in-law, though such attributes are not, as a rule, so strikingly evident to outside observers."[23]

Slotkin's 1942 survey of 183 Jewish-Gentile couples showed that 80 per cent of Jewish intermarrieds felt "partially or entirely accepted" by their own parents, and 73 per cent of Gentile intermarrieds felt "partially or entirely accepted" by their Jewish in-laws. Gentile parents tended to accept the intermarried couple somewhat more freely.

Table 4:1. Percentage of Intermarrieds "Partially or Entirely Accepted" by Parents and In-laws[24]

N=183 couples

Gentile intermarrieds accepted by their own family	84%
Jewish intermarrieds accepted by their own family	80%
Jewish intermarrieds accepted by family of spouse	77%
Gentile intermarrieds accepted by family of spouse	73%
Intermarried partner accepted by both families	57%

Compared with Slotkin's 1942 figure of 20 per cent, for Jewish parents who could *not* at least "partially accept" their child's intermarriage, Mayer reports that 11 per cent of his intermarried Jewish respondents (or 5 out of 45) "were warned that the marriage would mean the end of their relationship with their parents." ("My parents made it clear that if I persisted, they would disown me." "They threatened never to associate with me again, and said they'd never forget or forgive what I had done." "They said they would never walk into our home after we were married.") [25] Presumably no such warnings were uttered by parents of Mayer's *Gentile* intermarrieds.

But for a very sizeable majority, parental objections are partially or wholly overcome, and success breeds success. One of Mayer's respondents said she was willing to face her family's opposition to intermarriage because she regarded it as a temporary unpleasantness; she had seen a similar family crisis in her neighborhood quietly and quickly resolved. ". . . Two weeks after the wedding, [the young intermarried couple] were home living with the in-laws and everything was just fine. Her father even took him into the business."[26]

Exploration and retreat. Dating and courtship give young people a proving ground for testing their capacities and preferences for a variety of role behaviors. In a mobile society adolescence and young adulthood is the time for much role-testing. There are many aspects to the quest for identity: it involves a search for an occupational identity, a social class identity, a residential identity, an ethnic identity. Mobility does not follow a simple upward or downward course; the person's movements are marked by exploration and retreat, setting goals and seeking compromises. Hard-won gains may fail to deliver the satisfactions one had so keenly anticipated, and the person willingly retreats to a more congenial milieu. (A current joke tells of a Negro civil rights demonstrator's lament that he "sat in" at an Alabama restaurant for six months, and when they finally would serve him he discovered that he didn't like anything on their menu.)

In social mobility the critical task is not to be a tireless and sure-footed climber, but to find a congenial plateau where gains can be consolidated and enjoyed, where one can find fellowship and trust, a sense of freedom and stability. A Jew who leaves his ethnic home may sometime later wish to return. Theodore Herzl, Ludwig Lewisohn, and Louis Brandeis tested "full assimilationism" before they chose to reclaim a Jewish identity; countless Jews have undoubtedly followed this pattern of experience with countless variations. Wessel's observation concerning Jews who move from a Jewish neighborhood to a Gentile neighborhood and finally settle in a mixed neighborhood demonstrates this phenomenon of exploration and retreat. (Note that the retreat is not a simple regression, one does not return to his starting point.)

Cases have been reported of converts to Judaism who eventually —or suddenly—revert to Church attendance themselves or send their children to Christian Sunday school.[27] Can a Jewish husband accept the unexpected renewal of his wife's Christian identity? Can a Gentile wife accept her "emancipated" husband's reversion to Jewishness? How frequently does this problem emerge in the lives of those who intermarry, and how is this conflict resolved? To what extent is the reaffirmation of old loyalties a life cycle phenomenon—a sign of middle-age conservatism—or is it more likely to occur as a response to changes in the cultural or political climate? (For the generation of Jews who lived through the Nazi era and the rebirth of Israel, this is an impossible question to answer. According to Wirth and Goldhamer, however, it it not uncommon for Negroes who pass completely while young to resume their Negro identity in later life.)

The inner tension of Jews who have through intermarriage committed themselves too irrevocably to a Gentile identity, is indicated by a most provocative observation reported by Hollingshead and Redlich. In their interviews with the highly intermarried New Haven psychiatrists, the investigators found that the greatest confusion and uncertainty over the religious education of their children was expressed by those "who either do not practice their ancestral religion *or have changed to another religion*."[28] (Italics added)

Harry

At the time of their marriage, Harry was an agnostic, emancipated from his Jewish background, and his bride was a practicing Catholic. As they grew older and raised a family of two boys, his wife became progressively less active a Catholic while Harry became increasingly absorbed with Jewish concerns, eventually transformed into a person "omnivorous for anything and everything Jewish." He could no longer view his boys' Catholic education with the old detachment. The balance of religious attitudes which served them so well when they entered into marriage no longer prevailed. A chronic tension hung over the family situation, which led his son to feel—as he wrote in an autobiographical essay—that he was living "on the margins of heresy, adrift between two religious communities."[29]

Samuel

Gordon documents his lengthy interview with *Samuel,* a professor of sociology who was raised by Russian immigrant Jewish parents on the East Side of New York City. While Samuel was a university student he met and married a Jamaican girl of Indian ancestry and Presbyterian church affiliation. It is interesting to compare the feeling of distance from Jewishness with which he characterizes his college days, with the emergence of a poignant ambivalence over his Jewish identity.

"It wasn't unusual for me to date Christian girls," Samuel explains in his interview with Gordon. "I never bothered to ask, or even think, about it because just about everyone was doing it." Samuel adds that his mother "objected strenuously, but frankly . . . I just had to decide whether I was going to live my own life or someone else's."

Samuel further underscores his distance from Jewish life. As early as age twelve "I made it clear that I was anxious to stop going to Talmud Torah . . . the educational system was certainly not the best . . . it was a boring and wasteful process . . . [Also] many of the kids in my friendship group were not going. . . . As I look back upon the whole Talmud Torah experience, it was a damn lousy education they gave us. . . . I have no emotional attachment to Hebrew, the Synagogue, or the Talmud Torah."

During his four years as an undergraduate he recalls visiting the Hillel Foundation (the Jewish student center) "only about a half-dozen times . . . Judaism—what I knew of it—really didn't mean very much to me. I never belonged to any Jewish fraternity. . . . I don't believe that during my college days I ever went into a synagogue." When he and his wife decided to get married, Samuel emphasizes that he did *"not* ask her to convert to Judaism. I certainly wouldn't!" he adds.

By contrast with all of the foregoing negative and indifferent statements about his Jewish identity, a considerable amount of positive feelings, as well as ambivalence, comes to the surface as Samuel talks about his two children. He and his wife "decided a long time ago that nominally we would say that our children were Jewish if they had to fill out a form at school or anything like that. But my wife isn't happy about this decision and every now and then complains about it. Originally, we had decided that if there were a male child, he would be circumcised ritually and that he would also be christened. You see we didn't care too much about these things ourselves. We thought we would satisfy both our families in this way. . . . Out of regard for my mother, [I] would want some form of identification with the Jewish people [for my children]. . . . It isn't because I am such a devoted Jew, you understand. Well, maybe, what I am trying to say is that I would rather they would not be identified with any other faith. . . . [His wife feels otherwise, and Samuel admits that] the difference in religious background does seem to create a problem."

To answer Gordon's question about whether he would want his children to marry a person of a different color or of a different faith, Samuel answers: "I think that would have to be completely up to them."

"Now you may gather from this that I, for one, have no emotional attachment whatsoever, either to Judaism or to the matter of being a Jew. But that isn't altogether correct. Personally, I find that I do have attachments, indicated, for example, by my wanting to talk to my children about Hanukkah while my wife talks to them about Christmas. I find that on occasion I will sing a Yiddish song for them, or use certain Hebrew words so that they will learn the sounds, but it's very difficult for me to do much more than that. I would like them to at least be aware of the fact that I am Jewish and at least to have a little knowledge of Judaism. Unfortunately I'm really not the best one to give them the kind of Jewish content they should have because I don't know enough."

Samuel reflects: ". . . . It has always puzzled me that persons who are born into Jewish families, yet practice or observe almost nothing of Judaism, seem to be unable to accept the idea of mixed marriage. They simply get emotional about it. It is, to many of them, as if the bottom had dropped right out of their lives. I suppose to a large extent intermarriage signifies giving up the very core of identification with one's groups. . . . The final and last step, so people seem to think, is to give up [their social] identification by intermarriage. Perhaps they are right. I'm beginning to see what they mean."[30]

As a college youth and student of sociology Samuel presumably felt that the color difference need not (or should not) be a source of anxiety or uncertainty. As a husband and father, he frankly worries about this:

> She is brown and I am white. . . . She is not a Negro. She is Indian, that is, of Indian ancestry. . . . All her forebears were born in India. [Of his children's racial indentity, he explains further:] Whether or not the color problem will ever become a serious one for our children, I do not know. I do not think that it ought to be. They are Caucasians, you know. Indians are included in the Caucasian race. Yet many people unfamiliar with this anthropological classification of races may raise questions, for after all, Caucasians or not, there *is* a difference in skin color. . . . I am beginning to worry about it.

> You ask what my response would be if my children, when grown to adulthood, were to come to their mother and me and say "We would like to marry persons of a different color and a different faith from ours." I think that my wife and I would both respond by asking *"Which* other color? What other faith?"[31]

The experience of Samuel—an intermarried Jew whose indifference toward his Jewish background underwent a dramatic transformation when he became a father—is paralleled by the story Gertrude tells of her acculturated Jewish husband, agnostic if not atheist, and the unexpected plea he made to raise their boy as a Jew:

> [One day before their baby was born, Ben announced] that if it were a boy he would like to have it brought up as a Jew. If it were a girl, then I could 'stuff it full of Christian beliefs.' And he did not mean this unkindly.
> 'But, Ben,' I asked, 'Why, if it is a boy, do you want to make him race-conscious? You do not believe actively in the religion . . .'
> 'Well—er,' he fumbled, 'well, I was born a Jew, and I went to Hebrew school, and—er—well, I want him to be like me.' . . .
> But it eventually turned out [Gertrude continues] that his real wish was to please his mother. What that man wouldn't

do to please his mother! Of all sons, surely the Jews are the best and most loyal.[32]

Just as surely as youth is a time for action and rebellion, middleage is a time for reflection and conservatism. Fiedler conjectures that even the white Anglo-Saxon Protestant, as he approaches middleage, finds something appealing about the Jewish ethos, and through the Jewish American novel finds the fantasy material that enables him to become "an imaginary Jew."[33] As one begins to feel more Jewish, he probably begins to *look* more Jewish, for as Carleton Coon observed, the Jewish appearance is in significant part a matter of expression. Coon also observes that the "combination of [facial] features . . . found among many [Eastern European] Jews . . . becomes more pronounced with advancing age, when the nose and face grow longer and the nasal tip becomes increasingly depressed."[34]

Just as the self-consciousness of courtship and the honeymoon eventually gives way to the more relaxed give-and-take of married life—as one establishes himself in his social and occupational world, modelling his life after the norms of the Gentile majority may not seem quite so necessary or rewarding as it used to seem, and one might like to reclaim and reassert a portion of his Jewish identity.

Marcus Hansen has elaborated on the idea that "what the son [of an immigrant] wishes to forget, the grandson wishes to remember." Separation and reunion may also take place within a single lifetime, as an autobiographical interview with virologist Albert Sabin dramatically illustrates. Documented by Rabbi Kertzer, Dr. Sabin's experience encompasses what has been classically described as three generations of identity experience—the immigrant, the rebel, and the bi-cultural person.

Albert Sabin

Born in 1906 in a Polish village near Bialystok, the son of a weaver, Albert Sabin was 13 years old when his family came to America and settled in Paterson, New Jersey.

"My father was not observant, [Dr. Sabin recalls] and I was

never a religious Jew. But the phrase *Eretz Yisroel* [Land of Israel] brings me back to my early childhood. My grandfather used to take me to the synagogue on a late Saturday afternoon, and I would hear an old man spin tales about *Eretz Yisroel*.

"I married a Christian girl, and our daughters, who came late in our marriage, occasionally attended Protestant Sunday schools and observed the Christian festivals. My older daughter, Debbie, had few Jewish friends until she was admitted to Walnut Hills High School. It is a school for superior students, and a great many of them, brought in from all parts of Cincinnati, were Jewish. She asked if she could be confirmed and we enrolled her in the Rockdale Temple."

During World War II, Dr. Sabin was a lieutenant colonel assigned to the Army's Preventive Medicine Division. He was dispatched to Egypt on a special mission to investigate the cause of certain epidemic diseases.

"I journeyed by army vehicle across Sinai, retracing Moses' steps, but in a shorter time—eight hours. . . . I only spent ten days in Palestine and did not return for sixteen years. In 1959, the Israeli government invited me to the new state to look into a polio epidemic that was raging there.

"I realized that I was witnessing the enactment of the greatest chapter in the entire history of the Jewish people. I had never felt the need of being Jewish until then."

Dr. Sabin visits Israel two or three times a year. (He begins his conversation with the apology, *"L' daavoni ayneni mdaber ivrit*—I regret that I speak no Hebrew.") He is a member of the Board of Governors of Hebrew University, and in the past few years he has helped raise funds for the Haifa Technical Institute, the Weizmann Institute, and Bonds for Israel.

"Though the Hebrew Union College gave me an honorary degree, I don't feel that man's spiritual strivings need be articulated through symbolic observances. Intellectually and emotionally I'm a Jew, without the prescribed activities of organized religion.

"My Jewishness is expressed by the strong link that I feel to my heritage."

Dr. Sabin quoted an Israeli colonel who explained, when asked for a definition of a Jew, "You're a Jew when a Jew in Minsk is hurt and you feel the pain."[35]

Incidents and crises. Case studies of intermarrieds describe the unexpected appearance of ethnic traits and attitudes which had been either suppressed or unnoticed during dating and courtship. Bossard and Boll tell of a Gentile wife who discovered to her annoyance that her husband spoke with a Jewish accent. (Her husband was likewise irritated when they were in a restaurant and she ordered ham.) [36]

An intermarried couple met an observant Jew of the older generation who was also a painter of some reputation. The wife appealed to the artist to reconcile her Jewish husband to the fact that she had hung in their living room a painting of a village church: "You're an artist; please explain to Ben that a painting of a church with a cross on the steeple is not a religious object; it's a work of art." Perhaps if his wife had been *born* a Jew, Ben would have been quite unconcerned about the little church house in his wife's favorite landscape.

Delayed guilt. In her unique anti-intermarriage pamphlet, Rebecca Mack tells of a Jew who married an Italian girl in her church, and raised a family of three children. What appeared to be a good and happy marriage suddenly became an object of guilt and bitterness for the husband after his mother died of heart trouble.

> After his mother had been dead for a short while, the young man went to visit her grave. As he stood by the side of it he cried out, 'Mother, O Mother. I am sorry for what I have done. . . . Please forgive me!' . . . No more did he care about his home and family. No longer did he share their joy and happiness. . . . He blamed himself for the death of his mother. . . . He became very bitter toward life. He blamed fate. He blamed God. He blamed everyone but mostly himself and his selfish ignorance.[37]

The clinical and research literature likewise describe cases in which intermarried persons respond to life crises with sudden and overwhelming feelings of guilt over their intermarriage, or unexpectedly retreat into a conservative in-group role. At the death of his child, Tashman's intermarried physician reverted to long-neglected practices of Jewish ritual.

Bloom describes two cases in which a personal crisis leads to such a reversion.[38] Bossard and Boll tell at length of an intermarried Gentile woman whose seemingly happy life was shattered by several deaths in the family which came in painful and unexpected succession. Her reaction was marked by an obsessional guilt over her "sinful" act of leaving her faith to marry a Jew. Bossard and Boll explicitly infer that this guilt must have been lurking below the surface and troubling her all through the years of her seemingly happy married life.[39] Lewisohn conjectured that "an obscure cause of disharmony in mixed marriages is the repressed . . . consciousness of the sin of diminishing Israel."[40]

What of the children? Tashman tells of a Jewish physician and his Gentile wife who, like Gertrude and Ben, faced a crisis upon the birth of their first child. The wife was apparently quite unprepared to learn that her husband wanted the boy named Isador, and intended to have him circumcised "for cleanliness." In her unhappiness over her husband's demands, the inference she apparently drew was that in her husband's eyes *her* people were "unclean," and that a child who belonged to her husband's group could not really belong to her.[41]

Baber describes a Jewish wife who as a bride could agree to raise her children as Christians, but as a mother found herself emotionally incapable of carrying out her pledge.[42] Several other cases of dissension and resentment over religious practice are presented, including two cases in which the Jewish spouse suffers needless anguish over a false assumption that their mate would oppose giving the child a Jewish identity.[43] Even couples who claim to be indifferent toward religion, says Baber, experience frequent conflict over matters of religion, usually involving the upbringing of children.[44] Landis stated in 1949 that his research "supports Baber's conclusion that the chief source of friction [between intermarried couples] centers around the religious training of children."[45] Baber and Landis would probably question the Levinsons' generalization that "the religio-ethnic dilemmas of most intermarried families are not markedly different from those of inmarried Jewish families having similar educational and social values."[46]

Both Mayer and Gordon cite cases in which intermarried parents express anxiety over the ethnic identity of their children. A Jewish mother and wife of a Negro asked the interviewer: "Do

you think Roy [her son] could 'pass'? What do you think we
should do about his future?"[47] Another Jewish woman, who divorced her Negro husband and raised her daughter with the help
of the maternal grandmother reflected: "I shudder to think what
might have happened had my baby been born with a dark skin.
. . . Suppose that when I left my husband I had taken with me a
dark-skinned child. What would have happened? Would my
parents and friends have accepted her? . . . . Even having a light-
skinned daughter whose father was Negro was often upsetting
to me. I can't even tell you why."[48]

The Jewish mother's concern that her child be spared from
the Negro stigma may be paralleled by the anxiety of those Gentile mothers who hope to rescue their child from the stigma of
Jewishness. "I'm hoping our son will be thought of as Gentile,
and I will do everything in my power to make it that way. If I
have the money to put him through St. Marks, St. Paul's, or
Groton, he will be all right, and I won't have any trouble. But
if he goes to a public school, I don't know what I'll do. . . . I
don't think Richard will be thought of as Jewish, because he will
be brought up in my crowd. I want him to see as little as possible
of my husband's side of the family. Even now I don't like to receive them in our house. . . . I don't want Richard to know any
of his Jewish cousins."[49]

Back in the 1930's, George Sokolsky—speaking from personal
experience—warned partners in mixed marriages that those who
"dare assume the burden of fitting [their offspring] to meet the
certain difficulties that lie ahead of him" assume a terrific task.[50]
He recommended that children of mixed marriages be helped
to develop artistic talents and if possible enter the arts professionally, for "in the arts, nothing really matters but ability. . . .
In the arts, there is not only a genuine democracy in the sense
that all men of ability and genius are equal, there is also an
aristocracy in which the intellectually fittest survive. For the
child of a mixed marriage, then, the arts offer greater prospects
of the happiness that comes from achievement than does any other
field."[51] Sokolsky admits that genius cannot be implanted, but
advises parents to "be vigilant, providing the child with an atmosphere and environment to stimulate whatever talents he may

possess."[52] It should be noted that Sokolsky's wife was Chinese, and he was perhaps dealing more specifically with the problem of bi-racial marriage in the United States.

Thirty years after Sokolsky attested to the terrific difficulty of raising the offspring of a mixed marriage—and offered his pathetically restricted hope that in the world of the arts the child might find "genuine democracy"—Leslie Fiedler commented that intermarriage does not solve the problem of ethnicity for the new generation. "The children of such mixed marriages have still to make the choice of 'passing' or not . . . [The offspring are called upon to take sides in] choosing between Mother and Father . . . or are chosen for one side or another before they have a chance—in the most desperate of psychological games."[53]

Albert Memmi (who, like Sokolsky, is the Jewish partner in a mixed marriage) describes in detail the inner conflicts and misgivings of a Jewish parent over the exercise of his responsibility for influencing his child's ethnic identity. The shared responsibility for raising children usually strengthens a marriage partnership, says Memmi, but in the case of a mixed marriage, parenthood brings into the foreground unresolved differences between the partners, and activates each partner's inner conflicts over his ethnic identity. "What of the children?" expresses the man on the street's objection to mixed marriage. However clumsily put, says Memmi, "the objection is well-founded."

Memmi suggests that parenthood forces the couple to take a stand on the very issues they had hoped, through a mixed marriage, to avoid. "Suddenly all theoretical options which had been relegated to the background and left in a convenient and equivocal shadow require urgent attention and threaten to materialize by themselves and at random. Should the boy be circumcized? According to religious law, there are only eight days to decide after which the boy will remain uncircumcized. Should the girl be baptized? It must be done within a year or it will never be done. What upbringing should they be given? A religious upbringing or not? How do you present them with the fact of being Jewish? I still don't know what I should tell my children about Jewish history. Besides, is it exactly *their* history? Should I decide that it is and that they will be Jews? . . .

"Once started down this path a little voice whispers: 'And if you decide to make them into non-Jews? Why push them in one direction rather than another?' The little voice becomes more insidious: 'Why not spare them a dangerous destiny? Why deny them a salvation to which they are already half entitled . . . ?' But immediately my heart begins to beat more quickly. In answer to the little voice comes this loud cry which I have so often heard uttered by so many partners of mixed marriages: 'I do not want to become a stranger to my children.' Of course this is valid for both partners. Of course it is a question of irrational fears, an often unfounded anxiety to which time will fortunately give the lie. But there is, at the heart of most mixed marriages, a real obsession with exclusion.

. . . .

"So what do you do? Do you do nothing, so that the child is drawn toward neither side? This would seem to be the most honest solution, the one to which the least prejudiced mixed couples most often turn. But let's not pull the wool over our eyes: in this case, to do nothing is a decision with the probable consequence that the children will become part of the majority. There is in the so-called neutrality of the non-Jewish partner a not always unconscious hypocrisy, 'Let's not influence the child, neither of us. Let him choose for himself and decide when he can.' This also means: Let society have its way—the school, the neighborhood, the surrounding culture. This is really playing it safe; the entire society will do the job. The reader may answer that many, perhaps the majority of Jewish couples today contribute nothing to the Jewish upbringing of their children either, but this is absolutely not the same thing. A young Jew of Jewish parents, even if these parents are indifferent to Judaism, will be Jewish because it will never occur to him to be anything else. . . . Jewish parents feel this and can envisage the future of their children, and their common future with them, without affective anguish, in spite of the uncertainty of this future.

"Paradoxically, the Jew who makes a mixed marriage feels a greater anxiety concerning his children. He shoulders a supplementary anxiety and complicates further an already complex future. In most cases, an unnamed apprehension gnaws away at the partners of a mixed marriage, its presence manifested by small compromises, petty bickering and little tricks which would be distasteful if they weren't so laughable.

" 'I insisted on calling my son Emmanuel,' I was told by a Jewish friend who had married a Catholic. 'On thinking it over, I sincerely believe that I wouldn't have done so if I had married a Jew. I don't particularly like the name, but I spontaneously felt that in this way the child would somehow be more mine.'

"In Tunisia, the French wives of Moslems picked ingenious Moslem names which might one day be adaptable if the child were to live in France: Saphia (Sophie), Hedi (Eddy), or Nédié (Nadia), etc. . . .

"Sometimes all this degenerates into an open struggle, and in this more or less artful wrestling for the children, the grandparents are not the least tenacious or the least ferocious. Approaching death, more concerned about the species than about the individual, they will use the most unfair methods if necessary—clandestine baptism, masses and catechisms for each occasion, or secret visits to temples. My own mother fought as hard as she could, alternating tragic sighs with enticing smiles, offering her services to organize the ceremonies, etc. I can't even hold it against her; it was her world and she thought it was ours, that of my childhood. She could not agree to let a child, born in part from herself, be torn from her.

"In short, the children, far from being a bond, might well become the prize. And when you think of the fragility of these little creatures, and how badly they need this unique being called Papa-Mama! How dismayed they are when faced with dissension between their parents and how extraordinarily they can sense the slightest discord. Certainly a healthy stomach can digest anything, and stable children can in the end overcome anything. But why place an extra obstacle in the already long and arduous road to adulthood? Isn't it better for them to start out on a solid ground, leaving difficult adventures for later on, should they discover in themselves the desire and courage for them? I don't know what the statistics are, but I would not be surprised if a greater percentage of troubles, failures and defeats are not to be found in children of mixed marriages than in children of other marriages," Memmi conjectures.[54]

Idealization of the *mischling*. The offspring of a mixed marriage has been chosen as an object of pity, a creature without an ethnic home—but he has also been idealized as the harbinger of a new race, as an orchestration of two ethnic melodies. Writing in the Jewish press in 1928, Charles Recht hailed the *mischling* as "a more esthetic and healthy type than the old products of the ghettos," and a testimony to eugenics. "We will not go back and swear that the dusky acquiline nosed Semitic types with ball jointed knees, are the better types than the children of our intermarriages, who resemble the figures of angels," Recht rhapsodized.[55] During the same era, A. A. Brill noted that in his experience the offspring of intermarrieds "are always either extremely brilliant or exceptionally neurotic," depending on whether they are able to transend the conflict between the Oriental and Occidental aspects of their psyche.[56] Folklore must eventually give way to reliable knowledge; there is much to be learned about the adjustment patterns of children of mixed parentage.

Bart

Bart bears the surname of an old Protestant family. He was raised and is still living in a three-generation household—with his parents, an older brother, and his paternal grandparents. Bart's father is an intellectually gifted person with a literary flair. He seems to have a talent for throwing away opportunities. He has never made a good living, hence his wife and family settled down permanently in his parents' home. Bart's mother holds a steady job and quietly counteracts her husband's extravagances so that by Christmas time there is somehow a little extra money available for gifts and family entertainment.

Bart himself vacillates between going to college and working for a magazine publisher. When he was a student, there were semesters when he made very good grades, and there were semesters when he neglected his studies almost totally, and flung himself into *la dolce vita*. In his choice of career he has vacillated between medicine and journalism. In each case it seemed to Bart that he had to choose between a Jewish way of life and a Gentile way. Although Bart could claim a great-grandfather who had been professor of medicine at a famous Eastern university,

Bart felt uneasily that medicine would too obviously match the goal of his Jewish friends, and was therefore not right for him.

Bart attributes this pervasive, internalized conflict to the fact that many of his high school friends were Jews, and he had spent much time with their families. Instead of acquiring a feeling of familiarity about his Jewish surroundings, they were a source of acute and uncanny embarrassment. Bart recalled his painful embarrassment when a friend's mother chose to compliment Bart on his good school grades by telling him, "You're a good Jewish boy." On another occasion, Bart adamantly refused to get some corned beef at the neighborhood delicatessen for Christmas dinner: "Imagine the ribbing I'd get from my friends when they saw me shopping at a Jewish delicatessen on *Christmas!*" (Perhaps Bart's friends had taken notice of his special sensitivity about "behaving Jewishly" and might indeed have teased him for this altogether normal act.)

The meaning of Bart's "Jewish complex" became clear to his counselor when Bart's physician advised that Bart be circumcised to get rid of a recurring irritation around the foreskin. Bart's father objected violently to this prescription. "No man in *my* family," he shouted, "has ever been circumcised!" To explain his father's pronouncement, and the emotional meaning behind it, Bart divulged a family secret: that although his mother was raised in a Lutheran boarding school, her father was a Jew.

Roy; an Autobiographical Essay

Mother had just lit the Hannukah candles and went to the oven to take out the pork roast. (She knows I don't like pork.) "Mother," I asked, "Do you think you know *why* you lit the candles tonight?" "Of course I know," she answered. "Because God divided the Red Sea." "Ha-ha!" I teased her; "That's Pesach." "Oh, Roy," she sighed with a familiar air of exasperation; "You always know better."

This glimpse into my home life illustrates the casual patchwork of Jewish and Gentile influences which make up my background as the eldest son of a Jewish mother and a father who was raised as a German Lutheran. I could have chosen a moment from our Easter dinner, our Pesach dinner, or our

Christmas celebration to illustrate the same point. (Let me just add that I do have a special affection for Christmas. It has always been the major holiday in our house. On Christmas we entertain relatives from both sides of the family. We make merry and exchange gifts, but I think we also sense its more spiritual meaning. I think it is a time when people *do* try to shake off their pettiness, and share with others some of their innate goodness.)

I will not pretend that a love of the Christmas spirit is the only instance in which I speak up for my German Lutheran identity. I am not now an adherent to the Lutheran Church, but I admire Martin Luther immensely. He believed that all men should be taught to read the Bible in the vernacular so that they could interpret it for themselves. Luther was in part responsible for the decline of the aristocracy in Europe, which led to the founding of this country upon democratic principles. I also love German beer, wine, folk songs, poetry, and most of all, its music. I believe Beethoven to be the penultimate in human feeling and expression.

My father was converted to Judaism under the threat of my mother's family that they would disown her if she did not marry in the Jewish faith. He was raised as a Lutheran but does not seem to hold any deep religious interests. He only went as far as sixth grade in school, and makes a decent living as an office worker. He is a quiet and compassionate man; he is a good father and he lets Mother run the house. Mother's parents are Russian Jewish immigrants. They forced her to quit high school and go to work, though the financial need was not great, and in other ways she seems to have had an unhappy upbringing. She is more intelligent and better informed than my father, and also more sensitive and sympathetic. Mother is closer to her sisters, I have always noticed, than Father is to his family.

It was to please my grandfather that I prepared for bar mitzvah, and it was he who taught me Hebrew, showed me how to put on the phylacteries and utter prayers in a language I did not understand. I'm sure that if I said I did not want to learn Hebrew and become bar mitzvah, they would have left me alone. Nobody forced me.

In grammar school I was not much aware of differences between Jews and Gentiles. When I was ready for high school we moved into a highly polarized neighborhood where I felt caught in the cross-fire of Gentile anti-Semitism and Jewish exclusiveness (which I dislike intensely to this day).

In high school I made Gentile friends and Jewish friends, and the truth is that I tended to like the Gentile boys better. Whether to escape from my Jewishness or to learn something of my father's background, I enrolled on my own in a Lutheran Sunday School and attended Lutheran church services for about a year or so of my middle teens. My family did not question me or interfere. I liked Lutheranism very much. I read up on its theology and probably knew more about the hows and whys of the Church than most of its members. I frankly never believed in the Christ-as-God theory. But their idea of universal brotherhood appealed to me. I liked the music. The people were nice to me; a few people I met there are still my friends. What really crushed and angered me, however, was to hear the boys in my Sunday School class make anti-Catholic and anti-Jewish remarks. Though I might say I left the Church on philosophical grounds, on the emotional side I simply couldn't hold back my anger when I heard a minister or Church member make an anti-Semitic remark.

In college I hoped I could make both Gentile and Jewish friends; I fancied that I might serve as a kind of go-between for Jews and Gentiles on campus. I thought I could get along with Jews on the basis of the fact that my mother is Jewish, and get along with Gentiles on the basis of the fact that my father is German. It seemed to me that my Jewish acquaintances really wanted me to obliterate my German background. Someone would force into a conversation—a propos of nothing—a remark about the Nazis, as if he was goading me to renounce my German identity. Once I flared up at these continual insinuations and mockingly played along with their absurd notions that I had Nazi leanings, but my little joke backfired disasterously. I felt ostracized and tormented in both obvious and subtle ways. Perhaps my reaction was exaggerated because at that time I was going through a rather severe emotional crisis on other counts— school work, marriage, sex, family, *Weltschmerz,* and what to do with my life in general. I felt quite bitter that my Jewish friends

turned against me at a time when I could least afford to be cut
off. I guess I could be very bitter about them, but it was a
Jewish therapist who helped put me back on my feet again.
My therapist, by the way, insists that he did not *give* me my
present Jewish identity; that if I had not had a positive feeling
toward Jewishness I would not have accepted him as a therapist
in the first place.

Yes, I do have positive feelings about my Jewishness. They
flare up most dramatically when I hear an anti-Semitic remark.
I have lost more than one Gentile friend because of such a
sudden resurgence of my Jewishness. But I sometimes feel deeply
Jewish in a quieter way. The Jewish side of my family are not
educated people, yet they have always provided me with books.
When I graduated from college the event seemed much more
important to my Jewish relatives. My intellectual interests and
compassion for the underdog gives me something in common
with Jews. I've always been a soft touch for people in trouble—
sometimes at considerable personal sacrifice of time and money.
This too is part of my Jewishness.

Recently I was in a group of temporary Christmas season
workers in a shipping room, and one day at lunch everyone said
something about his ethnic background. When it came my turn,
I said my mother is Jewish and my father is German. "But
what are *you*?" someone asked. As usual I felt angry at being
forced to take sides, and the badgering continued:

"Did you say you were German?"

"I said I was half German."

"That's your *better* half." (Laughter.)

Must I renounce one side of myself or the other? I cannot
stomach anti-Semitism, but neither can I believe that all Germans—including Richard Wagner, Beethoven and Nietzsche—
are responsible for the Nazi crimes (whose victims included
Gentiles as well as Jews). My feelings are definitely mixed in
the matter of my identity, but so are the feelings of many of my
Jewish friends. They continually strive for acceptance by Gentiles
and at the same time they are clannish and non-accepting of
Gentiles.

To me, the chosen people theory and the master race theory
are equally unacceptable. I want to live in a world of tolerance

and acceptance in which an individual is appraised according to his character and attributes, regardless of his racial background or ethnic origin. If, to satisfy my Jewish friends, I just gave up the German side of my identity and called myself a Jew, I would be ashamed to look my father in the face. If we are to have tolerance in this world, let us begin by tolerating me—Roy Huber—half-German, half-Jew.

Bruce

Devereaux documents the case of a young man whom we shall call Bruce, whose mother is described as "a frustrated white school teacher married [to] an industrious but almost illiterate Indian farmer. . . . Frustrated even further by her *mésalliance,* she put considerable pressure on her son to live and behave like a white man." Devereaux interprets the son's behavior as an outward compliance with his mother's demands, disguising a "compulsive downward identification"; outwardly he goes along with mother, inwardly he identifies with his father.

"This intelligent young man . . . entered one of the best American universities and did well scholastically. However, during his second year in college, his parents found it difficult to keep paying for his education. At this point his father's sister, an uneducated but relatively well-to-do farm-wife, offered to pay for his schooling. Refusing help from a 'lousy Indian,' the young man dropped out of college, took a job in a factory, and married. His mother having warned him against marrying a 'blanket-Indian girl,' [i.e., an uneducated person] the young man—in scrupulous *mock*-compliance with his mother's wishes—married an extremely uneducated and even stupid white farm girl, who was as unsuitable a spouse for a person of his intelligence as the least educated Indian girl might have been. Last but not least, when, because of his education, the management proposed to make him a foreman, he refused the promotion, on the (unvoiced) grounds that, as a foreman, he would have to entertain at his home other foremen and even factory officials, who would consider his (in reality perfectly adequate) home as a 'dirty Indian hut.' The result of all these *superficial* compliances with his mother's attempts to make him identify with whites (upward identification) was that he chose not to get a college degree, if it meant that he had to accept help from his 'lousy Indian' aunt; that, instead of an educated Indian girl, he married a completely uneducated white girl, and that he remained a mere factory worker, instead of accepting promotion to foreman. The neuroticism of this man's compulsive downward identification, disguised as a striving for upward identification, hardly stands in need of discussion."[57]

Tonio Kröger

My father . . . had the temperament of the north: solid, reflective, puritanically correct, with a tendency to melancholia. My mother, of indeterminate foreign blood, was beautiful, sensuous, naive, passionate, and careless at once, and, I think, irregular by instinct. The mixture was no doubt extraordinary and bore with it extraordinary changes. The issue of it, a *bourgeois* who strayed off into art, a bohemian who feels nostalgic yearnings for respectability, an artist with a bad conscience.[58]

In his 1903 novella *Tonio Kröger*, Thomas Mann writes—in autobiographical style—the story of a poet whose father was a proper German businessman and public official married to a Mediterranean beauty. At the literary and philosophical level, the story expresses a conflict between the world of practical affairs and the realm of artistic experience, between logic and feeling, between the life of action and the life of reflection. Below the surface, however, Mann has set down the inner conflict of a *mischling* who cannot integrate his Mediterranean physique and temperament with a masculine sex-role identity.

Tonio recalls his father as a dignified and respectable personage, "a tall, fastidiously dressed man with thoughtful blue eyes, and always a wild flower in his button hole." His beautiful black-haired mother, who expressed her romantic spirit by how wonderfully she played the piano and mandolin, was "absolutely different from the other ladies in the town." How she differed from Herr Kröger is revealed when Tonio comes home with a poor report card. Father is troubled and angered that Tonio does not show a proper sense of duty; Mother reacts with the same "blithe indifference" that gets Tonio in trouble with his school masters. Tonio silently reproaches himself for yielding to his "gypsy" tendencies:

His thoughts . . . would run something like this: 'It is true enough that I am what I am and will not and cannot alter: heedless, self-willed, with my mind on things nobody else thinks of. And so it is right they should scold and punish me and not smother things all up with kisses and music. After all, we are not gypsies living in a green wagon; we're respectable people, the family of Consul Kröger.' And not seldom he would think: 'Why is it I am different, why do I fight everything, why am I at odds with the masters and like a stranger among the other boys? The good scholars, and the solid majority . . . their thoughts are all about things that people do think about and can talk about out loud. How regular and comfortable they must feel, knowing that everybody knows just where they stand! It must be nice! But what is the matter with me, and what will be the end of it all?[59]

It is clear that Tonio resembles his mother in physique as well as in temperament: his "brunette face with the finely chiselled features of the south; [his] dark eyes, with delicate shadows and too heavy lids, looked dreamily and a little timorously on the world."[60] He recalls an adolescent crush on Hans Hansen, "uncommonly handsome and well-built, broad in the shoulders and narrow in the hips, with keen far-apart, steel-blue eyes."[61] At fourteen years of age, Hans and Tonio had little to say to each other as they walked home from school together. "Tonio did not speak. He suffered. . . . . . The truth was, Tonio loved Hans Hansen, and had already suffered much on his account. . . . . . He loved him in the first place because he was handsome; but in the next because he was in every respect his own opposite and foil. Hans Hansen was a capital scholar, and a jolly chap to boot, who was head at drill, rode and swam to perfection, and lived in the sunshine of popularity."[62]

At sixteen, Tonio's heart "throbbed with ecstasy" for the blue-eyed daughter of Dr. Holm, and Tonio worshipped her from a distance in their weekly dancing classes ". . . blond, jolly Inge, who most assuredly despised him for his poetic effusions."

Silently he vowed to love her as long as he lived, and placed her on a "sacrificial altar, where flickered the pure, chaste flame of his love. . ."[63]

Now in his thirties and a person of reputation in the world of letters, Tonio had "no regard for himself as a human being but only as a creator . . . like an actor without his make-up, who counts for nothing as soon as he stops representing something else."[64] He confesses to a woman friend and fellow artist, ". . . I am sick to death of depicting humanity without having any part or lot in it. . . . Is an artist a male, anyhow? Ask the females! It seems to me we artists are all of us something like those unsexed papal singers . . . we sing like angels; but—"[65] He travels, searching for peace and quiet along the sea coast, in meadows and forests where he enjoys a "profound forgetfulness" as he hovers "disembodied above space and time; only now and again his heart would contract with a fugitive pain, a stab of longing and regret, into whose origin he was too lazy to inquire."[66]

At a Danish resort Tonio suddenly encounters Hans and Inge (or is it their Nordic prototypes?) together, and beholds them "with a sudden pang of home-sickness" and pathetic envy:

This was the blond, fair-haired breed of the steel-blue eyes, which stood to him for the pure, the blithe, the untroubled in life. . . . He looked at them. Hans Hansen . . . lively and well built as ever, broad in the shoulders and narrow in the hips; Ingeborg . . . laughing and tossing her head in a certain high-spirited way she had. . . . To be like you! To begin again, to grow up like you, simple and normal and cheerful, in conformity and understanding with God and man, beloved of the innocent and happy. To take you, Ingeborg Holm, to wife, and have a son like you, Hans Hansen—to live free from the curse of knowledge and the torment of creation, live and praise God in blessed mediocrity!

. . .   .

. . . You blond, you living, you happy ones![67]

That night Tonio lay in bed and whispered into his pillow the names of Ingeborg and Hans, those "chaste northern syllables that meant for him his true and native way of love, of longing, of happiness; that meant for him life and home, meant simple and heartfelt feeling. He looked back on the years that passed. He thought of the dreamy adventures of the senses, nerves, and mind in which he had been involved; saw himself eaten up with intellect and introspection, ravaged and paralyzed by insight . . . exhausted by frigid and artificially heightened ecstasies; erring, forsaken, martyred, and ill—and sobbed with nostalgia and remorse."[68]

A puritanical Nordic father, and a sensuous Mediterranean mother with whom he sees a physical resemblance and feels a kinship of temperament, somehow fixed in Tonio's mind the dictum that he is not a man and cannot be a man because he does not have the stern blue eyes of his father. What he cannot be, he idealizes, he worships. We conjecture that the intensity of his adolescent crush on Hans—so blond, so normal, so manly—leads Tonio to fear that in addition to the "gypsy" taint he is also a lover of men, a homosexual. Now he must carry the burden of "things nobody else thinks of." At school, how he envies those boys whose thoughts "are all about things that people do think about and can talk about out loud."[69] Tonio is not a homosexual, but he must expend much energy controlling a fear of homosexuality and avoiding homosexual fantasy. His talent permits him to transform his psychic suffering into works of artistic beauty, but he feels sure that his talent "is a very dubious affair and rests upon extremely sinister foundations."[70]

The Kröger complex. What do we see of Tonio Kröger in the life stories of Bart, Roy, and Bruce? In each case the son of a mixed marriage has chosen a culture style which bears a closer resemblance to that of his mother. In each case his efforts are dissipated by the eruption of inappropriate counter-tendencies. It is as if by choosing his mother's culture style he forfeits his masculinity. To ward off such an imaginary (but emotionally threatening) catastrophe, Bart shifts his role from scholar to playboy, Roy eulogizes German Kultur, Bruce turns from an intellectual career to take "a man's job" in a factory.

Certainly we must not suppose that the Kröger complex overtakes every *mischling,* or that the sons of inmarrieds are immune to it. Let us say that a boy of mixed parentage who tends toward his mother's cultural identity—either by natural inclination, through parental or cultural influences—finds himself in a life situation that lowers his threshold (or "raises his susceptibility") to doubt and confusion about his sex-role identity. Where other factors contribute to this susceptibility (perhaps an unsatisfactory relationship with his father, or lack of normal play opportunities) we may expect a fear of homosexuality, and an ambivalence toward his chosen cultural style. Variations in the outcome of the Kröger complex range from an outwardly quiet reduction in personal efficiency—as energy is diverted to an inner struggle—to a life of manifest conflict and vacillation.

The Harvard mischlings

The study of normal, successful college students who happen to be the offspring of Jewish-Gentile parentage should provide a welcome contrast to the study of those *mischlings* who seek help in psychological clinics, or are projections of a novelist's fantasy. In 1960 Philip M. Rosten completed an honors thesis devoted to a psychological study of 15 Harvard and Radcliffe students (nine males and six females) each of whom was the offspring of Jewish-Gentile parentage. Rosten included in this pioneer study two control groups—18 all-Jewish students and 21 Gentile students—to better identify the unique characteristics of the *"mischlings,"* as Rosten calls the sons and daughters of a mixed marriage.

The Jewish parent. For 12 of the 15 *mischlings*, the Jewish parent was the father (the classic sex-bias of Jewish-Gentile marriages) . Rosten describes the majority of these Jewish parents as "assimilated Jews" without formal ties to the Jewish community. Some could be described as seeking "to escape from their heritage"; two had no close Jewish friends—so far as their children knew.[71] Three had been formally converted to Christianity, and two others attended a Christian church fairly regularly. "In four cases, the Jewish [parent] openly advocated a Gentile religious training for their children, although . . . no *mischling* could recall even the slightest desire by their Jewish parent for them to attend Hebrew school or a temple." Two of the three Jewish mothers represented in this group—and none of the 12 Jewish fathers—influenced their family to observe the High Holy Days in even a "quasi-Jewish fashion."[72]

The Gentile parent. Typically, the mother of a Harvard *mischling* is a Protestant of Old Yankee stock, a seventh-generation American. (Three Catholic parents were of more recent immigration.) Of the 12 Protestant parents, five traced their lineage to 1750 or before. In this regard, Protestant parents of Rosten's *mischlings* were virtually identical to the Protestant control group.[73] "Only one Gentile parent [had] converted to Judaism," Rosten reports, "and she later drifted back into [a] Christian religion." Religiously, the Gentile partners are more active than their Jewish mates. At least two of the three Catholic parents raised their children as devout Catholics. All 15 families observed Christmas, and "seven observed it as a religious ceremony. . ."[74]

Family background and home environment. Nine of the 15 *mischlings* reported that their parents had faced family opposition to their marriage, on one or both sides. In six cases there had been "open hostility to the matches." Typically, however, the initial antagonism has "virtually disappeared":

> My [Gentile] mother is closer to my father's mother than Dad is, although I remember once being told they didn't exactly love each other at first.[75]

The *mischlings'* parents clearly followed the Gentile majority in their choice of residential neighborhood. While 53 per cent of Rosten's Jewish control group described the neighborhood of their upbringing as predominantly Jewish, only *one* of the *mischlings* was raised in a predominantly Jewish "neighborhood" —a 15-story Manhattan apartment house. One-third of the *mischlings* grew up in neighborhoods where there were *no* Jewish families, so far as they knew. (Not a single member of the Jewish control group—by contrast—had been raised in an all-Gentile neighborhood.)

Our description of the *mischling's* parental and home background thus far would lead one to suppose that the *mischling* would move surely and steadily toward a Gentile identification.

Table 4:2. Ethnicity of Neighborhood; Mischlings vs. Control Groups[76]

Respondent's description of neighborhood in which he grew up	Mischlings (N=15)	Gentiles (N=21)	Jews (N=18)
All Gentile	33%	43%	0%
Predominantly Gentile	60	57	47
Predominantly Jewish	7	0	53

Actually, only three of Rosten's 15 *mischlings*—one out of five—regarded themselves as Gentiles. Why 80 per cent of this group did *not* so regard themselves may be accounted for by three factors in their social experience: the cultureless home, Gentile unfriendliness, and the allure of Jewishness.

The cultureless home. Rosten sensed that many of his *mischlings'* parents tried to maintain a home atmosphere which was *neither* Jewish nor Gentile—in the words of one of his respondents, a "cultureless" atmosphere:

> There was no attempt to make any culture dominant. Nobody in our family ever thinks in Jewish or Gentile terms. Our home is sort of a cultureless thing—I guess you'd say our culture is liberalism rather than any religious or national culture.[77]

In her study of intermarried couples, Maria Levinson likewise observed a characteristically "cultureless home atmosphere."[78]

Only one *mischling* acknowledged that cultural differences were important to his parents. About half of the group shared the feeling "that the harmony was not easily attained and that much of what passed as natural unconcern was . . . conscious suppression of cultural loyalties which, if openly expressed, might disrupt the ethnic congeniality."[79] One topic which seemed to stir up the parents' old ethnic loyalties was their children's marriage plans:

> . . . There's a funny thing about my [Gentile] mother. I've always been curious about her reaction to my sister's marriage —she married a Presbyterian. I wondered if [my mother] didn't really like the idea because maybe she felt inferior to my father because he has the status, so that she looks upon the marriage as a victory for her side.[80]

> I think my [Gentile] father objects to my mother calling me Jewish. He won't say so, but Mother—when she's planning my marriage, and she thinks I'm going to marry a Jew—I think so too—and so she thinks in terms of a religious marriage and my father keeps saying, "Do you really want to get married in a synagogue?"[81]

These momentary recrudescences of ethnic feeling were apparently the exception in the *mischling* household, where there was "almost always a total disregard for anything which contained even a trace of ethnic identity . . . [a] policy of indifference . . . [which was apparently intended to bring] cultural harmony to the family. . ."[82]

A home which censors the expression of ethnic attitudes—positive and negative—places its children at a disadvantage in several ways. First, the *mischlings* "did not know how their Jewish parent felt about *his* Judaism because the subject was so rarely mentioned at home. Nor . . . in many cases did they know how their Gentile parent felt about his past:

> My parents are both agnostics. We have no ceremonies at all, no attachments to any heritage. It's so independent, so realistic, it's disgusting. *My mother might have been Jewish and my father Gentile for all it matters to them.*[83]

Their home experience did not prepare them to share the norms of either the Gentile majority or the Jewish minority—did not prepare them to accept the profound significance attached to ethnic group membership in the world outside their home. The posture of indifference to ethnicity gave the child "a false impression of what it means to be a Jew or a Gentile in the world beyond the home," and left the *mischling* particularly vulnerable to his first encounters with anti-Semitism.[84]

Gentile unfriendliness. Like his Gentile peer, a *mischling* destined to become a student at Harvard or Radcliffe is likely to grow up in a status-oriented upper middle class Gentile neighborhood. Early in adolescence—sometimes sooner, sometimes later—the *mischling* discovers that those whose acceptance and friendship he has been trained to seek do not share his conviction that he is no different than they are:

When I was twelve and had never been confronted with any anti-Semitic problems, I was left out of a birthday party because, as my parents told me, I was Jewish and the boy's parents didn't approve of it. In fact his mother didn't approve of it so much she had incited my friends into wrecking my bike and beating me up. I was confused and hurt.[85]

I was requested to withdraw my application from a riding club. I was fifteen at the time. It was very painful because it took away friends.[86]

I never got invited to the first-class dances. The second-class, yes, but not to the big ones. The line was fuzzy but it was there all right. (When did this first occur?) Not until high school when the girls I knew started throwing deb parties. I'd get invited to some, but there were always a couple around Christmas time that I never went to.[87]

I never got into a final club here at Harvard, although I think I might be able to get into one or two now. However, whether or not I was actually rebuffed many times because I was Jewish I don't know. I have always felt, however, that I was or would not be accepted for this very reason.[88]

Among their Gentile peers, the *mischlings* discovered something they had not learned at home—that "the wider American community . . . tends to regard the *mischling* as part of the Jewish community. . . . *All but one* of the 15 *mischlings*," Rosten reports, confirmed this fact, "that society as a whole regards a half-Jew, half-Gentile as a Jew, regardless of the individual's own preference":

Society looks upon any person like me as a Jew. They use the same damn attitudes they use against a Jew. I can't say as though I like it, although I guess I wouldn't want them to think of me as a pure Gentile either. But at least there's less bigotry.[89]

Rosten presents the case of Meg as an interesting example of how a Jewish father makes a girl Jewish in the eyes of the Gentile elite. Meg was born to Gentile parents, was "raised in a Gentile church, had gone to a Gentile private school . . . was raised in a predominantly Gentile atmosphere, and viewed herself from a Gentile vantage point in life. . ." When her father died, Meg's mother married a man who was "Jewish in past only and had not tried to instill any sense of his culture into his new daughter." According to Rosten's scrutiny, Meg had no more Jewish characteristics than her Gentile friends. But, said Meg, "people are inclined to think of me as Jewish when they know of my father's background. I've run into it a couple of times when I've proclaimed my heritage and had people say, 'Oh, I thought so!'—as though they were making a great discovery."[90]

It is significant—and how ironical—that Rosten's *mischlings* reported far more anti-Semitic suffering than the Jewish control group. The Jewish sample, according to Rosten, had almost nothing to report by way of social ostracism.[91]

Early recollections. Most *mischlings* recalled with vivid detail the experience which gave them their "first understanding" of what it is to be a Jew in a Gentile world. "All but three recalled eposides which had occurred before they were nine or ten."

I was young—seven or eight. There was a little girl who came over to play with me and we were running on the hillside and she said, "Let's pretend we're Nazis trying to kill Jews." Well here I was and I knew my mother was Jewish but I didn't know what a Jew was. So I went to ask her and she told me. I was aware of it before I was seven years old . . . but it never impressed me until then.[92]

All of a sudden I realized that some people didn't like Jews. I never knew before that there was any real difference between being Jewish or not. It was just a word which I associated with my father in some vague way.[93]

Rosten reports that "many [of his *mischling* respondents] were embittered against their parents because they had not prepared them sufficiently" to deal with the attitudes of their status group toward Jews and toward *mischlings*. This was, in fact, their *"principal criticism . . . about the way their parents had raised them."*[94] (Italics added.)

(Suppose you were your own parent—would you have done anything differently?)

I think my parents were too protective to me when I was younger. I think I wasn't sufficiently aware of what both sides meant. I would have tried to make me more aware of what it meant to be even partially Jewish in what is essentially a Gentile society, and at the same time what it means to be a Gentile in a Jewish society. I'm not sure I'd know how to go about it.[95]

Friends. All 15 *mischlings* recalled having a Protestant friend in grammar school—an experience shared by little more than half of the Jewish controls. The majority of *mischlings* had friends who were Catholics—an experience shared by a minority of Jews. If their recollections are to be trusted, and if Rosten's Gentile control group provides an apt standard of comparison, the *mischlings* had *fewer* Jewish friends during grammar school than their Gentile peers! (See Table 4:3.)

Table 4:3. Ethnicity of Friends, Grammar School Age or Before[96]

Ethnic group membership	Mischlings (N=15)	Gentiles (N=21)	Jews (N=18)
Protestant	100%	96%	59%
Catholic	71	76	27
Jewish	33	38	100

According to Rosten's statistics, from grammar school to high school the number of *mischlings* who had "a great deal of contact" with Jews *quadruples,* a shift in group affiliation unmatched by either control group. (See Table 4:4.) This finding suggests that during adolescence a growing unfriendliness of the Gentile elite leads the *mischling* to increasingly seek and accept the companionship of Jewish peers. One of Rosten's respondents reflects upon the adolescence crisis of *mischling*hood:

[Being a *mischling*] is fine when you're young, when you don't realize there are religious differences and bigotry, and it's

fine when you're old and have your feet on the ground . . .
when you realize what matters is you and what you make of
yourself. But during adolescence and the first year of college
it's really a problem because you find yourself without any
ground to stand on.[97]

Table 4:4. Ethnic Groups with which They Had "A Great Deal of
Contact" at Two Age Levels (Grammar School and High School)[98]

Percentage of respondents who recall "a great deal of contact"
with that group

Ethnic group	Mischlings (N=15)		Gentiles (N=21)		Jews (N=18)	
	Grammar school	High school	Grammar school	High school	Grammar school	High school
Protestant	87%	93%	76%	96%	33%	61%
Catholics	47	33	42	38	11	22
Jews	13	60	19	38	95	88

Rosten offers no statistical tally of friendships by ethnic groups
at Harvard, but his interview citations make frequent references
to Jewish-*mischling* friendships. Even Sam Abraham (whose case
is discussed later in this chapter), staunchly Episcopalian and
certain he would want to raise his children as Protestants, quietly
notes that he has been dating a Jewish girl.

The allure of Jewishness. By contrast with their encounters of
Gentile unfriendliness, the Harvard and Radcliffe *mischlings*
seem to experience a feeling of belonging and social intimacy in
the company of their Jewish peers:

It's nice to tell Jews you're half-Jewish when you're alone
with a group of them. It makes you feel a part of them.[99]

[Said a *mischling* girl:] I always feel that when I go out with
a Jewish boy he doesn't feel at ease with me until I tell him
I'm half-Jewish.[100]

The *mischling* discovers that when his Jewish parentage becomes known to a Gentile group, he loses status; when it becomes
known to a Jewish group, he *gains* status as a social intimate.

I get a little annoyed at the Gentiles who think that unless
. . . you have a good WASP name you're less than they are.
It used to bother me when I knew I was going somewhere
where they thought I was a Gentile—it made me feel ill at ease
a little bit.[101]

Group identification, like love, can thrive only if it is reciprocated, if the individual's claim to full membership is fully
endorsed by the group to which he wants to belong. But the
mischling learns that he is *not* fully welcomed into the Gentile
society toward which his parents have oriented him, and this
experience gives him something in common with his Jewish
peers—the sting of anti-Semitism. The *mischling* finds that Jews
may also take a guarded, skeptical attitude toward him,[102] but
he learns through experience that Jews are more likely to accept
him as an intimate friend, to sympathize with his marginality.
The *mischling* can better tolerate Jewish joking about his Gentile parentage than Gentile joking about his Jewish parentage.
The security he feels among Jews who accept him as a member of the tribe undoubtedly leads the *mischling* to regard his
Jewishness as a valuable personal resource, to wish he knew more
about his carefully suppressed Jewish background, to feel an
extra measure of pride in his Jewish parentage, to feel a sense
of loyalty toward those Jewish peers who welcome him as an
equal.

I sort of feel guilty if I don't [tell of my Jewish past] when
I should. I don't feel Jewish like a Jew should. I don't look
Jewish. What the hell, I'm *not* Jewish! But I couldn't live with
myself if I weren't honest, and I couldn't face Dad. [More
importantly, perhaps, he couldn't face his Jewish friends
either.][103]

Himself a *mischling*, Rosten recalls with pride what he learned
about his Jewish forebears:

I remember hearing my father or his mother reminiscing about
their pasts—how my great-grandfather was the most renowned
scholar of the Torah in the . . . village, or how my grandparents worked twelve hours a day, six days a week, so that

my father and his sister would have a chance to have the best education—and feeling that what they said was part of me.[104]

Ignorance of the Jewish tradition becomes a source of shame to the *mischling*, and an occasion for resentment toward his Jewish parent:

> . . . I feel a little guilty that I don't feel pride with Judaism and then I realize that there's no good reason why I should because of the way my father brought me up.[105]

A heritage hidden, and revealed. We have already noted that only one of Rosten's 15 *mischlings* had been given any Jewish religious education, compared with *nine* who had been given some religious education in a Christian church—in four cases with the explicit encouragement of the Jewish parent. To describe the *mischling's* home atmosphere as "cultureless," therefore, would overlook a strong and explicit parental bias in favor of placing their children into the Gentile mainstream of society. Not a single *mischling* "could recall even the slightest desire by [his] Jewish parent for [their children] to attend Hebrew school or a temple."[106] According to their children's testimony, "the Jewish parent was unmoved to give his child even a rudimentary awareness of Judaism's more tangible features."[107] Four *mischlings* expressed regret over their lack of knowledge of the Jewish tradition:

> My father never seemed to care—he had no desire at all that I become a Jew. . . . I wish I had learned more about it earlier, because it wasn't until I got to college that I really began to learn something of what the Jewish religion was like.[108]

Four of Rosten's *mischlings* said that most of what they knew about Judaism *they learned from their Gentile mother.* "Dad hardly ever mentioned it."[109] Despite this curtain of silence, the *mischlings* felt and incorporated a Jewish "sense of being" as part of themselves. All but two said they acquired this awareness very early in life—"they were 'always aware' of their Jewishness."[110] Undoubtedly the *mischling's* upbringing was enveloped by many subtle Jewish influences—in spite of the posture of culturelessness, in spite of the guidance toward a Christian religious affiliation. Six of the 15 bore family names which were either distinctly Jewish or "might be Jewish."[111] "While the *mischling* lived in a predominantly Gentile neighborhood and did not have much contact with Jewish peers, his parents had many Jewish friends,"[112] and through the voluntary maintenance of these Jewish social attachments they undoubtedly communicated their sense of kinship with their fellow Jews, their "sense of attachment to a unique existence."[113] Contact with Jewish grandparents and other Jewish kin added something to the casual and unintentional influences through which the *mischlings* felt and incorporated a Jewish "sense of being" as part of their identity.

Though none of the 15 considered themselves Jews, all but two said they acquired an awareness of their Jewishness very early in life; it was something "they were 'always aware' of . . ."[114] The personal meaning and value of this awareness was shaped— we hypothesize—by the individual's direct social experience. Apart from a felt respect for his Jewish parent, the *mischling's* positive interest in Jewishness was nurtured by his discovery that Jews were more likely to accept him as a friend, an equal, an intimate, than Gentiles. In the individual experience of the *mischling*, Jewishness was first encountered as a family mystery, next as a social burden, and then as a bond of fellowship.

To pass or not to pass. By upbringing, by religious education, by parental encouragement and design, the *mischling* has been groomed for membership in Gentile society. In adolescence he discovers that in order to validate this membership he must conceal his Jewish parentage, he "must constantly repress any trait that might even hint at his hidden background. . . . He might well be plagued by . . . [a] fear of 'being discovered,' for if he is, he may feel that he has disqualified himself from falling back on the Jewish community for support."[115] The anxiety associated with the tactic of passing is described by the *mischling* who commented:

Guys who don't [tell of both sides] are sitting on a powder keg. They'll always be wondering what happens if their little lie gets known. People are going to treat you worse if you hid one side and they found out. This is one thing I don't have to worry about.[116]

Rosten judged that the majority of his *mischlings,* from the standpoint of name, appearance, and behavior, "*could* have passed as Gentiles if they had wanted to. . . . Only four . . . felt that people regarded them as Jewish [even] when their parentage was not known." Having been raised as candidates for the Gentile elite, Rosten's *mischlings* were often tempted, in one way or another, to underplay what society regarded as the flaw in their lineage. Sons of seventh generation Old Yankee mothers, their claim to membership in the elite was—to them—based on something quite real:

> I would listen to my mother recount the time her grandmother ran into the streets before the charging horses of Confederate soldiers to rescue the American flag, or tell of her mother's lineage which extended back into British nobility, and feel . . . that this too was part of me.[118]

The *mischlings* resolved the problem of passing in a variety of ways. Only one insisted "that he has never hidden one side of his background."[119] One *mischling,* who seemed particularly insecure about his status (*see* the case of Sam Abraham) seemed to seek out occasions to broadcast the fact that his father was Jewish. Three-fourths of the group made no serious and consistent effort to pass. About four shared a policy described by Ralph, who—according to Rosten—was able to maintain so effective a "Gentile veneer"—without recourse to "overt hypocrisy"—that only three or four of his Harvard friends shared his secret. Ralph explained:

> My policy is pretty well set. If somebody asks me point blank I'll tell him, as honestly and truthfully as I can. If no one asks I just don't mention it.[120]

Ralph describes his life in a Gentile world "heavily impregnated with anti-Semitic elements:"

> I belong to an organization outside of school I'd never have got into if they had known my father was Jewish.

He admits that he feels "a marked anxiety . . . in a situation when I know people would be prejudiced against me if they knew I was half-Jewish."[121] The three *michlings* who had adopted a policy similar to Ralph's had permitted a somewhat larger number of intimates to share their secret.

The majority of Rosten's respondents were known as *mischlings* "to fairly close friends. . . . Their dual heritage [becomes known] only after a period of friendship, or more rarely, during religious discussions."[122] In more casual social contacts, however, they are tempted to pass if they can do it without direct lying. Characteristically, the *mischling* negotiates situational passing by "skirting the issue through half truths, and [the episode is] almost always accompanied by feelings of guilt or shame":[123]

> This is sort of embarrassing. I'd find myself tellings people my father was Russian and sort of neglect the Jewish part. I'm ashamed of it now because I know this would hurt him if he knew, and I felt guilty about it. I'm just beginning to grow out of it now.[124]

> [Said Rosten's singularly candid and volatile Karl:] I'm not above calling myself an Episcopalian, for strictly dishonorable reasons—it's socially acceptable.[125]

> I suppose I've [hid my Jewish side] . . . No, I *know* so. But I never lied about it; just sort of . . . well, you know, forget to mention it when I should have. I'm not terribly proud of it.[126]

Apart from their aspirations to status in the Yankee elite, Rosten's *mischlings* were tempted to pass in order to spare themselves the sting of anti-Semitism:

> [Ralph:] When I got to high school I saw that there was real prejudice against the Jews and then all of a sudden I began to think that this prejudice could be directed against me . . . [I decided that] if somebody was going to be adamantly anti-Semitic he wasn't going to pick on me and nobody ever has.[127]

> [Sam:] Father said he wanted me to be an Episcopalian because he wanted me to avoid a lot of trouble that Jews have . . .[128]

Rage and confusion. Some of Rosten's *mischlings* show real difficulty in coping with a world that refuses to validate their Gentile self-image. Their reactions run the gamut from Sam Abraham, who tries very hard to deny any feeling of resentment, to Karl, who readily verbalizes his bewilderment, frustration, and isolation, his sense of injustice and resentment against Jewish and Gentile society alike:

> I've had many qualms about my identity. . . . Until I got to college I sort of resented in a way my father because he was Jewish, and that because he was a Jew I was going to be an outsider. . . . You can't hide from it—you've just got to face up to it. . . . *I think it's affected my entire personality.* In many ways it tends to make you feel you're never really accepted . . . and it makes you feel you never really belong to either group either, and you . . . hate them and you hate your old man, too.

> . . . I probably always resented my father a little bit just be- cause Jewish religion is not the accepted religion and I never really belonged to one group or the other . . .

> . . . When I hear an anti-Semitic comment I sometimes feel like joining in—sometimes I do and then I wonder why the hell I did that. Sometimes I just want to knock the shit out of them. . . . In some ways it makes you more prejudiced. . . . Other people who are prejudiced against Jews act for no good reason, without any basis whatsoever. *I'm prejudiced against Jews and I got plenty of reason* and it's all inside. I have no external things, just things inside my own personality.

> I would feel better if society would just sort of reduce the whole impact of religion and forget about the whole thing. It's here to stay, though, and we've just got to live with it. But I wish there was no such thing. . . . Life would be a helluva lot happier if it weren't.[129] [Italics added.]

Like Karl and Ralph, a minority of Rosten's respondents, to whom a Gentile identity meant a great deal, saw their *mischling* status "almost completely as a detriment, an unwanted burden which they basically resented":

I feel it's a dirty trick played upon me—I always have. [It's] a dirty deal I don't really deserve. . . . The anxiety I feel seems to me just to be imposed for no reason. I have no identity with the Jewish faith at all.[130]

Others confess that they are confused and indecisive about where their Jewishness ends and their Gentileness begins. In the words of a Radcliffe *mischling:*

I consider myself half-Jewish, but I don't know. When I think of my background I think in terms of Jewishness, but when I do something I often think of myself from a Christian viewpoint. Yet even when I think of my background I get a little confused. I'm completely without any identity in an ethnic sense.[131]

Of Rosten's 15 *mischlings,* only one claims a Gentile identity without qualification. Not one regards himself as a Jew. The majority "tend to feel they live in a limbo between the two groups, not a Jew, not a Gentile, but a unique combination of both."[132]

Learning the bicultural ropes. Learning to live in a world which does not validate the status for which they were groomed, the *mischlings* try to fashion a new role—"an identity where they will not have to abandon either side of their heritage. . . . In so doing, they have to fall back upon their own resources almost completely, being both teacher and pupil." They have to overcome what Rosten calls "the deleterious effects of their parents' attitude of ethnic indifference. But even had [their parents] tried to show their children what it means to be a Jew or a Gentile in the greater world, they could not have assuaged the *mischling's* feeling of uncertainty, for neither was a *mischling* himself."[133]

To the extent that it requires the avowal of contradictory attitudes, the dual ethnic role must be an uncomfortable one. In an autobiographical footnote, Rosten describes his own vulnerability to hurt and bewilderment—when, for example, his identification with his Jewish father fills him with anger and frustration that an acquaintance should denounce Senator Wayne Morse as "that goddam kike," and when his regard for his Protestant-born mother makes it painful for him to hear a Jewish friend cynically generalize on the moral looseness of *shikses.*[134]

The *mischling's* inner life becomes more of a battleground than a symphony—in Rosten's words, an internalized replica "of the whole sociological phenomenon of ethnic group interaction. . . . Because of his position the *mischling* can never face these influences with group support." His interview findings lead Rosten to conclude that the *mischling* "lacks a clear sense of where he belongs. . . . He is ethnically isolated from most of mankind."[135] Said one of his respondents: *"I'm a lonely crowd. I guess I don't fit in anywhere."*[136]

Degrees of conflict over mischlinghood. The majority of Rosten's respondents view their social role *not* "as an incidental factor in their lives . . . but as something which has affected their entire being in both positive and negative ways." They "constantly view life through a prism of two cultures. Some have experienced a great deal of conflict over their stance in life, while to others it has caused only minor instances of ethnic uncertainty. All, however, have felt the bewilderment and hurt of never really 'belonging' to any ethnic group at some point in their lives."[137]

Scientific study means measurement, and in an effort to gauge the degree of conflict his respondents had experienced, Rosten posed the question, "Has the fact that you come from a mixed religious marriage ever been a problem to you?" Twelve of the 15 responded in a way that added up to Yes. (The three "detached" *mischlings*—those whom it had "never bothered"—will be described later.) After listening to their stories, Rosten judged that eight of these 12 suffered *"moderate to high conflict,* either [currently] or during adolescence, over their dual ethnic status in life." At the acute extreme were those who feel severely handicapped by their status:

> I don't really belong anywhere. . . . I never really have belonged to any group. . . . It's something you always have with you which makes you an outsider all the time, something which you can never erase.[138]

In addition to the eight "conflicted" *mischlings* and the three "detached" ones—for whom mixed parentage was not a problem —Rosten identified a group of four "aware" *mischlings;* they felt the influence of their marginal status but had experienced "only minor or momentary conflict" because of it.[139]

Rosten hypothesized that the uncertain, conflict-laden status of a *mischling* would lead him to become more deeply aware of his inner life—more soul-searching, introspective, or self-doubting than the average person. Because society provides no ready-made set of attitudes for the *mischling*—because he can adopt neither a Jewish outlook on life nor a Gentile outlook—he must work out of his *own* outlook on life, and must therefore exploit his inner resources more intensively than others. Such was the line of reasoning that justified administering a set of Intraception Scales devised by Myron Sharaf to each of the *mischlings,* and to the control groups.

Each of three scales consisted of about ten items dealing with some aspect of intraception defined as "a syndrome of personality traits including empathy, self-insight, and the ego-defense mechanism of intellectualization."[140] The Scales are described in Table 4:5.

Table 4:5. Summary Description of Sharaf's Intraception Scales

Name of scale	Sample item	Significance of extreme scores
Rejection of intraception	I like to put myself in someone else's place and imagine how I would feel in the same situation.	Low score: Very intraceptive; person favors empathy, self-insight, and intellectualization as a way of viewing life.
Self-deception	At times I have made cruel and inaccurate remarks about other people who were not present to defend themselves.	Low score: person shows readiness "to acknowledge value-violating and emotionally painful aspects of the self."[141]
Self-acceptance	I usually have the feeling that I am working successfully toward my life goals.	High score: general satisfaction with the self—feeling of moral worthiness and effectiveness.
		Low score: feelings of "self-rejection, incompetancy, guilt and shame."[142]

Inspection of Rosten's results shows that on two of the three scales, the "detached" group tended to match the adjustment pattern of the Gentile control group. (The sub-sample size is admittedly small, and statistical significance cannot be claimed for this observation.) In Table 4:6, the "conflicted" and "aware" groups are combined into a group of 12 "subjectively marginal" *mischlings,* for comparison with the "detached" minority and the controls.

Table 4:6. The Mischling as a Soul-Searcher

	Average Score by Group			
Scale	Subjectively marginal mischlings	"Detached" mischlings	Gentile controls	Jewish controls
	(N=12)	(N=3)	(N=21)	(N=18)
Rejection of intraception	26.5	26.7	30.2	33.2
Self-deception	38.3	47.7	44.0	41.3
Self-acceptance	45.2	53.8	52.6	51.4

On the basis of these test score differences, Rosten concludes that *mischlings* show "a greater uncertainty about [their] own moral worth and effectiveness, and . . . are more prone to feelings of self-rejection. . . . They are also *less* inclined to be self-deceiving (i.e., more prone to acknowledge 'value-violating and emotionally painful aspects of the self') " than either their Jewish or Gentile peers.[144]

The "detached" ones. Of all 15 *mischlings* who were asked, "Has the fact that you come from a mixed religious marriage ever been a problem to you?" only three gave convincingly negative answers, and the remainder of their interviews indicated a relative absence of conflict or uncertainty over their ethnic status. These three were somehow able to fully identify with a Gentile reference group, and their scores on the Intraception Scales tended to match the Gentile control group better than the subjectively marginal *mischlings.* (*See* Table 4:6.) Of the entire group of 15 *mischlings,* only two had been raised as Catholics, and both fit into the "detached" group:

I was raised as a Catholic and came to think of myself solely as a Catholic. My identity to Judaism ended with the word. I never even identified my father with it.[145]

It never bothered me. It never really could because it had no meaning for me. I was raised as a Catholic and always thought of myself as a Catholic.[146]

The one non-Catholic member of the "detached" trio was a young man who "was raised in an academic community in which he never experienced the consequences of anti-Semitism." His father was Protestant, his mother Jewish. Of all of Rosten's 15 *mischlings*, this faculty offspring displayed a unique conception of his social status. Asked, "Where would society place a person if all they knew about him was that he was half-Jewish, half-Gentile?" he responded:

I guess they'd tend to think of him as a Gentile just by weight of numbers. If the person identified with one or the other I think they'd tend to treat him as he himself did.

Rosten comments: "No other *mischling* felt that society would categorize a *mischling* as a Gentile, or felt it would unequivocally accept a *mischling's* own [choice of ethnic] identity."[147] Perhaps the academic community has norms all its own.

Rosten's study leads to the conclusion that Harvard and Radcliffe *mischlings* who experience the greatest conflict of identity are the offsprings of Jewish fathers and Protestant mothers of Old Yankee stock, who grew up in a fashionable (and non-Jewish) Yankee environment—or in an upper middle class Midwest environment—attended private schools or high status high schools, sought their dates and close friends in the "social set" of the Gentile community.[148] Of the four *mischlings* whose bicultural identity was attained with a minimum of conflict—Rosten's "aware" group—two had a Gentile father and surname, and the other two were raised in communities where anti-Semitism seemed less prevalent—one in the Upper South, the other in the Southwest. Of the three "detached" respondents—those whose identity was most thoroughly Gentile—two had been raised as Catholics, and one in an academic community.

It's not all bad. Rosten asked whether there may not be advantages as well as disadvantages to the social role of the *mischling*. Although the *mischling* lacks the security of full group membership, he has partial access to *two* groups with which he can directly experience a degree of belonging "which no Jew or Gentile can experience." Rosten reports that most *mischlings* cherish this mobility "as deeply as they deplore their ethnic uncertainty," and use their *mischling* status as a passport to "wander between the two groups with a unique mixture of subjective participation and objective observation . . ."[149]

> I think it's given me wisdom. . . . I can look at things, people . . . [and situations] with a little more circumspection than most people because I've been forced to view things from two different sides of the . . . coin, and I've been accustomed to look at just about everything in more than one way. . . . But I've lost security—the kind of security of being born into one religion.[150]

> Sure I've missed something. I've missed the sense of belonging to one group, and I know that I never really will have this feeling. When I was younger it meant a lot to me. But life isn't composed just of backgrounds, and I like the freedom to travel between groups. It's been a very broadening experience and I wouldn't want to give it up. But it wasn't very easy or pleasant for me. Overall, though, I'm glad I had it.[151]

Sam Abraham

Rosten centers his discussion of the conflicted *mischling* around the case of a short, plump, boyish Harvard junior whose manner throughout the interview was one of careful propriety and lack of feeling.

> . . . He appears to be the epitome of the blasé, unconcerned college student. . . . His whole character [reflects an] air of one indifferent to life's fluctuations. He speaks in a quiet, almost fixed monotone . . .[152]

> I first met him when I went to his room for the interview. He met me at the door and ushered me into one of the most immaculately kept apartments I have ever seen, almost the antithesis of the usual student room where books and clothing are strewn about with general carelessness. Although it was late in the evening, Sam wore a neat, button-down collar shirt with a

conventional tie to match his conventional gray flannel slacks.[153]

After the usual introductions, I began the interview. In contrast to the average interview which lasted from forty to fifty minutes, my talk with Sam took less than half an hour. He was congenial throughout and his answers are, I feel, an honest attempt to convey his own impressions of his life. During the interview Sam rarely raised his voice, and his speech was almost devoid of emotion. He sat relatively motionless, and except for an occasional shrug of the shoulders or movement of the hands, his appearance was virtually expressionless. He only laughed twice—short, almost forced chuckles—and he never smiled. Even when he was describing the more intimate aspects of his past—such as his father's or mother's character—he displayed this same lack of subjectivity.[154]

. . .   .

Sam spoke as though he were analyzing an alien intellectual concept rather than [his own] personal history. No other *mischling* even approached this lack of affect.[155]

Sam describes his father as "a very, very liberal Jew [who] goes to church with Mother all the time—that's the Episcopal church. . ." Sam says quite candidly that Father "wanted me to be an Episcopalian because he wanted me to avoid a lot of trouble that Jews have." Father is described as friendly and hard working. In Sam's eyes, Father is "not very religious . . . [and] his family isn't very Jewish."[156]

Sam's loyalty to the Episcopalian church ("I've been very, very happy in it") [157] must withstand the tension of an antagonism toward his church-oriented mother, and a degree of felt rejection by "the social people" of his Gentile community:

I don't like my mother. She's very social, very high-strung and interested in social position because of security for the family. Very domineering. I love her but I don't like her, if you know what I mean. She's very, very high Episcopalian—her background is high Episcopalian. . . I don't like low Episcopalians; they are all just in it for the social thing.[158]

My hometown is a very, very, very social place. . . . *Most of*

my friends turned out to be Jewish. I don't know. . . . I'm
basically a very friendly person. I try to make friends with
everyone, and *the people who accepted my friendship were
Jews mainly.* . . . Maybe the Jews are more desirous of having
friends than the social people; maybe the social people stay
away from me because I'm Jewish.[159] (Italics added.)

Eager for his son to be a good Episcopalian ("He's always
urging me to go to church") ,[160] Sam's father is frankly dissatisfied
that most of his son's friends are Jews. ("My father keeps urging
me not to have Jewish friends—certainly not [to befriend them]
because they are Jewish."[161] "My father got annoyed when talking to me about the fact [that] all my friends were Jewish. . . .
He wanted me to make new friends. Probably for awhile it did
[make me anxious] but I really don't know.)[162]

> In high school, most of my friends were Jewish. It was a
> very social place, and as I was half-Jewish maybe—although I
> really don't know—I was shunned.[163]

> As I say I have always felt insecure. As most of my friends
> were Jewish I felt left out, in one way, but not in a way that
> mattered.[164]

Asked if he has encountered any problems on dates, Sam responds, "No—I'm going with a Jewish girl now." He admits that
for him marriage poses "a ticklish problem. . . . Somehow it
seems to me I wouldn't want to marry a Jewish girl, but I'm not
prejudiced and I really can't answer my feelings about it other
than the same reason my father wanted me to become an Episcopalian—he was afraid of prejudice. He didn't want that to
occur and I wouldn't either. I'd certainly raise my kids as Protestants," says Sam, and adds—incongruously—"all my friends are
reformed Jews."[165]

In the interview situation, Sam responds to Rosten's probing
questions with a good deal of awkwardness and denial. Asked if
he would accept an important job if he knew the employer was
"violently anti-Semitic," Sam replied, "It would depend on the
job. I would tell him I wasn't anti-Semitic." As for accepting a
job with an *anti-Gentile* employer, Sam replied, "I probably

wouldn't accept [it] because there would be some prejudice toward me."[166]

Asked how he thinks society regards a person who is known to be half-Jewish, half-Gentile, Sam replies, "That's a hard question because I never came in contact with it except for my social home-town. I never really stopped to consider why my friends were Jewish. I suppose I may have shied away. Personally, it [my background] never affected me. . . . My friends wouldn't think about it—they don't think about it except as a joke. . . . I suppose [society] would discriminate against him because he is Jewish. I never thought much about it. . . . I'm basically insecure—I need friendship." Sam volunteers the comment that when he hears an anti-Semitic crack, "I get aggravated . . . [because] *most of my friends are nice guys."* (Italics added.) [167]

At the close of the interview, Sam volunteered the summary comment: ". . . I've always been an Episcopalian. . . never a Jew, but here at college I'm beginning to wonder about it. It never caused me any problem, although socially there may have been some effect—I'm not sure."[168]

Rosten links Sam's emotional insecurity to the strong indications of ambivalence implied in the behavior of his father, to whom Sam shows a close and positive relationship. Sam's father urges his son to be a good Episcopalian and cultivate Gentile friends. Yet, according to Sam, father's five best friends are all Jews. His father has befriended the Episcopal minister, attends Episcopal services, but declines to join the church. He wants his son to be an Episcopalian so as to "avoid a lot of trouble that Jews have," but refuses to change a very identifiably Jewish family name, and has raised his son in a "very, very social" hometown where he attended a "very social" high school, and where assimilation into a Gentile environment would seem to be particularly difficult.[169]

Sam describes his mother as a domineering, driving person. He says he "is not and has never been" close to her; he does not like her. Her life is centered around the church, and her five best friends (so far as Sam knows) are Protestant. His parents probably do not get along on a basis of mutuality, and consider their parental role something of a burden. Sam is an only child, born ten years after his parents were married.

The incongruities of Sam's family relations are paralleled by
the incongruities of his relations with his social milieu. He regards himself as a life-long confirmed and practicing Episcopalian, but his society treats him like a Jew. He tries to be
friendly with everyone, but is befriended mainly by Jews, in
whose company he feels like an outsider. Having been raised in
a community that puts a high premium on eligibility for upper
middle class Protestant society, Sam has been so often shunned by
his co-religionists, he will probably never feel quite secure in an
all-Gentile community. As Rosten sees him, Sam is "caught in a
personally painful social situation . . . and his frequent denials
and disavowals of his predicament indicate that his situation is
so painful that he cannot really face it."[170]

The search for "the average mischling." Rosten's sample may
very well match the average *Harvard mischling,* and thereby
represent a specific variety of *mischling* adaptation. The average
offspring of mixed parents may no more resemble the Harvard
mischling than the average American college student matches the
norm of a Harvard man.

Goldstein and Goldscheider's Providence (Rhode Island) survey gives quite a different picture of *mischling* upbringing in the
American culture. In their random sample of Jews in and around
Providence, in 42 per cent of all mixed marriages the non-Jewish
spouse converted to Judaism, and of 136 offsprings of such marriages, *all* were being raised as Jews. Of those *mischlings* whose
non-Jewish parent did *not* convert, over one-half (84 out of 144)
were being raised as Jews. A Camden (New Jersey) survey, according to Kertzer, showed that in one-third of mixed marriages
the children were being raised as Jews.[171] In a Deep South community studied by Sidney I. Goldstein, on the other hand, a majority of families headed by mixed parents (10 out of 16 such
families) send their children to Protestant Sunday School. There
seem to be a number of local and regional norms for *mischling*
upbringing, and no characterization of an "average *mischling*"
can be meaningful unless it is related to some particular social
group.

The childless intermarriage. One solution to the problem of
how to raise children of mixed parental background is to have no
children. Baber tells of a Jewish woman "of a good family" who

married a Negro lawyer only after she had promised her "heart-broken . . . mother that they never would have any children."[172] Baber noted the low fertility rate of mixed marriages, and concluded that "undoubtedly one reason is the realization of the hardships imposed upon the children of such unions. . . . Such comments as "they didn't feel that they should have any children," "they agreed that they ought not to have children," or "they are definitely against having children" occur with special frequency among inter-racial couples.[173]

In 1938 Koenig made a study in depth of 31 Jewish-Gentile families in Stamford, Connecticut. A majority of 17 were childless, 12 had only one child, and only 2 couples had two or more children. Engelman, who studied Jewish-Gentile intermarriages in Germany between World War I and the Nazi era, reports that childlessness was widespread among mixed Jewish couples. In 1927 the average number of children per intermarried family was 0.5. [174] (In a group of ten couples, such an average would be obtained if one couple had two children, three couples had one child each, and the remaining six couples were childless.) In their 1966 study of Jewish and intermarried couples in Providence (Rhode Island), Goldstein and Goldscheider report that 26 per cent of intermarrieds were childless, compared with a 10 per cent rate of childlessness for inmarried Jews. Intermarried women past childbearing age averaged 1.6 children, compared with 2.2 children for the average inmarried Jewish woman.

It is probably an oversimplification to say that intermarried couples choose to remain childless because of the complications and risks involved in bringing up children of mixed parentage. Would a person for whom raising a family was important enter into a marriage which did not lend itself to raising a family? Voluntary childlessness is not unique to mixed marriages. What do the childless couple and the intermarried couple have in common? Entering into marriage at a later age is certainly one common factor. A high degree of involvement in a professional or social career may likewise favor both intermarriage and childlessness.

Engelman infers from the prevalence of childlessness among intermarrieds a confession of disappointment, that the couple does not feel as secure as they had hoped, that they are living with a social handicap which they dare not bequeath to their children.[175] To what percentage of intermarrieds this description applies, we do not know. As behavioral scientists we have much more to learn about both intermarriage and voluntary childlessness.

The misunderstanding. Cross-ethnic partners sometimes discover that their mutual attraction is based on conflicting goals; the Jewish partner wants to get out of the Jewish group and the Gentile partner wants to get into the Jewish group. This conflict of purposes may become apparent when a Gentile fiancee agrees upon conversion to Judaism. As Rabbi Rubenstein has observed, the Jewish husband-to-be may suppose that his fiancee makes this "concession" to appease his parents' wish for a Jewish marriage. He may react with confusion and resentment to his discovery that his fiancee really *wants* to take on the identity of an observant Jew. (See also the case of Cora and Barney, Chapter 3.) Rabbi Rubenstein's experience in counseling proselytes led him to conclude that this situation "can frequently lead to much bitterness and misunderstanding" between a secular Jew and his unexpectedly philo-Judaic fiancee.[176]

A Gentile who must give up well-practiced habits of religious devotion cannot tolerate "a religious vacuum," says Rabbi Rubenstein. If she converts to Judaism she must replace her old religious rituals with new ones. The convert's newly acquired "religious commitments and attitudes . . . which have considerable intensity . . . [may] threaten the Jewish partner . . . who really wants a non-Jewish mate . . ."[177]

The Gentile fiancee who reaches out for a Jewish identity at the same moment that her Jewish husband-to-be retreats from it has become a classic *quid pro quo,* and rabbis who encounter this situation again and again undoubtedly learn to exploit its humorous or didactic possibilities:

"About *your* becoming a good Jew, my dear, I am not worried. But what about your husband; do you think we can make a Jew out of him?"

Responding to a young lady's inquiry about conversion to Judaism, a rabbi began to explain the various steps she must take to become an observant Jew. Her fiance impatiently demanded to know why his future wife had to become a *religious*

Jew. "Why can't she be like me?" His fiancee interjected, "But Honey, I can't be like you; you're a *born* Jew. I was born Italian. The only kind of Jew I *can* become is a religious Jew."

The new convert finds herself in an uncertain position, and overcompensation may be viewed as a way of coping with feelings of insecurity. The overscrupulous convert is a familiar figure in human experience, comparable to the overzealous adopted citizen so amply described by Stonequist in *The Marginal Man*. Whether the convert expresses her Jewishness in religious observance, organizational activity, social life or other aspects of the Jewish style, "Jewish attitudes can be acquired in a surprisingly short time by those who come to participate in the Jewish situation," Rubenstein observes.[178]

Linton Freeman observed the occurrence of an analogous "misunderstanding" in Oriental-Caucasian partnerships between students at the University of Hawaii. He describes Caucasian students who rebel against the dominant culture, pursue an interest in Oriental culture, language or philosophy, may affect Oriental manners and even assume a quasi Oriental name. The rebel idealizes the Oriental woman and may hope to meet and someday marry a "typical" Chinese or Japanese girl. Such a girl is by definition not available to a Caucasian; family and peer pressures operate against inter-ethnic dating. As a consequence, the "Caucasian man looking for an Oriental wife would generally find an Oriental girl [who is a rebel against *her* culture, is therefore] seeking a Caucasian husband."[179]

The misunderstanding begins to unfold; "while the Caucasian tried to be Oriental, the Oriental was attempting to appear to be Caucasian. Very often each was more typical of the other group than were many of that group's members. This led a Japanese-American girl to make the following statement about her Caucasian fiance:

> He really hates Haoles [Caucasians]. He won't have anything to do with them. So did the boy I went out with before. Yet I'm almost a Haole myself. I act like one. Why does he bother with me?[180]

The rebel's search for the "perfect stereotype of the new culture" seems all but impossible to realize. Since it is characteristic of lovers to overidealize each other, this tendency may postpone their recognition of the irony that each is seeking what the other is rejecting. Sometimes the couple is married before this "disillusionment" occurs. In such cases "there followed a long and difficult process in which the participants gradually got to know each other as individuals rather than as stereotypes. Adjustment was sometimes difficult, but as time passed it tended to moderate the rebellion of both partners. A Caucasian man with a Japanese wife described their relationship in the following terms:

"I had an antagonism toward my own culture and race. I was constantly fighting something. But with marriage I've lost a great deal of that. My wife is interested in Western culture and I'm interested in Eastern, and we sort of complement each other."[181]

Bill, a fragment of a case

Bill, a graduate student of Jewish background, came into counseling with feelings of deep insecurity about his relationship with his fiancee Agnes. Bill is the eldest of four children in an upper middle-class family. Both parents are native born and hold professional degrees. He describes a highly ambivalent relationship with his mother, who is overprotective, controlling, puritanical, compulsive. He describes his father as submissive to his wife's control, and neurotically insecure over his job. According to Bill, his father continually nags, depreciates, and frustrates him. Bill retells the story he has heard that when he was born his father was deeply and openly upset over the extent that his wife now ignored him in favor of the baby. Only the counsel and pleading of Mother's father, according to family legend, held the marriage together through this crisis.

Bill's earliest recollection is of a time when, at age four, he was playing with his lead soldiers and reluctant to heed Mother's call to come to dinner. Father angrily threatened that if Bill didn't come to the table immediately Father would stamp over the toy soldiers and crush them to bits.

Bill can recall several close friendships with Jewish girls with whom he maintained "brother-sister" relationships. But he has always preferred to date Gentile girls. His current fiancee is Agnes, an attractive blond college girl of Protestant background. Until she went away to college she lived as the only child of her widowed mother, a strong-willed woman who showed signs of both high intelligence and deep emotional disturbance. They lived in semi-poverty in a deteriorated neighborhood.

Bill admits that one of the things he found appealing about Agnes was that when he first met her she looked so much like a simple little country girl, so unlike the "mature" and fashion-conscious Jewish girls he knew (and avoided). When they became engaged, Bill responded to Agnes' worry about her lack of adequate winter clothing, and opened up charge accounts for her at several stores. Her spending became uncontrollable, and her tastes strongly favored Saks Fifth Avenue. Agnes began to dress with elegance and adopted a modish coiffure. Her dormitory friends found the transformation so sudden and complete, they began to playfully refer to her as "Annie Weiss" instead of Agnes White . . .

Their relationship deteriorated into a chronic round of bickering, abuse, and frustration. Bill finally sought a counselor to help him resolve the unreasonable burden of guilt that prevented him from breaking an engagement that had obviously gone sour.

5

Jewish Attitudes Toward
Intermarriage

Rabbi Gordon asks, "What impels Jewish parents [who have no religious affiliations] to oppose intermarriage? They seldom enter a synagogue from one year to the next. They do not observe the dietary laws or any of the ritual of Jewish life. Their relationship to the Jewish community is only nominal. They do not know Hebrew and can hardly use the language for prayer. Why do they get so disturbed about the possibility of their son or daughter marrying a non-Jew? They sit before me with tears in their eyes and literally cry out, 'Rabbi, you've got to save my child!' "

Gordon admits that this phenomenon appears paradoxical only so long as one supposes that Jewish identity depends upon the practice of Jewish ritual in the same sense that one would call himself a Catholic only so long as he practiced the rites of the Roman Catholic Church. Jewish identity, however, may run very deep in a person for whom religious ritual is far less important than a feeling of belongingness to an extended Jewish family, and to a Jewish community. He opposes intermarriage because he sees it as a threat to the solidarity of his group, and as a threat to his status within that group.

Does the above argument provide a *logical* basis for Jewish opposition to intermarriage? Back in 1918, Rabbi David De Sola Pool approached this topic from the position that one cannot argue with feelings. "A feeling has its own justification and it seldom yields to logic. The feeling which the Jew has toward his Judaism and his Jewish people is something which he can often hardly explain to himself. His brain may tell him that he is not an observant Jew . . . and that perchance he has few Jewish connections. Yet, suffusing his whole being is a strong feeling of warm sympathy with and pride in his religion and people.

"Let anyone but insult Judaism, or the Jews, in his hearing and it will at once be seen how strong and how real is his almost undreamed-of feeling for his religion and his people."[2]

To Bohannan, a contemporary anthropologist, "Judaism is still a tribal religion . . . because it demands—an gets—a specifically social allegiance that (with the possible exception of Mormonism) even the most strict sects of Chrisianity do not require."[3] Various survey findings show that Jewish identity is bound up with family loyalty. As Heiss demonstrated, Jews who intermarry show a life history of alienation from their extended family (while Catholics who intermarry show a history of alienation from the Church) . Likewise, Maier and Spinrad found that Jewish college students say they owe their greatest loyalty to their family or to "people" (in contrast to Catholics and Protestants, who say they owe their greatest loyalty to God). In choosing a mate, the Jew takes a loyalty test—not to his religion, but to his people, his group, his tribe.

THE INVISIBLE BONDS OF KINSHIP

A 1960 study by Landis "found that Jewish children were closest to their parents, with Catholics next, and Protestants in third place." In this study only 12 per cent of Jews "from devout families" would intermarry (though males showed more willingness to intermarry than females) , while 72 per cent of the Catholics declared a willingness to "marry outside of their faith."[4] A 1958 community survey in Trenton (New Jersey) comparing the attitudes of Jewish youth with their elders' indicates that

opposition to intermarriage does *not* seem to depend upon adherence to traditional religious practices. Comparing the two
generations in that Eastern city, adherence to Orthodox Judaism
showed a decline from 81 to 17 per cent; but on the question
of whether Jews ought to continue as a distinct group, 95 per
cent of the younger group agreed (compared with 93 per cent
of the older generation!) .[5]

Family solidarity is highly valued by the Jewish group. Jewish
families are less frequently broken by divorce and desertion than
non-Jewish ones.[6] According to a Detroit survey by Lenski, and
a suburban Chicago survey by Winch, Greer, and Blumberg,
Jews are least likely to migrate to another community and most
likely to maintain close ties with their extended family.[7]

Another indication of Jewish family solidarity in the United
States is provided by the observation, reported by Orlansky, that
Jewish patients at state hospitals "are visited more often, and
by more visitors, than other patients."[8]

Kramer and Leventman found that of North City's third
generation respondents (median age 29.8), 90 per cent had immediate family in the city, and 94 per cent of those who do "visit
or keep in touch with them regularly . . . Over half of the respondents continue to consult their parents on such major
decisions as large purchases, moving, jobs, and education of
children. They take for granted a continuing closeness with the
family, seeking aid from them when the need arises."[9] (Unfortunately, no comparison was made with a Gentile control
group.)

According to Hurvitz, many "sociologists and students of the
family report on the solidarity of the Jewish family."[10] The
sociologist W. I. Thomas learned to read Yiddish and analyzed
letters sent to the advice column ("Bintel Brief") of the *Daily
Forward*. According to Bressler's report of Thomas' unfinished
study, "the key motif expressed . . . is the effort to preserve the
solidarity of the family. Thomas conceives of the Jewish family
as consisting of both the immediate and extended kinship group,
and he says that 'the individual seems to possess a high degree
of emotional involvement, an intense consciousness of solidarity,
and a strong awareness of the standards of obligation with reference to both these groups.' "[11] Hurvitz defers to the prevalence of

Jewish "family clubs" as further evidence of extended family solidarity.[12]

Writing in 1940 on *The Jewish Fate and Future,* Ruppin correctly perceived the Jewish endogamous bias as the expression of a *community* loyalty rather than a religious attitude *per se:*

> Even Jews who have become indifferent to their religion often remain averse to marrying outside their community; this is perhaps the last remnant of their national consciousness. They feel that, although they have dropped the Jewish ritual, they will remain Jews so long as they and their children intermarry with Jews, and that only a mixed marriage would finally separate them from their people.[13]

Emancipation or exile? Intermarriage and separation from the Jewish community may go together for more than one reason. As *Milton* candidly explained, intermarriage may represent the choice of a Gentile milieu in preference to a Jewish social world. Or, as *Ezra* seemed to argue, a Gentile wife may be inevitable for the Jew who in his youth happens to have taken up residence in a Gentile community. Or, as *Gertrude* was led to conclude, staying away from one's Jewish in-laws (and from one's Gentile in-laws as well) seems to evolve as a practical way of sidestepping the conflicts and irritations that mixed couples are vulnerable to. The Levinsons refer to neurotically intermarried Jews who avoid family contacts out of feelings of shame or guilt, that their families would not (or should not) forgive or accept them. To dissuade an errant offspring, parents may explicitly threaten ostracism; they may elect to carry out their threat, or find that they have been taken at their word.

French novelist and essayist Albert Memmi agrees with *Gertrude* that mixed couples do well to break off family ties. "The best advice which can be given to a young mixed couple is not to live in either the husband's or the wife's native city. . . . The number of young couples who are totally ruined by beginning their lives together in the midst of family and friends is enormous."[14] A Tunisian Jew by birth, Memmi insists that his views on mixed marriage are based not on firsthand experience alone (his wife is French Catholic) but on conversations with a great number of mixed couples. Memmi's novel of inter-marriage—*Strangers*—is brief and strife-ridden. It begins wistfully, and ends on a note of sadness. Memmi comments on mixed marriage more explicitly and at length in his essay, *The Liberation of the Jew*. In these comments, he shows a special sensitivity to what a mixed marriage does to the Jew's relationship to the Jewish community, and what it does to his inner sense of Jewishness:

Albert Memmi

I was twenty and I fell in love . . . I was Tunisian, Jewish, poor, unknown, having just arrived in Paris, the city I had dreamed of for twenty years. I married a blonde, Catholic French girl whom I had met at the Sorbonne. (The only thing I forgot was money—she had no more than I, but I was, in this respect, totally unconcerned.) By my marriage, in one fell swoop I created solid and multiple ties which joined all my disparities to this prestigious universe I was burning to conquer. I might add that in a way I succeeded, because I made the best marriage possible considering what I was and what I still am.

I have had to conclude, however, that mixed marriage is no solution to the difficulty of being a Jew. It was experience that convinced me of this; and not only my own. I have discussed the problem with dozens of men and women who have lived the same adventure; I have witnessed many dramas in which this conjugal difficulty was the basis of all conjugal difficulties. On the other hand, I have almost never seen a mixed marriage alter an oppressed condition and very rarely have I seen it sub-jectively help someone.

I will not again go into the conflict which inevitably arises with the original group. No visible attempt at assimilation—and mixed marriage is obviously one—can be accepted without anger by the Jewish community. Is the community wrong? Perhaps; I have already said that I don't consider assimilation a catas-trophe. On the other hand, it would be hypocritical of me not to state the facts: mixed marriage means disappearance in the long run, or else it is a futile effort. This explains the agreement between believing Jews and atheist Zionists in condemning it.

. . . .

The best advice which can be given to a young mixed couple is not to live in either the husband's or the wife's native city. Once the first blush of enthusiasm passes, the number of young couples who are totally ruined by beginning their lives together in the midst of family and friends is enormous. But moving from one's home town is obviously a serious step, and why get into a situation which requires such an extreme remedy? If I had to choose between the safety of the group and the happiness of the individual, by temperament and by philosophy, I would choose happiness. Had I been convinced that mixed marriage could procure peace for the soul of the Jew, an end to his anxiety, and a better adaptation to the non-Jewish world, I would have extolled the virtues of mixed marriage, no matter how serious this choice. But all things considered, I have not noticed that it simplifies the fate of the Jew, nor that it helps him in bettering his relations with other men—Jews or non-Jews—or with himself.

. . .   .

Every marriage is a drama; the highest hopes are placed in it, and therefore it must always fall somewhat short. Every marriage brings together beings who are separate and distant from one another; that is why each marriage is a difficult and perilous undertaking. For this reason, wouldn't it be better not to further complicate it? Isn't it wiser to shorten the inevitable distance as much as possible in the beginning? Every marriage is difficult, and it is a simple fact that a mixed marriage is much more difficult than others.

. . .   .

One cannot know in advance how greatly such apparently trivial details in cooking or bed-making methods may disrupt domestic life. And the newness of the situation is certainly more disturbing when the distance is increased by differences in such important and unavoidable institutions as religion or language. While adolescent strength is still intact, one can joyously brave everything for long periods and then one day suddenly weaken and sigh with nostalgia. I must admit that I have sometimes dreamed of a Passover evening, of Purim, if for no other reason than their picturesque qualities; waiting for the prophet Elijah, the door open to the night; the story of the traitor Haman, hanging on the gallows. . . . Childish pleasures, perhaps, but why deny oneself forever all recourse to childhood? Why weigh all one's anchors? . . .

Couldn't I have solicited my wife's help from time to time in satisfying my nostalgia? Or, failing that, I might have set out alone to quench my thirst at some source outside our home; or, better still, taken my wife with me to friends or relatives. Wouldn't she have agreed, if only out of love for me? Of course, and especially in the beginning of our marriage she went along with the best will in the world. It was I who quickly came to feel it was an imposition and a lack of human respect toward her. Why should I have insisted that she mimic my ghosts? I also sensed that it was a danger for our union. Wasn't I emphasizing our cultural differences, insisting on the fact that we did not share the same memories, the same inner universe? In seeking reassurance for myself, wasn't I running the risk of wounding her?

. . . The vast majority of non-Jews who marry Jews deliberately accept a difficult future. . . . But human beings are made of more than good intentions and a concerted desire to do the right things. Sooner or later they learn that though one can give a great deal, one cannot and must not be completely submerged in others. . . . Although they might not hold their own people in great esteem, they had not totally disowned them, though they might have thought this to be the case . . . their attitude stiffens and, if they do not retreat, they at least begin to exist for themselves, with a kind of painful shock. In general they are not even able to go back. Beset, since their marriage, by the suspicion of their own group, mortified by their own failure after so much defiance, feeling guilty themselves, they no longer even try to confide in anyone. Many young women, having abandoned any hopes of integrating themselves into their husband's group, end up by withdrawing into a final and complete solitude.

      . . .   .

Mixed marriage, seemingly an ideal ground for synthesis and harmony, for an opening and for reciprocal generosity, more often turns out to be a dangerous crossroad, open to currents from every direction and offering every opportunity for all kinds of collision. The mixed couple, instead of becoming an ideal oasis, a neutral zone between mutually devouring groups, is often transformed into an arena in which the whole world erupts. . . .

It is paradoxical, but I have seen it many times: mixed marriage revives Jewishness, makes one more aware of the Jewish fate and awakens solidarity in people who have never before felt it. As in the case of conversion, it is after a mixed marriage that many Jews become the most sensitive about their Jewishness. These men, who so badly wanted to open their arms to others, suddenly turn violently against them. This is, of course, because they feel guilty towards their own people. Thus these Jews feel they must furnish their people with proof, march in the front line of combat and be among the most orthodox or at least the most obedient. . . .

I have noticed that the husband is often outdone by the wife who, not content with merely embracing the cause of her husband's people, reproaches everyone for lack of vigor and combative zeal. One of my Zionist friends married a Parisian who literally dragged him to Israel. Another, a woman whose husband was a very active F.L.N. militant, finally accused her husband of weakness and ended up participating alone in some very dangerous missions. In short, it was not enough for them to stop being adversaries; they had to become accomplices, alter egos; they had to identify totally with their new role. Saints, in short; but I must admit that I mistrust saints and situations which give rise to them.

In any case, the result is too often an unhealthy, confused situation in which each difficulty becomes complex, filled with every kind of malaise, without anyone knowing clearly what caused what (if, for example, the partner is fought through the intermediary of the group or the group is fought through the intermediary of the partner); a situation in which almost everything is blown up, aggravated by so many diverse problems, weighted down by the historical and social conjuncture.

. . . .

Strangers was not our story, that of my wife and myself, nor even a true story. It was a condensation of hundreds of stories, reduced to their essentials and dramatized to make a single, coherent work which would command the reader's attention.

But we had at least a presentiment of all these fluctuations of the heart and mind, and we had anticipated all these upheavals and to some extent lived through them. Only a steady, positive desire for happiness and intelligence, a determination to maintain self-control and health allowed us to forestall, disarm and exorcise them. In short, if we have, as I hope, been successful in this important venture of our life, our marriage, it is *in spite* of its mixture.

. . .   .

As soon as mixed marriage is mentioned, most people immediately bring up general ideas of politics and morality, philosophy and religion. And mixed marriage does have this extra significance which deserves careful thought. It is not enough for me to hope that mixed marriage might hold the key to so many difficult problems; I want to know if I myself can find in it the solution to my problems of integration in a difficult world. It is not enough for me to think that mixed marriage is socially moral or historically desirable. I want to know what it will cost me and if this price does not exceed my strength.

. . .   .

It is difficult enough to live when one is Jewish. Why exclude any possible way out of the many difficulties if one can thereby find happiness, or simply peace. Had I discovered that mixed marriage was a passable or even partial solution to the Jewish problem, I would have considered it favorably. But I have been convinced, by my own experience, by all that I have seen and heard, that a Jew who marries a non-Jew resolves nothing either for himself or for his children. As a Jew, that is. Obviously a mixed marriage can be a good marriage, but only to the extent that it can be separated from the quality of being mixed and to the extent that the Jewish fate can be disregarded.[15]

COLLEGE ATTENDANCE AND INTERMARRIAGE

It is easy to view college as an experience which weakens the bonds of kinship and fosters assimilation into the privileged majority. It is also true that many Jewish parents, especially in smaller towns, view college as an opportunity to increase the probability that their youngster will find a suitable Jewish mate, by selecting a college that has a sizeable Jewish enrollment. In this regard, college residence serves a function similar to that of the regional youth conferences periodically held in those parts of the country which have a sparse Jewish population—to foster ethnic endogamy by facilitating community exogamy.

To what extent do Jewish college students display attitudes of ethnic loyalty? In a 1957 college survey conducted by Maier and Spinrad only 10 per cent of his Jewish sample expressed a readiness to marry outside their own faith, compared with 27 per cent of his Catholic sample, and 45 per cent of his Protestant sample. In a 1951–52 survey that covered nine Midwestern universities, Teitelbaum likewise found that students who declared themselves in favor of intermarriage number between 10 and 15 per cent of Jewish respondents. (*See* Table 5:1.) Students at metropolitan universities seemed more definitely opposed to intermarriage, however, than students at a fashionable private university; at the metropolitan university significantly more students were opposed, and fewer students were either uncertain or failed to respond to the question.

Table 5:1. Responses of Various Groups of Jewish Students to the Question, "What is your attitude to mixed marriages (or intermarriages) between Jews and Gentiles?"[16]

	Students Attending Metropolitan Universities (N=117)		Students Attending State Universities (N=207)		Students Attending a Private University (N=210)	
	(N)	%	(N)	%	(N)	%
Opposed	(69)	59.0	(114)	54.8	(77)	36.7
Uncertain	(35)	29.9	(65)	31.2	(93)	44.3
In favor	(12)	10.3	(28)	13.5	(32)	15.2
No response	(1)	0.8	(1)	0.5	(8)	3.7

In the above findings no distinction is made between the sexes, and each of the above groups presumably included an equivalent percentage of males and females. Consistent sex differences in resistance to intermarriage show up in the results of a 1966 survey conducted by Berman. About 300 urban university students were asked to make a 5-choice response to the question: "How important is it that your husband (wife) have the same religious background as yours?" Of the survey population 261 respondents followed instructions and could be classified in one of eight sex-ethnic categories shown in Table 5:2. Within each of the four ethnic groups, women tended to respond in a more in-group direction than men. In the context of this discussion, a most important finding is the fact that Jewish men and women are the *only* groups for which "extremely important" is the most popular response category. (The number of Jewish men and women—16 and 12—was too small to satisfy tests of statistical significance, except for differences between Jewish men and Negro men, Jewish women and Negro women, Jewish women and white Protestant women—in all of which cases a statistical significance of .01 *was* attained, using the chi square test with Yates correction.)

It would be incredible to suppose that Jewish youngsters born and raised in a pluralistic American society, with its explicitly democratic ethos, should develop an in-group loyalty as intense as that which prevailed in the Pale of Settlement of Czarist Russia, where intermarriage required conversion of the Jewish partner to Christianity. The foregoing findings do show that American Jewish college students express a stronger sense of family and ethnic loyalty than their Gentile contemporaries, and this difference seems to be greater for Jews attending urban and state universities than for those attending a prestige private university.

PARENTAL SUFFERING

The opposition of Jewish parents to intermarriage carries a charge of distress and alarm that sometimes comes as a shock to the Gentile partner, as the following two citations from Mayer indicate:

"I learned about their feelings a month before we were to get married. Five months before they had come to our engagement party, so I was really shocked and upset when all these feelings came out. . . . I gave him back his ring and told him I didn't want to fight his mother."[19]

Table 5:2. How 261 Urban University Students Answer the Question: "How important is it that your husband (wife) have the same religious background as yours?"[18]

Response Category	Women								Men							
	Jewish (Mean=4.25)*		White Catholic (Mean=3.97)		White Protestant (Mean=2.91)		Negro Protestant (Mean=2.89)		Jewish (Mean=3.87)		White Catholic (Mean=3.64)		White Protestant (Mean=2.76)		Negro Protestant (Mean=2.20)	
	(N)	%	(N)	%	(N)	%	(N)	%	(N)	%	(N)	%	(N)	%	(N)	%
5. Extremely important	(6)	50**	(15)	27	(0)	0	(5)	11	(5)	31**	(13)	30**	(1)	5	(1)	2
4. Very important	(4)	34	(23)	41**	(5)	22	(8)	18	(3)	19	(11)	25	(5)	24	(3)	7
3. Somewhat important	(1)	8	(10)	18	(13)	56**	(16)	35**	(4)	25	(13)	30**	(7)	33**	(12)	27
2. Not very important	(1)	8	(7)	12	(3)	13	(9)	20	(1)	6	(5)	11	(4)	19	(16)	37**
1. Not at all important	(0)	0	(1)	2	(2)	9	(7)	16	(3)	19	(2)	4	(4)	19	(12)	27
	(12)	100	(56)	100	(23)	100	(45)	100	(16)	100	(44)	100	(21)	100	(44)	100

* Mean computed from numerical equivalent shown at left of each response category.
** Modal response category.

"... When there was this hue and cry from his family ... I was upset because they weren't going to come to the wedding—so we called the whole thing off and decided not to get married. This was a very trying situation. ... I felt it would be too difficult with his parents."[20]

In his survey of Jewish-Gentile intermarriages, Slotkin found that the family of the Gentile partner was predictably more accepting of the couple than were the Jewish in-laws.[21] From interviewing his group of intermarrieds, Mayer observed that the Gentile partner was sometimes surprised to learn that there was *any* degree of opposition felt by the prospective in-laws, but the Jewish partner was "more apt to suspect" that his prospective in-laws harbored antagonistic feelings.[22]

The Jewish parents' deeply "tribal" hostility toward their child's prospective mate has been noted with dismay by Rabbis Bamberger and Eichorn. "The non-Jewish fiancee," says Rabbi Bamberger, "is regarded by many a Jewish parent as an interloper, almost a kidnaper, who has trapped a precious and innocent lad."[23] [Sklare (1964) echoes this attitude in attributing the rise of intermarriage to the fact that Gentile girls know that Jews make good husbands.][24] Rabbi Eichorn voices regret that to many Jewish parents a convert to Judaism is still a "Gentile," and Jewish parents react to the convert according to their prejudices rather than in keeping with the teachings of Judaism:

> The fact is that many Jews are so ignorant of Jewish teachings about conversion and harbor such deep prejudices toward converts that in their minds, a marriage between a born Jew and a converted Jew is still an intermarriage.[25]

Parental anxiety about intermarriage is sometimes described as part of the emotional climate of the Jewish community. Dean quotes a Jewish father interviewed during the Cornell group's Elmira study:

> The basic worry of every parent is that their son will marry a *shiksa*. Some mothers live in constant dread of it. When two mothers with marriageable sons get together you can be sure sooner or later they'll talk about it. They don't worry so much about their daughters. I guess they're more sure of them.[26]

In the literature on intermarriage, the parent who opposes intermarriage is described as prejudiced, ignorant, guilt-ridden, frantic, stirred by "racial feelings" or "tribal loyalty" rather than religious values. Rarely are the parents' fears and forebodings represented in print with compassion. An 1877 pamphlet on intermarriage, *Le Mariage Mixte,* written by the Belgian Jewish educator, Lehman Kahn, candidly expresses the feelings and attitudes of Jewish parents of that era. The author forewarns the parents that a mixed marriage will not unite the families of the bride and groom into one larger family according to the enduring tradition of the Jewish community. Kahn shares the parents' apprehension that the Gentile son-in-law "cannot feel a real filial piety" toward his Jewish father-in-law, but may regard him as somewhat "illegitimate" *(beau-père contrebande),* and may view his Jewish mother-in-law as a vaudeville comic figure. It seems as if Kahn is saying that one cannot expect a Gentile to understand the matricentric role of the Jewish woman.

Kahn continues: "The new in-laws will certainly not respect you for your position in the family *per se.* They will respect you for your higher social position, for your occupational status, for your personal integrity, but they will not give you that kindly, unconditional, and unguarded affection *(cette douce affection, cet abandon charmant)* that prevails among [Jewish] relatives." And somewhere in the family of the Gentile spouse there will be the troublemakers who will want to hurt you, and who will condemn you for permitting the marriage to have occurred:

You will always be considered a stranger, an intruder, and they will remind you of it first by pin-pricks and later by sword-thrusts, and if it's not the closest relatives who cause the wounds it will be the more distant ones. There are in every family one or two persons who are narrow-minded and closely bound to their religion. They will be angry with you, her father, referring to you as a stranger, because of your ambition and presumption. They will be angry with your son-in-law for his act of betrayal, and with his parents for their condescension and weakness. The sacrifices that will be imposed on you, the anguish that you will have endured, the tortures that your soul will have suffered upon finally giving your consent to the union, will not be held in your favor. On the contrary, they will hold you responsible as if to so many crimes committed by you in a spirit of pride. They will reproach you for having depended upon hesitation (rather than use your authority to oppose the marriage) , and they will not condemn you less for having yielded at the end.

These people will never pardon you for the shame that, according to them, you have thrown on their family. They will work on the minds of the other members of their family to set them against you, to estrange them from you and to alienate from you the remainder of their good feelings and their esteem, to erase the last trace of friendly relations.

The affection that you receive from your son-in-lay may give you consolation from the disdain you suffer from his family. You will think that this affection will be yours forever, and who can deny you this consoling thought?" [But Kahn is not quite sure that this hope will stand the test of experience.][27]

Rarely in the literature on intermarriage does one find so poignant an expression of the inner doubts and fears of the Jewish parent who faces the prospects that his child may take a Gentile mate.

The distressed parents may seek help from a rabbi, but get little sympathy or comfort from him. Did they give their child a Jewish education? Do they observe the customs of the Jewish religion? How often do they attend the synagogue? It becomes apparent that the parents are concerned with something other than religious values *per se*. The rabbi may feel embarrassed that the parents express such tribalism and racial pride,[28] prejudice toward convert, or ignorance of Jewish teachings.[29] The rabbi may feel that the parents are interfering unduly in his discussions with the prospective mates. Instead of giving the couple a chance to decide whether they honestly want a Jewish wedding, the Jewish parents may demand one and thereby coerce the couple into making promises they are not ready to commit themselves to. Instead of letting the Gentile partner decide whether he wants to convert, the Jewish mother's tears may induce a "shot gun conversion . . . odious and meaningless" to rabbi and convert alike.[30]

Underneath the parents' bitterness, says Rabbi Rubenstein, is an "unspoken feeling of guilt that, somehow, it was all their fault," that somehow they had failed as parents and now faced a situation that was "basically degrading."[31] Psychiatrist Abraham Franzblau reminds rabbis that one of their functions is to help parents "cushion the shock. . . . They ought to be helped to see that their lifelong relationship with their child is a precious asset. Too harsh or drastic behavior on their part might destroy it and only drive the couple into each other's arms. . . . Psychiatric help may also be advised to help parents take the strain. They are often more likely than the young couple to accept such help."[32]

The rabbi may well discover that his sympathies are with the young couple who seem honestly and wholesomely in love, rather than with Jewish parents who are full of bitterness and injured pride. Moreover, since the Gentile bride may show far more interest in Judaism than either the husband or his parents, the rabbi may find himself counseling and protecting the convert, pleading to the Jewish community to accord her a decent and friendly reception. He may comfort the convert wife with the truism that even daughter-in-laws who are born Jews have difficulties with mother-in-laws, and console her with the thought that her in-laws' wounded feelings "can at least be mollified when parents become grandparents."[33]

To the parents and to the community, the rabbi may express assurance that "intermarriage does not necessarily destroy Judaism or the Jewish community":

> Judaism represents a very special value in American life. The creative use of alienation attracts many non-Jews to Judaism. With surprising frequency, it can result in conversion. Oddly enough, the loss of fixed dogma and explicit disciplines in modern Judaism has not created an end to conversion. It is often the person for whom all religious symbols have become transparent who converts to Judaism—in reality, he or she adheres to the Jewish situation which he recognizes as the institutionalization of his own. He does not accept a new set of dogmas to replace others which can no longer be accepted.[34]

Rabbi Mordecai Kaplan asks Jews to accept the fact that "whenever the members of different civilizations come into social con-

tact with each other . . . that contact results in intermarriage,"
and calls upon Jews to make Judaism vigorous enough to claim
the offsprings' loyalty:

> [When intermarriage occurs] and children are born, the
> more vigorous civilization will be the one to which the chil-
> dren will belong. For Judaism to accept intermarriage between
> Jews and Gentiles as legitimate from its standpoint, it must
> be infinitely more sure of itself than it is at present. . . . It
> must be able to imbue the Jewish partner to a mixed marriage
> with the willingness to maintain a Jewish home. . . . Judaism
> should meet all situations that might lead to mixed marriages
> not fearfully or grudgingly, but in the spirit of encountering
> an expected development. . . . With a belief in the integrity
> and value of his own civilization the Jewish partner to the
> marriage could achieve moral ascendency, and make Judaism
> the civilization of the home.[35]

Jewish young people know that such philosophical thoughts
may have little meaning to their parents. Shanks asserts that for
many young people parental objection is a most powerful
obstacle to intermarriage:

> I have no objection to intermarriage for myself or anyone else,
> but my parents object violently to any mention of it. That is
> the only thing that would discourage me from entering into it.

> I could not intermarry while my parents or close relatives were
> alive. However, I see nothing wrong in intermarriage . . .

Shanks concludes, perhaps hastily, that "the actual brakes on
intermarriage stem from community disapproval and parental objection, rather than from the individual's conviction."[36] Franzblau agrees that young people who might have no strong convictions against intermarriage may "completely reject the dictates
of their own hearts because they know their parents would be so
violently opposed."[37]

Gordon and Mayer's respondents recall in detail parental
opposition to intermarriage. (Their data include expressions of
Gentile as well as Jewish disfavor over intermarriage.)

Flora

"My mother was very upset about it. And so was my father. They equated it with a kind of moral transgression, as though I were going out with a married man or having an illegitimate child. . . . They felt that it was a disgrace for a Jew to marry a Gentile—it just *is*, and they didn't give any reasons. They said things like they were glad their parents were dead, rather than have them know what I was doing. They never said that I couldn't be happy with him, but it was just morally wrong."[38]

"What was it about her being a Gentile," Mayer blandly asked a Jewish husband, "that your parents objected to?" "There were social and family reasons. . . . The whole idea that one should marry within his group was very deeply ingrained in them. They just believed it all their lives. It is the same as asking us—why do you believe that it's wrong to rob a bank?"[39]

"My mother said it was making her sick, that it was killing her, and that I did not care for her. It was mostly a kind of bludgeoning. They said I should do something for my parents."[40]

Samuel

Gordon records Samuel's description of the family crisis precipitated by his marriage to a Jamaican Indian. His mother, a Russian immigrant described as observant of Jewish customs but not Orthodox, knew that her son had been dating non-Jewish girls. "She objected strenuously, but frankly I did what I wanted in this respect. . . . Mother kept asking how could I do this sort of thing to her? . . . She really became very emotional and cried. . . . It was hard for me to take because I have a warm feeling for my mother, but I just had to decide whether I was going to live my own life or someone else's."

He discussed his marriage plans with his mother "as much as one can, I suppose." A few days before he actually got married (he was living at a distance from his family) he wrote a letter to his brother and sister and sent "a very carefully worded letter" to his mother. His sister "intercepted my mother's letter for a number of weeks in the hope that she would save her some anguish. I'm sure that she did it with every desire to keep my mother from being hurt. After our marriage, I phoned my sister to get her reaction and to find out how my mother had taken it. It was then that I found out that she didn't even know about it. By this time some of my friends had heard from me and I felt that it would be most unfortunate if my mother heard about my marriage from someone other than me. So I flew to New York with the purpose of telling her about my marriage.

"Well, I spent a couple of hours that were really difficult. There were copious tears and much emotion generally. She cried hysterically for a long period of time. Some of the things she said made sense, some did not, but she was certainly the most distressed human being I had ever seen. I guess I spent a couple of days trying to talk to her, to make her understand that this was a good marriage and to get her to see that the world had not come to an end. By the second day she had calmed down somewhat—not that she was really calm, but she was considerably changed from the way she had been, and then, suddenly she went to a trunk, opened it, and pulled out a white tablecloth which, she tearfully told me, I should take back home as a present to my wife and myself. And then she gave me some advice: 'She's your wife; treat her well. Don't run around. Be a good husband' and words of counsel like that. She seemed to be coming around at least to the point of recognizing that we were really married."[41]

In describing a Jewish parent's distress over his child's intermarriage, the parent is often described (as in the foregoing case) as "a Russian immigrant," as unacculturated, or provincial. In Drachsler's 1920 description of the immigrant parents' dread of "losing their children through intermarriage" the impression is inescapable that this is an attitude peculiar to "the older generation . . . the immigrant group:"

> The fear of . . . losing the children haunts the older generation. It is not merely the natural desire of parent to retain influence over child. Nor is it simply the dread that the wayward offspring will mar the good name of the immigrant group by abuse of his newly found freedom. It is a vague uneasiness that a delicate network of precious traditions is being ruthlessly torn asunder, that a whole world of ideals is crashing

into ruins; and amidst this desolation the fathers and mothers picture themselves wandering about lonely in vain search of their lost children.[42]

Surely Drachsler would have predicted that some thirty years hence the children and grandchildren of these immigrants—especially those who had become well-educated, affluent residents of a prestigeful Midwestern suburb—would express quite a different attitude toward their children's choice of a marriage partner. On the contrary, Sklare and Greenblum report that among Lakeville respondents of Eastern European Jewish origin *"the reaction of the third generation hardly varies from the second or first;* only about one in five in each generation would be indifferent to an intermarriage in their own family and *none* would be happy with it."[43] (Italics added.) Only about one-third express confidence that their child *will* marry a Jew.[44] The majority live in doubt and discomfort. Though parents say they would do "everything within their power" to prevent an intermarriage, they seem to recognize that they would, in fact, be virtually powerless to do anything about it:

I would make every effort to show him the error of his ways. Then I'd accept the situation, but I'd be brokenhearted.

I'd accept it, but my heart would bleed.

I'd do everything in my power to make them see the light. Then if they did marry non-Jews, I'd accept it. But I'd be disappointed; you'd almost blame yourself.[45]

Sklare and Greenblum describe the reaction of a wealthy lawyer and father of two sons, to the question of how he would react to his child's hypothetical intermarriage:

Initially I'd be very hurt. I'd do everything I could to discourage it before it happened. I'd convey to them the problem of whether their child would have a christening or a *pidyon ha'ben.* But if it occurred, I'd have to make the best of a bad situation.

"As he responded to our question on intermarriage," the

authors add, "his college-educated wife sat in tears at his side."[46]

In contrast to those who spoke with such candor and feeling, it seemed to Sklare and Greenblum that a sizeable percentage of his respondents were trying hard to *understate* their felt opposition to intermarriage. It seemed as if they "seek to advance [an] image of sweet reasonableness on the intermarriage problem . . . [as if they had] judiciously weighed the evidence and reluctantly come to the conclusion that an interfaith difference intrudes such a strong disharmonious element in marriage as to place an otherwise sound relationship in jeopardy."[47]

These articulate, well-educated, highly acculturated members of a suburban community with an active program of Jewish worship and education, talking leisurely and candidly to a Jewish interviewer—why should these parents feel under such pressure to deny their loyalty to a basic rule of Jewish life (to which they themselves conform)? Why did so many seem to work so hard to present "an image of sweet reasonableness" on an issue of deep personal significance? Sklare and Greenblum touch upon various factors which may help account for this incongruity:

First, Lakeville's Jewish parents share the view of enlightened people, in the individual's "right to freedom of marital choice." Secondly, they believe overwhelmingly that a marriage choice should be guided by love. (Only 5 per cent say they would rather their child take a Jewish mate in marriage without love, than to marry a Gentile with whom he was in love.) [48] Thirdly, they realize that their opposition to intermarriage is *not* grounded in loyalty to religion or peoplehood *per se*. (Only 14 per cent give the survival of the Jewish people or the Jewish religion as the basis for their concern.) [49] Fourthly, they sense that the willingness of a worthy Gentile to take a Jew in marriage may symbolize a socially and morally desirable event—the ultimate act of interfaith acceptance. And finally, their liberal ideology would be outraged if their opposition to intermarriage were but a mask for prejudice against other minorities (or fear of the proud majority). One Lakeview parent was moved to declare: "I'd welcome my son's wife with open arms, whether [she were] white or black, Jew or Christian, Caucasian or Mongolian."[50]

What, then, were they afraid of? So far as they could express it, Lakeville's Jewish parents were afraid that an intermarriage would fail to bring their child happiness. About nine out of ten parents "stress that discord is inevitable in an interfaith marriage; they maintain that a Jewish-Gentile marriage is inherently an unstable union and therefore an unhealthy one. . . . In addition to emphasizing disturbed relations between husband and wife . . . about three in ten [emphasize] difficulties which are created for the offspring . . . and [about three in twenty mention] the problematic relationship of the married couples to relatives, friends, and society at large."[51] An unhappy mixed marriage would not only deprive the parents of *nachas,* but leave them with the haunting feeling that the parents themselves must somehow be at fault. (". . . You'd almost blame yourself.")

Jewish parents and Gentile parents. Since Mayer had asked both Jewish and Gentile intermarrieds to recall the manifestations of parents' opposition, it is possible (though Mayer had no reason to do so) to compare the antagonistic attitudes attributed to Jewish parents with antagonistic attitudes of Gentile parents. Only Jewish parents are quoted to assert that intermarriage is "morally wrong."[52] While social disapproval was occasionally anticipated by Gentile parents ("If he didn't look so Jewish, it wouldn't be so bad! What will our friends and neighbors think?"),[53] it was the Jewish parents who seemed to feel deeply threatened by ostracism.

Gentile parents expressed distress over more purely *religious* considerations: "My mother regarded my marrying a Jewish person as not taking religion seriously. To her, her religion was the only correct one."[54] "My mother wept. She was upset because I wasn't marrying a Catholic girl. She was upset because there would not be a church ceremony with all its significances. The greatest shock of all was that my parents had to come to grips with reality: I wasn't still a Catholic."[55] Mayer quotes a Catholic husband: "Mother feels she is a failure because I intermarried and will have nothing to do with the Church."[56] "Mother . . . said I was making them a laughing stock and that I was turning my back on the religion that they had taken such pains to instill in me."[57] "My mother didn't really believe I was an agnostic," remarked a Protestant daughter. "She felt that I would get more religious as I got older, and that this would be a problem."[58]

Gentile parents expressed discomfort that their descendants might bear the physical and social stigma of Jewishness. ("My mother was horrified at his being Jewish. . . . The children would not have the advantages I had had. . . . She felt they might be born with Jewish features or revert back to Jewish ancestry."[59] "My mother said, 'You have an old family and a fine one. You should marry someone of equally good family—don't taint the blood! Governor ———— was an ancestor of yours!' "[60]

On both parental sides there was expression of anti-Semitism or fear of anti-Semitism. (A Jewish daughter recalled her mother's prophecy: "When you and your husband argue after you are married, he'll be sure to denounce you as a Jew—in his heart he probably hates Jews.") [61] On both sides there were personal attacks on the would-be partner's appearance, behavior and profession. On both sides there were expressions of disgust and derision over the manners and morals of the out-group.

To summarize, Jewish parents seemed to express deeper personal anguish and showed more violent and prolonged opposition, which they attempted to justify on moral grounds and fear of ostracism; they also threatened more severe sanctions against the offending child. Gentile parents—particularly Catholics, it would seem—raised more purely religious objections to their child's intermarriage plans and expressed concern over the prospect that their grandchildren would belong to a disadvantaged class.

Fathers and mothers. A Jewish father's chronic ambivalence toward his Catholic daughter-in-law was reflected in his customary greeting to his grandsons: *"Vos machstu,* boys? . . . And how is the *shiksa?"* "I was fifteen," his grandson recalls in an autobiographical essay, "before I discovered that *shiksa* did not mean 'mother.' "[62]

"My mother-in-law," recalls Mary Ruth Bondarin, ". . . had been reared in a Jewish tradition which was violently opposed to intermarriage. Slowly, as I proved that I was sincerely dedicated to the Jewish way of life, she was able to be more genuinely supportive of our marriage. Now she extolls me to her friends as being 'closer than a daughter' to her, although she still feels that I am an exception among converts."[63]

Does the Jewish father suffer more deeply than his wife at

the prospect of their child's intermarriage? Our limited array
of interview material suggests that mothers react more violently
but recover more quickly when actual experience reassures them
against their fears and forebodings of ostracism and destruction
of family ties. Fathers more often show a deeper, more lasting,
and more personal anguish, as if the crisis aroused their own
feelings of ambivalence over sexual involvement with the out-
group.[64] There is nothing in the admittedly scanty literature
on parental reactions to match Doris' statement that her father
has had "nothing to do with her" for all the seventeen years
of her married life:

> It's as if I didn't exist. . . . My father will not talk to me.
> When my grandfather died and I went to the funeral and
> tried to talk to him, he told me to move away from him. That's
> how it is. But I still send him cards on Father's Day, on his
> birthday or an anniversaries. Nothing will move him. It's as if
> I didn't exist any longer.[65]

In the case of *Fred* (summarized in Chapter 3), the mother
of his Jewish girl friend shielded the romance from her husband
as long as she could. When the father learned that his daughter
was engaged to a Gentile boy—who was preparing himself for
conversion to Judaism—"father responded . . . with a hysterical
display of anguish, utttered thoughts about suicide and heart
attack, and absolutely forbade that Ethel have anything further
to do with Fred."

Gordon's case of *Joe* similarly draws a contrast between a
Jewish mother's unhappiness and a father's morbid brooding:

Joe

"I informed my parents that, although I had tried to forget
Ruth, I could not and I wanted to marry her. I further asked
them to invite her to be our guest for a few days when I arrived
home, before going into the army. . . . Shortly after I received
word from my parents that they had extended the invitation to
Ruth, but it was clear that they did so with heavy hearts. I heard
later that about this time my father was talking about suicide.

However, my mother even though very unhappy, was doing her best to calm him down. I know they thought Ruth was a fine person. They also knew that Ruth was preparing for conversion to Judaism. If only she had been *born* of Jewish parents! I cannot understand the reason for this emphasis. They wouldn't have asked about a Jewish girl's religious tendencies. Somehow, although my parents really didn't observe very much of Jewish ritual themselves, this idea of my marriage simply played havoc with them. What is it that caused them to respond this way? Was it fear of what others in the family or certain Jewish friends would say? Was it a sense of shame? Did they think I ever planned to give up my identity as a Jew? Had you been around my parents during those days when I returned from the West Coast, you would have noticed their attitude immediately. Now my parents are good people, wonderful people. Why did this happen to them?

"Now my father isn't a very talkative person. He doesn't say much, but he thinks a great deal. When he heard about Ruth, it was as if someone had hit him with a sledge hammer. I felt that he was just going to go to pieces. My mother was shocked too, but she was worrying most about the way my father was taking the news. I knew that my parents simply did not want me to marry a Christian girl. I knew that it might break their hearts, so you can imagine the state of mind I was in . . ."[66]

After two years of marriage, Joe's memory of his own suffering is apparently quite keen, for the advice he said he would offer a friend "about dating someone of a different religion [is] . . . *'Stop now if you possibly can.* Stop, because if you're not sure that you love each other, no intermarriage can be successful. Don't create problems for yourself. Don't prolong the agony!' "[67] (Italics added.)

6

Intermarriage and the Social Order

ENDOGAMY AND THE INCEST TABOO

Anthropological study presents an image of man capable of patterning his social relations with almost infinite variation; what is shameful in one society is laudable in another, what is wasteful in one society is prudent in another, what one society requires another society taboos. In the anthropologist's universe of relativity there seems to be at least one "absolute" and that is the incest taboo, the rule which restricts sex relations within the nuclear family to married parents. Says Murdock: "Incest taboos apply universally to all persons of opposite sex within the nuclear family. The data from our [sample of] 250 societies . . . reveal not a single instance in which sexual intercourse or marriage is generally permissible between mother and son, father and daughter, or brother and sister. Aside from a few rare and highly restricted exceptions, there is complete universality in this respect."[1]

Societies enforce many taboos but few are enforced with the "peculiar intensity and emotional quality" of the incest taboo. Murdock concedes that the various taboos have not been widely compared by any objective measure of "intensity," but he holds that "any impartial reader of the ethnographic evidence will [reach] the same conclusion. Again and again there will be brought home to him something of the sense of grisly horror with which most peoples invest the very idea of incest. He will be impressed by the frequency of an invariable death penalty for this breach of the mores. Even more convincing, however, is the fact that there is often no legal sanction at all; the taboo is so strongly internalized, the idea is so deeply repressed, that the act is considered simply unthinkable, and, if it occurs, is attributed to supernatural intervention and its punishment left exclusively to inexorable fate or divine vengeance." ("The emotional quality attaching to prohibitions of fornication and adultery is usually quite different," Murdock adds.) [2]

Because the incest taboo is virtually universal, it is easy to regard it as instinctive. Frazer shrewdly observed, however, that if avoiding incest were just as natural to man as avoiding fire, no prohibitions or punishments would need to be set up against it.

> We may always safely assume that crimes forbidden by law are crimes which many men have a natural propensity to commit. . . . Instead of assuming therefore, from the legal prohibition of incest, that there is a natural aversion to incest we ought rather to assume that there is a natural instinct in favor of it, and that if the law represses it, it does so because civilized men have come to the conclusion that the satisfaction of these natural instincts is detrimental to the general interests of society.[3]

Other theorists, including Havelock Ellis and Westermarck, conjectured that the experience of growing up in the same household dulls any sensual attraction of persons brought up together and renders them incapable of experiencing erotic excitement toward each other.[4] Murdock points out that this hypothesis is inconsistent with four important lines of evidence: (1) The taboo frequently applies with equal force to kin brought up in different households. (2) In some cultures marriage with a house-mate, or with a member of the extended family, is permitted and practiced. (3) Living together as husband and wife leads to enduring attachments and sustained sexual interest, in most societies, rather than "sexual indifference and ultimate aversion" as the Westermarck-Ellis theory would suggest. (4) "Above all, the theory flagrantly overlooks, and even inverts, the vast body of clinical evidence which shows that incestuous desires are regularly engendered within the nuclear family and are kept in restraint only through persistent social pressure and individual repression."[5]

Westermarck and others have theorized that the incest taboo has been maintained to prevent injury to the species through inbreeding. Freud argued that this attributes to preliterate cultures an unwarranted sophistication,[6] but Lindzey has recently brought together evidence that incest myths frequently contain the theme of infertility, or deformed offspring; and that observed cases of the offspring of human incest matings show a *high* incidence of abnormalities.

Neither psychoanalytic theory, learning theory, sociology nor anthropology—taken separately—can provide a satisfactory interpretation of incest taboos, Murdock argues. One must bring together principles from *all four* of these fields of study for the development of "a complete and adequate theory . . . [Otherwise] the phenomenon remains mysterious and unexplained."[7]

From the standpoint of sociological theory, any conflict within the family weakens its effectiveness in performing those functions which society assigns to the family: economic cooperation, and the bearing and raising of children. Probably no form of intrafamily conflict would be more disruptive than sexual competition and jealousy:

> The imperious drive of sex is capable of impelling individuals, reckless of consequences while under its spell, toward behavior which may imperil or disrupt the cooperative relationships upon which social life depends . . . [Family living] can ill suffer the strain of the frustrations and aggressions inevitably generated by indiscriminate competition over sexual favors. . . . Possibly in man's long history there have been peoples who have failed to subject the sexual impulse to regulation. If so, none have survived, for the social control of sex is today a cultural universal [of which the incest taboo is an outstanding feature].[8]

It is hard to imagine that parents could maintain the solidarity of their partnership, maintain authority over children, secure cooperation among adolescent and adult siblings without ruling out sexual rivalry and competition from the nuclear family itself. "Incest prohibitions have a social value of such unquestionable importance," Murdock asserts, "as to account for its presence in all known cultures and for their enforcement by all known societies."[9]

An important by-product of the incest taboo is that each marriage links together two nuclear families, thereby fostering group solidarity and broadcasting the most adaptive family inventions and practices. (A society which practiced incestuous marriages would presumably lack the necessary cohesion to meet social crises, and eventually be destroyed or absorbed by a rival culture.) "The social advantages of incest taboos," Murdock concludes, "are enormous."[10]

Psychoanalytic theory has called attention to "the peculiar emotional intensity of incest taboos," and has likewise focused on a universal condition of human survival—the infant's direct dependence upon his mother[11] for gratification of his needs. This relationship, experienced as a bond of affection, determines the emotional tone which the taboo acquires—that incest is not merely strange or ridiculous, but is dangerous, ghastly, disgusting.

Murdock asks, What are the specific episodes "that lead the maturing child to inhibit the direct expression of his sex drive within the family?"[12] (His analysis of infant experience is guided by Hull's reinforcement theory. In the light of more recent psychological theory and findings, more use might well be made of the infant's curiosity, exploratory tendencies, or need for new and novel experience.) [13]

Learning theory and the incest taboo. The normal infant is actively affectionate and curious. He craves physical contact with other persons. His curiosity about the world expresses itself in his explorations of his own body, and of persons inside the home environment. The child learns through experience that while members of the family may fondle, cuddle, and stimulate almost any part of his body, stimulation of his genitals tends to be avoided. Likewise he learns that he may physically stimulate or show curiosity about the physique of others in the family, and elicit a pleasant or playful gesture in return. The child learns one outstanding exception to this rule; if he reaches toward his parent's or sibling's genitals, no playful response is forthcoming. The fun is over; something went wrong.

From the standpoint of learning theory, one might ask whether it is necessary for the parental figure or sibling to *express* horror, disgust, or threaten punishment, in order for the child to acquire an attitude of horror, disgust or anxiety toward incestuous behavior? Or is it enough that the "forbidden gesture" stops the fun, abruptly terminates the giving of tactile pleasure and the receiving of affection? An ingenious animal experiment conducted in Pavlov's laboratory has some relevance to the above question.

Konorski trained a group of dogs to regularly expect that a given stimulus (like a bell) would be followed by the presentation of food. After this classical conditioning was well established, Konorski taught the dogs that if a certain bodily movement occurred after the bell was sounded, no food would be forthcoming. This "lesson" was taught by placing one of the dog's hind legs in a harness so that the experimenter could occasionally raise the dog's hind leg by means of a string-and-pulley arrangement. Thus the animal learned that only "if he didn't make the wrong move," could he expect this orderly sequence of signals and rewards. Konorski observed that after a period of such training, "the animal begins to resist the passive flexion of the leg *by actively extending it.* After a time the animal performs an active movement of extension to the [bell] itself. . . . Finally the movement of extension becomes so strong that we are almost able to raise the animal into the air by its extended limb . . . " Konorski reports.[14] (Italics added.) Remote as this animal conditioning study may seem from a human's inner horror over incest, this experiment dramatically illustrates the organism's capacity for acquiring a powerful compensatory habit of its own, to cope with a threat to its regular supply of gratifications.

Murdock supposes that the child learns to inhibit his incest strivings "in consequence of frequent rebuffs, frustrations and punishments. . ."[15] The Konorski paradigm suggests that direct punishment may be *not at all necessary* for transmitting the incest taboo. It is quite possible that "frequent rebuffs, frustrations, and punishments" would implant not a normal incest avoidance habit, but an exaggerated, overgeneralized discomfort which would flow *over* the boundaries defined by the incest taboo.

The incest taboo everywhere seems to flow over the boundaries of the immediate (or nuclear) family. According to Murdock, "exogamous restrictions of whatever sort seem clearly to be extensions of the sex taboos between parent and child and between brother and sister. . ."[16] In some societies the overflow touches only cousins, aunts, uncles, nieces, and nephews; in other societies the taboo flows out to cover distant relatives as well, and in societies that practice the rule of exogamy the incest taboo covers the entire tribe. Are there principles of habit generalization that can account for the vast differences in the total area covered by the incest taboo—account for differences between cultural norms, and for differences between individual attitudes? Can these principles help explain why one young man feels no excitement about his nubile sister, another feels no excitement about his sister, cousins, or any of their girl friends, and another feels no great excitement about *any* young woman of his social milieu? Stating the problem from a different angle, why is the *exotic* a more necessary condition for the arousal of romantic sentiment and sexual excitement for some persons than for others?

Outside the realm of the neurotic or clinical, men who maintain conventional marriage partnerships sometimes regard a woman of low status or loose morals as sexually exciting. Kinsey assumed that a married man's preference for a prostitute may be attributed to the fact that she provides "the sort of coitus" he prefers.[17] There is, however, both clinical and theoretical justification for the hypothesis that in such a case, preference for a prostitute represents not so much an attraction to a more congenial sex object, as an aversion to his wife as a sex partner (or an ambivalence over sex relations with a woman who "but for the grace of God" could be his sister). The Southern tradition of "sacred white womanhood" purges those who are cast in this role "of every honest and authentic female emotion," Hernton asserts, and renders them unfit as sex partners in marriage. "Even when white women are married and become mothers, Southern white men still refer to them as chaste!"[18]

In the experimental laboratory, the phenomenon of "stimulus generalization" follows certain well-established regularities. Let us look into two laboratory studies in human conditioning, in which habits were acquired under varying degrees of punishment (i.e., electric shock).

Bersh, Schoenfeld, and Notterman established a conditioned "involuntary" heart response in two groups of human subjects by pairing an electric shock with a tone of 1920 cycles per second. One group was trained with a relatively weak (20 volt) shock, and the other with a relatively stronger (28 volt) shock.

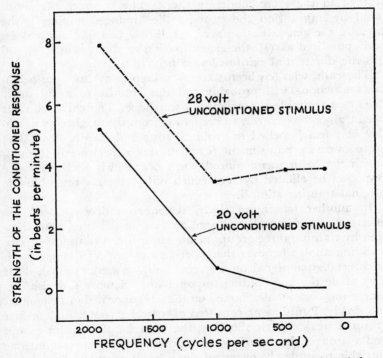

Figure 6:1. Generalization gradients for the conditioned heart response in man following training with relatively weak (20 volts) and relatively strong (28 volts) UCS[19] (Bersh, Notterman, and Schoenfeld, 1956).

After the conditioned response was well established, both groups were tested by measuring their response to the original tone, and to three other tones of progressively lower pitch (1020, 480, and 180 cycles per second).

Results of this experiment demonstrated two characteristics of the acquired "alarm" reaction: (1) new stimuli arouse the acquired "alarm" response to a greater or lesser degree depending on how closely the new stimulus matches the original conditioned stimulus—the training stimulus; (2) the group trained by means of the stronger shock gave the conditioned response to stimuli more dissimilar to the training stimulus than the group trained to the more moderate shock. The stronger the shock (and by implication the stronger the "induced anxiety") the broader the generalization gradient. These two findings may be conceptualized as (1) the generalization gradient principle, and (2) the differential reinforcement principle.

The child who has been warned to keep away from the neighbor's watchdog will probably feel the impulse to avoid other dogs that resemble the neighbor's watchdog. The child who has been trained *too severely* to keep away from the neighbor's watchdog may feel impelled to avoid all sorts and sizes of dogs. The more severe the punishment (threatened or experienced) through which the habit was acquired, the more readily will avoidance responses be elicited by cues which only remotely resemble the original training stimuli.

In another laboratory study, Rosenbaum demonstrated the effects of experimentally induced anxiety on stimulus generalization by training three groups of human subjects to quickly move a sliding knob whenever the experimenter projected a standardized rectangular signal on a screen. Subjects were "punished" if they made the knob-sliding response when a more squarish rectangle was occasionally flashed on the screen, or if they responded too slowly. Punishment consisted of a buzzer sound for the first group, a weak electric shock on the wrist for the second group, and a stronger shock for the third group. Thus the experimenter was able to study the effects of three levels of induced anxiety.

Rosenbaum found that subjects trained with strong shock showed a more broadly generalized response habit than subjects trained to either the weak shock or buzzer. He concluded that "experimentally induced anxiety shows the energizing function of a drive in elevating generalization gradients."[20]

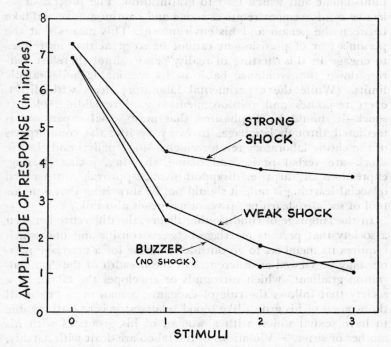

Figure 6:2. Gradients of response amplitude for the three levels of experimentally induced anxiety in normal Ss[21]

Habits are not functional unless they show *some* degree of generalization. (For example, children are taught table manners at home in hope that they will also use them away from home.) It is the *degree* of generalization that makes a habit either too weak (e.g., the child who uses his table manners *only* at home) or too strong (e.g., the child who cannot enjoy eating with his fingers at a picnic). How, in the laboratory and in everyday life, is the degree of generalization regulated so that a habit matches a given norm?

In the experimental laboratory, the gradient of generalization is reduced through "selective reinforcement"; the habit becomes nicely discriminated as the person learns which situations lead to punishment and which lead to gratification. The process of selective reinforcement requires active and continual give-and-take between the person and his environment. This means that the person's fear of punishment cannot be so great that he refuses to engage in this "testing of reality" and cannot therefore narrow down the avoidance habit to its reasonable and realistic limits. (While the experimental laboratory deals with direct, overt responses and reinforcements—e.g., lever-sliding, electric shock—it should be emphasized that most social experience is mediated through language. In everyday life, the counterparts of the classic laboratory reinforcements—food pellets and electric shock—are verbal praise and blame, shaming, joking, teasing, expressions of surprise, disappointment, approval. Since much of social learning is talk, it should not be surprising that a major tool of social re-learning—psychotherapy—is also talk.)

In the language of conditioning theory, the difference between a society that permits marriage between cousins and one which requires its members to go outside the tribe for a marriage partner may be viewed as differences in the breadth of the "generalization gradient" which surrounds or envelopes the taboo. In a society that follows the rule of exogamy, a man must "treat all the women of his group like blood relatives; it is as unthinkable to have sexual union with a woman of his group as with his mother or sister."[22] Violations of the taboo are dealt with harshly, sometimes by death. Sexual union with a member of one's own tribe may be "avenged by the whole tribe as if it were a question of warding off a danger that threatens the community as a whole or a guilt that weighs upon all."[23]

Viewed in this light, the phenomenon of "neurotic exogamy," e.g., the Jew who feels sexually inhibited toward Jewish women and avoids any steps which might lead toward marrying a Jewish woman, is following a private rule of exogamy. This phenomenon follows Freud's insight that "the psychology of the neurotic" parallels the manners and customs of preliterate societies. (As Freud put it, remnants of primitive man's "ways of thinking . . . survive in our own manners and customs," and particularly in the behavior of neurotics.) [24]

The principle of differential reinforcement would suggest that in societies that follow the rule of exogamy (i.e., maintain a broad generalization gradient) parental roles are more likely to be defined as authoritarian and punishing, and that in societies that follow the rule of endogamy (i.e., maintain a narrow generalization gradient) parental roles are more likely to be defined as benign and sheltering. Let us look for anthropological evidence which may have some bearing on this hypothesis.

MATRILOCAL RESIDENCE AND ENDOGAMY

Of all communities represented in the Yale Cross-Cultural Survey files, 171 could be classified as tending toward exogamy, endogamy, or neither. In only *one-fifth* of these communities was endogamy the prevailing rule. The remaining four-fifths were evenly divided between those which tended toward exogamy, and those which were neither exogamous nor endogamous.[25] Since the Yale Cross-Cultural data show exogamy to be twice as prevalent as endogamy, overgeneralization might seem to be a common by-product of incest taboo reinforcement. What are the distinguishing characteristics of an endogamous society, and does this minority-group (!) of communities have something in common with the endogamous Jewish minority group? (And is it possible that this "something in common" tends to be *absent* in the family experience of Jews who "revert" to the more common marriage practice of mankind?)

Murdock's analysis of the foregoing 171 communities reveals that endogamy is significantly linked with a *matrilocal rule of residence*, i.e., endogamous societies tend to follow the custom that a newly married couple establishes residence in or nearby the parents of the wife. (Western society would be described as neo-local, designating that newly married couples establish residence separate from both parental homes.) Residence rules have important consequences for the organization of the family, and the matrilocal character of endogamous communities may provide important clues toward solving the riddle of neurotic exogamy.

A woman's world. The matrilocal rule gives a definite advantage to the wife, who settles down to married life "surrounded and supported by sympathetic kinsmen."[27] It is for her to enjoy the

Table 6:3. Endogamy, Exogamy and Rules of Residence[26]

Rule of Residence	Community Exogamy or Tendency Thereto (N)	per cent	Community Endogamy or Tendency Thereto (N)	per cent	Local Community Neither Exogamous Nor Endogamous (N)	per cent
Patrilocal	(54)	77	(7)	21	(40)	59
Matrilocal	(5)	07	(17)	51	(2)	03
Other*	(11)	16	(9)	28	(26)	38
Total	(70)	100%	(33)	100%	(68)	100%

*—Includes matri-patrilocal, avunculocal, bilocal and, and neolocal.

security of familiar physical and social surroundings; the local norms and customs of family living are her norms. Her children, brought up in a matrilocal extended family, can readily see their mother's attitudes validated in the behavior of their closest neighbors and kinsmen.

The role of the husband in a matrilocal society is quite different, and more difficult. He "must break with the past in some measure, and establish new social ties." Especially are his habits disrupted "where marriages are *exogamous* with respect to community," and he must move out of the community of the matrilineal relatives of his mother, to those of his wife. Under such circumstances the young man enters upon his new status in life "living among comparative strangers to whom [he] must make new personal adjustments and upon whom [he] must depend for the support, protection, and social satisfactions which [he] had previously received from relatives and old friends." In a matrilocal society, therefore, the husband finds himself "at a considerable psychological and social disadvantage in comparison with [his wife]."[28] One thing his old and familiar environment has in common with his strange new habitat: they are dominated by women.

It should not be surprising that the patrilocal rule of residence is more prevalent in societies at large. The division of labor usually requires that men work far from the dwelling, and calls upon men to possess "a thorough knowledge of the environs of the community and of the location of all its useable resources." Women are usually assigned to activities in or about the house, and a familiar environment is therefore less important for dealing with her everyday work. The practice of both community and ethnic endogamy would reduce the hardship of matrilocal residence to the husband; he need not give up entirely his accumulated knowledge of his natural habitat.[29]

Patrilocal residence rules are most clearly favored where the principal means of subsistence put a premium on physical strength and endurance; hunting, herding, domestication of animals and ownership of slaves. In such societies collaboration between male kinsmen is at a premium. A warlike way of life likewise enhances the importance of men. A high level of political integration favors men since they are invariably the holders of political power, and use this power to control property and augment their prestige.[30]

Social conditions which favor a matrilocal rule of residence, therefore, include (1) a relatively high status of women in property and other rights, (2) dependence upon women's activities for subsistence, (3) the absence of moveable property, (4) relative peacefulness, and (5) a relatively low level of political integration.[31]

Thus it appears that a matrilocal society is one in which brute strength is unlikely to be an important masculine trait. (Hunters, warriors, and slaveholders maintain a patrilocal rule.) Killing and violence (e.g., the slaughter of animals, the conquest of enemies, the subjugation of slaves) are outside the culturally patterned repertory of masculine skills. The skills and weapons of violence would therefore be alien to our modal matrilocal society.

Since women play a dominant role in a matrilocal society, the rearing of children (including the transmission of the incest taboo) is undoubtedly more significantly under maternal control. We begin to see the outlines of a society of strong mothers and gentle fathers. To whatever extent that father symbolizes the "power" by which the incest taboo is enforced, the severity of the "threat" would seem to be at a minimum in a society in which father's prestige does not rest upon physical strength, in which father brandishes no instruments of violence, and is unpracticed in the arts of violence.[32]

We are led to hypothesize that in a matrilocal society the nature of the "threat" by which incest avoidance is established and enforced would be not so much a threat of physical harm (or loss of property) as a threat of *loss of love*. It is this threat which uniquely fits the maternal role. Furthermore, mother's high status in the family and community augments the power of her love, makes her love and affection a more valuable and necessary aspect of the child's inner security.

This completes our network of hypotheses concerning the special characteristics of the incest taboo in an edogamous, matrilocal society; basing our conjectures largely on Murdock's anthropological findings. Now we must address ourselves to the questions: How well does the Eastern European Jewish culture fit the above formulation, and in what ways has this culture changed in the course of its transplantation into the Western world?

MARRIAGE CUSTOMS OF THE *SHTETL*, THEIR SOCIAL AND PSYCHOLOGICAL SIGNIFICANCE

In her field work amongst the tribes of New Guinea, Margaret Mead unexpectedly discovered that the Arapesh husband had a considerable emotional investment in the fact that through marriage he and his wife's brothers become, as if by natural law, gardening and hunting companions. Describing the Arapesh viewpoint on marriage, Mead writes:

"So the father, in choosing his son's wife, considers her brothers and her cousins, who will be his son's friends in the years to come. It is well if there are many of them." She describes the misfortune of Aden, condemned to a life of loneliness because his parents had been cousins and members of "vanishing lines." To make matters worse, Aden's two wives were sisters. Reflecting the Arapesh viewpoint, Mead continues: "That was a foolish thing to do for a man so precariously placed as Aden. He thereby lost the chance of acquiring a second set of brothers-in-law and was completely dependent upon his one set. When his one little child, Sauisua, grew up, no one would be anxious to choose for a daughter-in-law a girl with so few relatives." From the Arapesh viewpoint, marriage is defined as an occasion for increasing "the number of people whom one can love and trust" and actively affiliate oneself with.[33]

Marriage and the cultivation of yichas. The above citation parallels rather amazingly the *shtetl* attitude toward marriage as an occasion for enlarging and enriching the *mishpocho,* or extended family. This attitude reveals itself in the great importance attached to the question of how well the bride and groom are balanced in status or *yichas,* for only such a match can be a source of pride to the families of both the bride and groom. How well the bride and groom's *parents* are matched on status is also a matter of much importance for only amongst equals is there likely to develop warm and amicable relations as befits good *machotonim.* (*Machotonoshaft,* meaning in-lawship, and *machoton,* meaning in-law, are common household words in Yiddish and connote an intimacy and emotional investment foreign to their English language counterparts.)

As Zborowski and Herzog point out in their anthropological study of the *shtetl,* the Jewish small town of Eastern Europe was both a very cohesive and highly stratified community. "The people in the *shtetl* are keenly aware of each individual's position in the social spectrum."[34] "Within a community the *yichas* (status) of every member is generally known to the last detail, and to recite one's *yichas* to new acquaintances is an integral part of an introduction."[35] In everyday social behavior distinctions between persons of highest and lowest status are of course most obvious: "If a learned man appears [in the market place], he walks among the stalls like a visitor from another land and is greeted with deference by those he meets there. He passes by, hardly aware of the piled-up merchandise over which they haggle, for he inhabits a world of the mind."[36] On the Sabbath each man is seated in the synagogue according to his status; on the wooden bench at the rear of the synagogue sat the common lot, the *prosteh yidn.* The East Wall, the wall which faces the holy city of Jerusalem, was reserved for the aristocracy, the *baal yichas.*[37] The man of learning and wealth "is called more often to the reading of the Torah, and receives the passages that are valued the most."[38]

The criteria of social status included both inherited and ac-

quired characteristics. The man of great learning enjoyed a high
level of acquired status *(yichas atsmo)*, and the descendants of
men of great learning were accorded a measure of hereditary
status *(yichas ovos)*. Wealth was of course a source of status when
money was used according to the traditional values of the community: for charity, religious study, and community service. Occupation was an important criterion of status, which stigmatized the shoemaker, tailor, butcher, musician, and locksmith,[39]
and favored those whose work required the exercise of literacy,
social or verbal skills, and also favored the self-employed.

Marriage was a most important instrument for preserving,
consolidating, and enhancing family status. A marriage might
also debase the family's social position. "Since the standing of
the whole family is involved, the complicated rules of who-mar-
ries-whom are subject to infinite debate within the family circle
and in the *shtetl* at large."[40] The matings of the eldest children
may significantly alter the younger children's status as prospective
mates. Thus in a family in which the eldest daughter was homely
or the eldest son was stupid, the younger children might well find
themselves disadvantaged, for children must be married off according to age. "Many a girl has been forced to renounce her
beloved because to marry beneath her *yichas* would 'put a spot
[i.e., a blemish] on the family name.' "[41] Among the aristocrats
of the *shtetl* "the feeling about choosing a mate on one's own social level is so strong that marriage between an aristocrat and a
plebian has been referred to as 'intermarriage,' [though] such
usage is extremely rare," Zborowski and Herzog admit.[42]

Learning and the enhancement of yichas. We have already
noted that learning served as a potent instrument of status, perhaps the most potent in *shtetl* society. "The intellectual attainments of a penniless youth are expected to win him the daughter
of a *nogid,* rich and respected, with a handsome dowry and some
years of support in the home of her parents while he continues
his studies. . ."[43]

The upbringing of a boy is interwoven from infancy with preparing him for marriage. In the circumcision ceremony at the
eighth day of birth they bless and dedicate the infant "so that
he may enter into the Law, the nuptial canopy, and into good
deeds. . ."[44] "From infancy the boy is guided and prodded toward

scholarship. In the cradle he will listen to his mother's lullabies:

> Sleep soundly at night and learn *Torah* by day
> And thou'lt be a Rabbi when I have grown grey."[45]

A boy acquires prestige in proportion to the progress he makes at school. . . . A boy who is known as a genius, *iluy,* will be shown the same deference as a learned adult. . . ."[46] A boy is usually named after a deceased grandfather or an ancestor, and preference is given to the learned. The namesake will be reminded constantly to follow his example and become a *lamdn,* a *ben torah.* Thus, learning is a frequent topic of family conversation, of mother's lullabies, of wishes and exhortations that the child receives from day to day.

"Once he starts school, the boy is the 'jewel' of the family. Every Saturday, when the father holds his weekly 'hearing,' while the teacher sits by, the mother feels her fate too is involved. If he does well she will be proud because she is 'bringing up a good Jew.' "[47]

"Nothing must interfere with school. 'I remember that I didn't have any high boots and the mud came up very high that year. So mother used to carry me on her back to *cheyder,* but I had to go to *cheyder.*' "[48]

Nothing enhances a youth's status like outstanding scholarship. Not merely for its own sake, but because the attainment of learning implies intelligence as well as high moral standards and correct social behavior. A learned man knows "the rules of behavior, which are the commandments of God, [and is therefore expected to] behave in accordance with them." It is therefore "assumed that a learned man will be a good husband and father."[49]

Thus every advantage is "attached to scholarship—status, prestige, a rich wife, [all in addition to] the joy of study itself. . . . The student is the pride of his family, and more. He brings honor and joy, sheds on them the reflected glory of his *yichas*"[50] which is socially validated through marriage into a family of wealth, good deeds, and learning. A young man who is a serious candidate for an arranged marriage might first be quizzed by the "father and perhaps the uncles of the bride . . . to determine his knowl-

edge of the Talmud and his adroitness in scholarly discussion.
If the father is not equal to the task he brings with him a learned
teacher. . . ."51

Kest. The degree of prestige accorded the bridegroom was represented by the duration of *kest,* a period of time during which
the young couple is maintained in the home of the bride's parents. The duration of *kest* was inscribed in the marriage contract;52 it might last for several months, "through any number
of years to *ebige kest* or [permanent] maintenance." During this
period the young husband was free from economic responsibilities
and expected to complete his scholarly studies. At the termination of *kest,* the young man might be helped into business by his
father-in-law, unless the young husband found a scholarly post
for himself. "In some cases the wife chose to undertake the economic support of the family herself, in order that her husband
might continue to live a life devoted to study."53

The custom of "paid *kest*" facilitated marriage between the
daughter of a scholar and the son of a *nogid.* For such a balancing
of *yichas,* the father of the young husband would pay his *machoton* to maintain the young family and help the young husband complete his education. Thus the matrilocal rule of residence could be observed even when it required financial support
of the husband's father.54

An exception to the matrilocal rule of residence was allowed
if a young husband was an only son and his parents did not want
to part with him. In such a case, *kest* could be provided in the
home of the husband.55

How widespread and how long-established was the matrilocal
rule of *kest* in the Jewish culture? In the *shtetl,* writes Yudel
Mark, the question of for how long a period "the father of the
bride would support the young couple" was a major consideration in the arrangement of a marriage, second in importance
only to the matching of bride and groom on *yichas.* Implying
that kest was the prevailing custom, Mark recalls that "when a
daughter married, the son-in-law was taken into the house and a
little room was partitioned off for the couple."56

According to Abraham Cohen—British rabbi and scholar, translator of Maimonides and author of *Everyman's Talmud*—kest
was practiced in ancient times to accommodate the Jewish belief

—codified in *Pirke Aboth*—that a man is ready for marriage at the age of eighteen, but is not ready to seek a livelihood until the age of twenty.[57] Hence, said Rabbi Cohen, "the bridgeroom used to live in the house of his bride's father during the first years of marriage."[58]

It would be useful to know just how frequently the matrilocal rule of *kest* was practiced in the *shtetl* and in earlier eras of Jewish life. Though at a particular time and place only a minority of marriages might involve practice of kest, we would hypothesize that these instances, though small in number, would enlist the most glamorous figures in *shtetl* life: the sheltered daughter of a *nogid* who travelled far and wide to find a jewel of a young man, an *iluy* for whom no question of religious lore was too subtle or complex. *Kest* therefore involved the natural leaders of the *shtetl*: persons of wealth, and men of learning—and their matrilocally patterned behavior might well have served as models for the *shtetl* at large.

Kest and social norms of the shtetl. Let us attempt to enumerate the social functions and consequences of *kest*. First, *kest* held out a reward for scholarly diligence and offered promotion in social rank to intelligent and thoughtful young men, and to their families; *kest* articulated the lofty ideals of religious scholarship with the more basic drives toward economic security and sexual fulfillment. Secondly, *kest* added dignity to earned wealth, and must thereby have added dignity to business enterprise itself. Thirdly, *kest* dispersed and distributed scholarly minds through the *shtetl* culture, and thereby effected a mingling of practical and intellectual values within the culture, such as cannot prevail in a culture where a monastery or university wall divides the world of thought from the world of action. Finally, a custom which brings together the extended families of scholars and businessmen counteracts the forces that divide the rich from the poor, the intellectual from the practical man, and *kest* might therefore have served as a most important cohesive force in a culture of antagonistic values.

Kest and sex-role patterning. We have already pointed to Murdock's observation that a matrilocal rule of residence is a rarity in human society; it places the new wife in familiar and supportive surroundings while her husband starts married life in a strange household where he must adapt to the ways of his wife's kinsmen. Such a custom, according to Murdock, is likely to evolve in a relatively peaceful society in which women enjoy high status and men are without strong political organization. Over generations of practice, the matrilocal rule further augments the status of women—following the familiar self-reinforcing cycle of cause-and-effect—and from this culturally patterned situation evolves a tradition of privileged wives and "wonderful husbands," strong mothers, and gentle fathers.

Viewed from this perspective, the strong mother and gentle father may be seen as by-products of a marriage custom that facilitated early marriage, rewarded religious scholarship, distributed men of learning throughout the extended families of the *shtetl*, and thereby added a cohesive force to the *shtetl* community.

Marriage and mishpocho. A prospective bride is judged by the social status of her parents, her dowry, her physical attractiveness, her knowledge of the dietary laws, and her household skills, though the bridegroom is more likely to be judged "almost as if he were a disembodied intellect. . . ."[59]

The equitable matching of bride and groom by all the determinants of *yichas*—in a way that preserved established status, rewarded earned status, gave no undue advantage for good looks or recent wealth, imposed no undue penalty for homeliness or deformity, strengthened and enriched kinship bonds—such a task called for a knowledgeable, disinterested and diplomatic arbiter, a role which was fulfilled by the *shadchan* or matchmaker.

The *shadchan* was a person of importance for he defined his client's status by the candidates he would recommend. "Whether he modestly confines his activities to one *shtetl*, or is an ambitious traveler between city and town, he picks up an array of gossip and information that makes him both welcome and feared. Even families who know each other well often call upon his services for arranging a marriage . . . Anyone in the *shtetl* may be an amateur *shadchan*, and most are. A favorite subject for gossip, especially among women, is potential pairs. . . . But the *shadchan* with his inevitable umbrella is the one who does what they merely talk about."[60]

Expansion and enhancement of the *mishpocho* is attained

through marriage, and "the anxiety of . . . parents is proverbial," especially over the marriage of their daughters. "From the moment a girl is born, her parents begin to ponder her *shiddach,* her marriage arrangements. As she approaches adolescence, she is reminded to act with decorum: 'You are a *kaleh-moyd* now,' a bride-girl. Fond relatives, pinching her cheek, will say archly, 'Soon the *shadchan* will be coming.' She herself may wonder anxiously if perhaps she will be [a spinster, described as] a *farzesseneh,* 'one who is left sitting.' "[61]

In Jewish life, as elsewhere, distance lends enchantment. The daughter of a *nogid* might dream of a handsome stranger, a jewel of a young man from some far-off place, whom her father will give her as a husband. A talented and ambitious young man might dream of being invited to join, through marriage, an aristocratic family in a distant land, and start life afresh in a new and elite milieu. In the Eastern European culture, contacts leading to such marriages were made by traveling businessmen, by traveling *shadchanim,* and at regional fairs.

A traveling businessman whose daughter was approaching a marriageable age might go out of his way to visit a *yeshiva* and enlist the aid of the director in finding a worthy son-in-law.[62] Traveling *shadchanim* were the aristocrats of their profession, who, unlike those whose work was restricted to local matchmaking, might cover the entire Eastern European world—Russia, Poland, Lithuania—through personal visits, correspondence, and conferences with other traveling *shadchanim.* Written in elegant Hebrew prose, a *shadchan's* letter might open the door of a most elite household. A *nogid* might encourage a *shadchan* to make a special effort on his behalf, by advancing the *shadchan* "travel money" or "postage money" to meet the expenses of his search for a worthy candidate.[63]

A seventeenth-century rabbi described the fairs held at Lemberg and Lublin as meeting grounds for marriageable youth, their parents, and teachers:

He who had a son or a daughter to marry journeyed to the fair and made a match, for everyone found his like and his suit. At every fair, hundreds of matches were made up, sometimes thousands. . . .[64]

Weyl quotes another description of summer fairs in Polish towns and cities, "where thousands of students of the Talmud assembled and engaged in public disputes open to everyone. 'The keener intellects received wealthy brides as a reward for their mental exertions. Rich parents took pride in having sons-in-law educated in Talmudic schools, and sought them at the fairs.' "[65]

"A person who is in good spirits will be told, 'You look as if you had married off all your children.' A favorite toast is 'a good match for your daughter,' even if the prospective bride is only three or four years old." Family status requires that a suitable dowry be offered, even when bride and groom have fallen in love and the involvement of their families is only ceremonial. "Relatives will forego immediate comforts, or even place themselves in debt for years to come, so that the bride, and they, 'should not be ashamed before his family.' "[66]

"Before the wedding feast is under way the *chossen* will give his speech, the *drosheh*. Usually it is 'a little piece of Torah,' a discussion and interpretation of some complicated text relating to marriage."[67] A highlight of the wedding celebration is " 'the quarreling dance' by the new mothers-in-law, who stamp, grimace, and lunge at one another, dramatizing a mock quarrel. Finally they rush into each other's arms and embrace."[68] Thus do the new *machotonim* celebrate the happy fusion of the values of learning, prudence, charity, business acumen and *mishpocho*.[69]

From the standpoint of the *shtetl* society, marriage to an outsider—a Gentile—destroys and repudiates social values which have been cultivated and nurtured through a lifetime of work. Intermarriage not only destroys the status of the Jewish marriage partner but lays a pall of social humiliation over the entire *mishpocho*. Parents are disgraced, and denied the pleasures of *machotonoshaft*, unmarried sisters may feel the threat and shame of spinsterhood, and brothers share the suffering and stigma of the family. Perhaps it is significant that intermarriage is not even discussed or indexed in Zborowski and Herzog's otherwise detailed study of life in the *shtetl*. Perhaps this omission communicates the sense of horror aroused by this travesty on the *shtetl* concept of marriage.[70]

In *shtetl* society, marriage to an outsider was lamented as an insult and a catastrophe. Parents would act out the seven days of

mourning that customarily follows the death of a Jew. Undoubtedly, exercise of the extreme sanction of sitting *shiva* for
the defector facilitated the expression of both the hostility and
the anguish that intermarriage evoked in the *shtetl* family.

The endogamous tradition of the Jews has expressed itself at
various times by placing marriage with a Jew of another nation
in the category of "intermarriage." According to Baron, the
Sephardic Jewish communities of Holland, France, and England
for centuries opposed marriage of their members to Jews of Eastern Europe. About the end of the eighteenth century "if a Portuguese Jew in England or Holland married a German Jewess he
would, of course, lose all his prerogatives, be no longer reckoned
a member of their synagogue, forfeit all civil and ecclesiastical
preferments, be absolutely divorced from the body of the nation
and not even be buried with his Portuguese brethren."[71] In past
generations of life in the United States, Sephardic Jews have condemned "intermarriage" with German Jews, German Jews have
deemed it unseemly for their offspring to marry Russian or Polish
Jews,[72] and Russian Jews have felt loathe to see their child marry
a Hungarian Jew, especially if the Russian Jewish parents would
face *machotonim* who spoke not Yiddish but Magyar.

THE EXTENDED FAMILY IN THE
JEWISH CULTURE

Undoubtedly the chagrin and frustration with which Jewish
parents view intermarriage implies something about the importance attached to maintaining and enhancing a cohesive extended family. Jessie Bernard reports that to the immigrant
German Jews in America, as to Jews of the *shtetl* tradition, intermarriage was viewed with anguish because "it meant the absence
of interfamily ties which bound in-laws so close in the older
generation:"

To the immigrant generation nothing was worse than intermarriage. . . . Intermarriage meant the flaunting of everything
the community stood for. It meant bringing a strange person
into the intimacy of the family circle, a stranger who would
look upon all the ritual of the family with an outsider's eyes.[73]

Perhaps the position of the Jews as a minority group attached a special importance to community solidarity, and interfamily ties —effected through marriage alliances—were regarded as the links that held the Jewish community together. In their observations on the culture of the Hopi Indians, Sargent and Williamson note that "the tightly knit [extended] family group provides the individual with a sense of security."[74] One might suppose that the *mishpocho* likewise contributes to the psychological survival of the Jew in an unfriendly or uncertain world. Bohannan draws upon a biological analogy in theorizing about the survival value of kinship groups:

> Kinship groups can fulfill all the social needs of mankind. In that sense, the kinship group is the least 'specialized' of all human groups. Students of biological evolution assure us that the least specialized organism—that which can adapt itself most readily to the widest variety of demands in the widest variety of environments—has the greatest chance of survival.[75]

Bohannan implies that although nonkinship groups (e.g., lodges, labor unions, bridge clubs, hospitals, banks, churches, schools, employment agencies) can fulfill certain specialized social needs more efficiently, only the kinship group is flexible enough to serve any and every social need. Just as one enjoys financial security not by using a savings account but by having it, the individual may draw emotional security from the knowledge that in a crisis—any kind of crisis—he has a family to turn to.

Reik refers in detail to the "intimate and insoluble ties of the Jews."[76] One of Freud's early patients was "a middle-aged Jewish man from the lower East Side of New York. When Freud first explained to him that most of his neurotic conflicts had their roots in his relationship with his family, the patient was not as astonished as one would have expected. He said: 'But I always knew that. We all suffer from *mishpoch'itis.'* "[77] The acculturated Jew's internalized conflict between loyalty to his extended family and identification with the dominant culture is well illustrated in the following joke—told between the World Wars in Berlin, when it was considered a mark of sophistication in certain Gentile circles to understand Yiddish expressions:

'Wissen Sie was bedeutet eine Mishpocho?'
'Ist es etwas zum essen?'
'Nein, es ist etwas zum kotzen!'

'Do you know what a *mishpocho* is?'
'Is it something to eat?'
'No, it's something to throw up!'

A significant portion of the Gentile observer's difficulty in understanding the Jewish culture (or the Jew's confusion when he views himself through Gentile eyes) may be assigned to a failure to grasp the concept of extended family membership, and the deep personal meaning it holds for its members, for according to Murdock the only type of family recognized in American society—"to the exclusion of all others"—is the nuclear family, consisting of parents and their offspring.[78]

Unlike the matrilocal rule of residence, the extended family is the norm "among the majority of the peoples of the earth. . . . Nuclear families are combined, like atoms in a molecule, into larger aggregates," writes Murdock, either through plural marriage or as an extended family, which "consists of two or more nuclear families affiliated through an extension of the parent-child relationship . . . by joining the nuclear family of a married adult to that of his parents. . . . Three generations, including the nuclear families of father and sons, live under a single roof or in a cluster of adjacent dwellings."[79]

Of the 192 societies of the Yale Cross-Cultural samples ("for which sufficient information is available") 47, or something less than one-fourth, "have normally only the nuclear family," the great majority being either extended or polygamous.[80] American behavioral scientists tend to overlook the deviant position of our own society and accept it uncritically as a standard by which other groups are to be judged. It is ironic, for example, that in a book dedicated to the thesis that a psychotherapist must understand the cultural background of his client, the author fails to grasp the significance of the Jewish extended family. To Georgene Seward, the Jew who "clings to his family for emotional support" is displaying an "exile neurosis."[81]

A check of the current social psychology textbooks shows virtually nothing on the topics of extended family, grandparents,

aunts, uncles, or cousins—but much discussion, for example, on
the influences of television. One finds nothing on the role of
the extended family in our culture, in the social psychology texts
of Newcomb, Krech and Crutchfield, Kimball Young, or Sargent and Williamson. Doob deals with extended family nomen-
clature in various cultures as an anthropological curiosity (to
demonstrate "the limits of human plasticity"), but has nothing
to say about the role of the extended family in contemporary
Western society.[82]

Kimball Young's discussion of parental influences on personality development emphasizes the point that overprotectiveness carries the risk "that the child remains in a state of protection far beyond the time when these relationships are essential
to the child's growth. . . . Protection and affection which may
be quite pertinent to the first few months [!] and years of life
may later become a serious handicap to the development of the
child's personality."[83] Apparently a family is something that
must be quickly outgrown, and the sooner this is accomplished
the better. Sargent and Williamson offer a fifteen-page analysis
of family influences on personality development in our culture,
without a single reference to anyone except parents (or foster
parents) and siblings.

Talcott Parsons has argued that the extended family does not
fit into our society, and perhaps the majority of behavioral
scientists share this viewpoint. (When one reads that the extended family does not fit into *our* society, that it has, in fact,
been "obliterated or assigned peripheral tasks," such scholarly
observations seem to describe nothing so well as a faculty enclave
in a college town.) Litwak questions the evidence from which
this view of the extended family was drawn, and points to observations closer to the mainstream of American life which
ascribe a more significant and positive role to the extended
family.[84] In a 1967 publication, Winch, Greer, and Blumberg
likewise question the validity of the classic sociological generalization on the demise of the extended family in urban society. The
authors present survey data on extended family life in an upper
middle class suburb of Chicago, and note that *mishpocho* ties are
particularly strong among the Jews. The authors point out that
their findings do *not* support the common-sense assumption that
Jews maintain stronger extended family ties because they are

non-migratory, but rather suggest "that they are non-migratory because they are familistic."[85] That is to say, Jews seem to *resist* pressures to migrate, because they want to maintain their extended family ties.

Unlike the nuclear family, an extended family is never outgrown; the person is a member of his extended family for his entire lifespan. Disturbances in his adjustment to his extended family are felt as personal problems. Deep emotional disturbance is likely to be reflected in disturbed extended family relations. It is interesting to note that in Georgene Seward's second book on the topic of culture conflict and psychotherapy, three cases of Jewish clients are presented, and in all three of these cases the extended family is significantly involved:

Itzhak

Born into an Orthodox Jewish subculture on the East Coast, Itzhak was overprotected by his mother and pampered by his relatives "as the only child in a large [extended] family."[86] His parents took him to the West Coast in an effort to better their economic condition, and settled in a mixed neighborhood. As family life was further disrupted by father's overwork and mother's part-time employment. Itzhak's behavior became increasingly dependent, and infantile. His disturbance is interpreted as a disruption of "his integration with the extended East Coast family. . . . He enjoyed sharing their religious observances and their holidays and longed nostalgically for them in his loneliness out West. He expressed his *Heimweh* symptomatically by the headache which told him he must get back there before Friday sundown."[87]

Seymour

Disillusioned in her effort "to make her husband develop more into the intellectual and sophisticated person she desired," Seymour's mother chose her brother-in-law, a successful lawyer and politician who lived in the same neighborhood, "as the real model for her child. Seymour thus from his earliest years heard endless tales of how Uncle Arnold would or could do this for one, or that one must behave in a certain way to impress him. Comparisons between Seymour and Arnold's son, Monroe, [who were about the same age] were constantly voiced. The family atmosphere in which Seymour found himself thus consisted of an extreme emphasis on achievement through intellect, on fierce competition for social status and prestige" within the context of an extended family.[88]

Ilona

A cultured and educated Hungarian Jew, Ilona at age thirty-five fled to the United States as a refugee. Suddenly a stranger and an outcast, "she attempted to meet the crisis by throwing herself into a hasty marriage with a man alien to her in cultural background, language and religion. By her precipitate behavior, she hoped to acquire the protective coloration of the new group."[89] A series of relocations, required by her husband's job and his recurrent drinking problem, aggravated her feeling of insecurity; "she was lost in the mobile, breezy ways of her American-Western husband. . . . She longed for the intimate closely knit circle of relatives and friends so characteristic of the European-Jewish life in which she had grown up and so utterly unfamiliar to her Gentile husband with his casual acquaintances. She felt that she could never bridge the cultural gap between them no matter how much Burt might admire culture and look up to her for help in attaining it."[90]

How important is the extended family—*mishpocho* and *machotonoshaft*—in contemporary American Jewish life, and how significantly does it bear upon the solidarity of the group and the emotional security of its members? Direct evidence on the relationship between endogamy and extended family solidarity is offered by the Heiss finding that Jews who intermarry are less likely to have lived with grandparents, less likely to have had active ties with cousins, aunts, and uncles. From Maier and Spinrad's survey we have learned that Jewish college students characteristically affirm that they "owe their greatest loyalty" to family or to people (unlike their Gentile classmates, who say they "owe their greatest loyalty" to God). *Loyalty to people* calls for an interiorization of their standards, and a loyalty to the norms that strengthen the bonds of peoplehood.

7

Jews in America — Conflict and Congregation

We have taken the position that we can learn more about Jewish attitudes toward endogamy and intermarriage by dealing with this topic *not* as a religious issue but rather as an expression of the individual's ethnic identity—or as an expression of his concern for the solidarity of the Jewish community, and for his security and status within the community. In this chapter we shall survey evidence on group cohesion in the American Jewish community, examining both historical materials as well as recent survey data. We shall also look for evidence of distinctive patterns of Jewish adjustment to life in the United States, focusing upon social practices which are likely to influence tensions toward intermarriage—residential choice, occupational choice, and dating.

THE JEWS OF DETROIT

A 1958 community survey conducted by Gerhard Lenski offers some valuable insights on how the Jews of Detroit (Michigan) compare with their Catholic and Protestant neighbors on atti-

tudes and practices related to group cohesiveness and intermarriage. Lenski's investigation is based on interviews of 656
Detroit adults selected on the basis of probability sampling
methods. His interview schedule covered 155 questions, and dealt
with the influence of religious affiliation on political, economic,
and family life.

Although his Jewish sub-sample numbered only 27 individuals
—and his reported percentages must therefore be taken as approximations—their general characteristics match up quite well
with the expectations of those who are acquainted with the
Jewish community of Detroit. Compared with their Catholic and
Protestant neighbors, Detroit Jews are politically liberal, middle
class, well educated, economically successful—with a uniquely
high rate of self-employment. (Nearly half of 27 male heads of
Jewish families were self-employed, compared with only 7 per
cent of male heads of non-Jewish families.) [1] Only 12 per cent
claim to attend temple or synagogue services on a regular weekly
basis,[2] but their places of residence are more concentrated geographically than any other ethnic group.[3]

On church attendance and intermarriage norms, Detroit's Jews
and Catholics stand in bold contrast. Catholics are loyal church-
goers (more than 70 per cent attend Mass at least once a week),
but "30 per cent of all those who were raised as Catholics married
someone who was raised a non-Catholic." A mere 12 per cent of
the Jews, on the other hand, report regular weekly attendance at
religious services—but each and every one of the 24 married
Jews in Lenski's sample "were lifelong Jews married to a lifelong Jewish spouse."[4]

Given this difference in marriage practices, it is not surprising
that Catholics and Jews also differ in the ethnic characteristics
of their relatives and friends. "Whereas 96 per cent of the Jews
reported that all or nearly all of their close relatives were Jewish,
only 79 per cent of the Catholics reported that all or nearly all
of their close relatives were Catholic. There is an even more
pronounced discrepancy with respect to ties of friendship.
Whereas 77 per cent of the Jewish respondents reported that
all or nearly all of their close friends were Jewish, the comparable
figure for Catholics was only 44 per cent."[5]

In addition to their actual rate of intermarriage, Lenski appraised his respondents' attitudes toward intermarriage by asking:

"As a general rule, do you think it is wiser for Protestants (Catholics, Jews) to marry other Protestants (Catholics, Jews), or not?"

A positive response was given by 75 per cent of the Protestants, 81 per cent of the Catholics, and 92 per cent of the Jews.[6]

A most worth while aspect of Lenski's report consists of various estimates he made of the individuals' ties to their extended family and to the community. *All* of his middle-class Jewish respondents said they had relatives living in Detroit, compared with 71 per cent of his middle-class Protestants.[7] Restated, almost one out of three white middle-class Protestants had no relatives living in Detroit (excluding immediate family living in the same dwelling unit), a degree of separation from kin which was nonexistent in the middle-class Jewish sample.

It would follow, of course, that Jews tend not to migrate (except to places where they will find *mishpocho*). Almost half of the Jewish respondents were natives of Detroit, and in this respect they were similar to the Catholic sample. Of the white Protestants, on the other hand, *less than one-third* were natives of Detroit. The Jews apparently do not play the game of occupational mobility according to the rules of the sociologists, who cherish the principle that geographical mobility normally accompanies occupational mobility—or, that people who want to better themselves must be willing to relocate. It seems logical enough that "people whose ties with kin bind them to their community of birth are necessarily at a disadvantage in the competition for advancement. This factor may well contribute to the different rates of mobility for Catholics and white Protestants," Lenski concludes—but it does not appear to handicap the Jews.[8]

Lenski asked his respondents how often they visited relatives. Since Jews are most likely to have relatives in the city, it is not surprising that they were most likely to visit relatives every week. Not only do Jews happen to have relatives living in the city, but three out of four see their *mishpocho* at least once a week.

Percentage visiting relatives every week:[9]

Jews	75
White Catholics	56
White Protestants	49
Negro Protestants	46

As another test of group cohesion or solidarity, Lenski asked his respondents whether they thought any of their friends or relatives would be at all unhappy or disturbed if they attempted to join another faith. More than any other group, Jews "expected some objection if they sought to shift their allegiance." Lenski submits the following percentage figures:[10]

Jews	96
White Catholics	87
White Protestants	75
Negro Protestants	28

A study of residential patterns of Detroit's ethnic groups indicates that Jews are even more highly concentrated geographically than Negroes. Lenski employed a statistical measure of association between area of residence and socio-religious group (Tau_b). Results ranked the four major groups as follows:

Jews	.39
Negro Protestants	.37
White Protestants	.10
White Catholics	.07

Lenski commented: "The fact that the coefficient for the Jewish group was even higher than for the Negro Protestants is especially remarkable since Negroes are so severely limited in their choice of residential area both by finances and by out-group hostility. . . . One can only conclude that the magnitude of this coefficient is one more indication of the strength of the communal spirit of this group."[11]

To summarize, this recent study of a large urban community shows a uniquely high degree of group cohesiveness in the Jewish group, compared with their Protestant and Catholic neighbors. The maintenance of extended family ties is indicated by a relatively low rate of migration, and a norm of frequent and regular visits with relatives. Geographical congregation and a commitment to endogamous marriage—both in principle and in practice —also distinguishes the Jews of Detroit from their Gentile neighbors. Although synagogue attendance falls far below the norm for Catholic and Protestant church attendance, the investigator concludes that "the vigor of Jewish communalism more than compensates for the weakness of the religious associations."[12]

It is regrettable that the above findings are based on a sample of only 27 Jews (compared with 267 white Protestants, 230 white Catholics, and 100 Negro Protestants) . Because there were no intermarrieds amongst the 27 Jewish respondents should not lead us to suppose that intermarriage is unknown in the Detroit Jewish community. In adherence to the endogamous norm, as well as in other measures of group cohesiveness, the Jewish community of Detroit probably shows a strong resemblance to the Jews of North City, the Midwestern Jewish community of 20,000 studied by Kramer and Leventman—where the intermarriage rate (as reported in 1961) was about two per cent for Jews of the second generation, and seven per cent for Jews of the third generation. Similarly, Goldstein and Goldscheider's 1966 Providence (Rhode Island) study shows an intermarriage rate of 1.3 per cent for older Jews (aged sixty or more) , and a rate of 9 per cent for Jews under thirty.

Community studies of Washington, D.C., and San Francisco have shown an altogether different picture of Jewish life in the United States, and reports of intermarriage rates as high as 40 per cent have sent a wave of alarm throughout the Jewish community. We do not arrive at an understanding of the over-all situation by "averaging together" Washington, San Francisco, Detroit, and North City. We would do better to recognize the difference between a stable, cohesive home town, and a mobile, cosmopolitan gathering place for salaried professionals—and look for adherence to the rule of endogamy where we see other signs of Jewish group solidarity.[13]

The test of a tradition. It would grossly oversimplify history to view the cohesive Jewish communities of the United States as transplanted *shtetls* of Eastern Europe. Such solidarity as now prevails represents the resolution of many crises and confrontations between successive waves of immigration, and represents the test of a tradition that says *Chaverim kol Yisro'el*—all Jews are comrades.

In the middle of the nineteenth century, American Jews were largely of German origin—a small minority group living a comfortable middle-class life, continuing a tradition practiced in America since Colonial times when "the few Jews who had settled in the colonies had many relations with their neighbors." German Jews were regarded by the dominant group as Germans, and they were indeed German in their language, customs, and habits. "There was considerable intermarriage, and it was not a great issue in Jewish life." According to Glazer, they "found acceptance in society, to the extent that they wished it. . ."[14]

Aside from the fact that they were too small a minority group to arouse suspicion, the German Jews enjoyed two important advantages as settlers in America—advantages which the next wave of Jewish immigration could not claim. The German Jews had come to America as Westerners, and with a background of relatively friendly relations with the Gentile world. "In Moravia," wrote Stefan Zweig, "the Jews lived in little villages on friendly terms with the peasants and townsfolk. They showed neither the inferiority feelings nor the ceaseless opportunism which characterizes the [oppressed] Jews of Galicia and the East."[15]

When the wave of Eastern European Jewish immigration hit American shores, toward the close of the nineteenth century, the acculturated German Jews were shaken from their comfortable niche in American life, and unhappily identified with a mass of strange, impoverished slum-dwellers—noisy, dirty, and hopelessly "foreign." As early as 1840 a letter appeared in the Berlin *Allgemeine Zeitung dem Judentum* from an American Jewish correspondent: "The Polish Jew is the dirtiest of all creatures, and thanks to him the word 'Jew' is here too coming to be used as an insult."[16] In the 1880's a "B'nai B'rith lodge in Chicago explained that it declined to accept Polish and Russian Jews as members because . . . they are not yet civilized, were inclined to Orthodoxy, and did not seem fit to belong to a respectable organization of American Jews."[17]

At the end of the nineteenth century German Jews and the Jews from Eastern Europe lived as two distinct communities in Rochester, New York, as they did elsewhere. German Jews "were prepared to defend their Russian co-religionists publicly, [though] privately they had come to regard them as a threat to their own secure position in America." In 1889 the United Jewish Charities of Rochester declared that immigrants from

Eastern Europe "are a bane to the country and a curse to the Jews."[18]

The new immigration threatened the security of the German Jewish community for a variety of sociological reasons. (1) German Jews—long regarded as Germans by their American neighbors—were now linked up with a strange and improverished immigrant class from Eastern Europe. (2) More important perhaps was the sheer increase in Jewish population represented by the new immigration. Just as anti-Negro prejudice is greater in the delta country of the deep South where their relative number is greatest (while in the border states Negroes constitute a small and more readily tolerated minority), the new mass immigration placed the Jew in a more competitive position vis-a-vis his Gentile neighbor. Regardless of whether the mass of newcomers were Easterners or Westerners, educated or ignorant, dirty or fastidious, there was bound to develop an increase in tensions between Jew and Gentile in the United States.[19]

Kramer and Leventman offer an illuminating example of the status loss suffered by the German Jews as a result of the Eastern European immigration. Prior to World War I German Jews of North City "participated in the organizations of the general community. But the mass influx of Eastern European Jews brought with it systematic exclusion of Jews from the social life of the larger community. . . . *The Athletic Club, for example, passed a resolution excluding from membership the sons of Jews who were members at the time.*" (Italics added.) [20]

The Jewish tradition of "peoplehood" was put to a severe test by the conflict and tensions between the acculturated German Jew and the impoverished, strange immigrant from Russia or Poland. Though they might privately regard each other with mutual disdain, German Jews took responsibility for the unseemly newcomers through immigrant aid societies and community charities. German Jews served as arbitrators and mediators in the labor union struggles in the New York garment industry (though it should be noted that the "exploiting bosses" might also have been German Jews).

American sociologists noted with amazement that the more successful Jewish immigrants "not only live without exploiting their own people, but sincerely devote their abilities and resources to the improvement of the mass of their race." In other immigrant groups, Park and Miller observed, such leadership as arose tended "to exploit the simpler members of their own group. . ."[21]

During the twenties and thirties the German Jew in America was becoming, in effect, a "displaced person," as they lost their parents' status as "100 percent Americans," and as the acculturated descendants of the Eastern European Jews assumed leadership of the Jewish community. Some called themselves Hebrews, to distinguish themselves from the majority of Jews. Some sought to establish a more congenial identity as Episcopalians, Unitarians, Christian Scientists, or Roman Catholics. Among New York's German Jewish elite, "mixed marriages were suddenly fashionable, and when they occurred, it was usually the Jewish partner who converted . . ."[22]

A segment of the German Jewish community made a considerable effort to use the Reform movement as a vehicle for separating themselves from the Jewish majority, by defining their conception of Judaism as a *religion* designated by a Credo to which its adherents must subscribe. Reform Rabbi Stephen S. Wise in 1933 pleaded with his "co-religionists" (as Reform Jews liked to call each other) against borrowing too heavily "from the alien church ideal of Western lands." The dichotomy of church and state, warned the Rabbi, is an "utterly alien and un-Jewish dichotomy," and violates the immemorial Jewish tradition which regards "people and synagogue or people and religion as one and inseparable." To define Judaism as a "religion" and set up a Credo to which its adherents must subscribe, makes a false and misleading emphasis; it is un-Jewish and untraditional, "repulsive and expulsive to a great number of Jews . . . [who, however, ignorant of Jewish scholarship, correctly intuit] that they are members of a fellowship, not communicants of a sect or church."[23]

Descendants of the Eastern European Jews gradually moved into positions of leadership of the Reform movement itself, found a place in its services for Eastern European lamentation, and an increasingly firmer place in its ideology for the concept of peoplehood. (One of Gordon's respondents complains about the infiltration of Eastern influences into the practices of Reform Judaism.)[24]

The rise of Hitlerism in Germany confronted the German Jewish community in the United States with its second identity crisis. German Jews became understandably ambivalent over their proud German identity, and welcomed the opportunity to close ranks with the acculturated descendants of the Eastern European Jews. Just as two generations before, German Jews organized for the relief of the Eastern European refugee of the Czarist pogroms, now the Eastern European Jewish community organized relief and rescue work on behalf of the Jews of Germany, and wherever Jews were the victims of Nazi terror.

Segregation—or congregation? Meanwhile the Jewish community in the United States moved toward further harmony-in-diversity, and displayed a cohesiveness which appeared somehow to violate the sociological laws of acculturation, and to somehow imply a rejection of the "American way of life." Epithets of "closed community," "gilded ghetto," and "self-segregation" suggest that the observers are looking at the Jewish community "through Gentile eyes." Erich Rosenthal, for example, asserts that the aim of Jewish education seems to be "to implant Jewish self-consciousness rather than Judaism . . ." He quotes a rabbi from Chicago's North Side who ascribes the voluntary segregation of Jews in his community to the fear that the free mingling of their children with a Gentile majority would lead to inter-marriage.[25] Glazer likewise laments the fact that today's Jews live in a "closed community" and attributes the "enormous system of organization" to a fear of intermarriage, "and the consequent desire to supply a full social life within the Jewish community, for one's children":

The structure of Jewish organizational life has, in recent decades, expanded to the point where a Jewish organization exists to parallel almost every non-Jewish one. Thus, Jewish children may go to a Jewish nursery school, school-agers will attend Sunday and afternoon schools, and an ever-growing proportion attend Jewish day schools; the high school element will be urged to attend dances and participate in Jewish youth groups. The college element . . . has all-Jewish fraternities and sororities and Hillel centers. After college, where the opportunity for meeting non-Jews is greatest in contemporary American Jewish social life, the network of associations closes in again. After marriage, there are country clubs, synagogues, charitable organizations, social organizations—all Jewish.[26]

Glazer expresses something akin to a romantic nostalgia for the comfortable niche enjoyed by a relative handful of Spanish and German Jews in America prior to the Eastern European immigration. There is likewise a note of discomfort in Rosenthal's description of the "self-segregation" of Jews in the United States. Cahnman disagrees with the Glazer-Rosenthal viewpoint, suggesting that the term "congregation" better describes the residential habits of a group which maintains "voluntary association with [their] own kind."[27]

Cahnman reviews Rosenthal's study of Jews in the Chicago area, pointing to their preference for residential congregation. Some want to live near Jewish institutions, especially synagogues, some want Jewish neighbors, some presumably want Jewish shopping facilities. The Jew's attraction to suburbia represents less a wish to live among Gentiles than an orientation toward a high-status neighborhood; if a high-status Jewish neighborhood is available, the Jew accepts it or may even prefer it. Suburbia, says Cahnman, symbolizes the [Jew's] desire to enjoy the best of two worlds.[28]

Anticipating Cahnman's viewpoint, Greifer observed in 1955 that the settlement of Jews in suburban Philadelphia followed a pattern of *congregation*, "as friend followed friend, and relative moved near relative. . . . I know of several pioneering Jewish families," Greifer adds, "that settled in new suburban communities but after a few years moved back, at great personal loss, to localities more heavily populated by Jews. Apparently the failure of additional Jewish families to settle in the new communities isolated the pioneers from Jewish contacts and communal institutions."[29]

Wessel describes the experience of upper middle class Jews who first escape from Jewish neighborhoods, and later begin to seek residence near each other:

Is it that a close, warm community offers security for children

and for families who have suffered from discriminatory conduct? "We made a mistake bringing up our children in
Gentile communities; they have been hurt. The early friendships don't count. When returning from college, they do not
know where to turn for friends."[30] . . . [Wessel says she] has
heard this same comment in New Jersey, in Connecticut, and
in England from families in which all members had presumably achieved complete acculturation; indeed, had planned
family life to achieve it without denying membership in a
Jewish religious community.[31]

Like Glazer and Rosenthal, Tumin attributes the rise of elite
Jewish residential areas to *negative* feelings between Jews and
Gentiles. To Tumin, elite Jewish suburbs house "rejected as-
pirants" to membership in the elite groups, whose opportunity
to join the elite groups "has been illegitimately cut off."[32] Other
observers of Jewish life (Cahnman, Wessel, Greifer, Gans, Lewin)
would probably insist that this view overlooks the *positive*
feelings that bring Jews together—for Jews have habits, attitudes,
values, and goals which can be fully understood, shared, ap-
plauded, and appreciated only by other Jews. It is too easy to
say that ethnic neighborhood patterns are the result of fear
and rejection. Gans asserts that "no one has ever studied why
one community or subdivision gains Jewish residents while another area is avoided."[33]

Community size and conformity pressure. In Kramer and
Leventman's study of the highly organized Jewish community
of a Midwestern American city dubbed North City, the investigators feel sure that the 20,000 Jews of North City "live in
a more highly structured and clearly delineated community than
do the majority of [big city] American Jews. . ." North City
is large enough "to permit the development of a complex institutional structure parallel to that of the larger community, but
not large enough to allow many to escape the network of
institutional affiliation" and take their identity for granted.[34]
Glazer had earlier observed that "in the smaller cities Jews have
always been a captive audience for each other . . .

In Nashville, for example, with less than three thousand Jews
and three synagogues, one-half of the families are members

of more than one synagogue (many, of all three). . . . There
are so few Jews that most of them know each other and any
individual finds it hard to resist the pressure, from those few
involved, to help (or save) a Jewish institution.[35]

Glazer warns against an uncritical use of "conformity" as an
explanatory concept. ". . . The existence of a captive audience
. . . in which each Jew lives his life among other Jews, is only
part of the story. There must be some bond of feeling among
all Jews before some of them can arouse the guilt-feelings of
others and so gain their support for some Jewish institution.
Unless this bond of feeling exists, the principle of the captive
audience will not operate. . . . There would be no conformity
if there did not exist this bond that makes Jews feel part of the
same group."[36]

Even in the smallest communities in the United States, according to a survey by Shosteck, the spirit of congregation is evident in
Jewish life through the vehicle of organization life. "Where towns
are too small to support an organization or a synagogue, it is the
common practice for Jews to affiliate in nearby places, or for Jews
of several neighboring towns to combine in the support of an
organization."[37] Seven out of ten respondents (small town B'nai
B'rith members) belong to at least one more local Jewish group
in addition to B'nai B'rith; either religious, Zionist, or Jewish
War Veterans. The tendency to hold membership in Jewish organizations was correlated directly with age, income, and educational attainment.[38]

America is different. One measure of the cohesiveness of the
larger Jewish community of the United States is the number of
channels of communication which are kept open through periodicals addressed to various segments of the Jewish group. In
1956 a study conducted by the Common Council for American
Unity "listed 228 periodicals—ranging from weeklies to quarter-
lies and publications of irregular frequency, not counting mimeographed leaflets and bulletins—published by or for ethnic groups
in English. Fully 128 of these were put out by and for Jews, which
meant that the Jews alone had a larger press in English than all
other ethnic groups *combined*. Of the 75 ethnic weeklies appearing in English, Jews had 50."[39]

Sherman makes the point that for other ethnic groups in the United States, the acquisition of English brought an end to their group identity. For the Jews of the United States, on the other hand, the acquisition of English served to unite a group of "previously fragmented, separate Jewish colonies," Spanish, German or Yiddish speaking, ". . . into a consolidated Jewish community."

Among all other ethnic groups, language was the very heart of their ethnic culture; in Jewish culture language never occupied so important a position. This is why it has been possible for the Jews to be the only group in this country to create its own ethnic culture in English.[40]

Belief and belongingness. In 1966 *Commentary* published a symposium on "The State of Jewish Belief," consisting of statements by 38 leading American rabbis, who had been asked to comment on such *religious* issues as (a) the Torah as divine revelation, (b) the Jews as the chosen people of God, (c) the distinctive qualities of Judaism as a religion, and (d) the relevance of the "God is dead" issue to Judaism. The explicit intent of this symposium was to focus on Judaism as a system of belief and practice, to *counterbalance* the widespread current emphasis on Jewishness—"that is, Jewish identity, understood historically and sociologically. . . ."[41]

Despite the editors' efforts to direct their contributors' attention away from the topic of Jewishness, at least twelve of the contributor rabbis (or approximately one-third) used the occasion to register their conviction that there can be no meaningful separation between Jewish belief and belongingness. A sampling of such statements follows:

[Judaism] would lose immeasurably by severing its essential connection with the life and experience of the Jewish people. . . . To be a Jew is not merely to assent to a creed . . . [One] must identify himself . . . with all Jews in the world today, whatever they believe or practice, even if they renounce belief and practice.[42]

[Judaism] is not realizable by the individual, but only by a group, a people, a community that makes its realization a

communal responsibility. . . . Judaism had to become a religion of a people, if it was to be at all.[43]

Peoplehood is the constant element in Jewish civilization.
Within its context, religion evolves.[44]

In this age of waiting there is really one task for Jews, as a
continuing community of believers. It is to eschew theological
or ideological definitions of Judaism, which are particularly
impossible in a period of general intellectual confusion and
uncertainty, and to turn to the two things Jews can do: to
reforge the link of personal knowledge and experience of the
inherited Jewish learning and to maintain the Jewish community in being, as a distinctive entity.[45]

[In Judaism] the basic unit is not the individual, but the
group into which he is born . . . [and through which he de-
velops] his fundamental value system, his basic attitudes, and
his general outlook on life. It is the group which provides him
with the emotional support he requires, and which helps develop within him a sense of responsibility for his actions.[46]

The entire people of Israel is entered into the moral covenant with God. . . . The individual . . . cannot function without the community. His very communion with God can be
achieved only through his community. Neither the solitariness
of individual salvation nor the rootlessness of abstract universalism fulfills the terms of the covenant.[47]

The greatest danger to Judaism is that so many Jews have
lost their sense of Jewish particularity . . .   . . . Jewishness,
like the Jewish religious act, is the concrete reality from which
Judaism arises. Ultimately it is the *mitzvah*-performing Jewish
community which will determine the nature of that abstract
scheme of values which men call Judaism.[48]

Judaism has been rightly defined as 'religious ethnicism,'
but this does not form a mixture that can be isolated into two
distinct components. Instead, we are confronted here with an
organic whole that cannot be broken down into its constituent
parts without destroying the very life of the organism involved.[49]

Elaborating on Rabbi Arthur Hertzberg's warning against "theological or ideological definitions of Judaism . . . in a period of general intellectual confusion and uncertainty" (see fourth citation above) , Rabbi Harold M. Schulweis deplored theological preoccupations with "sin and salvation, redemption and eschatology . . . [as] a weakening of Jewish communal consciousness in favor of personal encounters . . . [as a] theological effort to purge Judaism of 'Jewishness' . . . [and therefore a serious threat] to Jewish self-understanding and conduct. For beneath the attack on Jewish 'ethnicism,' " Schulweis warned, "lies the threat to the unifying role which peoplehood plays and to the civilizational character of Judaism . . . . . . The social advantage of making Judaism a religion like all other religions," he concluded, "is the newest mode of unhealthy collective assimilation which threatens the uniqueness and authenticity of Jewish religious civilization."[50]

It seems clear, therefore, that the distinction made by the *Commentary* editors—between Jewishness as a sociological or historical phenomenon, and Judaism as a system of belief and practice—is an artificial and misleading one in the judgment of a substantial group of contemporary rabbis (Orthodox, Conservative, and Reform) who seem convinced that without a feeling of peoplehood the practice of Judaism is impossible. We must therefore note that Jewish group solidarity—which would tend to discourage intermarriage—is not only a historical and sociological phenomenon, but is defined by contemporary rabbis as a religious imperative.

COMMUNITY SOLIDARITY IN THE UNITED STATES

The present-day Jewish community in the United States is overwhelmingly a native-born, English-speaking population, of which it is estimated that 90 per cent are of Eastern European origin.[51] In 1957 the Bureau of Census asked a nationwide sample of the population to voluntarily state their religion. Results showed 93 marriages in which both partners gave their religion as Jewish, for every seven Jewish-Gentile marriages.[52] Sklare has correctly observed that this figure of seven per cent should hardly be taken as a *current* rate of intermarriage since the Census tally included couples who were married half a century ago in Czarist Russia "as well as people living in the wide world of the fourth generation." He conjectures that the current rate is at least double that of the Census Bureau's cumulative rate of 7.2.[53]

Compared with Sklare's estimate of 15 per cent as a current rate of Jewish-Gentile intermarriage, Rabbi Gordon estimated that the national average would reach 10 per cent by the late 1960's.[54] To Gentile investigators, the Jewish group shows "an amazingly high degree of endogamy—more so than is attained by any other white minority group in America. . . . Even if the intermarriage rate were to increase to 20 or 25 even 30 per cent," Kennedy has pointed out, "this would still mean that 80 or 75 or 70 per cent of all Jewish marriages were in-marriages—and this also would, I feel sure, still be the highest degree of endogamy reached by any other white minority group."[55]

While Gentile observers view with amazement the contemporary Jew's high degree of endogamy, Jewish observers view the present state of affairs with alarm, as if their standard of comparison was not "any other white minority group in America," but the norms of the *shtetl*, where complete enforcement of endogamy was the standard, and intermarriage was an abnormal and rare occurrence, and either illegal or accompanied by apostacy. While Gentile observers may regard the Jews as a religious group, Jews regard themselves as members of a community—and view intermarriage not as the diffusion of a religion but as the weakening of a community.

Statistics on intermarriage, moreover, cover only *mixed* marriages—those in which only one spouse claims to be Jewish. But the "intermarriage problem," as viewed through Jewish eyes, also includes marriage partnerships between a born Jew and a convert to Judaism, marriages which are tallied in the statistical surveys as endogamous. Marriage between a born Jew and a convert to Judaism—"the religiously endogamous intermarriage"— has the full sanction of Jewish religious authority, yet such a marriage is part of the intermarriage problem because it is viewed by the community as a deviation from the endogamous tradition.

Commenting upon Kennedy's New Haven study, Glazer and Moynihan note that there has been no increase in intermarriage in New Haven since 1930 "although in this period the Jews of

New Haven became much more acculturated and prosperous. This pattern sharply distinguishes the Jews of the United States from those of other countries in which Jews have achieved wealth and social position, such as Holland, Germany, Austria, and Hungary in the twenties. There the intermarriage rates were phenomenally high."[56] The above observation appears to support Glazer and Moynihan's thesis that "the ethnic group in American society [must be regarded *not* as] a survival from the age of mass immigration but as *a new social form*."[57]

RELIGION VERSUS KINSHIP

Although the Jews are not an actively proselytizing group, Jewish religious law is far more congenial to the induction of a sincere convert—*ger tsedek*—than is the Jewish community congenial to intermarriage between a born Jew and a convert to Judaism.

"Although mixed marriages are prohibited . . . a member of another faith who desires to be converted to Judaism must (according to traditional ritual) appear before a rabbi and state his desire to be converted. The rabbi will then provide for his instruction in the elements of Jewish law, belief, and practice. Before admitting him to the Jewish fold, the rabbi must warn him of the severe discipline of Judaism and the difficulties involved in adherence to the Jewish faith. If the applicant persists in his desire to enter the Jewish faith, the rabbi will arrange for the ceremony of proselytization. A male applicant must be circumsized. According to the traditional ritual followed by Orthodox and Conservative Jews, both male and female applicants become proselytes by immersion in a pool of running water, declaring that they are performing the ceremony in order to be admitted into the Jewish faith, and reciting as they emerge from the water the benediction, 'Blessed art Thou, O Lord our God, King of the Universe, who didst sanctify us with Thy commandments, and has commanded us regarding the ceremonial immersion of the proselyte.' "[58]

Reform rabbis offer an easier route to conversion, and some Reform rabbis defend a policy which permits them to officiate at mixed marriages.[59] One can point to various places in the Hebrew

Bible in which mixed marriage is forbidden or denounced,[60] but one must also acknowledge that the book of Ruth is a eulogy to the faithful convert to Judaism. Jewish law makes no distinction between the proselyte and the born Jew. The faithful convert must be "welcomed as a spiritual son of Abraham," writes Rabbi Israel Porush. "It is explicitly forbidden to vex him in any way on account of his descent. 'One may not say to the descendant of proselytes, Remember the deeds of your fathers, for it is written, "And a stranger thou shalt not wrong, nor shalt thou oppress him." ' "[61]

But adherence to the religion of Judaism does not make a person authentically Jewish in the eyes of the Jewish community, which (a) makes an implicit distinction between Judaism and Jewishness, and (b) defines Jewishness according to how thoroughly one's kinship is bound up with other Jews. By this implicit standard, the intermarried convert to Judaism is at best only half Jewish because only half of his extended family is Jewish. Hence the distress of those converts to Judaism who discover that despite their best efforts to lead a thoroughly Jewish life, they are not recognized as being "really" Jewish.

IS IT GOOD FOR THE JEWS?

Our survey of Jewish life in the *shtetl* and in America should give us perspective by which we can evaluate popular interpretations of Jewish attitudes toward intermarriage. Rabbi Gordon expresses the widely held view that ascribes Jewish opposition to intermarriage to "memories acquired through historical and contemporary events in which Jews suffered physical and psychological pain and anguish at the hands of non-Jewish persecutors. . . . Intermarriage with persons whose ancestors or families had directly or indirectly been responsible for such acts was generally regarded as equivalent to treason to the Jewish people."[62]

While the above argument has a ring of plausability, it does not account for the application of the intermarriage taboo to members of other persecuted groups, *e.g.*, Negroes, Orientals, or Armenians. In the context of the *shtetl* heritage, it would seem that the Jews' negative feelings about intermarriage stem more directly from a value system according to which marriage is by no means a private affair—marriage is a partnership between two members of a community, and it is also an alliance between their extended families, who look upon the marriage of their offspring as a unique and precious opportunity to enhance family prestige, enrich family life, and strengthen the bonds of community solidarity. (From this point of view, intermarriage is not so much an act of "treason to the Jewish people," as it is an insult to one's *mishpocho*.)

In the Jewish tradition it is a great *mitzvah*—an act of special goodness—to sponsor the marriage of an orphan. Aside from his lack of dowry, the orphan is disadvantaged as a marriage partner for his lack of *mishpocho* in a society in which *machotonoshaft* is a prized by-product of marriage. A devout convert—a *ger tsedek* —might to this extent be likened to an orphan, in that his marriage is not likely to establish harmonious extended family relations, and is unlikely to contribute to the cohesiveness of the Jewish community. To the Jewish in-laws it may be as if the convert's family "did not exist," a fact which may be of little moment from a Western standpoint, but from a Jewish standpoint may evoke a sense of loss and isolation.

A Jewish professor recalls: 'Three years ago my neighbor's only son fell in love with a Gentile girl who was quite willing to convert to Judaism. His parents were distraught, and came to me, a fellow Jew and a college professor, for help. I told them that their religious obligation was to receive a faithful convert on the same terms as a born Jew. The couple married and moved to another city. The old father died. His widow lives a solitary, lonely life. If her son had married a born Jew, the young couple might still have moved to another city, the old father might still have come to the end of his days, but the widowed mother might now have someone to relate to as machotonim, and this would be good for her.'

The Gentile partner of a mixed marriage, Getrude confesses that she finds the in-group behavior of her husband's family irritating, and would rather not visit them. It seems only fair, in her mind, that she should therefore not expect her husband and children to spend much time with *her* family. Accordingly, it appears that Gertrude and her husband have worked out a tacit agreement that they play no favorites and visit with neither of their families.[63]

A Jewish parent is entitled to feel some uncertainty over a young Gentile who in the best of faith has taken on the new roles of marriage partner and convert to Judaism. Who can but guess at the depth and durability of his Jewishness, of his ability to function as a Jewish spouse, a Jewish parent, and member of an extended Jewish family? Conversion to the religion of Judaism follows a well-established and explicit program of acts, but there are no well-defined norms to guide induction into the ethnic community, and this transition becomes the occasion for embarrassment and uncertainty on both sides.

This concern over how the stranger will fit into the life of the group is not altogether a *shtetl* survival. The concept of peoplehood is a biblical concept, and the modern rabbi quotes *Pirke Aboth* when he says, "Do not separate thyself from the community." When viewed through Gentile eyes, Jewish group loyalty may be seen as neurotic dependency. Thus clinical psychologist Georgene Seward regards the Jew's reluctance to cast off his ethnic identity as evidence of "a heritage of persecution [which binds the Jew] forever to 'his people.' "[64] (Students of American Negro life recognize the sad truth, however, that oppression cannot be depended upon to generate group cohesiveness.) Seward admits that "the so-called exile neurosis" is poorly understood and she therefore issues a call for psychological research on "relationships between social levels, Jewish practices . . . family structure, personality structure, and goal strivings."[65]

The cohesiveness of the Jewish community is an enduring social phenomenon, sustained by a tradition of thought and behavior peculiarly adapted to minority group living. Group solidarity is a source of security, recognition, and personal fulfillment to its members. It serves as an alliance against the threat of a sometimes unfriendly and occasionally hostile majority, but to say that organized Jewish life is maintained in the United States to oppose intermarriage would be something like asserting that the government of the United States is maintained to block Red China.

Kinship feelings in all its manifestations—*nachas, machotono-*

shaft, mishpocho, congregation, community, peoplehood—lies at the heart of the Jewish ethos (and may even be a mental health resource rather than an aspect of neurotic suffering). From this standpoint, Jewish opposition to intermarriage can be accounted for without regard to racial purity or individual salvation. An opposition which seems so uncanny, unreasonable, and illiberal, becomes quite understandable when viewed as a by-product of that most familiar Jewish norm: *group solidarity.*[66]

JEWISH GOALS IN AMERICA: PARADOX OR DILEMMA?

Several investigators and observers of the Jewish group (Bamberger, Barron, Kirshenbaum, Glazer, and Shanks) have expressed concern (if not alarm) over the spectacle of an energetic and intelligent people struggling for mutually incompatible goals. Can the Jew champion both integration and separation in his adaptation to the American social environment?

To Shanks, American Jews face "the problem of being led to waters but forbidden to drink. We have encouraged the cultural and social contacts which lead to intermarriage while condemning the intermarriage itself. It is ironical indeed that the very programs so favored by the Jewish group to reduce prejudice and anti-Semitism also have the latent function of increasing the temptation of intermarriage . . ." Shanks amplified his argument with specific examples:

Campaigns to abolish religious restrictions in fraternities and sororities; to abolish college quota systems (instead of setting up Jewish colleges) ; pressure to eradicate gentlemen's agreements on real estate covenants,[67] country club memberships, and resort restrictions; interfaith cultural and social activities —all have the beneficial result of helping the Jew and Gentile understand each other . . . [but also increase] the social and cultural contacts that lead to intermarriage.[68]

"The problem of living in and associating with a Gentile world without being absorbed by it is faced by no group so directly as by unmarried Jewish young men and women. The psychological toll which this problem exacts from the minds and hearts of these young people should not be underestimated," says Shanks. "It is a problem for which there are no blanket answers. Each individual case must find its own best solution."[69]

We return now to a question we posed at the outset of this study: are these observers pointing to a paradox of Jewish life— a puzzle that can be solved by looking below the surface; are they pointing to a dilemma—an arduous decision which must somehow be faced; or might they even be pointing to a self-defeating ambivalence—like the behavior of a young man who courts a girl and at the same time supplies her with good reasons for rejecting him?

The balancing of opposites. The manifestation of a contradiction in Jewish group life will not surprise those students of the Jewish tradition who see "the balancing of opposites" as a unique characteristic of Jewish thought and action. Child of tradition and rebel against it, skeptic and mystic, intellectual and sensualist, businessman and philanthropist. There is something strongly Jewish about choosing to cope with contradictions, striving to *transcend* the dualities of life, rather than accept a discrete choice between alternatives.[70]

In *American Judaism,* Glazer points to a number of contradictions, incongruities, and dilemmas in Jewish life. American Jews fight for conditions which lead to intermarriage, yet strive to maintain themselves apart.[71] When the Reform movement strove to recast Judaism as a religion without tribalism, its leaders carefully deleted from its prayer book all references to exile, all prayers to restore the Jews to the Holy Land, replaced the concept of peoplehood with the concept of co-religionists. "Even in the formulated positions of Reform Judaism," comments Glazer, "there were interesting anomalies indicating that Reform rabbis were still held back by some kind of primal attachment to the Jewish people."[72] He cites the Reform positions on both intermarriage and circumcision as positive evidence of "a simple unreflecting attachment to the Jewish people" untouched by the rational spirit of Reform.[73] In the Eastern European immigrant group, many Jews were incongruously "both religious and radical. . . . It was not uncommon for a Jewish worker to read an antireligious Yiddish newspaper, vote Socialist, join a socialist union, and yet attend the synagogue weekly, or even daily, and observe most of the Jewish law."[74]

The contemporary philosopher of Jewish mysticism, Abraham Joshua Heschel, asserts that "Jewish thinking and living can only be adequately understood in terms of a dialectical pattern, containing opposite or contrasted properties.

> ... [a *polarity* of contrasting ideas and events] lies at the very heart of Judaism, of *mitzvah* and sin, of *kavanah* and deed, of regularity and spontaneity, of uniformity and individuality, of *halacha* and *agada,* of law and inwardness, of love and fear, of understanding and obedience, of joy and discipline, of the good and the evil drive, of time and eternity.[75]

"Jewish tradition contains many tensions," Malin observes.[76] Jewish writers, he continues, "are torn by dualities—exile and Land, head and heart, past and present." They do not accept the Jewish God but they give their readers that "sense of mystery" and "legacy of wonder" which Heschel identifies with the Jewish religion.[77] The "transcendence of polarities" is identified as an underlying theme in the poems of Karl Shapiro, who (in "The Confirmation") for example "counterpoises masturbation to divinity."[78]

According to Malin, Leslie Fiedler offers a theory of literary criticism which describes Isaac Rosenfeld, Karl Shapiro, and Franz Kafka as bearers of "a new faith which attempts to rise above dualities . . . [a faith which] *cares* about the healthy union of opposites, suggesting that Joy results from exposure to Wholeness."[79] Malin conjectures that as Jewish writers "rebel against spiritual moments" they paradoxically *affirm* them. Once again he quotes Fiedler's comment that Jewish-American writers, like Simone Weil, "teach the uncomfortable truth that the belief of many atheists is closer to a true love of God and a true sense of his nature, than the kind of easy faith, which, never having *experienced* God, hangs a label bearing his name on some childish fantasy."[80]

Acculturation without assimilation. In her psychological theory of occupations, Ann Roe expresses dissatisfaction with concepts of "adaptation" or "survival" as a basis for understanding the complexity of man's occupational structure. One must hypothesize, Roe suggests, some sort of drive for exploring one's capacity for mastering progressively more complex modes of living.[81] If the tension of uncertainty increases the feeling of gratification that comes with success, this would indeed lead to a progressive rise in the person's subsequent "level of aspiration." (As Alfred Adler put it, success gives one courage to seek greater successes.)

Shifting from the occupational adjustment of the individual to the social adjustment of a group, let us note that the Jews have overcome many complex and tension-laden tasks of social adjustment. Given this cultural history, does the Jew *need* a more complex and challenging social goal than simple retreat into the safety of separation, or full assimilation into the dominant group? Perhaps the striving for both integration *and* identity represents a peculiarly Jewish goal, a more fitting challenge for the Jew's resourcefulness and creativity in his adaptation to a Gentile world.

Participation without absorption has been proposed as a goal for Jews in the United States by a number of students of Jewish life and leaders of Jewish groups. The argument has been made that by maintaining their ethnic identity Jews not only sustain something of value for themselves but also maintain a source of enrichment for the American culture. Rabbi Mordecai Kaplan expresses confidence that

> Judaism can be rendered so rich in content and so inspiring in purpose that it can afford to encourage complete cultural and social integration in the life of the non-Jewish majority.

> Reconstructionism is intent upon bringing Judaism to that high point of development which will enable Jews to live comfortably in two civilizations. It is convinced that the Jewish tradition and culture . . . can . . . contribute much of value to the totality of American life . . . [and] that American culture . . . [can] make an important contribution to the totality of Jewish life, as other cultures with which Jews came into contact did in earlier epochs of Jewish history.[82]

A generation ago Reform leader Rabbi Stephen Wise expressed

his deep misgivings that the Jews in America "developed too deep a passion to be like unto the majority people in the midst of which [they] lived. Too much that was Jewish was forsworn; and under the aegis of liberation or emancipation, too much that was un-Jewish was assimilated." Only as a distinct group, the Rabbi argued, can the Jews make their distinct contribution to American life; assimilation is therefore "treason" to the Jews' creative capacity:

> The time is come for us to behold the truth that we are not to suffer ourselves to be consumed and devoured, overborne and assimilated. Rather are we to be a constitutive and creative factor, a transforming force in American life. We must cease to think of finding shelter in America and begin to think of our people as enrichers and not beneficiaries of America. As a people, we too have been docile and acquiescent instead of being inflexibily self-insistent as Jews.

> Never was there [a] less valid figure or illustration than the figure of 'the melting pot' applied to America. To accept it were treason to our capacity for contribution to the treasures of American life. We would be more than Jewish clay in the hands of alien potters. We would be potters shaping the vessel of our fate as men and Jews.[83]

Some thirty years after Rabbi Wise's impassioned and eloquent appeal, Sklare matter-of-factly ascribes to American Jewry the "dual ideal of full participation in society and the preservation of Jewish identity." Perhaps the cultural climate of the United States provides the unique opportunity for the Jews to implement this design for living. In Europe "assimilation was the price demanded from the Jews for their legal and social emancipation."[84] America is different; from its beginnings it has been ethnically diversified,[85] it has given haven to religious minorities; even its old Anglo-Saxon immigration branched into distinctive regional types: New Englander, Southerner, Midwesterner, Westerner. Jews are also different from other immigrant groups. Their historical experience and group cohesiveness enables them to accomplish "through accommodation and adaptation" an adjustment to a culture which other groups can achieve only through assimilation.[86]

The goal of acculturation calls for the adoption of the manners and customs of the majority, even in the conduct of religious ritual. The Reform movement has been criticized for going too far in patterning its ritual after a Protestant model. The Conservative movement in America, according to Sklare (1955), has likewise been mainly concerned with incorporating Western standards of *decorum* into the traditional synagogue ritual. In his novel *Remember Me to God*, Kaufmann describes this touching episode: a suburban Jewish congregation lets their assistant rabbi go because he talks with a "Jewish accent"; they did not want their Gentile guests to hear the nasal voice of this foreign-born rabbi intone, "We inwoke Dy diwine blessing."[87] Even an Orthodox congregation, it must be supposed, would to some extent choose its leaders according to how they look when seen through Gentile eyes.

THE MIXED NEIGHBORHOOD: COMPROMISE OR SYMBOL OF A BI-CULTURAL LIFE STYLE?

How does this ideal of acculturation without assimilation, identity without identification, integration without absorption operate in contemporary Jewish life as social scientists observe it? Belth interprets the Cornell Middletown studies to demonstrate that the Jew "can live happily only if he learns to become a 'comfortable participator' in both the Jewish and general community."[88] Kramer and Leventman's North City respondents expressed a preference for living in an ethnically mixed neighborhood. What these third-generation Jewish respondents describe is *not* a compromise between the comfort of an in-group enclave and the challenge of seeking membership in the majority group; they seem to attach a positive value to learning to live as Jews in a Gentile world.

I prefer not to be in a single racial area. It's ridiculous to be with Jews only; you meet them anyway.

Children get a better outlook on life from mixed neighborhoods. They have to learn to deal with non-Jews in life.[89]

Kramer and Leventman affirm the observation of Wessel that Jews who have lived in Gentile neighborhoods come to prefer mixed neighborhoods. "Although many [of North City's third generation respondents] were brought up in Gentile neighborhoods, only one of them prefers to live in one now. They believe their own children will be happier if they have Jewish friends in the neighborhood, something they missed in their own childhood . . . They justify their preference with a recollection of earlier experiences in Gentile neighborhoods:"

You feel a certain isolation in a Gentile neighborhood.

You're only a neighbor [in a Gentile neighborhood], not friends. It doesn't matter to me, but the children will need friends and these are likely to be Jewish.

I want the kids to have some affiliation with a Jewish community, some tradition such as drive for college and certain occupations. These are the good parts of the heritage and are found more easily when you live with Jews.[90]

His study of small-town New York State Jews leads Peter I. Rose to a conclusion which parallels that of Kramer and Leventman. Rose emphasizes the difference between the classical marginal man who lives on the periphery of two antagonistic cultures, and the *bi-cultural* man who "wants to remain a hyphenated American," wants to internalize the best of two cultures:

He is more a part of his community than he is apart from it. He is far more assimilated to the Gentile milieu than his urban cousin. But . . . he remains a Jew.
. . . He enjoys the advantages of sharing two "cups of life" and, in a word, is bi-cultural. This duality (rather than marginality) causes the majority of respondents to come to agreement with one who stated:

You see, we feel we have the best of both . . . Judaism with all its traditions, its stress on culture, on learning, on freedom. . . . And the fact that we live in a small town with nice people and good, clean air. . . . We wouldn't trade either for the world.[91]

Rose's respondents appeared to express "a firm conviction that Jewish identity should not only be maintained but intensified. Thus, while a high degree of informal interaction is practiced, the small-town Jews, like their urban co-religionists, are anxious for their children to keep the faith and to marry Jews. As a result they send them to Jewish summer camps and, when they are through with high school, encourage them to attend large, metropolitan universities."[92]

It seems safe to say [Rose concludes] that the small-town Jew is similar to the city-dwelling Jew to the extent that he wants his children to remain Jews. He is firmly opposed to inter-faith marriage. To him this represents either the confrontation of too many social problems or alienation from Judaism; both are considered highly undesirable. Complete assimilation into the Christian community is not the goal of the American Jew.[93]

To live comfortably in two civilizations, to prefer a mixed neighborhood to either a Jewish or Gentile neighborhood, to want both Jewish and Gentile friends; in the language of Kramer and Leventman the bi-cultural Jew lives in two social universes and addresses himself to two status audiences. According to their analysis, the immigrant generation of North City Jews addressed itself to the problem of survival, the second generation to the problem of security, the third generation to the problem of status not in the Jewish universe alone but in the eyes of the Gentile world as well.

Having chosen a mixed community, the bi-cultural Jew has thereby chosen to share the standards of his non-Jewish neighbors. He wants to adopt the norms that invite his neighbor's approval. He seeks to share a style of life with non-Jewish peers, and willingly subjects himself to the judgments of the larger society.[94] He would like to be an "equal" among Gentiles as well as a Jew among Jews. This calls for a kind of "social invisibility," identity without identification.

Kramer and Leventman inferred from the career outlook of North City's third generation Jews, a desire to adopt a more Gentile attitude toward earning a living and making money. A number of their respondents explicitly *contrasted* "their own philosophy of material gain with that of their fathers." Ambition for economic success seemed notably lacking in this group of 84 young men (average age 29.8 years, 82 per cent married). One-third expected to continue in their present occupational status. "Most of the rest want either to advance in their careers, to establish themselves independently in their professions, or to take over the family business. *Less than five per cent want to start their own businesses . . ."* (Italics added.)

They want to have "jobs they enjoy, and . . . sufficient time left over to spend with their families. . . ." Kramer and Leventman wonder how to interpret this "decline of economic tensions," these "lowered economic sights" of the third generation. Does it reflect their greater economic security, or does it betoken an insecurity that any display of aggressive ambition would violate the norm of the Gentile majority? As Kramer and Leventman see it, the third generation Jew of North City "concentrates on spending his money and finding out what it can do for him rather than on enlarging his income. This permits him to avoid incurring the hostility of his non-Jewish peers."[95]

"Social invisibility" and name-changing. Hyman Kaplan can strive diligently toward Americanization, but can his namesake hope for "social invisibility?" We are once more reminded of Kugelmass' interview study, reported in Chapter 1. Twenty-five respondents who had changed their name from an identifiably Jewish name to a distinctly Gentile one expressed—without exception—disappointment and chagrin over their name-change. "Life had not changed," and some reported that it now seemed clear to them that they had exaggerated the influence of anti-Semitism on their professional or business vicissitudes. While they had all had at least one year's experience with the new name, perhaps the majority of the respondents were still in an awkward period of transition. Or does the adoption of a boldly Anglo-Saxon name in itself indicate unrealistic hopes about quick alteration of identity? (Perhaps a more satisfied group of name-changers could be found among those who had traded Rabinovitch for Robbin rather than for Rayburn.)

Kugelmass reports an estimate that only one-half of Jews in

America bear recognizably Jewish names, and reports the astonishment of rabbis serving as military chaplains, at how frequently Jewish dog-tag identification is worn by men who bear distinctly non-Jewish names.

"Social invisibility" also requires that one's physical appearance not be unequivocally Jewish. In Kaufmann's novel, Richard's father chides his wife for boasting that their pretty teen-age daughter doesn't look at all Jewish. Mrs. Amsterdam responds with annoyance, "So go find me a Jew that wants to look Jewish. . . . You should be Jewish in the heart, not in the face."[96]

Variations in the bi-cultural experiment. The problem of living in two social universes—with both Jewish and Gentile friends and group affiliations—is complex and its resolution allows for a good deal of variation. Who knows what actually constitute the implicit values of the Gentile status audience, and which of those values are worth striving for? One must decide to what extent he has the aptitude to meet the social requirements of the elite group. In practice one finds much variation in the extent to which third generation Jews commit themselves to the behavioral standards of the majority group.

One need not wait for access into an elite group to share its status rituals and style of life. Dean observed within the Jewish community of Elmira "the occasional parallel development . . . of organizational forms or activities in emulation of the majority group. If Jews are not accepted in the Junior League, The Women's Council may adopt projects that are remarkably like those of the Junior League." It is too easy to leap to the conclusion (as Dean seems to do) that parallel group practices occur "because of restrictive majority group practices."[97] Undoubtedly there are Jews who would prefer to act out the status rituals of the elite within the comfortable surroundings of their own group, just as there are Jews who would prefer a smoked meat that *tastes* like bacon but is actually made from kosher beef.

How much to retain of Jewish norms and practices, and how to incorporate them into one's everyday life is another complex problem for the dweller in two civilizations. Sanua tells of a visit with a well-known scholar at Columbia University, to illustrate how "contradictions are constantly juxtaposed" in the lives of Jews who live in two worlds:

As the interviewer was about to take a few notes the scholar, with some embarrassment, observed it was the Sabbath and said he would not want his children to see anyone writing, since this would set a bad example. According to Jewish tradition any work, including writing, is prohibited on the Sabbath. . . . While opposing writing as a bad example, the scholar allowed his own children to watch a televised football game, against religious injunction. Although the pencil was taboo, television was not.

On the basis of his own observation, Sanua describes individuals whose adjustment to living in two worlds makes them "indistinguishable from non-Jews as long as they are outside their own milieu. But once they are in their own homes" they adopt the behaviors and rituals of the Jewish tradition.[98]

Rabbi Zalman Schachter comments sympathetically on the private compromises Jews make between Jewish and Gentile norms of behavior:

When someone who eats in a non-kosher restaurant orders beefsteak instead of pork chops because he 'keeps kosher,' I can no longer laugh at him. His choice was occasioned by a sort of low-level, yet very genuine, concern not to eat of 'impure beasts.' When he asks that his steak be well done—so that he can obey 'eat no blood'—I respect him even more. When he refuses butter on it and milk with his coffee because of "seethe not the kid in its mother's milk," I respect him still further. And if he orders a scale-bearing fish instead of meat, I see him struggling honestly to do [God's] will.[99]

Gentile friends. Contrary to the formulations of Newcomb, Krech, and Crutchfield et al., Kramer and Leventman found that North City Jews who maintain Gentile friends find their status *enhanced* in the eyes of their fellow Jews. This means, of course, that their fellow Jews share the norm that Gentile friendships are desirable. One upper-stratum North City Jew explained,

"Jews should honor such a person. It is about time we Jews got around and found out what *they* are like." Another added that it was the duty of Jews to break down anti-Semitic stereotypes by "letting *them* know that we're human too." The desire for Gentile friends was also couched in terms of personal achievement: "I could use a few Gentile friends, they'd help my business." "My friends would think I was pretty great if I had some Gentile friends."[100] North City's upper status Jews usually meet their Gentile friends through organizations. They "do not feel socially accepted by their Gentile neighbors unless they have already met as members of the same organization. . . . It is [therefore] small wonder that they view these memberships as a key to social acceptance."[101]

Kramer and Leventman report a steep rise, from the second to the third generation of North City Jews reporting that they have both Jewish and Gentile friends (18 to 70 per cent).[102] On the basis of their Lakeville study, however, Sklare and Greenblum found that Jews who refer to their "Gentile friend" are frequently referring to a person of Gentile origin who is a member of a Jewish clique, or to a convert to Judaism who has a Jewish husband and Jewish children. Sklare and Greenblum considered it "most remarkable . . . that in spite of being more acculturated than their parents and moving in a more mixed environment, [Lakeview's Jews] make their close friendships with Jews virtually as often as did their parents. Thus, while 87 per cent of the parents had most or all of their close friendships with Jews, the same holds true for 89 per cent of [the] respondents."[103]

In accounting for their all-Jewish friendship pattern, only one out of ten attributed it to Gentile exclusion. Typically, they had had many Gentile friends during adolescence. (". . . Almost four in ten . . . report that in adolescence only half, or less than half, of their circle of close friends consisted of Jews.") They considered it natural, normal, self-evident that Jewish adults befriend other Jewish people. Some emphasize common religio-ethnic heritage, others emphasize life styles and manners, common interests and standards, social tastes, closer family and home ties:

> My association with non-Jews has been good. But there's a warmth amongst Jews that couldn't be in a Gentile. A Gentile can't be as warm; he would have a different philosophy.[104]

We have Gentile friends, but we'd never think of mixing them. It wouldn't work. We're very small drinkers. We like to have a nice dinner and play cards. We'd feel self-conscious, especially if they'd lose.[105]

[A woman who as an adolescent had close Gentile friends, and still has Gentile acquaintances, says of her Jewish clique:] They wouldn't be able to speak as freely about politics and religion if non-Jews were present.

You can have difficulty when you have a non-Jew in the group. You can't use Jewish words without having to tell him all the time what they mean. . . . And sometimes you might give a kibitz about Gentiles, and this would be embarrassing.[106]

Respondents describe their feeling of self-consciousness in Gentile company—which Sklare and Greenblum interpret as a feeling of responsibility to enhance the Gentile image of the Jew:

'I have to be careful with my manners, my dress, my expressions,' says a middle-aged lawyer. He is active only in nonsectarian organizations, but he claims no close Gentile friends. 'I'm always on my guard as to whether I laugh too loud or my voice is too shrill,' says a minimally observant woman whose close friends are all Jewish. 'I feel that I have to count my words,' says a chemist's wife who observes hardly any religious practices, but has a predominantly Jewish friendship circle.[107]

. . . An unobservant businessman . . . observes about Gentiles, 'You have to be on guard and careful about subjects you discuss. I don't have the freedom of personality I have with Jews.' . . . A thoughtful young housewife . . . completely alienated from Jewish organizational and religious life . . . one of those respondents constituting the 7 per cent who do not have a predominantly or all-Jewish friendship circle . . . confesses, 'I'm less comfortable with non-Jews because you feel that they think of you as a Jew. Jews don't really think of you as a Jew.'[108]

Lower status Jews of North City "see no value in Gentile friendships for either the community or themselves. . . . 'We don't need *them,* we have our own friends.' . . . To cultivate Gentile friends is considered degrading by some [lower status Jews]. 'Are we ashamed of being Jewish?' "[109]

Marginality of the high-status Jew. Kramer and Leventman pinpoint a "major source of tension for high-status Jews," namely the discrepancy between their upper class position in the Jewish community and their relative lack of status in the Gentile world. The basis of this discrepancy is not anti-Semitism *per se,* but involves a difference in the standards of upper class membership. In the Jewish community of North City upper class membership is open to persons of *yichas atsmo*—persons who have earned this position through their own talents and earnings, who lavish their wealth on charities and otherwise satisfy the standards of the Jewish community for prestige and social leadership.

In the Gentile community, however, upper class membership is defined by a somewhat different set of determinants, including length of local residence (favoring the "old families") , old wealth, or prestigeful occupations. The upper class Jew therefore suffers the social insult of being treated as a social inferior by high status Gentiles. Dean quotes a rebuffed aspirant to recognition by the Gentile elite: "I sometimes feel like a prostitute. They'll call on me to lead their community chest campaign or help in the Red Cross. But when it comes to the country club, I'm not good enough for them."[110]

It is incorrect to suppose that the resentment which high status Jews feel toward Gentile society indicates "a desire for integration into that community." Kramer and Leventman argue that the upper status Jew is probably more interested in the likelihood that high-status treatment in the Gentile world would further enhance his status among high-status *Jews.*[111] In any case, it becomes apparent that the high-status Jew has a special need for the Jewish community, and is likely to represent a conservative force in Jewish community life.

The salaried professions. A significant difference between second and third generation Jews is the frequency with which the latter is a salaried professional, who must compete for advancement with Gentile colleagues. Unlike the world of business or the independent professions (e.g., medicine, law, dentistry, accounting), the salaried professions (teaching, engineering, journalism, advertising, science) place the Jew in a predominantly Gentile world where status tensions lead him to adopt the characteristics of his Gentile colleagues. This may designate finding Gentile friends, dating Gentile girls, and perhaps eventually acquiring a Gentile wife.

Does this sequence of experiences occur by design or by drift? It is quite likely that the salaried professions constitute a major avenue of departure from Jewish life. More often than business or the independent professions, the salaried professions require relocation, take their recruit away from his extended family and into the Gentile world. For those who seek separation from the Jewish community (what Slotkin, the Levinsons, and others have called "emancipation") entering a salaried profession provides an unequalled opportunity, and this motivation may also show itself in the choice of a Gentile mate. Undoubtedly there are men in the salaried professions who regard relocation as an unacceptable interference with their mode of life, and are tempted to accept the best local employment they can find rather than sever their Jewish bonds of kinship. (One would expect, for example, that Jewish professors teaching in institutions of their home-town would be more highly *in*married than their more geographically mobile Jewish colleagues.)

Identity and self-identification. Is it possible that as Jewish college students become increasingly acculturated, as they become better able to conceal their Jewish identity, they increasingly choose to identify themselves openly as Jews? Teitelbaum was led to believe so, when he compared the results of his 1950–51 survey with a study reported by Nathan in 1932. Polling 941 Jewish college students, scattered through 57 institutions, Nathan found that only one-third expressed the desire to reveal their Jewish identity openly. Teitelbaum's Northwestern survey showed that over one-half of Jewish students there "were unreservedly open about their Jewishness." Jewish students at urban and state universities polled by Teitelbaum in 1952 indicated by an overwhelming majority (80 to 92 per cent) that they openly identified themselves as Jews.[112]

Comparing his findings with those of Nathan, Teitelbaum observes that in 1932 Jews were "more marginally American than they are now." They "were living in the twilight zone of two, perhaps three, worlds." Teitelbaum asserts a belief that "the new generation of Jews that has arisen since 1932 is more secure in its Americanism. Besides," he adds, "the lesson of Hitlerism and fascism, namely, that the concealment of one's Jewishness is unavailing, has not gone entirely unlearned."[113]

The status orientation matrix. The negative chauvinist or assimilationist addresses himself to a Gentile status audience only. (Or as Rose and Rose put it, with a touch of humor, the negative chauvinist is " a Jew who will associate only with those Jews who will not associate with other Jews.") [115] The in-group Jew addresses himself to a Jewish status audience only. The bi-cultural Jew addresses himself to both a Jewish and a Gentile status audience. The marginal man—that classic figure in social psychology—might be described as a Jew who lives in chronic ambivalence over his Jewishness (cannot do without a Christmas tree but would rather call it a Hannukah bush) and feels rejected by Jews and Gentiles alike because of his uncertainty and inconsistency.

The various types of adjustment available to the Jew might be summarized in a status orientation matrix, adapted from Dean. Note that two cells are occupied by the assimilationist, and two by the bi-culturals—to designate that their bid for acceptance by a Gentile status audience may or may not succeed.

In the status orientation matrix, two sets of cells are separated by a broken line to represent the fact that for both the bi-cultural Jew as well as the assimilationist success or failure is a matter of degree and occasion. According to Kramer and Leventman, cell A is the most coveted position in the eyes of the high status Jews of North City.[117] The matrix oversimplifies reality, of course. For example, even the most in-group Jew feels some concern about "not offending the Gentiles."

In the center of the matrix, cell D, appears the "marginal man" who holds ambivalent and basically unsatisfying relations with both Jewish and Gentile groups. This group has received a great deal of attention by theorists and observers since the development of the concept by Stonequist. Antonovsky's study assigned only 14 per cent of his respondents to this classic status of cultural marginality—unstable, uncertain, and in perpetual conflict over his position. To recapitulate Antonovsky's findings —reported in Chapter 1— the classic "assimilationist" attitude, just short of hiding one's Jewish identity, held for about three per cent of his sample. One third of his sample showed a clearly

Table 7:1. Responses of Jewish Students to the Question, ". . . [How] do you respond or react to your Jewish identity?"—Compared by Type of University and by Sex[114]

	Students Attending Metropolitan Universities (N=117)				Students Attending State Universities (N=207)				Students Attending a Private University (N=210)			
	Males		Females		Males		Females		Males		Females	
	(N)	%	(N)	%	(N)	%	(N)	%	(N)	%	(N)	%
"Open about it"	(44)	80.0	(57)	91.9	(72)	80.9	(104)	87.4	(60)	48.0	(56)	66.0
Reserved*	(11)	20.0	(5)	8.1	(16)	19.1	(15)	12.6	(65)	52.0	(29)	34.0

* Pre-coded ("multiple choice" type) questionnaire response read, "self-conscious or uncertain about it, prefer not to mention it or to conceal it."

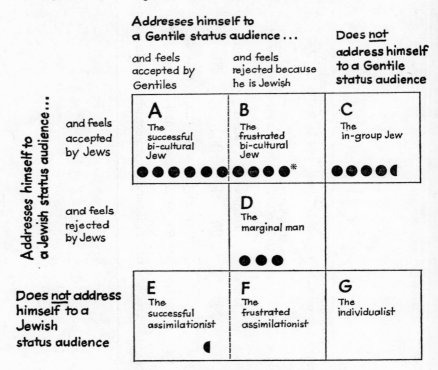

Figure 7:2. Status Orientation Matrix[116]

*Cells are weighted according to the observed incidence of each adjustment pattern in a population of married Jewish males of New Haven, Connecticut, according to an interview study by Antonovsky. (Each dot represents five per cent of Antonovsky's population.)

in-group adjustment, and the remaining one-half of his respondents were described as holding passive, moderate, or unproblematical attitudes toward Jewish identity. At the risk of oversimplifying Antonovsky's findings, cells A through E of the orientation matrix have been weighted to approximate the distribution of adjustment patterns in Antonovsky's sample of New Haven married Jewish males.

What are the underlying attitudes of those who occupy cells

E and F of the matrix, the assimilationists? Rose and Rose ask their readers to maintain a distinction between Jews "who advocate assimilation because of a rational belief [or at least a belief strongly advocated in social psychology textbooks] that it is the best solution to the minority problem and the person who advocates assimilation because he personally would like to escape being a member of the minority group."[118] The Levinsons describe the assimilationist as an "emancipated" person who has achieved a pluralistic identity. (Slotkin also uses the term "emancipated" to describe those who have given up their Jewish affiliation.) To Newcomb, Krech, and Crutchfield *et al.* he is the courageous and healthy rebel, who knows that his future lies with the dominant group. To Lewin he is a victim of self-hatred. To Drachsler, he is a person whose group ties have snapped and set him "adrift in a vast sea upon which float countless similar 'kin-wrecked' folk." He is the most likely to intermarry, Drachsler observed; lacking the bonds that once tied him to a group and its tradition, mate selection follows the simpler rule of propinquity and physical attraction.[119]

Who is neutral? What of cell G in the matrix; does anybody live there? Are there Jews who seek acceptance by *neither* a Jewish nor a Gentile status audience? Dean thought so, and reserved this position for persons whose self-esteem is bound up with some professional or ideological group. Artists, scientists, labor leaders—their work places them in a group where they "need not be confronted with decisions on 'Jewishness,' " Dean argues.[120] The radical of the thirties presumably also rejected both Jewish and Gentile reference groups.

Writing an autobiography of his career as a professional radical, Paul Jacobs seems convinced in retrospect "that for me one of the unconscious pressures toward radicalism was that the movement provided an atmosphere in which I could reject being Jewish without any feeling of guilt. . . . One of the first rituals in the radical movement was the adoption of a party name by which one was to be known in the organization. . . . Even granting the legitimate need we felt to change our names in order to escape possible consequences," Jacobs asks, "why was it that so many of the Jewish radicals took as their cover names ones that were conspicuously non-Jewish? No comrade Cohen ever adopted Ginsberg as a party name; instead, he became Green or Smith or Martin, or something equally bland."[121]

Riesman makes a special plea for a brand of individualism that rejects all forms of Jewish group life, and calls upon his reader to find within himself "the courage to face aloneness and the possibility of defeat in one's personal life or work without being morally destroyed."[122] Maslow calls upon him who would nurture his creativity to *resist* acculturation, to "wear the cloak of conventionality lightly," to maintain a "detachment from the culture," and to cherish his autonomy and privacy.[123]

Who can participate with everybody and identify with nobody? Is this an attainable attitude, is it an ideal, or is it a self-defeating posture? When Riesman, for example, compares a caricature of Jewish marketplace behavior with an idealized portrait of a Christian gentleman whose affairs of business are guided fastidiously by the Protestant ethic, one begins to wonder if the observer is an Individualist or an imaginary Puritan.[124] Perhaps nobody stands on neutral ground; nobody whose life is mingled with the Jews can be quite neutral in his attitude toward Jewishness.

Dating norms. In an advice column of the Boston *Jewish Advocate* the mother of a college girl confesses her failure to prevent her daughter from dating a non-Jew. How can a mother exercise responsibility for influencing the dating practices of a daughter who is away at college? The columnist, Dr. Rose N. Franzblau, advises the mother to give her daughter the opportunity "to learn about others and their beliefs through friendly associations with them":

> To teach loyalty to your faith and what it stands for, and also to assure that she will carry it on to the next generation, you must show faith in your youngster.
>
> To impose such severe limitations on her association with youngsters her own age is to foster what will appear to her like emotional bigotry. This can only make a youngster feel like a prisoner who is innocent but has been sentenced unfairly.
>
> Your daughter needs to learn about others and their beliefs through friendly associations with them. When given the freedom to be herself, she will stay true to her own faith.[125]

Rabbi Victor Weissberg expressed public disagreement with the permissive dating standard advocated by Dr. Franzblau:

> Oftentimes children seeking the novel, do not understand their primary allegiances and where the enduring sources of their happiness lie. . . . The encouragement of our children to inter-date must inevitably encourage them to intermarry.[126]

Shanks tends to agree with Rabbi Weissberg that a norm which permits cross-ethnic dating encourages the social contacts that "lead to intermarriage while condemning the intermarriage itself." Inevitably, says Shanks, this leads to conflict, and such turmoil "strikes at the heart of the problem of Jewish life in America, the problem of being integrated without being absorbed":

> . . . The conflict . . . is rehearsed nightly at one Jewish dinner table or another, the problem of whether Dave may ask the girl next door, a Gentile girl, to the prom; the problem of whether Joan may accept a date from the captain of the football team, who is not Jewish; or the problem, as father says, "How long is this going to go on?"—meaning his son's or daughter's continued dating of a non-Jew; or the problem of whether to "run around" in an all-Jewish crowd or a mixed crowd; or the problem of whether to move into the largely Jewish dorm or the other one where the Jews are fewer and living mostly with Christian roommates; or the problem of whether to date Sally again when you begin to become a little more than usually attracted to her. The individual situations are endless.[127]

According to Rabbi Ralph Weisberger, who worked as Circuit Rabbi for the North Carolina Association of Jewish Men, the prevailing norm for Jewish-Gentile relations among small town Jews follows the admonition: "Dating yes, marriage no."[128] Freeman and Kassebaum studied cross-ethnic dating in a Southern city, and observed that because of their economic status, Jewish men tend to have "high dating desirability."[129] The rule of "dating yes, marriage no" may work better than the reflections of

Weisberger or Shanks would suggest. Of North City's sample of third generation Jewish men, only seven per cent were inter-married, only ten per cent said they would give their parental blessing to intermarriage (or at least accept it for their children), yet two thirds of these men said they had once dated Gentile girls.[130]

The young men of North City seemed to accept the norm of "dating yet, marriage no" without attempting "any clearly formulated reasons. . . . This is simply the way things have always been, as far as they are concerned":

I was brought up that way in my environment. It's just not kosher to marry a Gentile and I never thought differently.

I have irrational feelings about intermarriage. It's just not done, I almost married a superior type of non-Jewish nurse myself, but I decided against it and I'm not sure why . . .[131]

North City's third generation seems to demonstrate that a group which has learned to cope with many other paradoxes and tensions can also adapt to the norm of "dating yes, marriage no." The degree of success with which this norm is maintained is probably a reflection of the cohesiveness and stability of the Jewish community of North City. Shanks would ask, "What is the psychological toll for maintaining this norm?" and to this question there is at present no answer.

Community exogamy. The practice of community exogamy has deep roots in the Eastern European Jewish culture. The fairs of Lemberg and Lublin, the work of traveling *shadchanim* and businessmen (described in Chapter 6) united families from every part of Eastern Europe. According to Rappaport, every elite Jewish family in Eastern Europe was linked by marriage with families in Lithuania, Poland, or Russia. In contemporary America, opportunities for travel are infinitely greater than they were in the world of the *shtetl,* and this state of affairs is often regarded as a disruptive influence in Jewish life. It is sometimes true that when a Jewish youth leaves home he gets lost in the Gentile world—but it is also true that Jewish youths leave home to accomplish for themselves exactly what the traveling *shadchanim* and *nogidim* did for the young people of their time; to find a mate who combines the intimacy of ethnic endogamy with the enchantment of geographical distance.

Jewish parents may worry about the intermarriage risk of sending their children away from home, but Jewish parents also urge their children to choose a campus where they will find good opportunities for Jewish dating and courtship. (A poster on the University of Wisconsin campus reportedly reads, "Meet Your Spouse at Hillel House.")

Like college campuses, Jewish vacation resorts serve as a gathering place for marriageables. Strictly *kosher* resorts serve the special needs of Orthodox Jews, for whom it is not enough for a partner to be of Jewish parentage—the prospective mate must also fit into a traditionalist way of life. Rabbi Kertzer tells how the fairs of Lemberg and Lublin have been replaced by vacation resorts in the Catskills and Miami Beach:

> . . . Each week [at Grossinger's] finds a good number of college students, young doctors, psychiatrists, physicists, and an equal number of girls from the sororities of Northwestern, Pennsylvania, and Ohio State, all with one thing in common: their Orthodoxy, and all with the common objective of meeting other young men and women who will keep kosher homes and rear their children in traditional fashion. These young traditionalists are products of all-day schools, children of well-to-do parents, whose quest for a mate is limited in spring and summer to the few select Northern hotels catering to a kosher clientele, and to the Sterling Hotel in Miami Beach in the winter. . . .[132]

In small towns especially, Jewish parents attach special importance to extending the social opportunities of their youth, beyond the limits of their own community. From his interviews with 260 small-town Jews, Shosteck describes his respondents' plans for helping their youngsters find a Jewish mate:

> A great many of the parents expressed the hope that they would be able to see their youngsters safely through high school. They would then send them to a college or university with a large Jewish enrollment, where they could make suitable social contacts, especially through a B'nai B'rith Hillel Foundation.

Many parents with close relatives in nearby cities sent their youngsters to live with these kin so that they might attend big city high schools. Wealthier persons generally sent their boys and girls to preparatory schools which had satisfactory Jewish representation in the student body.

Parents encouraged the building of friendships with Jewish youth in nearby towns and in big cities that were not too distant [through organized social events or educational activities]. In a number of communities the rabbis took a hand in holding conferences with Jewish teen-agers to discuss problems of courtship and marriage.[133]

Weisberger likewise reports that small-town Southern Jews attach considerable importance to choosing a college in which their child will have a better chance of finding a Jewish mate.[134] Freeman and Kassebaum similarly report "conscious parental pressure [for girls] to select a college with a relatively sizeable proportion of Jewish students."[135]

Few of Shosteck's respondents expected their children to marry a local member of the Jewish community "even in towns where there were a number of young men and women in the same age group. . . . As a number of parents put it, 'Familiarity breeds contempt.' These children had been brought up together and looked upon their Jewish playmates and chums more as brothers and sisters rather than future spouses."[136]

Bernard Rosen's description of the social life of 55 adolescents who comprise the younger generation of the Jewish community of Elmira, New York—a highly organized group with "a vivid sense of identity"—conveys a social atmosphere in which neighbors do indeed interact like brothers and sisters. Rosen describes attitudes of spite and rivalry amongst these 55 adolescents, strongly suggestive of brother-sister quarreling. "The mutual contempt between the sexes may . . . spring from the fact that they have played together since early childhood, and no romantic mysteries remain." (Adults express great fear of intermarriage, "especially of their Jewish boys marrying Gentile girls.") [137]

In his study of the small Jewish community of Urbana, Connecticut, Mandelbaum likewise describes the "family atmosphere"

as counter-romantic, and indicates that young people do not
expect to marry a local person:

Young men are averse to keeping company with local girls
and young women seek their husbands from other places. A
group as small and compact as is Urbana Jewry comes to
take on the aspects of an extended family. Its members are
so familiar with each other's history and foibles that there is
little room for romantic interest. Moreover, young men desiring to be fetter free, feel themselves enmeshed by local gossip
if they pay particular attention to an Urbana girl.[138]

Mandelbaum's observations parallel those of Barron, who
studied the Jewish community of Derby, Connecticut. "It is rare
to find the individual Derby Jew marrying another Jew of the
same community," Barron observes—attributing this phenomenon to "the almost incestuous repulsion against marriage with
members of the in-group with whom contact has been intimate
and prolonged."[139] The counter-romantic atmosphere of a family-
like Jewish peer group is likewise apparent in Melford Spiro's
study of the *sabra* youngsters who grew up together at *Kiryat
Yedidim*. Spiro reports that *without exception* these young people
choose their marriage partners from outside the *kibbutz*. Having
been raised communally with their peers, Spiro concludes, they
regard "endogamous marriages . . . as incestuous."[140]

The results of these concerted efforts—by parents and young
people alike—are expressed in Shosteck's statistics, showing 60
per cent of those of his 260 respondents with married children
reporting that their son- or daughter-in-law came from a community over 50 miles away. "The smaller the Jewish community
and the greater its distance from a larger Jewish center, the
larger the proportion of children finding spouses in distant
places."[141] The above findings fail to indicate whether Jews who
find an out-of-town mate are less likely to intermarry than those
who marry "the girl next door." Fortunately, a recent bit of
survey evidence sheds an interesting light on this issue. In a 1967
report, Christensen and Barber use Indiana marriage statistics
to compare 200 Jewish inmarriages with 176 Jewish-Gentile
marriages, on the question of whether the couple listed the same
county or different counties as their place of residence. A higher

percentage of the inmarrying Jewish couples were found to be residentially heterogeneous, than were the Jewish-Gentile couples (17.5 per cent *versus* 11.9 per cent). This statistical finding therefore agrees with the considerable body of anecdotal reports that community exogamy is a prevailing practice for maintaining the Jewish tradition of ethnic endogamy. Is this practice mainly a small town phenomenon, or does it hold for Jews in larger communities as well? That, we do not presently know.

8

Sex Role Patterning in the Jewish Family

"The notion, widely held among non-Jewish women, that Jewish husbands are cherishing helpmeets and faithful providers," writes Rabbi Louis I. Newman, "leads to many happy marriages which cross the boundaries of creed and ethnic origin."[1] The topic of Jewish-Gentile intermarriage often begins by noting the appeal of Jewish men to Gentile women, and proceeds to the question: "What's wrong with Jewish girls?" When viewed through Gentile eyes, Jewish boys seem to have been raised right but Jewish girls seem to have been raised wrong. A major thesis of our study is the proposition that the Jewish family structure designates a pattern of sex roles which better fits its men than its women for sharing the norms of Western middle class society. If true, this state of affairs could shed a significant light on tensions leading to intermarriage.

It has been claimed that in the Gentile world proverbs about women focus on their weaknesses—their fickleness and faithlessness, for example—whereas in the Jewish culture proverbs about women emphasize their *power*:

A wife sets you on your feet, or knocks you off them.

A wife can turn a man into a bald fool.

If the wife wears the pants, her husband must rock the cradle.

If the wife wears the fur-cap, her husband wears house slippers.

When a wife dies, she gets even with her husband because she shows what a fool he really is.

When God wants to turn someone into a fool, He takes away an old man's wife.

A mute woman hurls curses with her hand.

A woman makes of her husband what she will.

Whenever a woman runs things, people get run over.

As much as the wife is a queen, so much will her husband be King.

Women persuade to good or to evil, but they always persuade.

A mother is a cover—she hides her children's faults and her husband's vices.

A house without a woman is like a wagon without wheels.

Hide me, Pa—here comes Ma![2]

Writers on life in the *shtetl* give ample emphasis to the dominant role of women in that milieu. The heroic image of the infinitely resourceful, adaptable, good humored, foresighted, strong willed, nurturant, compassionate, emotional but level-headed, naive but shrewd wife and mother is celebrated in the characterizations of Gertrude Berg's Molly Goldberg, Thomas Wolfe's Esther Jack, and S. J. Wilson's Frances Hirshman. Each of these fictional characters illustrates the character structure implied in the familiar Jewish concepts of the *yiddishe mammeh,* the *balabosteh,* the *berieh.*

Landes and Zborowski, in their study of the *shtetl* family structure, conclude that "the wife is the actual head of the household and responsible for its 'Jewish way of life.' "[3] Yudel Mark emphasizes the dependency of the *shtetl* family upon the wife and mother for their economic survival:

The *shtetl* woman had a hard lot. The poorest of them were market women. The food peddlers who sold hot beans to schoolboys, the seamstresses or the bakers (typical occupations of the working woman). Many were storekeepers. Their husbands helped out on market days or at the fair, but most of the time they spent their days studying in the *bes-medresh*. It was the wife who operated the business, talked the language of the peasant and knew how to deal with the customers. Even if the husband wanted to help, he was clumsy and helpless in the business world.[4]

According to the norms of the *shtetl*, the ideal husband is "both learned and successful in business," but the idealized image of a husband-scholar designates that he "delegate the family's economic responsibilities to his wife. . . . [She] is expected to be fully responsible in mundane affairs." Such responsibility gives the *shtetl* wife "latitude and opportunity for movement, to conduct business, seek employment, and visit relatives in other parts." Women are presumed to be more emotional than men, "to quarrel more violently," and take general command over the household. "The father . . . becomes like a child to her in the home, except when he is studying or performing ritual acts; only outside the home, in the synagogue or in business, does he enter upon a fully adult role. Mother is frequently described as 'a loving despot'—always busy, always nagging. . . . Generally her conduct is understood, tolerated, loved . . . [and] in retrospect it is idealized. . . ."[5]

When a wife becomes too quarrelsome or demanding, her husband "withdraws psychologically, silently picking up a book, or bodily, silently leaving for the synagogue. . . . By her conduct the woman manipulates her traditionally subordinate status [in the synagogue] to win some advantages; in many directions, she thus persuades her husband and son to do her will."[6]

In the Jewish tradition, the husband is the religious authority of the household but he is dependent upon his wife to carry out the ritualistic practices necessary for maintaining a Jewish home: observing the laws of *kashrut*, e.g., "lighting and blessing the Sabbath candles, offering God a portion of the dough from the Sabbath loaf."[7] Likewise, the Law of Moses holds the husband responsible for his wife's happiness and sexual fulfillment ("Her food, her raiment, and her conjugal rights shall [her husband] not diminish"), but he must depend upon his wife to go promptly and regularly to the ritual bath or he literally may not touch her.[8] Jewish religious law thus vests the husband with responsibility and the wife with power and privilege.

The religious imperative of early marriage likewise inducts the young man into the role of husband before he has become economically self-sufficient—a tradition of scholarship designated a matrilocal family structure and the practice of *kest,* which enhanced the economic power of the wife, and placed the husband in the role of a dependent and an "outsider."

In the matrilocal extended family, the wife is surrounded and supported by her sisters and mother. In the *shtetl,* adult sisters maintain a solidarity "little known to brothers." Thus "it often happens that the mother's relatives are the ones best known to her children, even, in cases to the entire ignorance of the father's kin. Informants born and reared in the *shtetl* area have told us," report Landes and Zborowski "of never having met paternal grandparents, especially the paternal grandfather, until the age of thirteen or fourteen."[9]

Parent-child relations in the shtetl. Landes and Zborowski describe the relationship between *shtetl* mother and son as "the most striking instance of ethological variation."[10] To her son, "mother is the embodiment of warmth, intimacy, food, unconditioned love, security [and] practical reality. This inclusive libidinal character . . . is in complete contrast with the spiritualized, remote character of the father. Father's life is as dedicated to the study of the Law as mother's is to material comforts for the family . . . [and affection for her sons]."[11] The influence of a mother-centered household is contained in the proverb, "A son always takes after his mother's brother."

"There is no avoidance between mother and son, except that intercourse is forbidden."[12] "A young son often sleeps with her, unlike her husband who is prohibited by sacred law [concerning menstrual uncleanliness] for remaining in her bed. . . . Although displays of endearment between husband and wife are frowned upon, regarded as vulgar whether in speech or gesture, a great deal of demonstrativeness is allowed between mother and son, which mothers encourage. . . . It seems to us," Landes and Zborowski add, "that though the marital obligations are fulfilled with the husband, the romance exists with the son."[13]

"We have found the involvements between mother and son to

be so far-reaching and intense as to constitute a kind of adoration. . . . Even though she may choose his wife, the feeling [of jealousy and resentment] is such that there is a folk saying, 'When a son marries, he gives the wife a contract and the mother a divorce.' "[14]

"The son's adoration of his mother . . . [stems from] her great concentration of loving, admiring attention on him. . . . To no one else will he ever be so desirable and important, no where else will he receive the indulgences shown a helpless child. . ." The harsh treatment, deprivation and separation occasioned by his schooling—which may start at age three—sharply contrasts with his mother's endless love and attentions. . ."[15]

"It appears characteristic of Jewish males to regard the mother as a retreating figure of shelter, a most desirable warm figure always just out of reach, a poignant symbol of tenderness. . . . Indeed we believe that the Jewish man hopes to find a mother again in his wife, and is happiest in his marriage when this search is fulfilled.[16] Besides, the culture aids him, for in the time of arranged marriages his mother selected his wife, and a proverb states, 'Every daughter-in-law has something of her mother-in-law.' "[17]

According to Kazin, "the real drama behind most Jewish novels and plays [of the 1930's], even when they are topical and revolutionary in feeling, is the contrast between the hysterical tenderness of the Oedipal relation and the 'world' [of harsh realities]. . . . Jews don't believe in original sin," Kazin reflects, "but they certainly believe in the original love that they once knew in the *shtetl*, in the kitchen, in the Jewish household—and after *that* knowledge, what forgiveness?"[18]

Landes and Zborowski recall a folk tale which describes the Jewish mother's devotion to her son:

A young man begs his mother for her heart, which his betrothed has demanded as a gift; having torn it out of his mother's proffered breast, he races away with it; and as he stumbles, the heart falls to the ground, and he hears it question protectively, 'Did you hurt yourself, my son?'[19]

A girl's "affectionate tie is with her father. . ."[20] Although the father is "unwantonly demonstrative to his daughter, [he is] less so than the mother to her son."[21] The daughter "is peculiarly his. . . . She is the one family member in whose company he can relax; and when she marries, he finds joy in her husband [whom the father by custom may select] that he cannot find in his own son."[22]

"Rivalry between father and son is a familiar theme, expressed in large and small ways, privately and publicly. It is a commonplace that a man prefers his son-in-law to his son, and a proverb says, 'Every son-in-law has in him something of his father-in-law.'" Another proverb adds, "One's son is given, but one's son-in-law is chosen."[23] An idealization of the gentle father role is contained in the *Hasidic* story of a father who complained to the *Baalshem* that his son had forsaken God. "What, Rabbi, shall I do?" "Love him more than ever," was the *Baalshem's* reply.[24]

"The mother-daughter relationship contains more rivalry and even hostility than do the other family couplings. . . . She nags at her daughter in a consistently hostile manner. . ."[25] She shows much ambivalence over teaching her daughter housewifely responsibilities. "Her negativism is in striking contrast to the emphasis of many other cultures where girlhood is also the mandatory period of training for housewifely responsibilities. . . . This can be interpreted as the mother's jealous protection of the adult status she acquired by marriage. . ."[26]

To what extent does the patterning of family life in the *shtetl* help account for observations on American Jewish family life, particularly those observations which have some bearing on motivation toward intermarriage? The following analysis will focus upon role behavior of the Jewish woman.

"WHAT'S WRONG WITH OUR GIRLS?"

The role relationship of strong mother and gentle father, patterned by the derivatives of a matrilocal rule of residence, is somewhat of an anomaly in human culture just as the matrilocal system itself is a cultural anomaly. To what extent these norms have survived in the post-*shtetl* Jewish culture (or how they have become distorted) is a question of considerable importance in understanding the tensions present in contemporary Jewish life—of which the "intermarriage problem" is but one manifestation. There is a difference between a strong mother and a "castrating" neurotic woman; there is a difference between a gentle father and a masochistic or "castrated" male. Perhaps the delicate balance between the strong mother and the gentle father may require the traditional value system of the *shtetl;* perhaps this norm does not transplant well into the soil of the Western world. For whatever reasons, post-*shtetl* Jews continue to ask each other, "What's wrong with our girls?"

How much of the Jewish woman's *shtetl* role has survived the transplantation of the Jewish community to the United States? Let us see how much we can piece together from various sources, what facts and impressions we can gather which have some bearing on this question. On the survival of the matricentric tradition, Cahnman reports:

> The overwhelming majority of my Jewish students at Hunter College, a few years ago, reported that they live in more or less close proximity to their maternal families while they have little contact with relatives on the paternal side.[27]

Cahnman is led to conclude that the matricentric tradition has indeed survived, and he asks whether "the mother-in-law centered Jewish family . . . [has become] a deterrent to survival, or at least an instrument of ambivalence" for the prospective Jewish husband. Cahnman judges that Jewish men "feel oppressed by the expectation of the relentless pressure of the obligations to which they will be subjected in the families of prospective Jewish spouses," a burden which he need not shoulder if he married "a simple Gentile girl." It is not the Jewish girl herself who is so demanding, Cahnman seems to say; it is the solidarity of the girl's kinsmen and their thoroughness in looking after her rights.[28]

Cahnman continues his troubled thoughts about Jewish girls: "Reports which I have received from college campuses over the years indicate that Jewish mothers sensitize their daughters more to their rights than to their obligations, so that they insist that their future husbands be conveniently docile in the home, inordinately 'ambitious' in the marketplace and capable of satisfying the highest material expectations of 'happiness.'" Cahnman warns that Jewish girls must "compete more effectively" or face a situation in which "a considerable number of Jewish boys prefer Gentile girls."[29]

Rabbi Kirshenbaum likewise judges that the tendency for Jewish girls to "grow up spoiled and arrogant" provides "one of the cardinal reasons" for mixed marriages between Jewish youths and Gentile girls. The rabbi takes the common sense view that Jewish girls are spoiled by doting parents who "often extend themselves beyond their financial ability to give them every advantage and indulgence." He proceeds to spell out the unhappy result of such an upbringing:

When they grow up and are ready for marriage they seek a husband as complaisant and indulgent as their parents were. Their behavior is that of a child-aristocrat. Their greatest ideal is fine clothes, expensive jewelry, and an elaborately furnished home, and they do not hesitate to let this be known to the young men who court them. Many are frightened off by the sheer unreality (as far as they are concerned) of this fantasy of many Jewish girls. They fear they cannot cope with the demands of that kind of life. This has the effect of driving them into non-Jewish circles. Here they find friendships among non-Jewish girls who may appreciate the personal character of the Jewish boy rather than his ability to provide them with a life of luxury.

A Jewish young man, who was intermarried for a few years and later divorced, complained to us bitterly, blaming Jewish girls for his own unhappy marriage experience.

'I am a good tradesman,' he said. 'I earn a decent income. When I took out a Jewish girl she would ask to be brought only to the most expensive places. She would talk of a wealthy home, costly furs, and a luxurious life. Her mother constantly mentioned that she hoped her daughter would have a better lot in life than she had had. They scared me off. I felt that with my earnings I could make a comfortable and decent home for a wife, but not the kind the mother and daughter had pictured. Most Jewish girls whom I took out were more interested in my income than in my person.

'I became acquainted with a Gentile girl whose outlook was more modest and limited. She did not ask for too much and did not look for a life of ease and luxury. She was more interested in me than in my money, and she struck me as making a better wife than any of the Jewish girls I knew. When we fell in love I saw no obstacle whatsoever to our union. At first I really felt happy. As it happened, later we decided through our experience that people of different religions were people of different worlds; that when one is raised in a certain religion, even though one may be no believer, nonetheless the cultural implications and the way of life of the religion are deeply ingrained—and we decided to part. This is something we did not think of or anticipate at the time of the wedding. But the fault [of] my unhappy and broken married life is that of the Jewish girls and their exaggerated demands on life. They do not want to understand that most Jewish young men who seek marriage want friendship and a faithful partner who will know how to manage a modest household and be able to establish a sound foundation for a happy future.'

We cannot generalize that this applies to all Jewish girls, [Rabbi Kirshenbaum concludes], but it remains true in large measure that many Jewish young women are attracted by outward appearance, dazzled by luxurious dress and pleasures, extravagant in their behavior, and expect far too much personal and material satisfaction from marriage.[30]

In a Letter to the Editor, a reader of *Commentary* echoes Rabbi Kirshenbaum's complaint that Jewish girls are too materialistic and conservative. (The letter was instigated by Sklare's 1964 *Commentary* article, in which he expresses alarm over the high rate of intermarriage among Jewish faculty at the University of Illinois at Urbana.)

. . . No 'properly' reared Jewish girl would consider a professor for a husband when she might have a lawyer or a doctor—or even a dentist! Where is that politically liberal, intellectual . . . avant-garde Jewish [graduate] student to find his mate? Among the potential officers of suburban Hadassah?[31]

That this is not exactly a new problem is indicated by an 1877 pamphlet on intermarriage written by the Belgian Jewish educator Lehman Kahn, and published in Brussels. Jewish girls have such tastes for luxury and comfort, Kahn notes with regret, that "today, the young man who intends to establish himself and to start a family, has to think twice before taking a chance."[32] Kahn attributed this problem to the simple fact that Jewish girls were being given a leisure-class education which of course unfitted them for the humbler role of housewife. Secondarily, he referred to parental pressure to find a husband of wealth and status.

Our girls, those of the middle class, actually receive a more complete education than in former times, they learn many things related to making family life pleasant and to enrich it; but this education by the nature of things renders future wives pretentious and demanding.

They are not easily satified with the simple cozy pleasures of home life; they are not pleased with their humble role of housewife; their education, they believe, owes them a better fate. When one knows how to play the piano, it is below one's dignity to cook. When one has learned ancient mythology and modern science one can't stoop down to the work of scrubbing floors, washing dishes; when one knows how to weave tapestry and to embroider, one can't stoop to sewing and mending. How can one expect an educated woman, versed in several languages, to go to the markets and speak the vulgar tongue of the shop keepers? When one has a higher education, one doesn't marry to work but to enjoy life; the struggle belongs to the husband; it is up to him to earn a living. And if the 'evil' stopped here—if the refinement of education and extravagant habits simply doubled the cost of living—the husband wouldn't have too much cause for complaint. But still another and more expensive consequence of education is the fact that an educated women adopts the standards of fashionable society and requires personal and household luxury on a scale that quadruples the cost of living.[33]

Kahn appeals to Jewish parents to raise their daughters "modestly and in simplicity, to prepare them for all positions in life, especially for the humble roles. . ." He implores the Jewish parent not to ask a hard working, intelligent suitor "the size of his pay check, nor worry about how brilliant a social position he commands":

. . . In the choice of a husband for our daughters, our duty is to look more to the character of the suitors than to their fortune, to their honor rather than to their profession. . . . Let us consent to give . . . our daughter in marriage [to an intelligent, sober, hard working young man], to prefer him to a rich and titled but depraved or skeptical young man. . . . The struggle for a living doesn't humiliate or degrade a man; on the contrary, it ennobles him and lifts him in his own eyes; moreover, it exercises his wits and strength, gives temper to his courage and renders him capable of practicing all the virtues.[34]

As a final and perhaps essential piece of advice to parents, Kahn urges them to give the young couple as much financial help as they can afford "to help them establish themselves and start a young family."[35] Thus did Kahn hope to reconcile the norm represented by the French proverb, "Poverty is not a vice," with the Jewish maxim that suffering is no virtue. (*S'iz kein chiev mutshin.*)

The conservative sex. Are Jewish girls more conservative than Jewish boys? If so, does this mean they are more satisfied with their minority group status, that they are more timid about challenging the status quo, or that women in general are more conformist than men? From the dean of women at an Eastern university, Wessel learned that "Jewish girls do not seek Jewish room mates during the freshman year, but do so in later years. Why," asks Wessel, "are these girls withdrawing from the wider community?"[36] One of Mayer's intermarrying Jews complained about the conservatism of Jewish girls, characterizing them as ". . . too concerned about how their actions would appear to others. Their behavior was controlled by what others might think."[37]

From a variety of sources come facts which point to the conservative attitudes of Jewish women, compared with Jewish men. Teitelbaum's 1953 study of Jewish undergraduates at Northwestern University pointed to several ways in which coeds were more conservative than college men; coeds more frequently indicated that they openly identified themselves as Jewish, more frequently expressed opposition to intermarriage—for themselves or for others—and more frequently profess to the habit of private prayer.[38]

In 1955 Leon Feldman compared Jewish college men and women, and reported that women were "more home-oriented, more concerned with family guidance, and at the same time less fearful of social or vocational discrimination by the larger world. Accordingly, she accepts and avows her Jewishness more openly than her Jewish brother and college man, and she participates more in Jewish organizational activity, feeling more secure as a Jew."[39]

Does the Jewish woman's more conservative orientation, better structured role, make her a "better adjusted" person than her male counterpart? Orlansky reports a Cleveland area study by Kieth Sward which led him to conclude that Jewish women have "better adjusted temperaments, on the average, than Jewish men because they are in a more sheltered social position."[40] Sanua's Rorschach study (reviewed in Chapter 11) likewise indicates that Jewish girls are better adjusted than Jewish boys. Sanua, like Sward, ascribes the girl's advantage to her better-defined and more traditional role. (The author is reminded of an Orthodox rabbi of his acquaintance who has given his two daughters Old Testament names, and his two sons Anglo-Saxon names.)

Are women everywhere more conservative than men, is this a Jewish phenomenon to any degree, or is it the mark of a minority group that its women should be more conservative, more loyal to their culture? Abel and Hsu studied the Rorschach responses of a group of Chinese [students?] in the United States, and concluded that the women were the better adjusted sex. Burma notes that in the Negro group it is mainly the men who attempt to pass; women who could pass if they tried "can usually do better for themselves by remaining in the Negro group."[41]

It may well be that Jewish wives are more conservative and in-group because middle-class women in general are like that. Minnis studied a sample of 177 (of a total of 379) organized adult women's clubs in New Haven, and found that 90 per cent were racially exclusive, and 76 per cent were religiously exclusive. (College alumnae associations and veterans organizations' auxiliaries provided the exceptions.) Minnis found Caucasian garden clubs, Gentile literary clubs; "division according to religion . . . [was] found to take place even when the type of associations and the services rendered are not of a religious nature."[42]

The Jewish wife appears to exert conservative, in-group influence on the social life of the married couple. Belth refers to a Cornell study which sampled 150 Jewish families and found that 85 had all-Jewish social circles. Belth judges that it is the *wife* who "sets the social pattern" of the exclusively Jewish social group. Of 70 men surveyed by the Cornell group, only 12 belonged exclusively to Jewish organizations, but 34 of their wives (or about three times as many) maintained this exclusion. The limited number of Jewish-Gentile friendships which do develop result mainly from organizational contacts—presumably from fraternal organizations of which the husbands are members. "Neighborhood contacts seem to be . . . least productive of social mixing."[43]

Although Kramer and Leventman (in their North City's Jewish community study) interviewed men only, their respondents described their wives as a conservative, in-group influence.

After school, I drifted away from my old friends. I made friends with my wife's friends who are all Jewish.[44]

. . . It's hard on the wife in a Gentile [neighborhood], where they just say 'nice day' but aren't friendly or neighborly. They're clannish.[45]

A significantly higher proportion of wives' organizational membership, 76 per cent [compared with 63 per cent of third generation husbands'] are Jewish ones, suggesting their more limited contact with the general community. Fewer of their organizational memberships are non-Jewish, and more wives than husbands belong to no organizations at all.[46]

Wives who express social ambitions rarely "desire to loosen the family's ties to the Jewish community. . . . The wives have less contact with Gentiles than their husbands. . . . They have fewer organizational and fewer, if any, occupational sources for meeting Gentiles. Any college friendships with Gentiles have not survived married life and a divergence of communal interests. . . . [Their] range of interests and social relations is confined to the in-group."[47]

Vance Packard held some presumably candid conferences with members of the social and business elite on the bases of discrimination against Jews for executive positions. Among various factors cited by his respondents, it was asserted that "wives of Gentiles and Jews often raise barriers between the two groups. There seem to be higher barriers separating the women than the men."[48]

Working outside the home gives the husband access to more opportunities for acculturation, and to more substantial rewards for acculturation, than the wife is likely to encounter. The Jewish tradition, on the other hand, gives the wife a relative advantage with regard to her status as mother and wife. It is quite possible that the dominant group of middle class women maintains a more closed society than do their husbands. These various factors seem to indicate that Jewish women tend to prefer the shelter of the Jewish way of life, and give priority to a husband whose vocational goals (i.e., business ownership or an independent profession) are consonant with a Jewish way of life.

The Jewish mother: portrait vs. caricature. The clinical literature abounds with references to overprotective, overanxious mothers.[49] Loewenstein asserts that Jewish mothers, in their devotion and attachment to their children, overnourish their children and make them "overfearful in the face of physical danger. This maternal attitude discourages the normal childhood desire to seek parental approval through a show of physical strength and prowess."[50] What Georgene Seward describes as the "exile neurosis" of the Jew who "clings to his family for emotional support"[51] is undoubtedly linked to the overprotective maternal attitude.

[Freud did not overlook the positive aspect of maternal affection, and his observation may contribute something to our understanding of Jewish personality. In an essay on Goethe, Freud once commented, "... He who has been the undisputed darling of his mother retains throughout life that victorious feeling, that confidence in ultimate success, which not seldom brings actual success with it."[52]]

When we go beyond the clinical literature, we find that Jewish mothers do indeed tend to be more affectionate toward their children, and that this attitude is positively correlated with the mother's self-esteem and with esteem for her husband. These findings emerged from a large-scale study of child-rearing practices conducted in New Haven by Sears, Maccoby and Levin. (The study involved the families of 198 middle-class mothers, of whom 64 were Jewish.)

Sears, Maccoby, and Levin defined affectionate warmth as "a pervasive quality [involving] love, acceptance, enthusiasm, an outgoing of affection. Is is not a dimension that a mother can discuss easily," the investigators admit, "nor is it one on which she can be measured by her answer to a single question. Nevertheless . . . the quality of warmth does stand out in her discussion of other matters."[53] For example, "there was a clear tendency for mothers who were delighted over pregnancy to be warmer to the infant after it was born."[54] The investigators carefully rated each mother on "emotional warmth to her child,"[55] and at the middle class level, Jewish mothers were rated significantly higher than other ethnic groups.

Contrary to the clinical literature—which blurs the distinction between warmth and overprotection, and describes the overprotective mother as insecure and frustrated—Sears, Maccoby, and Levin found that mothers who were affectionate toward their children also tended to show high self-esteem and were more likely to hold their husbands in high esteem, than mothers rated low on emotional warmth toward their children. "On the average, those mothers who held their husbands in high esteem were much warmer in their relationships to their children than were those who felt less enthusiasm and respect for their husbands. . . . Likewise her warmth was greater when she had a high degree of satisfaction with her current life situation."[56] (Perhaps this explains why Jewish mothers categorized as lower class showed significantly *less* maternal warmth than middle-class mothers.)

Are Jewish mothers more controlling and neurotic, as seen through the eyes of their children, than mothers of comparable groups? In 1966 Berman included in a family background questionnaire given to a large group of college freshmen the following question: "What about your mother's personality do you *dislike* the most?" Written responses were categorized by blind analysis, and frequencies were tallied for 15 males and 15 females,

Table 8:1. "What about your mother's personality do you *dislike* the most?" Frequency of Responses of 45 College Freshmen, by Sex and Ethnic Group[57]

| | Jewish group | | Gentile groups | | | | Combined groups | |
| | | | Eastern European | | Western European | | | |
	15 M	15 F	15 M	15 F	15 M	15 F	45 M	45 F
Too strict. Set in ways, stubborn, old-fashioned, prejudiced	2	2	2	3	0	3	4	5
Overcontrolling. Nags, interferes, is suspicious.	3	1	2	2	3	1	8	4
"Hysterical." Childish, irrational, fussy. Gossips, talks too much.	1	3	3	2	1	0	5	5
Argumentative. Loud, mean, violent. Bad temper.	2	3	1	0	1	2	4	5
Ignorant. Stupid, incompetent.	0	0	2	3	0	1	2	4
Nervous. Irritable, impatient, touchy, worrisome, excitable, hypersensitive	1	3	3	2	1	0	5	5

randomly chosen from each of three ethnic groups. As shown in Table 8:1, the descendents of Eastern European *Gentiles* are somewhat more likely to describe their mothers as "hysterical," nervous, or ignorant. Jews are somewhat more likely to describe their mothers as argumentative. Sons of all groups are more likely to describe mother as nagging, and daughters are more likely to see mother as ignorant. Samples are too small to satisfy criteria of statistical significance, but this study of 90 non-clinical college freshmen casts doubt upon the proposition that an overcontrolling or nervous mother is a special burden of Jewish youth.

The affectionately aggressive (or aggressively affectionate) Jewish mother, the daughter who identifies with her, and the men who acquiesce to the women's domestic maneuverings, are nicely portrayed in the case of a patient described by Reik. As he reconstructs the case, Reik lets the young woman tell her own story:

Lenora

"I was then secretary in a company and I heard that a young man from Detroit would get a leading position in our New York office. When he arrived, I immediately fell in love with him. All the girls in our office were setting their caps for him. He took many of them out. They said he took girls out as soon as he learned to walk. He also invited me for dinner several times, but I had decided to give him a run for his money and told him I had other dates. He stopped asking me then. What could I do? I couldn't invite him, could I?

"Once we stepped into the elevator at the same time and I casually said 'You invited me to dinner; when will you take me?' 'Tomorrow, if you are free.' I was free, of course, and I had already decided to get him, if it was the last thing I did. He took me to dinner each Friday, but Mama always asked me to bring him home. Finally she decided I should not go out with him again before he had been in our house for dinner at least once. When he asked me the next time I said I could not go. I then said I had to ask Mama first. That was in his office and he pointed to the telephone and said 'Speak with her!' I called her, but she was adamant.

"He did not hear what she said, of course, but he must have guessed it because he said, 'Oh, I am going to be inspected.' Then I rang up Mama again and told her that he would come on Friday evening. He asked me before that whether we would have to stay there a long time after dinner or if we could go to a movie afterward. You see, he was afraid that he would be bored with my family. We even agreed upon a signal: if he wanted to leave and go to a movie or dancing with me, he would yawn. He never did. He liked Mama very much. I played the piano for him and my father and my brother talked business with him. He stayed until after midnight.

"When he left, Mama said: 'You live alone, don't you? I will give you something to eat that you can take home.' She went to the kitchen and filled some jars with knishes and meat loaf. He came many times to the house. Once when he was there, my father whispered to me: 'If you don't get him, Mama will.'

"Then he had to go to a convention in Milwaukee for two weeks. I asked him 'Will you write me?' He promised to write, but I never got a card or even a post card from him.

"When he returned, he called me into his office. 'Why?' I said, 'I thought you were not interested in me any longer.' 'Why should you think that?' he asked, 'You did not even write me even once,' I said. 'I did,' he said and took from his pocket some post cards with my address on them. He had not sent them. 'How could I?' he said, 'You don't write this on post cards. Will you marry me, Lenora?'

"When I came home that evening, I went straight to the bedroom of Mama and Papa and said: 'I shall marry.' And they both had only one thing to ask: 'When?' "

Reik comments: "We see here that the new member is as completely absorbed by the family as a foreign body by an amoeba.

"What interest me are rather the potentialities of this family solidarity than its achievements. Is it not imaginable that the best features of it will one day be transferred from its narrow circle to the family of man?"[58]

The male ego in a matricentric milieu. If in a normal population affectionate mothers tend to hold themselves and their husbands in high esteem (as Sears and his colleagues have demonstrated), it is plainly evident from clinical experience that overprotective, oversolicitous and "seductive" mothers develop and perpetuate a neurotic mother-child relationship. Although Jews are not the sole heirs of maternal overcontrol, Jewish humor frequently strikes a note of protest against living in a culture dominated by women.[59] The endless procession of shadchan jokes catalog the weaknesses, imperfections and failings of Jewish women:

'Is that the girl you want me to marry? She's cross-eyed,' the young man protests in a whisper. 'You can talk louder,' replies the shadchan. 'She's also deaf.'

The Jewish mother is also the target of much joking, gently ridiculing both her possessiveness and her unworldliness. Since education has traditionally been a male monopoly, the naivete of the Jewish mother is a favorite target. George Jessel's telephone conversations with his mother (popular during the days of radio comedy) clearly belong to this tradition:

> [Jessel tells his mother] that he is sitting with Wendell Wilkie. ("No, mama, not Mendel—Wendell,") who is talking about the four freedoms. Mother wants to know what he said about her neighbors upstairs, the Friedmans. The son tells her that he will browse around the art gallery this evening, and had to assure her that this is a respectable place. . . . He promises that he will bring Whistler's Mother home for the living room, but mother says there is no place there and Whistler's mother would have to sleep with George's sister. The son explains that it is a picture. When he tells her that he picked up a Reubens, she believes that he means Rubin, the delicatessen man. When she is told that Reubens is a painter, she would like to know how much he would charge to paint the kitchen.[60]

Maternal possessiveness and naivete are blended into the themes of the following Jewish jokes:

> A mother gave her son two neckties as a present. The son, who wants to show his appreciation, wears one at their next meeting. Noticing it, the mother says, 'What's the matter? Don't you like the other one?'[61]

> [Reik recounts the familiar anecdote of] the desperate mother who frantically runs along the beach, her arms stretched out to the sea, yelling 'Help! Help! My son, the doctor, is drowning!'[62]

> A Jewish mother confides to a friend that she is taking her boy to a psychiatrist who tells her that the boy's trouble has something to do with an Oedipal Complex. 'Oedipal-schmedipal,' her friend reassures her, 'so long as he loves his mother.'

One might even conjecture that the importance which the Jewish male traditionally attaches to participation in synagogue worship, study, community life, and business or professional success stems partly from the fact that the Jewish tradition does not allow him to be the boss at home. A Jewish husband who accepts this culturally patterned role as "natural and normal" might say: "Why should I want to strut around like a big shot at home and order the wife and kids around anyway? My wife is perfectly capable of handling the kids and managing the house; if I want to be a hero, I've got my business (or my profession) to do something with." Indeed, the Jew may feel that he *must* do well in his work in order to fit graciously into the domestic role of a good Jewish husband and maintain his self-esteem.

The decline of the synagogue as a source of masculine self-esteem (where girls may now become *bas mitzvah,* where women now sit among the men and on occasion even lead the services!) may make work and community service all the more important to men as vehicles for personal achievement and social recognition. Alas for the Jew who can find no worth or dignity in the synagogue, who feels bound to a dull and ungratifying job, who has lost the security of his extended family ties, who has not made for himself a dignified place in the community, and whose major share of the Jewish cultural heritage is a bossy wife!

Jewish women and community leadership. Warner and Srole observed that in Yankee City "the Jewish wife emerged into a participating role in her community earlier than did the wives from other ethnic communities." The authors found no counterpart among other ethnic groups to the Jewish Ladies' Aid Society, which had been organized by women of the immigrant generation, and was performing "the charity function for the entire community." This was not a society for distributing Holiday food baskets to the local poor; the J.L.A.S. was conducting its charities on an almost world-wide basis, "extending to needy families in Boston, New York, Denver, Poland, and Palestine. The influence of the J.L.A.S. [had] reached even to the male-directed synagogue and Hebrew School, where it [acted] as a fund-raising unit."[63]

The more acculturated generation of immigrant women (those who emigrated at an age of eighteen or under, and designated by Warner and Srole as the P^2 generation) were dominant in the Hadassah organization, through which they organized the community around the Zionist program, described by Warner and Srole as "a more important community function than any performed by the Jewish male associations."[64] The authors were even more impressed by the fact that this acculturated immigrant generation of women "not only represent[ed] their families in important association structures of the Jewish community but also represent[ed] the Jewish community in certain special structures of the total Yankee City social system. This had occurred specifically in the Yankee City Health Center and on the Yankee City Community Welfare Board, both privately endowed charitable institutions serving the entire city, where Jewish . . . wives [were] members of the Board of Directors."[65]

Warner and Srole also attribute the break with the Orthodox tradition of segregation of women in synagogue seating, to the insistence of the acculturated immigrant wives. (One respondent recalled that she warned her husband that she would not go to the new synagogue "unless I can sit with my husband and children. And a lot of other people are going to hold out until the changes are made. You watch and see!")[66] The investigators emphasized the significance of this change: "The synagogue was the only structure in the Jewish community system in which the P[2] wife had made no advance. . . . If [she] could have broken through the partition to invade the sacred area of the congregation which, by Hebraic Law, is a community only of males, she would have reached, symbolically at least, a status in the sacred community equivalent to that of her husband. . . . This was the last and most difficult barrier keeping her from equality with her husband," and the barrier was of course breached.[67]

The authors made no attempt to account for the ready support which the P[2] wives gained from their husbands in changing the seating arrangement. The husbands "were in a position to enforce the traditional seating modes . . . had they been of that mind. They were in control of the executive committee and they had the power of the sacred law, from both of which there was no possible appeal. Yet *they battled with their own elders on behalf of the reform.* (Italics added.) They have offered no resistance to the ascent of their wives even into the final sanctum of the 'holy of holies.' "[68]

In a more general way, Warner and Srole were somewhat at a loss to account for the "highly important position of the . . . Jewish wives in the community,"[69] perhaps because the authors had so strongly committed themselves to the viewpoint that the Jews originally shared the patriarchal family structure characteristic of all the other ethnic groups of Yankee City—the French, the Irish, the Greeks, the Italians, Armenians, and Poles—a system which called for "almost complete subordination of wife and children."[70] Since the matricentric tradition of the Jews and its influence upon family role relations went completely unnoticed by the investigators, they looked elsewhere to account for what they considered a "revolutionary change in the traditional personality type of the Jewish wife."[71] They pointed to the bourgeois class background of the Jews, which was unlike the agrarian background of other ethnic groups. They pointed to the middle-class status of the Jews. Overlooking the long history of matrilocal practice and its influence on the status of women in Jewish society, Warner and Srole could do no better than observe that leisure was "the immediate single factor" in accounting for the unique position of Jewish wives in the community system.[72]

The matricentric norm in contemporary Jewish society. There is no shortage of conjectures and generalizations on the matricentric norm in contemporary Jewish life, but research data on this topic are hard to come by. A rare and recent finding is that of Winch, Greer, and Blumberg, who asked 241 suburban housewives whom they would want to raise their children if they were orphaned. Almost three-fourths of the Jewish wives designated a maternal relative as the foster parent—compared with 31 per cent of Protestants and 48 per cent of Catholics who designated a maternal relative. (See Table 8:2.)

Table 8:2. Responses of 241 Upper Middle Class Chicago Suburban Housewives to the Question: "If something happened to you and your husband, who in the Chicago area would you want to see raising your children?"[73]

Percentage distribution by ethnic group

Response	Protestants (N=58)	Catholics (N=46)	Jews (N=137)
Relatives of wife	31%	48%	73%
Relatives of husband	17	30	12
Friend or agency	19	9	6
No one in Chicago area	33	13	9
Total	100	100	100

Kertzer offers the following observation of matrilocalism in present-day Texas:

> Owners of successful business establishments [in Texas small towns], with real-estate investments to enhance their security ... maintain as much as possible their contacts with other Jews and Judaism. Unlike many of their Northern coreligionists, they close their stores on the holy days. They dispatch their children to college, not only to get an education, but, they will tell you, to meet "a nice Jewish boy or girl." Sometimes the young people never return, but frequently their daughter marries a boy who is willing to enter the family business. I have seen more three-generation homes in Texas than in New York.[74]

Leichter and Mitchell's 1967 publication, *Kinship and Casework*—summarizing the results of a large-scale interview and questionnaire study of extended family relations of family service agency clients—presents a rich array of evidence on matricentrism in the lives of contemporary, U.S. born Jewish adults:

> Whatever its source, there is a definite skewing in interaction and sentiment toward the wife's side of the family, particularly for the wife. The husband is most intensely involved with his own kin in some areas, particularly family businesses, which are specifically his activity, but he is more closely tied to his wife's kin than she is to his.[75]

These two very recent studies suggest that much more may be learned about matricentric familism in contemporary Jewish life, as behavioral science researchers begin to recognize the significance of this phenomenon for personality theory and for counseling practice.[76]

9

Sex Norms and Practices in the Jewish Culture

Kinsey describes contemporary standards of sexual morality as the product of an "original Judeo-Christian code," a reflection of "the Hebraic and Christian concept of the reproductive function," a survival of "the tradition of the Judaic law and Christian precept."[1] "The lower frequencies of sexual activity among Orthodox Jews," says Kinsey, "will occasion no surprise to those who understand the pervading asceticism of Hebrew philosophy."[2]

While it is true that the Talmud and present-day legal codes agree on the question of what modes of sexual expression are to be sanctioned and what modes are to be censured, it would be misleading to suppose that (a) the ascetic spirit *pervades* the traditional Jewish attitude toward sex, or that (b) there is only a negligible difference between Jewish and Christian standards of sexual morality. Psychoanalyst and Jewish scholar Henry Raphael Gold insists that "fear of sexual desire and shame and guilt about its very existence are alien to the classic Jewish tradition, as expressed in the Bible and in the Talmud."[3]

Redeemer versus creator. In the Christian tradition, man's earthly life tends to be undervalued in favor of a promised Heavenly reward. Renunciation of earthly pleasures betokens one's dedication to the world of the spirit. The life of self-sacrifice and self-denial, the ascetic life, becomes a natural model for the good Christian life. The Christian depreciation of sex is represented by the words of St. Paul: "It is well not to touch a woman . . . [though] it is better to marry than to burn." Likewise did St. Augustine identify sex with sin: "The act of generation is sin itself and determines the transmission *ipso facto* of the sin to the new creature."[4]

The Christian tradition emphasizes the role of Christ the Redeemer, who rescues man from the bondage of sin—who transports man above and away from earthly temptations. The Jewish tradition centers around God the Creator, who charges man to exercise his generative powers, to be fruitful and multiply. The sexual function becomes man's instrument for fulfilling the first divine commandment: to add to the stream of life.

In the Hebrew language, the sex drive is called *yetser ha'ra,* a term which could be literally translated as "the evil impulse," and is used more broadly to refer to the violent passions. Since the precept of propagation and the command to give one's wife "a full portion of her conjugal rights" makes the sex act a sacred duty, rabbinical scholars explain, the sex drive might be called an "evil impulse" only in the sense that it is easily misdirected.[5] The rabbis speculated that each and every human activity (if it was "in accordance with the intention of the deity") is accomplished through an angel, a messenger, an intermediary of God. Thus, argued Maimonides, there must also be an angel "in charge of lust," one which produces "the force of orgasm."[6] In the Jewish culture, sex is a precious and powerful and complex phenomenon. Jewish laws and rabbinical speculations deal explicitly and in great detail with the creative function of sex, the power of the sexual passion, the pleasures of sex, and above all— the management, mastery and regulation of the sexual passion.

On the eighth day of life the infant boy is circumcised and his reproductive organ becomes a symbol of his membership in the covenant between God and Israel, as well as an instrument for fulfillment of the divine command. The benediction dedicates the newborn to the Law *and to the nuptial canopy:*

O give thanks unto the Lord; for he is good; for his loving-kindness endureth for ever. This little child, may he become great. Even as he has entered into the covenant, so may he enter into the Law, the nuptial canopy, and into good deeds.[7]

Sex and marriage. As it is written in the *Shulchan Aruch,*[8] the precept of propagation "becomes obligatory on a man when he reaches the age of eighteen; at any rate he should not pass his twentieth year without taking a wife."[9] If after ten years of marriage they remain childless, the husband is required to divorce her and seek another wife.[10] When a man has fathered a son and a daughter he has fulfilled the precept provided his offspring prove to be fertile. If either son or daughter die without leaving an offspring, the precept has not been fulfilled. Though both may die, if each has left at least one offspring and there are both male and female among them, the commandment has been fulfilled.[11]

If a man knows that he is "ungenerative," he should seek "a wife who is not prolific."[12] "Even if one has fulfilled the commandment of propagation, yet should he not remain without a wife, and, if possible, he should take one who is prolific."[13] "If one has many children and on account of that he is afraid that if his wife should be prolific, quarrels and dissentions may arise between the children and the woman, he is permitted to marry a woman who is not prolific, but he should not stay without a wife because of this apprehension."[14]

The pleasures of sex. Just as the worldly pleasures of eating and drinking were woven into the Jewish culture, through festivals and benedictions and blessings, so were the pleasures of cohabitation worked into the context of Jewish life. In the *Song of Songs* the loved one sings:

O that you would kiss me with the kisses of your mouth!
For your love is better than wine . . .
And her lover replies:
You have ravished my heart, my sister, my bride,
    you have ravished my heart with a glance
        of your eyes,
    with one jewel of your necklace.
How sweet is your love, my sister, my bride!

>how much better is your love than wine,
>   and the fragrance of your oils than any spice!
>Your lips distil nectar, my bride;
>   honey and milk are under your tongue. . . .

As if to fill in a pause in the impassioned dialogue, the poet intones:

>Eat, O friends, and drink:
>   drink deeply, O lovers![15]

The traditional prayers and benedictions over the bride and bridegroom acknowledge the sacred and spiritual aspects of marriage, but they also explicitly celebrate the sensual side of marriage, the "joy and gladness . . . [the] pleasure and delight" that bride and bridegroom find in each other:

>Blessed art thou, O Lord . . . who has created joy and gladness, bridegroom and bride, mirth and exultation, pleasure and delight, love, brotherhood, peace and fellowship. Soon may there be heard in the cities of Judah . . . the voice of joy and gladness, the voice of bridegroom and the voice of the bride, the jubilant voice of bridegrooms from their canopies, and of youths from their feasts of song. Blessed art thou, O Lord, who makest the bridegroom to rejoice with the bride.[16]

Intercourse with a virginal bride is preceded by a prayer which reads as follows: "Blessed be he who placed a nut-tree in the Garden of Eden, a lily of the valley, that . . . she preserved in purity the powers of love . . . Blessed be he who chooses the children of Israel."[17]

According to the *Code,* "it is a religious duty to make the groom and the bride rejoice, also to dance before the bride and to says that 'she is beautiful and graceful.' " It is also recorded that Rabbi Judah ben Illai used to dance before the bride.[18]

"He who espouses a maiden should rejoice with her seven days," prescribes the *Code.* "The groom should abstain from work and he should not buy and sell in the market place, but he should eat and drink and rejoice with her, whether he is a bachelor or a widower. Even if she releases him, he is nevertheless forbidden to do work. . . . If one marries a widow or a divorced woman . . . the rejoicing is required to last only three days; but if he is a bachelor, some authorities hold that he must rejoice with her seven days. . . . In this particular instance the woman may relinquish her right to rejoicing."[19]

"He who has taken a wife is required to stay in town for an entire year, in order that he may rejoice with her. . . . The woman may, however, relinquish such right."[20]

Frequency of cohabitation during the married years depends upon the health and vigor of the husband, the wishes of his wife, and the nature of the husband's work, according to the *Code*. "Men of strong constitution who enjoy the pleasures of life, who have profitable pursuits at home and are tax exempt, should perform their marriage duty nightly. Laborers who are employed in the city where they reside, should perform their marital duty twice weekly, but if they are employed in another city, once a week should be appointed for the performance of their marital duties. Merchants who travel into villages upon asses to bring grain to be sold in town, and people like them, should perform their marital duty once a week. They who convey baggage on camels from distant places, should have an appointed time once in thirty days. The time appointed for the learned men is from Sabbath Eve to Sabbath Eve."[21]

" 'And know,' writes a rabbi whom Jews call holy, 'that the sexual union achieved in the proper manner and the proper time and entered into with the right spirit, is a matter pure and sacred; let no man think that there is anything ignoble or ugly in it.' "[22] It is written in the *Zohar*,[23] "The pleasure of cohabitation is a religious one, giving joy also to the Divine Presence."[24]

The rabbis speculated upon both the spiritual and the sensuous attitudes toward sex, and gave a degree of sanction to both. On the spiritual side, it was argued that the lofty purpose of the sexual function—the creation of life—made it unseemly to exercise this act for carnal pleasure. Perhaps the voluptuous sensations were provided by Providence to stir those who might otherwise be reluctant to perform the divine commandment. But "the pious need no driving to do the will of God," and will therefore engage in the sexual life without frivolity or gluttony.[25]

The mystical meanings of sex. In addition to fulfilling the commandment to propagate, the sexual embrace also was taken to symbolize the union of life's dualisms: the union of matter and spirit, God and man, the infinite and the finite, the Creator and his universe, Judgment and Grace. The rabbis speculated that "just as the universe is a dualism seeking unity, so was man himself originally dual; for God created man . . . double-sexed, and cut him asunder into male and female. Ever since that separation was accomplished, neither man nor woman has been complete alone. To realize one's self, to find completion and harmony, he must seek union with his mate of the opposite sex."[26] When man is in union with a woman he partakes of God's oneness, and "the Creator dwells in him." Because the Creator is one he can only dwell "in him who is likewise one."[27]

The sexual act also symbolizes God's love of Israel. God "chose Israel as his bride . . . [and] entered into a union with his glory."[28] In song and ritual the Sabbath meal is described as a wedding feast. "The Sabbath is the bride and Israel is the groom." Pious Jews sing a traditional Sabbath song which describes "the magnificence of the feast . . . the details of the wedding, [and] tells how the husband embraces the bride 'and does what is pleasing to her by continuous grinding.' "[29] (Tradition allows for a non-sexual interpretation of this voluptuous phrasing.) "The law is beloved by Israel as sexual intercourse is by other peoples. Therefore," taught the rabbis, "he who has not known passionate love for woman cannot attain love for God."[30] Glasner attributes to the *Zohar* the statement that "wisdom will not come to the virgin."[31]

B. Z. Goldberg cites a passage in the Hebrew Bible supported by a commentary by Rashi,[32] to the effect that on the walls of the Temple of Jerusalem, there were decorative images of some sort representing "male and female in union," thus symbolizing the union of God with Israel.[33] Knight Dunlap has suggested that the superimposed triangles which make up the star of David symbolizes sexual union, the upright and inverted triangles representing the characteristic pubic hair pattern of male and female respectively.[34]

Fulfillment of woman's conjugal rights. The woman's right to sexual fulfillment is established in the Mosaic command that "her food, her raiment, and her conjugal rights shall [her husband] not diminish." According to the *Code*, "it is the duty of every man to visit his wife on the night she had performed the ceremony of immersion [following the menstrual period of enforced abstinence], also on the night preceding the day he is about to set out on a journey, unless he goes out on a sacred mission. When one observes his wife making an endeavor to please him and making herself attractive in his presence so that he should pay his attention to her, he is bound to visit with her even when not at the time appointed for the performance of the marital duty, and their descendants will then be worthy." The husband must observe and respond to his wife's unspoken and indirect expressions of sexual desire, for if she makes a direct verbal proposal she behaves with "a brazen shamelessness . . . like an adulterous woman whom he must not keep."[35]

The husband's moral duty to give his wife sexual fulfillment is also derived from the fact that the precept of propagation is obligatory upon the man but not the woman.[36] It therefore becomes the husband's task to "seduce" his wife into helping him fulfill his religious obligation to propagate. It is up to him to so "ingratiate himself with her to the end that she will not only consent to the union but even be passionately desirous of having him."[37]

The husband is "obligated to perform his marital duty also when [his wife] is pregnant or nursing. One should not deprive her of her rights unless by her consent, and when he already fulfilled the obligation of propagation. If he deprives her thereof to distress her, he violates a . . . commandment, for it is written: 'And her duty of marriage shall he not diminish.' "[38] Cohabitation during the middle and end of pregnancy was also considered good for the embryo, and "during the last three months, it is good for the woman as well as for the child, for because of this the child will come out clean and fast."[39]

Restraint and modesty. "If there is a famine in the land . . . one is forbidden to have intercourse unless on the night of her immersion." (But "they who are childless are permitted to cohabit at any time.") "One should not consort with his wife unless it be with her consent . . . nor should one have intercourse with his wife when she is actually asleep, or while he or she is intoxicated." "It is forbidden to have cohabitation in market places, or public squares, in gardens or in orchards . . . in order that it resemble not fornication." When one "has no need for it, but simply awakens his lust in order to satisfy it, [he] is following the counsel of the Satan."[40] He should not cohabit in a spirit of levity with his wife, nor should he befoul his mouth with ribald jests even in private conversation with her . . ." Cohabitation should take place in private and in a darkened room, screened off from either moonlight or candle light.[41] "It is forbidden to glance at that place, for whoever glances there possesses no shamefulness and . . . one who is bashful is not apt to sin. . . . Certainly one who kisses that place violates all this. . . ." "When having intercourse one should think of matters of the Torah or any holy subject, and although it is forbidden to utter the words with the mouth, yet thinking is permissible, even meritorious. . . ."[42]

Restraint is also required for the preservation of one's health, for "semen is the strength of the body and the light of the eyes, and when it effuses in abundance the body weakens and life is shortened. He who indulges in having intercourse ages quickly, his strength weakens, his eyes grow dim, a bad odor proceeds out of his mouth, the hair of his head, eyelashes and brows fall out, and many pains besides these befall him. The learned physicians said that one out of a thousand die from other diseases, while one thousand die from excessive cohabitation; therefore a man should be very careful about it."[43] This grim, ascetic warning sounds strangely out of place in the *Code*, and represents the diversity of viewpoints compiled into the *Code of Jewish Law*.

The sexual taboos. The command to propagate, the obligation to give one's wife a full portion of sexual gratification, and the idealization of sexual passion as a religious experience are counterbalanced by two major taboos: cohabitation during the menstrual period, and masturbation ("to cause in vain the effusion of semen.") [44]

The menstrual taboo. "Unto a woman in her menstrual uncleanliness," commands the law of Moses, "thou shalt not come near."[45] Both partners to a violation of this command are punishable by ostracism, and the man who touches an unclean woman "in a caressing manner . . . is punishable with stripes."[46]

So great is the revulsion against cohabitation with an unclean woman, the rabbis expressed confidence that a husband would surely overcome any "evil inclination" to violate this taboo.

Nevertheless, a considerable number of prohibitions were spelled out to effect a literal enforcement of the commandment that one "not come near" an unclean woman. Accordingly, "any kind of coming near her is forbidden: they should not laugh at each other, he should not carry on with her conversations of levity even about things that bring about sin. . . . He is not permitted to come in contact with her, even with her little finger; he should not hand over anything to her, be it even a long thing, nor should he receive aught from her; he is forbidden to throw anything from his hand into her hand, neither is she permitted to throw aught from her hand into his hand."[47]

"He is not allowed to sleep with her in the same bed . . . even if each of them are wearing clothes. . . . It is forbidden even if they lie in two separate beds but the beds touch one another. . . . He should not look at any part of her body which she is accustomed to generally cover, but is permitted to look at the always uncovered parts although he derives pleasure therefrom. . . . He is forbidden to hear her sing. . . It is proper for her to wear special clothes during the days of her uncleanliness so that both of them be ever reminded that she is menstrually unclean. With difficulty was she permitted to powder, paint and adorn herself with colored clothes during her menstrual period in order that she may not become repulsive to her husband."[48]

A woman "is considered menstrually unclean until she counts seven days [after the menstrual flow] and takes the proper bath of immersion." The *Code* provides detailed instructions for self-examination for menstrual flow, and for dealing with irregular periods. The wife must tell her husband if she sees or feels any evidence of menstruation. If during the very act of cohabitation "the woman had perceived that she had become menstrually unclean, it is her duty to tell her husband immediately, saying 'I have become unclean.' He should then not separate from her before his virile strength is exhausted, for this very act affords him pleasure, but he must raise his body supporting himself on his hands and feet and not upon her; he should be filled with fear and trembling because of the sinful happening, and on its exhaustion he should separate from her. He should then consult a Rabbi who will instruct him what penance he should do for his sin."[49]

What was the influence of the menstrual taboos on the sex attitudes of the Orthodox Jew? Wolfenstein has argued that the traditional taboos lead to a generalized inhibition of sexual potency. To Solomon Maimon—who was no defender of the Orthodox tradition!—it appeared that the menstrual taboo tended to *increase* the Jew's interest in his wife as a love object:

> Every month the husband is wholly separated from his wife for a fortnight (the period of monthly purification in accordance with the rabbinical laws) ; they may not so much as touch one another, or eat out of the same dish or drink out of the same cup. By this means satiety is avoided; the wife continues to be in the eyes of her husband all that she was as maiden in the eyes of her lover.[50]

The masturbation taboo. "To cause in vain the effusion of semen . . . [is more offensive] than any of the violations mentioned in the Torah," and is compared by the *Code* to the crime of murder. Those who "commit fornication with their hands" are to be banned. As further punishment for their sin they may suffer poverty, their children may die young or become wicked. Masturbation serves none of the purposes of cohabitation, neither propagation nor gratification of a woman, neither the experience of dualism seeking unity nor the passion of God's love for Israel. The *Code* views with horror this defiance of the divine command, the wasting of semen which is "the strength of the body and the light of his eyes," the source of man's health and physical powers.[51]

Masturbation was punishable by natural means (loss of strength), by social sanctions (ostracism) and by divine retribution. *The tendencies to violate this taboo must nonetheless have been very strong,* for the *Code* elaborates at some length on how one might avoid the thoughts, feelings and physical sensations which lead to the forbidden act. Moreover, the *Code* refers to a book entitled *Y'sod Joseph* listing many remedies and acts of penance for persons who have violated this taboo "copied by the author from various holy books and ancient authorities."[52] Rabbi Glasner agrees that "the detailed precautions against [masturbation] that are prescribed in the Talmud and elsewhere lead one to suspect that it must have represented a very difficult problem of social control."[53]

Regulation of the sexual passion. A passion which leads men to risk natural, social, and divine punishment presents an awesome task for individual mastery. Renunciation or denial of one's sexual impulses was inappropriate from the standpoint of the Jewish culture because the sexual act was instrumental to fulfillment of divine commands, and the rabbis attached to the sexual act the most profound religious values. To renounce sex as alien to the spiritual life, to tolerate it as an animal vestige might fit a Christian concept of the good life, but the Jewish culture required that the sexual impulse be directed and regulated. This could not be accomplished by a deeply interiorized guilt mechanism, by an "act of will," by holy vows and prayers alone, but seemed to call for a detailed control of one's everyday life so as to maintain an environment in which a good sex life is available, and circumvent situations which lead to moral transgression.

Early marriage. The primary instrument for the regulation of sex is, of course, early marriage. The *Code* required that a man marry "when he reaches the age of eighteen; at any rate he should not pass his twentieth year without taking a wife." If marriage would interfere with his study of the *Torah,* and he is studying "with great diligence . . . he may delay marrying, provided he is not passionate."[54] A father is required to find marriage partners for his sons and daughters "immediately [as] they approach maturity, lest, if he neglect them, they may come to the commission of adultery or to the thinking of it. . . ."[55]

According to Jacob Katz, in the Middle Ages "a person's eligibility for office in general and for the rabbinate in particular . . . depended, first of all, on his age. *This was calculated from the time of marriage rather than from the date of birth. . . .*"[56] (Italics added.) The Talmudic view of human nature implied that it was necessary to be married in order to lead a moral life. "A Jew who was bred on this outlook was left with no alternative but to arrange as early a marriage as possible both for himself [and] for his sons. . . . Sixteen was considered the proper age for a girl and eighteen, at the very latest, for a boy. Parents who arranged a match—or even married off—their daughter of thirteen or fourteen or their sons of fifteen or sixteen were considered praiseworthy [in Jewish society of the Middle Ages] and were certainly not criticized."[57]

Avoidance rules. The regulation of sex requires the avoidance of perceptions and acts which may lead to sexual excitement at times when normal gratification is unavailable, according to the *Code of Law*. One "should guard his mouth against obscene talk . . . and should likewise guard his ear against hearing such things."[58] "One should not look when either animals, beasts or fowl are having intercourse."[59] One should not eat too much, for when a man is satiated he becomes sexually hungry, and when he is hungry he is sexually satiated.[60] Fats, cheese, eggs, garlic and wine "warm up the body."[61] If one is married, "his wife is in town and she is [ritually] clean," he may hold his penis while urinating, for it is unlikely that this will stimulate him to think of intercourse. Otherwise "it is forbidden to hold the penis while urinating."[62] A husband "should not manifest his love . . . for his wife . . . in the presence of others, [nor should he permit his wife to show him affection] so that the looker-on should not come to bad thoughts."[63]

The mastery of sex requires the avoidance of social situations which might arouse sexual temptations. The *Code* forbids a man "to be alone with any woman," Jewess or Gentile, relative or stranger; except that a husband may be alone with his wife, a mother with her son, and a father with his daughter. "One need not scruple to be alone with a woman whose husband is in town, because the fear of her husband is upon her." But a Jewess may not be alone in the company of non-Jews. "One woman may be alone with two virtuous men, but in a town and in the daytime; but in the field or at night even in the town, it is necessary that there be three virtuous men. . . . One man should not be alone with two women. . . . It is permissible for a man to be alone with a female child if she be less than three years old, also for a woman to be alone with a lad who is less than nine years of age."[64]

The mastery of sex through the avoidance of temptation is further prescribed in the rule that "he who has no wife shall not be a teacher for minors, because their mothers visit the school and thus he will be alone with them. There is no need that his wife live with him at school, but as long as she is in town, even if she be in the house and he be at school. But a woman

shall not teach children even when her husband is in town, unless
he lives with her in the same house, because of the fathers who
bring their children."[65]

Provocative words, sights, and gestures likewise threaten man's
mastery of the sexual passion. "A man should avoid women, thus,
he should not make gestures either with his hands or feet, nor
wink to them, nor jest with them, nor to act with levity in their
presence, or to gaze at their beauty [or to scent their perfume].
. . . It is forbidden to gaze at the colored clothes of a woman
with whom he is acquainted, although the clothes be not upon
her lest he come to think of her. If he encounters a woman on
the street, he should not walk behind her, but he should run
so that she be either alongside of him or behind him. . . . One
who gazes even at the small finger of a woman with the intention
of gratifying his desire is guilty of a serious crime. . ." "It is permissible and highly proper for one to look at the woman he is
to make his wife, to see if she pleases him, but he should not
regard her with lascivious eyes. . ."[66]

To avoid physical sensations which may arouse an impulse
to masturbate, "it is forbidden to ride on an animal without a
saddle,"[67] one "should be careful not to sleep alone in a room,"[68]
nor should two bachelors sleep together. To avoid erection "it is
forbidden to sleep on one's back . . . or to sleep with his face
downward, but sleep on the side. . ."[69] As if relief from anxiety
were recognized as a motive for masturbation, the *Code* advised
that one "also be careful to fulfill his vows and not to worry
too much."[70]

If one comes to "the thought about women . . . he should divert
his attention from trivial matters to matters of the Torah which
is a favorite wife and full of grace. The thought of fornication
[and therefore the temptation to masturbate] only comes into
a mind devoid of wisdom." Before bedtime one should recite the
first chapters of the Psalms. As a remedy for breaking the habit
of masturbation, the *Code* prescribes that one "awake in the
midst of the night to perform the ceremony of weeping for the
destruction of the Temple," and during the day perform his
religious duties "energetically and with haste so that his entire
body be heated up." He is asked to give generously to charity,

to perform acts of penance and humility, to serve as godfather in the circumcision rites of the poor, "to honor and love those who study the Torah, to pray with devotion and weeping . . . raise an orphan in his house and treat him the way he treats his own children . . . to love peace and pursue peace."[71] In this prescription for the restoration of self-respect one sees the familiar ingredients of emotional catharsis, physical exertion, intellectual distraction, and the development of satisfying interpersonal relations.

Control without inhibition. Freud deal in detail with the injurious effects of "civilization" on the sexual potency and pleasure of marriage partners. The majority of people, Freud argued, are "constitutionally unfit for [pre-marital] abstinence" beyond the age of twenty. The restraint required before marriage and the restrictions on sex in marriage itself, so impair sexual enjoyment that after "three, four or five years, marriage ceases to furnish the satisfaction of the sexual needs that it promised." This "spiritual disappointment and physical deprivation . . . [which becomes] the fate of most marriages" not only "dissipates the physical tenderness of the married couple for each other," but also undermines "the mental affection between them which was destined to succeed the originally tempestuous passion . . ."[72]

Society's "double code" permits the husband to find some substitute for his conjugal disappointment (in an exotic woman?), but women do not enjoy this sanction and therefore suffer more severely from "the disappointments of matrimony . . . [and a] severe, lifelong neurosis [may affect] the whole course of their lives . . ." It is in this context that Freud warns his male reader not to marry a neurotic woman:

A girl must be very healthy to 'stand' marriage, and we earnestly counsel our male inquirers not to marry a girl who has been neurotic. . . . The more strictly a wife has been brought up, the more earnestly she has submitted to the demands of civilization, the more [is she likely to] seek shelter in a neurosis. Nothing protects her virtue so securely as illness. The conjugal state, which is held out to the youthful among civilized people as a refuge for the sexual instinct . . . fails to compensate for the earlier abstention.[73]

Freud is arguing that strict taboos lead inevitably to generalized avoidance habits; just as the incest taboo leads to
exogamy, a prolonged pre-marital taboo leads to impotence and
frigidity. How does a society which enforces a long catalog of
sex taboos prevent the pernicious by-product of stimulus generalization, and instill a repertory of well-discriminated habits
instead of a vague and disabling avoidance attitude?

Once again we return to Murdock's impression that "societies
fall into two groups with respect to the manner in which they
handle . . . sex taboos"; one group depending upon internalization so strong that the taboos become "second nature," while
the other group depends on avoidance rules. It is eminently
clear that the *Code* regulates sex behavior mainly through the
explicit control of overt social behavior, rather than through the
internalization of deep and disabling feelings of guilt. (Murdock supposes that avoidance rules are resorted to when internalization methods "don't succeed." We would argue that strong
internalizations—deep feelings of guilt—run the risk of overgeneralization and would therefore be dysfunctional in a culture
which specifies a repertory of carefully discriminated sex habits.)

We have distinguished between internalization and avoidance
as the method of guilt and the method of shame. We might also
look upon them as the individual approach *versus* the social approach. The concept of an "avoidance taboo" has a strongly tribal
connotation; indeed, the effectiveness of an avoidance taboo
would seem to depend upon a society small enough, well-inte-
grated and stable enough so that "good behavior" is maintained
by the process of "keeping an eye on one another." The method
of shame would seem to belong to the family, the tribe, the *shtetl,*
where "good behavior" can be enforcd with a minimum of disabling guilt.

The use of sexual fantasy. In Judaism the concept of *Shekinah*
describes the felt presence of God. The term came to imply a
radiance, and in works of art the *Shekinah* is represented by
rays of light descending from on high. The concept of radiance
points to a similarity between the ecstasy of religious mysticism—
the glow of beatitude, the discovery of a "radiant core" of
human experience[74]—and the heat of sexual passion. A source
book of the mystical Jewish tradition, the *Zohar* explicitly casts the

Shekinah into the role of a celestial Female, who finds pleasure in sexual union, presides over the sexual union of man and wife, and may serve as man's celestial companion while he is away from his wife.

"When a man leaves home, as for example a student who must go to a strange city to study at a scholarly academy . . . he must pray God to send the *Shekinah* to him . . . to live with [him] *so that he can unite himself with her* while he is away from his wife. The prayer for such a granting of the *Shekinah*, however, must be made while a man is still . . . living with his wife; and when he returns, he must at once have intercourse with his wife, since it was 'she who procured for him this heavenly partner.' " (Italics added.) [75]

"A scholar who is away from his wife during the week but returns on the Sabbath must on that day give her this pleasure in order thus to glorify his celestial companion, the *Shekinah*. Similarly, when the wife returns to him after the menstrual separation, he must 'procure for her this pleasure which constitutes a meritorious work, celestial pleasure.' The proper performance of the earthly duty is that *a man during union with his wife have his mind on the Shekinah,* for union with the one is an image of union with the other. Let no one think that the relation with the *Shekinah* is more pure when the human intercourse is not involved, the author says, for the *Shekinah* by no means leaves because of the presence of the human wife. . . . The *Shekinah* is as vividly and truly present during human intercourse as when a man is having intercourse with her in solitary mysticism." (Italics added.) [76]

All of the foregoing suggests that the Jewish mystical tradition served to *direct* and *pattern* man's erotic fantasy rather than divert or inhibit it. This convention served more than one psychic purpose: (1) It not only sanctioned solitary involvement in sexual thought, but sanctioned moments of soaring passion as the act of uniting one's self with a celestial companion. (2) It protected man's sexual potency from the inhibiting effects of guilt and anxiety. (The renunciation of sexual fantasy undoubtedly reduces a person's capacity for giving and receiving sexual pleasure.) (3) It linked together a man's sexual fantasy and his conjugal experience, by defining the *Shekinah* as a gift from his

wife, and by asking him to have his mind on the *Shekinah* while
he is in union with his wife. (This fusion of opposites—spiritual
craving and carnal desire, private fantasy and conjugal intercourse—stands in bold contrast to the Christian distinction between sacred and profane love.)

The sensuous woman. Note that the *Code* permits a woman
to be alone with two virtuous men, but does not permit a man
to be alone with two women. Note also that a distinction is
made between a *virtuous* man and others, but no such distinction
is made for women. Both these facts point to the "tendency from
the Bible down through the later Jewish literature to regard
the sexual drive in women as greater, more constant, and more
aggressive than that in men. One frequently finds it asserted
that it is women who lead men into sexual misconduct. . . . The
Bible cites numerous examples of women who took the initiative
in sexual misdemeanors."[77]

Pointing to woman's carnal nature, the Book of Proverbs
says:

> Three things are never satisfied;
>   four never say, 'Enough':
> Sheol [the abode of the dead], the barren womb,
>   the earth ever thirsty for water,
>   and the fire which never says 'Enough.'[78]

Edwardes and Masters quote from the Talmud: "A woman prefers one measure of luxury and sexual indulgence to nine measures of luxury and continence."[79]

Paradox and diversity. Sexual needs seemed to require that
sexual intercourse between husband and wife be sanctioned "even
where conception could not possibly result—for example, where
the woman was already pregnant or not capable of having children." Katz acknowledge that such sanction "seems to run counter
to the severe condemnation of masturbation . . . [but] scholars
who pointed out the discrepancy managed to solve it dialectically;
in practice the sanction was never doubted."[80]

Although religious law and ethics emphasize the husband's
obligation to fulfill his wife's marriage portion, the wife is also
"admonished to attract her husband's attention to the point of
completely monopolizing his erotic impulse."[81]

Judaism has known extremist movements at both ends of the spectrum: the Essenes "preached asceticism and practiced continence," while in a later era the Sabbataians and Frankists "endorsed all sorts of sexual excesses as divinely ordained measures for hastening the advent of the Messiah."[82]

Rabbi Glasner aptly comments: "It is difficult to generalize about Jewish sex attitudes and sex practices. The picture that emerges, however, seems to lean in the direction of a frank, nonpuritanical attitude of acceptance of sex, accompanied by a rather rigid, self-imposed discipline of sexual restraint."[83] Around this norm one must conceptualize a sanctioned diversity of valuations, ranging from a sort of puritanism to a view that eulogized the sex act as a mystical experience of God's love of Israel, and encompassing also the viewpoint that woman is sensuous by nature and needs a good deal of sexual gratification for her psychic well being.

Sex talk and curiosity. A sacred obligation, an evil impulse; a physical thrill, a mystical experience; exhausting to men, insatiable for women; an appetite which is satiated when man goes hungry, but hungers when man is satiated; sex has always seemed too important, too puzzling and fascinating a topic for Jews to ban from discussion and speculation.

The Jewish view of sex as a most complex and challenging aspect of man's impulse life, of his relation to people and to God, helps account for the observation that Kinsey found so puzzling: that Jews "discuss sexual matters publicly with less restraint than most other groups," and thereby give the misleading impression that they are sexually more active. Kinsey was surprised to discover that "the freedom with which [Jews] record the details of their own sexual activities and the freedom with which they discuss those details, not only with us but with many of their fellows and with utter strangers, has . . . little relation to the extent of the overt activity in their individual sexual histories."[84] When he talks about sex, the Jew is carrying on a dialogue on man's mastery of his passions, over which rabbis and scholars have openly pondered for many hundreds of years.

"It is told by Rabbi Eliezer that he used to have cohabitation with such awe and fear that it appeared to him as if a demon was forcing him to do it."[85] The Talmud tells of a scholar, Rab Kahana, whose spirit of inquiry on the nature of sex moved him to hide under a friend's bed. When he heard his "subject" chattering with his wife "and joking and doing as he required," Rab Kahana spoke up, to his friend's surprise: "One would think that [you] had never tasted of this dish before!" [Rab Kahana's friend] said to him: 'Kahana, is that you there? Get out! It's rude!' Then [Kahana] replied: 'It is a matter of Torah [i.e., the pursuit of knowledge], and I need to learn.' "[86]

This perennial dialogue on the place of sex in the good Jewish life is marked by the open-minded, speculative diversity that is so characteristic of Jewish thought. At the ascetic end of the gamut one may quote Maimonides, who wrote: "We ought to limit sexual intercourse altogether, hold it in contempt and desire it only rarely. . . . The act is too base to be performed except when needed."[87] Nachmonides, who (according to Rabbi Glasner) was almost equally renowned, chided Maimonides for adopting a "Gentile" attitude toward sex; Maimonides presumably borrowed his ascetic view from Aristotle. "The act of sexual union," Nachmonides argued, "is holy and pure. . . . The Lord created all things in accordance with his wisdom, and whatever he created cannot possibly be shameful or ugly . . . When a man is in union with his wife in a spirit of holiness and purity, the Divine Presence is with them."[88]

Sex talk in religious ceremony. The extent to which the Jewish culture sanctions talk about sex is illustrated by the content of "Achad Mi Yodeyah," a traditional children's song contained in the Passover *Haggadah,* handbook for the *Seder* feast of liberation. For many hundreds of years Jewish children have concluded this annual family celebration by singing this repetitious counting song in which each number, from one to twelve, is associated with an important aspect of the Jewish world view. *One* stands for the Lord himself, *two* stands for the tablets of the Law, *three* stands for the patriarchs . . . *eight* stands for the days preceding circumcision, *nine* stands for the months of pregnancy, *ten* stands for the ten commandments. . . . It is interesting to note that when the *Haggadah* is translated into English, references to circumcision and pregnancy usually disappear. In a translation prepared by the Jewish Reconstructionist Foundation, *eight* stands for the Hannukah lights and *nine* stands for the half-holidays of the year. The editor explains in a footnote that these verses "do not correspond to the Hebrew, but are adopted to appeal to the interest of the child."[89] The *Haggadah* of the Reform Jews is likewise expurgated to conform to Western standards of prudery. [A Yiddish proverb might reassure the *Haggadah* editor— *Fun zogn vert men nit trogen.* (Talk doesn't make one pregnant.)][90]

That it appears unseemly to let children sit around the Seder table and sing about circumcision and pregnancy reveals an unnoticed but perhaps significant consequence of the Westernization of Jewish ritual. This becomes a matter of some importance because all that we know about the dynamics of learning (as spelled out in the first portion of Chapter 6) indicates that whatever fosters attitudes of prudery tends to inhibit potency toward an in-group partner, and tends to foster neurotic exogamy.

To incorporate into the wedding ceremony a song about the sensuous delights of a young man and his bride ("Your lips distil nectar, my bride; honey and milk are under your tongue. . ."), to read in the Bible about the sexual lapses of kings and elders, to sit at the Seder table and sing about circumcision and pregnancy—such is the cultural tradition that predisposed Kinsey's Jewish respondents to talk about sex with a frankness and freedom that seemed incongruous for a group whose sex habits are circumspect. Kinsey was surprised to learn what a careful distinction Jews make between talk and acting-out: *Fun zogn vert men nit trogen.*

Sex joking in the Jewish culture. Reik's book on *Jewish Wit* illustrates how frequently sex themes appear in Jewish humor. In *Hooray for Me,* nostalgic novel of the childhood of a third-generation Jew in New York City, S. J. Wilson skillfully conveys the manner in which sex joking is woven into Jewish family life, and even serves as a vehicle of the mother-son romance.

Frances Hirshman

In *Hooray for Me,* the protagonist's mother, Frances Hirshman, is portrayed as an intelligent, compassionate, witty, and educated woman. She is also an authentic Jewish mother—*not* a comic figure of the Molly Goldberg genre (lampooned in Greenburg's *How to Be a Jewish Mother*) . Frances is the dominant figure of the Hirshman household, abundantly affectionate toward her favorite son, Bobby. The style with which she weaves sex joking into her conversation may be conveyed through the following citations:

On the first day of school, she awakens five-year-old Bobby by kissing his eyes and saying: "Wake up, Mr. Schmeckel-Peckel." "What kind of a name is that?" Bobby asks. "It's a love name," his mother replies.[91] Bobby's older brother teases Bobby for acquiring this sobriquet, and Bobby makes his mother promise not to call him that in the presence of his friends.

Bobby's mother is amused at her boy's story that he spoke up in class saying he liked his classmate and neighbor Libby Jackson "because she has lullaby eyes." Frances turns to her husband and jokes: "If he can think up something like lullaby eyes now, just imagine him when he's grown up. I can hear the cherries popping all over the neighborhood." "Fran, watch what you're saying," Father replies with embarrassment.[92]

When Bobby sticks his adolescent brother in the buttocks with a pin, Mother jokingly consoles him by saying: "It will heal by the time you get married. And if it doesn't, your wife will kiss it and that will make it better." Her adolescent son blushes, runs to his bedroom, yelling: "How did I ever get into this crazy, crazy family?" Mother retorts: "Einstein has been working on that problem for some time now. He should have the answer any day now."[93]

When Bobby is displaced from his bedroom to accommodate a neighbor boy whose mother has been hospitalized, Bobby jealously insists: "I want to go to bed right now." Mother distracts him with the response, "Congratulations. That's the first time you ever said you wanted to go to bed. Most people wait until they're married before they ever say it. See how smart you are?"[94]

In Bobby's milieu—a New York Jewish neighborhood in the 1930's—the idea of marriage is never too far in the background. When a little girl misbehaves, her mother says she'd be happy to marry her off to almost anyone. When Bobby bears a grudge against a neighbor women, she tells the five-year-old: "So you won't invite me to your wedding. I'll save on the present I was going to give you."[95]

Reik includes several sexual jokes in his book on Jewish wit. Western sensibilities might be shocked to hear Jewish jokes on the absurd theme that women enjoyed being raped during a pogrom:

> After a pogrom, a husband remarks ruefully to his wife, 'I know you couldn't escape from the soldier's grip; but did you have to wiggle your behind?'[96]

> A lusty soldier dives toward a young woman as her children scream in terror. 'Quiet down a little,' she orders. 'A pogrom is a pogrom.'[97]

Singing, speculating, and joking about sex may be viewed as culturally patterned verbal behaviors which serve to counterbalance the influence of the taboos (according to the principle of discrimination learning). Talk is therapy in the Jewish culture; talk is also prophylaxis.

To the Western reader there is something incredible about the place of sex in the Jewish culture: How is it possible for a society to maintain so many sexual taboos (against incestuous play, against masturbation, against exogamous marriage, against intercourse during periods of ritual uncleanliness, etc., etc.) without serious risk of overgeneralization; i.e., without seriously disturbing sexual potency in the remaining sanctioned areas of sexual expression? How can one culture enforce such a variety of sex taboos and at the same time expect the husband to give his wife a full share of "her conjugal portion?"

It begins to seem clear that the Jewish customs related to sex and marriage have their place in an over-all way of life that was maintained in the *shtetl*. The acculturation of the Jew to Western society has of course replaced *shtetl* customs of avoidance and sexual joking with Western standards of decorum and conscience, on a widespread scale. These alterations have undoubtedly introduced new strains and tensions, the influences of "civilization" on Jewish living, of which neurotic exogamy[98] and sexual inhibition are two symptoms.

Sexual irregularities. Jewish law does not oblige an unmarried couple to obtain the blessing of a rabbi in order to become man and wife. According to the Talmudic tractate on marriage, *Kiddushin,* the act of sexual intercourse itself binds a couple in marriage as validly as a written marriage contract or an exchange of dowry. In Christian thought, the term adultery—and its connotations of deep moral wrong—is freely applied to any sex act between persons married or unmarried, if they are not married to each other. Jewish thought has preserved the biblical distinction between fornication (disregard by an unmarried couple of the obligations implicit in sexual intimacy) and adultery, which is condemned as a breach of the marriage contract and a threat to family life.

The Jewish concept of illegitimacy is likewise more restricted than the Gentile concept. In the Jewish tradition, a child "born out of wedlock" is not a bastard unless the child is the "offspring of a union that would not have been permissible in marriage, such as incestuous or adulterous relations, or relations between a member of the priestly class and a divorcee."[99]

Although the *Code* prescribes early marriage and all manner of avoidance rules to minimize sexual irregularities, the *responsa* literature in every generation and in and every locality deals with cases of sexual misbehavior. "Involuntary bachelorhood, unattached widows and widowers, bachelor teachers, travelling salesmen, and itinerant beggars; by the very nature of their lives, all these groups were suspect of sexual transgression. They also served as a constant temptation to possible deviation on the part of others. To be sure, even marriage was no absolute guarantee against the evil inclination. As the Talmud so realistically puts it," Katz adds, " 'There is no guardian against unchastity.' "[100]

"Though Judaism was definitely intolerant of sex perversions," writes Henry Raphael Gold, "it accepted the idea of the existence of a variety of individual sex expressions."[101] Irregularities were regarded as temporary lapses. The *responsa* literature abounds with "inquiries regarding ways of doing penance for sexual sins, ranging from masturbation to adultery. . . . The concept of *ba'al tschuva* (a penitent) was applied almost exclusively to persons who had committed a sexual offense . . ."[102]

Jewish sex norms. This author has found virtually no documentation dealing directly with the implicit norms, or actual practices, of premarital or extra-marital sex in the culture of the Eastern European Jews[103]—how much or what kinds of sex play occurred in the Jewish community, or to what extent dalliance with the peasant girl was sanctioned. A familiar Yiddish proverb says, "If there are no maidens, one dances with *shikses*." *(Az es iz nit du kein meyden, tanst men mit shikses.)* Another proverb instructs the Jewish daughter on how to fend off a seducer: "For a pat, give a rap—for a kiss, give a slap." *(Far a tap, a klap—far a kish, a potch.)* Jewish proverbs likewise remind the young and amorous that sexual intimacy should wait for marriage: "One must't eat the *challa* before reciting the blessing" *(Men tur nit essen di challa far der ha'moytse)*— and "Don't eat the noodles before the Sabbath" *(Ess nit di lokshen far shaboss.)*

Describing the sex and marriage practices of Jews in a small town in New England, Barron reports that sexual dalliance with Gentile girls of a nearby city was widely practiced. The following "stag party" ditty was sung by this group in Yiddish, and presumably goes back to the *shtetl* culture:

> In the holy books 'tis said
> A *shiksa* may you take to bed;
> If she doesn't let you make her
> Then let the devil take her.[104]

The Ehrmann study. Over the period 1947–1950, Ehrmann collected data on the sex and dating habits of students at a large university, enrolled in the course Marriage and the Family. Data were collected through questionnaire and interview methods. Findings are reported for 841 students, which include about 58 Jewish males and 35 Jewish females, and show quite clearly that "more Jewish than non-Jewish boys had had or were having sexual intercourse or some form of [heterosexual] genital activity in their current behavior."[105] Among Jewish girls, however, coital experience was relatively rare (although the size of the female samples were too small for statistical significance). Those few college girls (Jewish or Gentile) in Ehrmann's study who were having coital experience frequently explained that they were engaged.

Experienced male subjects, on the other hand, characteristically described their partners as gainfully employed unmarried women—office workers, waitresses, factory workers, nurses, technicians, or professional women. College girls were often deliberately shunned as sexual companions:

> Several males emphasized the fact that it was either unwise or unprofitable to try to seduce fellow coeds. . . . 'If you get a coed to go to bed with you, she's on you like a leech; and she wants you to marry her.' . . . 'Coeds are definitely out.'[106]

In their dating experience with coeds, college men did not depend on the girl to determine the point at which their petting activity would stop; the males knew where they wanted to stop, *and this was especially true of Jewish males and of males who dated Jewish coeds.*[107] Male respondents describe their tactics and strategy as follows:

> 'I'm afraid to go too far with a girl I've known for a long time because her parents might find out and cause difficulties for both of us.' . . . 'I don't want to lead a girl astray, but if she's already gone astray, I am not hurting anything by pegging along.' . . . 'I wouldn't do anything with some girls because I'd worry too much about what the girl would think of me.' . . . 'There are two kinds of girls that I know well: those that I am not going to be in love with and those that I might be or have been in love with. I don't go out with girls with whom I am not going to be in love unless it's to have intercourse. With girls I have been or might be in love I am going to save that until marriage. If I did it to them I would have a terrible feeling of shame and a guilt complex.'[108]

Which of the above comments were made by Jewish males is not recorded, but a significantly higher percentage of Jewish males (52 per cent) were reporting current coital experience than their Protestant (38 per cent) or Catholic (33 per cent) male classmates. Ehrmann feels sure that there must be something outside the Jewish religious tradition itself to account for this difference:

> In the particular region in which this study was made, [Jews] are a close-knit minority community. Sexual access to the females in their own group is handicapped by a virtual

chaperonage system through constant scrutiny of peers and elders and by a very strong supposition of possible marriage with more than a perfunctory relation in dating. Their superior economic status and their greater sophistication enable them to obtain partners elsewhere. Being partially denied women in their own group seems to act as a spur, rather than as a deterrent, to sexual activities. Under similar conditions it seems more than likely that Protestant and Catholic males would react the same way.[109]

In the interviews, and through notes added to the questionnaires, Catholic respondents and Protestants of most denominations often volunteered explanations on the principles of sex morality conveyed by their religion. *"By contrast, not one Jew, male or female,"* offered a comment relating their sex standards to the teachings of their religion. Ehrmann finds this surprising in view of "the overwhelming evidence from the [questionnaire] schedules, from the interviews, and from many years' clinical experience . . . that the restraints imposed upon Jewish girls by the Jewish culture is in the local situation one of the most powerful forces limiting sex activity of any investigated in this study."[110] What Ehrmann found, one might say, is that his Jewish respondents regard the sex code of their group *not* as a religious teaching but as an unwritten "law of the tribe."

Some findings of Kinsey. The sexual life of Jews in America fell under the scrutiny of Kinsey and his co-workers, who found that "the sexually least active individuals in any age and educational group [rated by frequencies of total sexual outlet] are the Orthodox Jews."[111] The Orthodox Jewish adolescent avoids masturbation, in keeping with "Hebraic laws on this point, and the often lower rates of the religiously inactive Jewish boys indicate that even they are not entirely free of the ancestral codes."[112]

While "it is not unusual to find even devoutly religious Protestants or Catholics who have become involved in the homosexual without any clear understanding of the church's attitude on the subject" (presumably to avoid "the sinfulness of masturbation and of pre-marital intercourse") . . . "the homosexual among Orthodox Jewish groups appears to be phenomenally low."[113]

". . . Data on the lower frequencies of sexual activity among

Table 9:1. Incidence of Coital Experience in a University Student Population by Sex and Religious Group (N=841) *

| | Males (N=576) ** | | | | | | Females (N=265) *** | | | | | |
| | Prot. (N=460) | | Catholics (N=58) | | Jewish (N=58) | | Prot. (N=212) | | Catholics (N=18) | | Jewish (N=35) | |
	(N)	%	(N)	%	(N)	%	(N)	%	(N)	%	(N)	%
Have had *any* coital experience, before or during time of study	(294)	64	(35)	61	(51)	88	(25)	12	(4)	21	(4)	11
Coital experience reported at time of study	(175)	38	(19)	33	(30)	52	(19)	09	(2)	16	(3)	08

* All members of the sample are white, single, and not previously married. Numbers attributed to Protestant, Catholic, and Jewish subgroups are approximations based on report, given by percentages only. *See* Ehrmann, pages 88-89.
** Sample included 302 World War II veterans, median age 22.9; 274 non-veterans, median age 20.0.
*** Median age 19.7.

the Orthodox Jews will occasion no surprise to those who understand the pervading asceticism of Hebrew philosophy. Nondevout Jewish groups, even including those who observe none of the Orthodox customs and who may be removed by several generations from ancestors who ever attended the synagogue, may still be controlled to a considerable degree by the Talmudic interpretations of sexual morality."[114]

Perhaps Kinsey's major finding on *Sexual Behavior of the Human Male* was that *educational level* was the major correlate of sexual control, regulation, and inhibition. We are *not* dealing here with the *effects* of higher education, for as Kinsey pointed out, among high school boys the few who were oriented toward college led a distinctly more inhibited, restrained sex life. As Glazer commented, postponement of sexual pleasure is one aspect of the middle class orientation of foresight, care, and sobriety.[115]

Because the "average Jew" is an urban middle class person his frequency and variety of sex outlets are more restricted than those of the "average Gentile" whose group covers a wider socio-economic range. When, however, Kinsey compared marital intercourse of Jews with Gentiles matched on educational level, it appears that Jews give their wives a slightly fuller share of their "conjugal portion."

Table 9:2. Median Frequency of Marital Intercourse of Protestants and Jews, Education Level 13 Years or More[116]

Religious Group[1]	Median frequency at various age levels							
	Age 21-25		Age 26-30		Age 31-35		Age 36-40	
	f[2]	N[3]	f	N	f	N	f	N
Protestant, active[4]	2.19	(91)	1.85	(123)	1.75	(109)	1.56	(73)
Protestant, inactive[5]	2.51	(280)	2.13	(346)	1.86	(270)	1.59	(187)
Jewish, inactive	2.88	(86)	2.47	(109)	2.12	(84)	1.90	(62)

[1] Only those religious groups are included for which Kinsey had accumulated a sufficient number of cases of married men at educational level 13 years plus.

[2] f=frequency (per week).

[3] N=number of cases on which median is based.

[4] Religiously "active" designates regular attendance or active participation in organized church activities.

[5] Religiously "inactive" means practically no church attendance or activity.

As we approach Kinsey's statistics on *female* sex activity, we might ask how consistent are his findings with Ehrmann's campus survey, and with the complaints of Mayer's intermarried Jewish men—that "Jewish girls are more moral, and it's harder to have a good time with them"; that Jewish girls are puritanical and sexually inhibited. (Perhaps the inmarrying Jew holds the same opinion but attaches a more positive value to virginity.)

It is in the nature of the incest taboo that a Jewish male's sexual inhibitions should be more readily elicited by a *Jewish* girl—and the Jewish male would be no more than human to place some of the blame on the girl, for his relative lack of sexual arousal. If a Jewish girl arouses his ambivalence toward intimacy, he may in turn arouse her anxiety and thereby set in motion a vicious cycle which inhibits sexual adventure.

It is also possible that the Jewish male is comparing Jewish girls of his own social class with Gentile girls he may meet at public dances or bars. *He* may not worry about uncontrolled variables, but the scientific observer cannot afford to overlook the point that in this case *social class,* not ethnic group membership, would appear to be the critical factor. It is true that Jews tend to rise out of the lower class, and even lower class Jews tend to adhere to a middle class ideology. A similar bias would be involved if one compared Jewish girls who are at least "moderately religious" with Gentile girls who are "religiously inactive," since Kinsey has shown that degree of religious devoutness is a most important determinant of predisposition to pre-marital sex activity.[117]

From the standpoint of this study, one of Kinsey's major findings is that Jewish girls who do engage in pre-marital sex begin to do so *at a later age* than their Gentile counterparts. The percentage of girls who have experienced coitus by age fifteen is quite small for all ethnic groups, but at this age level the percentage is about five times greater among Catholic girls (and four times greater among Protestant girls) than among Jewish girls, according to Kinsey's statistics. By age twenty, the difference between Catholics and Jews narrows to a ratio of three to two, and by age twenty-five the difference is further reduced to a ratio of four to three.

Kinsey's data may contain all sorts of sampling errors and yet

Table 9:3. Percentage of Girls Who Have Engaged in Pre-Marital Coitus at Successive Ages, and by Religious Background[118]

	Protestant			Catholic			Jewish		
Age range	Moder- ately devout	Reli- giously inactive	Median	Moder- ately devout	Reli- giously inactive	Median	Moder- ately devout	Reli- giously inactive	Median
Adoles- cence to 15	3%	5%	4%	7%	12%	10%	—*	2%	—
20	19	25	22	24	41	34	11	27	22
25	33	44	39	—	54	—	23	42	36

* Where a dash is shown in place of a percentage figure, not enough cases were collected for that subgroup to justify computing a percentage.

be useful as a rough estimate of the phenomenon surveyed. Whether the "true difference" in accumulative sex experience by age fifteen is seven times or three times is not the issue; whether by age twenty-five *almost* as many unmarried Jewish women are sexually experienced as are religiously inactive Catholic women, or whether slightly more Jewish women are sexually experienced, is also not the issue. Granting a considerable range of possible error, it seems highly probable that Jewish women follow a culturally patterned schedule of sexual activity, of which the "accumulative incidence of pre-marital coitus" may be only one index. In all likelihood, Jewish girls do engage in all the activities that lead to coitus, approximate or substitute for coitus, but tend to begin at a later age than Protesant or Catholic girls. (It should of course be noted that "pre-marital coitus" does *not* mean promiscuity. In about half of the cases in which women acknowledge pre-marital experience, intimacy was confined to relations with the fiance.)

The Jewish girl apparently *earns* her reputation for being sexually inaccessible, puritanical, moralistic, by postponing her sexual involvements during adolescence. During the high school period, Kinsey's statistics would indicate that Gentile girls (except for the religiously devout) are more active sexually than Jewish girls, and this fact may leave many men with the lifelong (though erroneous) impression that adult Jewish women are more puritanical than their Gentile counterparts. The postponement of the Jewish woman's "emancipation" may be attributable to social controls (parental or cultural influences—including the prudence exercised by Jewish boys!) or to conscious choice, rather than psychic inhibition, since by young adulthood she comes close to matching the Gentile norm.

Let us compare Kinsey's findings on female sex experience, with the Ehrmann study reported earlier in this chapter, and with a 1940 report by Landis *et al.* As Table 9:4 indicates, results of these three studies consistently show that Jewish girls are less likely to engage in premarital coitus than their Gentile peers.

Table 9:4. Percentage of Young Women Who Have Had Pre-Marital Coital Experience; Three Studies Compared

Date of publication	Principal investigator	Ethnic Groups					
		Protestant		Catholic		Jewish	
		(N)	%	(N)	%	(N)	%
1940	Landis*	(71)	45	(65)	29	(159)	19
1953	Kinsey**	(1740)	22	(206)	34	(930)	22
1959	Ehrmann***	(212)	12	(18)	21	(35)	11

* Psychiatric women patients from upper Manhattan and Bronx—age range 15-35, 101 single and 41 married—combined with a control group of 153 matched on age, religion, nationality, educational, socio-economic, and marital status, recruited through women's clubs, adult education agencies, recreational societies, and the like. From Landis, 1940, pages 17, 19, 312.

**Age level 20 selected for this Table. Numbers and percentages are for combined "moderately religious" and religiously "inactive" groups. ("Devout" groups eliminated from this summary.) From Kinsey, 1953, Table 89, page 342.

*** University students, median age 19.7. Numbers approximated from author's findings reported by percentage only. From Ehrmann, 1959, pages 88-89.

As Ehrmann noted, the cultural restraints imposed upon Jewish girls are observable from clinical experience as well as survey data. Ehrmann's observation that Jewish males are more likely to set their own limits to petting (rather than let the girl decide where to stop) indicates that this group norm is interiorized by both sexes, and that both sexes share responsibility for the maintenance of this norm. Unlike Protestants and Catholics, who view their sex code as a *religious* principle, Jews seem to regard the sex code of their group as an unwritten "law of the tribe"—a *social* code enforced through social sanctions. In the candid words of one of Ehrmann's college boys:

I'm afraid to go too far with a girl I've known for a long time because her parents might find out and cause difficulties for both of us.[119]

10

Jewish Traits

There is a difference between assimilation and acculturation, and to Jews this difference is all-important. When a person so thoroughly identifies with a culture—in habits, attitudes, and values—that he can be completely absorbed into its dominant group, that is assimilation. When a person adopts the language and customs of a culture—and understands its values sufficiently well to participate in it—that is acculturation. By such a definition, an assimilated Jew is in the process of phasing out his Jewishness as thoroughly as his own resources and social conditions permit. An acculturated Jew, on the other hand, shares the habits and customs of the dominant group, while preserving an inner core of attitudes and values that are distinctly Jewish. (Many of these inner values may happen to coincide with significant values of the dominant society. The Liberty Bell is inscribed with a line from the Hebrew Bible; respect for secular authority is invoked by the Halachic law *Deena al malchusa deena*—The law of the land is the law.)

The distinction between assimilation and acculturation may be clearer in theory than in practice; it is always possible that in the process of adopting the habits and customs of the dominant group, one may at the same time acquire the core values of the Gentile world. One might say of such a Jew that he feels like a Gentile and thinks like a Gentile; he sees the world through Gentile eyes, and judges Jews by Gentile standards. If so, he is likely to feel more at ease among Gentiles, and it would be surprising if he did *not* marry a Gentile.

Is it *really* true that Jews think and feel differently from Gentiles? Orlansky's 1946 critical review of research on Jewish personality traits led him to conclude that findings have been "erratic, disparate, and occasionally contradictory." In the interests of reliable knowledge, he called for comparisons between adequate samples of Jews and non-Jews—rather than "clinical observations on maladjusted individuals, and unchecked generalizations from personal experience."[1] An up-to-date scrutiny of research in this area might show little further progress over the last twenty years. So great is the importance of this topic to an understanding of the intermarriage problem, however, that we cannot be diverted from probing into it because of a scarcity of well-established data. This chapter consists largely, therefore, of hypotheses, hunches, intuitions, and field observations—it is *not* a summary of well-validated findings.

Whether Jewish personality traits exist for behavioral scientists or not, they certainly do exist for intermarrieds. Mayer's intermarried Jewish respondents justify their choice of a Gentile mate by pointing out that Jews have certain characteristics which they consider undesirable: girls don't "behave properly . . . [don't] have any manners," Jewish boys are brash smart-alecks, "loud and boisterous." Gentile mates, by contrast, seem remarkably well-behaved. Jewish women describe their Gentile suitors as polite, shy, gentlemanly, and deferential. Jewish men describe their Gentile dates as calm, modest, unselfish, well-mannered and acquiescent. As Rabbi Rubenstein has so richly observed, the intermarrying Gentile girl finds something refreshing and alive in the Jewish norms of non-puritanical candor, directness, and audacity. What a puritanical Jewish girl finds offensive in Jewish men may have an irresistible appeal to the more enlightened Gentile girl, disenchanted over the hypocrisy and aridity of what she has learned as the rules of good behavior.

In raising a Jewish child, there are no well-defined rules

for facilitating acculturation while precluding a tendency toward assimilation. It seems quite possible, for example, that politeness, prudery, and deference to authority may be so strongly implanted in a Jewish child, that he will forever feel ill-at-ease in a society marked by its informality, audacity, and non-puritanical ethic. Reflections of Jewish parents of intermarrieds sometimes contain a dawning recognition of the possibility that their child's marriage choice was really consistent with how the child had been brought up:

> My daughter is marrying a Gentile, and I really can't say I'm surprised. When my husband and I moved to Campustown, we knew we'd have very few Jewish neighbors, and yet that's where we wanted to live and raise our daughter. There were exactly three Jewish boys in Alice's high school class, and every one of them was "fast" [sexually aggressive], and they spent so much money on dates it was disgusting. None of Alice's high school crowd went in for expensive dating. The Gentile boys were gentlemen. Alice preferred them. I guess that's how we raised her.

> Our son-in-law isn't Jewish but he is a wonderful young man. The truth is, our daughter tried dating Jewish boys, but *dammit* they wouldn't leave her alone; they wouldn't keep their hands off her. The Gentile boys were the only ones who treated her like a lady.

A girl whose upbringing was guided too strictly by Victorian standards of decorum will be unable to make a distinction between joking and lechery, between foolishness and prurience. She may have faithfully attended temple Sunday school, studied Jewish history and ritual—but to the extent that she has interiorized a puritanical superego, she unfits herself for the enjoyment of Jewish in-group participation. To her, polite and distant Gentile company seems more congenial, more comfortable, safer —less embarrassing, less confusing. She may not intermarry, but she experiences the kind of tension that leads to intermarriage. A girl who understands the Jewish ethos, on the other hand, is not surprised by candor, joking, or boldness; she feels neither endangered nor insulted by the direct expression of affection.

(*Far a tap, a klap—far a kish, a potch.* For a pat, give a rap—for a kiss, give a slap.)

Jewish ethos and the masculine sex-role in Western society. Returning to the observations of Mayer's intermarrieds, one may observe an interesting similarity between some of the traits which intermarrying Jewish men *dislike* in Jewish women (demanding, self-centered, puritanical, socially conformist, materialistic) , and traits which Gentile women *admire* in Jewish men (ambitious, successful, intellectual, cultured, sober) . What is the significance of this parallel?

Restating the above observations, Jewish women are *demanding* and *materialistic,* but Jewish men are *ambitious* and *successful;* Jewish women are *puritanical,* but Jewish men are *sober.* (Readers of Sydney Harris' newspaper column, "Strictly Personal," will be reminded of Harris' occasional theme "Antics with Semantics.") It begins to seem as if a Jewish upbringing produces character traits which are more favorable to men than to women as the sex-roles are defined in the Gentile world. (Analogously, Japanese norms seem to better fit the feminine sex-role as defined by Western standards; self-effacing politeness seems charming and altogether fitting in a woman, but a bit ludicrous in a man.) If true, this statement may tell us something important about the tensions which lead to intermarriage.

"Jewish men make wonderful husbands" for the same reason that "Japanese women make ideal wives"—because their cultural tradition instills certain personality traits which Western society attaches to a particular sex-role. Jewish boys are more likely to win the applause of Gentile status groups, gain social experience which better qualifies them for living in a Gentile world, and once more we encounter the familiar self-reinforcing cycle whereby success breeds success. This interaction between the Jewish ethos and the sex-role standards of the Gentile world, we hypothesize, gives the Jewish male easier access into Gentile society, and a better opportunity to participate in the Gentile world. He senses somehow that a Gentile wife would fit more naturally into his new milieu, that a *man's* Jewishness is better appreciated in the Gentile world than a woman's Jewishness. He may not intermarry, but he experiences the kind of tension that leads to intermarriage.

AN UNPOPULAR TOPIC

If the foregoing paragraphs make the reader feel uneasy—or bristle with indignation—perhaps it is because we have embarked upon an almost forbidden topic: Jewish traits. In 1942 Riesman observed that it is considered illiberal to suppose that Jews are in any way different from anybody else. In 1948 Samuel Koenig argued that research on Jewish personality traits would be unwelcome since educated Jews place so much emphasis on acculturation, or adopting the traits of the dominant group.[2] In a 1951 issue of *Commentary,* Freedman describes the classic Jewish student types of the 1920's and 1930's, but agrees with other observers of the American college scene that Jewish students "are becoming much like other middle-class young Americans."[3]

In a rare published analysis of "The Jewish Ethos," its author prefers to remain anonymous.[4] To the extent that one might ascribe to Jews personality traits which perchance compare unfavorably with Gentiles, one might be accused of playing into the hands of the anti-Semite, for *"anti-locution, or the use of unfavorable terms to characterize Jews"* is a recognized form of anti-Semitism.[5] Thus when Peter I. Rose found that a sizeable majority of small-town New York State Gentiles agreed with the statements: "Jews tend to be more money-minded than most people . . . Jews tend to be shrewder business men than most people . . . [and] Jews tend to be more aggressive than most people," he interpreted these findings as evidence of *"prejudice against Jews"* (italics added), though he admitted that these statements were consistent with what small-town Gentiles *saw* of Jews:

> Many of the small-town Jews in New York State do, in fact, fulfill several of these classic stereotypes. . . . They *are* frequently in business. They *are* more liberal politically. They *do* tend to possess an urbane demeanor. . . . And their children, being strongly motivated, *do* tend to do especially well in school [which, from a Gentile point of view, may constitute aggressive behavior].[6]

"The practice of ascribing to the Jews unalterable qualities, mostly evil ones," wrote James Fuchs in the Jewish press of

1928, "is of such ancient standing . . . that it forms a standing snare and temptation to wayward genius." In the same article he wrote, "Generally speaking, the literature of racial traits, outside of Germany, is stupid but amusing—in Germany it is not only stupid but ponderously tedious as well."[7]

The study of national character has thus been derided as ethnic insult masquerading as science. The concepts of "inherited, unalterable qualities," "collective unconscious," or "racial soul" are of course quite unnecessary and even irrelevant to the study of national character if we define it as the distinctive personality structures which are commonly observed in a given society.

From a behavioral science point of view, national character is regarded as a product of social learning, as the prevailing patterns of social adaptation, or as Linton has phrased it, "as that personality structure which is most congenial to the prevailing institutions and ethos of the society."[8] As Inkeles and Levinson point out, a society need not be marked by a single character style, but may give rise to several modes of adjustment. (Analogously, an economic environment does not lead to a single "best" mode of adaptation, but generates a whole set of interacting and complementary economic roles: land owner, peasant, miller, implement maker, trader, baker, etc.)

Anthropologists have proved much more receptive to the study of national character, according to Inkeles and Levinson, than psychologists. "Extraordinarily few psychologists have shown interest in the study of national character, and the attitude generally manifested toward the relevant work done in other disciplines has been predominately cold if not hostile."[9]

During the 1920's and early 1930's social psychologists concentrated their energy "on attacking generalizations about the psychology of groups. Such generalizations were associated with race theory and were opposed as being unscientific stereotypes . . . or as rationalizations of our own social structure."[10] To defend the thesis that the only legitimate psychology was a study of *individual* consciousness or *individual* behavior, it was argued that since there is no such thing as a group brain, there can be no such thing as a group mind or group consciousness, and therefore no such thing as a social psychology.

The social psychologist denied that there was anything necessarily mystical about his subject-matter. Individuals *as group members,* and under group influences, think and act differently than they do in the absence of group influences. The subject-matter of social psychology can be just as empirically grounded, it was argued, just as scientific as the subject-matter of individual psychology.[11]

The accusations of mysticism and racism which have been directed against the study of national character bear a striking similarity to the charges which were once directed against social psychology, and in each case it has been amply demonstrated that neither mysticism nor racism have any essential place in these areas of the behavioral sciences.

In 1951 Linton declared that "the existence of different personality norms for members of different small culturally homogeneous societies seems to be well established. . . . Although the work leading to these results has been done almost exclusively on the so-called primitive societies, it seems highly probable that the same techniques can be applied to the study of culturally homogeneous societies within modern nations."[12]

"Cultural homogeneity" is, of course, a matter of degree. In the last three chapters we have examined a number of distinctive and enduring characteristics of the Jewish culture: the norms and values of the *shtetl* (which figures in the family background of perhaps 90 per cent of American Jews), the sex norms of the Jewish group which (Kinsey to the contrary) diverge from the Christian tradition, a matricentric family pattern with its implications for sex-role patterning and transmission of the incest taboo. If personality traits are acquired (rather than inherited) then a distinctive social environment should foster distinctive personality norms. Human societies have so much in common, we can expect that most personality traits will show up in all societies; a society may be considered distinctive in how a given trait is distributed within it. Is it a rarity or is it common? Is it assigned to a particular age or sex group, or social class? Is it nurtured, tolerated, or frowned upon?

Freud believed that his personality was profoundly Jewish. In the Preface he wrote for the Hebrew edition of *Totem and Taboo,* Freud contemplated the paradox that though he had long been "completely estranged from the religion of his fathers," he nonetheless "feels that he is in his essential nature a Jew and . . . has no desire to alter that nature. If the question were put to him: '. . . What is there left to you that is Jewish?' he would reply: 'A very great deal, and probably its very essence.' He could not now express that essence clearly in words but some day, no doubt," Freud concluded hopefully, "it will become accessible to the scientific mind."[13]

A Conversation with Freud

Freud's thoughts on "the essence of Jewishness" come to light in the report of Joseph Wortis, who as a young American psychiatrist met with Freud over a period of months in 1934 for the purpose of training analysis. During one analytic session, Wortis confesses that he is somewhat puzzled by the fact that Einstein appeared to champion a spirit of Jewish nationalism. "I wish I could clear up the problem for myself," said Wortis candidly. "I have no strong Jewish feelings, and up to recently was satisfied to think of myself mainly as an American. How far ought I to let my allegiance to the Jews bring me?"[14] Wortis documents the conversation that ensued:

" 'That is not a problem for Jews,' said Freud, 'because the Gentiles make it unnecessary to decide; as long as Jews are not admitted into Gentile circles, they have no choice but to band together.'

" 'But how about the program for the future?' I [said Wortis] would like to see the Jews become assimilated and disappear, and Einstein talks as if they ought to be preserved forever.'

" 'The future will show how far that is possible,' said Freud. 'I personally do not see anything wrong in mixed marriages, if both parties are suited to each other, though I must say that the chances for success seem greater in a Jewish marriage: family life is closer and warmer, and devotion is much more common. My married children have all married Jews, though it may be that they simply did not have access to the best Christian circles. There is no reason why Jews ought not to be perfectly friendly with Gentiles; there is no real clash of interests. But a Jew ought not to get himself baptized and attempt to turn Christian because it is essentially dishonest, and the Christian religion is every bit as bad as the Jewish. Jew and Christian ought to meet on the common ground of irreligion and humanity. Jews who are ashamed of their Jewishness have simply reacted to the mass suggestion of their society.'

" 'But I don't know what the Jews stand for,' [Wortis] said. 'I can pledge allegiance to a scientific group, or a political or cultural group because they represent certain ideals, but what does Judaism stand for; in what way do its ideals differ from other group ideals?'

" 'Ruthless egotism is much more common among Gentiles than among Jews,' said Freud, 'and Jewish family life and intellectual life are on a higher plane.'

" 'You seem to think the Jews are a superior people, then,' [Wortis replied.]

" 'I think nowadays they are,' said Freud. 'When one thinks that ten or twelve per cent of the Nobel Prize winners are Jews and when one thinks of their other great achievements in sciences and in the arts, one has every reason to think them superior.'

" 'Jews have bad manners,' [said Wortis,] 'especially in New York.'

" 'That is true,' said Freud; 'they are not always adapted to social life. Before they enjoyed emancipation in 1818 they were not a social problem, they kept to themselves—with a low standard of life it is true—but they did not go out in mixed society. Since then they have had much to learn. In countries where they have enjoyed real freedom, however, as in Italy, they are indistinguishable in this respect from Italians. The old saying is true: "Every country has the Jews that it deserves." America certainly hasn't encouraged the best kind of social conduct.'

" 'It is also said that Jews are physically inferior,' [Wortis said].

" 'That is no longer true either,' said Freud, 'now that the Jews have access to outdoor life and the sports, you find them the equal of Gentiles in every respect, and we have plenty of champions in all fields.'

"[Wortis then said] 'The Jews are over-intellectualized; it was Jung who said, for example, that psychoanalysis bears the mark of this Jewish over-intellectualization.'

" 'So much the better for psychoanalysis then!' said Freud.

'Certainly the Jews have a strong tendency to rationalize—that is a very good thing. What Jung contributed to psychoanalysis was mysticism, which we can well dispense with. . . . But all this,' said Freud, 'is not psychoanalysis; however it is worth discussing because I see you have a sincere interest in the problem.' "[15]

Reik believed that Freud was indirectly describing "the psychology of the Jewish people" in the Jewish jokes and stories Freud incorporated in his *Wit and its Relations to the Unconscious.* (Ernst Simon attempted to summarize the Jewish traits covered by these stories.) In *Jewish Wit,* Reik attempts more deliberately to analyze Jewish jokes "as a contribution to the comparative psychology of the Jewish people";[16] hoping to "cast a new light on the psychology of these strange people, on their character and temperament . . ."[17] Reik's *Jewish Wit* is perhaps the only book-length treatise on the Jewish personality. Reik offers many penetrating insights into the Jewish ethos, which will be referred to in the following paragraphs, as we attempt a more systematic discussion of Jewish traits.

A SURVEY

As we canvass the literature for clues on Jewish traits, we should not regard each finding as one more piece of a jig-saw puzzle which will eventually delineate *the* Jewish personality. The cultural environment of the Jews permits too much diversity to shape its members into a single personality type. The problems of minority group living allow for a variety of solutions, and we should expect a study of Jewish traits to suggest a variety of modal personalities, not one.

A better understanding of Jewish traits can shed light on the intermarriage problem by affording a more detailed picture of how Jewish traits match up with sex-role norms in the middle class Gentile world—accounting for the differential aptitude of Jewish men and women for participation in the Gentile world. This survey may also shed some light on the classic topic of "Jewish nervousness" and the search of the intermarrying Jew for a calmer, "healthier" mate than he might find amongst the daughters of Israel. Our survey should map out in more detail the points at which Jews and Gentiles are most likely to differ in their attitudes toward sex, authority, and aggression—and therefore suggest what conditions of upbringing (entirely apart from religious instruction *per se*) may predispose the individual to cross the ethnic line in order to find congenial company.

Jewish audacity. "Ruthless egotism is much more common among Gentiles than among Jews," Freud assured young Wortis; elsewhere Freud defined the peculiar quality of Jewish egotism as "audacity without arrogance." Jewish *chutspa* has not, however, been universally admired. From Arthur Schopenhauer to David Riesman, Jews have been chided for their bad manners. As one of Mayer's respondents put it: "There was just something about [Jewish girls] that I did not like. . . . I just didn't think they behaved properly, they didn't have any manners. Frankly I was embarrassed when I was in their company." There is a considerable diversity of opinion among observers on the historical and psychological sources of this trait.

Social mobility. Bad manners, selfishness, love of ostentation and luxury are classic criticisms of the *parvenu* or *nouveau riche*, whether Jewish or Gentile, and might therefore be viewed as by-products of the phenomenal upward mobility of the Jews in the United States. ("Jewish wives start complaining the minute they're pregnant and sit home all day. . . . As soon as the baby is born, they start playing mahjong all the time, instead of keeping a clean home and cooking good meals for their husbands.")[18]

Audacity and aggression. Various observers have held that by his "lack of respect" the Jew strikes back at his oppressor. If we Jews push and crowd "with obnoxiously indecorous haste," Browne addresses himself to the Gentile world, ". . . you must expect that. After all, if you won't be fair, how can we be decorous?"[19] Reik ascribes Jewish "contrariness in thought" to the fact that "other kinds of critical and aggressive actions were impossible" for them to exercise.[20] David Riesman refers to "strident and greedy" Jews who use anti-Semitism as a license: "If Jews cannot be the most popular, they must be the most disliked," goes their logic.[21] When Freud remarked to Wortis that "Every country has the Jews that it deserves," he apparently meant that the Jew feels entitled to display bad manners because he has endured generations of suffering and deserves some "compensation for the wrong or injury life has inflicted upon him."[22]

On the topic of "Some Character Types Met with in Psychoanalytic Work," Freud refers to cases in which an early traumatic experience or physical handicap leads the person to claim that he is an "exception who is exempt from the necessities of life and for whom the common regulations do not hold. . . ."[23] Reik calls attention to Freud's meaningful aside, that he chooses not "to go into the obvious analogy between deformities of character resulting from protracted sickliness in childhood and the behavior of whole nations whose past history has been full of suffering."[24]

Jewish skepticism. It is not surprising that behavioral scientists regard Jewish skepticism as an aspect of minority group adjustment. "The skepticism of the Jews," says Loewenstein, "is bound up with their insecurity . . . a fear of being betrayed."[25] Erikson likewise sees Jewish skepticism as part of a minority group role —an attitude that keeps the Jew "from wholehearted participation in either the enthusiasms or the prejudices of the nation of which he is a citizen." Jewish skepticism, Erikson continues, "is by no means directed only against non-Jewish ideals. Jews show similar skepticism toward their own."[26]

On the other hand, Emanuel Rackman—an Orthodox rabbi— regards skepticism as something closer to a core value of the Jewish ethos: ". . . Judaism encourages doubt even as it enjoins faith and commitment," he writes. "A Jew dare not live with absolute certainty not only because certainty is the hallmark of the fanatic and Judaism abhors fanaticism, but also because doubt is good for the human soul, its humility, and consequently its greater potential ultimately to discover its Creator."[27] Rabbi Herbert Weiner retells a conversation between the celebrated Hebrew poet Chaim Nachman Bialik and Chaim Greenberg, in which the poet argues that the attitude of doubt is intrinsic to the Jewish mode of thought:

> The poet meets a little blond Aryan girl on the train, and muses out loud about adopting her. He jokingly speculates that this little girl, if brought up in his house, would become a fine Jewish lass, just as the Vilna Gaon, idol of rabbinic Jewry, would have grown up to be a good Tartar if kidnapped as a child by the Tartars. Greenberg is shocked by this light treat-

ment of the essential Jewish soul, and Bialik tells him that he
must learn 'the mystery of rhythm.' He illustrates his point by
telling how Sholom Aleichem's Tevya the Dairyman repudiates
his daughter when she marries out of the faith. One day, Tevya
sees his daughter waiting on the road but, his heart breaking,
he drives his milk wagon past her without a word. Then there
comes a summer twilight when Tevya is again riding in his
wagon and speculating, 'Why did God create a divided world—
Jew, Gentile, my faith, your faith? Wouldn't it have been better if we were all alike?'

Tevya understood the mystery of rhythm, said Bialik. He
understood that one must not be reconciled with a daughter
who is an apostate, and yet that it was necessary from time
to time to pass into a sphere of thought where all these things
'aren't worth a plugged nickle.' Any Jew, concludes Bialik,
who is incapable of ridding himself of his nationality from
time to time, and then returning to his roots, to his environment, and its spirit—to his tribe if you please—such a Jew is a
sick person.[28]

The religious tradition of the Jews glorifies transgression of
the law. "In the Talmud Resh Lakish blesses Moses for having
summoned up the courage to break the tablets of the Law in
order to prevent the children of Israel from putting them to
wrongful use."[29] The story is told of a Hasidic rabbi who was
chopping wood on the Sabbath for a poor widow. He died, and
"by this sacrilegious action, they said, he ascended even higher."[30]
In the Old Testament the Jews are described as "a stiff-necked
people." Says Reik: "Since Jacob wrestled with God, they continue to challenge their deity towards whom they remained un-
failingly recalcitrant."[31] Gilbert Murray described the Jew as "at
once the child of tradition and a rebel against it."[32]

In Jewish humor nothing is sacred, not even the sacred. Sholom
Aleichem's Tevya the Dairyman remarks, "With God's help I
starved to death."[33] Reik tells of an elderly Jew who "speaks to
his children who surround him before he dies: 'My whole life I
endeavored to live according to the Law and deprived myself of
most pleasures and had a poor and miserable existence. I was
always hoping that I would be rewarded in the beyond. I would
laugh if there was nothing in the beyond.' "[34] A Jew reaches

heaven and pleads that God tell him why he lived a life of such
unrelieved poverty though he prayed not only regularly but fer-
vently three times a day. God answers: *"Du host mir tsu fiel
ge'nuddet."* (You pestered me too much.) Hershel Ostropolier
(The Tyl Eulenspeigel of Yiddish folklore) was confronted with
the statement: "It is said that you don't believe in God." *"Whoever* said that?" "Well, people are talking—" *"Why listen to what
people say?* Why not ask the Lord Himself?"[35]

Audacity and a "nerve of failure." Searching for "A Philosophy
for 'Minority' Living," David Riesman calls upon his reader to
find within himself "a 'nerve of failure' . . . the courage to face
aloneness and the possibility of defeat in one's personal life or
work without being morally destroyed."[36] Riesman's call will be
recognized by his Jewish readers as a call for *chutspah* in a world
of uncertainties, and recalls the death bed reflection of Reik's
pious old Jew: "I would laugh if there was nothing in the beyond."

For all that has been written about "Jewish masochism" (personified in Jewish humor by the *Shlemiel*) , "Jews also manifest
in marked degree the opposite tendency," says Loewenstein. "The
will to live and to succeed in life . . . is demonstrated by the
remarkable facility with which Jews 'bounce back' when they
get a chance; in fact this very resilience has been the target of
much anti-Jewish criticism. And the fact that they have survived
as a group in spite of all the odds against them is proof of their
tenacious, stubborn will to live."[37]

In the context of the hardships and uncertainties of ghetto
life, a Jewish proverb advised: "A man should live if only to
satisfy his curiosity."

A painful embarrassment and a precious gift. In the process
of acculturation to American life, says Riesman, "certain elements in Jewish ethics . . . often tend to become distorted. . . .
Irreverence toward authority degenerates into an indiscriminate
disrespect for convention, whether that convention is an exploita-
tive device or a crystallization of decent standards of personal
intercourse. This Jewish irreverence may also appear as a cynicism that seeks money and power without the conviction that
they represent the fruits of virtue or that they are genuinely
important ends—or even the means to such ends."[38]

But on the other hand, Riesman expresses his conviction that "the critical attitude which subjects to principles and to reason all claims of power and all demands for loyalty, [is] an attitude which I believe to be among the significant contributions of Jewish ethics to the general problem of the powerless minority and the small nation."[39] (Riesman uses this argument to oppose political Zionism as anti-Jewish.)

Reik also considers skepticism a core trait of the Jews. Erik H. Erikson holds that Jewish relativism finds "its highest expression in revolutionary scientific discoveries which have upset theories previously accepted as absolute truths."[40]

Skepticism and creativity. Maslow describes the self-actualizing person as one who gets along with his culture in various ways, but "in a profound and meaningful sense they [have] resisted acculturation and maintained a certain inner detachment from the culture in which they were immersed."[41]

The self-actualizing person wears the cloak of conventionality very lightly and easily casts it aside when it would "hamper him or inhibit him from doing anything that he considers very important or basic. . . ." Self-actualizers have "selected from the American culture what was good in it by their lights and rejected what they thought was bad in it."[42]

Maslow's and Riesman's hero share several interesting characteristics. They resist full identification with the dominant culture, they have the courage to face aloneness, they wear the cloak of conventionality lightly, and do not let it interfere with their significant work. Riesman acknowledges that his definition of a man of courage draws upon the Jewish tradition, but Maslow says nothing about the Jewishness of his self-actualizing man.[43]

The theology of chutspa. There is nothing in the Jewish ethos like the Christian emphasis on self-sacrifice as "inherently desirable and worth while," asserts *Critic*.[44] The ethical command of Christianity, he explains, has been to *reverse* man's natural impulses; to transform egoism into altruism, to transform self-seeking into self-sacrifice. Emily Post expressed the Christian viewpoint when she said that "good manners consist in toning down one's behavior so as not to offend others, and of doing everything in one's power to please them."[45] *Critic* quotes the noted Jewish essayist Ahad Ha'am (1856-1927) to point out that the Jewish ethical orientation sanctions a more direct assertion of one's rights. Jewish moral law "makes no distinction between the 'self' and 'others.'" Justice has an abstract, objective quality. All men are equal "before the throne of justice," all lives have the same value, and *life* has a higher value even than self-sacrifice or mercy. Let each man preserve and value and develop his life "and at the same time . . . help his neighbor attain that goal, so far as he is able. Just as I have no right to ruin another man's life for the sake of my own, so have I no right to ruin my own life for the sake of another's. Both of us are men, and both our lives have the same value. . . ."[46]

In making these comments, Ahad Ha'am is responding to the difference between the Golden Rule as given in the New Testament ("Whatsoever ye would that men should do to you, do ye even so to them"), and the Jewish counterpart as stated by Hillel ("What is hateful to yourself, do not do to your fellow man.") The New Testament version stresses self-sacrifice and altruism, Hillel stresses equality (". . . your *fellow* man") as a basis for justice.

In his treatise on the Jewish religion, Rabbi Milton Steinberg underscores and amplifies Ahad Ha'am's thesis: "I owe myself respect for the divinity with which I am touched and for the singularity of my being. But my neighbor is exactly in my case . . . I may not withhold any of the reverence, solicitude, and freedom I claim for myself.

"To this there are no exceptions . . . [and] there are no limits. I cannot respect my fellow excessively. On the contrary, since he contains something of God, his moral worth is infinite.

"Translated into concrete terms, this means that I may not . . . injure him in any fashion, oppress, exploit, humiliate him, or deprive him of anything to which he is entitled. Nor may I deceive him or withhold the truth from him, since, as the rabbis pointed out long ago, oppression may be through words as well as deeds. Finally, I may not restrain or inhibit his self-fulfillment according to his talents, inclinations, and conscience.

"In all this I have the right to expect him to behave toward me as I seek to behave toward him. No less a child of God than

I, he is no more. 'A man,' say the rabbis, 'is his own next of kin.'
If then I ought to stand in defense of his rights and dignities I
should stand no less resolutely in defense of my own.

*"By Jewish lights, I am under no obligation to turn the other
cheek, especially not if I have been unjustly slapped to begin
with.* The theory that evil should be endured rather than resisted [is both unnatural and] . . . also immoral in that it urges
acquiescence to injustice. And *injustice is never to be acquiesced
in, no matter whom or where it strikes, not even if it strikes me."*[47]
(Italics added.)

Critic worries about this difference between the Christian emphasis on humility, self-denial, "the beauty of . . . self-sacrifice,"
and the Jewish demand for justice; and he wonders if there is
room to hope for genuine harmony between Jew and Gentile.
"In actual practice there are probably among Jews and non-Jews
equally numerous cases of self-sacrifice."[48] It is not a question of
whether Christians are more moral (or less moral) than Jews,
but whether a difference in ethos generates differences in social
habits and models of good behavior, so that seen through Gentile
eyes the Jew lacks humility, and seen through Jewish eyes the
Gentile lacks audacity.

Loewenstein holds that by reason of his upbringing a Jew
cannot express "true submissiveness and humility." Fear may
elicit a display of obsequiousness based on the "desire to placate
an all-powerful enemy. . . . It has an undertone of derisive irony,"
Loewenstein adds, "which is why non-Jews find it particularly
objectionable."[49]

Chutspa and the social order. Religious tradition is not the
only basis from which one can derive the difference between Gentile and Jewish norms of self-sacrifice. Political and economic
realities in the Gentile world demanded that the individual interiorize habits of obedience, allegiance, loyalty, courtesy, and
self-abasement toward those who controlled his political and
economic destiny. Expressions of politeness are interwoven with
deference to status: "Your lordship . . . sire . . . m'lady . . . master
. . . I am your humble servant . . . your obedient servant." Within
the Jewish community of Eastern Europe status differences prevailed, and they were well-defined, but they were *not* based on
the harsh realities of political or economic power. Unlike the

feudal or industrial world beyond the Pale, self-employment was the norm within the Jewish village. Allegiance was felt toward the extended family, toward the community and its leaders; awe and reverence were felt toward God—but habits of obedience, acquiescence, and self-abasement were simply not required by the social order of the Eastern European Jewish village.

In the *shtetl* culture there were Great Rabbis, charismatic leaders who were treated like holy men. But the average rabbi was primarily a teacher, respected for his learning, but not accorded the homage which the Gentile world gave its priests and bishops. As a young Orthodox rabbi explains in Blankfort's novel, "We rabbis don't have special Grace or position. We are not intermediaries between man and God. We may feel a sense of mission but it is to teach. Actually a rabbi is merely one among equals. . . . You know, any ten Jews thirteen years or over can form a congregation. They don't need a rabbi. They can read the prayers by themselves. They can preach, study, read from the Torah. It is our tradition. We are essentially a religion without hierarchy."[50]

In their relations with the outside world, Jews "learned to remain unimpressed by Gentile temporal power," as Riesman puts it. "Since the Jews' ethical scheme placed no great premium on material power or on material success, the majority was not looked up to with envy and admiration; hence its verdicts, both as to the ends of life and as to the value of the minority itself, did not echo in the Jews' self-consciousness."[51] The Jew learned to cope with the political authority of the outside world but did not identify with it.

Contrary to the psychoanalytic viewpoint of Kardiner, who describes the adult culture as a "projective system" shaped by the prevailing practices of child-rearing, we are here dealing with the historical viewpoint argued by David Potter, that the political and economic order shapes the socialization process; that within the family setting children are taught social habits that will equip them for membership in the political and economic community, that parents tend to relate to their children as persons of high status relate to lower status persons in the prevailing culture. (A good example is provided by the peasant culture of Southern Italy, in which the father seems to take on the role of the all-powerful padrone, treating his children as if they were his peasants, insisting—for example—that they owe him their wages just as he himself is obliged to deliver his crops to the *padrone*.)

Honesty versus politeness. By traditional Jewish norms it is more important in everyday social conversation to tell the truth than to be polite.[52] A Yiddish proverb says, "Better an honest slap than a false kiss." A common Yiddish exclamation is *Yoysher!*— Let's be honest! A common rhetorical question is *Emes?*—Is that the truth? Conspicuous politeness, on the other hand, carries the negative connotations of evasiveness, distance, or lack of self-respect. This discrepancy between Jewish and Western norms provides an endless source of inner conflict and social misunderstanding.

During the whirlwind of rush week at a large midwestern university, Sandra, an attractive Jewish freshman, had been invited to join several Jewish sororities, as well as a Gentile sorority (which was presumably liberalizing its membership requirements). Unreflectively she chose the Gentile sorority, then she began to ask herself why she had made that choice. Home for the weekend, Sandra confided to an old friend:

"One night I couldn't sleep at all; I had to know *why* I chose Gamma Gamma instead of one of the Jewish sororities. I kept thinking about it, and finally I decided that this is how it happened: At the Jewish sororities I knew right away which of the girls liked me and which of them didn't; they didn't try to hide it. At Gamma Gamma *all* the girls acted as if they liked me. Of course they couldn't all really like me, but they made it seem that way, and it felt so wonderful to be with a group of girls where it was as if everybody liked me. I guess that's why it felt so much more pleasant at Gamma Gamma than at the Jewish sorority houses."

Melford Spiro's observations of the *kibbutz* pioneers at *Kiryat Yedidim* underscores the commitment of this group to unvarnished honesty in their face-to-face relations, a norm which to the Western observer would seem to violate the ordinary rules of politeness:

. . . With some few exceptions, the *chaverim* are exceptionally straightforward in their relations with their fellows. Just as they do not attempt to conceal their thoughts or behavior—because of the futility of attempting such concealment [in such an intimate society]—so they do not attempt to conceal their opinions of their fellows. It is expected that people will treat others with candor, and with little evasion or circumlocution. Indeed, the *chaver* who does not employ such candor is not trusted. One person, for example, has been given positions of responsibility in the kibbutz because of his exceptional talents. Nevertheless, the chaverim generally dislike him because he is not *yashar*, literally, straightforward.[53]

Kertzer describes the arbitration procedures of the predominantly Jewish diamond industry, to illustrate how the principle of yashar facilitates an easy, informal trading in very costly and nonstandard merchandise:

In the diamond world, a deal is consummated by Jews and the few Gentile strays alike with a handshake and the words *mazel and brochoh* [good luck and blessing]. The elaborate machinery of arbitration [written into the Constitution of the Diamond Dealers' Club] stems from the nature of the business. Diamonds vary greatly in quality, and involve large sums of money. An honest mistake in judging the quality of a handful of gems can cause a miscalculation entailing a loss of thousands of dollars. A clerk may send a wrong shipment to Minneapolis, and the misshipped gems may be sold at the wrong price. If the arbitrators are persuaded that it was an honest error, they will suggest a compromise to seller and buyer: "Pay him what it costs him." The principle of *caveat emptor* is not operative. *Yashar*—equity—the principle of Talmudic law is invoked.[54]

In his Detroit interview study, Lenski asked his respondents "whether they would pay a fine resulting from a minor traffic violation if they knew they would not get caught." Seventy-two per cent of the Negro Protestants, 63 per cent of the white Protestants, and 61 per cent of the Catholics said they would pay the fine regardless. But only 31 per cent of the Jewish respondents said they would pay such a fine.[55] Surely this deviation from the majority group norm connotes some kind of audacity in respondent behavior—but what kind of *chutspa* is this? Is it the daring to reveal what one would actually, honestly *do,* rather than pay lip service to the conventional norm of good citizenship? Or does the Jewish norm betoken a lack of awe for authority *qua* authority?[56] In either case, Lenski's Jewish respondents seem to have been guided by the Jewish tradition of *chutspa.*

An incident from the author's counseling experience is appropriate here in so far as an extreme example is sometimes useful in describing a phenomenon which is almost too subtle and elusive in its everyday manifestations:

Bessie

A lower middle class Jewish girl, native born, Bessie is a freshman majoring in physical education. (She plans to teach gymnastics in Israel some day.) Bessie came to the counselor on the stern advice of one of her instructors to "go talk things over with a counselor," to resolve a "clash of personalities" which has put Bessie under the threat of disciplinary dismissal.

Last week Miss Roberts, her physical education instructor, had asked Bessie to serve as a judge at a high school basketball tournament to be held the following Saturday at a distant suburban high school. Bessie complied readily, for the task represented good training experience. When she arrived at the high school, however, she discovered to her bewilderment that her name was not listed on the mimeographed program. Miss Roberts, who was present, explained to Bessie that she was serving as a substitute, in case one of the listed judges failed to show up. Bessie felt quite frustrated over having made a long trip for nothing, and she also felt offended that Miss Roberts had not told her fully and honestly that she was seeking a volunteer to serve as a *substitute* judge.

Sensing Bessie's inner turmoil, Miss Roberts prevailed upon the other teachers and judges to change the roster, and came back to tell Bessie that she was now definitely scheduled to judge one of the games. "No thanks," Bessie replied archly, "I've already decided to go back home." Miss Roberts was too embarrassed to go back and undo the changes which the other had so courteously submitted to. She was aghast at Bessie's insolence, and raised the question of whether Bessie had good enough manners to be a candidate for the teaching profession. This was the background of Bessie's "forced" visit to the counselor's office.

The counselor listened to Bessie's story, and then engaged her in a discussion about the rules of polite behavior as they apply to relations between college students and their professors. Did she judge that her interests lay in observing these rules or not? Would she be willing to tell Miss Roberts that she was sorry to have caused her the embarrassment of last Saturday's incident? Bessie agreed that it would indeed be in her interest to do so, but half-whispered with a mixture of pride and guilt: "My mother taught me *not* to be a *tochos-lecker*."[57]

Richard and Stuyvesant: a Conflict of Goals and Generations

Myron S. Kaufman's novel *Remember Me to God* describes the consuming drive of a Harvard student and third generation Jewish New Englander, Richard Amsterdam, to escalate his friendship with a proper Bostonian into full membership in the Yankee elite. A crisis occurs when Stuyvesant Gold, an in-group New York Jew, son of an immigrant delicatessen owner, wants to join the staff of the Harvard *Lampoon,* of which Richard is currently the only Jewish member. Richard vacillates between carefully avoiding the ill-mannered interloper and transforming him into a Harvard gentleman:

"I want you to concentrate on developing a more gentlemanly demeanor, so you won't stick out like a sore thumb. . . . It's not going to be easy [because] the average Jewish guy isn't 'to the manner born,' so to speak, and he hasn't had it taught in the cradle and had the benefit of good schools all his life. Probably his parents never had a chance to go to college, and probably his grandparents were immigrants from eastern Europe. It's going to take a lot of hard, discouraging work to unlearn all these foreign mannerisms and New Yorky mannerisms of yours and set up some new brain patterns so you'll have some polish. . . . Keep an eye on Bill Hodge. You learn what a gentleman is by watching

one. And study the guys from Groton and St. Mark's. Their facial
expressions. How they modulate their voice. It's always clear and
distinct and pleasing to the ear. An American should be proud
of his language and handle it with respect, because it's the
language of Shakespeare. . . ."

[An angry exchange follows, in which Gold attempts to reduce
Richard's argument to the conflict between the rich and the poor,
and the question of whether one is willing to be identified as a
Jew or must try to pass as a Gentile. Gold makes it clear that
his bid for membership on the *Lampoon* is based strictly on his
talent as a cartoonist, and that he makes no claim to "fancy high
class manners"]:

"Look . . . if a cartoonist does good work people enjoy it. They
don't ask about his jacket or if he shoots grouse. They judge his
work. All right, so he doesn't stand so debonair! What's the harm
in that?"

". . . The word is 'harm,' Stuyvesant. Not 'horm.' "

"Aw, lay off already! Have a heart, will ya!"

"And the word is 'heart.' Not 'hort.' "

"The way you say it, it sounds like 'hat.' "

[At their final encounter, brief and strife-ridden, Gold de-
nounces Richard as a more contemptible stinker than the worst
of all the Yankee snobs he is trying so desperately to emulate]:

" 'All Jews should be Republicans'—what kind of stuff is that!
What are you giving me! 'Jews should be Republicans.' 'Jews
should drink whiskey.' "

"I never said 'all Jews should be Republicans!' That's just the
opposite of what I said! I said they shouldn't form a bloc! I said
they shouldn't all pile into one party and look conspicuous—
that's what I said! I never said they should 'all be Republicans.'
. . . I can see you don't understand my theory at all," Richard
said grimly.

"No. It's a lousy theory. I never saw a hebe like you before.
You don't seem Jewish to me. I'm starting to think you're the
worst stinker in that whole bunch. . . ."

Richard tries out the argument that in order to overcome prejudice one must first make himself acceptable to prejudiced people:
"The wild-eyed so-called liberal that goes in for grand gestures,
and yelling slogans and waving his arms on a soap box isn't a

liberal. He's just a Don Quixote. He charges with his head against every brick wall like a damn fool and kills himself on it and accomplishes nothing. . . . To change society, you have to know how to influence it. And to lead it or influence it, you have to . . . be part of it. You have to be in it, not just a jerk on the outside with no connections. . . ."

"It's a bum theory!" Gold exploded. "I'm not kissing their behinds! I'm not afraid to walk right up to Congressman Rankin or Senator Bilbo with a Hebrew newspaper sticking out of my pocket and spit in his face! . . .   . . . You're a disgrace to your religion! You're a *tochos-lecker* for the goyim, that's what you are! When I look at you I'm sorry I belong to the same race as such a disgusting character!" [Lapsing from his Yankee gentlemanliness, Richard retorts]: ". . . When I look at you I could vomit!"[58]

Jewish aggressiveness. Is Jewish aggressiveness mainly a situational phenomenon (a well-reinforced parvenu habit, a compensation for feelings of insecurity or inferiority, as Lewin and others have asserted) or does this trait express a more enduring aspect of the Jewish ethos? Reik recalls the Jewish proverbs "Wash my fur but do not wet it," "To kill a chicken and not hurt it." Reik comments on the latter proverb: "To us children it meant, of course, not to inflict pain on an animal unnecessarily. It was only many years later that we found out the real meaning of this phrase: that to attain a definite goal one must not have an exaggerated delicacy of feeling. Qualms must not deter you if you are bent on success."

As a child it seemed somehow objectionable to hear his parents say "He who is kind to himself, is kind to others." Reik explains: "We had been taught not to try to promote our own welfare, but that of others, and to suppress in their favor our own self-seeking interests. This proverb recommended almost the reverse. It took us a long time to comprehend the psychological justification of the words. The study of one's own life and of the lives of others proves that it is impossible to neglect one's own interest to an excessive extent in favor of that of others. Too much consideration for others, a tendency to self-sacrifice, must lead to an inordinate desire to revenge one's self on those others for such self-denial and sacrifice that were too great. Unconsciously, free play will then be given to evil and revengeful impulses.

"... It is ... a warning originating from the inner perception and coinciding with the findings of psychoanalytic practice. Human nature being what it is—our own included—we must be tolerant towards our egotistical impulses, too, to a certain degree, lest we treat our fellow-men badly. Well-considered self-interest was also served in the advice we heard given: 'One must not push anybody away, only gently put him aside.' "[59]

Jewish aggressiveness and vitality was well documented in a 1935 survey in which one out of every ten youths in the city of New York was interviewed. The investigator reported that "the principal recreational activities of Jewish and non-Jewish youth are the same, but *more* of the Jewish than the non-Jewish had participated in them. . . . *More* of them had participated in athletic games, had gone swimming, played tennis or golf, attended concerts and lectures. *More* (though the differences were not so great) had hiked, gone to dances, and visited museums."[60] (Fewer Jewish youths spent any time on manual or mechanical diversions.) Jews are likewise more active in voluntary organizations, as various surveys have shown.[61] In political activity likewise, a 1945 New York City study "showed that low-income Jews wrote more often to their Congressmen than did even high-income Protestants and Catholics."[62]

"Jews get (or used to get) better marks in school . . ." Glazer observes. "Jews work (or used to work) harder at getting an education. It is also believed that they work harder in their trades, in their professions [and] in business."[63] As Jerome Singer puts it, the Jew's "striving for 'good marks' . . . persists throughout life, well beyond the school years."[64]

Ethnic dominance in intermarried families. Where husband and wife have different cultural backgrounds, whose standards are likely to dominate their household? The husband's—because the man is the head of the family? The wife's—because she has most intimate contact with the children? The Gentile partner's—because that represents the dominant and therefore more prestigeful culture? The Jewish partner's—because "a child who's half Jewish is considered a Jew anyway?" There are 'good reasons' for any of the foregoing alternatives.

What are the known facts? Baber studied 130 Jewish-Gentile marriages, in 83 of which the Gentile partner was Catholic. Of 54 cases in which the husband was Jewish and the wife Catholic, the Jewish culture dominated in almost a 3 to 1 ratio. Of 29 cases in which the husband was Catholic, "the husband's culture barely predominated (ratio of 6:5)." Jewish husbands showed more dominance over the cultural atmosphere of the home than Catholic husbands "in spite of the fact that on an attitude-toward-religion scale the Catholic husbands were somewhat more religious than the Jewish husbands." Baber adds that "in *both* groups the children were brought up in the Jewish faith a little more frequently than in the Catholic faith."[65]

Aggressiveness and Western sex roles. Social aggressiveness would seem to be more handicapping to a woman than to a man, according to the sex-role standards of Western society. A number of Mayer's intermarried Jewish husbands complained that Jewish girls were too brash and forward. ("Jewish girls have the attitude: 'Here I am, *do* for me! Buy me a Cadillac and a mink coat.' " "Jewish girls *want*—Gentile girls don't demand so much." "Jewish wives start complaining the minute they're pregnant and sit home all day. . . . As soon as the baby is born, they start playing mahjong all the time, instead of keeping a clean home and cooking good meals for their husbands.") [66]

Undoubtedly traits linked with upward mobility better fit the masculine sex-role as defined by the Gentile majority. The Jewish male is more likely to be admired for being serious-minded, hard-working, ambitious, intellectual; he may be more readily forgiven for his aggressiveness and social awkwardness. All these traits clash more sharply with the Gentile conception of the feminine role. The implication that upward mobility traits are less appropriate to the personality of the woman than to the man is contained in the rule of Chicago's Gold Coast society, as described by Zorbaugh, that a *man* may rise into the social elite (through brains, ambition and a "brilliant marriage,") but a woman must be *born* into the top layer of society if she is to achieve a position of leadership in the society of the elite.[67]

Does aggressiveness reduce a woman's fitness for marriage, as defined by the norms of Gentile society? This hypothesis is suggested by a finding reported by Havemann and West, on marriage rate of college graduates. While college men are actually *more* prone to marry than their non-college counterparts, 31 per cent of women college graduates were unmarried, compared with 13 per cent ratio for all adult women in the United States.[68] Are college women "the self-sufficient type," are they "too choosy" or do they deliberately "shun the role of housewife and mother" in favor of a career?[69]

A clue to this mystery is contained in the "strong correlation between spinsterhood and *earning one's way through college.* . . . The girls most likely to marry are those who were supported through college by their parents. . . . The girls who had to rely mostly on their own resources, however, earning from more than half to all their expenses, are much more likely to remain spinsters. Even among those thirty and over, nearly half [45 per cent] are unmarried career women, compared with only 31 per cent of the thirty-and-over women who were supported by their families"[70] ("Among the men graduates, however, working one's way through school seems to have no effect whatever on marriage prospects. Indeed while the proportion of all married male graduates in [Havemann and West's] sample is 85 per cent . . .the figure for the men who earned more than half their own expenses is 86 per cent.) [71]

It would seem that the girl who worked her way through college is likely to be ambitious, resourceful, hard-working, intelligent, upward mobile; an admirable person but perhaps a bit too pushy to match the Gentile norm of a gentle and acquiescent wife.

Intimacy. "Personality is the core, the heart, of Jewish culture," as *Critic* observes. "From Jesus to Spinoza to Freud, and through them all, has run this intense interest in personality. In the family, in the community, in social life, in the arts and sciences, in economic life—everywhere the emphasis is on the relationship between persons. The giving and receiving of intense personal response to people is one of the main channels of activity in Jewish culture. . . . Argument, controversy, debate . . . rather than impersonal discussion. . . ."[72] The Gentile's involvement with gadgetry and tinkering, says *Critic,* is paralleled by the Jew's involvement with people and with their inner life.

What Reik describes as the Jewish trait of "intimacy" comes very close to *Critic's* definition of "the giving and receiving of intense personal response." To Reik the following joke describes the distinctively Jewish feeling of intimacy: "A Polish Jew . . . was sitting in a railway compartment with an unknown gentleman and . . . behaves very shyly and conventionally until he realizes by some remark of the other that he is a Jew too. Whereupon he immediately stretches his legs on the seat opposite with a sigh of relief: '*Azoi.*' [In that case . . .]"[73] The Jew places a special value upon the kind of intimacy that approximates the "confidentiality and cordiality existing between members of a family," an intimacy which excludes the need for formalities of deference or respect, an intimacy akin to "the feeling of belongingness and closeness between members of a Jewish family . . . [sharing an] awareness of common descent and of the same fate. . . ."[74]

Even argument and unsparing ridicule seem to serve the purpose of dispensing with pretense and posturing, so that people can deal with each other on a basis of equality and intimacy. To know each other intimately is more important than to be distant though friendly. Reik tells a Jewish joke which revolves around "the commandment to ask friends and foes for forgiveness on the High Holidays: after the service a Jew reconciles himself with his worst enemy, telling him: 'I wish you everything you wish me.' Whereupon the other Jew indignantly replies: 'Do you already begin again?' "[75]

According to Tumin, the Gentile elite sometimes justifies their denial of membership to an aspirant by claiming that he lacks the proper "emotional toning" for membership in the elite.[76] Lewisohn, in his 1928 novel *The Island Within,* tells of an incident in which the expression of Jewish intimacy is viewed through Gentile eyes as an act of inexcusable rudeness:

[Lewisohn's protagonist muses over the story of a Jewish physician] . . . introduced into the Gentile milieu of his betrothed and behaving abominably. Poor Dr. Bergmann, afraid of seeming distant and a stranger, had, out of the depth of his Jewish conception of the family, been overintimate. He had asked questions which would in Jewish circles have been taken as a

warm and gracious sign of interest on the part of so new a
member of the clan, but which here sounded and, in truth,
were excessively prying and rude.[77]

Psychoanalysis and Jewish intimacy. Hollingshead and Redlich's study of New Haven psychiatrists reveals not one but two
groups of professional workers—a predominantly (83 per cent)
Jewish analytic group, and a predominantly (81 per cent) Gentile group of directive-organic physicians.[78] In the Jewish tradition of intimacy, the analysts impress the interviewers as being
"more 'inner-oriented,' introspective, and psychologically sensitive than their directive-organic colleagues," who place a Yankee
faith in what they can *do* for their patients—through drugs, shock
treatment, persuasion, suggestion, etc. When asked to reflect on
their professional satisfactions and disappointments, the analytic
group reveals the priority they give to psychological intimacy:

> . . . The analytically oriented physicians emphasized the per-
> sonal gratifications they gained from understanding the com-
> plexities of human behavior; the directive-organic physicians
> stressed the opportunities their training and ability opened
> to them to help other people. In the area of professional dis-
> appointments, the analysts regret how little they know about
> individual motivation of behavior; this did not bother the
> directive-organic group. They are more concerned with the ad-
> ministrative tasks of their practice and the economic obstacles
> their patients face when they try to obtain psychiatric care.[79]

Intimacy and child-rearing practices. Sears, Maccoby, and
Levin, in their study of *Patterns of Child Rearing* in New Haven,
Connecticut, discovered that middle class Jewish mothers, compared with other ethnic groups, are more likely to use "isolation" as a technique for controlling their child (rather than
resort to physical punishment, deprivation of privileges, or
withdrawal of love). The investigators defined isolation as
"sending the child away from people; his being alone is the
punishment."[80] Perhaps the choice of isolation as punishment
implies that a particularly high value is placed on social intimacy.
Intimacy and dating. A classic hazard of dating (and a familiar

theme in romantic comedy and humor) is that the girl seems
to be getting too seriously interested in an ambivalent but
tantalized young man, and seems predisposed to transform a
dating situation into a courtship relationship. The conventions
of dating designate the enjoyment of a person's outward attractiveness ("nice to be seen with") and resourcefulness for "having
a good time" without seeking a deeper interplay of personality,
without getting too seriously interested in each other.

The proposition that one can enjoy the company of another
person by "having fun doing things together" without really
getting to know each other is somewhat foreign to the Jewish
norm of social relations. In a dating situation, a need to "get
to know each other" is more easily utilized by the male, for
whom it may become an instrument of flattery, control, or
seduction. Expressed by the young woman, however, this attitude
may be regarded as "getting too serious," and contrary to the
Gentile norm of dating as an occasion for "having a good time"
without getting too deeply interested in the other person.

Intimacy and the conflict of the generations. Park quotes a
1917 interview with a Jewish immigrant who expresses consternation and disbelief over how America has transformed and de-
humanized his children: they refuse to argue with him, to involve
themselves with him or with his concerns. They have become
spectators and consumers. They not only dance to a machine (i.e.,
a phonograph), they themselves have become "machines," and
"a terror possesses him" when he thinks that these are his children:

Yosl

I am a live man and I have a soul, despite my age. They are
machines. They work all day and come home at night. What
do they do? Nothing. Wait for supper. During supper they
talk about everything in the world—friends, clothes, money,
wages, and all sorts of gossip. After supper they dress up and
go out. Where to? Either the theater, banquet or movie. Or
else their friends call and they drink, eat and play cards; or
they start the machine [i.e., the phonograph] and it plays and
they dance. The next day again to work and so on for the
rest of their lives. . .

They have all been to school—educated people; but just try, for the fun of it, to ask them if they ever read a book. Not on your life. Books have nothing in common with them; Judaism has nothing in common with them; Jewish troubles have nothing in common with them; the whole world has nothing in common with them. They only know one thing— work, eat, and away to the theater. How can they do this? I am asking you; how can one lead a life like that? [And in his voice there was a deep anger ...]

[His voice grew louder and he became very angry.] And I— I cannot live like that. I am no machine. I like to think. I like to be in [a] good mood, I want to talk to people, I want to get an answer to my questions. When I live among shoe-makers [i.e., ignoramuses] I know that the shoemaker is a blind man, but when I live among educated people, then I expect them to be *Menschen*.

When I first came here I used to speak and argue with them. But they did not understand me. They would ask: "Why this and that? This country is not Russia. Here everybody does as he likes."

Gradually I realized that they were machines. They make money and live for that purpose. When I grasped the situa-tion a terror possessed me and I did not believe that these were my children. I could not stand it to be there; I was being choked; I could not tolerate their behavior and I went away. . .[81]

The bittersweet taste of intimacy. When intimacy manifests itself as a lack of privacy, even a proud and devout Jew will admit to a feeling of exasperation. Rabbi Kertzer recalls the following restaurant episode: "I had discussed a serious problem with a couple about to terminate their engagement. We spoke in low voices, but apparently not low enough. A man who had been sitting at the next table walked up to us, check in hand, and asked, 'Do you want my advice?' "

Kertzer once recalled the foregoing anecdote to Isaac Bashevis Singer, who assured Kertzer that his irritation over Jewish lack of privacy was justified. Singer added this story: "Once, at the Writers' Club, I was involved in a confidential conversation when another writer walked up to our table. I told him that what we were discussing was secret. His response was, 'With me, I have no secrets.' "[82] Discussing intimacy as a Jewish trait, Kertzer writes:

I have tried in vain to find the Yiddish or Hebrew equivalent for the word "privacy." There are obscure, unused phrases covering the meaning, but privacy is not a much-sought-after quality in Jewish life. In the most concentrated Jewish communities in the world, Tel Aviv, or parts of Manhattan's Lower East Side, or Brooklyn's Flatbush, no one ever heard of privacy. A visitor on a bus in Israel who asks directions to a certain street will get his answer not only from the bus driver but from a score of passengers as well. Someone else will ask whose house the traveler is seeking. Another voice will announce that she knows the family well, and they are old and respected residents of the neighborhood and still others will offer loud assent.

Several years ago, on a hot, crowded bus going from Haifa to Acco, I felt a hand rubbing my shoulder. Turning around, I discovered a middle-aged woman gliding her fingers on my upper arm. In response to my quizzical look, she asked, in a most matter-of-fact way: "What kind of material is that shirt made of? Is it that new thing called nylon?" As the bus plunged along the overheated highway, a small crowd gathered around us, expressing delight at the wonders of the new fabric, and speculating on how long it would take for Israel to produce such excellent material. In Israel, privacy is the rarest of commodities.

America's most eminent rabbi of the twentieth century, Dr. Stephen S. Wise, once remarked that the world's greatest sin was not difference, but *in*difference. Instant intimacy, pronounced among Jews, and fairly typical of Americans, may have its drawbacks. But on the other hand, it reveals a people who care for other people.[83]

Among the third generation of Jews of North City (interviewed in depth by Kramer and Leventman) 34 per cent admitted that they prefer Jewish friends, and seemed to show some self-consciousness over maintaining such an "old fashioned" or provincial point of view. Some attribute this attitude to a lack of opportunity to meet non-Jews. Others refer to "the comfortable intimacy they find with other Jews."[84]

I prefer Jewish friends because I like them better. Those I like have a certain sensitivity and quality—a cynicism combined with compassion, a humor and irreverence. Only some Gentiles, who are really misplaced Jews, share this quality. And they also prefer to associate with Jews.[85]

Worldliness and the Jewish tradition. Critic contrasts the Western European's ambivalence between asceticism and orgiastic excess, with the Jewish "Apollonian" tradition of temperate sensuosity, fostering the enjoyment of good food, fine clothing, and comfortable living.[86] Kutzik emphasizes the point that the traditional Jewish practice of charity aimed not merely at the preservation of life or the amelioration of suffering; charity was for "the *enhancement* of life," for sharing "the pleasures and comforts of life." The Talmudic rabbis espoused a principle of *hadar mitzvah,* "commanding that whatever is done in observance of the Jewish holidays must be done beautifully and is more worthy the more beautifully it is done."[87]

It's only money. In the Jewish tradition, says Loewenstein, "worldly success is by no means displeasing in the sight of God."[88] Before Jewish New Year cards underwent their inevitable acculturation, they would customarily wish the recipient "A Happy *and Prosperous* New Year." Among Eastern European Jewry the man of wealth, the *nogid,* was a heroic figure. (He was not an expoiter of workers; there were no large-scale employers. He was not a rapacious landlord; Jews were not permitted to own land.) The *nogid* was a valuable community resource. He supported the synagogue and charities, he paid the taxes which were levied against the community, he imported bright young scholars to marry his daughters and give lustre to their adopted community. "Money is dirt," says a Jewish proverb, "—but dirt is not money."

Reik recalls the Jewish proverb: "*Kovod* on the left, money on the right." (*Kovod* means honor, appreciation, deference.) To Reik the proverb warns that one should "not strive too ambitiously for appreciation [which may well be accompanied by poverty], but to look for a comfortable life."[89] This author offers the following interpretation: "Beware of confusing honor with earnings for one can not replace the other."

The Jew as a liberal. Sifting through the 100 (or so) articles he could locate on Jewish personality, Orlansky found a mass of contradiction and ambiguity, with one notable exception: "All studies with which the writer is acquainted agree that Jewish students are more liberal and radical than non-Jewish students in their attitudes on political, social, and religious matters."[90] Orlansky admits that "here for once, psychological tests lend unequivocal support to a conventional stereotype" of innovator, radical, liberal, skeptic, iconoclast, eternal dissenter.

The Jewish emphasis on social justice, on the enhancement of life, on preservation of the community have oriented the American Jew to the liberal wing of American politics.[91] As Fuchs has put it: "By its emphasis on this worldliness and the enjoyment of life here and now, the Jews have been made more receptive to plans for a better life, for reconstituting society, for remaking man's environment, for socialism, for millenialism. . . . The non-asceticism of the Jews has, along with their insecurity, helped produce a distinctive [and liberal] Jewish political style. . ."[92]

Worldliness vs. puritanism. In 1926 Upton Sinclair "called the Jews 'sensual' and accused them of corrupting the American stage by the mass introduction of sultry stage erotics." A writer in the Jewish press, James Fuchs, castigated Sinclair for engaging in a meaningless generalization, for dabbling in the tedious and stupid literature of racial traits.[93] A generation later, *Lawrence* Fuchs apparently felt no misgivings about comparing America's "bleak puritan heritage" with the "free acceptance of physical pleasures that one finds in the Jewish culture. . . . The case can be made that Jews have been disproportionately influential in the de-puritanizing of America because of the special place of Jews in Hollywood, the legitimate theater, advertising, publishing, and the ladies' garment trades."[94]

"While the Jews loathe drunkenness, they do like to drink. . . . In fact, the Jews are enjoined to drink at various festivals and ceremonies." "Most Jews are sensuous about food. There are few vegetarians among them. In short, the Jewish spirit and temper are non-ascetic because of the value which most Jews have always placed on the enjoyment of life's pleasures."[95]

A worldly folklore. Of the following two folk tales, one attempts to identify the aptitude for making money, and the other

asks men of wealth and power to be humble in their hearts
and not in their affectations.

There is a story to the effect that a poor man asked his
rich brother: 'Why are you wealthy, and I am not?' The
brother answered: 'Because I have no scruples against doing
wrong.' The poor brother began to misconduct himself, but
he remained poor. He complained of this to his elder brother,
who answered: 'The reason your transgressions have not made
you wealthy is that you did them not from conviction that it
matters not whether we do good or evil, but solely because
you desired riches.'[96]

A king was told that a man of humility is endowed with
long life. He attired himself in old garments, took up his
residence in a small hut, and forbade anyone to show reverence
before him. But when he honestly examined himself, the king
found himself to be prouder of his seeming humility than
ever before. A philosopher thereupon remarked to him: 'Dress
like a king; live like a king; allow the people to show due
respect to you; but be humble in your inmost heart.'[97]

Permissiveness. Since Jewish law holds that anyone who was
born to a Jewish mother is a Jew, there is a very considerable
latitude about how one may interpret or practice his Jewish
identity: through worship, study, social affiliation, political action, philanthropy, gastronomy, nationalism, aesthetic experience, mysticism, or tribal loyalty.

The religious and the non-religious. To the three major religious groupings—Orthodox, Conservative and Reform—one
must add the Jew who for whatever reason does *not* maintain
religious affiliation. (It is estimated that only one-half of New
York City's Jews hold synagogue membership.) The unaffiliated
Jew, Bezalel Sherman argues, does not necessarily lack interest
or pride or involvement in his Jewishness; he is not necessarily
drifting into the Gentile majority. "Nothing in the Jewish faith
makes it mandatory for a Jew to belong to a synagogue. . . .
The unaffiliated regard themselves, and are often regarded by
others, as loyal Jews and good members of the Jewish community." (Even the most secular of Jews, however, are expected

to call upon a rabbi for the traditional Jewish rites of circumcision, wedding, and funeral.) [98]

The unaffiliated Jew, Sherman argues, is a manifestation of the traditional "diversity of Jewish expression." Since he may maintain active membership in a variety of Jewish organizations—service, fraternal, educational, cultural, community relations, or social welfare— the term *unaffiliated* is in itself somewhat misleading. "Most unaffiliated Jews," Sherman adds, "vigorously affirm the human values that have been cherished over a long period of Jewish history."[99]

Herbert Gans defines an informal variety of Jewish practice in which tangible symbols of Jewish culture are employed to express an affection for the Jewish tradition and help socialize the children into an awareness of their Jewish identity. "Symbolic Judaism," as Gans labels it, designates the collecting and displaying of Israeli religious objects, Jewish household decor, Jewish phonograph records. In addition to the enjoyment of Jewish cuisine and entertainment, Gans sees the practice of "symbolic Judaism" closely linked with a "preoccupation with the problems of being Jewish in America . . . concern over anti-Semitism, irreligiousness, intermarriage, community apathy, cultural or social assimilation . . ."[100] From a psychological standpoint there is a vast difference between collecting Israeli copperwork and a "preoccupation with the problems of being Jewish in America," for only the latter implies a sense of identity with the Jewish people. If, as Gans holds, the two traits are closely linked, his "symbolic Jews" are—from a psychological standpoint—very real Jews.

The principle of change. Kramer and Leventman found little religious conflict or rebellion amongst the third generation Jews of North City. Their parents had already adapted religious practices to American life and, more importantly, had "incorporated the principle of change. It requires little effort to adapt them further. Any tensions that occur in the religious sphere are resolved by simply changing the religious institution, modifying its demands to suit new styles of life.

"Since members of the third generation find that they can be both Jewish and successful (at least as much as they want to be), they feel no need to shed a religious affiliation that does not restrict their life chances. They do, however, continue to

modify their religious patterns in the direction of greater conformity to those of the dominant society. . . . Sentiment exceeds
commitment in the third generation, sufficing to assuage the
conscience without isolating the Jew from the general community."[101]

Solidarity through permissiveness. Arthur A. Cohen expresses
consternation over the fact that "American Jewish leadership has
not seen fit to encourage the examination of the theological bases
of Jewish faith. In fact," he continues, "the leading rabbinical
seminaries teach little Jewish theology as such, give scant attention to Jewish philosophic literature, and have allowed the
apologetic comparison of religiou beliefs to become a moribund
discipline." Cohen suspects "that some Jewish leaders fear—
perhaps not unjustifiably—that . . . they have no theology at all."

"The major Jewish argument against [developing a] Jewish
theology," says Cohen, "is that it is a Christian pastime—that it
may, by insinuation and subtle influence, Christianize Judaism.
In this view, Christianity is a religion of faith, dogma, and
theology and Judaism is a religion which emphasizes *observance*
of God's Law, not speculation about it."[102] It is certainly true
that the Jewish tradition, as Cohen's mentor Rabbi Steinberg
phrased it, "is far more concerned that men shall act rightly than
that they shall speculate in some approved fashion."[103]

Rabbi Steinberg's comment suggests more directly the bases
of the Jewish bias against a Jewish theology: (1) that it would
lead to schisms and cleavages which would threaten Jewish
solidarity (Protestantism can afford to divide itself into dozens
of denominations, the Jews cannot) ; (2) it would over-emphasize Judaism as a religion and thereby neglect the concept of
Judaism as a community; (3) it would run counter to the
Jewish tradition of *open-ended* speculation and skepticism.

A distinction between *faith* and *folk* parallels the Christian
dichotomy of Church and State, argued Rabbi Stephen S. Wise,
leader of Reform Judaism a generation ago. For Jews to adopt
such an "utterly alien and un-Jewish dichotomy [would be] a
tragic blunder . . . [violating the] immemorial Jewish tradition
[which holds] people and religion as one and inseparable."[104]
The Credo of Jewish Reform, he argued, places "a major em-

phasis upon the Jewish church [and] a minor emphasis upon
the Jewish people." Even the most ignorant Jews, Rabbi Wise
insisted, dimly and correctly sense "that they were members of
a fellowship, not communicants of a sect or church."[105] A credo
is a segregationist device, Rabbi Wise seemed to argue, which
threatens the solidarity and therefore the survival of the Jewish
community. A credal test violates the Jewish tradition of unconditional brotherhood.

Varieties of Jewish experience. Reik refers to the Jews as "a
community of destiny."[106] To Herberg the Jews are a covenant-
folk.[107] Irving Feldman describes the Jews as "a society of imagination" since it extends in time and space far beyond one's own
biographical circumstances.[108] Another definition of Judaism is
contained in the *bon mot* of the Jew who explained, "Of the
Jewish holidays I observe only the Jascha Heifetz concerts."[109]

Loyalty to Jewish food habits take on a special significance
as a vehicle for maintaining ethnic solidarity. In *This Is My God,*
Wouk asserts that "food laws are social instruments for keeping
the Jewish nation alive and psychological instruments for preserving the identity of individuals."[110]

Reik tells of a Jew who, not long after he had been baptized,
"comes once again into the delicatessen where he enjoys chopped
breast of goose and sighs regretfully: 'And from such a religion
one should separate oneself!' "[111] (Both the baptism and the
chopped goose breast give the joke a Viennese flavor.) Rabbi
Weisberger tells of a Jewish officer of the U.S. Navy whose ship
was docked at an Australian port. It was Friday and he "felt
homesick, so he took a walk aimlessly about the port. Soon his
sense of smell was directing his steps. A familiar odor drew him
on. Finally, he stopped where he smelled it strongest, knocked
on the door and asked, 'Would you by any chance be cooking
"gefilte fish," and are you Jewish?' The response was in the
affirmative, to both queries."[112]

The existentialist theme in Jewish life. In 1953 Podhoretz
argued that theology has never flourished in the Jewish culture
because theology attempts "to understand the problem of evil
in rational terms . . . to make sense of a classically senseless
situation." Wrote Podhoretz:

[A] conception of reality as insanely irrational is common
to the comic literature of oppressed peoples. We have lately
seen it in Ralph Ellison's novel about the Negroes, but it has
a long history behind it. With varying degrees of success,
Defoe, Smollet, Disraeli, and Dickens all work from such a
conception when they write the comedy of the poor. What is
unusual about Sholom Aleichem is that he makes the absurd
malevolence of the world all part of the fun and richness of
living. This is a way of accepting life even when life is most
niggardly in its gifts. And this is an attitude that strikes me
as quintessentially Jewish. . . . If there is no answer [to the
problem of evil], one can either rage like Dostoevsky, or laugh
[like] Sholom Aleichem. . .[113]

Judaism as a community of the alienated. "Judaism represents
a very special value in American life," comments Rabbi Richard
L. Rubenstein. Many non-Jews are attracted to Judaism precisely
because of its freedom from fixed dogmas. "It is often the person
for whom all religious symbols have become transparent who
converts to Judaism—; in reality, he or she [affiliates with] the
Jewish situation . . . as the institutionalization of his own. He
does not accept a new set of dogmas to replace others which can
no longer be accepted."[114]

Belongingness and responsibility. "A person whose near relative behaves capriciously or foolishly will sometimes react to the
amusement of others in a [typically Jewish] manner and say:
'I would laugh too, if the fool did not belong to me.' "[115] Here
again we are confronted by the tribal spirit that says all Jews
belong to each other and must take care of one another. "In the
traditional Jewish view," says Kutzik, "there is no individual
per se: the individual is seen as an organic, inseparable part of
the community."[116]

Communalism as the dominant Jewish value is represented,
says Kutzik, in Hillel's injunction: "Separate not thyself from
the community," and in Baron's statement that "in theory and
practice, the Jewish group recognized the superiority of the
communal over individual rights."[117]

"In spite of the grating sound it makes in the liberal ear, it
must be stated," Kutzik continues, "that 'the dignity of the individual' is not a Jewish value. This is so in spite of the widely

recorded and readily observable fact that the individual is highly valued by the Jews. For the Jewish valuation of the individual derives from and is inseparable from his worth as a member of the community. . ."[118]

"What really matters in the Jewish religion," writes Salo Baron, dean of American Jewish historians, "is not the immortality of the individual Jew, but that of the Jewish people . . . the eternal life of the nation. Hence the extraordinary attachment to life manifested by Orthodox Jews. Life on earth, the care of the sick and the poor, the duty of marriage and increase in family—all these are repeatedly stressed that the race and the people may be maintained until the end of days."[119]

Likewise the late Chief Rabbi of the British Commonwealth and spokesman of world Orthodoxy, Joseph Hertz, declared: "Israel's faith is a religion of *life*, not death, a religion that declares man's humanity to man as the most acceptable form of adoration to God."[120] The Jew's culturally patterned compassion for the needy and underprivileged, his commitment not merely to the preservation of life but to its enhancement, makes him a natural candidate for political liberalism, the tradition with which he is thoroughly identified in American political life.

In America's smaller communities where Jews are too few to play an active role in local politics, Jews are notably active in community services and in community fund raising. Belth observed a peculiar "inverse law" operating in the middle-sized towns which came under the scrutiny of the Cornell University studies in intergroup relations: "the more that Jews are excluded from socially elite organizations and residential areas, the more they seem to be in positions of civic and social service leadership."[121] Denied the privileges of upper class status in the dominant group, the Jew accepts a role closer to the traditional function of the Jewish elite.

Intellectualism. Observers unfamiliar with the Jewish cultural tradition are likely to interpret the Jew's academic striving as a neurotic "compensatory effort." It is ironic that in a book dedicated to the thesis that the psychotherapist must understand the cultural background of his client, the author fails to grasp the status accorded to learning in the cultural tradition of the Jews. Georgene Seward thus chooses to interpret the American Jew's academic achievement as a "compensatory effort" to deal with his "exile neurosis."[122] Sargent and Williamson likewise interpret the "tendency to do better than the majority group, as often seen among the study habits of American Jews" as an aggressive reaction to discrimination.[123]

The foregoing interpretations fail to take into account many centuries of cultural experience in which the highest value was attached to an aptitude and desire for intellectual learning. Norbert Wiener conjectures that the selection of husbands on the basis of scholarship has been practiced over enough generations in the Jewish culture to make its mark on the genetic pool of the Jewish community.[124] Loewenstein says "there is no doubt that constant encouragement of the intellectual capacities of a child favors their development."[125]

On the survival of intellectual exercise, Erikson conjectures that when Bettleheim was subjected to the horrors of life in a Nazi concentration camp, he "preserved his life and sanity by deliberately and persistently clinging to the historical Jewish identity of spiritual and intellectual superiority over a physically superior outer world; he made his tormenters the subject of a silent research project which he safely delivered to the world of free letters."[126] ("A man should live if only to satisfy his curiosity.")

The Jewish experience with intellectualism, skepticism, and alienation are all brought into focus in the reflection of Freud that "Because I was a Jew, I found myself free from the prejudices which restrict others in the use of the intellect; as a Jew, I was prepared to be in the opposition and to renounce agreement with the majority."[127] Paraphrasing the Duke of Wellington's statement that the victory of Waterloo was won on the playing fields of Eton, Reik asserts that "the many intellectual victories of modern Jewish scholars and explorers were achieved in the Talmud schools, the *Yeshivot* of Eastern Europe where . . . their ancestors studied."[128]

Developed in a religious context, Jewish intellectualism has become a strong secular tradition in Jewish life.[129] Jews are more likely to attend college, and more likely to earn a college degree. Jewish students (especially males) apparently work harder than non-Jews; they tend to receive higher grades than non-Jews of equal aptitude scores.[130] "In New York City, two studies, in 1948 and 1953, showed that one-sixth of the Jews over eighteen had completed college, compared with a little more than one-twentieth of the non-Jews—and this even though considerably fewer of the Jews were native-born. In other cities, with smaller percentages of foreign-born Jews, the percentage of college graduates was even greater."[131]

Western culture over-emphasizes the difference between the practical man and the "egghead." As Jessie Bernard points out so nicely, the immigrant businessman's curiosity and eagerness to learn and discuss the subtleties of the American business world took on a "graduate seminar" quality, and clearly belongs to the Jew's intellectual tradition.

> Whenever [immigrant businessmen] get together they discuss business. They talk over their own and others' experiences and analyze the reasons for success or failure. And in this way they teach one another and each learns from the experience of his fellows. It is a school of business as truly as though it were formally organized. The sons of these men, years later, were to pay high tuition fees to analyze business experience under university professors, in much the same way as their fathers did informally. Mr. F., for example, tells his fascinated listeners how Jake has managed to swing a million-dollar deal with only fifty thousand dollars. The intricacies of mortgages, loans, incorporation privileges, liens, and the like are vividly explained by means of this concrete case and the information thus acquired is put to good use by the hearers when the opportunity arises.
>
> These are men of the first generation, untrained in any school but that of experience.[132]

Glazer has likewise pointed out that the Jewish character has through centuries of cultural experience been stamped with the values that make for good businessmen and intellectuals: foresight, care, moderation, sobriety, consciousness about one's time, one's education, one's personality and way of life. "The dominating characteristic of his life is that he is able to see that the present postponement of pleasure will lead to an increase in satisfaction later."[133]

THE SELF-ACTUALIZER AND THE MENSCH

Abraham Maslow reports on his "holistic analysis" of 45 persons whom he chose to study because their lives seemed to demonstrate the kind of psychological health that is betokened by "the full use and exploitation of talents, capacities, potentialities, etc. . . . They are people who have developed or are developing to the full stature of which they are capable," says Maslow, who regards the process of "self-actualization" as a better index of psychological health than prevailing concepts of "adjustment," or the mere absence of pathology.[134]

In Maslow's detailed discussion of traits and attitudes which distinguish self-actualizing people, it is interesting to note the extent to which these characteristics overlap with what have been described in the literature as *Jewish* traits and norms. We shall summarize from Maslow's discussion of "healthy people" what seems to this writer to describe a Jewish style of life.

Life is with people. Self-actualizers show an intimacy, an intensity in their interpersonal relations—which has been described by *Critic,* and others, as central to the Jewish ethos. Self-actualizers "have deeper and more profound interpersonal relations than any other adults. . . . They are capable of more fusion, greater love, more perfect identification, more obliteration of the ego boundaries than other people would consider possible." They have especially deep ties with rather few individuals. . . . The ones that they love profoundly are few in number. . . . One subject expressed it [thus]: 'I haven't got time for many friends. Nobody has, that is, if they are to be *real* friends.' "[135]

Self-actualizers are democratic and humanitarian, in the Jewish tradition. "They have a genuine desire to help the human race . . . . . . However far apart he is from them at times, he nevertheless feels a basic underlying kinship with these creatures. . ."[136] A profound though subtle trait of self-actualizers is their "tendency to give a certain quantum of respect to *any* human being just because he is a human individual." "They love or rather have compassion for all mankind."[137]

Resistance to enculturation. Maslow's self-actualizers express what might be interpreted as a Jewish impatience with Western standards of politeness and decorum: They show a distaste for artificialities—"cant, guile, hypocrisy, front, face, playing a game, trying to impress in conventional ways: these are all absent in themselves to an unusual degree."[138] They likewise show "a relative lack of the disgusts and aversions seen in average people . . . e.g., . . . disgust with body products, body odors, and bodily functions."[139]

Jewish skepticism cannot be too different from what Maslow describes as the self-actualizer's "inner feeling of detachment from the culture. . . . They very frequently seem to be able to stand off from it as if they did not quite belong to it."[140] Maslow compares them "with the oversocialized, the robotized, or the ethnocentric. . ."[141] Self-actualizers "get along with the culture in various ways, but of all of them it may be said that in a certain profound and meaningful sense they resist enculturation and maintain a certain inner detachment from the culture in which they are immersed."[142] These sojourner-citizens either do not seek or do not value full membership in the proud majority.

My son the self-actualizer. As he describes the self-actualizer's love of privacy, and his creative use of detachment, it occurs to Maslow that this freedom from any need for immediate approval, love, and respect suggests that self-actualizers "have been given plenty of this very same love and respect in the past."[143] Here we see how the warm and supportive Jewish mother launches the career of a self-actualizer. Maslow's comment clearly echoes Freud's reflection that "he who has been the undisputed darling of his mother retains throughout life that victorious feeling, that confidence in ultimate success, which not seldom brings actual success with it."[144]

The enjoyment of living. Self-actualizers talk and behave like "good and lusty animals";[145] they consider it desirable to enjoy life and have a good time,[146] a familiar theme in discussions of the Jewish ethos. The basic experiences of life are for them a source of "ecstasy, inspiration, and strength."[147] If they do not recite the traditional blessings when they behold the beauties of nature and the joys of living, they apparently experience the feelings that are expressed by these traditional Jewish blessings.[148]

Attitudes toward sex. It seemed to Maslow that self-actualizers were "considerably more free and casual and unconventional than the average" in their readiness to talk about sex,[149] an observation which Kinsey directed specifically at his Jewish respondents. For self-actualizers, sex is far more than a source of "passing pleasure"; they seem to draw from it something "strengthening and revivifying" which makes it akin to the mystical experience that some people derive from music or nature.[150] To these urbane hedonists "the orgasm is simultaneously more important and less important than in average people. It is often a profound and almost mystical experience, and yet the absence of sexuality is more easily tolerated by [self-actualizing] people. This is not a paradox or a contradiction," Maslow insists. ". . . Loving at a higher level makes the lower needs and their frustrations and satisfactions less important, less central, more easily neglected. But it also makes them more wholeheartedly enjoyed when gratified."[151]

But self-actualizers do not overidealize sex. ". . . It may be a delicate pleasure rather than an intense one, a gay and light-hearted, playful sort of thing rather than a serious and profound experience or even a neutral duty. . ." (It is as if the self-actualizers have interiorized the Mosaic command that the wife's "conjugal rights shall [her husband] not diminish.") Self-actualizers can "lightly and mildly enjoy sex as a titillating, pleasant, playful, enjoyable, tickling kind of experience instead of a plumbing of the most intense depths of ecstatic emotionality."[152]

In sexual foreplay and style of lovemaking, self-actualizers "made no real sharp differentiation between the roles and personalities of the two sexes. . . . They did not assume that the female was passive and the male active. . ." Maslow argues that they were able to diverge from the Western norms of sex-role behavior because they were "so certain of their maleness or femaleness."[153] Perhaps they diverged from the Western norm because they were governed by a somewhat different norm, a Jewish norm.

Sex object choice. The healthy person, says Maslow, is romantically intrigued by strangeness, but does not need the exotic or outwardly beautiful for sexual attraction.[154] ". . . Novelty in the sexual partner is very exciting and attractive, especially for neurotic people, but . . . [this generalization does not hold] for self-actualizing people."[155]

As one becomes more of a self-actualizing person, he feels attracted to a partner less on the basis of outward characteristics (e.g., "good looking, good dancer, nice breasts"), and more on the basis of characterological traits (e.g., "compatibility, goodness, decency, good companionship"). A successful love partnership improves with time.[156] Partners who deeply and intimately know and accept each other become progressively less concerned with trying and striving, with maintaining defenses and roles. "There is a growing intimacy and honesty of self-expression, which at its height is a rare phenomenon. The report of [self-actualizers] is that with a beloved person it is possible to be oneself, to feel natural. . ."[157] "They can feel psychologically (as well as physically) naked and still feel loved and wanted and secure."[158] For self-actualizers, Maslow observes, psychological intimacy is more conducive to sexual fulfillment than the excitement of the strange and exotic. Maslow admits that this conclusion "contradicts folk wisdom and also some of the more esoteric theorists on sexuality and love. . ."[159]

The balancing of opposites. This familiar theme in discussions of the Jewish ethos (introduced in Chapter 7) is given a prominent place in Maslow's description of self-actualizing people. "For example the age-old opposition between heart and head, reason and instinct, or cognition and conation seem to disappear in healthy people where they become synergic rather than antagonists, and where conflict between them disappears because they say the same thing and point to the same conclusion . . .

The dichotomy between selfishness and unselfishness disappears altogether in healthy people because in principle every act is *both* selfish and unselfish. Our subjects are simultaneously very spiritual and very pagan and sensual. Duty cannot be contrasted with pleasure nor work with play when duty *is* pleasure, when work *is* play, and the person doing his duty and being virtuous is simultaneously seeking his pleasure and being happy. If the most socially identified people are themselves also the most individualistic people, of what use is it to retain the polarity? If the most mature are also childlike? And if the most ethical and moral people are also the lustiest and most animal?

Similar findings have been reached for kindness-ruthlessness, concreteness-abstractness, acceptance-rebellion, self-society, adjustment-maladjustment, detachment from others—identification with others, serious-humorous, Dionysian-Apollonian, introverted-extroverted, intense-casual, serious-frivolous, conventional-unconventional, mystic-realistic, active-passive, masculine-feminine, lust-love, and Eros-Agape. In these people, the id, the ego, and the superego are collaborative and synergic; they do not war with each other. . . . The higher and the lower are not in opposition but in agreement, and a thousand serious philosophical dilemmas are discovered to have more than two horns, or, paradoxically, no horns at all. . . . *Is it necessary to choose between the good woman and the bad . . . when we have found that the really healthy woman is both at the same time?*[160] (Italics added.)

Self-actualization as a Jewish style of life. Maslow prefers to regard his self-actualizers as "not simply another subcultural group, but rather less enculturated, less flattened out, less molded" than the average person.[161] Yet Maslow goes to considerable lengths to show that they *do* tend to abide by a norm, they *do* share common attitudes toward themselves, toward people, toward life—and on close scrutiny this self-actualizing style of life shows a number of parallels with the Jewish ethos.[162]

To what extent does the core concept of self-actualization itself reflect the Jewish ethos? For those who hold full membership in the proud majority, perhaps it is enough to settle back and enjoy this happy accident of status—to get along, to take his good fortune humbly, graciously, comfortably. But for one whose people has endured centuries of oppression and exclusion, he is not a real person unless he makes intelligent use of opportunities to develop and exercise his capabilities. In the Jewish tradition, moreover, humility and self-denial are not idealized; the good life is attained not by purging one's soul of desire, but by doing what is necessary so that the work of the Creator can unfold, can be fulfilled, can be actualized. Maslow's concept of self-actualization has much in common with the energetic, achievement-oriented spirit of the Jews—which is a source of pride to the philo-Judiac, and is viewed as a threat by the anti-Semite.

Not only does the Jewish ethos predispose the individual toward achievement, but—if there is a degree of validity in our discussion so far—it directs him toward particular areas of achievement. The Judaic emphasis on social responsibility and the enhancement of life supports whatever other motives direct the individual toward the study of medicine[163] or to the clinical applications of psychology, or to social work. The Jewish emphasis on Torah as knowledge supports academic achievement leading to teaching, research, and scholarship. The Jew's relative lack of culturally patterned guilt about money promotes achievement in business. Much has been written about the extent to which the Jewish tradition predisposes the individual to be a skeptic, an innovator, a challenger of the status quo. (Diametrically opposed to Reik's conclusion that skepticism is at the heart of the Jewish ethos, is the argument of Glazer and Moynihan that the Jew has been an innovator and an *avant-gardist* in America because as a latecomer he has been obliged to seek professional opportunity in new and undeveloped fields, rather than seek entry into the more conservative and stable areas of the Establishment. Glazer and Moynihan conjecture that "even had its founder been a German anti-Semite," psychoanalysis would have a special appeal to Jews because of the vast and unmet need for professional workers.) [164]

Freud and Lewin as Jews

Freud felt sure that his Jewishness enabled him to stand apart from the comfortable majority, and thus prepare him for the role of innovator and founder of psychoanalysis;[165] just as Bakan seems convinced that the Jewish mystical tradition provided the raw materials for the development of psychoanalytic theory. Contradictions and inconsistencies in Freud's work and character take on new significance when viewed as an expression of the Jewish theme of "the balancing of opposites," to which we have already referred.

Freud was a bold theorist but also a dedicated practitioner; he was trained as a physician and neurologist but he called himself a psychologist; he was dedicated to the scientific method but he did not conceal his private superstitions; he described himself as an atheist but claimed that the "very essence" of his character was Jewish; he was a rebel against puritanical sex taboos but his intimates describe his personal standards and tastes as Victorian and Orthodox.[166] Freud dared to think that he could throw light on the most hidden motives of men, though in everyday life Freud was not considered a good judge of character, and much of his difficulties with his disciples was attributed to Freud's limitations as *ein Menschenkenner*.[167]

In the field of social psychology, Kurt Lewin was not only a bold innovator, but was likewise notable for his "balancing of opposites": individual and group, mathematical logic and quasi-mystical concepts like "we feeling" and "group atmosphere," basic research and social action, the formulation of universal laws of social behavior and attention to the particular problems of Jews in America.

After he had established himself as a theorist of first rank, Lewin called for "research on the conditions and effects of various forms of social action, and [for] research leading to social action. Research that produces nothing but books," said Lewin, "will not suffice."[168]

Lewin rejected the notion that action-research "is in any respect less scientific or 'lower' than what would be required for pure science in the field of social events . . . [but believed] the opposite to be true."[169] "Socially, it does not suffice that university organizations produce new scientific insight. It will be necessary," Lewin insisted, "to install fact-finding procedures, social eyes and ears, right into social action bodies."[170] In his dedication to the concept of action-research, which he did much to popularize, Lewin was clearly speaking in a tradition that sees truth, morality, and social needs as separable aspects (but not separate bodies) of a unitary reality—stated in a more traditional and figurative language: *Torah,* God, and Israel are one.

The self-actualizing woman in Western society. We return to our observation that the energetic, achievement-oriented spirit of the self-actualizer better fits the *male* sex-role in Western society, that the Jewish ethos and matricentric tradition generate

ethnically patterned behaviors which put the Jewish woman at
a relative disadvantage when "viewed through Gentile eyes."
Thomas Wolfe describes a self-actualizing Jewish woman whose
wealth of talents raises her above any cultural stereotype. In
this sense, Esther Jack is an exception, and yet there is much
we have said about Jewish traits, about the matricentric woman
(and much about the folklore of the stranger-woman, which is
a topic of Chapter 9) which is clearly recognizable in this
ficationalized character study.

Esther Jack

Based on the character of Thomas Wolfe's "constant companion" for a period of five years (he was twenty-five and she
was forty-three when they first met), Esther Jack is the Jewish
patroness and mistress of George Webber, artist-protagonist of
The Web and the Rock. Wolfe describes George's ambivalent
fascination over the inscrutibility which he attributed to this
exotic woman:[171]

. . . smiling gently, and with that musing and tranquil expression . . . which already had power to wound his suspicion and
to awaken in him a jealous curiosity.

It was a somber, dark, and passionate look that transformed
her merry and eager face with an expression of brooding intensity . . . a masklife grief, an almost Slavic and undecipher-
able passion to her face, and he was pierced with a bitter desire
to know the secret of this look. . . .

. . . An inner and remote absorption from which the world
was excluded. That look had in it so much perplexity and
pain, so much dark grief and brooding passion, that it
awakened in him a feeling of bitter mistrust.

He felt tricked and cheated and baffled by a cleverness and
subtlety of living that was too old, too wise and crafty, for him
to fathom or contend with. He wondered if her . . . merry and
rosy face . . . were not merely some apparatus of concealment
and escape from this secret thing that dwelt in her, if they

were not merely an appearance calculated to deceive the
world. . . .[172]

The voluptuous stranger-woman. Wolfe describes how George's
wild and sensuous fantasy transformed this "nice-looking woman,"[173] this "matronly figure of middle age, [this] creature with
a warm and jolly little face, a wholesome and indomitable energy
for every day"[174] into "the most beautiful woman that ever lived.
. . ." Filled with the "triumphant joy and power" of his love for
Esther, George would now "rush out on the streets like a lover
going to see his mistress." Now he found the women on the streets
of New York "more beautiful than flowers, more full of juice
and succulence than fruit . . . a single music of breast, buttock,
thigh, and lip and flashing hair. But not a one, he thought, as
lovely as his Esther."[75]

> [To rich Jews and poor Jews alike, George ascribed this
> voluptuous, sensuous, exotic appeal. The women of] . . .
> wealthy and cultivated Jews . . . were very elegant and fash-
> ionable, beautifully gowned, dark, tall, some of them exotically
> lovely. . . . Some of them valued fine intelligence and the ability
> to create more than they valued money, but most of them had
> both.[176]
>
> The Jews loved what was beautiful and pleasant in life.
> Rich Jews and poor Jews were full of life and curiosity. . . .
> They had a glorious time. . . .
>
> As for the poor Jews . . . they swarmed, they fought, they
> haggled . . . they ate, drank, and fornicated with a will. The
> poor Jews also enjoyed life.[177]

George describes a fellow Anglo-Saxon who for the past ten
years "had turned more and more to certain Jews in New York
for companionship. His mind, with its hunger for the rich and
sumptuous, drew back wearily and with disgust from the dry
sterility and juiceless quality of his own Puritan inheritance."[178]
When George's feelings toward Esther became twisted by fear
and suspicion, he fantasied Esther as a menacing, irresistably
voluptuous siren, smouldering "with all the slumberous and in-
satiate passions of the East. . . .

Again and again, a mad, distorted picture blazed within his mind. He saw a dark regiment of Jewish women in their lavish beauty, their faces melting into honey, their eyes glowing, their breasts like melons . . . their proud bodies opulently gowned and flashing with somber fires of ancient jewels as they paced with the velvet undulance of an intolerable sensuality the proud and splendid chambers of the night. They were . . . the living cross on which the flesh and marrow of Christian men had been crucified.[179]

The matricentric woman. It seems clear from the beginning that Esther fulfills George's yearning for a warm and sheltering, powerful and inspiring woman. Esther fulfills this yearning more boldly than George can tolerate; she fulfills it to a degree that threatens his feeling of Christian manhood and autonomy. (It is interesting to note that before he found Esther, he had lived with an erotic fantasy in which his partner was a wealthy, voluptuous widow.)[180] He recognizes that in Esther he has found one of those rare people whose "energy of joy and delight draw other people to them as bees are drawn to ripe plums." George sees himself by contrast as typical of most people, with "little power for living in themselves, they are pallid and uncertain in their thoughts and feelings, and they think they can derive the strength, the richness, and the character they lack from one of these vital and decisive people. For this reason people loved Mrs. Jack and wanted to be near her: she gave them a feeling of confidence, joy, and vitality which they did not have in themselves."[181]

George could enjoy the fusion of Esther's maternal and erotic qualities, as he watched her prepare dinner:

There is no spectacle on earth more appealing than that of a beautiful woman in the act of cooking dinner for someone she loves. Thus the sight of Esther as, delicately flushed, she bent with the earnest devotion of religious ceremony above the food she was cooking for him, was enough to drive him mad with love and hunger.[182]

Esther's boundless love and emotional support gave George "a kind of frame, design, and purpose to life that it had never had before."[183] The author elaborates: "It was not merely that he was in love with her. In addition to that, through his association with her it seemed to him that now at last he had begun to 'know' the city. . . . She was the city's daughter just as he had been the product of the town."[184]

Before long, George began to feel Esther's powerful and sheltering influence as something terrifying and threatening to his sense of integrity.

> She was now central, like an inexorable presence, to every action, every feeling, every moment of his life. . . . Had she dwelt there in the courts of the heart only . . . she could perhaps have been expelled by some effort of the will. . . . But she had entered in the porches of the blood, she had soaked through all the tissues of the flesh, she had permeated the convolutions of the brain, until now she inhabited his flesh, his blood, his life, like a subtle and powerful spirit that could never be driven out, any more than a man could drive out of him the blood of his mother. . . .[185]

The self-actualizing mistress. Esther's success in her profession and as a person, which had fascinated and even inspired George, began to gnaw at his self-esteem as it became apparent that public recognition of *his* work as a writer was still a long way off. Sitting one night in a theatre where Esther's scenic and costume work was on brilliant display, George "suddenly had a strange, uncomfortable feeling of something closing in on him, as if a magic and invisible ring had been drawn round him, encircling him, shutting him in, making him against his will a part of this world to which he belonged."[186]

George felt trapped, fearful, suspicious. He came to realize that "a love which made him so dependent on her, which made him feel, without her, hopeless, helpless, and a thing of no account, was for such a man as he, a prison of the spirit—and . . . now [he] began to hurl himself against the bars."[187]

Brooding over his deep ambivalence over Esther, he was moved to elaborate a paranoid fantasy of Jews who plot "the castration of the spirit of a living man."[188] George now felt both fascinated and disgraced by Esther's enormous creativity and work output.

This sudden perception of Esther's indomitable courage and energy, her power to work, and her balanced control over all the decisive acts and moments of her life, in contrast to the waste, confusion, and uncertainty of his own, smote him a hammer-blow of shame and self-contempt.[189]

After their separation, after his fury had spent itself, he again idealized Esther as "the best and truest friend I ever had . . . the noblest, greatest, and most beautiful woman that I ever saw or knew . . . the woman that I love."[190]

The balancing of opposites. Wolfe places an enormous emphasis on the fact that Esther was at home in an environment that terrified George: *the city.* Under her sheltering wing, he could also feel at home in the city. What gave this simple fact its immense emotional significance? To a town boy, the city is not only large and strange, it is also a center of dazzling luxury and wealth and social power; it is a place where men pit themselves against each other in the fiercest of competitive struggles over the command of these prizes. What fascinated George was to see how thoroughly but without ostentation or arrogance Esther enjoyed the luxury and pleasures of the city, to see how boldly Esther competed without becoming "strident and metallic," to see how enormously Esther worked without becoming "harrassed and driven."[191] The enjoyment of living, psychological intimacy, ambition, and seriousness of purpose, the audacity to assert her taste and judgment—these Jewish traits Esther displayed with style and verve.

As the woman talked, a feeling of immense joy, peace, and certitude entered his spirit. He got from her a sense of strength, ease, and happiness which he had not felt before, and the doubts and confusion of a moment before had vanished. Suddenly the life of the city seemed opulent, glorious, and full of triumph for him, he felt able to conquer and subdue any obstacle, he forgot his horror and fear of the swarming life of the streets, and the terrible loneliness and impotent desolation of a human atom threading its way among millions. . . .

This little creature had found a way of life that seemed to him full of happiness and success: she was strong, small, and competent, she was also full of joy, tenderness, and lively humor, and she was immensely brave and gentle. He saw plainly that she was a product of the city. She had been born in the city, lived in it all her life, and she loved it; and yet she didn't have the harassed and driven look, the sallow complexion, the strident and metallic quality that many city people have. She was the natural growth of steel, stone, and masonry, yet she was as fresh, juicy, and rosy as if she had come out of the earth.[192]

. . . In Mrs. Jack, he beheld a natural and happy product of the environment that terrified him, and in her warm little stories he began to get a picture of the city America he had not known, but had imagined. It was a world of luxury, comfort, and easy money; of success, fame, and excitement; of theatres, books, artists, writers; of delicate food and wine, good restaurants, beautiful fabrics and lovely women. It was a world of warm, generous and urbane living; and it all seemed wonderful, happy, and inspired to him now.[193]

The woman really loved the city. She loved it not with ostentatious show, self-consciously nor coldly. . . . The city was . . . her field, her pasture, and her farm; and she loved it so because she was herself so much a part of it, because she knew and understood it so, because it was the stage and setting of her own life and work.

For her, the city was a living, breathing, struggling, hoping, fearing, loving, and desiring universe of life. It was the most human place on earth because it had the most "humanity," . . . to her the city *was* America. And in all of this, of course, because this vision and this understanding was so healthy, sound, and true, Mrs. Jack was right.[194]

George contrasted Esther's *Jewish* New York against the repelling and depressing sight of those "surly, sour, and petulant" faces which betokened lives without daring or dignity or beauty, lives that "stretched back through a succession of grey and ugly days into that earlier [and more Gentile?] New York of which he could get no picture except that it was dreary, and barren, and dull."[195]

The physical pleasures. Esther's non-Puritanical outlook, her straightforward and Jewish love of life delighted George. She "wanted what was best and most beautiful in life, she was always on the lookout for it, and she never failed to know and appreciate it when she found it. In everything, she wanted only the best."[196] With pungent humor she mocked the "smallness and meanness" of the Puritanical world, the tastlessness and joylessness of Gentile food.[197]

One of the finest elements in the Jewish character [Wolfe commented] is its sensuous love of richness and abundance: the Jew hates what is savorless and stingy in life, he will not stand for bad food or dreary discomfort, he will not make jokes about them, or feel it a fine thing to cheat the senses. He feels there is something mean and degrading about poor living, he loves warmth and opulence, and he is right.[198]

Chutspa and self-actualization. Esther's enormous self-confidence and zest for work fascinated George. He listened to her rapturous outpouring on "the most wonderful and exciting thing that goes on inside me" when she worked as a designer. "He was somehow delighted by the joy she took in her skill and knowledge; her boastfulness was so gay and good humored that no one could be displeased with it, and he felt sure now that it was entirely justified."[199]

It was as worker and as doer that this woman was supreme. The true religion of her soul, the thing that saved her and restored her from . . . the insane excess of self-adornment, the vanity of self-love . . . was the religion of her work. It saved her, took her out of herself, united her life to a nobler image, which was external to her and superior to the vanities of self. There was no labor too great, no expenditure of time and care and patient effort too arduous and too exacting, if, through it, she could only achieve 'a good piece of work.'

And of all the things she hated most, the first one was a shoddy piece of work. To her this was original sin. She could overlook the faults and errors of a human personality, excuse its weaknesses, tolerate its vices, and the flaws it could not help. But she could not, would not, stand for shoddy work, for there was no excuse for it. An ill-cooked meal, an ill kept room, an ill-made dress . . . meant something more to her than haste or carelessness, something more than mere forgetfulness. They meant a lack of faith, a lack of honesty, a lack of all integrity —a lack of everything 'without which,' as she said, 'your life is nothing.'

And that is what saved her in the end. She held steadfast to the faith of honest work. This was her real religion, and from it all the good things in her life and person came.[200]

The Yeshiva College Freshman

The most highly developed and widely used objective-scoring personality test is the Minnesota Multiphasic Personality Inventory, devised by Hathaway and McKinley at the University of Minnesota. The MMPI consists of 566 statements which the respondent scores True or False, to indicate how that statement applies to him. (The respondent is advised to skip any item which does not apply to him, or "if it is something that you don't know about." Over the past 20-odd years the MMPI has been given to thousands of normal adults, as well as to mental hospital patients of known diagnostic categories, to various student groups, and others.

Between 1956 and 1958 Boris Levinson gave the MMPI to 169 Yeshiva College male freshmen and compared their Yes-No frequencies with men in general. He found that the Yeshiva group answered about one out of six items (or 99 out of 566) differently from men in general, to an extent that could not be reasonably attributed to chance.[201] These "99 differences" do not follow any of the familiar clinical syndromes, according to Levinson. Yet, certain consistencies do seem to emerge as one inspects these "99 differences," consistencies which underscore what we have already said about Jewish traits. Here are five or six categories into which about half of these "99 differences" seem to fit:

Audacity. Yeshiva College men are more likely to respond to the following items in a direction contrary to Western standards of modesty or politeness; these seem, in other words, to indicate a culturally patterned attitude of *chutspa.*

When I take a new job, I like to be tipped off on who
should be gotten next to. (True) [202]
I am an important person. (True)
I like to know some important people because it makes
me feel important. (True)
Criticism or scolding hurts me terribly. (False)
When in a group of people I have trouble thinking of
the right things to talk about. (False)
If given the chance I could do some things that would
be of great benefit to the world. (True)
I am often so annoyed when someone tries to get ahead
of me in a line of people that I speak to him about it.
(True)
I do not try to correct people who express an ignorant
belief. (False)
I am often inclined to go out of my way to win a point
with someone who has opposed me. (True)
I would like to wear expensive clothes. (True)

Intellectuality. Yeshiva College students shun physical exploits, and are predisposed to intellectual activities to an extent
which opposes the general male norms on the following items.

I like or have liked fishing very much. (False)
I would like to be an auto racer. (False)
I would like to hunt lions in Africa. (False)
I very much like horseback riding. (False)
I like mechanics magazines. (False)
I think I would like the work of a librarian. (True)
I like poetry. (True)
*I think I would like the kind of work a forest ranger
does.* (False)
I would like to be a soldier. (False)
I think I would like the work of a building contractor.
(False)
*If I were a reporter I would very much like to report
sporting news.* (False)

Manhood versus masculinity. Seven of the eleven items listed
directly above *and italicized* are scored on the Masculinity-Fem-

inity Scale of the MMPI (Scale 5) to indicate "feminine emotional makeup."[203] Yeshiva freshmen likewise *oppose* the general masculine norm by their tendency to respond "True" to the following MMPI items:

> *I like dramatics.*
> *I like to cook.*
> *I liked "Alice in Wonderland" by Lewis Carroll.*
> *I think Lincoln was greater than Washington.*
> *I like movie love scenes.*
> *I would like to wear expensive clothes.*
> *I have often felt that strangers were looking at me critically.*

Yeshiva men also oppose the masculine norm by responding "False" more often than men in general to the following Scale 5 items:

> *My feelings are not easily hurt.*
> *It does not bother me that I am not better looking.*
> *I am entirely self-confident.*

Scale 5 items are regarded as particularly lacking in subtlety; it seems obvious that they deal with sexual identification, with the "endorsement of culturally feminine occupations, and the denial of culturally masculine occupations."[204] It is therefore easy for a respondent who wants to give the impression of masculinity to do so. Yeshiva freshmen are apparently not attentive to the standard of masculinity as defined by the male groups on whom Scale 5 was standardized.[205] Boris Levinson concludes, in fact, that "the present MMPI norms are not functional" for persons living in a traditional Jewish cultural environment.[206]

Yeshiva freshmen tend to disavow such "masculine" pursuits as fishing, auto racing, lion hunting (!), horseback riding, as well as the work of forest ranger, soldier, building contractor, and sports reporter. Compared with the general male norm, Yeshiva men tend to like library work, poetry, dramatics, and cooking. It appears that their concept of manhood is congenial to the role of a good Jewish husband, and a gentle Jewish father.

Sexual interest. Although Yeshiva men oppose the general norm for their sex by responding True to the statement "I have never been in love with anyone," they deviate from men in general in their response to the following four items, which suggests a greater degree of tolerance for sexual feelings:

> I am embarrassed by dirty stories. (False)
> I am attracted by members of the opposite sex. (True)
> Sexual things disgust me. (False)
> I like movie love scenes. (True)

This finding is of course consistent with the non-puritanical Jewish attitude toward sex.

Self-consciousness. The Yeshiva College student responds to the following MMPI items in a way that indicates a sensitivity to criticism that deviates significantly from general male norms. (Is this degree of self-consciousness a by-product of social marginality, or does it stem from the in-group tradition of maintaining social norms through the use of "shaming" and "avoidance rules?")

> I do not mind being made fun of. (False)
> My feelings are not easily hurt. (False)
> What others think of me does not bother me. (False)
> It does not bother me that I am not better looking. (False)
> I have often felt that strangers were looking at me critically. (True)
> Often I cross the street in order not to meet someone I see. (True)
> Sometimes I am sure that other people can tell what I am thinking. (True)

Symptoms of stress. Compared with men in general, Yeshiva College students answer the following statements in a way that indicates some sort of psychic suffering.

> Most of the time I feel blue. (True)
> Most nights I go to sleep without thoughts or ideas bothering me. (False)

I am entirely self-confident. (False)
I have very few fears compared to my friends. (False)
I find it hard to keep my mind on a task or job. (True)
Religion gives me no worry. (False)
At periods my mind seems to work more slowly than
usual. (True)
I am made nervous by certain animals. (True)

The Yeshiva College student apparently worries more about
his physical well-being than men in general, another sign of
psychic suffering.

I wake up fresh and rested most mornings. (False)
I seldom worry about my health. (False)
The sight of blood neither frightens me nor makes me
sick. (False)
I do not worry about catching diseases. (False)
I am neither gaining nor losing weight. (False)
I have never had any breaking out on my skin that has
worried me. (False)
My eyesight is as good as it has been for years. (False)

To summarize, comparison of MMPI responses of 169 Yeshiva
College male freshmen, with norms for men in general, reveals
that the Yeshiva group differs significantly in 99 items. Inspection
of these items suggests that the Yeshiva men describe themselves
as significantly more self-conscious (7 items), more anxiety-rid-
den—including anxieties about physical well-being (15 items)—
predisposed to intellectual rather than physical or mechanical
activities (11 items), more tolerant of sexual feeling (4 items),
and predisposed to indicate an attitude of *chutspa* (10 items).
The Yeshiva freshman's concept of manhood permits a disavowal
of interests closely linked with masculinity in the American
culture (e.g., hunting, sports, mechanics, outdoor pursuits), and
allows for more emotionality and aesthetic interests than the
masculine sex-role designates in the American culture.

To what extent the Yeshiva freshman group matches or deviates from their Jewish age-mates in general, we do not know.
More importantly, we do not know the extent to which Yeshiva

College freshmen differ from college freshmen in general, since Levinson made his comparisons from a group of "normal Minnesota males" (on which the MMPI was standardized) in which college men were in a small minority.

Jews Without Gentiles

Are Jewish traits adequately accounted for as reactions to environmental pressures of an urban minority group (an "exile neurosis") ; or are they behavioral compromises between what the Jewish culture itself would elicit, and the social realities of the Gentile world? What would happen if a group of Jews were transferred from an urban Gentile world to an agricultural colony in which they could live without direct contact with Gentiles? If Jewish traits are a reaction to Diaspora pressures, the transferees and their children should become progressively less Jewish. If Jewish traits are an expression of a Jewish culture, the absence of dampening Gentile influences should make our transferees and their children *more* Jewish than their Diaspora forebears. What is happening in Israel, to Jewish immigrants and their offspring, is therefore of special interest. The following report deals specifically with an agricultural colony studied in depth by Melford Spiro:

Around 1920 a band of about 90 young intellectuals separated themselves from Eastern Euorpean Jewry to establish a utopian agricultural colony in Palestine. They evolved a Marxist-Zionist ideology according to which anti-Semitism was an inevitable by-product of a capitalistic society because capitalism must have a scapegoat. They believed that the capitalistic system forces the Jew to live a debased, corrupt life so that—in effect—he deserves the anti-Semitic scorn of the offended majority. To these young rebels the *shtetl* was an unhappy by-product of an ugly social system and its religious values could be dismissed—according to their Marxist philosophy—as "prescientific superstition." The pioneers might therefore be described as rebels against *both* the *shtetl* and Western society.

The colonists worked out an explicit system of "collective education," a program of communal child rearing which transferred responsibility for the upbringing of children from parents to community. Children were to be raised in dormitories by nurses and teachers responsible to the community, and according to procedures which would imbue the child with the values of a collective society—responsibility, cooperation, fellowship—and spare him from the "capitalistic" attitudes of exploitation, individualism, and self-glorifying competition.

Thirty years after the founding of this utopian colony, the pioneers had transformed the land from a malarial swamp to a mechanized and prosperous agricultural settlement producing dairy products, poultry, meat, fish, and vegetables. What were the effects of their separation from the Gentile majority, of their renunciation of Judaism as a religion, of their adoption of a radical program of child rearing, of their agricultural way of life on their own social adjustment, and on the modal personality traits of their offspring? In what ways does the Palestinian-born generation—the *sabras*—reveal what we have already defined as Jewish traits? In *Kibbutz; Venture in Utopia,* Melford Spiro describes the social adjustment of the pioneers themselves. In Spiro's second volume, *Children of the Kibbutz,* he describes the system of "collective education" at Kiryat Yedidim as it governs the life of its members from birth to graduation from high school. In his second volume, Spiro richly documents the behavior and attitudes of the children, their nurses, parents, and teachers—to delineate the actual results of the "collective education" program.

The behavioral science view of man, with its emphasis on the Darwinian concept of behavior as adaptations to an environment, would lead us to expect that after 30 years' separation from the Diaspora, the pioneers and their offspring would be significantly less Jewish than their kinfolk in the Gentile world, whose minority group status perpetuates the "Diaspora personality." Let us comb through Spiro's study to see which Jewish values were preserved in the culture of the *kibbutz,* and in what ways the *sabra* manifest Jewish traits of personality.

Parental affection. The socialization system of Kiryat Yedidim "did not merely evolve as an adaptation to a pioneering mode of living," Spiro observes; "it was deliberately fashioned on the basis of certain ideological convictions. . . ."[207] In Western society the economic power of the father places him in a position of authority and control over his children, and to this state of affairs the pioneers traced "the ambivalence and hatred that were the special characteristics of the traditional family."[208] Accordingly, the pioneers hoped that by divesting the father of his authority over the child, not only would it be unnecessary to train the child in attitudes of subservience to a "power elite," but parent and child would be free to develop and enjoy a bond of love uncontaminated by the ambivalences generated in the traditional family setting. Spiro's analysis of the educational philosophy of the pioneers make it clear "that the elimination of the authoritarian character of the father was motivated, not only by a desire to ensure the emotional well-being of the child, but also by the desire of the parents to achieve and maintain his love."[209] To Spiro it seems clear that this desire "to retain the affection of their children represents the preservation of an important value of the [Eastern European] parents against whom [the pioneers had] so strongly rebelled."[210]

Spiro describes in detail how the pioneers directed much of their energies and sacrificed much of their resources for the comfort and well-being of their children—as if to fulfill the guiding principle of the *shtetl* that *"nachas fun kinder* is the epitome of Joy."[211] The children's quarters had conveniences and facilities (e.g., toilets, showers, hot water, modern kitchens) which the adults could not afford for themselves. During a period of acute food shortage for all Israel, the contrast between the diet of adults and children at Kiryat Yedidim was marked. Few adults "ever left the dinner table with full stomachs. The children, on the other hand, always had as much food as they wanted, and their meals exhibited greater variety and possessed a higher quality than those of their parents. For the children there were always fresh fruits and sweets at the evening meal; but there were often months when the *chaverim* had no fruit, and sweets were always a rarity."[212]

Kibbutz parents "are very proud of their children, brag about them to others, and compete with other parents in praising their merits. A mother tells others about the words her infant is speaking, and other mothers immediately give examples from their own children to show that they are even more advanced in this regard. A girl is praised for her ability in climbing olive trees, and a father says that his daughter is even better."[213]

"The one characteristic of all kibbutzim, on which all observers are in unanimous agreement," says Spiro, "is the attachment of parents for their children. Kiryat Yedidim, like other kibbutzim, is a child-centered society, par excellence. Children are prized above all else. In observing the kibbutz and from interviewing parents one receives the distinct impression that no sacrifice is too great to make for the children. . . . Adults work long hours in the fields with brief annual vacations, while their children receive a high school education . . . and enjoy a three-month summer vacation."[214] Spiro emphasizes the point that "there is no *necessary* relationship . . . between this attitude toward children and the system of collective education—other attitudes are equally compatible with it."[215]

Intimacy and demonstrativeness. Observing the nurses assigned to groups of children, Spiro found that with few exceptions the nurses were not merely conscientious and responsible, but "warm and loving toward the children . . . [and] genuinely devoted both to their work and to their charges."[216] While carrying out the many details of their daily routine, the nurses were observed to hug their infant charges, kiss them, coo and jabber to them, and express words of endearment and praise.[217] It seemed to Spiro that in addition to the genuine affection the nurse felt for the children with whom she was in constant contact, her demonstrativeness served at least two other purposes—it expressed her feelings toward a child's parents, as well as an anxiety about winning and holding the children's love. "Not all nurses are anxious about the children's love," says Spiro, "but so many of them are that one cannot escape the conclusion that this anxiety is a basic feature of the nurses' behavior."[218]

Nurses not only express physical affection toward the children, they also teach or encourage children to show "physical expressions of love and warmth" to each other. "A nurse, for example, may ask an aggressor to 'make nice' to his victim, by embracing or kissing him. Or, with no prior provocation, she may request a child to embrace or kiss another child. And, of course, the nurses often request the children to embrace or kiss them."[219]

Parents likewise lavish boundless affection on their children—
with play and pampering, words of endearment, pet names, hug-
ging, petting, caressing, stroking, and kissing. "Babies and tod-
dlers are kissed on any part of the body—chest, belly, arms, legs,
forehead, cheek, head (except the mouth, buttocks, and genitals).
Older children are generally kissed only on the cheek or forehead. Parents always kiss and/or hug their children when they
greet them; and when they leave they always kiss or hug their
children in farewell. In general, when a parent greets his child
he is almost always effusive in his affection and, in some instances,
the physical affection displayed by the parent reveals clear erotic
overtones."[220] Spiro further observed that intense exchange of
physical affection is "almost always between parent and child of
opposite sex." He records the following "seductive routines" as
examples of not uncommon parent-child interactions:

> Ahuv (four years) and his mother are playing on the grass.
> He lies between her thighs, and she caresses his hair, kisses his
> face, embraces him tightly.

> Father of Pnina (two-and-one-half years) plays with her
> while waiting for the nurse to undress her. . . . He kisses her
> many times on the body—the chest and stomach, which evokes
> much laughter from Pnina. She is very excited, giggles and
> laughs, asks her father many times to repeat this.[221]

The children's hour. As if to mitigate the hardship imposed
on parent and child by a socialization system that separates them
for most of the day, a two-hour period is observed every evening
as "the children's hour." This period is "set aside by the parent
to be devoted exclusively to his child and to whatever his child
wishes to do."[222] "If the child wishes to take a walk, the parents
take a walk; if the child wishes to visit a friend, they visit a
friend; if the child wishes to hear a story, they tell him a story.
In short, the child controls the situation."[223]
Spiro notes that "for many parents this represents a sacrifice,
since these hours are often the only ones they might otherwise
employ in pursuing their own interests, such as reading, studying,
or conversing. But no parent would think of making other plans
for the children's hour."[224] In order to make room for an early

evening "children's hour," the entire kibbutz "works during the heat of the day even in the summer, instead of taking a long afternoon siesta and beginning the afternoon work after the hottest part of the day has passed."[225]

The children's hour is sacred; "nothing is allowed to interfere. . . . All activities in the *kibbutz* come to a standstill; one wit has observed that if the bordering Arab state were to attack the *kibbutz* at that time, it would win a handy victory, since the *chaverim* could not be induced to leave their children."[226]

Permissiveness. A policy of permissiveness is codified in the group's philosophy of education, and guides the behavior of nurses and parents. Nurses are usually permissive about noise and confusion at mealtime.[227] Toilet training does not begin until the ages of fifteen to eighteen months, and is gradual and permissive in implementation. Nurses express disapproval or disgust over incontinence, and lavish praise on children for making good use of their chamber pots, but *"no nurse . . . was ever observed to scold a child for not sitting on the chamber pot or for wetting or soiling during the training period."*[228] (Italics added.) "Thumbsucking is not viewed with alarm by the nurses, so that the children may suck with impunity. Not one child was observed to be punished or reprimanded for thumbsucking. . . ."[229]

Children were raised in mixed dormitories from birth through adolescence; boys and girls dressed, undressed, sat on chamber pots, showered, and slept together. The official ideology of the group regarded sexual manifestations in young children as normal, and banned any attempt to interfere or punish childhood sexuality.[230] Spiro describes undisguised masturbation, sexual contact of various kinds (both homosexual and heterosexual) between young children, deliberate exhibitionism and voyeurism.[231]

> . . . Nurses and teachers report activities [of children age seven —nine] which they perceive to be consciously sexual in intent and sensation. The boys . . . like to wrestle in bed, either in the nude or in their undershorts, covered with a sheet. They especially like to do this with one particular boy who is big and fat. The nurses report similar "homosexual" behavior among the girls of the second grade [age seven]. Miri and Shula, for example, like to roll on the floor together and to

lie on top of each other. This they do with considerable laughing and giggling. Two other girls, moreover, have been seen
sleeping together by the nurse when she entered the school in
the morning.

. . . The nurse is confident that boys and girls often get into
bed with each other at night, but she does not know how often
this occurs, nor does she know what [these seven through nine
year olds] do. These children frequently play "clinic," a game
in which the boys "examine" the girls, who are nude. Moreover, boys and girls often lie on top of each other, and hug and
kiss each other in public, even in the classroom and in the
presence of the teacher, "with no sense of shame."[232]

Spiro "never observed a nurse to prohibit any sexual act on
the part of a child, much less punish the child. There is not one
instance in the entire sample of nurse's interference in the sexual
activity of the children."[233]

Audacity. The pioneers' educational theorists hoped to shape
a character with a love for collective living, with a deep sense
of responsibility toward the group—but independent and skeptical, a person without fear of authority. The pioneers' description
of a model *chaver* has much to say in praise of *chutspa:*

[The person reared in the kibbutz will be] . . . independent,
original in his ideas, insists on his opinion but tries to understand everything before he accepts it; he will be revolutionary,
a negator. It will not be easy to lead him, although he will be
amenable to reason. He will love the collective and be ready
to do a great deal for it. He will be forceful and will want to
take his fate in his own hands. *No external, ruling authority
will have an influence on him.* He will do nothing out of fear,
and will not recognize the authority of any person except
from an inner attitude. . . .[234] (Italics added.)

Spiro asked *kibbutz* parents to rank in order of importance
thirteen values "which they hoped to inculcate in their children."
From the results, one would conclude that parents assign relatively low priority to traits related to decorum and obedience.[235]
Spiro's observations of classroom activity would lead one to conclude that children of the *kibbutz* have little concern for decorum

or obedience; they expect insolence to be tolerated, and audacity to be rewarded. The following three episodes are offered as examples:

A meeting was called to discuss the case of Yehuda, who had stolen the marbles he had lost to Giora. The teacher decries stealing as 'a very bad thing' and contrary to the principle of *kibbutz* living. She offers Yehuda a chance to talk, to explain. He refuses to talk or apologize. When questioned, he admits that he has taken the marbles. He sits without moving, eyes straight ahead. The teacher catalogues all the 'wrong' things Yehuda has done that week, and expresses a hope that the school will yet draw out Yehuda's better impulses (*yetser ha'tov*). Yehuda laughs. The nurse then asks Yehuda directly whether he will continue to steal, or stop. Yehuda does not answer. The nurse now makes the point that marbles should be played for enjoyment, not for keeps, and suggests that Giora (from whom Yehuda had stolen the marbles) give five marbles to Yehuda. Teacher and nurse then suggest that all children who have marbles should distribute some to those who have none, and the meeting is adjourned.[236]

Sixth grader Ahuv tried to run away from the *kibbutz,* and after he was located and returned to safety, a meeting was called to discuss what Ahuv had done. Teachers and nurses were determined to punish him, but the children voted against punishment. The teachers insisted that Ahuv be confined to his bedroom for one day. 'The children opposed this decision, and throughout the day they brought food to Ahuv, and spelled each other in staying with him, so that, in effect, he was never alone.'[237]

Competitiveness is considered contrary to *kibbutz* philosophy; high school examinations are disguised as 'questionnaires,' and no course grades are given. 'One of the very few personal competitive events in the high school is the literary competition sponsored by the student newspaper. Prizes (books) are awarded to the winners.' In the year of Spiro's residence at the *kibbutz,* first prize was awarded to a senior whose essay argued *'that prizes should not be awarded in the high school.'*[238]

Audacity is encouraged in the classroom by an explicit policy
of informality and a ban on punitive methods. "Even in the
grammar school . . . the teacher chooses a project only after consultation with the class." Children feel free "to criticize the
teacher when they feel he is wrong." Children "leave the classroom at will—to get a drink, to go to the toilet, or for any other
reason they deem important. Similarly, they may leave their
desks without permission—to get supplies from the cabinet, to
sharpen a pencil, and so on. They may talk among themselves
both during oral lessons and while working privately at their
desks; some hum or sing to themselves while writing or studying."[239] Often the commotion reaches the point of utter chaos,
and the teacher is unable to restore order. Spiro describes numerous examples of classroom disruption in which the students apparently "know that the teacher desires order, yet they refuse to
comply with his request."[240]

> The teacher (female) of the eighth grade and I enter the
> class, and she explains that I have come to observe. The chil-
> dren begin to shout and scream, and she cannot get their at-
> tention. When the geography lesson finally begins, each child
> talks at will, insisting that he be heard above the shouting of
> the others. She cannot discipline them. . . . After the inter-
> mission, the children enter the classroom with great shouting.
> They cannot be calmed. Teacher asks questions, and they all
> answer at once. She refuses to continue until there is quiet, but
> there is no quiet. The children blurt out whatever idea they
> have as soon as it arises. . . . One boy becomes angry because
> the teacher calls on another when he—so he insists—had his hand
> up first. . . . Teacher reprimands boy for disturbing, and he
> laughs. Another boy beats a rhythm on the desk. Teacher
> shouts at children but cannot control them. (At least half of
> her time is spent trying to obtain order.) [241]

"Students are not only disobedient; they are also insolent,"
Spiro reports. "A universal characteristic of the *sabras,* according
to almost all observers of the kibbutz movement, is their *chutspa*
or insolence, a characteristic we found in the grade school students as well [as in the high school]. The *sabras* have little respect for authority, per se, and they have few compunctions about

criticizing authority figures."[242] Spiro cites a number of classroom incidents to show that his characterization of *sabras* as insolent is not undeserved:

> Girl is not listening, and teacher (male *kibbutz* member) of the ninth grade tells her to do what the rest of the class is doing. She says that she *is* doing what the rest of the class is doing—wasting time!

> Girl is disturbing ninth-grade class in English and teacher tells her to be still. Girl says, 'What for? You haven't taught us a thing all year anyway.'[243]

Spiro richly documents the name-calling, derision, and insults which punctuate the everyday conversation of sabra adolescents —and behavior which a Western observer can only describe as rude and ill-mannered. Sabras "seldom observe such simple amenities as greeting a fellow student with a 'hello,' or saying 'thank you' when some courtesy has been extended them."[244] The parental generation apparently made little effort to teach their children decorum, and undoubtedly did teach them— through everyday example—the fine art of *chutspa*.[245]

Intellectuality. In their philosophical orientation, the pioneers attach a spiritual value to agricultural labor, and imply a negative attitude toward sedentary middle class occupations. They are raising their children to work in an agricultural economy, to become farmers. One would suppose that in such a setting, the high school would offer courses in animal husbandry, crop management, farm machine mechanics, home economics, dairy production, irrigation. *Not at all!* The entire high school curriculum is devoted to academic and intellectual subjects—humanities, social science, foreign language, physical and biological science —"and could well constitute the curriculum of a private school in the United States."[246]

Moreover, graduates of the *kibbutz* high school show a real attachment to the values of a liberal education. "Almost all the *sabras* interviewed mentioned additional study as their most important ambition."[247] When they become parents, *sabras* "are very much concerned that their children become 'cultured' adults and that they have an opportunity both for creative growth and for the expression of intellectual talent. Typical is the comment of a *sabra* mother," says Spiro, "when, due to a shortage of workers in the *kibbutz,* some of the *chaverim* had suggested drafting the students. She was vehemently opposed, concluding that "My child will study even if I must starve.""[248] Members of this agricultural settlement spend much of their precious free time in reading and study, and use their small cash allowance to buy books, according to Spiro. Literature and foreign languages are favorite subjects. ". . . The pictures that hang on their walls, the music to which they listen, their interest in and attendance at concerts and plays, all betoken a high intellectual level."[249]

Sabras have been so thoroughly indoctrinated with the value of intellectual attainment, they feel uncomfortable when they compare themselves to Western-educated or city-bred persons. "One *sabra,* whose job takes him outside the *kibbutz,* said that he felt inferior to his colleagues in the city because they knew more than he did. He blames his ignorance on the *kibbutz* school system, which did not compel him to study when, at sixteen, he lost interest in academic matters. Now he would 'do anything' to study. A younger *sabra* reported that more than half his class felt ignorant, despite their formal education, and are now eager to study more. Another *sabra,* engaged in study in the city, said he felt 'ashamed' that he knew so little compared to the city students."[250]

The paramount position given to agricultural labor in the *kibbutz* hierarchy of values stands in conflict with the importance attached to academic and humanistic studies in the high school curriculum. Some *sabras* express a keen inner conflict between these contradictory value stystems. The usual resolution, it seems, is to suppress one's artistic or intellectual aspirations—either matter-of-factly or with some bitterness over the fact that "in the *kibbutz* itself only the worker is respected. . . ."[251]

Sexual adjustment in adolescence; non-Puritanical restraint. We have already described the permissive policy of the pioneers toward sex behavior of infants and young children; nothing is forbidden, and sex play of various kinds can be freely observed.[252] In adolescence, children continue to live, sleep, and shower in mixed company, but their sex behavior becomes highly circumspect! The *sabra* have been taught "that the sex drive is normal and natural, that it is neither sinful on the one hand, nor of overwhelming importance on the other."[253] Sexual intercourse, however, is taboo for the high school group—and it was Spiro's impression that "there seem to be no violations" of this taboo. To account for such thorough observance of this taboo, some claim an "absence of great sexual tension." One former high school student recalled to Spiro, "We simply did not feel a need for it." Another high school graduate speculated that high school girls were "opposed to sexual affairs as a kind of 'instinct of self-preservation.' " For whatever reasons, Spiro conjectured that "most students are virgins when they graduate from high school."[254]

A philosophy that regards sex as a natural appetite—neither evil nor sinful—but staunchly opposes sexual intercourse among high school students, is defended by the high school authorities in the following way: The many extracurricular group activities sponsored by the high school are as intrinsic a part of the educational program as the classroom work itself. "Were sexual intercourse permitted or encouraged, it is felt, students' interests and energies would be withdrawn from their studies and from the many group activities which are such important preparation for their future lives. By discouraging sexual behavior, therefore, the authorities seek to channel adolescent energies in these culturally important activities. Nevertheless, should a couple be genuinely in love, the authorities will not interfere with their sexual activities. Such couples are left to themselves unless their relationship proves to be socially and/or emotionally disruptive. When the latter happens, students, as well as teachers, may take action" to censure their behavior.[255]

High school students follow an incredibly heavy daily regimen of morning classroom activity, afternoon work in the *kibbutz,* and evening extracurricular activities. Their round of group activities begins at 6:45 A.M. and ends at 11 P.M., a regimen which commits many to chronic fatigue, and affords almost no opportunity for privacy.[256] High school authorities argue that this program, strenuous as it is, provides a "strong moral and social force" for the student society, and also prevents them from indulging in sleep, smoking, drinking, sex, or "just wasting time."[257] The norm of non-puritanical restraint maintained by the kibbutz bears a strong resemblance to the sex code of the *shtetl,* where the norm was maintained by religious ritual, and early marriage. In the *kibbutz,* the norm is maintained by a highly structured group life, and early marriage. In the *kibbutz,* as in the *shtetl* and among Orthodox Jews elsewhere, homosexuality "seems to be entirely nonexistent; the author observed no manifestations of it, nor did any respondent or informant reports its existence."[258]

It should not be supposed that only a compulsive round of group activities spares the *sabra* adolescent from the sexual conflict and turmoil manifest by adolescents in Western society. Spiro believed that "the sexual conflicts that are frequently at the core of adolescent turmoil in our own society do not seem to be strong in the [high school group]. The socialization system precludes morbid curiosity about the body. ". . . Obsession with sex, which often results from viewing it as a great mystery or (as among certain groups in our own society) as sinful or dirty, does not occur among these students." The sexual titillation of magazines, movies, advertising, and cosmetics are either unavailable or taboo. No girl need worry about having a date or being popular in a society in which every adolescent has a place in a prescribed round of social activities. "Since dating does not exist [for the high school group of the kibbutz], a major obsession of American adolescent culture, and the whole host of anxieties and tensions that derive from it," Spiro concludes, "are absent as well."[259] (Spiro feels quite sure that the "dating and rating" complex represents "a major sociological determinant of sexual maladjustment in our society," a phenomenon which simply does not exist in the *kibbutz.*)[260]

Shtetl-kibbutz continuities. Again and again, Spiro feels impelled to acknowledge a continuity of values between the *chaverim* and the *shtetl* against which they ostensibly rebelled. They believe in "the moral value of the group. The group, in *kibbutz* culture, is not only a means to the happiness of the individual; the group and group processes are moral ends in their own right."[261] Spiro quotes from Zborowski and Herzog's description of *shtetl* attitudes toward group experience, asserting that it "applies, without qualification, to Kiryat Yedidim."[262] They shared with the *shtetl* an intense affective relationship to their children and a readiness to sacrifice for their children's well-being. They shared a deep commitment to intellectual development, to the moral value of learning. They shared with the *shtetl* an anti-puritanical restraint, a pride in work, an abhorrence of physical aggression, and a broad tolerance for verbal aggression.

Spiro identifies as a "most significant continuity . . . *the degree to which the daily routine is regulated.* The lives of their fathers were regulated in even their minutiae by the compendium of rabbinic law, known as the *Shulchan Aruch* [referred to in Chapter 9 as the *Code*]. The daily lives of the *chaverim* are regulated to almost the same degree by the rules of The Federation. These rules govern such diverse aspects of their lives as the number of children permitted within a dormitory, the nurse-child ratio, the number of hours to be worked in a day, the length of the annual vacations, the minimum housing facilities, the minimum amount of furniture for each room, the leisure time to be provided a pregnant woman or nursing mother, and a host of others." (Italics added.) [263] These are agricultural pioneers but they are also a people of the Law.

The matricentric tradition survives in their perennial concern with "the problem of the woman." In its beginning, the group denounced bourgeois Western society for the inferior role to which it relegates women and dedicated themselves to the creation of a society in which women were to be the equals of men in all matters. The dominance of the woman in *kibbutz* marriage partnerships is suggested by Spiro's finding that in those cases in which a family decides to resign from the *kibbutz,* the decision is almost always "instigated by the women. . . . Most of the tension in the *kibbutz* is caused by the women. . . . With the exception of politics, nothing occupies so much attention in the kibbutz as 'the problem of the woman,' *ba'ayat ha'chavera.* This phrase, constantly on the lips of the *chaverim,* was the subject of a number of town meetings during the writer's stay in Kiryat Yedidim. It is no exaggeration to say," Spiro adds, "that if Kiryat Yedidim should ever disintegrate, the 'problem of the woman' will be one of the main contributing factors."[264] The pioneers channel much energy and express much concern for the well-being of their women, as if an unexpected and continuing crisis has occurred because of the status loss their women have suffered in shifting from a matrilocal extended family society to a communal society of agricultural workers.

A culture of contradictions. One cannot summarize Spiro's observations without noting the contradictory values imbedded in the way of life chosen by the pioneers of Kiryat Yedidim. They glorify agricultural labor, *but* foster intellectual values. They want their children to love collective living, *but* also want them to stand fast against the influence of external authority. They decry "self-glorifying competition," *but* encourage audacity and tolerate socially disruptive insolence. They espouse an anti-religious Marxist ideology, *but* celebrate the Jewish holidays and in the education of their children reserve a significant place for Bible study. They teach a philosophy of sexual freedom, *but* enforce a taboo against premarital sex. They dispose of anti-Semitism as a by-product of a decadent society, *but* structure their own society in a way that seems to painstakingly avoid what might be offensive to the anti-Semite. They raise their children for the life of agricultural workers, *but* indulge them with luxuries the parents cannot afford for themselves.

The explicit philosophy of Kiryat Yedidim defines the goal of "collective education" as the development of the "synthetic personality." This concept undoubtedly suffers gravely in translation; what the *chaverim* mean to designate is a personality that *synthesizes* into a balanced or harmonious whole "an attachment to the soil, a joy in work, and an appreciation for—if not creativity in—art, science, and literature."[265] The ideal *chaver*, therefore, is one who has found a way to integrate and harmonize the antagonistic habits, attitudes, and values of agricultural worker and intellectual. This tolerance for contradiction, this engagement in a balancing of opposites, is a phenomenon we have encountered before as a characteristic of the Jewish ethos.

Though they adopted a Marxist atheism and held the culture of the *shtetl* in contempt, the *chaverim* emerge from Spiro's study as profoundly Jewish, as conveyors of the Jewish ethos—a "sense of being" which, we are surprised to discover, is *not* bound up with a sedentary urban life or minority group status. Although they explicitly rejected their parents' way of life (as their parents objected to their errant children's emigration) the pioneers none the less showed a deep sense of Jewishness in their decision to settle in the ancient homeland of their people. "One might speculate," says Spiro, "whether the choice of Palestine rather than Uganda, for example, was not motivated by an unconscious desire to identify with their fathers in the very process of rebelling against them." By establishing a society of comradship in their ancient homeland, the rebels effected "a closing of the circle rather than . . . a widening of the gap"—a paradoxical attainment worthy of a people of paradoxes.[266]

As we reasoned at the outset of our overview of the *kibbutz*— if we think of Jewish traits as a mode of adaptation to minority group status in a Gentile world, then we would expect the *sabra* (as well as the pioneers) to be less Jewish than the Jews of the *galut*.[267] If, on the other hand, we think of Jewish traits in the Western world as a compromise between the traits designated by the Jewish culture itself and the contradictory demands of Western society, then we would expect the children of the *kibbutz* (as well as their elders) to be *more* Jewish than their Western cousins—since in Kiryat Yedidim there are no Gentiles to offend. Our analysis of Spiro's observations on the pioneers and their *sabra* offspring[268] most certainly reveals the salience of norms and values—an intensity of parental affection, a permissiveness in child rearing practice, a non-puritanical restraint in sex conduct, an audacity, an intimacy, an intellectuality, a group cohesiveness, and a tolerance for contradiction—which we have already encountered as characteristics of a Jewish way of life and a Jewish "sense of being."

CONCLUDING COMMENTS

The topic of Jewish traits is an almost forbidden area of discussion and borders on the sin of anti-locution. We have accepted this risk for the sake or pursuing certain hypotheses about the interrelationships between Jewish traits (*i.e.,* the imprint of Jewish norms on the individual) and tensions leading to intermarriage. We examined the popular concepts of the "exile neurosis" and "Diaspora personality" to see whether the evidence indicated that the Jewish ethos required an urban, persecuted minority group status—or whether the values and attitudes of the Jewish group have an autonomy and integrity of their own. And if so, how does this Jewish "sense of being" differ from the norms of middle class Western groups?

We hypothesized that the Jewish ethos fosters traits which better fit the *male* sex-role of middle class Western society—in consequence of which Jewish males and females develop an unequal aptitude for participation in Gentile society— *i.e.*, Jewish boys are more likely to be regarded as "culture heroes," and Jewish girls are more likely to be viewed as domineering, bold, strong-willed—unacculturated and in-group oriented. We hypothesized that this "unequal welcome" attracts Jewish males and females into Gentile society at unequal rates, which induces tensions leading to intermarriage.

If Jewish and Gentile upbringing instill different attitudes toward sex, aggression, and authority, then a person whose upbringing was atypical for his own group might discover more congenial company in another milieu. A culturally divergent life history undoubtedly leads some Jews to develop a personality which matches the Gentile norm, and some Gentiles somehow develop a "Jewish personality." When they discover that they feel more comfortable, more at ease in cross-ethnic company, they are natural candidates for intermarriage.

One may look at Jewish traits as a hodgepodge of "survivals" or as a system in equilibrium which can be thrown off balance by a disturbance in one of its critical areas. From the latter position, we see in the bowdlerization of the *Haggada* and in the expurgation of Sunday school Bible readings an endorsement of Western sex norms; and in the interiorization of Western sex norms we see a tension toward intermarriage unwittingly aggravated by the guardians of Jewish survival!

Our analysis also implies something about the advantage of a pluralistic and open society, where individuals who find psychic unrest in their inherited status group are free to cross the ethnic line and seek a more congenial social environment.

Our survey of observations and hypotheses concerning the Jewish ethos has been guided by its bearing upon the phenomenon of intermarriage, and in the conduct of this survey we have touched on many questions which are only partially answered, or almost totally unanswered—but they are not unanswerable. We hope, therefore, that while dealing with problems of some practical interest, we have also pointed to some promising areas of behavorial science research.

11

Mental Health and Impairment in Jewish Life

Among Jews who intermarry, men and women offer a common observation about their Gentile mates: they are calm and quieter. Does the blander temperament of the majority reflect the emotional security of membership in the dominant group? Perhaps the high rate of intermarriage amongst the Jewish psychoanalysts of New Haven suggests that their search for a "healthy" woman led them to choose a Gentile partner. (Freud warned that "a girl must be very healthy to 'stand' marriage, and [he earnestly counselled his] male inquirers not to marry a girl who has been neurotic. . . . The more strictly a wife has been brought up, the more earnestly she has submitted to the demands of civilization, the more [is she likely to] seek refuge in a neurosis.") [1]

". . . One thing can be said with certainty," writes Loewenstein; "The one definitely psychopathological tendency of Jews is to react with anxiety in many situations. . . [Normal anxiety is] moderate, temporary and adequately under control. . . . Intense and permanent [anxiety reactions] . . . unquestionably belong in the framework of mental pathology. Jews tend to react with anxiety, and with deeper and more lasting anxiety than non-Jews, in the most varied psychological situations."[2]

In his 1946 review of the literature on "Jewish Personality Traits," Orlansky concluded that "psychiatric opinion holds that Jews are more . . . anxiety ridden than non-Jews."[3] In their 1965 textbook on intergroup relations, Rose and Rose ascribe "a high degree of mental disorder and suicide" to the Jewish group.[4] If Jewish group membership exacts so high a toll on the individual's psychic well-being—or if it is believed that such is the price one pays to be a Jew—this fact would justify the tactic of looking outside the Jewish community for a "normal" mate, or the decision to get out of the Jewish group through intermarriage.

Sources of strain in Jewish living. There is hardly a more familiar in-group expression than "It's hard to be a Jew." Perhaps it is worth asking: What are the emotional problems that burden the Jew?

Existential insecurity. Living for generations under the menace of pogroms and persecution has built into the Jewish culture a "state of apprehension," says Loewenstein, that is acquired in the normal process of growing up as a Jew.[5] Srole and Langner likewise hypothesize that Jewish anxiety "may historically have been established as a conditioning pattern of the Jewish family structure," and is in contemporary life "generated in the Jewish family."[6]

Stonequist and others have stressed the Jew's cultural marginality as an additional source of insecurity. Lewin has described the feelings of inferiority and "self-hatred" which are a costly by-product of striving to attain full identification with the majority. Since anxiety marks the worldly as well as the provincial, acculturation and assimilation may be important aggravators of an anxiety which is rooted in something more basic to minority-group living. Perhaps it may be said that Jews suffer not necessarily from neurotic insecurity but from an *existential* insecurity. As Milton Steinberg viewed Jewish social behavior in the 1930's, he regarded both medieval Orthodoxy and radicalism, both Zionism and cynicism as by-products of frustration and disillusionment toward a polite Gentile world which seems to invite assimilation but doesn't really.[7]

The pathogenic family. The exceptionally close ties within the Jewish family, and particularly between mother and son, have been described as a source of Jewish neurosis. According to Srole and Langner, the Jewish family structure is "one factor often hypothesized by psychiatrists as potentially pathogenic. . ."[8] As Freud's patient jested: "We all suffer from *mishpoch'itis*."

Jewish patterns of neurotic behavior. Let us now shift our emphasis from *sources* of emotional conflict to their *manifestation* in the behavior patterns of Jews.

Hypersensitiveness. Browne describes hypersensitiveness as "the first and most pervasive symptom" of the Jewish manner. "We Jews are quick to see a slight, so quick, indeed, that often we see one where none is intended. But that is not to be wondered at," he adds. "So long as we continue to be attacked or disdained, so long must we remain a chip-bearing people. . ."[9] The insecurity of living even in a benign Gentile world is described by Dean as "the feeling that Gentiles will 'treat you well enough until the chips are really down,' at which point their true anti-Semitic feeling will emerge."[10]

"Sometimes, under the pressure of agonizing and humiliating racial memories," says Loewenstein, "Jews develop such an insurmountable terror of anti-Semitism that they are prone to feel themselves insulted and attacked whenever a Gentile so much as pronounces the word 'Jew,' and the mildest anti-Jewish remark may throw them off balance, plunging them into outraged silence or excessive rage. Only rarely are they able to meet such remarks calmly or to parry them with a humorous reply."[11] An excellent example of such an interaction is reported by Dean:

It was necessary for a Jewish Community Center to raise the rents of tenants of its building, among them, the Chamber of Commerce. A member of the Chamber expressed his regrets to the president of the Center that the rent of such a worthwhile organization as the Chamber had to be raised. The president mentioned the Center's deficit, and remarked that if an organization composed of businessmen could not pay a fair rent, it ought to go out of business. The Chamber of Commerce man suggested a compromise. The president of the Center answered that the period of negotiations was over and that the increase would have to stand. The man from the Chamber then said, 'Now I know how Christ felt on the cross.' The president of the Center was stunned into speechlessness.[12]

On the topic of Jewish hypersensitiveness, Nock recalls how a member of one of New York's clubs once defined the problem:

> When we are playing Kelly pool downstairs, if A [an Irishman] wins a big pot on an awful fluke, I can say, 'Isn't that a dirty Irish trick?' If B does it, I can say, 'Isn't that just what you'd expect from a conniving, swindling Massachusetts Yankee?' But if C does it, I can't say, 'That's a dirty Jewish trick,' for it would hurt him—it really would—and everybody in the room would feel uncomfortable and a little shocked to hear me say it."[13]

Bowman warns the Gentile who would contemplate intermarriage that there is something contagious about this feeling of "fear, suspicion, and apprehension" by which a persecuted minority is infected. The Gentile partner may be too unaccustomed to the hypersensitive atmosphere of Jewish living, and may find the strain too great.[14]

Hyperactivity. Is Jewish hyperactivity to be viewed as an anxiety symptom? Lewin thought so, and implied that the Jews of Israel would lose this quality of Jewishness when they become securely established as a dominant group in a country of their own.[15] Browne likewise sees Jewish "intensity" as a by-product of living in an unstable environment:

> We Jews are anything but an easy-going, leisurely folk. On the contrary, it is characteristic of us to attack life with a rush and fury. . . . Whatever we attempt, be it the amassing of wealth or the measuring of stars, characteristically we attempt it impatiently. Of course, that does rob us of grace at times; it does sometimes make us a bit over-aggressive. But we simply have to be that way. . . . For two thousand years we have been involuntary gypsies, forever driven from city to city and land to land.[16]

Motor inhibition. "The Jewish child is discouraged by his parents from any use of force," says Loewenstein.[17] "If there is

anything peculiar to the Jewish mind," Lowenstein says elsewhere, "it would seem to be the special way in which the ego
deals with the aggressive drives."[18] In evolving their cerebral
way of life, "the Jews shut off the normal channels of aggression,"[19] which led to the acquisition of obsessive and compulsive
traits which serve as "defense mechanisms against physical aggression."[20]

Loewenstein and Meyerson agree that the Jew's emotional
problem has been aggravated by his traditional exclusion from
manual and outdoor occupations: "the most basic and normal
channels in which human aggression can be employed."[21]

From his observations at *Kiryat Yedidim,* Spiro reports that
members of the *kibbutz* freely express interpersonal aggression
through gossiping, criticism, quarreling, and complaining, but
the expression of physical violence—even in a moment of towering
rage—seems to be taboo:

> The shower room . . . [is] the center for many arguments,
> and the conflicts over the distribution of manpower or machin-
> ery often occur in the men's shower room. These arguments
> may assume serious proportions, and the author not infre-
> quently saw *chaverim* burst into rages and become blue with
> anger in the course of such conflicts. These arguments remain
> on a verbal level, however, and never break out into physical
> clashes—at least, the author never observed any.[22]

Neurotic aggressiveness. According to Maslow, Jews are not
neurotic in the ordinary sense of the term. A neurotic person
is apt to be lacking in *both* self-esteem and security. Perhaps we
could say the neurotic lacks both self-confidence and social acceptance; he feels both unloveable and unloved, unworthy and
unwanted, helpless to cope with an unfriendly world. The seclu-
siveness, withdrawal, and masochistic behavior of neurotics result
from the *interaction* between low self-esteem and low security,
according to Maslow's "holistic-dynamic" theory of personality.

What of the person who is low in only *one* of these traits and
high in the other? Catholic women, for example, are often low
in self-esteem but high in security. The result, says Maslow, is
a person who is "quiet, sweet, or serving. . ." humble and dependent, but not neurotic. In Jews, on the other hand, "there is

a tendency to be simultaneously high in self-esteem and low in security. . ." Such a person, says Maslow, is likely to "use his strength to hurt, to dominate, or to assuage his insecurity . . . [to be] openly hostile and aggressive. . ."[23]

To Maslow, the influence of security on the canalization of self-esteem is remarkable. "A person with high self-esteem, who is also secure, shows this feeling of strength of self-confidence in a kind, cooperative, and friendly fashion. The person who is high in self-esteem and is also insecure is interested not so much in helping weaker people as in dominating them and hurting them. . . . In extremely insecure people [of high self-esteem] . . . it may have the quality of hostility, aggressiveness, and nastiness."[24]

The paranoid attitude. Reik assigns a "paranoid character trend [to] the majority of Jews," (adding that this is a result of their social history rather than any fixed hereditary condition). Reik quotes a character in a novel by Schnitzler who tells his Jewish friend: "It's a mania of yours that you have quite lost the capacity for seeing anything in the world except the Jewish question."[25]

Moral masochism. A familiar character in Jewish folklore is the *Shlemiel,* the pathetic fellow for whom nothing ever turns out right. He is characterized by such self-descriptive epigrams as "If I should undertake to sell candles, the sun would never set; if I should deal with shrouds, no one would ever die. . ." His lack of talent for dealing with ordinary life situations is expressed by the proverbs: "When a *Shlemiel* kills a chicken, it walks; when he winds up a clock, it stops." Reik describes the *Shlemiel* as "a masochistic character who has the strong unconscious will to fail and to spoil his chances."[26]

Riesman describes the masochistic attitude of those who try too hard to avoid the stereotype of Jewish aggressiveness: "Are Jews pushing? Very well, we will be retiring. Are Jews over-critical? Very well, we will swallow our protest."[27] But one may also detect a need for punishment—or certaintly a bid for rejection—in those Jews who seem to select the very traits "that are detested in the majority stereotype. . . . Are Jews pushing? Very well, pushing is nice, and we will push. Are Jews critical? Very well, let us exploit this fine cultural resource."[28] In 1942 Riesman had acknowledged the existence of those "strident and greedy" Jews who use anti-Semitism as a license: "If Jews cannot be the most popular, they must be the most disliked."[29] Behavior which invites disparagement and contempt may also be labelled masochistic.

Classical masochism seeks punishment by a loved one; for the moral masochist the source is unimportant, "it is the suffering itself that matters."[30] Another distinguishing mark of moral masochism is that the person seeks not physical pain but humiliation and failure.[31] As Freud put it, the moral masochist "always holds out his cheek wherever he sees a chance of receiving a blow."[32] This need to maintain a certain quota of suffering is suggested, Freud says, by patients whose masochistic neurosis ("which has defied every therapeutic effort") "may vanish when the person has become involved in the misery of an unhappy marriage, has lost his fortune, or has developed a dangerous organic disease."[33]

Perhaps the masochist solves the problem of anti-Semitism by making himself worthy of the anti-Semite's contempt. His identification with the aggressor takes the form of acting out the anti-Semite's stereotype of Jewish behavior. He solves the problem of moral integrity by behaving like a "helpless, dependent . . . naughty child."[34] Fenichel sees in masochistic behavior "an accusing, blackmailing tone." The attitude " 'Look how miserable I am' typically stands for 'Look how miserable you have made me.' "[35] Riesman warns against the temptation to luxuriate in sentiment over "the weaker sides of Jewish life in America."[36] To Reik the "cruel and shameless self-abasement" that one sometimes encounters in Jewish wit portrays the Jews who cannot "take revenge upon their oppressors, and . . . [therefore] introject the object of hate and . . . enjoy the expression of witty malice and verbal revenge against the enemy of the self."[37] (In this respect the *shlemiel* parallels the self-defeating American Negro who has too deeply interiorized the negative racial stereotype.)[38]

The masochist has presumably learned that the direct expression of aggressive impulses is wicked, dangerous, alien, and must be repressed. The unconscious stirring of aggressive impulses arouses feelings of guilt, which give rise to the need for punishment that is served by masochistic symptoms: feelings of inferiority, "lack of dignity and self-respect,"[39] or "an obsequiousness, and lack of fighting spirit."[40]

The repression of aggressive impulses in the Jewish culture is reflected in relative infrequency of Jewish involvement in crimes of violence, accidental deaths, and juvenile delinquency. Among the Orthodox it is considered un-Jewish for one's kitchen knives to be very sharp.

Sophia Robison studied the juvenile delinquency rate in New York City, and concluded that 'if Jewish children were delinquent in correct proportions to population size there should have been almost ten times as many Jewish delinquents as there were in actual fact.' Kennedy quotes Robison to say that 'it is doubtful whether any religious group in New York can rival the Jews as regards to infrequency of delinquency.'[41]

In Jewish humor, the repression of aggressive impulses is represented by jokes on the military, and by jokes in which wit triumphs over brute strength. The alien and frightful quality of physical aggression in the Jewish culture is perhaps well expressed by the fact that the cry for "Help!" in Yiddish is "Gevalt!" (which means "physical force," i.e., "I am being threatened by violence!").

Reik offers the following two Jewish jokes on the military:

In 1914, at the beginning of the First World War, a Jew came by chance upon a territory on the Russian border which was guarded by a sentry. The soldier raised his gun when he saw the man approaching, and shouted: 'Halt or I shoot!' The Jew made an irritable gesture and said: 'Are you *mishugge*? Put that gun away. Don't you see that here is a *mensch*?'[42]

A Jewish recruit is asked by his officer: 'Why should a soldier sacrifice his life for the Fatherland?' 'You are quite right, Lieutenant! Why should he?'[43]

The establishment of Israeli police departments inspired jokes about the incongruity between the Jewish tradition and police force. One story is told of a policeman who knocked on a citizen's door and announced that he was under arrest. The citizen asked his fellow Jew to kindly leave him alone. The policeman, in anger and frustration, shouted: 'I swear by my mother and father and also by my wife and children, that I *will* arrest you!' 'Aha!' the citizen countered slyly; 'you're taking me by force?' *('Du nehmst mir mit gevalt?')*

Obsessive-compulsive symptoms. Loewenstein points to a "resemblance between certain types of obsessive neurotics and devout Orthodox Jews, punctillious in the observance of the rites and ceremonies of their religion . . . obsessed with what is pure and impure, just and unjust." Loewenstein interprets obsessive-compulsive symptoms as "defense mechanisms against physical aggression." Neurotic preoccupation with money is likewise seen as a derivative of the inhibition of the aggressive drives.[44] To Loewenstein, "if there is anything peculiar to the Jewish mind, it would seem to be the special way in which the ego deals with the aggressive drives, and the defense mechanisms the Jews have elaborated [to fit] the peculiar circumstances of their [non-Jewish] social environment. . ."[45]

According to Sargent and Williamson, "clinicians often report that a major or minor factor in a Jewish person's maladjustment is his reaction to his unfavorable ethnic status."[46] This generalization should be tempered by Charlotte Buhler's reminder that "culture provides a most convenient scapegoat" for a person's difficulties with life.[47] A person who is in conflict with his impulses and at the same time in conflict with his culture is not likely to keep those two battles very neatly separated. A good rationalization gives the ego more comfort than a poor rationalization. This does not detract from the inevitable conclusion that "it's hard to be a Jew." Loewenstein puts this conclusion in the following words:

> The capacity to carry Jewishness well depends on the absence of factors predisposing to neurosis. There is no getting away from the fact, however, that even for the most well-adjusted, it is not easy to be a Jew. Many have been psychologically damaged by feelings that they are not like other people. Others again have benefitted by their 'exceptional' status, and through it have developed a breadth of vision and a depth of human understanding that have made them in truth exceptional. But even these outstanding Jews are not proof against anguish and self-torture, nor immune to the ambivalent reactions of the Gentile world.[48]

Incidence of neurotic symptoms and impairment in Jewish society. Until quite recently, research on ethnic differences in mental health has yielded ambiguous, inconclusive, and inconsistent results. State mental hospital populations over-represent the lower classes, hospital out-patient clinics over-represent urban groups, Jewish private practitioners attract Jewish patients; there seemed to be no way to secure a valid appraisal of ethnic differences in mental health.[49]

The New Haven census of psychiatric patients. In a pioneering study, Myers and Roberts conducted a census of all persons residing in the metropolitan area of New Haven who were under treatment of a psychiatrist on December 1, 1950. They report that two and one-half times as many Jews were in treatment for neurotic disorders—per capita—as Catholics or Protestants, and that this significant disproportion could not be accounted for by class differences.[50] Catholics showed the highest rate for alcohol and drug addiction, and organic illnesses were most frequent, per capita, among Protestants. Of approximately

Table 11:1. Distribution of New Haven (Conn.) Psychiatric Patient Population by Diagnostic and Ethnic Group[53]

	Catholic		Protestant		Jewish		(Totals)
	(N)	%	(N)	%	(N)	%	
Control Group*	(6,736)	57.5	(3,869)	33.0	(1,108)	9.5	(11,713)
Total patient population**	(1,059)	57.0	(576)	31.0	(223)	12.0	(1,858)
Neurotic disorders	(189)	46.2	(122)	29.8	(98)	24.0	(409)
Alcohol and drug addiction	(61)	68.5	(28)	31.5	(0)	0.0	(89)
Organic disorders***	(36)	53.8	(29)	43.4	(2)	2.8	(67)
Other psychiatric disorders****	(773)	59.7	(397)	30.7	(123)	9.6	(1,293)

* A 5 per cent sample of the general population of New Haven.

** Based on comprehensive census of all patients living in metropolitan New Haven who were under treatment of a psychiatrist on December 1, 1950.

*** Excluding epilepsy and disorders of senescence.

****Including schizophrenia, affective disorders, psychosis with mental deficiency, disorders of senescence, and epilepsy.

2000 persons under psychiatric care in New Haven on the census date, not one Irish Catholic was in psychotherapy,[51] and not one Jew was to be found among the alcohol and drug addicts.[52]

The Midtown Manhattan Study. A more recent milestone in mental health surveys, The Midtown Manhattan Study, conducted a Home Interview Survey of 1,660 adults systematically selected from a residential section in Manhattan. An elaborate and carefully constructed interview was conducted by the Study's "sensitive, psychologically knowledgeable interviewers," who recorded and summarized the respondents' answers to specific mental health-related questions, interviewer's observations of respondent behavior (e.g., verbal elaborations and asides, appropriateness of replies, signs of tension or ease, mannerisms, dress), and treatment history. Summaries were rated by two psychiatrists, which placed each respondent in one of the following six categories:

Unimpaired
1. Well
2. Mild symptom formation
3. Moderate symptom formation

Impaired
4. Marked symptom formation
5. Severe symptom formation
6. Incapacitated

Adjusted for age and socio-economic origin, the mental health distributions by religious origin give Jews the lowest rate in *both* extreme categories (Well and Incapacitated), and show Jews to be "more heavily concentrated than Protestants and Catholics in the subclinical range in between, above all in the most populated mental health category, namely, 'mild' symptom formation."[54]

When the lower socio-economic stratum—the group having the highest concentration of mental morbidity—is examined separately "respondents of Protestant, Catholic and Jewish origin have almost identical 'well' frequencies, but their 'impaired' rates are 32.0, 30.5 and 19.4 per cent respectively." This finding leads Srole and Langner to forward the hypothesis that Jewish respondents "tend to reflect some kind of impairment-limiting mechanism that operates to counteract, or in some degree contain, the more

Table 11:2. Distribution on Mental Health Classification of Catholic, Protestant and Jewish Respondents[55]

Mental health categories	Religious origin		
	Catholic	Protestant	Jewish
Well	17.4%	20.2%	14.5%
Mild symptom formation	34.5	36.4	43.2
Moderate symptom formation	23.4	19.9	25.1
Impaired	24.7*	23.5	17.2*

Survey based on 832 Catholics, 562 Protestants, and 213 Jews, age range 20-59. Data from Table 16-4, page 305, *Mental Health in the Metropolis,* by Srole, Langner, *et al.*
* t=2.6 (.01 level of confidence).

extreme pathogenic life stresses during childhood. This hypothesis appears to be consistent with the repeatedly confirmed relative immunity of Jews to such self-impairing types of reactions as alcoholism and suicide."[56]

This important finding—the Jews' lower frequency of marked or severe mental impairment—led the investigators to look for possible "hidden sources" of mental health in Jewish cultural life. Two hypotheses were put forward:

First, the strong Jewish family structure, "often hypothesized by psychiatrists as potentially pathogenic . . . may conceivably be eugenic on balance, in the specific sense that powerful homeostatic supports are brought into play at danger points of crisis and stress that in other groups may be unbalancing for the family and impairing for the individual."[57] *Mishpocho* membership may seem like a costly form of mental health insurance but perhaps it is somewhat effective against whatever leads people to utter despair, demoralization, and self-impairment.

Secondly, the Jews' chronic anxiety comes in for re-examination by Srole and Langner. Perhaps this "alertness to danger" is learned through the normal process of growing up in a Jewish family and somehow immunizes the Jew against "the more severe pressures and traumas of existence."[58]

The Jews' low rate of marked or severe impairment is in all likelihood related to this group's special readiness to obtain psychiatric service. Of all respondents rated "impaired," "Jews have a current out-patient rate of more than twice that of Protestants and approximately *ten times* that of Catholics."[59] (These differences cannot be accounted for by ethnic differences in socio-economic status, the investigators assert.)

What is the cultural meaning of the Jews' readiness to obtain psychiatric help? Does it reflect the aggressiveness and vitality of the Jew, or the emotional and material support of the extended family? Does it reflect the religious value placed on the enhancement of life?[60] Or does it have something to do with a culturally patterned *willingness to talk* about intimate and troubling matters?

The latter possibility is suggested by an unexpected finding of Kinsey's investigators: Jewish respondents seem unusually free in recording the details of their own sexual activities, and show an unusual willingness to discuss those details, "not only with us but with many of their fellows and with utter strangers." This *willingness to talk,* however, "has surprisingly little relation to the extent of the overt activity of their individual sexual histories." Jews give the impression that they are sexually more active, Kinsey asserts, because of their willingness to "discuss sexual matters publicly with less restraint than most groups."[61] The Jewish culture perhaps trains its members to think and speculate and joke and *talk* about matters close to their inner life; these habits may themselves have a therapeutic value, as well as prepare the person to relate effectively to a psychotherapist.

Paper-and-pencil test studies of mental health. Sanua summarizes the major finding of a total of ten published studies in which Jews and Gentiles were compared on scores obtained on personality tests following the questionnaire or "paper-and-pencil" format. (The ten studies were located through "an exhaustive study of the psychologically oriented literature.") Sanua summarizes and compares these studies in tabular form, and demonstrates that the results are contradictory and therefore seem inconclusive: "some of the psychologists report that Jews seem to be more unstable, while others report the exact opposite."[62] Sanua arrives at a special insight into these seemingly unsystematic findings when he observes that the direction of Jewish-Gentile differences in adjustment correlate with *date of publication!* With one exception, "all the Jewish groups show poorer adjustment" in studies published prior to 1938. "Most of the results of studies after 1938, however, show an opposite trend. In the later instances, Jews show better or at least an equal degree of *social* adjustment as do the non-Jews." Sanua attributes this trend to differences in acculturation and change in generational status.[63]

Social adjustment versus inner tensions. Sanua followed the hunch that the tests following the questionnaire format left something important unmeasured. He therefore decided to give a large number of Jewish youngsters both the Thurstone Personality Schedule (a questionnaire format test) and a form of the Rorschach inkblot test adapted for group administration (the Rorschach Multiple Choice Test). Both tests were given to 730 high school students in 17 New York City high schools, selected so as to include an adequate number of Orthodox, Conservative, and Reform Jews, as well as persons of the first, second, and third generations. (A total of 630 were Jews, 100 were non-Jews.)

Consistent with the trend Sanua had observed from ranking published studies chronologically, scores on the Thurstone Personality Schedule improved with generational status. Third generation Jews approximated the scores obtained from a group of "long-established Protestants."[64]

"The most striking finding in this research," says Sanua, "is the ascending 'inner maladjustment' shown by Jewish boys from the first to third generation on the Rorschach Multiple Choice Test. Socio-economic status and specific type of synagogue affiliation [Orthodox, Conservative or Reform] seem to have very little effect on such scores."[65]

Non-Jewish boys give a significantly less neurotic score than the Jewish sample on the Rorschach (6.78 and 9.80, significant at better than the .01 level of probability). The same trend holds for differences in mean Rorschach score for Jewish and non-Jewish girls. This finding led Sanua to conjecture that "the Jewish male tends to be influenced to a greater degree by social and cultural forces than Jewish females, who tend, in turn, to have a more well-defined role within the Jewish family in general."[66] The ascending "inner maladjustment" of Jewish boys from the first to third generation may be interpreted as outcomes of (1) progressive differences in upbringing, or (2) differences in life goals.

Undoubtedly if the immigrant Jew is more likely to have been raised in the traditional Jewish extended family, it is probably more likely that he continues to maintain close ties with grandparents, aunts, uncles, and cousins in the extended family tradition. It is also likely that he more fully accepts the norms of Jewish family relations, that is to say he feels less conflict between the sex role and family relations norms of the Jewish culture and those of the dominant group. For each succeeding generation, we would hypothesize that extended family ties weaken, and the conflict between Jewish and Gentile norms become more difficult to resolve. For each generation an improvement in outer security is counterbalanced by an increase in "inner marginality." (Here again we encounter the proposition that the extended family may be an important survival mechanism for minority group living.)

The other line of interpretation is followed by Hurvitz, who points out that each generation has it unique goals and problems. The earlier generations cope with their tensions and anxieties by channeling their energies and investing their hopes for themselves and their children in *achievement*. The third generation is the beneficiary of this struggle. Life for him is relatively comfortable; the inner tensions and anxieties are still there but they are not so readily directed toward achievement. "This may help explain why the shift of American Jews from concern with achievement has resulted in a concern for adjustment," says Hurvitz.[67]

Kramer and Leventman offer a somewhat more elaborate interpretation of the differences between the life goals of the generations. The first generation addresses itself to the task of *survival,* the second generation orients itself toward *achievement,* the third generation seeks *status* in the eyes of the Gentile community. Each poses a more difficult and uncertain task; each poses a task which brings the person into increasing conflict with Jewish norms and values; each places him in a more ambiguous and ambivalent relationship with the dominant group.

The superiority of women. Sanua's finding that Jewish females tend to be significantly less neurotic than Jewish males is consistent with the findings of Keith Sward, and calls to mind the observations of a rabbi who worked for a period of seven years as Jewish chaplain at a large medical center:

> Jewish women usually do a better job of coping with a medical crisis than Jewish men—whether as a patient or as the spouse of a patient. Women usually bear up better under the psychological stresses of severe illness, pain, and disability; and they are more likely to show courage when facing death. Jewish men are more often the petty complainers; illness and pain is for them a much more disorganizing and distressing experience. They are more likely to act the role of what in Yiddish we call a *kvetch*.
>
> Also as the spouse of a patient, Jewish women are more resourceful, more adaptable. The Jewish husband who accompanies his wife to the medical center for treatment often doesn't know what to do with himself when he is not at his wife's bedside—except to sit and bite his fingernails, and smoke. The Jewish woman who accompanies her husband to the medical center for treatment usually holds up better. Although she is a stranger in town (almost all of our patients are), she will find people to talk to, she will do a little shopping, she will find something to do when she is not at her husband's bedside.

Our review of the evidence on parents' reactions to intermarriage (Chapter 5) likewise indicated that Jewish fathers are more likely to lapse into a chronic state of anguish. Their wives show a better capacity for recovery from this psychological crisis. Does this sex difference in psychological stamina mean that the burden of minority group living falls more heavily on the shoulders of men than of women? Is the Jewish parent-child relationship more likely to implant neurotic tendencies in boys, and more likely to give a sense of security and self-esteem to girls? Or is it the culturally patterned husband-wife relationship that gives Jewish girls a greater sense of psychological well-being? However one may try to account for this sex difference, the fact that it prevails would seem to mean that Jewish males tend to be more restless and dissatisfied with things as they are. (Jewish girls are more likely to be satisfied with their present status. Since to them the status quo is more satisfying, they are more conservative, more conventional.) These observations put the classic question "What's wrong with Jewish girls?" into a new perspective, and round out our survey of tensions leading to intermarriage.

12

Sexual Inhibition and the Lure
of the Exotic

For the stranger-woman's[1] lips drip with honey
　　And her mouth is smoother than oil;
But in the end she will turn bitter as wormwood
　　And will cut like a two-edged sword.
Her feet lead the way down to death,
　　Her steps come surely to Sheol,
She gives no heed to life's path,
　　Her tracks stray whither she knows not.
So now, my son, listen to me,
　　Depart not from my instructions:
Keep far away from her,
　　Approach not the door of her house,
Lest you give up your honor to others
　　And your worth to one without mercy,
Lest strangers devour your strength
　　And you must toil in an alien's household.
Until at last you bemoan your fate
　　When flesh and body are wasted—
Saying, "Why did I resist discipline?
　　O why did I resent reproof?

I did not heed the voice of my teachers,
    Nor pay attention to my instructors;
Now I am facing final ruin
    In the [judicial] assembly and the community.
[As the saying is], "Drink water from your own cistern,"
    And fresh water from your own well,
Lest your springs overflow in public
    Like rivulets in the open street—
Springs which should be yours only,
    Not to be shared with strangers.
Be grateful for your own fountain,
    And have pleasure with the wife of your youth;
A loveable doe! A sweet mountain goat!
    May her breasts always intoxicate you!
    May you ever find rapture in loving her!
Whatever you do, she will help you;
    When you lie down to rest she will cherish you,
And when you awake she will talk to you.
Why should you swoon over the fruit of a strange woman,
    And clutch the bosom of a foreigner?[2]

The eternal shiksa. The lure of the exotic love object is a familiar theme in the Old Testament, in mythology, in pornography, in folk lore, as well as in the observations of anthropologists, sociologists, social psychologists, and clinicians. As Franzblau puts it: "The exotic is erotic." In societies which follow the rule of exogamy, the choice of a strange woman is viewed as normal human behavior; in an endogamous society the lure of the exotic woman becomes a temptation to do what is forbidden.

The "stranger-woman" as a fascinating, mysterious, many-splendored person is touchingly portrayed by Albert Jay Nock, in his recollection of a Jewish girl with whom he made a brief and passing acquaintance:

She was the only girl I ever saw who seemed to me the acme of everything desirable, with no offset that I could discover—everything in nature and disposition, education, beauty and charm, cosmopolitan culture and manners. . . . What especially interested me was my complete certainty that with the best will in the world on both sides I should know her no better at the end of a hundred years of close companionship than I did at the end of those eight days. I never saw or heard of her afterwards, nor tried to do either. I have often thought, however, of what would happen if some rash and personable young Occidental fell in love with her—no one could help doing that—and married her. If he were sensitive, how distressed and dissatisfied he would be as he became aware of the vast areas of her consciousness from which he was perforce shut out forever; and on the other hand, if he were too insensitive to feel he was shut out from them, how intolerable her life with him would be.[3]

In pornographic writings it is often a woman of a "heathen race" or dark skin who excites a man to rare and wonderful feats of potency, or delights him with sexual pleasures that are beyond the repertory of "civilized" women.[4] (In both the Cupid and the Lohengrin legend the strange love partner is the *male*, who appears mysteriously to a beautiful maiden and offers his love on condition that she must not know his identity.) [5]

To a Jew the exotic woman is a lighthearted *shiksa*, to a Southern white . . . a sensuous Negress, to a Negro . . . a white angel, to a Gentile . . . a voluptuous Jewess, to a Northerner . . . a passionate Mediterranean, to an Italian . . . a fun-loving Irish girl, to an American . . . a sexy French girl or an acquiescent Fraulein.[6]

Slotkin says he was "often assured by Gentile men that Jewesses are more voluptuous than Gentile women. . ."[7] He quotes a Gentile whose intermarriage resulted from a greater feeling of ease with Jewish women:

"I went with Jewish women mainly, and that's how I met my wife. The opportunity for meeting Christian women was there, but I wasn't interested. I was only interested in two things —company and a bed partner. The Christian women I knew were sisters of my friends and so on, and I didn't want to get entangled like that."[8]

It is interesting to compare Child's rebels and in-group members on their attitudes toward girl friends. The rebels tended to avoid Italian girls and expressed a frank preference for non-Italian girls as dates and prospective wives. The conservative in-group, on the other hand, though they were virtually unan-

imous in their "preference for an Italian wife,"[9] seem to get
"more fun" out of dating non-Italian girls:

"The French girls are more fun than the Italians. The Italian
girls are more like home girls. You go out two or three times
and they want to go steady. The others know it's just for fun.
I've found French girls the most enjoyable."[10]

"Irish girls are more fun than Italian girls. The Italian girls
have more old-fashioned ideas."[11]

Child interprets the in-group Italian American's attraction to
the non-Italian *"shiksa:"* "Partly because these informants are
planning to marry Italians, going with an Italian girl is more
likely to arouse ideas of marriage in the man as well as in the
girl. He is more likely to consider her strictly as a 'good' girl.
Consequently, it is easier to obtain gratification from rather
irresponsible companionship with girls of other nationalities. . . .
It is probable, moreover, that because of differing cultural standards for young women's behavior, girls from certain other nationalities will generally provide more gratification in a casual
relationship than will Italian girls."[12]

Whyte describes the sex code of adolescent and unmarried
adult males in "Cornerville," an Italian slum district in "Eastern
City." In this sub-culture "the most desirable woman for non-
marital sex relations is the girl of old American-stock background,
preferably blond, who has a higher status than the corner boy.
"Once," Whyte recalls, "I was walking through the aristocratic
section of Eastern City with a corner boy, when we passed a
tall and stately blond, fashionably dressed, and very attractive.
My companion breathed deeply as he said: 'The old Puritan
stock'. . . . The real McCoy! Wouldn't I like to give her a belt!'"[13]

Linton Freeman observed and interviewed a group of students
at the University of Hawaii who identified with an exotic culture—embracing its philosophy, language and customs—and restricted their dating to members of the "adopted" culture. Reports Freeman:

Members of the opposite sex particularly were idealized,
and the desire to find a mate within the new group became
important. Fantasies were constructed depicting the ideal mate
an archetype of the new culture. He or she was the possessor

of all the positive features attributed to the culture itself and individual differences were ignored. Potential mates were classified categorically. They were positively stereotyped and seen initially at least as eminently desirable. On the other hand, potential mates from the individual's own people were categorically negatively stereotyped. They were considered undesirable regardless of their actual characteristics.[14]

Lust and inhibition. Like the Protestant American at the University of Hawaii who idealizes the womanly charm of Hawaiian (or Japanese) women, many Jews feel quite sure that "Gentile girls are hotter." Perhaps the man who says "Jewish girls leave me cold" comes closer to the truth. (If a Jewish girl arouses a young man's incest horror, her only fault may be that she reminds him of his sister or mother.) Sartre offers an anecdote to this point:

> I have heard several anecdotes on this subject, but shall cite only one of them which I have heard directly from the person to whom it happened. A Jew goes to a house of prostitution, chooses one of the women, and goes upstairs with her. She tells him she is a Jew. He finds himself impotent, and very soon is overcome with an intolerable sense of humiliation that expresses itself in spasms of vomiting.[15]

Sartre attributes his informant's reaction to an offended racial pride; here we shall regard the informant's uncontrollable revulsion (impotence, vomiting) as an expression of incest horror. It is as if he inhabits a world in which there are three sexes— men, women and Jewish girls (as represented graphically by the following set of diagrams borrowed from *Playboy* magazine.)

Figure 12:1. The Three Sexes

Kinsey observed that in societies where pre-marital coitus is strictly prohibited for "decent" or "respectable" girls, males "find it difficult to have coitus with their wives, because they hold them in something of the same respect that they held their mothers, sisters, and all 'decent' girls before marriage. Consequently some males in such cultures [Oriental, North African, Continental European, Mediterranean and Latin American] may continue to secure much of their coitus after marriage from prostitutes or mistresses, rather than from their wives."[16]

Since in the Jewish tradition it is immoral to deny a wife her "conjugal portion," the Jew who feels sexually inhibited toward a woman of his own group may feel impelled as a Jew to seek a woman "who pleases him." In the case of Abram (presented in Chapter 3), we encounter a religious Jew who approaches middle age before he finds a woman "who pleases him." Although she is Catholic, it is in a deeply significant sense an expression of his Jewishness for Abram to take her as a wife. The finding of Heiss, that Jews who intermarry do so at a later age than Jews who marry within their group, suggests that Jews who intermarry have had some difficulty in finding a more conventional mate.

So widespread is the appeal of the exotic woman, theorists of an earlier generation did not hesitate to suppose that this attitude had an instinctive basis. Park was satisfied to believe that "the disposition of men to go abroad for wives and of women to welcome these roving strangers is probably part of original nature. Human beings are naturally exogamous," he believed.[17] Reuter likewise theorized that "the existence of some racial differences between populations closely associated operates rather definitely as a sex stimulant. Moderate differences in racial type appeal . . . to the universal wish for new and stimulating experience. The familiar holds no illusions and makes slight appeal."[18]

Park observed that "in a society where a caste system, or something approaching it, prevails there is always a tendency on the part of the women of the lower caste to become the concubines of the men in the higher caste."[19] The appeal of the stranger manifests itself in a wide range of social settings. As Reuter observed, the adolescent boy naively finds something especially

appealing about "the girls outside his village or immediate circle.
. . . The nubile girl idealizes the strange man. . . . The essence
of romance is illusion. The psychological basis of exogamy as
well as of the taboos on incest lie in the romantic possibilities of
the strange and unexplored."[20]

To Reuter "the essence of romance is illusion." Is it possible
to translate this statement into terms which are more psychologically explicit? We begin with the observation that early social
training inhibits sexual play and may even repress sexual fantasy
(both of which are included in the concept of "romance"). The
more familiar the person, the more strongly she elicits feelings
of sexual inhibition. The Levinsons' concept of the "contrast
choice" suggests that feelings of ambivalence toward sexual expression can be overcome by finding a partner whose characteristics
are sufficiently novel so as *not* to arouse one's acquired inhibitions, and whose characteristics are at the same time sufficiently
familiar to match one's positive fantasies about sexual pleasure.
(Reuter warns that "the range of difference may not be great
else the offended aesthetic sensibilities overshadow the sex appeal. . . . The tendency to avoid contacts may be greater than
the tendency to court advances.")[21]

The folklore of the exotic woman regards her as a "sex
stimulant," mediated by some sort of instinctive mechanism.
Clinical experience, however, suggests that when certain conditions of upbringing inhibit the male from enjoying the sexual
potential of an in-group partner, he may be predisposed to seek
an "outsider" in order to experience normal sexual gratification.
The seeking of a "contrast choice" takes on the character of an
adjustment mechanism, according to the Levinsons. To so resolve
one's inner conflicts about marriage, the Levinsons insist, "is
not in itself neurotic, and it has useful adjustive functions."[22]

Gradients of contrast. How might one distinguish between a
"normal" contrast choice and a "neurotic" one? Perhaps one significant factor is the *degree* of contrast required in order to elicit
sexual arousal and fulfillment. Franzblau introduced the concept
of appraising the "religious distance" between an intermarried
couple. (There would be little "religious distance" between a
Reform Jew and a Unitarian; a considerable "distance" between
a secular Jew and a devout Catholic.) Franzblau hypothesized

that the smaller the "religious distance" between the couple, the more favorable are prospects for a successful marriage. To make an unrealistic marriage choice, one improbable of success, is almost by definition a neurotic act.[23]

Franzblau offers the clinical judgment that even neurotic marriages (including neurotic intermarriages) may help alleviate the partners' emotional problems, rather than create or aggravate them. "When the unconscious needs of a couple meet and match, a tight union may be formed and there may be a lasting marriage." If a couple stays together, even though they seem unhappy about their marriage partnership, they may be assumed, says Franzblau, to be "held together by their unconscious needs."[24]

The "bad woman." For some men the mate must not only be different, she must also be of a lower order than women of his own group. Freud referred to men who feel attracted to women about whom there lurks an aura of "the forbidden." She may be a woman about whom there is some "faint breath of scandal"; she may be a prostitute.[25] "Passionate attachments of this kind are repeated many times over with [women possessing] all the same peculiarities—each an exact replica of the others—in the lives of those [men] belonging to this type. . ."[26]

Reik tells of a patient who was impotent except when he addressed his wife in vulgar sexual terms.[27] If he cannot degrade her, Reik comments, he cannot imagine that she should be sexually available. Until he degrades her, she is made of "sugar and spice," she belongs on a pedestal, not in bed.[28]

Kubie likewise refers to "the familiar yet perplexing phenomenon of a man who loses his potency with any women he loves and respects, but who can be potent with one he scorns. I had a patient," he recalls, "who had had a happy affair with a woman for many years, during which his wife was hopelessly ill. He married his mistress eagerly after his wife's death, only to become impotent with her on their wedding night and thereafter. Comparable reactions occur in women as well; in anyone, in fact, in whom the taboo on sex is so deep-seated that [sex can be enjoyed] only extra-legally or in the gutter."[29]

Hernton tells of a white college professor who presumably "discovered" his full sexual capabilities after a drinking party where he had observed, with revulsion and anger, his wife being openly seductive to a Negro graduate student. When the graduate student met the professor's wife the next day "she had a black eye. . . . She told me her husband beat her and made love to her like he never had before."[30]

For one to choose a mate whom he looks down upon "contradicts the normal tendency to seek a mate whom one can overidealize," Franzblau reflects. But "for some people marriage is impossible unless the loved one has a blemish, whether physical, psychological or moral. . . . They cannot marry the untouchable goddess. The woman they marry must be blemished. . . . A different race or religion, especially if it should chance to be found in an inferior person, constitutes a blemish of exactly the kind some people choose to make marriage permissible and which makes it possible for them to fall in love."[31]

The search for a strange or "blemished" partner with whom one can lay aside his sexual inhibitions recalls a statement by Freud that psychic impotence is after all a matter of degree, and that some degree of psychic impotence is the prevailing condition of civilized peoples.[32] Psychical impotence is one of the most common disorders which the psychoanalyst is called upon to remedy—far more widespread than is generally supposed.[33] Many men who *can* perform the sexual act "perform it without special pleasure" and therefore may be said to suffer from a more limited kind of psychical impotence.[34]

A man may discover that his virility fails "only with certain women, whereas it never happens with others. He knows then that the inhibition of his masculine potency is due to some quality in the sexual object, and sometimes he describes having had a sensation of holding back, of having perceived some check within him. . . . What this inner opposition is, however, he cannot guess, or what quality in the sexual object makes it active."[35]

"In only very few people of culture," Freud believed, "are the two strains of tenderness and sensuality duly fused into one; the man almost always feels his sexual activity hampered by his respect for the woman and only develops full sexual potency when he finds himself in the presence of a lower type of sexual object. . . . Full sexual satisfaction only comes when he can give himself up wholeheartedly to enjoyment, which with his well-brought-up wife, for instance, he does not venture to do. Hence comes his need for . . . a woman ethically inferior, to whom he need ascribe no aesthetic misgivings, and who does not know the rest of his life and cannot criticize him. It is to such a woman that he prefers to devote his sexual potency. . . . It is possible, too, that the tendency so often observed in men of the highest rank in society to take a woman of low class as a permanent mistress, or even as a wife, is nothing but a consequence of the need for a lower type of sexual object on which, psychologically, the possibility of complete gratification depends."[36]

In the above citations, Freud makes several contributions to the discussion: (1) that some degree of psychic impotence is the prevailing condition of civilized men—well-brought-up persons of culture and social rank; (2) that disabling impotence is one of the most common disorders which brings patients to the psychoanalyst; and (3) that this disability must therefore be traceable to the influence of "civilization" on habits formed during infancy and childhood.

Mother-son affection and the incest taboo. This leads us, of course, back to an analysis of the affectionate bond between mother and son, and to the transmission of the incest taboo. The boy's initial object of affection is his mother. He learns that he may direct toward her affection, adoration, tenderness, but that he must confine his physical curiosity or thrill-seeking to the limits prescribed by the incest taboo. At the time of puberty his sexual drive becomes dominant and normally the boy begins to transfer his expressions of affection, adoration, and tenderness from his mother to girls of his own generation, with whom he can also engage in certain sensuous exploration, or at least whom he can fantasy as a sex partner in his daydreams or during moments of sexual arousal.

In this normal adolescent period, feelings of tenderness and affection become interwoven or integrated with his sexual passion. For example, he finds that displaying affection and tenderness to a girl whose esteem he values may lead her to invite him to come closer to her, accept or welcome his gentle caresses and reciprocate with pleasantly stimulating gestures. The sharing and mingling of intimate feelings leads to mutual trust; sharing glimpses and foretastes of each other's sexual charms and powers elicits pleasant fantasies of fuller gratification. As tenderness leads to sensuous forepleasure (if not gratification) and sensuous forepleasure leads to a deeper trust and admiration, the adolescent grows into manhood prepared to exercise a capacity for love which brings tenderness and lust together.

Fluegel describes the adolescent who is unable to experience the normal process of falling in love because his love impulses are unconsciously fixated on his mother.[37] We would translate this to say ". . . because his love impulses are unconsciously inhibited by an overgeneralized incest taboo."

The result of this inhibition, says Fluegel, may be a young man who is "content to live quietly at home. . . . If sexual relations are attempted, psychic impotence or frigidity—relative or absolute—may result; marriage will frequently be avoided or will be entered into from motives other than those of real affection . . ."[38] Or this inhibition "may manifest itself not merely in relative indifference to the attraction of [women] but more violently, in active dislike of persons of that sex," and perhaps to the choice of a homosexual outlet.[39]

To a normal adolescent, incest is forbidden, but to an adolescent who has overgeneralized the incest taboo, *sex* is forbidden. He therefore tends to avoid situations which may lead to intimate contact with girls of his own group because this may lead to something forbidden. To discharge his shameful feelings of lust he may masturbate, and accompany this act with fantasies of a shameful women—loose, immoral, or at least "different" from members of his group. He may also fantasy that they perform shameful or perverse acts. All this reassures him that he is *not* violating the incest taboo (his mother or sister certainly wouldn't carry on like that). So closely may the act of masturbation be associated with the fantasy of an *immoral* woman, that a boy may "call up the image of some girl whom he sincerely loves in order that he may the better resist the temptation to practice masturbation."[40]

When masturbation or erotic fantasy is regularly accompanied by the fantasy of an unworthy partner "women of an inferior type come to be firmly associated with the more directly sexual aspects of love,"[41] and women who may be regarded with affection or tenderness are correspondingly dissociated from the sexual side of life. Marriage to a proper young lady is marred by diminished potency.

The use of prostitutes also enables a man to exercise virility without tenderness, a lustful engagement without emotional intimacy. Men sometimes justify the use of prostitutes or "outsiders" on the basis that these women will offer various kinds of foreplay, and perform variations of the sex act which a well-brought-up wife will have no part in (so they suppose). Freud judged that a man's wish for substitutional or perverse acts stems from his need to see the partner degraded. Before he can experience full sexual potency he needs this reassurance that his partner is indeed a "bad" woman.[42]

Masturbatory fantasies, says Freud, may utilize a disguised image of mother, giving sex an even more forbidden aura. The sex impulse becomes a creature of one's fantasy life, unsuited for expression in the real world.[43] This "retreat into fantasy" postpones further any attempt to integrate affectionate and sensuous feelings (a process which requires some amount of real-life social experience), heightens incest-guilt which the person seeks to undo by finding a partner who is decidedly remote from his "forbidden" love object.

Affection remains attached to the mother, while sensuous interest is directed toward the "outsider." In his sexual life the person wants "no reminder of the incestuous persons forbidden to it; the impression made by someone who seems deserving of high estimation leads, not to a sensual excitation, but to feelings of tenderness which remain erotically ineffectual. The erotic life of such people remains dissociated, divided between two channels, the same two that are personified in art as heavenly and earthly (or animal) love. Where such men love they have no desire and where they desire they cannot love. . ."[44]

Sexual inhibition and the culture of the shtetl. In an earlier chapter we examined the evidence that the *ideology* of the *shtetl* eulogized sexual expression, and that the social practices of early marriage and *kest* minimized the postponement of sanctioned sexual activity. What of the significant but indirect influences of the *shtetl* culture on the sexual capabilities of the individual? What were the distinctive features of modesty training in the *shtetl*—the vehicle through which the incest taboo is transmitted?

Did a *shtetl* upbringing tend to foster sexual adequacy or inhibition?

Freud attributed sexual inhibition to two factors: (a) degree of emotional attachment to mother, and (b) the period of delay between sexual maturity and the availability of a sanctioned sex partner.[45] We have viewed the problem of sexual inhibition from a slightly different angle, asking what we believe is the more basic question: How deeply charged with dread and horror is the incest-avoidance habit? Over how wide a range of stimulus-generalization does this habit operate?

Our analysis of Murdock's anthropological materials indicates that conditions which favor a matrilocal rule of residence tend to favor the practice of endogamy, and this suggests that a mother-centered household favors the transmission of a relatively benign and specific incest-avoidance habit. In a mother-centered household, modesty training is more likely to be guided by the "maternal" controls of giving or withholding affection, than by the "paternal" controls of physical punishment, or the threat of physical punishment. Using the hyperbole of psychoanalysis, let us say there are two mechanisms by which the incest taboo can be transmitted—maternal "seduction," or paternal "castration-threat."

If a boy must have the freedom to fantasy sexual fulfillment with a woman who resembles his own sister or mother, then the incest taboo cannot have been implanted in his psyche too severely—for the same disabling guilt that inhibits his fantasy will later inhibit his efforts at overt sexual expression. To avoid the unwanted by-product of generalized inhibition, therefore, modesty training must be benign and specific; the child must learn that incest is forbidden but he must not come to regard it with an unspeakable (and unthinkable) horror.

Did the culture of the *shtetl* follow this rule in its modesty training procedures? According to Landes and Zborowski, modesty training in the *shtetl* proceeded largely through keeping boys and girls apart—through actual segregation, through shaming, and through exploiting the normal potentialities for conflict between brother and sister. The manager of this learning program was, of course, the mother.

Boys spent their day at *cheder;* girls spent their day at home.

If a boy is found playing with his sister, he is reminded that he is a boy, and that "it is beneath him to play girls' games."[46] Just as brother and sister are shamed into avoiding each other as playmates, they are subjected to other avoidance devices, such as "full body covering and segregated seating of the sexes except on rare formal occasions. . . . Avoidance seems to increase with the maturity of brother and sister, as does the tension between them," which expresses itself in nagging, quarrels, and silent anger. Mother "insists on functioning as their intermediary," and the better she accomplishes this role, the more effectively she may perpetuate their avoidance.[47]

Shame versus guilt, and incest-taboo generalization. This glimpse into the incest-taboo maintenance procedure recalls Murdock's statement that "societies fall into two groups which respect to the manner in which they handle incest and other sexual taboos. One group seems to depend primarily upon strong internalizations of sexual prohibitions during the socialization process. The taboos are so thoroughly instilled by precept and sanction that they become 'second nature.' The very thought of violating them arouses a sense of guilt in the socialized individual, with the result that the society can afford to depend mainly on the consciences of its members to prevent deviations. The other group of societies apparently *succeeds less well* in internalizing sexual prohibitions. Consequently they cannot rely upon individual conscience for the enforcement of taboos, and are compelled to bulwark these with external precautionary safeguards such as avoidance rules."[48] (Italics added.)

These two incest-taboo maintenance methods might be labelled the method of guilt and the method of shame. The reader will surely recognize the method of guilt as the prevailing norm in middle-class America,[49] while the method of shame summarizes what has been observed about modesty training in the *shtetl.* Perhaps it is misleading to say that the latter method "succeeds less well in internalizing sexual prohibitions"; perhaps it was important to that culture *not to go too far* in internalizing and generalizing the incest taboo! Perhaps shaming, precisely because it is less efficient from the standpoint of an exogamous society, is more functional in an endogamous society.

Incest fantasy in the Jewish culture. While the method of guilt surrounds the *idea* of incest with disgust, revulsion and loathing, the method of shame focuses upon the suppression of incestuous *behavior*. The incest theme, as a consequence, is a distinct rarity in the sacred or secular literature of the West (except for frankly pornographic writings),[50] but it is not hard to find incest references in the literature of the Jews—where the topic is more often treated with awe and fascination than with loathing.

Each year, at the close of the High Holy Days—on the afternoon of the Day of Atonement—tradition requires a reading of Leviticus 18, "the incest chapter," which also catalogues various other sexual taboos: adultery, homosexuality, bestiality, and intercourse with a woman who is menstrually unclean. But the emphasis is on the incest taboo, and in its explicitness this ceremonial reading seems to suggest that the Jewish attitude toward incest is different from the norm for most human societies, in which one cannot find an explicit rule against incest—"the taboo is so strongly internalized, the idea is so deeply repressed, that the act is considered simply unthinkable."[51] Each *Yom Kippur,* however, the Jew in the synagogue is reminded that it is not unthinkable to "uncover the nakedness of his sister," but it is indeed forbidden.

> And the Lord said to Moses . . . 'None of you shall approach any one near of kin to him to uncover nakedness. . . . You shall not uncover the nakedness of your father, which is the nakedness of your mother . . . you shall not uncover her nakedness. You shall not uncover the nakedness of your father's wife; it is your father's nakedness. You shall not uncover the nakedness of your sister, the daughter of your father or the daughter of your mother. . . . You shall not uncover the nakedness of your son's daughter or of your daughter's daughter, for their nakedness is your own nakedness.
>
> You shall not uncover the nakedness of your father's wife's daughter . . . since she is your sister. . . . You shall not uncover the nakedness of your mother's sister. . . . You shall not uncover the nakedness of your daughter-in-law; she is your son's wife. . .[52]

Landes and Zborowski note that "in the Talmud . . . dreams of incest with mother and sister are described coolly as 'opening the way to wisdom.' "[53] "To see one eye kiss another" is described in the Talmud as a dream symbol of incest.[54] Bakan cites a tale from the *Zohar,* in which Rabbi Abba and Rabbi Jose in their travel meet a man who bears a mark on his face because he transgressed "the Law against illicit intercourse." Recalls the repentant stranger: "I was once traveling with my sister, and we turned in to an inn, where I drank much wine. All that night I was in company with my sister . . ." The stranger describes his weeping and repentance. Rabbi Abba pronounces over the stranger the verse from Isaiah, "And thine iniquity is taken away and thy sin purged," and asks the stranger to repeat it three times. The mark vanishes from his face, he vows "from this day to study the Torah day and night," and Rabbi Abba sends him away with a blessing.[54]

Bakan observes the ambiguity contained in a passage from Leviticus: "If a man taketh his sister, his father's daughter or his mother's daughter, it is *hesed.*" *Hesed* literally means loving kindness, but in this context it is usually translated to mean shameful. The *Zohar* explains that incest was *hesed* "at the beginning, in the hidden development of the world"; that is, the children of Adam had to engage in incest, "but subsequently human beings who behave so 'shall be cut off before the eyes of the children of their people.' "[55] "The Talmudic and Midrashic rabbis state that Cain killed Abel for the possession of one of their sisters."[56]

The incest theme appears in various guises in the secular Jewish literature. Landes and Zborowski describe the occurrence of provocative horseplay between brother and sister in the Yiddish theater. The incredible discovery of a married couple that they are actually brother and sister has provided a theme for European Jewish films (produced in Warsaw prior to World War II), and for stories in the Yiddish press.[57] It appears as if the method of shame, while prohibiting the *act* of incest, leaves room in the person's fantasy life for the exercise of awe and fascination over the possibilities of accidental or unintended incest. This suggests that in the Eastern European Jewish culture the socialization pattern, utilizing shame rather than guilt, transmitted a less generalized incest taboo than prevails in Western society—and thereby maintained a norm more adaptive to an endogamous society which placed a high moral value on unimpaired sexual functioning.

Disturbances of the mother-son relationship. Neither in the *shtetl* nor in any other milieu is normal development assured for each and every individual. If, as Freud held, a man's sexual inhibition is betokened by too great an emotional attachment to his mother, what are the conditions which lead up to this state of affairs? It is too easy to say that excessive attachment results from excessive mothering. What is "excessive mothering?" (Let us recall the observation of Sears, Maccoby, and Levin that maternal warmth was *positively* correlated with emotional health of the mother.) Pathologically excessive mothering, like excessive eating or excessive masturbation, is probably symptomatic of some underlying emotional tensions in the family situation. Let us consider certain disturbances of the husband-wife relationship that are likely to "contaminate" the normal bond of affection between mother and son—lead to manifestations of excessive or seductive mothering, and inhibit the normal emotional development of the son.

The dictatorial father. In his analysis of the problem of middle class sexual inhibition, Freud gives *no* attention to the influence of the tyrannical father whose harshness communicates (perhaps unconsciously) a "castration threat," attaches to the incest taboo the dread of unspeakable retribution, and thereby contaminates the affectional bond between mother and son with feelings of guilt and anxiety, and gives a seductive aura to mother's normal expressions of maternal affection.

The weak son of the tyrannical father is a classic figure in drama and in the novel, and seems to represent the risk that harsh paternal treatment may "break the will" of the offspring. When a boy must cope with the incest taboo in an atmosphere of maternal seduction *and paternal harshness,* the sex drive may become inhibited to a degree which severely limits his capacity for enjoyment of endogamous sex relations.

A culture which prescribes a dictatorial role to the father may evolve an allowed preference for an "outsider" sex partner; i.e., one who stands outside an overgeneralized incest-avoidance gradient. This preference may be served by exogamy, or by an allowed "double standard" which gives the husband access to a mistress, prostitute, or other extra-marital partner.

The jealous father. If father because of his own emotional insecurity feels threatened by the affectionate bond between his wife and son, father may deal punitively with the boy. We hypothesize that a punitive father tends to make his son more fearful of violating the taboos which are normally learned in the home situation. Paternal jealousy may likewise cast a forbidden, seductive aura over the affectionate relationship between mother and son.

Franzblau refers to the Jew who intermarries out of a repressed hatred for his father. "When it comes to marriage, he can retaliate in a way that is truly punitive. He punishes the hated father, and also 'gets even' with his people, his faith, and if you will, with God, by marriage. . . . The ultimate step in this type of unconscious rebellion is conversion to the religion of the mate."[58]

We have already demonstrated that a matrilocal rule of residence seems to require a benign and gentle father role, and we have hypothesized that this in turn helps maintain an endogamous tradition. The inhibiting influence of a tyrannical father provides an interesting example of how one modification of family role relations may upset a whole network of culturally patterned behaviors.

The demoralized, rejected, or weak father. When viewed through Western eyes, it may be difficult to differentiate between a gentle father and a weak father, but the difference is undoubtedly an important one. If mother tends to reject father as a failure in life, or as unworthy of her love, the results of this attitude importantly influence the emotional relationship between mother and son, and the capacity of the boy to identify with his father. Both these alterations in the emotional life of the boy lead to sex-role confusion and, therefore, inhibition of his normal sexual capabilities.

A woman who cannot direct affection toward her husband is likely to seek a substitute object, and her son becomes a likely candidate. She will dote upon him and confide in him beyond what is considered normal and prudent, to the boy's felt discomfort. She may even behave "seductively demonstrative" to the boy in father's presence, as an insult to her disaffected husband. ("Look," she silently communicates, "your four-year-old son is more of a man than you are.") The boy's open expression of tenderness toward mother may thereby take on a guilt-laden aura.

Malcolm Helper conducted an ingenious study of 50 families of high-school students, securing self-ratings of the children themselves, as well as objective measures of each parent's approval of the other as a model for the child. Results supported the conclusion that a boy is more likely to assume a similarity to his father *if mother approves of the father as a model for the child.* "In other words, a boy is more likely to see similarities between himself and his father if his mother wants him to be the kind of person his father is." (Father's approval of the mother as a model for the child did *not* relate significantly to emulation of the mother on the part of either boys or girls . . .") [59] Maternal approval of the father as a model seems to be especially important for the boy's emulation of father's characteristics and ideals, which is the normal basis for the establishment of a masculine sex-role identity.

Gil

In the case of Gil we encounter a Jewish youth whose father displays characteristics of both the tyrannical and the weak father. An engineering student, Gil is a tall, thin fellow who speaks just above a whisper in a somewhat whining tone. He had sought assistance from his family doctor and college counselor in dealing with chronic fatigue, headaches, and an unreasonable fear of hurting someone. His family doctor found no physical basis for Gil's complaints, prescribed tranquilizers, and recommended psychiatric treatment.

Gil says he has always gotten along very well with his mother, but has always feared his father—whom he describes as a man with a bad temper which he displays in open fights with his wife. Conflict between Gil and his father has recently centered around Gil's car. Father criticizes Gil for not taking good care of it. Last summer while Gil was away on vacation, his father "taught Gil a lesson" by selling his car.

Gil's mother encourages her son to take a passive, child-like adjustment to life. When he tells her how difficult college work is, Mother responds, "Why don't you try something easier?" Gil feels unable to compete in life, unable to exercise initiative. Competition seems to him not like a rule of social living, but like the *violation* of some unspoken rule. Competition is related in his inner thought to father's harshness, bad temper, and rejection. He recalls that at age twelve or thirteen he got some books on television servicing, and asked his father—who is a television repairman—to help him learn. Father laughed at him and re-buffed him, Gil recalls.

An electronics technician, Gil's father had also hoped to become an engineer but was unable to stay in college. Whether he quit because of academic difficulties or "because Mother wanted to get married" seems unclear. Father openly expresses skepticism about Gil's vocational goals: "You'll never be an engineer," he tells him. "Oh, you might have a better job than I do, but you'll never *really* be an engineer." In his fits of temper, Father tells Gil he's crazy and belongs in an institution.

Gil has always felt socially awkward, and feels particularly awkward with girls. To Gil, making a good impression means that "you have to act like somebody else." He has not been dating girls, but last summer he permitted a young lady to strike up an acquaintance with him in the college library. After seeing her a few times, she seduced him into sexual intimacy. Three attempts ended in premature ejaculation, and left him with profound worries about his sexual capabilities. The girl still shows an interest in him but Gil feels that he has disgraced himself.

He has started to date a Gentile woman fifteen years his senior. He sees her every Saturday night, and attaches much importance to the fact that by going steady with her he maintains control over her. They have light petting sessions, at which times she will turn aside and weep. At times she seems to be stimulating him sexually, at other times she acts moralistic and inhibited. She is periodically moody. He feels confused and upset about her, and has noticed a loss of appetite when they are together. Disenchanted with her, he has started going out with other girls, Gentile girls he meets at public dances; they are usually older than he is.

Gil's feelings of "not belonging" express themselves in his living arrangements and in his use of professional help. He moved away from home because it was too noisy; he has two younger brothers. He rented a room near campus but it was too lonely. He moved back home, but moved out again to board with a family that lived not far from his parents. He discusses his emotional problems with the family doctor, has seen two psychiatrists—breaking off with each because they seemed "not interested in him." He saw a counseling psychologist at the university for three months, broke off and later returned for another two months. His avoidance of Jewish girls seems to express a like attitude of alienation, of not belonging, as if he has been "cast into exile" by a rejecting and threatening father.

The seductive mother in case histories. The meaning of "maternal seduction" may be clarified by the presentation of the following cases (and case fragments) :

Rolf

Rolf, a white youth of Catholic background, sought out a Negro prostitute for his first sex experience but reacted with severe inhibition. He has subsequently sought sexual involvement with older men, a middle-aged white woman, and a Negro girl of college age. The oldest child, Rolf has two younger sisters. His father died while Rolf was still an infant. Undoubtedly his mother transferred to her son much of the affection and attention she would normally direct toward a husband. Mother always made a ritual of sending Rolf and his sisters to the toilet before they left for school, so that they would not have to use the school washrooms. Why the school washroom was "taboo" was never made clear; it seemed as if there was something dangerous about exposing one's sex organ. Mother taught Rolf that sexual thrill-seeking was sinful, but she talked romantically about the beautiful and spiritual aspects of sex as practiced in marriage. Rolf recalls that his mother would give him these "sex education" talks on weekend mornings when he—at about age ten—and his mother were lying together in her bed.

Will

Will is a tall, blond college freshman of Jewish parentage, who entered personal counseling beset by feelings of inferiority, doubts about his vocational future, and troubled feelings about girls and sex. His good appearance and boyish manner make it easy for him to get a first date, but girls quickly lose respect for him, Will believes; some have even told him he's mixed up. As a student he is concentrating in language study. He thinks of the glamorous possibilities of the diplomatic service, but recognizes that he is more apt to find work as a high school foreign language teacher, and be forever short of money. He thinks of teaching as a job for men "who can't do anything," and was geuinely surprised to have met a few male students who actually took pride in their choice of teaching as a career.

Home is the scene of Mother's chronic suffering and nagging over Father's failure to earn a decent living. At fifty, Father is vocationally unsettled. He has worked as a draftsman, an insurance salesman, and a clothing salesman. Will sees his father through his mother's eyes: weak willed, irresponsible, and socially inept. Will worries that this taint of failure is hereditary, and that he may never satisfy Mother's hopes that at least Will might someday bring some pleasure into her drab life.

Mother is disappointed not only over her husband, but over her eldest son and youngest daughter as well. Will's older brother quit high school, went to work on a laundry route, and is engaged to a Gentile girl. His younger sister has likewise chosen a Gentile high school crowd. "They're laying me into my grave," Mother laments. To calm her down, Will has volunteered the promise that he won't marry a Gentile, but he finds that he drifts toward Gentile dates, since he thinks of them as more available sexually, and wants desperately to overcome his feelings of sexual inadequacy.

Will is emotionally unprepared for normal sexual intimacy. His positive feelings toward girls are contaminated by over-idealization and fear. None the less, he feels driven by his friends to participate in their sexual exploits. Repeatedly he discovers that the erection which comes so readily when he masturbates simply fails to appear when a promiscuous girl makes herself available to him. He trembles and quakes, and with much maneuvering can at best elicit a token sexual response. His emotional unreadiness for adult sexual intimacy is also revealed by his maturbatory fantasies of engaging in perverse acts with "a real low-class dirty girl," or he imagines that he is watching a nameless man and woman in sexual union.

It seems evident that Will's parents are emotionally estranged, and that Will's mother seeks from her son some compensation for her disappointment in her husband. She seeks Will's attention, his sympathy, his confidence, and his emotional response. She has confided to Will about his father's sexual intimacies with a crippled woman. He feels embarrassed when his mother sometimes engages him in sexual joking, and blushes when she brags openly about how well he is doing in college. The seductive aspect of her behavior likewise comes out in her expression of regret that Will is seeing a counselor; she tells Will she's sorry he can't tell all his troubles to her.

Will is painfully aware of his inability to be aggressive in sports or in his social life. He is sure that, like his father, he will never be a good salesman. He recalls reacting with guilt when he would beat his older brother in a game. He feels that his trouble with girls is that he can't treat them rough. Instead he begins to tell them his troubles and even seeks sexual favor out of pity for his difficulties in proving his virility. Will contrasts his shy, clumsy, selfish, pity-seeking manner with the leader of his gang, whom he describes as "a real Jew"—clever, aggressive, self-assured, and geuinely interested in helping others. Other members of his gang maintain a competitive, provocative interest in sexual exploits. Will feels driven to keep up with them, but confesses to his failures and allows himself to become an object of pity and ridicule.

Will feels that, like his brother and sister, his social inferiority drives him into the company of Gentiles. "My brother and sister can't make it with Jews. My brother says Jewish girls are stuck-up and gold diggers. My sister doesn't rate with Jewish girls—they wouldn't have her." Will thinks of Gentile girls mainly as potential sex partners, and feels some shame about being seen with a Gentile date in public. On the other hand, like his brother and sister, he feels more dominant and socially adequate in the company of Gentiles. "When I go to a party with Gentiles, I'm the center of attraction. I joke and clown and I'm the life of the party. With Jews I'm just another guy. Jews are rich, they're smart, they've got nerve, they're competitive. Sometimes I actually hate Jews, and yet I like them." It is clear that Will feels he lacks the personality resources to keep his place in a competitive, upward-mobile Jewish group.

Will's sexual difficulties are aggravated by the coercive influence of his peer group, which he relies on too much as a basis for identity, whose members force Will into ventures that expose his sexual confusion. His mother's emotional attachment to Will reduces his potential for relating to a young woman in a normal way. He has reason to feel much doubt about whether he can satisfy any woman, but he feels especially intimidated by the thought of having a Jewish wife. However one may analyze Will's problem, we find him enmeshed in a troubled family situation which has made it difficult for him—as for his brother and sister— to share the life of his Jewish peers.

Bill

Bill, a graduate student of Jewish background, confines his dating to Gentile girls. Though he feels somewhat ambivalent over this practice he cannot shift away from this pattern. His mother seems very fond of Bill, but cannot express her feelings openly, perhaps because of her husband's longstanding jealousy. Bill likewise feels inhibited about expressing affection toward his mother. This gives their relationship the aura of a forbidden, secret romance. He phones her daily, ostensibly to ask what came in the mail. To his counselor Bill admits that the mail is unimportant to him, but he cannot bring himself to let his mother know that he calls just to be in touch with her. Since he does not eat home regularly, on occasions when he does have dinner with the family he will, as he leaves the table, sometimes tell his mother, "Thanks for the wonderful dinner." She replies shyly, "Don't thank me. I'm your mother."

Bill's mother, American-born and college-educated, is puritanical to an extreme with regard to Bill, although she is openly romantic toward her husband. Bill once placed on his desk at

home two note pads with "pin-up girl" covers. Later he noticed
that the covers had been torn off, apparently by his mother while
she was cleaning his room. At a time when he was officially engaged to Agnes, Bill brought to his room a book on sex in marriage. After his mother had cleaned his room, the book was
missing. Bill didn't want to ask mother about it, (a diffidence
which is in itself a commentary on their relationship) but a
week later Bill found it buried in a stack of old books deep inside
his closet.

Bill recalls that he once overheard his mother talking over the
phone about her children. During the conversation she said, "Yes,
of course Bill has always been my favorite," When she later
realized that Bill had overheard her, she responded with extreme
embarrassment.

Seymour

Jerome Singer presents the case of a Jewish young man in
whose life history a "seductive mother" and a passive father are
important features. The patient entered psychotherapy at age
twenty-three: "At the time of his first interview, Seymour was
dressed in a most untidy fashion, was unkempt and unshaven,
and his finger nails were bitten down to raw skin. . . . Tall, extremely thin, with black hair and a sallow complexion . . . rather
handsome, [he] possessed a certain dignity in his mien even in
his obviously depressed state. His reasons for coming were expressed in an extremely halting manner characterized by painful
blocking in speech: 'I feel I've had a kind of breakdown. . . . I
can't move. I don't seem to be able to do anything and I've messed
up everything I've tried to do in the past. I've been married for
six months and it seems like six years. I feel overwhelmed by my
wife, by school, by life in general. I've thought of suicide, of a
mental hospital. I feel myself to be a terrible failure.' "[60]

Mrs. C, Seymour's mother, was the daughter of a rabbi who
assuaged his disappointment over having no sons of his own
"by demanding an unusual degree of Hebrew scholarship from
his [three] daughters," though they did not secure a higher
education. The eldest daughter, Mrs. C. felt under pressure to
marry when her two younger sisters seemed ready to marry

promising sons of families prominent in their father's congregation. She chose to marry a "relatively uneducated . . . but extremely hard working and successful" businessman. Mrs. C. "quickly became disenchanted with the possibilities of a rapid transformation of her husband into a man somewhat in the image of her scholarly father. Her frustration was aggravated by the persisting competition with her sisters."[61] Mrs. C. chose her brother-in-law Arnold, a successful and politically potent lawyer, as a model for Seymour, who "from his earliest years heard endless tales of how Uncle Arnold would or could do this for one, or that one must behave in a certain way to impress him." Seymour was moreover spurred on to excel his cousin, Uncle Arnold's son, in intellectual achievement.[62]

"Seymour's earliest and most frequent memories involved a constant repetitive emphasis from his mother on his speaking properly, memorizing poetry and elocutions, and performing before intimate circles. He recalls constant closeness with his mother who spent long hours with him attempting to teach him recitations, caring for his physical needs devotedly, but attacking him in scathing terms if he seemed reluctant to continue his memory efforts. The endless references to Uncle Arnold and Cousin Monroe which were dinned into his ears served to develop in him a strong competitiveness and a need to show off but at the same time must have aroused a deep sense of futility for he recalls telling his mother at the age of eleven, 'Don't count so on me—I don't think I'll be able to live up to your hopes.' His mother wept when he said this, he recalls, but she continued her efforts."[63]

Seymour was enrolled in elocution classes, a children's theatrical troupe, and in various music courses. In adolescence he was forced "to take evening classes in business practices, typing, bookkeeping, public speaking, accordion playing, and a large number of other self-improvement programs. His mother took Seymour visiting with her on many occasions and often went away over weekends or for longer vacation periods with him, leaving her husband behind. Her emphasis was constantly on the boy's performing before friends and family, preparing him beforehand for each encounter in a tense briefing, and boasting afterward about his latest accomplishment."[64]

"Seymour's conscious reaction to this situation was one of acceptance. This was the way things were—[his mother] meant only the best even if she did act silly about it sometimes. He tried his best in all the courses,"[65] though he was a mediocre student at school. "His grades were fair and he was never in difficulties but his enthusiasm waned quickly and he could not concentrate well."[66]

Seymour's father apparently "felt honored and happy" that an uneducated person like himself could have an intelligent wife with a fine family background. In his view, "if he worked long hours at his laundry and dry-cleaning business, his reward would be an opportunity to relax quietly at home, go to sleep early, and perhaps play some soccer or handball on Sunday morning."[67]

Seymour's feeling of failure was well established when at age fifteen he developed pneumonia and "spent a spring and summer practically bedridden. During this time, Seymour developed an even greater intimacy with his mother. . . . She had made him her confidant since childhood but now long intimate conversations took place daily. This unusual closeness unquestionably aroused difficult conflicts for the boy who felt all the more that gratification and attention would come from a woman if one were helpless and passive but that a great obligation for intellectual understanding and responsibility was a concomitant of this pattern. Upsetting incestuous tendencies were also fostered. Seymour, whose sexual development was just getting under way at that time, was shocked by several sexual dreams in which his mother appeared as a seductive yet threatening figure."[68]

After his illness, Seymour spent two years with distant relatives out West, where he attended his second and third year of high school, a furlough from home which "proved in many ways an extremely valuable and strengthening experience, restoring to him his sense of independent worth."[69] He was popular with the girls, active in school activities, and improved his physical health. With his return to his home in New York came "a deep feeling of despondency which he could not shake off for months. He felt a great sense of weariness and obligation to prove his success to his mother but found himself losing interest in school work with poor grades as a result. Again he felt that he had 'failed the family' and that his 'glory' was past."[70]

While attending a local college, "an attractive buxom girl slightly older than Seymour made obvious overtures to him. He was deeply flattered since she was popular and for the remaining years at college they were inseparable although he occasionally rebelled in a passively aggressive manner to her demands on his time. Seymour worked better at his school work and impressed Shirley with his productivity and the variety of his intellectual accomplishments."

"Shortly after his graduation they were married. . . . Seymour's family was pleased with the match. . . . Shirley's father was a dentist with a large practice and her mother was a well-known music teacher. . . . [When Seymour subsequently entered law school his] distress became more severe. The new responsibility of marriage put Seymour under more pressure to do well at school and also to prove himself sexually . . . [Shirley's] competence as a housekeeper and in her work became for him a constant source of distress in view of his competitiveness and self-doubt. . . . Occasionally he discussed some point in his [law] tests and found to his dismay that Shirley sometimes offered a more adequate interpretation. This drove Seymour further within himself and he brooded bitterly over his 'engulfment' by his wife. The obsessional rumination, inability to concentrate, and speech blocking became so marked that Seymour could not keep up with his assignments . . . [and] voluntarily withdrew from school."[71]

To his therapist "Seymour expressed fears concerning his sexual potency and capacity for sexual relations. Although this fear was not confirmed in his actual sexual behavior since he reported frequent and mutually satisfactory intercourse with his wife, Seymour felt under constant pressure to maintain a high level of frequency, to keep erections for extremely long periods, and to provide his wife with many more orgasms than himself. He kept track of frequency and became anxious about 'maintaining a high average.' The few instances of *ejaculatio praecox* or of temporary impotence were magnified as catastrophic proof of his ineptness with subsequent resentment of his wife whose very presence imposed a demand for performance on him despite her denial that this was her intention."[72]

In contrast to his real life, and the competent, intelligent wife toward whom he felt overwhelmingly competitive, Seymour maintained an "extensive fantasy life" in which he played the role of a soldier of fortune roving through Indonesia, Burma or India, unmarried but with "a native woman, attractive and sensual . . . always available to him."[73]

Other factors underlying the seductive attitude. Like the foregoing cases, the Levinsons' case histories also suggest that something more than unalloyed maternal affection goes into the "unusually close relationship" that creates a need for an "exotic woman." Something more like a deeply ambivalent relationship is called for—a mother who is *both* nurturant and tyrannical, lavishly indulgent and overcontrolling, affectionate but also insatiably hungry for affection. A woman who has rejected her husband is likely to displace her hunger for affection onto her son. Likewise the mother who is widowed or separated may give her son not only a full quota of maternal affection but something akin to wifely adoration and flirtation as well.

Thus the mother who has been cut off from a normal married life is likely to introduce a seductive contamination into her relationship with her son. The result is an emotionally charged, affection-laden but conflict-ridden relationship that is both cherished and avoided—for it has about it the uncanny aura of "something forbidden." The gradual withdrawal of affection, which is a normal part of growing up, carries with it the threat of uncovering the hostile aspect of this ambivalence. The son may feel unaccountably guilty about the shift of his affectionate interest from his mother to girls of his generation.

The amount of affection a mother directs toward her son is not altogether determined by "contaminations" of the family situation; to some extent it is probably influenced by the number, sex, and birth order of other children. An only child is more likely to be "spoiled." The findings of Sears, Maccoby, and Levin indicate that if a son is born after the parents have had one or several daughters, he is likely to receive a greater amount of maternal affection.[74] (Does this account for the Levinsons' observation on the prevalence of cross-sex siblings in the families of Jews who intermarry?)

Whatever its basis, a "seductive relationship" with his mother heightens the young man's unconscious anxiety over violating the incest taboo. Gordon quotes a psychoanalyst's judgment that "it is almost inevitable" that a Jewish boy who has grown up with a seductive mother "will go out with non-Jewish girls, and ultimately marry such a girl. A Jewish girl would make him think of his mother . . . [and it is her hold upon him] that he must break." Gordon's psychiatrist informant adds:

> When there is an unusually close rationship between father and daughter or mother and son, the likelihood is that they will either not marry or that they will marry someone outside of their group in order to escape from an incestuous situation.[75]

It is not easy for a young man to choose between a marriage which is socially approved but seems to inhibit his potency, and one which promises to unfetter his virility but disturbs the security of his group membership. In a matricentric society open conflict with mother may carry an especially intolerable threat. If mother speaks for the extended family, the threat of her withdrawal of love may be perceived as a threat of ostracism from the extended family as a whole.

The resolution of this problem depends on a subtle and complex interplay of forces, a topic which John Mayer has subjected to close analysis in his study of *Jewish-Gentile Courtship*. Mayer's observations are limited, of course, to cases in which the resolution of the conflict led to cross-ethnic marriage, since he selected his cases from intermarried couples.

The incest dream and its significance. The "lure of the exotic" is the promise of relief from guilt that a "civilized" man feels about making love to a woman of his own class. He feels burdened by this guilt because he has learned the incest taboo "too well." This formulation leads directly to Freud's significant statement about the attitude change which is required for the alleviation of sexual inhibition or impotence:

> It has an ugly sound and a paradoxical as well, but nevertheless it must be said that whoever is to be really free and happy in love must have overcome his deference for women and come to terms with the idea of incest with mother and sister [for there lies the origin of his feeling that the sexual act is]

something degrading, which soils and contaminates not only
the body.[76]

One is tempted to ask whether this is what the rabbis meant
by a mysterious statement which appears in the Talmud, that a
dream of incest with mother or sister "opens the way to wisdom."[77] Perhaps the rabbis meant that if a man's spirit is free
enough to *dream* of incest, then he is free enough in his waking
life to know the full measure of his potency as a husband and
lover.

How is sex experience related to wisdom or knowledge? Certainly it represents a special and intimate aspect of how well
lovers come to know each other. Only one who has experienced
the full charge of his sexual potency or responsiveness "knows
himself" in this special way. Beyond that, we can speculate on
the spiritual aspects of sex as they are described in rabbinical
writings. From sexual joy, said the rabbis, comes that mystical
knowledge of completion and harmony, of the union of matter
and spirit, God and man, finite and infinite. The Divine Spirit
dwells in him who can rejoice in sexual union, because the
Creator is one and he can only dwell "in him who is likewise
one." In this context, Jews find no difficulty in accepting Freud's
"genitality" concept of emotional maturity, nor in accepting
the fact that the Hebrew word for sexual union and for knowledge (*da'ath*) are one and the same.

13

Paths to Intermarriage — Additional Psychological Clues

Our study of intermarriage has differed from the more familiar sociological approach, which describes the various social factors (e.g., mobility, urbanization, propinquity) that raise or lower barriers to intermarriage, and assembles statistics on intermarriage rates at various times and in various places. We have used such data as a background for our study, but have placed our emphasis upon those habits, attitudes, and strivings of the individual which may have some bearing on his tendency to seek a cross-ethnic marriage partner. We have looked upon the family and cultural settings as learning situations, and have tried to identify—or frame hypotheses about—variations in the individual's social experience which influence his attitude toward intermarriage.

The focus of our analysis has been on the inner life of the individual, and in this chapter we shall discuss a variety of psychological concepts which probe further into behevioral tendencies which are somehow related to intermarriage. Somewhat arbitrarily we shall classify the following discussions according to whether the concept stems primarily from clinical, experimental, or social psychology. In each case we shall define the concept and demonstrate its relationship to intermarriage behavior.

CLUES FROM CLINICAL PSYCHOLOGY

Unconscious motivation. "Intermarriage . . . is often reluctantly entered into because circumstances brought together two young people whose love for each other developed before either was fully aware of what was happening."[1] "Many marriages can probably be traced back to the fact that certain premarital meetings 'just happened.'"[2]

"I came to this country alone and went to a town in Indiana. There were very few Jews there. . . . I felt lost, and went through a severe psychological crisis. My old ideas were turned topsy-turvy and I couldn't find myself."[3]

The layman may say "Anything can happen." The poet and mystic may rhapsodize over the unpredictability of life. The sociologist may be satisfied to regard a person's decision as the outcome of social forces more or less randomly applied over the entire population. But the psychoanalytically oriented observer is committed to look for inner purpose and planning in even the most casual and trivial everyday acts. From this point of view, set forth in Freud's *Psychopathology of Everyday Life,* entering into a marriage partnership is the result of a long series of choices and decisions. The choice of high school friends and clubs, choice of college, choice of living quarters, choice of clubs and cliques and dating partners, the choice of occupation and place of work; each of these moves—and more—enables the person to systematically direct himself toward marriage or away from marriage, toward endogamy or toward exogamy.

What then of *Ezra* (case presented in Chapter 2), who migrated from his Jewish village in Russia to settle in a small town in Indiana where he was "forced" to mingle with the out-group? One might suppose that he made a choice between the Hoosier town and the many urban centers where he would have had no difficulty in finding Jewish companionship. One is led to suppose that his choice of the Indiana town was an early manifestation of the identity crisis which to him seemed to be evoked by his new surroundings and strange friends.

What of *Vivian* (case presented in Chapter 2), who "happens" to fall in love with a Catholic boy at the time when she is in severe conflict with her parents? And in the course of psychotherapy, as she is better able to recognize and cope with her hurt and resentful feelings toward her parents, she "happens" to find a suitable Jewish boy who "happens not to look Jewish" at all. Here again we see at work the individual's capacity for selection of a love object, and the exercise of choices guided by the person's present needs and strivings. A rich and heterogeneous environment offers a wide range of choices; a barren or restricted environment may well be one in which the person has placed himself as an inadvertent act of choice.

The classic "accident" of pregnancy, which from a common sense point of view seems to "force" people into marriage as the only honorable course open to them, deserves to be re-examined from the psychoanalytic point of view. Severe and prolonged conflict over a marriage choice, the shame, guilt, and confusion over repeated vacillation, the burden of responsibility for making a free and deliberate choice which would offend or hurt one's parents; from such a tension-ridden "freedom" a person might deeply wish to escape, and let the decision be rendered for him by an "accident." The following two cases will serve as illustrations.

Gloria

An attractive, intelligent young woman in her early twenties, Gloria was working as a laboratory aide in a hospital where she met and fell in love with Ralph, a part-time employee who was a pre-medical student. They enjoyed each other's company and Gloria encouraged Ralph, who sometimes seemed too easy-going for pre-medical studies, to take his school work more seriously. She saw Ralph as occupying a much higher social position than hers. She doubted whether he would ever consider her a worthy partner for marriage. His parents were college graduates; hers were unskilled workers. Moreover, she was deeply worried that she had complicated her relationship with Ralph when she gave in to his sexual advances. Ralph would react with panic and resentment whenever Gloria would express worry over a delay in her menstrual period. She felt caught in a dilemma: she would hurt (and perhaps lose) Ralph if she said *no* to sexual intercourse, and she would hurt him if they continued.

A counseling interview revealed the following item of family history: both Gloria's older sister and their mother as well were pregnant at the time of marriage. While Gloria consciously worried and fretted about avoiding pregnancy, below the surface lurked the feeling that this would *have* to happen to her. In the safety of the counseling interview Gloria could also recognize and express her deep maternal feelings: "Of course it would be wonderful to have a baby. . . . Yes I would *love* to have a baby." (By coincidence, Gloria's appointment was cancelled one week and she learned that this interruption was occasioned by the fact that the counselor's wife had had a baby. At the next interview, as Gloria asked the counselor about the new arrival, she blushed and breathed the word "baby" with indescribable tenderness.)

Reflecting more openly on her feelings about Ralph, about pregnancy and motherhood, Gloria recognized that Ralph was indeed unprepared for fatherhood, and that they would get along better if they did not engage in sexual intimacy. She continued to see the counselor for a few weeks longer. Gloria reported that Ralph accepted her decision, their relationship now seemed more relaxed and Ralph was talking about introducing Gloria to his parents.

Gina

A talented pianist and music student, Gina was the younger of two sisters, in a middle class urban family. Her engagement to an industrial design student, Myron, was strongly opposed by Gina's mother, with whom Gina maintained a highly competitive and ambivalent relationship. Mother objected to Myron's "undependability": he had dropped out of college twice, though he was now enrolled and—like Gina—ready to enter his third year of studies. From Gina's point of view, Myron had dropped out to get practical work experience in industrial design and had used this time to good advantage. Mother's real objection, Gina was convinced, was that Myron's parents were lower-class immigrants, and that Myron himself lacked a certain social refinement.

Since they were both living on campus and spending much time together, Gina and Myron wanted to get married but Gina found it difficult to overcome the violent and unreasonable opposition of her mother. (Gina's older sister had married a successful lawyer and it seemed that Mother wanted Gina to find a husband of equally high status.) Gina found herself in a chronic state of tension which was further aggravated by anxiety over pregnancy. She knew that anxiety would upset her menstrual cycle, and the implication of an overdue period made her increasingly anxious. She and Myron were having intercourse "every so often." They were using no contraceptives although neither of them had religious objections to their use. Securing contraceptives would however mean that they were deliberately planning to have sexual intercourse, Gina reluctantly admitted, and they preferred to regard these moments of intimacy as uncontrollable flights into passion rather than as foreseeable and recurring experiences.

Gina admitted that pregnancy would indeed be a high price to pay for destroying her mother's opposition to their marriage (and shaming her as well). After discussing the hardships she and Myron would face when pregnancy did occur, and the cost of putting aside their plans to finish college, Gina reported to the counselor that she and Myron had finally decided to set a wedding date, her mother's opposition notwithstanding. They now more openly discussed with each other and accepted responsibility for more prudent management of their intimate life.

Denial as a mechanism of defense. A person who is deeply ambivalent over marrying a cross-ethnic partner finds himself in an intolerable state of tension. If the opposing forces are very strong and also very well counterbalanced, the person may find himself in a seemingly insoluble dilemma. He feels loyal to his group, and at the same time loyal to a marriage partner which his group disqualifies. He feels guilty about distressing his parents, and at the same time ashamed to give in to them. He feels physically attracted but socially threatened. Since motivations are influenced by the perceptual field, when he is in the company of his "forbidden" partner he is sure he has decided to overcome his resistances and get married. But when he faces his old group he begins to question his judgment and favor the other side of the argument. Such tension and vacillation makes the person feel weak-willed and confused. His self-esteem suffers, i.e., his vacillation is an insult to his ego, and the ego seeks a way out.

In such a situation a person is likely to discover his capacity for *denial*. As Anna Freud points out, every child is taught the stratagem of *denial*. "Much of the pleasure which adults give to children is derived from this kind of denial of reality. It is quite common to tell even a small child 'what a big boy' he is and to declare, contrary to the obvious facts, that he is as strong 'as Father,' as clever 'as Mother,' as brave 'as a soldier' or as 'tough' as his 'big brother.' It is more natural that, when people want to comfort a child, they resort to these reversals of real facts. The grown-ups assure him, when he has hurt himself, that he is 'better now' or that some food which he loathes 'isn't a bit nasty' or, when he is distressed because somebody has gone away, we tell him that he or she will be 'back soon.' "[4] The child learns to enjoy playing in a fantasy world in which reality can be denied and transformed, but he must also learn to keep his fantasies "within well-defined limits," so as to satisfy the demands of adult authority. ("A child who has just been a horse or an elephant, going about on all fours, neighing or trumpeting, must be prepared at a moment's notice to take his place at table and be quiet and well-behaved."[5] He also comes to value his "capacity to recognize and to test critically the reality of objects," and to this extent the denial of reality is inconsistent with a highly prized function of the ego.[6] (A person ordinarily defines his capacity for reality-testing as "sanity." If someone was sure that he saw something, or heard something, and later has reason to doubt it, he asks himself *"Was* it there a moment ago, or am I going crazy?")

Denial can therefore be used only sparingly by a normal adult. He cannot deny an observable or well-remembered fact without insulting his own intelligence, memory, and judgment. One cannot escape from his ambivalence by telling himself that his "forbidden" partner does not exist or that they have *not* been going steady for the past three months. He cannot assuage the insult to his conscience by so grossly insulting his sense of reality. Perhaps he would be willing to accept a small insult to his ego if it would give him relief from his state of tension. Such a "bargain" might be secured if he merely denied his intentions, for intentions are intangible; intentions are not directly observable, though they may be readily inferred from observable facts. Thus a friend may inquire, "Jack, you've been seeing Nancy every night for the past three months; have you set a wedding date?" Jack replies, "I have no intentions of marrying her. Nothing will come of it. Yes, I'm interested in her, but not involved." Jack does not deny that he has been seeing Nancy, nor does he promise to stop seeing her; he merely denies (to himself as well as to others) that he intends to marry this "forbidden" partner.

Mayer was surprised to discover that this is substantially what a number of his respondents had been doing for a period of months prior to their marriage: going steady but denying to themselves and to each other that they intended to get married:

"[Protestant husband]: For the first six or eight months I enjoyed going out with her, but had no serious intentions of getting seriously involved. . . . I was really kind of a snob. When I was first dating her, I felt I couldn't get interested in a girl without a college education or a Jew."[7]

"[Catholic husband]: About a month after we met, we went steady and we liked each other a lot . . . but I didn't think it would become serious. At the time, I didn't know this would happen. At the time, I was just going out and enjoying myself."[8]

"[Jewish husband]: . . . The matter of religion came up between the two of us. We never imagined that we would be married."[9]

"[Jewish husband]: I thought it was possible, but I did not seriously think it could happen. I had been going with Gentile girls, and I was aware that it could happen, but I felt that *I would not let it happen to me.*"[10]

"[Catholic wife]: From the beginning, he said he would never marry me, so relax and forget that angle."[11]

"[Unidentified] exogamous partner: We were not a big romance—we just drifted together as we got to know each other."[12]

Mayer described one Jewish husband who "did not seem to have any expectations whatsoever as to where his affair might

lead: 'I never had any thoughts about marriage. I'm quite serious—I never gave the matter any thought. As far as marriage was
concerned, I felt it was inevitable, like certain other things. I
felt that it was best just not to bother pondering about things
like this. . . . One day I just found myself trapped."[13]

Mayer was amazed at the prevalence of statements expressing
this attitude, "particularly since they were spontaneous and not
in response to specific questions we had posed."[14] He found it
"curious" that normal adults could be so "myopic," so "completely present-oriented";[15] that "they felt the relationship would
remain stationary. . . ."[16] From a clinical point of view we would
regard these statements as expressions of denial.[17]

We have referred to denial of intentions as a "small insult."
Let us try to define what the person pays for this stratagem, and
what it leads to. Society renders a negative judgment against a
person who drifts aimlessly into marriage, who lets himself be
"trapped into a marriage" about which he "hadn't given any
thought." Myopia is after all considered a defect, not a matter of
style or taste. In everyday language, the "present-oriented" person is likely to be addressed: "How innocent can you get; don't
you know what happens when you go steady with a girl for six
months?"[18]

As Mayer observed, despite their denial of any intentions to
marry, as a couple continues to see each other they get to know
each other better and become more deeply attached to each other.
They also "become increasingly cut off from other prospective
marital partners," and thus "become more dependent upon each
other."[19] Friends and family come increasingly to tolerate and
accept the fate which the partner himself has been loathe to
recognize. Instead of making a decision before an unfriendly
society, the person lets society establish its consensus, and then
needs only to conform to the expectations of others: "Everybody
says we're going to get married, so we might as well go ahead and
do it."

CLUES FROM EXPERIMENTAL PSYCHOLOGY

Our major use of experimental evidence and concepts was
made in Chapter 6, in our analysis of incest-taboo learning and

its by-products. Here we shall discuss some further contributions of experimental psychology to understanding intermarriage behavior.

The resolution of ambivalence through stimulus change. Either overweening affection or hostile distance between mother and son is easier to cope with than a conflicting mixture of love *and* hate. Ambivalence is the psychoanalytic term for such an internalized conflict—and describes a mother-son relationship in which the positive influences of closeness, indulgence, pampering, and "seduction" are contaminated by the negative influence of oppressive overcontrol, and the reaction of incest-horror. An ambivalent object is particularly frustrating because one feels at the same moment both attracted and repelled. The ambivalent object repeatedly evokes approach responses, vacillation, and retreat.

In the animal laboratory of Yale University, Miller and Kaeling demonstrated quite dramatically how ambivalence can be induced, and how it can be overcome through changing the stimulus-qualities of the object. Hungry albino rats were trained to run an alley maze, and at the goal box they were *both* rewarded and punished. Later they were tested in the same alley and in two unequally different alleys. When returned to the original maze, the rats hesitated to approach the goal. The more dissimilar the maze, the less the old conflict was reinstated, the more easily the organism was able to cast off his old inhibitions and direct his energies toward reaching the goal![20]

The resolution of ambivalence through stimulus-change bears a certain resemblance to the "contrast choice" phenomenon described by the Levinsons, who concluded from their interview and projective materials that the exogamous choice was in many instances guided by the man's wish to find a wife who differed from his mother with respect to traits (possessiveness, overprotectiveness, nervousness) which undoubtedly aroused much ambivalence.

In a wide variety of life situations, persons who feel burdened with ambivalence often seek relief through stimulus-change: a new job, travel, new surroundings, a new routine, new friends. It is as if they attach their hopes to the expectation that the new situations will be similar enough to afford the familiar satisfactions, but dissimilar enough to overcome the old ambivalences. H. S. Sullivan somewhere speculated that the Englishman's fondness for travel stemmed from the fact that he had to leave the British Isles to feel some relief from the effects of a repressive upbringing.

Fear of failure and the psychology of risk-taking. Statistics show that mixed marriages are more likely to end in divorce, separation, or desertion than endogamous marriages. This fact lends itself to the common sense inference that mixed marriages are burdened by unusual, unexpected, and severe difficulties which result in a high rate of failure. It is just possible, however, that some persons are "divorce-prone" in the same sense that others are "accident-prone," and that the divorce-prone person tends to involve himself in a poor-risk marriage.

The theoretical basis for the above speculation stems from the work of McClelland and Atkinson on fear of failure and risk-taking behavior. Under laboratory conditions, McClelland observed 58 young children (a) playing competitive games and (b) playing at games of skill (e.g., ring-toss) in which they were asked to forecast the results of their next trial. In the competitive games they were free to take consistently minimal, moderate, or wild risks. In the individual games of skill they were free to make unduly low, judicious, or wildly optimistic forecasts. Through the use of an independent measure of achievement motivation, the conclusion emerged that children who anticipate success tend to make judicious forecasts and take moderate risks, while poor forecasts and foolish risks—extremely low or recklessly high—tend to be made by persons who may be presumed to be burdened by fear of failure.

The timid player transparently reveals his fear of failure, but how to interpret the tactic of taking wild risks? Here we are reminded of Alfred Adler's insight that "laziness is a sign of ambition joined with discouragement." Perhaps wild risk-taking and unrealistically high forecasts of future achievement reduce the sting of failure, for the person can at least "give himself credit" for a bold try or an optimistic attitude. (Another interpretation of these results would hold that the failure-prone player is simply not motivated to make the careful discriminations, judgments, and controlled skill responses which are neces-

sary in order to achieve success. Since he is sure he will lose anyway, he plays the game carelessly or childishly.)

It is a popular idea that young people imagine what their
future marriage partner will be like. Undoubtedly they also carry
around with them a conception of what kind of marriage partner they themselves will make. How good a husband will I be?
How good a wife will I be? These are questions which we may
assume that every young person has asked and answered; his
adequacy as a marriage partner becomes part of his self-image.
The McClelland-Atkinson formulation would suggest that a
person who is fearful of failure in the marriage role would tend
(if he marries) to make either an extremely low-risk or a high-
risk choice. Perhaps a low-risk choice would be represented by
the man who marries a physically handicapped woman, or a
woman who marries an older man. A high-risk choice would
allow for a wide range of examples, but a cross-ethnic partner
would certainly qualify as one such example.

Cognitive dissonance. Facing the prospects of a cross-ethnic
marriage brings the person into emotional conflict with himself,
his primary group, and perhaps in disagreement with some members of the dominant group. Argument clashes with argument,
facts are contradicted by opposing facts, there appear to be excellent reasons on both sides, and the result is what Festinger has
labelled cognitive dissonance. In everyday language we would
say that when facts do not guide the person toward a reasonable
conclusion but instead pull him in opposite directions, the person is overwhelmed by feelings of confusion. Our inner security
depends too much on maintaining a good sense of reality, as we
noted in discussing the functions of the ego. We have learned
to use facts as a guide to action. Festinger has produced a series
of provocative experiments which demonstrates that when a
person is confronted by facts which contradict judgments he has
formed on the basis of prior facts, he tends to reappraise his past
experience, to alter or reorganize his judgments in a way that
reduces the "dissonance" of fact jarring against fact.

Likewise one prepares himself to resolve a conflict over an
exogamous choice—either carry it out or withdraw from it—by
restructuring or reorganizing his memories, judgments, and perceptions in a way that will fit his decision. Stonequist cites the

case of a Jewish college girl (whom we shall call *Marian*) who found herself "through incidental contacts . . . in love with a Gentile:"

Marian

"There was complete turmoil. I could not bring him home, had to lie when I saw him, listen to my parents' recriminations and . . . threats to completely disown me. I found myself poisoned and suspicious; I found that I hated the thought of having a child who might be big and blond and blue-eyed and phlegmatic and mechanically minded and slow. I could not have a Gentile child . . . and our romance ended. . . ."[21]

Falling in love with a Gentile had forced Marian to violate her standards of honesty ("I had to lie when I saw him") and threw her into intolerable conflict with her family ("I had . . . to listen to my parents' recriminations and horrible suggestions, and threats to completely disown me"). It didn't make sense to her that what she experienced as the joy of love she must simultaneously experience, through identification with her parents, as loathesome and contemptible. She extricated herself from this cognitive mix-up by shifting her attention to the thought of having a child who was stigmatized by every undesirable "Gentile" trait ("phlegmatic and mechanically minded and slow") and this thought made even the more desirable traits ("big and blond and blue-eyed") seem revolting, and she now found it possible to withdraw from her Gentile love object.

If, on the other hand, the play of psychological forces leads the person to decide in favor of intermarriage, subtle reorganization of his memory undoubtedly takes place to help resolve the conflicts and confusions generated by the crisis situation. Now Andrew remembers a bit more clearly the dissatisfaction he felt over his religious upbringing and feels glad his children's religious training will be different. Now Carlotta realizes that she wasn't really satisfied with Catholicism, though during her courtship with Abram "she was a very religious person [and] attended church every Sunday."[22]

Dissonance-resolution versus rationalization. Is this concept of "cognitive reorganization" any better than the more familiar

concept of "rationalization?" Perhaps it is, if cognitive reorganization reckons more explicitly with the fact that there are various
ways in which the same set of cognitions (perceptions, memories,
judgments) can be organized, and each way takes reality factors
more or less equally well into account. The concept of rationalization implies a shift from a painful-though-true perception of
reality, to a comfortable-but-distorted perception. The concept
of cognitive dissonance suggests that our memories and perceptions make up a jig-saw puzzle which, because certain pieces are
faded or shrunken or missing, can be put together equally well
in various ways (always leaving a number of pieces left over).
Under certain motivating conditions, the person shifts, so to
speak, from one set of rationalizations to another.

Once the person has firmly made his decision he not only feels
a sense of relief, he also feels a growing sense of "insight"; now
he understands how he feels, why he feels this way, and what his
social world is really like.

Festinger's theory of cognitive dissonance, first published in
1957, was anticipated by Krech and Crutchfield in a statement
that antedates Festinger by nine years:

"Since tensions are the product of the structure of the psychological field, including cognitive structures, it is evident that
tensions may also be reduced by appropriate cognitive restructuring. It may be assumed that—other things being equal—the
existence of frustration will tend spontaneously to lead to cognitive changes which help to reduce tension."[23]

"The meaning of the phenomenon of 'rationalization' has
been much misunderstood. It has commonly been regarded as
evidence for man's irrationality, whereas in truth it should rather
be taken as evidence of just the opposite. . . . The existence of
rationalization is one of the clearest demonstrations of the need
for and striving after the only kind of logic that is available to
the individual—the logic of his own psychological world."[24]

An early forerunner of this viewpoint was, in turn, Alfred
Adler, who in the first decade of the century observed how memory serves the present needs and values of the person.[25] In surveys which compare the early recollections of home life and upbringing of persons who intermarry and those who do not (e.g.,

Heiss), results are biased to an unknown degree by this tendency for recollections to align themselves with the person's *present* attitudes and values.[26]

Cognitive dissonance, minimal verbal reinforcement, and the counseling process. A person who seeks counseling at a time when he is in conflict over whether to enter into a cross-ethnic marriage is without question looking for *more* than an opportunity to ventilate his feelings. He is looking for a point of view, a sense of identity around which he can find his place in society. He is, in other words, seeking an opportunity to re-examine, clarify, sort out, and restructure his judgments and beliefs concerning the nature of society and his place in it. Perhaps we could say that the client is motivated to seek counseling because of the psychological discomfort generated by cognitive dissonance, and that he seeks the counselor's help in restructuring his cognitive world to replace a measure of anxiety-inducing dissonance with a degree of inner harmony.

Counseling theory, however, has little to say about directly helping a person evolve a mature and realistic point of view, a more adequate sense of identity. These are cognitive phenomena, and counselors have long been committed to the principle that the therapeutic interview must focus consistently upon the *feeling tone* of the client's verbalizations: uncovering, clarifying, and re-experiencing his feelings toward important persons and toward his own impulses. Counseling theory holds that when the person is no longer burdened by anxiety, guilt, and hostility he can then exercise his own capacity for working out his way of life. This formula calls for a degree of "middle-aged patience" that the younger client may simply not have at his command.

The disagreement between what the client seeks and how the counselor is prepared to participate in the therapeutic interview can lead at times to unexpected or unwanted results. Perhaps the client gives up prematurely and the counselor concludes that the client was "not ready for therapy." Perhaps the client adapts to the counselor's unwillingness to deal directly with values and viewpoints, by responding instead to the counselor's "silent language"—the values and viewpoints which are implied in the counselor's gestures, by his ebb and flow of interest as the client shifts from one subject to another, and by the counselor's silent expressions of approval, satisfaction, disappointment, or doubt.

Georgene Seward holds that the therapist's ethnic group loyalties do indeed influence the counseling process. If, for example, the therapist is a Reform Jew he "may unconsciously project his own conflicts about Judaism onto an Orthodox client and so fail to pick up significant clues in treatment. An Orthodox therapist, on the other hand, may arouse serious resistances in a patient suffering from hostility toward his in-group."[27]

Experimental psychology has delivered an impressive array of evidence demonstrating that in an interview situation, the subject responds spontaneously to the most subtle gestures of interest and approval, to the extent that such "minimal verbal reinforcement" inadvertently but surely channels and directs the subject-matter of the interview.[28] We suppose, therefore, that the counselor's attitude toward problems raised in counseling—intermarriage, for example—somehow "gets across" to the client and, if the counseling relationship is well-established, the counselor's point of view tends to influence the client's cognitive restructuring and hence his future course of action.

When a person seeks a counselor whose occupational role clearly designates a known point of view (e.g., a Reform rabbi or a Unitarian minister), it is likely that the client wants help in incorporating the counselor's known point of view. When, however, the counselor's viewpoint is not clearly designated by his institutional ties, the client probably listens to the "silent language"[29] for one or more interviews and establishes a counseling relationship if he feels that the counselor's viewpoint represents the view toward which the client himself is groping.

As the client describes the details of his experience, his thoughts, his plans, his hopes, his fears—the counselor's responses reflect and interpolate the feeling tone of the client's discourse (e.g., "That irritated you." . . . "So you began to feel sorry for yourself." . . . "You really wanted to apologize but you were worried that she wouldn't listen"). Observing how carefully the counselor avoids interjecting his own viewpoint into the interchange, the client probably searches the "silent language" of the counselor for clues to this "forbidden knowledge"—as if to say, "I like my counselor, I respect him, and I can go along with his idea of what counseling is. But I wonder what kind of advice he would give me if he *did* give advice."[30]

CLUES FROM SOCIAL PSYCHOLOGY

Exogamy and passing. Assimilation describes the process of giving up a traditional way of life and so thoroughly adopting the language, customs, attitudes, and appearance of the dominant group that one "acquires full membership" in the dominant society. Assimilation is conceptualized as an unconscious and gradual process which may cover a transition period of several generations from immigrant to "100 per cent American." (Perhaps it better describes the cultural adaptation of certain other immigrant groups than Jews—or non-whites.)

"Passing" is a term originally applied to persons born and raised as Negroes whose physical appearance is Caucasian and who exploit this natural advantage to represent themselves as members of the white community. This concept describes the deliberate effort to escape from minority group status and infiltrate the dominant group through subterfuge. This approach to claiming the social and economic advantages of membership in the dominant group implies, of course, that the norms of the majority would deny the person access to full membership however eagerly he might be to adopt their way of life.

"For a Negro to pass socially means sociological death and rebirth. It is extremely difficult, as one loses in the process his educational standing (if he has gone to a Negro school), intimate friends, family and work preferences. . . .

"For one who is not firmly anchored in the Negro community emotionally, there is much temptation to take such a step. At first he finds that the color line . . . seems to disappear for him. . . . Then more and more difficulties begin to arise. He begins to dread meeting old Negro friends while out with new ones. There are cases where daughters have refused to speak to their mothers on the street and sons have looked the other way, when accompanied by whites, upon encountering their Negro fathers. As the new job and the new friends become of more emotional importance, the individual has a constant, haunting fear of being discovered. There is the possibility that an old Negro enemy may turn him in, or that some white person may accidentally discover him and work vengeance on him."[31] Stonequist (1937) cites from the experience of two Jews who tried to dissemble their way into the dominant group:

Dave

"Here in Chicago . . . I couldn't get a job in an office . . . because truthfully I said I was Jewish. This fact gave me quite a problem and worried me for some time. Gee! who would think that just because I was Jewish—regardless of qualifications—I was automatically excluded from society. Of course I could have gotten a job as a department store clerk or something like that, but for one who had ideals this would have been quite a setback. I plugged away in hopes of finding a job without having to lie. . . .

"I had been working all my life—and now nationality stood between me and starvation. I resolved to change my nationality and go to work—I went to another employment bureau, changed my name, nationality, etc., and got a job—right away, mind you! It was easy for me to get along as a Gentile as I had mostly Gentile habits—not having lived amongst members of my own race for any great length of time, and fortunately I looked like a German and that helped. . . . But I ran into some difficulties; some Gentile people can't stand an ambitious and hard worker and get jealous. . . . So the question was put to me: 'Dave, aren't you Jewish?' Those words at times made me inwardly mad but outwardly I displayed no change. To save my face I was obliged to deny this with my mouth, but in my heart I felt quite proud of my nationality. . ."[32]

Gregory

Through mistaken identity Gregory "found himself drawn into the comradeship of Gentiles who accepted him as one of themselves." He recounts the story of his subsequent experience in passing:

"Somehow I could not bring myself to reveal the truth about my own identity," he recalls. "I felt that they would learn sooner or later. I was too happy over being admitted into their small circle of companionship to persuade myself deliberately to ruin, as I felt I would by telling them, this short-lived satisfaction.

"I remember the day the boys learned that I was a Jew. I detected it in the atmosphere. Their attitudes, their greetings to me, their bearing in my presence seemed to undergo a perceptible change. I was still accepted as a member of the group but I felt I was on the fringe. . . . Occasionally remarks were made which were rather pointed. Toward the close of the year one of the group was pledged to a fraternity, the other two were introduced to the same fraternity by the first student—the matter was not even broached to me.

"Increasingly . . . I found myself becoming more sensitive to my racial heritage and to the 'stigma' (as I considered it) of a 'Jew.' . . . A factor that tended to increase the conflict was that the great majority of my Gentile acquaintances accepted me off-hand as one of them, never suspecting my racial identity until it was revealed to them."

As Stonequist summarizes Gregory's decision to pass: "He gave up Jewish practices . . . which were associated with an unhappy home life. . . . Gentile family life and Christianity appealed to him more and more as he came to experience them. . . . He determined to conceal his Jewish background. He joined a Christian denomination where he felt 'strangely at peace with myself and the world,' and decided to train for the Christian ministry. He entered the seminary and continued to pass as of Gentile origin. But the conflict concerning this grew deeper and deeper. . ."

Gregory began to wonder whether it was safe to continue this concealment, or whether it might be safer to divulge his secret: ". . . I was in the innermost group of the school life, an integral part of its life and activities. . . . I had been elected the President of my Senior Class; what mattered it to any one what I was born —the only thing that really mattered was what I was then; if I should tell I would be ashamed that I had not spoken sooner to those whose life secrets I had shared. . . . If it were known the world which I had found so friendly might turn on me—I had heard the boys speak slightingly of other Jews. . ."

With the encouragement of his fiancee and a sympathetic pro-

fessor, Gregory shared his secret with his closest friend. Six months
after graduation, Gregory—now established as a pastor—made
"the revelation" by letter to all his intimate friends. He was
heartened by their response. Years later "as a test to myself that
I had completely overcome [any lingering sensitivity about his
past], I preached a sermon on 'The Christian and the Jew' . . .
mentioning incidentally that the first half of my life had been
spent in a Jewish home. I speak freely on the subject now whenever I feel the occasion is appropriate. . . . I count it as part of
my responsibility wherever possible to dispel the prejudice that
is still abundantly evident. Within the last few years I have
formed several fast Jewish friendships (one rabbi among them)
who have helped to build up my interest in the problem of the
Jew and given me a new appreciation of liberal Judaism."[33]

Gregory's expression of dread that "the world which I had
found so friendly might turn on me" closely parallels Drake
and Cayton's description of the Negro passer's "constant, haunting fear of being discovered . . . that some white person may
accidentally discover him and work vengeance on him." Gregory's
physical resemblance to the Gentile majority also parallels the
Negro passer's necessarily Caucasian appearance. It is interesting
that Gregory chose the ministry as a career; a more thoroughly
Gentile identity would be hard to imagine.[34] But the choice of
the ministry was a two-edged sword; it affiliated him intimately
with the Gentile majority but it also placed a disturbingly high
premium on personal honesty and integrity. ("Almost every one
of my daily devotions brought into relief the conflict that was
ever present in my consciousness.")[35] Exposure, if it came, would
be far more damaging to a Christian minister than to a dentist,
an engineer, or a college professor.

Successful passing into the Gentile world probably calls for a
sub-clinically psychopathic personality, at least. Not only must
the candidate accept complete separation from his old primary
group, he must be able to enjoy and return the friendliness of
persons who "might turn on him" if they knew his "secret." He
must be willing to tolerate or even participate in certain forms
of anti-Semitism which represent the norm of his adopted culture.
The psychopathic personality is not burdened by guilt because
he is not much burdened by conscience, for only a person of

strong conscience can experience real feelings of guilt. He is not introspective and does not suffer from manifest anxiety. He finds a solution to life problems by rearranging his relations with the social environment, by adjusting to its demands. He behaves like a well-adjusted person except that he may reveal a certain lack of scruples and is unable to form intimate friendships.

Perhaps a most effective tactic for passing is marriage into a family which is strongly identified with the dominant group. Undoubtedly, passing would generate a powerful motive for exogamy. "Intermarriage is the swiftest avenue to repudiation" of one's Jewish identity, observed journalist George Sokolsky.[36] (For an anecdotal commentary on the concealment of Jewish identity through intermarriage and otherwise, see Chapter 2, "Jews that Pass" in Sokolsky's *We Jews*.)

Negro population figures cited by Stonequist[37] show a significantly lower number of mulatto men than women, suggesting that men are more likely to pass out of Negro society than women. The same sex difference would probably hold true for Jews, since the male sex role designates a greater degree of independence and justifies separation from one's family and primary group.

The ethnic convert. Rabbi Rubenstein observed that to Gentile college women who seek conversion to Judaism, membership in a Jewish *community* seems to be a significant motive; adoption of the Jewish religion is somewhat less important, he implies. Perhaps it would be useful to make a distinction between the religious convert and the ethnic convert, one who seeks to become an adopted child, a naturalized citizen of a new ethnic group. Gentiles who want to live as Jews are in this regard like Jews who want to live as Gentiles, Westerners who want to live as Orientals, Negroes who want to live as whites, or whites who choose to live as Negroes.[38] Not all passing is by stealth and dissimulation; there are those who make a more open and deliberate change in their ethnic group identity. For the would-be ethnic convert, intermarriage has high instrumental value.

The ethnic convert to the Jewish group becomes the marginal member of a marginal group, the object of veiled or open hostility by those Jews who regard converts as "opportunists," "adventurers," seducers of innocent Jewish lads, a threat to Jewish survival.[39] What are the consequences of these tensions between the convert and rejecting members of the Jewish community?

We have already noted the deep disillusionment of Carlotta, to discover that although she is living an exemplary Jewish life, to some of her Hadassah friends she is not a Jew. Those rabbis and others who oppose intermarriage tell of converts who after a few years revert to their former group membership. Many converts are undoubtedly unprepared for the indefinite probationary status to which a Jewish group may assign them, and for the discovery that their spouse's family may *not* fulfill their hope for a warm and supportive circle of kinship.[40]

Some converts meet the threat of rejection by deliberately and thoroughly involving themselves in Jewish societies and Jewish community life. As one of Wessel's respondents conjectured, "Perhaps . . . they feel the need of fortifying themselves." Their position demands, in fact, that they fortify themselves against discrimination from both the Gentile community, and from parts of the Jewish community as well. Years after she first immersed herself into the life of a Jewish community, a convert may discover that she was still on trial—and a moment's lapse of judgment may cost her dearly:

Isabel

Frequently mentioned in the sisterhood notes of the bulletin of a Conservative synagogue, Isabel had made a real effort to involve herself in Jewish life—and after 20 years as a Jewish wife and mother, her Catholic background seemed to have receded far into her past. Why suddenly was her name no longer listed in the sisterhood notes? Why did Isabel suddenly drop out of sight? The story of Isabel's fall from grace goes something like this. When Isabel's mother died, a number of Isabel's close friends—ladies of the congregation—offered to accompany Isabel to the funeral home. They sat in the chapel and watched their friend approach her mother's coffin. They were horrified and dumbfounded to see Isabel kneel and make the sign of the cross! Indignantly, they stood up and marched out. How could a Jewish wife and mother do such a thing? How could they ever face her again? What was her Jewishness worth, after all?

Isabel's mother had been a devout Catholic. Was it foolish for Isabel to want to address her mother's coffin with a gesture her mother would have understood? If so, it was a very costly bit of foolishness, for it cost her much of the good will and friendship she had labored for—and placed her under a cloud of suspicion in the Jewish community she thought she had become part of.

A convert may be tempted to pass as a born-Jew rather than accept the vulnerable and ambiguous role of a convert to Judaism. Wessel describes a young woman who chose this mode of adjustment to her status as the wife of a Jew:

> A young bride, blond and Nordic in type, married to a Jew— also blond and Nordic—who has accepted Judaism and is "passing," tells the following story: "When my friends say, 'You don't look Jewish,' I say, 'Neither does my husband.' "[41]

Physique and intermarriage. As Krech and Crutchfield have stressed, the likelihood that a person will arouse racial prejudice depends upon his observable characteristics. Warner and Srole based their "assimilation timetable" on the extent to which an immigrant group resembled the old Yankee community in *physique,* as well as in habits and customs. It seems plausible that the extent to which one is identifiable as a Jew would figure significantly in the likelihood that a person encounters the kinds of social experience that may lead to intermarriage.

The autobiographies of Dave and Gregory acknowledge the significance of a non-Jewish appearance in gaining a friendly access to Gentile society. Autobiographical accounts of how one happened to become affiliated with a Gentile group often begin, "Since I did not look particularly Jewish . . ." or "Since I do not have a Jewish name . . ." A portion of an interview with an intermarried Jewish husband, quoted from Mayer's study, will serve as an additional example:

> . . . When I was growing up, I was ashamed and embarrassed about being Jewish. There was a period I thought I didn't appear very Jewish. I was proud about this. . . . (Did you feel at all hesitant about becoming involved with your wife because she was Christian?) No, no. . . . For a young boy there was a

certain amount of titillation in becoming involved with something new, compared to middle class Jews I knew. Maybe there was even vanity in it—that a non-Jew should be attracted to me. I'm sure that was part of it.[42]

Undoubtedly some Jews feel a certain ambivalence over the fact that their appearance allows them to mingle in company which would be unfriendly to a more Jewish face. Bowman tells of a cross-ethnic romance which was aborted when the Jewish suitor was "complimented" on his non-Jewish appearance:

A Gentile girl was attracted to a Jewish boy. He was a brilliant student and had an agreeable personality. To both young people it appeared that their acquaintance was growing into love and neither of them was adverse to marriage. One day, in an unguarded moment, the girl said something to this effect, 'My, but I'm glad you don't look like a Jew.' The boy was surprised and taken aback. He asked whether it made any difference in their future relationship and her attitude toward him if he did 'look like a Jew.' She said it would. At the time she was not aware of the hurt she caused; but their courtship had lost something and they finally stopped going together. The boy realized better than she what her attitude might do to their marriage.[43]

In *Remember Me to God,* as Richard feels caught in a tangle of inner conflicts, family warfare, social embarrassments, and mixups over his efforts to convert and marry a high-status Protestant girl, he looks into his fiancée's somber eyes and says he wishes he had been born "with a real hook-nose type of a face. . . . 'I'd be better off,' he said. 'It was just my misfortune to look Gentile. If I didn't, I'd have fewer problems.' "[44] Autobiographical accounts of the conflict between asserting or denying one's Jewishness sometimes drop abruptly from a philosophical or moral level to the simple question of whether one is "hopelessly" stamped with the physique of Jewishness:

Eddie

"I possess unmistakable physical characteristics of the Jew. I have the round Jewish nose that you often see depicted in the cartoons or comedies. Dark wavy hair (not curly), and [I am] comparatively short of stature. At twenty-one, now, I appear almost predisposed to be stout. . .

"I am very restless and impatient. . . . My aggressiveness has led me into the highest student office of a Gentile school, aided by Gentile support. I am, I feel, too sensitive. My Jewish nose [makes me feel self-conscious]. . . . In any public place I foolishly sometimes avoid standing in a profile position."[45]

Ludwig Lewisohn similarly recalls his life as a graduate student in the America he had so passionately identified with, having been raised in a Southern town, in an acculturated German Jewish family. He was brooding over the question of how much his Jewish identity stood in the way of his hopes to find "a good position" as professor of English literature, as he wandered one afternoon through the streets of New York City. ". . . A numbness held my soul and mutely I watched life, like a dream pageant float by me. . . . I ate nothing till evening when I went into a bakery and, catching sight of myself in a mirror, noted with dull objectivity my dark wavy hair, my melancholy eyes, my unmistakably Semitic nose . . . an outcast. . . . A sentence arose in my mind which I have remembered and used ever since. So long as there is discrimination there is exile."[46]

The strict physical requirements for passing are implied by experimental evidence that prejudiced persons are significantly more skillful in detecting Jewish faces in a heterogeneous group of photographs than persons holding a more benign or friendly attiture toward Jews.[47] Undoubtedly the passer is concerned not so much over getting along with the more tolerant members of the dominant group, as with escaping the vigilance of the anti-Semite. For the Jew who seeks not to pass but to attain a more pluralistic identity, his physique may determine how friendly a reception he receives in the Gentile world.

Returning to Child's ten rebel respondents, one explained that strangers never direct against him the epithets "wop" or "guinea" because thanks to his appearance "he is never taken to be an Italian."[48] When the rebels were asked, "Do you think that, on the average, fellows of Italian descent are better looking or not as good looking as fellows of other descent?" two thirds of the rebels "compared men of Italian descent unfavorably with men of other nationalities." They expressed disfavor of Italians' "dark and oily" skin, "ragged features," short and stout physique.[49] They expressed admiration for the appearance of Germans and Swedes. (In-group respondents either asserted that there was "no difference" between nationalities, or asserted "very positively that both Italian girls and Italian men are better looking than those of any other nationality.") [50]

Child interprets the rebel reaction as indicating "a genuinely hostile attitude toward the Italian group,"[51] but to some extent the rebels may simply be expressing frustration over their inability to pass as "American." This interpretation gains support from the fact that the rebels did *not* extend their depreciation to the appearance of Italian *girls*.

The lovers. The childless intermarried couple suggests what has been described as "the Hollywood conception of marriage"— that it is the culmination of a romantic attraction, and is chiefly significant as a vow of faithfulness between two lovers. According to Bossard and Boll, textbooks used in college courses in marriage and family problems tend to support the viewpoint that "you marry solely for love."[52] Kent surveyed 52 male college sophomores on the traits they wanted in their wives. The three top-ranking traits were "physical attractiveness," "intelligence," and "sexually satisfying." Ranking twelfth in frequency of mention was "good mother." "Good manager" ranked thirteenth, "good family background" ranked fifteenth in a total list of 20 traits. To those for whom "the exotic is erotic," a high priority to sexual attractiveness in the choice of a marriage partner may favor intermarriage.

Richard

In *Remember Me to God*, Richard defends his wish to marry a high-status Protestant girl by asserting his right to marry the girl with whom he happened to fall in love, and toward whom he feels an overwhelming physical attraction:

> I can't go falling in love this way or that way for the sake of some tradition I hope is going to be around a hundred years after I'm dead. My love for Wimsy is living, and blooming.

I've got to live for when I'm alive, not for after I'm dead . . .[53]

. . . Did it ever occur to you [Richard asks his disapproving father] that it might be morally wrong to treat the human race as two different sets of animals that shouldn't marry each other? That it might be wrong for me to make ancient theological disputes an excuse for bottling up the natural feeling I have to reproduce with this girl? . . . We're all of one species, you know. If your point of view is right, why weren't people naturally made so that a Jewish man's sex organs would only fit into a Jewish woman. . . . They aren't. Everybody's sex organs are all standard. Any male fits into any female. That just shows how artificial it is when you say one bunch of people shouldn't marry another bunch of people.[54]

Richard argues that it is natural and even laudable to marry the girl toward whom one feels a most impelling sexual attraction, and that it is morally wrong to let "ancient theological disputes" frustrate one's "natural feeling . . . to reproduce" with that special person. Richard's disapproving father was forced to admit that "it's hard to express in words" just what it is about intermarriage that he finds so unacceptable. Fifty years ago, Reik suggests, a Jewish father could find a better answer to his son's declaration that he wanted to marry a girl because he had fallen in love with her. As the joke was told in Vienna during Reik's boyhood, the disapproving father countered: "What do you mean, you have fallen in love with her? Are you Sonnenthal?" (Adolph von Sonnenthal, Reik explains, "was the famous actor who had the leading lovers' parts in the Vienna Burgtheater.") [55]

The power of the sex drive is not, of course, a post-Victorian discovery. To Sumner, for example, "the passionate nature of the sex appetite, by virtue of which it tends to excess and vice," fully justified the enforcement of all the Victorian taboos and regulations. Chastity, decency, propriety, and modesty were, like the incest taboo, regarded as necessary "adjustments to facts of human nature and conditions of human life."[56] Neither does it betoken a specifically Victorian attitude to deny the highest priority to sexual attractiveness in the choice of a marriage partner. From the anthropological point of view, Murdock considers it "a *serious error*" to regard sexual privilege "as the sole factor, or even as the most important one, that brings a man and woman together in marriage and binds them into the family structure. . ."[57] (Italics added.) The four functions of the nuclear family are sexual privilege, economic cooperation, reproduction and child care, and the social training of children. Since the great majority of human societies (196 of the 250 represented in the Yale Index) allow some premarital liaisons between non-relatives, "sex certainly cannot be alleged as the primary force driving people into matrimony."[58]

A high priority to sexual attractiveness in the choice of a marriage partner might be a by-product, Murdock suggests, of the fact that our culture prohibits and penalizes any sexual intercourse outside the marital relationship. A cross-ethnic marriage may promise a fuller realization of one's potential for sexual gratification in a society in which the male is asked to put all his eggs in one basket. Given social conditions which inhibit sexual feelings toward the in-group, and at the same time attach a high value to sexual fulfillment in marriage and only in marriage, psychiatrist Franzblau sees nothing "abnormal" about an intermarriage based on a "voluptuary" advantage.

From a Jewish point of view, the *Code* deems it "permissible and highly proper for one to look at the woman he is to make his wife, to see if she pleases him . . ."[59] but the primary goal of marriage is of course the establishment of a family. A culture which places strong emphasis on the responsibilities and satisfactions of the parental role *(nachas fun kinder)* must frown upon a partnership which is poorly adapted to raising a family, whatever gratification the partners can uniquely offer *each other*.

Evolution of the social norms. If a Jew who is married to a Gentile woman is chosen to serve on the Board of a synagogue, if the president of a Temple sisterhood is a convert to Judaism, these facts point to a *result* of social change that is likely to cause *further* social change. This reinforcing spiral of built-in cause and effect (variously labelled "the vicious cycle" or "the beneficent cycle" depending upon one's value judgment) is worth examining in detail as it relates to intermarriage.

Success begets success, and successful intermarriage encourages further intermarriage. Of the Levinsons' sample of five Jewish women who intermarried, four had older brothers; and of these four, three had intermarried while their younger sisters were still single. The intermarriage of an older brother signifies the presence of certain factors in the family situation which tend toward intermarriage. For the younger sister, the intermarriage of an older brother adds still another factor that tends to further reduce the barrier to intermarriage. Parents may be shocked when the eldest child intermarries, but eventually exogamy achieves the sanction of something that "runs in the family." One of Gordon's Protestant respondents, Ruth, explained her willingness to intermarry, and the basis of her parents' readiness to accept a Jewish son-in-law, from the standpoint of family precedent:

Ruth

Frankly, it never occurred to me to ask about Joe's religion. You see, there have been many intermarriages in my family. We—that is my folks—are quite accustomed to them. My paternal grandmother was Catholic and my paternal grandfather was Protestant. My mother was a Catholic (although she isn't now), and my father is a Lutheran Protestant. My mother's brother married a Jewish girl. They brought up their children as Catholics. My mother's sister married a Protestant who was converted to Catholicism. My grandmother on my mother's side was Catholic. And my father's family were all Lutherans. So, you see, we have quite a history of intermarriage in my immediate family.[60]

Another of Gordon's respondents, a Caucasian Oklahoman married to a Nisei made it a point to explain that his father's first wife was an Indian (who died and was succeeded by the respondent's mother). ". . . It was not unusual for a white man to marry an Indian as my father had done. There were lots of Indians around. There wasn't a real prejudice against them as there was toward Negroes. As for Orientals [like the respondent's Nisei wife], there were so very few in our area that we didn't have any opinions about them."[61] It is interesting that although the respondent knew very little about his father, who died when the respondent was four, yet it seemed important to him to place his own marriage choice in the context of a family tradition.

In Weidman's novel *The Enemy Camp*, George and Mary, partners in a mixed marriage, talk about moving from their city apartment to a commuting suburb. Mary, daughter of a Philadelphia Main Line family, explains: "You always know where you stand with a commuting town long before you get there, or even try to get there. In our special situation, for example, if we tried to settle in Darien, anything that happened to us, well, don't get sore, but we'd deserve it. Darien is that kind of town, and they're not only not ashamed of it, they want everybody to know how they feel, so people like us won't make the mistake of trying to settle there. In Danville [where Mary's Bennington College friend Eileen lives with her Jewish husband], however, it wouldn't happen.

". . . The main reason Milton [Eileen's husband] is happy . . . is not because of the amount of work he gets done on the train. It's because of the kind of community Danville is. It's not one of those stuffy suburban towns, full of fake Tudor houses and restricted areas. Danville is full of artists and writers and actors and advertising men, the kind of people who don't have any special feelings about Jews or religion or that kind of thing. *There are a lot of mixed marriages in Danville,* just like our and Eileen's and Milton's, and the people are all friendly and pleasant, but the main thing, Eileen says, is that there is absolutely no anti-Semitism." (Italics added.) [62]

Elsewhere in Weidman's novel, a long-time business acquaintance of George's, Nick Perrini, confides in George that he is worried about his college sophomore daughter Violetta who "wants to marry a Jewish boy."[63]

" 'He's in medical school [Perrini goes on]. Wants to be a doctor. Comes from a good family, plenty of money. That's not the point. . .' [He is worried, Perrini explains, about what will happen when Violetta gets married and] 'goes away to live with him, with all those other Jews, his family and all. Violetta doesn't know anything about Jews. You're the only Jew I know, George, that's married to a Gentile. You're the only one I can ask.'

" 'Ask what?' George said.

" 'What will it be like for my Violetta?' Nick Perrini said worriedly. 'Living with all those Jews?' "[64]

The conversation continues, but we have quoted enough to demonstrate that while Nick Perrini was worried about his daughter's plans to marry a Jew, the fact that Perrini had access to a trusted and respected long-time acquaintance who could tell him from first-hand experience something about what a mixed marriage is like, may well have spelled the difference—for the father of the bride—between a manageable anxiety and an intolerable suffering. Perhaps, with unexpected results, Perrini had even made favorable comment at home about his hardworking Jewish accountant who had a Gentile wife.

As intermarriage becomes more commonplace, those who venture into it—and their families—will have an increasingly large fund of examples to guide and support them.[65] More and better research on intermarriage will not only document what has already happened, but will influence the marriage choices of the future. For example, the Levinsons report that in the eleven nonclinical cases they investigated, although a severe crisis was sometimes precipitated when a Jewish son declared his intention to marry a Gentile girl, "the difficulty was usually short-lived and . . . often the non-Jewish wife has become the favorite daughter-in-law and has strengthened the relationship between parents and son."[66] Surely this research finding (published in a journal of the Yiddish Scientific Institute) will alleviate just enough of some young man's apprehension about his parents' discomfort to embolden him to carry out his wish to marry the girl "who happens not to be Jewish."

One can almost hear a sympathetic and gentle rabbi address himself to the distraught parents who have just pleaded with him to "save their child" from intermarriage. "I understand your feelings of distress, my friends. I remember David's bar mitzvah as if it was yesterday. The fine speech he made about being a good Jew, and I believe he even wrote part of it himself. That was how long ago, fifteen years? David is twenty-eight years old now and if he tells you that he and Margaret are in love and are going to get married, then neither you nor I can really stop them, can we? Now sit back and let me tell you something that may come as a surprise to you. Margaret has already asked me to counsel her for conversion. . . . A converted wife sometimes becomes the favorite daughter-in-law. And (would you believe it?) a sincere convert can bring her Jewish husband closer to Jewishness and *closer to his parents* than he was before he got married. Don't be too surprised, Mrs. Jacobs, if your future daughter-in-law also teaches you something about Jewishness."

14

Summary, Conclusions, Discussion

At first glance, the topic of *Jewish-Gentile* intermarriage may seem too limited in its focus, too parochial in its scope, to provide a framework for scholarly analysis. We have argued that, on the contrary, the scientific approach favors the selection of a specific and identifiable phenomenon—and that reliable knowledge about intermarriage is more likely to flow from a close analysis of Jewish-Gentile intermarriages in the United States (using comparative materials for purposes of contrast or conjecture) than from a study covering everything or anything that can be labelled intermarriage.

Our study began by asking: What do behavioral science theorists, researchers, and counselors say about Jewish-Gentile intermarriage? What factors do they locate in society, or in the individual, to account for attitudes favoring intermarriage? Additionally, we asked: What can the history and culture of the Jews tell us to account for the attitudes of Jews toward their own group, and toward Gentiles—and of the attitudes of Gentiles toward Jews? What of the discrepancy between the Jews' eagerness and aptitude for intimate participation in the life of the majority, and their stern taboo against marrying into the majority group? What of the discrepancy between the Jews' general lack of concern for religious worship and doctrine, and their special concern for observing the rule of endogamy? Does this pose a *dilemma* for the Jews to resolve (for, as the saying goes, "You can't have your cake and eat it too") , or is this a *paradox* for the observer to understand?

These are the questions that have guided our study. If we were looking only for facts, our report could well have been briefer. But we were also looking for better ways of posing the questions, for promising avenues of thought and investigation, for research-able hypotheses for future testing, and for enlightened ways of thinking and talking about intermarriage—whether from the standpoint of behavioral science theory, clinical practice, Jewish group survival, or individual guidance.

What have been the results of this study? What facts have been uncovered, what relationships have been drawn, to change the reader's way of thinking about intermarriage, and of the role of Jews in our culture? What facts have been uncovered to enrich the counselor's understanding of the tensions that under-lie a client's manifest conflict over cross-ethnic dating or engage-ment?

As for the facts, Jews who intermarry—compared with those who inmarry—are more likely to have a history of broken homes and lack of contact with extended family (cousins, aunts, uncles, grandparents) than the inmarrying majority. On the other hand, intermarrying Catholics show a history of conflict with parents, and alienation from the Church.[1] Jews attending a prestige private university hold more favorable attitudes toward inter-marriage than Jews attending urban state universities.[2] Jewish *men* are more favorably disposed toward intermarriage, and are more likely to intermarry than Jewish women. Intermarrying Jews marry later in life than inmarrying Jews.[3] Oldest children are *least* likely to intermarry; youngest children and only chil-dren are most likely to intermarry.[4] Personality traits favoring intermarriage seem to be related to birth order: intermarrieds are venturesome, slightly unconventional persons who see them-selves as "exceptions" to the normal rules of society—shading into the hypomanic and manic personality types.[5]

Jews living in rural areas and small towns are more likely to intermarry than Jews living in cities.[6] Children of recent residents of small towns are more likely to intermarry than children of long-established residents.[7] Jews living in new communities are more likely to intermarry than Jews living in older communities.[8] Reform or unaffiliated Jews are more likely to intermarry than Orthodox Jews.

It has been vaguely sensed that college education and socio-economic advancement somehow increase the probability of inter-marriage, and our analysis of available statistics has clarified these relationships somewhat. Intermarriage seems to appeal to Jews whose socio-economic position places them at the periphery of the Jewish community, or outside of it. (This raises, of course, some interesting questions about cause and effect relationships.) Intermarriage is therefore likely to occur among the highly upward mobile members of the *salaried* professions; Jewish professors and government experts are more likely to intermarry than Jewish physicians, dentists, lawyers, and business owners.[9] Virtually ignored in the intermarriage literature (although published statistics direct attention to this phenomenon) is the relationship between intermarriage and *downward* mobility. The small town Jewish craftsman, foreman, or other blue collar worker is more likely to intermarry than the Jew who holds a position in business or the professions.[10]

The salaried professional must in most cases leave his home community and live in a geographically mobile Gentile world—unlike the doctor, lawyer, and business owner, who are under no such pressure to leave their community of birth. Intermarriage rates may therefore differ strikingly for town and gown—for Jewish academic faculties, and for Jews in the surrounding community.[11] Intermarriage rates likewise differ radically between Jews living in Washington, D.C.—an administrative center peopled by salaried experts—and Jews living in Detroit, Michigan, a hometown community of business owners and independent practitioners.[12] In arriving at an understanding of the intermarriage phenomenon, little is accomplished by calculating the average intermarriage rate for the country as a whole, compared with identifying the characteristics of Jewish communities in which intermarriage is a rarity, and those in which it has become a commonplace.

How shall we interpret the known relationships between occupational choice and intermarriage? Clinical experience and research interview materials point to Jews who feel at odds with the Jewish community. Some feel that they do not fit into business or the independent professions; that they will never earn enough to satisfy a Jewish wife, please Jewish in-laws, or keep up with Jewish neighbors. Others see a world of opportunity that lies far beyond the Jewish community—a world in which they can share the dignity, prestige, power, good manners, and freedom of the majority group—and escape from the burden of anti-Semitism. (To them, Jews live petty, neurotic, insecure, and provincial lives, and do not abide by the rules of polite behavior.) A Gentile spouse is a natural partner for one who addresses himself exclusively to a Gentile status group.

On the other side of the ethnic fence, we encounter Gentiles who see the Jew as a culture hero—steeped in a tradition of learning, sobriety, achievement, and family loyalty. To these Gentiles, Jewish skepticism, liberalism, audacity, and love of life offer a sane alternative to their kind of Christianity—puritanical self-denial, authoritarianism, and other-worldliness. Jewish intimacy in an unfriendly world seems better than Gentile "friendliness without friendship" (as Henry Murray once described the American culture). Clinical experience points to intermarrying Gentiles whose unstable or broken home background lends a special value to the Jewish tradition of family loyalty and group belongingness. While there are undoubtedly many cases in which conversion denotes little more than polite acquiescence to the wishes of Jewish in-laws, there is no shortage of cases (autobiographical and clinical) in which the search for a Jewish spouse was only one aspect of a larger search for entry into the Jewish community.[13]

One finds, on the other hand, mixed marriages in which both partners seem determined to cast their lot with the Gentile elite. Characteristically, the husband is a Jew who has attained a considerable degree of professional success. His wife is a member of the Protestant elite. The husband is likely to hold membership in a Protestant church, or at least attend church services. They live in an elite Gentile neighborhood, orient their social lives mainly around Gentile friends, raise their children as Protestants, and guide them into elite social groups.[14]

The intermarriage sex-bias—the preponderance of Jewish husbands and Gentile wives—is analogous to the sex-bias found amongst Negro-white couples and other mixed marriages in American society; the husband is usually a member of a minority group, and the wife a member of the majority group. Traditionally, Negro and foreign-born men of middles class status have been restricted to majority group wives of low status. (Merton accordingly hypothesized a "trading hypothesis"—the minority group male trades his middle class attainment for his wife's majority group status.)[15] To a significantly greater extent, Jews gain access to high status (or even elite status) Gentile wives— or at least this seems to be true for highly talented and achieving Jewish males. We have hypothesized that the sex-bias in Jewish-Gentile intermarriage is also influenced by the fact that Jewish norms of conduct (e.g., aggressiveness, audacity, intellectuality) match up well with the masculine sex role in Western society, and are incongruous—in many respects—with the feminine sex role in Western society. Hence, Jews are regarded as "wonderful husbands" for analogous reasons that Japanese are said to make "perfect wives."[16]

When the choice of a cross-ethnic mate indicates poor judgment at a practical level, or is accompanied by great inner conflict or reluctance, the clinician looks for neurotic drives toward intermarriage.[17] Classically—both in the folk tradition and in clinical lore—the choice of an out-group marriage partner (or pregnancy through an out-group partner) expresses hostility toward parental authority. There is no shortage of clinical evidence to support this formulation.[18]

"Neurotic exogamy"—as Abraham first labelled it in 1913— is described psychoanalytically as a derivative of the affectionate bond between the intermarriage-prone person and his cross-sex parent or sibling, a bond which inhibits his potency with a love object from his own group. Puritanical modesty training, parental seduction, father-son jealousy, and whatever else implants feelings of sexual inhibition, increases tensions toward intermarriage—for "the exotic is erotic," and the attractive stranger arouses more sexual interest than a partner who resembles one's parent or sibling. It may be argued (as the Levinsons do) that preference for a "contrast choice" is an adaptive mechanism for

those whose upbringing renders them inhibited to some degree
with a partner from their own group. The custom of finding a
Jewish mate who grew up in another town was practiced by
more affluent members of the Eastern European *shtetl*. Community exogamy has likewise been found to be the prevailing
norm among endogamous Jews of American small towns and of
at least one kibbutz in Israel.[19]

Problems of the intermarried may be defined so as to include
problems of the partners themselves, of their parents, and of
their children. Intermarrieds who adopt a Gentile identity must
cope with the inner tension of "self-hatred," as Lewin described
it—for adopting the Gentile way of looking at the world leads
one to look down upon the Jews. They must also face the uncertainty as to whether their children, despite the parents' best
efforts to groom them for the Gentile world, will be accepted
into Gentile society.

Intermarrieds face a special problem of mutual accommodation
when it becomes evident—as it sometimes does—that the partner
of Gentile origin is motivated to get *into* Judaism, while the
Jewish partner hoped his cross-ethnic mate would help him find
a way *out* of the Jewish community.

Jewish wives by conversion must learn to live on indefinite
probation, and withstand the skepticism and hostility of the more
hidebound members of their adopted community. The serious
proselyte often finds a natural ally and protector in the rabbi,
drawn into an intermarriage situation by parents who plead with
him to break up the match, and a Jewish fiancé who wants as
little to do with the rabbi as possible. The Gentile fiancée is
often the most cooperative member of the party, the most deferential to the rabbi, and the most appreciative of his primary
role—a teacher of Judaism. Intermarriage involves the rabbi with
parents and young adults whom the rabbi might otherwise never
meet, and confronts the rabbi with a bewildering array of responsibilities, frustrations, temptations, and opportunities.[20]

The impossible demands of distraught Jewish parents, who
insist that the rabbi show their offspring the error of his ways,
present the rabbi with an enormous temptation to castigate the
parents for backsliding in the practice of their faith, for failing
to maintain a thoroughly Jewish home, and for having neglected

the religious education of their children.[21] To the rabbi who sees intermarriage as a *religious* problem, it may seem absurd to behold such suffering by parents whose religious commitments are nil. The paradox melts away, however, when one views intermarriage *not* as the violation of a religious taboo, but as a threat to the community solidarity of the Jews, and to the emotional security of parents whose status seems to depend upon their contribution to the solidarity of their group. Available data, however limited, indicate that Jewish fathers suffer more deeply and chronically from this status insult than Jewish mothers. This fact may point to the peculiar emotional meaning of intermarriage to the middle-age Jewish male, or to the superior psychological resilience of women in the Jewish group.

After five or fifteen years of marriage, a person may have the same psychological needs but the *priority* of these needs may undergo considerable change, and an ethnic identity which seemed of little worth in young adulthood may assume a new and special value as one assumes the role of parenthood, as one approaches middle age, or as one copes with the crises of living. A regrouping of one's personal loyalties is difficult for the person who has committed himself too deeply to a fixed social position.

What of the children? Clinical materials point to conflicts in identity from which mischlings suffer—and this seems to be especially clear in the case of those boys who feel attracted to the cultural identity of their mothers—as if their choice creates a disturbing ambiguity over their sex-role identity. A study of mischling undergraduates at Harvard University shows widespread and pervasive insecurity over ethnic identity.[22] It appears that a majority of these youths were explicitly indoctrinated at home, in church, and in Sunday school, to regard themselves as Protestants—and were psychologically unprepared to be regarded by their peers as half-Jews. At the high school age level, the mischlings seemed to find their Jewish peers friendlier than the Gentile youth for whose company the mischlings had been so carefully groomed. (Ironically, the high school period is a time when Jewish youths begin to make Gentile friends, and when mischlings feel drawn into Jewish friendship groups.)

As college students, Rosten's mischlings may protect themselves against disclosure of their Jewish background, as they circulate among the Protestant elite—uneasy over the risk entailed in their social feint. They are more introspective and more sensitive to their own negative qualities than their Jewish or Gentile classmates. They would like to be both Jewish and Gentile, but this specifies a role for which there seems to be no available model. Compared with mischling boys, adoption of a Gentile identity seems to be easier for mischling girls—especially for those whose father is a born Catholic, who were themselves raised as Catholic, and brought up in a town where anti-Semitism is at a minimum.

Writers on intermarriage who show the widest range of viewpoints—from uncompromisingly anti-intermarriage to uncritically assimilationist—find one issue on which they can agree: *mixed marriages are not well adapted to raising children.*[23] A sizeable percentage of intermarried couples avoid the problem of mixed parenthood by remaining childless.[24]

A review of the textbook literature on acculturation reveals a viewpoint on intermarriage which does not particularly fit the available facts on intermarriage. A sampling of widely-used textbooks on social psychology[25] indicates an uncritical bias in favor of *maximal* assimilation into the dominant group, by every available means. To support this view, current textbooks cite a 1937–1938 interview study of Italian Americans, while many more recent studies in minority group living are ignored.[26] Virtually ignored in the social psychology textbooks are the classic and penetrating essays of Kurt Lewin on the topic of Jewish adaptation to a Gentile world. The pro-intermarriage bias of the behavioral science Establishment is perhaps most wildly evident in Anselm Strauss' interpretation of interview material obtained from a group of Japanese war brides. In a book intended to help close the gap "between research and its utilization by family-serving agencies and organizations,"[27] Foote and Cottrell pass along Strauss' conclusion that ". . . heteronomy now seems less likely than was formerly thought to interfere with marital harmony."[28]

What the social psychology textbooks say about intermarriage is largely by implication. What they say explicitly about the Jews revolves almost exclusively around the topic of anti-Semitism, perhaps because that is virtually the only aspect of the Jewish phenomenon that has been subjected to rigorous and extensive behavioral science research (undoubtedly because that is how research funds have been allocated). Accordingly, the college student of social psychology may learn a good deal about the personality structure and values of the tribesmen of New Guinea (thanks to Margaret Mead's indelible portrayal of the Arapesh, Mundugumor, and Tchambuli), but all the student learns about the Jews is that they tend to be disliked, and that social psychologists have devised ingenious ways of measuring the degrees, modes, and sources of this dislike.

What little the behavioral scientists have written about Jewish traits is rather directly related to anti-Semitism, demonstrating how the personality of the Diaspora Jew has been warped and blighted by the insecurity of minority group status, and the insult of anti-Semitism.[29] Perhaps David Riesman deserves a special commendation for the courage to set down explictly the negative attitude toward Jewish life which his behavioral science colleagues indicate by indirection.

Cahnman and Glazer are probably representative of their behavioral science colleagues in their preference for regarding the Jews as a *religious* group—as "Americans of Jewish faith"— and in explicitly counseling against the perpetuation of social norms which cannot be justified on religious grounds.[30] Their conception of Jewish life in America seems to be governed by what might fit neatly and unproblematically alongside the two major faiths—by what the prevailing American norms seem to "permit," rather than by what the integrity of the Jewish culture would seem to require.

In scientific discussion, *truth is more controversial than opinion.* In the absence of facts, anyone is entitled to whatever opinions he chooses to voice. But when facts are available and they are either distorted or ignored so as to favor certain cherished opinions, the seeds have been sown for a controversy of serious proportions. When all the available facts on intermarriage are assembled, they raise serious questions about how adequately the American behavioral scientist has been dealing with facts that conflict with his social ideology and with the prevailing norms of faculty society.

The Jews, who have survived so many adverse circumstances

over past centuries, will also survive the biases of contemporary behavioral scientists. That is not the problem. The problem is this: today's behavioral scientists are asking for (and getting) an increasingly important role in the formulation of social policy at many levels—in the administration of hospitals, schools, and universities; in the training of soldiers, teachers, executives, and other decision-makers; in the fulfillment of the American promise to Negroes and other disadvantaged groups; even in the reduction of international tensions and in the maintenance of world peace.[31] When the academic community embraces a particular social ideology or point of view, what happens to their capacity to deal critically with the entire range of available facts?[32] What happens to their interest in looking at facts that do *not* quite fit their ideology? For the intellectual community, this is probably the most basic and far-reaching question our study can pose.

As for the behavioral scientists' characterization of the Jew as a warped and neurotic creature, the question is not whether this is fair to the Jews (they have put up with worse than that), but whether this is fair to the student, and whether this is fair to the development of social psychology. The Jewish phenomenon is intrinsically too interesting, too rich a source of data on human adaptation, audacity, creativity, and group cohesiveness, to escape the serious and well-rounded study of behavioral scientists indefinitely. What they stand to learn from studying the Jewish phenomenon in depth will certainly be enriching, and may even be useful toward developing a theory of human adaptation to a world of uncertainty and change.

In an age of alienation, when group therapy offers "instant mishpocho," when the task of psychoanalysis has shifted from loosening too rigid an identity to firming up too diffuse an identity, when belongingness seems at least as important as autonomy, when the ability to acquire knowledge is more adaptive than craftsmanship or physical prowess; at such a time in human history, Jewishness is worth something. American novelists and essayists know this, the mass entertainment industry knows this, military historians know this, rabbis know this (from the number of Gentiles who seek access to Judaism without regard to intermarriage). Jews know this too; though they may find it impossible to explain *why* they value their Jewishness, they value it.

Sooner or later, behavioral scientists are bound to discover this too.

Those who look hopefully for some signs of progress in behavioral science thinking need not be entirely disappointed. The Leo Srole of 1940 who, with Lloyd Warner, predicted the disappearance of the American Jews in five generations[33] (and reported but was at a loss to explain the unique productivity of Jewish women), is not quite the same as the Leo Srole of 1960, who was willing to conjecture that Jewish family life "often hypothesized by psychiatrists as potentially pathogenic . . . may conceivably be eugenic on balance. . . ."[34] The Nathan Glazer of 1957, who could find no reason why ethnic groups should survive in America, and saw a future for Jewish survival in America only in the form of a religion, is not quite the same as the Nathan Glazer of 1963 who (with Daniel Moynihan) decided that the ethnic group in America is *not* a transitional phenomenon, but has become *a new social form.*

Throughout this book an effort has been made not only to describe what we know about the topic of Jewish identity and intermarriage, but also to sketch out areas of ignorance and ambiguity, and thereby point to various research problems. We need to know more about the prevailing norms of modesty training—the specific behaviors by which the incest taboo is communicated and maintained—and how they influence the individual's attitudes toward the entire gamut of possible sex partners. We need to know more about maternal warmth and maternal seduction, and the conditions under which one form of treatment shades into the other. We need to know more about the extended family —its role in the early socialization process, and in the lives of growing children, adolescents, and young adults. We need to know more about the Jewish "sense of being." We must move up from the anecdotal and clinical level, to a more systematic and empirical level of knowledge concerning life experiences that foster Jewishness as a source of self-actualization, and experiences that make Jewishness a burden and a handicap. We need to better define the "What's wrong with Jewish girls?" problem, and at least identify the prevailing patterns of sex-role adjustment in the Jewish group. We need to know more about intermarriages that lead to good partnerships and successful parentage. We need to know more about mischlings who, unlike the Harvard group, have been brought up as Jews. We need to know something about the influence of these successful families on the attitudes of their Jewish friends and neighbors. We need to know more about the interrelationships between attitude toward intermarriage and a variety of other variables: physical appearance, occupational choice, sexual adjustment, family experience, life goals.

Some of the most fruitful research findings on the Jews have emerged, as we have demonstrated, from larger community studies which describe Jewish life in its natural context—vis-a-vis the larger community. The Lenski study, for example, gave a unique characterization of Jewish group cohesiveness precisely because it compared the Jews of Detroit with their Protestant and Catholic neighbors, on various indices of group solidarity. The reader will recall, however, that some of Lenski's provocative findings lack the stamp of statistical significance because his total sample included fewer than 30 Jews. Veroff's pioneering nationwide sampling of thematic apperception test responses likewise showed provocative differences between Jewish and Gentile fantasy productions, but again (in the opinion of McClelland)[35] Veroff's Jewish sample was quite small. Gurin, Veroff, and Feld conducted a nationwide interview study to assess the mental health of American adults. When they turned to religious group differences, in the analysis of their data, they compared Protestants and Catholics—and simply set aside all those who did not belong to either of the "two major religious groups:" Jews, Buddhists, atheists, and others.

In each of the above three studies the populations were obtained through probability sampling methods, and the number of Jews drawn into the sample was roughly proportional to their representation in the population sampled. To double the number of Jewish respondents, however, would *not* necessitate doubling the entire study group; this could be accomplished through the established and familiar survey research procedure of over-sampling. If the investigators were interested in collecting data on Jewish attitudes and adjustment patterns, this could have been done without adding significantly to the cost of the research project. Entirely apart from what could be learned through special research projects, much more could be learned about the Jewish ethos from prevailing community studies—if behavioral scientists were interested in doing so.

The Jewish reader who hoped to find in this book a battle plan for fighting intermarriage, or a program for safeguarding the Jewish tradition of endogamy, may be dismayed that the author calls for research on good and successful intermarriages. It is the viewpoint of this author that intermarriage *per se* is not a threat to Jewish survival, though some of the conditions that lead to intermarriage are disruptive of Jewish group life. Throughout this book an effort has been made to identify those underlying conditions, so that the Jewish community can address itself more deliberately to its problems.

Jews who worry about intermarriage probably make too much of the fact that those Jews upon whose heads fell the worst blows of anti-Semitic savagery—the Jews of Germany—were a highly intermarried group. Simplism and uncritical moralizing have no place in the analysis of this complex and tragic phenomenon of our times. It should at least be borne in mind that the Jews of Poland, who adhered much more faithfully to the tradition of endogamy, were long subjected to a virulent brand of domestic anti-Semitism before Hitler introduced Nazi efficiency into the black art of persecution. And it may also be borne in mind that there have been highly intermarrying communities, like Italy, where anti-Semitism never really flourished.

What Rabbi Mordecai Kaplan once said about the Jewish view on restrictive real estate covenants must also apply to a sane view on intermarriage, or even mixed marriage. No Jew takes pride in a fellow Jew's preference for living in an all-Gentile neighborhood, but a Jew's right to live where he wishes (and with the marriage partner of his choice) cannot be denied in an open society. An open society where ethnic boundaries survive because they serve the individual's need for variety, for belongingness, for continuity, for identity, for authenticity—where ethnic boundaries are not prison walls—where those Jews who would rather be Gentiles and Gentiles who would rather be Jews are equally free to cross the boundary and find a more congenial ethnic home—that, in this writer's opinion, is a good society.

If this book fails to satisfy the alarmists or purists of the Jewish community, neither will it please the academic assimilationist. Assimilationism is without doubt a dominant viewpoint of members of the academic community,[36] and they indeed practice what they preach. Therefore, to cast doubt upon their theoretical position also brings into question their prevailing social norms. But what could be more self-limiting than a theory of man and society constructed around the particularities of the theorists' mode of life?

Throughout this book, the author—a counseling psychologist —has expressed a special concern over social psychological theory and its influence on the practice of counseling and psychotherapy. In this regard, this author finds himself in good company; at least two major figures in psychotherapy—Alfred Adler and Harry Stack Sullivan—pointed to social psychology as a most significant theoretical foundation for the art of psychotherapy. If social psychology is to fulfill its potential as a behavioral science, it must rediscover the social world its professors have left behind. That world has changed, but it is still there, and it is very much alive. It is an interesting world, and its people are real people.

Notes

The reader will observe that in the text, as well as in the footnotes, sources are referred to by author only; for complete citation, the reader is referred to the Bibliography. Where an author is represented in this work by more than one title, the source of a given citation is identified by author and year of publication.

CHAPTER 1

1. *Abie's Irish Rose*, by Ann Nichols, was published as a stage play in 1924, appeared as a novel in 1927, and subsequently was made into a movie.
2. The Jew's paradoxical attitude toward intermarriage is nicely delineated in Noah Gordon's novel, *The Rabbi*. The protagonist falls in love with a Gentile girl, a sensitive, spiritual person, and the daughter of a minister. Marriage to an idealistic young rabbi seems out of the question. Secretly the girl friend seeks out her beloved's old rabbi-mentor, and asks him to prepare her for conversion to Judaism. The old man's delight over his precious convert—a lovely, intelligent *ger tsedek*—is transformed into a sense of calamity and horror when he discovers that she plans to marry none other than the old rabbi's protege.
3. The use of intermarriage in the contemporary American Jewish novel is apparently quite different from the symbolic meaning attached to intermarriage in the novels of the 1920's. During that decade, according to Fiedler (1959, p. 15), the Jewish novel was marked by the "obsessive theme" of active assimilation. Intermarriage was seen as a vehicle for fulfilling the hope of assimilation, but with this promise came also "the threat of miscegenation." Kirshenbaum (p. 64) describes Asch's *East River* as "a paen in praise of intermarriage . . . [a] glorification of marriage between Jew and Christian." In the contemporary American Jewish

novel, intermarriage seeems to play a far more complex and subtle role —symbolizing the attraction of the Gentile toward Jewish values, the conflict between ethnicity and religion, the effort to loosen the grip of family obligation, the struggle against a fear of the Gentile world, and the classic conflict between sacred and profane love. In the recent novels of Philip Roth, Noah Gordon, Jerome Weidman, and Myron Kaufmann intermarriage is viewed as fraught with unexpected risks, problems, and disappointments. In 1964 Sklare expressed disappointment that in the contemporary novel "the stance taken toward the question [of intermarriage] is not in the least militant or didactic . . ." (p. 47). At least in the writings of the above-mentioned four, intermarriage is viewed as a problem, a dilemma, a paradox, or an irony—not as a design for living. Sklare (1964, p. 47) lists as novelists who have dealt with tendencies toward Jewish-Gentile intermarriage: Bernard Malamud, Saul Bellow, Leslie Fiedler, Bruce Jay Friedman, Herbert Gold, Jack Ludwig, and Neal Oxenhandler. Milton Barron lists the following recent novels on Jewish-Gentile intermarriage: Gwethalyn Graham, *Earth and High Heaven;* Norman Katkov, *Eagle at My Eyes;* and Myron Brining, *Footsteps on the Stair.* (1951, p. 249).

4. Kurt List has observed that the most popular musicals by Jewish composers and lyricists have dealt with the theme of intermarriage, broadly defined. *Show Boat, South Pacific,* and *The King and I* were cited by List. To these may be added *West Side Story, Golden Boy,* and *My Fair Lady. Fiddler on the Roof,* like the Sholom Aleichem story on which it is based, has an intermarriage crisis. Recent Broadway plays with an intermarriage theme include *Majority of One,* and *Two for the Seesaw.* In 1968 the Academy Award for "best screenplay" was won by the Stanley Kramer production, *Guess Who's Coming for Dinner.*

5. Quoted from Thomas, page 52. The same chasm between theory and practice is expressed in the following joke, which appeared in the pages of *Midstream*:

A Jewish girl calls up her mother, and the following conversation ensues:

"Mama, I'm married."

"Mazel Tov! That's wonderful."

"But, mama, my husband is a Catholic."

"So? Not everyone is a Jew."

"But, mama, he's a Negro."

"What of it? The world has all kinds. We gotta be tolerant."

"But mama, he has no job."

"Nu, that's all right."

"But, mama, we have no place to stay."

"Oh, you'll stay right here in this house."

"Where, mama? There's no room."

"Well, you and your husband can sleep in our bedroom, Papa will sleep on the sofa."

"Yes, but, mama, where will *you* sleep?"

"Oh, don't worry about me, darling. As soon as I hang up I'm going to drop dead." (Rosenberg and Shapiro, page 226.)

6. Hertzler, page 162.

7. Why should the Negro wish to survive as a distinct group? Podhoretz asked. The Jews claim an ancient heritage and a dream of redemption. "What does the American Negro have that might correspond to this? His past is a stigma, his color is a stigma, and his vision of the future is the hope of erasing the stigma by making color irrelevant, by making it disappear as a fact of consciousness.

"I share this hope, but I cannot see how it will ever be realized unless color does *in fact* disappear: and that means not integration, it means assimilation," Podhoretz continued. "I believe the wholesale merging of the two races is the most desirable alternative for everyone concerned." Podhoretz conceded that such a program was not "immediately feasible" on any programmatic basis, but insisted that "the Negro problem can be solved in this country in no other way." That was his reasoned conviction, however it might conflict with the "twisted feelings about Negroes" that had grown out of his personal experience:

> If I were to be asked today whether I would like a daughter of mine 'to marry one,' I would have to answer: 'No, I wouldn't *like* it at all. I would rail and rave and rant and tear my hair. And then I hope I would have the courage to curse myself for raving and ranting, and to give her my blessing. How dare I withhold it at the behest of the child I once was and against the man I now have a duty to be?'

Citations in text, and above, from Podhoretz, 1963, page 101. For quotations on Podhoretz's reappraisal of the article, and his recollections on public reaction to it, see Podhoretz, 1967, page 346.

8. Cahnman reports that during the six-year period of 1954–59, a Jewish child care agency in New York City had to find adoptive homes for over 150 offspring of unmarried Jewish mothers and Negro fathers, and in each case the child was placed with a Negro family "because no Jewish families could be found who would have been ready to receive them. . . . To continue the present practice would be unprecedented historically and unsupportable on democratic grounds," Cahnman argues. "I do not overlook the formidable difficulties which stand in the way of a satisfactory solution. All I can say," he adds, "is that between liberalism professed and illiberalism practiced there is a discrepancy which must be resolved." (Cahnman, pages 191–192.)

According to Rubenstein, the agency placement figures cited by Cahnman touch only a small fraction of the problem. Rubenstein estimates that "several hundred times each year . . . Jewish girls in New York City . . . have children out of wedlock with Negroes. These are the only children of Jewish birth who cannot be placed for adoption in Jewish homes." (Rubenstein, page 130.)

"Nor are racially mixed married couples readily accepted into the organized Jewish community," Cahnman observes (page 191) — a fact that Gibel documents from her personal experience.

9. Polish, 1964.

10. In dealing with a request to officiate at an intermarriage, Rabbi Polish pleads with his colleagues that they should not let their decision "be predicated on assuaging the feelings of in-laws or grandparents." He expresses regret over the occurance of " 'shot gun' conversions where only a Jewish mother's tears induced a Christian boy or girl to convert. . ." Such a conversion, Polish comments, is "odious and meaningless." (Polish, 1964, pages 34, 36.)

11. Kirshenbaum, pages 104 and 107.

12. The controversy amongst Reform rabbis on the question of officiating at mixed marriages, and the wisdom of requiring conversion as a condition for a Jewish wedding, is debated in a 1964 issue of *CCAR Journal* by Polish and Shulman.

According to Rabbi Kertzer, as late as the 1950's it was difficult to find a Reform rabbi who would participate in a mixed marriage. In the past decade "a startling shift" has occurred, he adds—so that in 1967 "perhaps one out of three would officiate, as long as the couple undertook to rear their children in the Jewish faith." (page 223)

13. In discussing Jewish-Gentile marriage partnerships, marriage between a born Jew and a convert to Judaism is sometimes defined as an *intermarriage,* while a cross-ethnic partnership in which husband and wife maintain their ethnic difference is called a *mixed* marriage. In practice, the distinction is not always useful. Whether the Gentile spouse converts may depend upon the demands of the Jewish in-laws, or the advice of the rabbi. A proselyte may maintain no contact with the Jewish community, and a technically Gentile spouse may become an active participant in the social and religious life of a Jewish community. Rabbis are often careful to limit their discussion to *mixed* marriages, since from a religious standpoint it is offensive to discriminate between a born Jew and a sincere convert. We shall use the term *intermarriage* to designate a marriage partnership between a born Jew and a person of Gentile origin, whether a religious conversion has taken place or not.

14. Bamberger, page 11.

15. Shanks, pages 374–375.

16. Shanks, page 375.

17. Barron, 1951, page 255.

18. Glazer, 1957, pages 9–10.

19. For a noteworthy effort to summarize the entire sociological and anthropological literature of intermarriage, see Albert I. Gordon, 1964.

20. A. I. Gordon, 1964, pages 2–3.

21. At a faculty lunch table, a professor of sociology unburdens himself of the tension he feels over his conference with a coed enrolled in one of his classes: "This sensitive, intelligent, lovely child says she is in love with a student who is Jewish. He brings her to meet his family; they will have nothing to do with her; they call her a *goya.* I tell you," the pro-

fessor says with a touch of desperation, "it is not the young people who need to be educated. It's their parents; *they* need to be educated."

22. Sherif, page 2.
23. *Ibid.*, page 200.
24. *Ibid.*, pages 85–86.
25. *Ibid.*, page 200.
26. *Ibid.*, page 202.
27. *Ibid.*, pages 143–144.
28. Glazer, 1957, page 9.
29. *Ibid.*, pages 9–10.
30. *Ibid.*, page 126.
31. *Ibid.*, page 126.
32. *Ibid.*, page 129.
33. *Ibid.*, pages 132–133.
34. *Ibid.*, page 142.
35. *Ibid.*, page 146.
36. *Ibid.*, page 147.
37. *Ibid.*, page 149.
38. *Ibid.*, pages 54–55.
39. Cahnman, page 187.
40. Cahnman, page 187. It may seem harsh to describe Cahnman's argument as a recommendation that Judaism be reshaped to fit the American ethos. Yet, where he sees the two traditions in conflict, his solution to the dilemma is to ask for a re-examination of the Jewish value to see whether it is not indeed outmoded, whether it has not lost its spiritual essence, whether it is "viable in a climate of democracy," whether it really has meaningful content—and to replace those values which cannot pass this scrutiny, with values (drawn from somewhere in the Jewish heritage) which are more congenial to the American spirit. For example, Cahnman proposes that the contemporary American Jew's reluctance to receive converts be replaced by the spirit of the *eighth* century Jews of south Russia, by whom "the conversion of non-Jews was eagerly sought." (pages 186–187)

"To maintain Judaism in the fluid environment of a democracy requires a new definition of the situation," Cahnman argues. "The dilemma is real. American Jews cannot give up their belief in democracy and the right of individuals to shape their own lives because that would mean denying that they are Americans and that they have a share in the hopes and aspirations which are the essence of America. . . . I cannot see America . . . permitting the founding fathers' device '*E Pluribus Unum*' to be interpreted . . . [as justifying] clearly marked-off ethnic groups, or ancestral communities of any kind, *or even huge religious blocks which are left standing forever.*" (pages 183–184, italics added.)

It is a delusion, says Cahnman, to suppose that a people with a mission "can remain shut up tight and clannish and be an example for all humanity at the same time. . . . If the concept of 'mission' should be meaningful, there must be an urge to excel in deeds and to accept fellows —and urge to influence and to missionize." (page 185)

41. Cahnman, page 187.

42. Doobs, page 45.
43. Sherif, page 16.
44. Foote and Cottrell, page 24.
45. A. I. Gordon, 1964, page 54.
46. *Ibid.*, page 55.
47. *Ibid.*, page 57.
48. *Ibid.*, pages 40–41.
49. *Ibid.*, pages 47–50.
50. *Ibid.*, page 97.
51. *Ibid.*, page 50. Gordon gives his source as Jacobson, page 153.
52. *Ibid.*, page 91.
53. *Ibid.*, page 51.
54. Franzblau, page 22.
55. A. I. Gordon, 1964, page 196.
56. Tumin, 1961, page 94.
57. Danglow, page 5.
58. A. I. Gordon, 1964, page 209.
59. *Ibid.*, page 51.
60. *Ibid.*, page 291.
61. Hertzler, page 80. Hertzler and Tumin agree that rate of intermarriage is a positive indication of intergroup harmony, but Engelman was able to marshal a considerable mass of statistical support for a contradictory thesis—that a climate of anti-Semitism exerts pressure on Jews to marry out of their group. John Mayer found evidence of this tendency in his interview study. While he did not find room for this evidence in his book on *Jewish-Gentile Courtship*, Mayer did document his findings on anti-Semitism as a factor in intermarriage, in a scholarly journal article (1961b).
62. From Stember, Table 40, page 106.
63. *Ibid.*, page 106.
64. *Ibid.*, Figure 41, page 107.
65. Zangwill, pages 198–199.
66. Quoted by Drachsler, pages 151–152 fn.
67. *Ibid.*, page 154 fn.
68. *Ibid.*, pages 40, 41.
69. *Ibid.*, pages 51, 52.
70. *Ibid.*, pages 94–95 fn.
71. *Ibid.*, page 210.
72. *Ibid.*, page 164.
73. Hertzler, pages 92–93.
74. *Ibid.*, page 98.
75. Writing in the early years of the Third Reich, Lewisohn asks, "Do they not know that the German Jews were the most assimilated group in all history, and that their penetration into German life and culture was the inevitable result of assimilation, if not the ultimate cause of their tragic martyrdom? We have in America, so far as I know, not a single highly articulate friend, like the late Lord Balfour and Josiah Wedgwood in England or Justin Godard in France or Jan Smuts in

South Africa, who thoroughly understands our plight." (Lewisohn 1936, page 54)

76. Steinberg, 1933, page 34.

77. Pettigrew's 1964 survey of psychological facts about the American Negro devotes Chapter 3 to an examination of the "genetic solution" to the problem of racial discrimination. Pettigrew advances the view of Curt Stein "that if panmixia—completely random mating with no regard to racial differences—were to take place in the United States, the darker skin shades of Negroes would be virtually eliminated, but there would be little noticeable effect on the skin color of Caucasians." (page 62) Quoting Stern, Pettigrew continues, " 'When complete fusion has occurred . . . [it might be asked]: "What became of the Negro?" ' " (pages 62–63)

"The United States . . . is as much a biological as a cultural melting pot," Pettigrew insists. (page 67) "Extensive racial intermixture has taken place from ancient times to the present. Modern technology has . . . so altered man's environment as to render racial adaptations to older environments largely obsolete." (pages 70–71) Pettigrew presents "the possibility that cross-mating may often be biologically beneficial . . . [reducing the incidence of] pathological conditions. . . . Not unlike the phenomenon of hybrid vigor in plant life, cross-group mating may result in especially sturdy specimens." (pages 63–64) As evidence of the salutory effects of cross-group mating, Pettigrew cites the finding of Hulse "that offspring from marriages of persons from different villages [in Switzerland] were on the average significantly taller and more robust than offspring from marriages of members of the same village." (page 64)

Significantly, the only arguments cited by Pettigrew in opposition to a "genetic solution" are the ethnocentric clichés of white supremacists. Social psychologist Pettigrew draws upon materials from anthropology, genetics, and medicine for his *Profile of the Negro American,* but he chooses to ignore the clinical and research literature on racially mixed marriages, psychological problems of group marginality (including the problem of "passing"), and attitudes of Negroes (especially Negro women) toward the "genetic solution."

At the 1966 meeting of the American Association for the Advancement of Science, biologist (and vice president of New York State University of New York) H. Bentley Glass forecast that race problems will disappear when race differences are eliminated. "Offspring of interracial matings are unimpaired, if not superior in vigor and fertility," he assured his colleagues. "The races are in fact disappearing, although the process will require thousands of years at present rates," Glass admitted. Psychologist Jerry Hirsch supported Glass' viewpoint: "We do not solve problems," said Hirsch. "We get over them. Old questions are solved by disappearing, evaporating." (Reported in Chicago *Sun-Times,* January 1, 1967, page 25.)

In a 1967 issue of *Life,* historian Arnold Toynbee (who has advocated assimilationism for the Jews) insists that American society must either accept extensive racial intermarriage—"fusion in its complete sense"—or move toward forcible separation of the races, as practiced in South Africa, in order to avert "a permanent state of civil war." *Life,* 63, No. 23, December 8, page 108-B.

78. This figure of speech elaborates the language of Curt Stern, as quoted in Pettigrew, page 62.

79. Krech and Crutchfield, 1948, page 507.

80. *Ibid.,* page 508.

81. *Ibid.,* page 508.

82. *Ibid.,* page 509.

83. *Ibid.,* page 509.

84. Simpson and Yinger, page 387.

85. "The second generation found a much more complex situation. Many believed they heard the siren call of welcome to the social cliques, clubs, and institutions of white Protestant America. After all, it was simply a matter of learning American ways, was it not? Had they not grown up as Americans, and were they not culturally different from their parents, the 'greenhorns?' . . . But alas, Brooks Brothers suit notwithstanding, the doors of the fraternity house, the city men's club, and the country club were slammed in the face of the immigrant's off-spring. . . . And so the rebuffed one returned to the homelier but de-pendable comfort of the communal institutions of his ancestral group . . . [living within] the realm of the sociologically possible . . . [cre-ating] social institutions and organizations within the ethnic enclave . . .

"Those who had for a time ventured out gingerly or confidently, as the case might be, had been lured by the vision of an 'American' social structure that was somehow larger than all subgroups and was ethnic-ally neutral. Were they, too, not American? But they found to their dismay that at the primary group level a neutral American social structure was a mirage . . . The desirability of whatever invitations were grudgingly extended [by white Protestant Anglo-Saxon institu-tions] could only become a considerably attenuated one." Milton M. Gordon, page 282.

86. Lewin, 1940, page 182.

87. Stonequist, 1937, page 102.

88. Bloom, pages 196–197.

89. Lewin, 1940, pages 182–183. Krech and Crutchfield refer briefly to Lewin's view on minority group members' adjustment, but judge that Lewin exaggerates the depth of their feelings of belongingness, exag-gerates their degree of ego-involvement in ethnic behavior patterns, and therefore exaggerates the risk involved in eliminating "sociological cues that identify [them] as . . . 'different' . . . ." (148, pages 508–509)

Lewin's viewpoint on the social insecurity of the assimilationist an-ticipated the research findings of Teitelbaum, discussed in a later sec-tion of Chapter 1, and Rosten, discussed in Chapter 4. In 1915 Brandeis expressed the hope that the Zionist movement would inspire Jews "to shake off the false shame which has led men who ought to be proud of their Jewish race to assume so many alien disguises. . . It is high time that the Jews should realize that few things do more to foster anti-Semitic feeling than this very tendency to sail under false colors and conceal their true identity." (Brandeis, 1915, page 23.)

90. Krech and Crutchfield, 1948, page 509.

91. Krech and Crutchfield, 1962, page 489.

92. Newcomb, 1950, page 539.

93. *Ibid.*, page 543.

94. *Ibid.*, page 543.

95. In his *Social Psychology* textbook, Doob preferred to speculate that Child's rebel had been "treated unkindly by his parents" and that his rebellion against the Italian culture represents a generalization of his rejection of his parents. (Page 477.)

96. Child, page 115.

97. *Ibid.*, page 77.

98. *Ibid.*, page 90.

99. *Ibid.*, page 96.

100. Newcomb, 1950, page 539.

101. *Ibid.*, page 544.

102. In his 1965 revision, Newcomb again offers the 1943 Child study "as a fairly recent example" of how children of immigrant's "faced marginal conflicts." (p. 406) Again ethnic marginality is defined as a variety of role conflict (especially persistent when the individual "has internalized the norms of both groups"). The *marginal man* is again described as one who holds membership in groups whose norms are so opposed to each other that it is "impossible [for him] to be regarded, or to regard himself, as a full-fledged member of either. If he finds it impossible to relinquish membership in either group . . . he is said to be *marginal* to both groups. Such persons are neither fish nor fowl, since they are not recognized as 100 percent members of either group." (p. 405)

103. See Krech and Crutchfield (1965), p. 498; Newcomb (1965), p. 405; Doob, p. 472, Seward (1956), p. 213. Since most of these authors use Child's sample as a model of the second generation American, this author invites the serious student to take a closer look at the facts from which the foregoing inferences and recommendations were drawn.

First, it should be noted that Child's study is based on field work carried out between July 1937 and December 1938—just prior to the outbreak of World War II—when Italian Americans were under continual pressure to defensively affirm, feign indifference to, or stoutly renounce their identity with an unfriendly Fascist power. Secondly— and aside from the political crisis—the Italian immigrant group did not respond to the economic and educational opportunity of the American situation, but tended "to accept a low economic position as inevitable. . ." (Child, p. 33) According to Child, they were committed to a frugal standard of living; an increase in earnings did not readily alter their "accustomed mode of living," but was used for savings or home ownership. (Child, p. 34.)

Child observed other norms of the Italian group which would make

American standards seem alien and threatening by comparison. The authoritarian role of the father designated control over the occupational choice of his children, the choice of his child's marriage partner, and obedience to the father's commands enforced by beatings if necessary. (p. 27) One of Child's respondents mentioned that he wasn't permitted to go out with girls until he reached the age of 22. (p. 140) An unmarried adult living with his parents was required to turn over all his pay to them. (p. 50) Children were "commonly expected to become full-time workers at a very early age." (p. 27) Immigrant parents showed "a great interest in having their children learn a craft or trade," (p. 33) norms which would tend to discourage higher education.

As Strodbeck has pointed out, in Southern Italian culture "school and book-learning environments were alien and remote from everyday experience. . . . Even in this country, the first-generation Southern Italian parents' attitude was, in part, negative to education. As an Italian educator reports: 'Mother believed you would go mad if you read too many books and father was of the opinion that too much school makes children lazy and opens the mind for unhealthy dreams.' Intellectualism, in itself, was not valued in Southern Italian communities. . . . Scholars were like monks: good men but not of the real world." (pp.150–151)

If, as Newcomb argued, "Italian Americans are in many ways typical of many marginal people," it now becomes abundantly clear that in a most significant respect the Italian Americans are quite different from that classic marginal group, the Jews. As Strodbeck has pointed out, "one of the most striking differences" between the cultural values of the Southern Italians and the Eastern European Jews is the value placed upon education and intellectual attainment. "The Jewish parent was expected to provide . . . as much education . . . as the sons showed themselves capable of absorbing." (p. 150)

Close examination of Child's data very strongly suggests that his ten "rebels" were not so much rebelling against their Italian identity *per se;* they were rebelling against parental norms which operated as barriers to social mobility. The rebels' striving for an education is a repeated theme. (pp. 82–85, 101–105) The rebel likes the movies because they teach him grammar (p. 104), wants a wife who is well-educated (p. 107), aspires to become a teacher (p. 102), resents the fact that his parents didn't contribute to his education (p. 107), models his expressive behavior after "high-class Italians, professional Italian-Americans." (p. 105) He feels ashamed of Italians because they are "poorly educated" ("whereas none of the apathetic or in-group informants mentioned" this trait!) He justifies his dislike for Italian girls because "most of them are ignorant." (p. 96) When he faces economic discrimination "it grieves me and makes me full of ambition to eradicate the feeling through self-education. It gives me an ambition to progress and to show cause that prejudice of that kind is unbased." (p. 82) The rebel shows other middle-class aspirations: He would like to travel (p. 78), he would like to marry "a girl who can talk about anything in life that we want to discuss—a show, opera, sports, news, politics . . ." (p. 109) Rebels express "unlimited aspirations for their children." (p. 109)

Child's rebels did *not* rebel against Italian characteristics which were consistent with middle-class values; on the contrary, more rebels were able to read standard Italian than either the in-group or apathetic group! (p. 103) One rebel was the leader of an Italian organization, (p. 101) most expressed a preference for Italian cuisine. (pp. 110–111) One so-called rebel "spontaneously attributes to himself certain characteristics which he traces to his Italian background . . . a love of detail and color in architecture and painting, a liking for certain kinds of music . . . and certain personal characteristics, particularly individualism." (p. 195)

It should also be borne in mind that Child's study was conducted during 1937 and 1938, the days of Mussolini and the Rome-Berlin axis. The most influential Italian language newspaper in New Haven followed the political line of the fascist government of Italy, according to Child, and that government "was acting . . . directly or indirectly, to encourage the cohesiveness of the Italian population in New Haven . . . . Public utterances of the Italian vice-consul in the city were a very clear call to the people of Italian descent to maintain a feeling of solidarity and loyalty to the idea of the mother country." (p. 47) Child's respondents were well aware that the Rome-Berlin orientation toward military conquest might soon involve them in a test of national loyalty: "[Can you read Italian?] I can, but my heart is not with Italy; therefore I don't enjoy reading Italian newspapers." (p. 103) "[If someone asks you what nationality you are, what do you say?] Well I know I'm a real wop. But I consider myself an Italian-American. If there was a war, I imagine I would go for this country, since I was raised here." (p. 152) Some in-group informants were pro-Mussolini, admired Fr. Coughlin and disliked Haile Selassie! (pp. 127–130) "All of the apathetic informants denied any interest in what goes on in Italy." (p. 165) When he responded to the question "Can you read Italian?" one rebel expressed his feeling of conflict between his wish to improve his Italian and his distaste for pro-Fascist propaganda: "I stopped reading Italian newspapers about two years ago. [Why?] I find the news earlier and more correct in the local papers. But I do miss it, and would like to preserve my knowledge of the language." (p. 103)

Undoubtedly the rebels felt alienated from the Italian group both because the old culture was in many ways *anti* middle-class, and was during the period of Child's field study becoming increasingly identified with a hostile foreign power. For both these reasons it is difficult to accept Newcomb's assertion that the Italian Americans, as represented by Child's study, "are in many ways typical of many marginal people." (Newcomb 1950, p. 542) As Linton has pointed out, a group adopts new ways "on the basis of their . . . compatibility with pre-existing culture patterns." (p. 3) Since the pre-existing norms of the Eastern

European Jews gave clear and high priority to education, to upward mobility and to middle-class urban values in general, one must seriously question the direct relevance of Child's data to the role behavior of the Jews in the United States.

What may we then conclude from the facts which Child's influential and pioneering study presents? The three groups—the rebel, the in-group and the apathetic—seem to emerge from a conflict between the values of the Southern Italian peasant culture and the middle class culture of the United States. The in-group has been predisposed to interiorize the parental values. (Perhaps their aptitude for mechanical or craft work significantly outstrips their aptitude for school work. Perhaps their appearance, temperament and general intelligence predisposes them to lower class in-group membership.) Their behavior is necessarily defensive both because of their minority group status and because of the international tensions which prevailed during the time of the investigation.

The rebel is primarily oriented toward middle class status, probably through early training in achievement motivation, and through specific encouragement from his parents "to respect and obey his teachers just as he did them." (Child, p. 193) Quite probably the rebels stand highest in verbal intelligence and have therefore had the most rewarding school experience. (In Child's protocols, the rebels display a distinctly superior command of English and speak at a higher level of abstraction.)

The apathetic group seems to be most clearly marked by *ambivalence;* they are the marginal persons torn between rebellion and submission to the authoritarian role of the Italian father, torn between loyalty to Italian fascism or to American democracy, torn between the security of lower class membership and the more uncertain rewards of middle class membership. We would hypothesize that the apathetic group is the most temporary and transitional of the three; that eventually its members take their place in either the conservative lower class in-group, or in a more acculturated and middle class Italian American group which, as they succeed to the position of the parental generation, need no longer play the role of the rebel. As Campisi has observed, the third generation of Italian Americans (the erstwhile rebels' children), feeling "more secure in their own status, can now afford to take a more tolerant view of their foreign parentage and reconcile some of the conflicting aspects of the two cultures." (paraphrased by Seward, 1956, p. 214)

104. Doob, page 472.
105. Seward, 1956, page 213.
106. Newcomb, 1950, page 539.
107. Krech and Crutchfield, 1948, page 509.
108. Lewin, 1939, page 164.
109. Lewin, 1939, page 164. In the Preface to his original *Social Psychology.* Newcomb professes a deep respect for his colleague Kurt Lewin, and acknowledges Lewin's great influence on Newcomb's viewpoint. (page. vii) In dealing with the social adjustment of minority

group members, however, Newcomb fails to acknowledge the fact that he and Lewin disagree sharply on this issue.

110. Lewin, 1939, page 164.
111. Newcomb, 1950, page 542.
112. Riesman, 1942, pages 48–49.
113. Warner and Srole, page 295.
114. Glazer, 1955, page 144.
115. *Ibid.*, page 141.
116. Anonymous author of "An Analysis of Jewish Culture," Chapter 9 in Graeber's anthology. The author will be referred to in this study as *Critic*.
117. Critic, page 255.
118. M. M. Goldberg, page 16.
119. Marden, page 403.
120. The argument that one cannot be both a full citizen of the American nation and of the Jewish nation is fallacious to the extent that it confuses two discretely different meanings of the word *nation*. *Webster's Collegiate Dictionary* offers no less than five definitions of the word, including "(1) A people connected by supposed ties of blood generally manifested by community of language, religion, customs, etc.," and "(2) The body of inhabitants of a country united under a single independent government; a state." Brandeis carried out the above distinction by referring to concept (1) as a *nationality*, and concept (2) as a *nation*. "A nation may be composed of many nationalities," Brandeis observed, "as some of the most successful nations are. An instance of this is the British nation, with its division into English, Scotch, Welsh, and Irish at home; with the French in Canada; and throughout the Empire, scores of other nationalities. Other examples are furnished by the Swiss nation with its German, French, and Italian sections; by the Belgian nation composed of Flemings and Walloons. . . . The false doctrine that nation and nationality must be made coextensive is the cause of some of our greatest tragedies. . . . As a nation may develop though composed of many nationalities, so a nationality may develop though forming parts of several nations. . . . There is no inconsistency between loyalty to American and loyalty to Jewry. The Jewish spirit, the product of our religion and experiences, is essentially modern and essentially American." (Brandeis, 1915, pages 19–20, 29.)

Brandeis's thesis, said Lewin, "is sociologically sound. . . . Every individual belongs to many overlapping groups: to his family, his friends, his professional or business group, and so on. He can be loyal to all of them without being thrown into a constant state of conflict and uncertainty." (Lewin, 1940, page 179.)

121. Anonymous, 1939a, page 43.
122. Glazer and Moynihan, page 16.
123. Adapted from Antonovsky, Table 1, page 59, and respondents quoted on pages 60 and 61.
124. Krech and Crutchfield, 1948, page 508.

125. Kugelmass, pages 147, 148. A. I. Gordon, 1949, lists three pages of name changes made by Jews of Minneapolis, from 1901 to 1945. (pages 318–320).
126. Davenport, page 151.
127. Teitelbaum, pages 2–3.
128. *Ibid.*, page 219.
129. *Ibid.*, from Table 1, page 31.
130. *Ibid.*, page 223.
131. *Ibid.*, from Table 36, page 110.
132. *Ibid*, pages 111–113.
133. *Ibid.*, from Table 3, page 32.
134. Hsu, 1961, page 224.
135. Kaufmann, page 87. Alfred Kazin describes *Remember Me To God* as "the most solid and most genuinely created novel of Jewish life in America." (Balzell, p. 67) By contrast, Nathan Rothman's review of the novel disposed of it as "a character study of a wretched hypocrite, without love, without integrity, without spiritual quality of any kind, and even without the will or the talent or the attractiveness to lend strength to his vulgar climbing." *Remember Me To God* "is not a story about a Jewish problem," Rothman insisted, but a picture of a despicable cad. (page 48)
136. Leslie Fiedler comments wryly on ". . . Jewish boys who gather in fraternities and dedicate themselves to athletics, hard drinking and sex, to make clear that they are by no means the joyless scholars, the bodiless 'brains' that Gentile fantasy would make them." (1954, page 120)
137. *Ibid.*, page 198.
138. Danglow, page 8.
139. Anna Freud, page 118.
140. Orlansky, page 379.
141. Lewin, 1941, page 198.
142. *Ibid.*, page 194.
143. *Ibid.*, page 188.
144. Slotkin, 1942b, page 38.
145. Bernard, page 271.
146. Rubenstein, pages 138–139.
147. *Ibid.*, page 138.
148. *Ibid.*, page 139.
149. Franzblau, page 23.
150. Reik, 1962, pages 175–176.
151. The following is a random sampling of items on the Sarnoff scale, agreement with which designates an attitude of anti-Semitism:

> The fact that Jews keep to themselves helps to intensify ill-feeling against them.

> I am generally not taken for a Jew by non-Jews.

Although we may get extremely angry when under verbal attack by anti-Semites, it would be dishonest for us not to recognize that much of the attack might have been avoided if we had not behaved in a way which invited it.

Despite the fact that I myself am Jewish, I can think of fewer things which upset me more than the sight of a typically boorish and bad mannered Jew trying to compensate for his feelings of inferiority.

Jewish college students would be doing the Jewish group a great service if they developed a bit more humility and reticence.

It is a strategic error for so many Jews to crowd into professions like teaching, law and medicine. It would be better for them to enter all types of occupations.

Imbedded in Sarnoff's A-S scale were the following items, agreement with which provided a measure of *assimilationist* tendencies:

I sometimes feel that if we mingled more with Gentiles they would learn to develop a more favorable attitude toward Jews.

Basically, Jews are only a group in the sense that they have a common religion such as Catholics and Protestants.

There are a lot of pros and cons about intermarriage; but, frankly, I would just as soon marry a non-Jewish girl as I would a Jewish one.

It is impolite to use any Yiddish expressions in the company of Gentiles.

I can see no objection to changing to a less Jewish-sounding name if it would be of help in getting me into jobs or schools which ordinarily discriminate against Jews.

When dealing with certain Gentiles it is best not to advertise the fact that one is Jewish.

152. Engelman, 1940, page 160.
153. *Ibid.*, page 166.
154. J. E. Mayer, 1961b, page 190.
155. *Ibid.*, page 190.
156. *Ibid.*, pages 190–191.
157. Anonymous, 1940, page 9.
158. *Ibid.*, page 9.
159. *Ibid.*, page 10–11.
160. *Ibid.*, page 11.

161. *Ibid.*, page 9–10.
162. Bernard, page 290.
163. Erikson, page 163.
164. Seward, 1958, page 279.
165. Fiedler, 1964, page 67.
166. An observer who is painfully aware of "the weaker sides of Jewish life in America" (Riesman 1954, page 68) finds it difficult to believe that American Gentiles can find something genuinely enjoyable in the Jewish style. Riesman conjectures that Gentiles who "overeagerly welcome all signs of Jewish folksiness from their Jewish friends [do so because they are] so afraid of being thought ethnocentric. . . ." (Riesman 1954, page 160)
167. Fiedler, 1964, page 65.
168. Tumin, 1957, page 33.
169. Fiedler, 1964, page 63.

The breakthrough of Jewish fiction to a dominant position on the American scene occurred, according to Ribalow, in 1956–57 when three American Jewish novels were high on the best-seller list: Herman Wouk's *Marjorie Morningstar,* Meyer Levin's *Compulsion,* and Gerald Green's *The Last Angry Man.* "This was the first time in American history," Ribalow noted, "that works of fiction by and about American Jews were read and accepted by so many non-Jewish Americans." (page 46)

Norman Podhoretz likewise identifies "the newly chic status of Jewishness" as a phenomenon of the 1960's. In his autobiography, he writes: "Even as late as the year 1953—how widespread, still, and not least among Jews, was the association of Jewishness with vulgarity and lack of cultivation." (page 161) In the 1960's "a startling transformation of attitude" emerged as American Jews suddenly "were replacing the Southern writers as the leading school of novelists and so dominating the field of serious fiction that a patrician WASP like Gore Vidal could complain whimsically of discrimination. . . ." (pages 309–310)

The theme of Podhoretz's 1967 autobiography, however, is that it is still necessary to defend the Jewish ethos. *Making It* is a bold and explicit defense of *yichas atsmo* in a world of affected noblesse, a plea for *yashar* in a world of Anglo-Saxon decorum, an unabashed celebration of *chutspah* in a world of feigned modesty. It is a bold repudiation of the old notion that a Jewish intellectual in America must affect the protective coloration of a facsimile WASP (or worse yet—reshape his thinking, his values, and his habits to fit an Anglo-conformist model) in order to find a place of dignity in the American community.

Podhoretz credits his mentors Robert Warshow and Moses Hadas with demonstrating by example "that it was possible to achieve cultivation without losing touch with oneself, without doing violence to one's true feelings, without becoming pompous, pretentious, affected, or false to the realities of one's own experience—without, in short, becoming a facsimile WASP." (page 149)

170. Fiedler, 1964, page 68.
171. *Ibid.,* page 68–69.
172. *Ibid.,* page 67.
173. *Ibid.,* page 68.
174. *Ibid.,* page 136.
"There is scarcely a father of an adolescent in the United States who is not presently becoming aware (though he may feel it as a pain, rather than know it as a fact) that his son is, in his whole life-style, his speech, his gait, the clothes he wears, the music he loves, as well as the vices he emulates, closer to the life-style of Negroes than *he* could have foreseen on the day of his son's birth. He may find him, in fact, in posture and in gesture, in intonation and inflection, perhaps even in the deepest aspirations, which, after all, control such outward behavior, closer to the great-grandfathers of his Negro friends, or at least to what those great-grandfathers have meant to the white imagination, than to their own great-grandfathers—Anglo-Saxon or Italian, Jewish or Greek, Scandinavian or German, Irish or Slav." Fiedler, 1964, p. 136.
175. *Ibid.,* page 135.
176. Bernard, pages 287–288.
177. Bamberger, page 14.
178. *Ibid.,* page 14.
179. *Ibid.,* page 14.
180. *Ibid.,* page 13.
181. The Jewish population, Dean explains, is spuriously conspicuous because of their concentration in retailing and other fields of public contact. In the city of Elmira, in which the Negro and Jewish communities each number less than three percent of the population, a group of white Gentiles were asked to guess the percentages of Negroes and Jews to the general population of the city. Respondents guessed on the average that Negroes constituted nine percent of the population, and Jews 27 percent. (page 249)
182. Rubenstein, page 140.
183. Brossard, page 154.
184. Rubenstein, page 135.
185. Bohannan uses the term *matricentric* to describe a family in which the relationships between a woman and her children is stronger than the linkage of the male in either the husband-wife or father-child relationship. The term seems to have been evolved to describe family patterns in societies which have had a history of slavery. (Bohannan, page 74) We have adopted the term matricentric to describe a society in which the household is dominated by women. In the culture of the Jews, this norm appears to be the derivative of a matrilocal rule of residence, *kest,* practiced in the Eastern European *shtetl* and in more ancient times. This topic is discussed in detail in Chapter 6.
186. Sklare, 1964, page 51.
187. Bondarin, pages 241–243.

CHAPTER 2

1. Lehrman, a psychiatrist who summarized his clinical experience with 30 patients who were or had been intermarried, concluded that as a group intermarrieds are "not very sick" compared with other patients who come for treatment. About one-third of Lehrman's sample sought consultation because of social pressures resulting from their marriage plans. In some cases at least, it is presumed that the parents insisted that their child talk with a psychiatrist before going ahead with his plans to intermarry.

The patients themselves, says Lehrman, were either oblivious or "only peripherally aware of the contributions of neurotic drives to their choice of mate." In the majority of his 30 cases, the patients were seen because of psychic suffering, and their mixed marriage emerged only as another facet of their conflicts. "With treatment, many mixed marriages have been saved," Lehrman adds—implying of course that many were worth saving. ". . . When divorce was inevitable, the next marriage had greater chance of success because of treatment." Pages 78, 80 fn.

2. Mayer offers as documentation: Romanzo Adams on Hawaii, Kurt B. Mayer on Switzerland, Louis Rosenberg on Canada, and Uriah Z. Engelman (1940) on the Jews of Germany, USSR, and Switzerland.

3. Rossman, summarized by Tumin, 1961, page 97.

4. Since this section deals with intermarriage statistics, it is well to point out that reported frequencies are ambiguous to the extent that respondents may differ in their personal definition of intermarriage, and collectors of statistics may not share a uniform definition of intermarriage. Should a convert designate his original religious affiliation, or his newly-acquired affiliation? Mihaly pleads that "no special term [be applied to] a marriage between a Jew and a non-Jew who has converted, since such a marriage is in every sense a Jewish one." (p. 86) Ordinarily, the term *intermarriage* refers to a marriage between persons of different ethnic *origin* regardless of acquired religious affiliation, and a *mixed marriage* describes a partnership in which each partner retains his own religious identity.

5. Erich Rosenthal, 1963, from Table 14, page 40.

6. Locke et al., from Table 1, page 330. Source given as The Official Catholic Directory (1955), New York: J. P. Kenedy and Sons.

7. The anomalously low rate of interfaith marriages in the West South Central region is undoubtedly related to the fact that a significant portion of Catholics in this area are persons of Mexican descent.

8. Cahnman, page 58.

9. *Ibid.*, page 64.

10. Louis Rosenberg, 1963, adapted from Table II, page 67.

11. Shosteck shows that in small-towns of Canada, "old timers" (residents of 21 years or longer) were more likely to hold Orthodox affiliations than "newcomers" (those with less than six years residence) :

	Percent Orthodox	Percent Conservative	Percent Reform
"Old timers"	40	35	25
"Newcomers"	10	40	50

Shosteck also demonstrates that intermarriage is more likely to occur among children of Reform Jews than among children of Orthodox Jews. (Of 260 small town Jews, percent of intermarriage among all married children was 14 for Reform Jews and 8 for Orthodox Jews.)

12. Trainin, page 170.
13. Sidney I. Goldstein, page 15.
14. Levinger, page 157.
15. Kramer and Leventman, page 212.
16. Slotkin, 1942b, page 37.
17. Rubenstein, page 123.
18. *Ibid.*, pages 139, 140.
19. Shanks, page 374.
20. *Ibid.*, page 374.
21. *Ibid.*, page 373.
22. Arthur A. Cohen, 1959, page 62.
23. Heiss, pages 50–51. Intermarrieds responded "Yes" to phrases quoted, to a significantly greater extent than control group—P exceeding .01 according to Heiss.
24. Maier and Spinrad, from Table 2, page 356. "Protestant" column totals 101% in authors' published findings; authors apparently neglected to follow the custom of "rounding off" percentages so that they total exactly 100.
25. Bernard, page 271. Kramer and Leventman suggest that through the Sunday School, the suburban rabbi plays a role similar to the Old World grandparent, inducting the child into religious observances toward which the parents themselves may have grown indifferent. One North City parent complained peevishly:

> The rabbi gets our kids in the palm of his hand and sends them home to make us feel ashamed of being irreligious Jewish parents. (page 83)

26. Levinson and Levinson, page 120. *Identification* is a key concept in social psychology, and a familiarity with this concept provides a basis for understanding such phrases as "a weakened identity" or "a pluralistic identity," such terms as assimilation, acculturation, marginality, and "emancipation."

Identification is the concept that seems to best describe the inner process that transforms the human animal into a member of society. In the family situation, a direct struggle for power and privilege would put the child at a hopeless disadvantage and generate the debilitating and divisive influences of hatred, resentment, and apathy. How does the human family become a cohesive and effective work group despite great differences in power and privilege among its members? Apparently the child adapts to his inferior social role, and also prepares himself for the future as a social animal, by extending his inner sense of identity to include his "rival" parent. The power and prestige of the parent becomes something for the child to enjoy rather than to fear and oppose. The normal experience of growing up in a family leads the child to identify with parental authority and thereby to interiorize the norms (customs, values, standards) of the society which his parents represent. This is the familiar "transmission belt" theory of socialization which describes the parent as the carrier of the culture from one generation to the next.

Identification with his culture means that the person judges his own sense of worth by how strongly he feels recognized and accepted by the group to which he claims membership. Cooley defined this need for group support as "social self-feeling," and called it "the mainspring of endeavor" for all normal persons. What Cooley describes as "social self-feeling" is by no means a sense of coercion or pressure to conform; he is describing the silent yet powerful influence of the group on the person's inner sense of worth:

> As is the case with other feelings, we do not think much of it so long as it is moderately and regularly gratified. Many people of balanced mind and congenial activity scarcely know that they care what others think of them, and will deny, perhaps with indignation, that such care is an important factor in what they are and do. But this is an illusion. If failure or disgrace arrives, if one suddenly finds that the faces of men show coldness or contempt instead of the kindliness and deference that he is used to, he will perceive from the shock, the fear, the sense of being outcast and helpless, that he was living in the minds of others without knowing it, just as we daily walk on solid ground without thinking how it bears us up. (Cooley, page 208)

> . . . The self that is most importunate is a reflection, largely, from the minds of others. . . . We live on, cheerful, self-confident, conscious of helping make the world go round, until in some rude hour we learn that we do not stand so well as we thought we did, that the image of us is tarnished. Perhaps we do something, quite naturally, that we find the social order is set against. . . . We find with a chill of terror that the world is cold and strange, and that our self-esteem, self-confidence, and hope, being chiefly founded upon opinions attributed to others, go down in the crash. Our reason may tell us that we are no less worthy than we were before, but dread and doubt do not permit us to believe it. . . . (Cooley, pages 246–247)

If a person is ready to give up his group identification, it must be supposed that his "self-esteem, self-confidence, and hope" is no longer founded upon opinions attributed to his group; feeling the support and approval of his group has ceased to be a source of his "inner sense of worth."

The tendency of a disadvantaged class to identify with the norms of the dominant group parallels the weak and helpless child's identification with parental power and authority. The French social philosopher Tarde set down as one of his "laws of imitation" the tendency of the masses to adopt the standards of the aristocracy:

> Given the opportunity, a nobility will always and everywhere imitate . . . its king . . . and the people likewise, given the opportunity, its nobility.
> Courtesy comes from the court, as civility comes from the city. The accent of the court and, later on, of that of the capitol spreads little by little to all classes and to all provinces of the nation. [Tarde pointed to] the influence of the upper classes upon the lower, of townsmen upon rustics, of colonial whites upon native blacks, of adults upon children, of upper classmen [in schools] upon lower . . . in the matter of accent . . . of writing, gesture, facial expression, dress and custom. (Tarde, pages 217–218)

A child who identifies too completely with the world of adults—one who always wants to act as if he is a grown up—shows an estrangement from his own world of childhood, and a predisposition to look with disapproval upon the normal activities of childhood. Similarly, a Jew cannot fully identify with the dominant group unless he has become estranged from—or is seeking to escape—his Jewish identity. Likewise, a Jew who identifies with the dominant group must be predisposed to disfavor Jewish attitudes, appearances, and habits. (The phenomenon of "negative chauvinism" was introduced in Chapter 1.)

27. Erich Rosenthal, 1963, page 29.
28. J. E. Mayer, 1961a, page 19 fn., citing Winch, q.v., page 406.
29. In Sklare and Greenblum's Lakeville study of 430 Jewish families in an affluent midwestern suburb, in those cases in which one spouse claimed to be of Eastern European descent, and the other of German descent, typically the wife was "a German girl who is younger and more advanced in generational status [married to] an older (and presumably occupationally successful) man of Eastern European descent who is less advanced in generational status." (page 33)
30. Cahnman, page 70.
31. Heiss, page 19.
32. J. E. Mayer, 1961a, page 83.
33. *Ibid.*, page 165.
34. *Ibid.*, page 134.
35. Heiss, page 53.
36. Adler, 1931, page 146.
37. McArthur, page 209.
38. Adler, 1931, page 146.
39. Wexberg, pages 188–189.

40. Adler, 1931, page 151.
41. Freud, 1915, page 320.
42. Lehrman, 1965.
43. Lehrman, 1967, pages 73–75.
44. *Ibid.*, page 114.
45. J. E. Mayer, 1961a, pages 60–61.
46. Sherman, 1961, page 189.
47. Levinson and Levinson, page 103.
48. *Ibid.*, page 109.
49. Franzblau, page 23.
50. Cahnman, page 183.
51. Sherif, page 197.
52. Kramer and Leventman, pages 18–19.
53. Seidler and Ravitz, page 12.
54. *Ibid.*, page 13.
55. *Ibid.*, page 11.
56. *Ibid.*, page 12.
57. *Ibid.*, page 13.
58. *Ibid.*, page 11.
59. Hollingshead and Redlich do *not* report how many of New Haven's 30 psychiatrists were psychoanalysts; only that 83 per cent of the psychoanalysts were Jewish; see page 155.
60. *Ibid.*, page 163.
61. *Ibid.*, page 164. In his 1962 Kober Lecture, Zigmond Lebensohn expressed concern over the influence of respectability on the composition of the psychoanalytic fraternity:

> The very respectability which psychoanalysis (and psychiatry) has achieved as a professional way of life now attracts to it young men of quite a different stamp than was the case in the early twenties. In those days psychoanalysis was suspected and derided. To practice it was a risky way of earning a living. In spite of this, and possibly because of this, the early psychoanalysts were a gifted, daring, creative and dedicated group. They instilled a spirit of hope, enthusiasm and scientific promise in an area which had become static, custodial and stale. But how different today seem the bright young men who enter the field! They have only to complete their training— no small feat in itself—to be assured of instant security, automatic prestige, financial bounty, and a long list of prospective patients. The course of training is hard, but the rewards are rich. And in the training process, can one doubt that the temptation is great to complete the requirements according to the book or to accept uncritically the methods and manners of the master?

62. Hollingshead and Redlich, page 163.
63. *Ibid.*, page 164.
64. Bossard and Letts, page 309.
65. A 1938 University of Chicago study by Robert Roberts uncovered 188 Negro-white marriages; in 147 instances (or 73 per cent of the

cases) the husband was the Negro partner. (Drake and Cayton, page 137) In Joseph Golden's interview study of 50 Negro-white couples in Philadelphia, the husband was the Negro partner in 44 instances (or 88 per cent of the cases). "It is this one-sided aspect of intermarriage that irks Negro women," write Drake and Cayton (page 136) and this displeasure leads to consistently higher "prejudice" scores for women when Negro men and women are compared on social distance scales of the Bogardus type. (Robin Williams, pages 266–267.)

Drake and Cayton recall a discussion overheard in 1939 among some Negro Communists "in which the whole question of intermarriage was being aired. A young colored Communist woman was protesting because a prominent Negro artist had married a white woman. She was rebuked by her husband for uttering sentiments unbecoming to a Communist Party member, and was threatened with 'party discipline' for giving vent to 'nationalistic deviations.' In self-defense, she flashed back with the charge that the white men in the Communist Party seldom married colored women, and that they could therefore be accused of 'white chauvinism.' Her critics were disconcerted, for no one could name a single male Communist in Midwest Metropolis who was married to a colored girl, although there were a number of cases in which Negro men had married white women. The general community pattern prevailed even within this radical sect." (pages 137–138 fn.)

66. Merton, pages 372–373.

67. Slotkin (1942) studied 100 intermarried Jewish husbands during the 1930's and estimated that 44 percent married below their class; only six percent married above, and the remaining one-half married within their class. (Of 83 intermarried Gentile husbands, on the other hand, only 9 percent married below their class, 19 percent above, and 72 percent within their class.)

Ethnic origin of intermarried husband	Wife's class position, compared with husband's			
	Lower	Same	Higher	(N)
Jewish	44%	50%	6%	(100)
Gentile	9%	72%	19%	(83)

Slotkin anticipated Merton's trading hypothesis with the comment that "Jews tend to marry Gentiles of a lower class due to the higher social status of the Gentile group in general."

How to account for the discrepancy between the class differences reported by Slotkin, and the more recent observations of the Levinsons and Hollingshead and Redlich? Slotkin conducted his study during a period of economic depression, with a less acculturated group, drawing his sample from social agency clientele. It is quite possible that an intermarrying downward mobile Jew tends to marry a person of inferior socio-economic rank, while the opposite trend applies to an upward mobile Jew.

68. A. I. Gordon, 1949, page 207.
69. Cavan, page 251.
70. See also McClelland et al., pages 19–20 for a summary of evidence on the upward mobility of American Jews.
71. Terman, page 298.
72. Sherman, 1961, page 198.
73. Bigman, page 206.
74. Shosteck; see Table 9, page 46.
75. Rubenstein, page 122.
76. A.I. Gordon, 1964, page 61.
77. *Ibid.*, page 77.
78. Kaufmann, page 407.
79. *Ibid*, pages 406–407.
80. Slotkin, 1942b, page 37.
81. J. E. Mayer, 1961a, page 23.
82. *Ibid.*, page 127 fn.
83. A. I. Gordon, 1964, page 51.
84. *Ibid.*, pages 216–218.
85. L. Freeman, page 371.
86. *Ibid.*, page 373.
87. *Ibid.*, pages 371–372.
88. *Ibid.*, page 372.
89. *Ibid.*, page 373.
90. Heiss, page 51.
91. Lewin, 1940, page 181.
92. Weidman, page 489.
93. Lewisohn, 1928a, page 244.
94. Weidman, page 92.
95. Hilgard, page 453.
96. Munroe, page 290.
97. Noyes, pages 330–331.
98. Gilberstadt and Duker, page 85.
99. Engelman, 1940, from Table 2, page 161.

CHAPTER 3

1. This is the expressed viewpoint of Levinson and Levinson, and of A. I. Gordon, 1964.
2. Israel, page 53. Rabbi Israel makes this statement by way of acknowledging the fact that not every intermarriage works out badly.
3. A. I. Gordon, 1959, page 244.
4. Trainin, pages 170–171.
5. Koenig, page 238.
6. Franzblau, pages 24–25.
7. Rubenstein, pages 123–124.
8. Hernton describes the mothering wife and dependent husband as typical of marriage partnerships between white men and Negro women:

Repeatedly I have witnessed Negro women virtually dominating their white husbands. . . . The woman . . . capitalizes on her Negroness and on her sex image by wielding a sort of Amazon mastery over the white male. In all but a few black women—white man relationships, it is the man who must do the adjusting—and what he must adjust to is nothing less than what is referred to as the Negro's "mode of existence," or the Negro's conceptualization of life in the United States. (page 162)

9. J. E. Mayer, 1961a, page 39. Mayer conjectures that where Jewish membership in a group (e.g., medical school) is deliberately restricted, the very few Jews whose distinguished qualifications enable them to gain membership will indeed constitute a special aristocracy of merit in the eyes of the majority! A by-product of discriminatory practices, therefore, are highly selected Jewish sub-groups which contribute to the image of the Jew as a superior person (page 26 fn.).
10. J. E. Mayer, 1961a, page 49.
11. *Ibid.*, page 59.
12. *Ibid.*, pages 133–134.
13. *Ibid.*, page 26 fn.
14. Gertrude, page 46.
15. Levinson and Levinson, page 115.
16. *Ibid.*, page 115.
17. *Ibid.*, page 119.
18. J. E. Mayer, page 50.
19. *Ibid.*, page 68.
20. *Ibid.*, page 68 fn.
21. *Ibid.*, page 50.
22. Abraham, 1913, pages 48–49.
23. Lehrman, 1967, pages 72–73.
24. Levinson and Levinson, page 112.
25. *Ibid.*, page 127.
26. *Ibid.*, page 128.
27. *Ibid.*, page 118.
28. *Ibid.*, page 112.
29. *Ibid.*, page 118.
30. *Ibid.*, pages 118–119.
31. *Ibid.*, page 117.
32. Hamilton and MacGowan, pages 157–158.
33. *Ibid.*, pages 157–162.
34. *Ibid.*, pages 157–158.
35. *Ibid.*, pages 153–155.
36. *Ibid.*, pages 151–152.
37. *Ibid.*, pages 151–152.
38. *Ibid.*, page 152.
39. *Ibid.*, pages 159–160.
40. Kramer and Leventman, page 204. The high intermarriage rate of Jews who work in the salaried professions is perhaps only a symptom

of a more basic and far-reaching problem of the Jewish community in America—the alienation of the salaried professionals from the Jewish community. Kramer and Leventman suggest that Jewish community leaders "are inclined, however reluctantly, to write this group off as a 'lost cause'. . . . They are relatively transient, and local community leaders are never certain that particular salaried professionals are going to be living in the community long enough to be worth 'cultivating.' Synagogues also find that members of non-Jewish occupations are unlikely prospects, unless they have children of Sunday School age. Even then, they can rarely be seduced into active participation." (page 203)

One wonders if the Jewish community is so highly organized around the talents and interests of its leaders—businessmen and independent professionals—that the salaried professional finds himself at a significant disadvantage as a participant in the activities of the Jewish community. Perhaps this is what Noah Gordon was trying to say in *The Rabbi*, in the episode concerning the alienation of the college professor over the building fund assessment which the synagogue demanded of him.

41. Kramer and Leventman, pages 204–205.
42. Rubenstein, page 138.
43. Kramer and Leventman, page 130.
44. *Ibid.*, page 140.
45. Quoted from Sklare, 1964, page 49.
46. *Ibid.*, pages 49–50.
47. E. Rosenthal, 1963, from Table 7, page 27.
48. *Ibid.*, from Table 17, page 44.
49. A. I. Gordon, 1964, pages 79–81.
50. J. E. Mayer, 1961a, page 36.
51. *Ibid.*, page 63.
52. *Ibid.*, page 37.
53. Kinsey et al., 1953, page 342. See Table 9:3 of this book.
54. In *Remember Me To God*, Kaufman contrasts the way Richard's Jewish girl friend Jeanie rules out premarital intimacy, with the unexpected acquiescence of his Gentile fiancee, Wimsy. After Jeanie has proved receptive to a prolonged session of petting, Richard moves boldly toward sexual intimacy. Jeanie tears herself away from him and squeals, "What are you trying to do to me . . . have you gone mad? . . . What's gotten into you?" (page 324) . . .

"You mean—just like that? Without getting married or anything? . . . I couldn't . . . I couldn't! I couldn't!" (page 325)

By way of contrast, Kaufman describes how Wimsy surrenders herself to Richard, in unexpected response to his sulking about postponing marriage until they can "straighten out his parents." Wimsy surprises him with the words, "I won't make you wait, dearest . . . you can take me. In sin." (page 382) When they are locked in sexual embrace Wimsy cries out, "Oh, ye saints in Heaven, save me! . . . Save me! I implore you!"

"What the hell are you praying for?" Richard mutters.

"We're in sin!" she says in his ear. "Isn't it the most thrilling ever? Mortal, deathly sin!" (page 384)

55. Shulman, page 30. Kirshenbaum, Pool, and Danglow have likewise expressed the attitude that engagement to a Jew at the time one seeks conversion to Judaism raises a doubt as to the candidate's sincerity.

56. Rubenstein, page 129.

57. Eichorn, 1963, page 119. Diametrically opposing Rabbi Eichorn's view that sincere converts are "a precious spiritual asset," is Rabbi Kirshenbaum's argument that even a sincere and devoted convert poses a threat to Jewish group survival: The proud Jewish parents, and the officiating rabbi, "praise the qualities of the new member . . . and tell all their friends. This has had the effect among families with no mixed marriages or converted Christians among their relatives" of weakening their defenses against intermarriage and presumably rendering them vulnerable to the designs of an opportunistic convert. (page 106)

58. J. E. Mayer, 1961a, page 107.

59. A. I. Gordon, 1964, page 170.

60. *Ibid,* page 77.

61. Rubenstein, pages 130–132.

62. *Ibid.,* page 141.

63. Schwartz, page 26.

64. Rubenstein, pages 127–128.

65. *Ibid.,* pages 135–136.

66. *Ibid.,* page 135.

67. *Ibid.,* page 136.

68. Price, pages 261–263.

69. C. Rosenthal, pages 265–268.

70. Lehrman, 1967, pages 70–71.

71. Bamberger, pages 13–14.

72. *Ibid.,* page 13.

73. A. I. Gordon, 1964, page 209.

74. Eichorn, 1963, page 120. Not every rabbi, of course, is so kindly disposed toward proselytes—or so hopeful about the long-term results of their conversion. Rabbi Kirshenbaum takes the extreme position that if a Gentile's outreach to Judaism coincides with his plans to marry a Jew, the convert is *ipso facto* not a righteous proselyte, and the children of such a marriage "with few exceptions . . . marry Gentiles and in time . . . disappear totally from the Jewish community." (page 107) Danglow concludes from 41 years' experience as a rabbi that "very few, if any, of such so-called converts—however 'nice' as they may be, subsequently evince any real interest or enthusiasm for the new faith they have professed to adopt from sincerity and without ulterior motive." (page 12) In 1918 Rabbi David De Sola Pool judged that in nine cases out of ten when a Gentile fiance undertakes conversion to Judaism, the act is "little more than a superficial form . . .

undertaken to please the Jewish husband or wife, or to satisfy the Jewish parents-in-law. . . . Of not more than the fewest of a small number can it be said that their conversion is sincere and that they constitute a real accession to the Jewish people." (page 13)

75. *Ibid.*, pages 119–120.
76. Eichorn, 1954, page 316.
77. Rubenstein, pages 133–134.
78. *Ibid.*, page 133.
79. Resnick, page 101.
80. J. E. Mayer, 1961a, page 176.
81. Eichorn, 1954, page 317 fn.
82. A. I. Gordon, 1964, pages 76–77.
83. J. E. Mayer, 1961a, page 23.
84. Bigman, page 138. See also A. I. Gordon, 1964, pages 205–206.
85. Linton Freeman, page 369.
86. J. E. Mayer, 1961a, page 110.
87. *Ibid.*, page 110.
88. *Ibid.*, page 116.
89. *Ibid.*, page 116.
90. A. I. Gordon, 1964, pages 284–288.
91. *Ibid.*, pages 290–293.
92. Can we conclude that 58 per cent of American-born white wives in interracial marriages are likely to be Jewish? Our confidence in Golden's finding as a *representative* (or "true") percentage of Jewish-Negro marriages falters when we examine the procedure by which he obtained his interview sample of 50 Negro-white marriages. Golden worked up a list of 141 Negro-white couples in Philadelphia by canvassing about 75 persons who were thought to know about interracial families in that area. He located his interview sample of 50 by telephone. Golden concedes that this procedure, since it eliminated all those who did not have listed telephones, led him to over-sample middle class families. One might also wonder if *Jewish* wives might be more willing to cooperate with a graduate student named Joseph Golden who telephones to say that he would like to interview a number of interracial couples.

We examine the facts behind the figures of Golden's study not because his procedures are any less adequate than those of many other investigators, but to give the reader a closer look at some of the practical problems involved in survey research, and to point in particular to the need for more adequate sampling methods.

93. Hernton, page 38.
94. Cahnman, pages 191–192. In a 1966 *Midstream* symposium on "Negro-Jewish relations in America," Leslie Fiedler broods over that disturbing by-product of the civil rights movement—increasing numbers of Negro babies born to unmarried Jewish girls. Fiedler describes this phenomenon in the context of Negro anti-Semitism, suggesting that by this means the Jewish girl—*a la* Queen Esther—makes love with the enemy of her people, as her Negro boyfriend acts out his towering

ambivalence toward the Jew. Some Negroes will marry their Jewish girl-friend "to escape Bohemia," says Fiedler, and then agree with a Negro poet's published statement that "Jewish girls only marry Negroes to emasculate them." The newest mythology, says Fiedler, is that love will save us—"not big theoretical, but small sexual love." Fiedler closes his comment on the gloomy note: "The disillusionment it will inevitably breed at least still lies ahead, and (if I am lucky) I may not live so long." (Pages 28–29.)

95. Gibel, page 13.
96. Drake and Cayton, page 142.
97. Hernton, page 53.
98. Hernton, page 53. See also Drake and Cayton, page 144 fn.
99. Hernton, pages 52, 53.
100. Gibel accuses Jews who oppose Negro-Jewish intermarriage of violating the Jewish tradition of compassion for the oppressed. She herself offers the statistic that of the nine or ten Negro-Jewish couples she knows intimately, *none* is raising their children in the Jewish faith (as she is). This is all the evidence one might need to oppose Negro-Jewish marriages as a disruptive influence on Jewish family life and on the Jewish community.
101. Hernton, pages 37–38.
102. *Ibid.*, page 49.
103. *Ibid.*, page 49.
104. *Ibid.*, page 44.
105. *Ibid.*, pages 43-45.
106. Devereaux, pages 82–83.
107. Hernton refers repeatedly to the neurotic white woman's search for a "stereotype Negro." If we turn, however, from Hernton's personalized and impressionistic report to Golden's more objective study, we learn that of the 44 intermarried Negro husbands he interviewed, Golden rated ten as persons who either could pass as white or were "almost passable." We may conclude, therefore, that Hernton's generalizations by no means fit *all* the known facts about Negro-white marriages.
108. Hernton, page 45.
109. *Ibid.*, page 40.
110. Devereaux, page 87.
111. The lure of the exotic lover is a classic theme in folklore and literature, and is the topic of Chapter 9.
112. Devereaux, page 87.
113. Gibel, page 14.
114. Buhler, page 514.
115. *Ibid.*, page 514.
116. *Ibid.*, page 511.
117. *Ibid.*, page 515.
118. *Ibid.*, page 510.
119. *Ibid.*, pages 509–510.
120. *Ibid.*, page 514.
121. *Ibid.*, page 522.

122. *Ibid.,* page 513.
123. *Ibid.,* page 522.
124. *Ibid.,.* page 524.
125. *Ibid.,* page 520.
126. *Ibid.,* page 521.
127. J. E. Mayer, 1961a, page 58.
128. *Ibid.,* page 59.
129. *Ibid.,* page 89.
130. *Ibid.,* page 89.
131. Mayer cites evidence to support his view that this sex difference in willingness to talk about personal matters has no special bearing on intermarriage. (*Jewish Gentile Courtships,* p. 68 fn.) It would indeed be worth ascertaining whether endogamously married men would speak more freely on the topic of "things about their partners that had especially appealed to them."
132. J. E. Mayer, 1961a, page 62. A first encounter with a stranger from a different milieu is more likely to elicit shy, polite, correct, somewhat formal and "serious" behavior than a first meeting with a person from one's own milieu. Undoubtedly there are young people of both sexes and of all groups, whose sexual inhibitions predispose them to feel more at ease in making a new acquaintance in an atmosphere of politeness and formality. Such a person might easily confuse in-group familiarity with sexual provocation or aggressiveness. Thus Lehrman notes with surprise that two of his female patients, one Jewish and the other Protestant, explained their attraction to cross-ethnic boys in almost exactly the same terms: Florence, a Jewish girl, sought out only Italian and Irish Catholic boys because they were warm, kind, gentlemanly, and not out to take advantage of her; precisely the reasons given by Gwen, a Protestant, for choosing Jewish boys! (Lehrman, 1967, page 75.)
133. *Ibid.,* page 62.
134. *Ibid.,* page 62.
135. *Ibid.,* pages 70–71.
136. *Ibid.,* pages 92–93.
137. *Ibid.,* page 83.
138. Anselm Strauss, page 104. Vorhaus describes a pattern of interaction between an active woman and a passive, reluctant male, in which the male finds himself undeliberately if not inadvertently "going steady" and getting married. To illustrate this phenomenon, Vorhaus (p. 79) constructs the following conversation between two buddies:
"When did you propose to her?"
"Come to think of it, I never did."
"You mean she proposed to you?"
"Of course not, she's not like that."
"Well, how did you *know?*"
"I don't know, it sort of happened. We just got around to assuming, to taking it for granted, that some time—when we could afford it—that we would get married."

139. It is interesting to note that a recent study of 64 American servicemen who had requested (and had been granted) permission to marry Vietnamese girls, shows a high incidence of broken homes, fatherlessness, limited education, sexual inhibition, and unaggressiveness—compared with a control group of 64 single American servicemen in Vietnam who were *not* applying for marriage licenses. The personality characteristics of the intermarrying group (based on Thematic Apperception Test and MMPI testings) show a clear resemblance to Strauss' Japanese-American wives' descriptions of their ex-serviceman husbands. (The Vietnam study, conducted by Army psychiatrist William F. Kenny and Army psychologist Albert Kastl, is reported in *This Week Magazine*, September 10, 1967, pages 4–5.)
140. Slotkin, 1942b, pages 36–37.
141. A. I. Gordon, 1964, page 280.
142. *Ibid.*, page 282.

CHAPTER 4

1. Levinson and Levinson, page 130.
2. What are the facts that guide Foote and Cottrell to the conclusion that "heterogamy now seems less likely than was formerly thought to interfere with marital harmony?" The reader who looks up Foote and Cottrell's reference for the above statement—"Strain and Harmony in American-Japanese War-Bride Marriages" by Anselm Strauss—encounters a most astonishing document, the declared purpose of which is to challenge the "assumption that Oriental-Caucasian marriages are subject to greater strain than the ordinary marriage." Strauss asserts that this assumption is "a substantial oversimplification," and contends that "the strains that occur in Japanese-American marriages are patterned and relatively predictable." As a matter of fact, Strauss advises the reader that "some Japanese-American marriages are . . . quite 'stable,' and . . . involve fewer major stresses than a great many marriages between native Americans." (Strauss, page 99)

Strauss' optimistic generalizations are based on an interview study of 45 Japanese war-brides living in the Chicago area. Most of the husbands were professional soldiers stationed in Chicago; others were ex-servicemen who had settled in Chicago "mainly because the wife needed Japanese companionship." (page 105) At least four cases of unusual and severe marital strife are reported—including the case of a wife who suddenly packed the family possessions and demanded that her husband resettle in Japan with her and adopt her family name, and the case of a war-bride who "killed her child and attempted suicide." (page 105) Still the author opposes "the usual assumption that interracial marriages . . . are peculiarly subject to strains and instability . . . [and assures his reader] that many strains indeed are less likely to occur in mixed marriages than in non-mixed marriages." (page 105)

As Strauss unfolds the facts which support his generalization, the reason why "many strains . . . are less likely to occur in mixed marriages" becomes alarmingly and astonishingly simple: many of the potential sources of strain in the lives of young couples involve gaining approval of each partner's close friends, maintaining good relations with in-laws and family on both sides, and resolving conflicts in institutional loyalties. These sources of strain do not exist for Strauss' couples for the same reason that the poor have no investment problems; Japanese-American couples of Strauss' study lead socially impoverished lives *without* old friends, *without* family ties, and *without* organizational affiliations except for a local war-bride club. (page 103) Their recreational life takes place in their own home or in the home of one of their war-bride friends. (page 103)

The other basis of these couples' marital harmony lies in the fact that the husbands are men without commitment to a profession, to a community, to family or to friends—and acquiesce to the limited though urgent requirements of their war-brides. According to Strauss, the husband's church attendance was "spotty or non-existent . . . and their ethnic allegiances are generally nil or weak." (page 101) Organizational affiliation of any kind is "a notable omission in the lives of these couples. . ." (page 103) Husbands show a willingness "to find their friends almost solely among other mixed couples." (page 104) "Some of the husbands are small town boys who have moved to Chicago mainly because the wife needed Japanese companionship." (page 105) The Japanese brides, Strauss reveals, also force their husbands out of the army if faced with overseas assignment and the need to make adjustments to still another culture. The husband "may never have been anything other than a professional soldier . . . so that he feels insecure in the civilian world and incompetent at non-army work." (page 104)

Separated from their friends, family, home town, and occupation, the husbands can draw comfort from the fact that their wives do not "exert much pressure upon their husbands to improve themselves occupationally or in status. . . . Unlike many American wives," Strauss notes, "they do not seem to make great demands, or successively increasing ones, upon their husbands to supply them with money for clothes and other status-symbols. . . . The lack of demand is reciprocal, for husbands do not require their wives to take up a career or to become mobility-conscious." (page 103)

Such are the factual details which support Strauss' optimistic report that many marriage strains "are less likely to occur in mixed marriage than in many non-mixed marriages," (page 105) and which underlie Foote and Cottrell's observation that "heterogamy now seems less likely than was formerly thought to interfere with marital harmony." (Foote and Cottrell, page 24.)

3. Barron, 1951, page 252, quoting from New York Times, January 31, 1950.

4. Danglow, page 10.

5. Rokeach, 1965, pages 10–11. Rokeach's index of pre-marital conflict was based on responses to questions: "Did parents object to the marriage? Had they themselves had doubts about it beforehand? Had they ever broken off their engagement?" For indications of marital conflict, Rokeach "asked questions about how often they quarreled, whether they had ever separated (if so, how many times), and whether they had ever contemplated divorce." (1965, pp. 10–11. A fuller description of this research is reported in Rokeach, 1960.)
6. Franzblau, page 22.
7. Bamberger, page 11.
8. Barron, 1951, page 250.
9. Bamberger, page 11.
10. Bossard and Boll, pages 117–118.
11. A. I. Gordon, 1964, pages 102–111.
12. Slotkin (1942a), page 227.
13. Bloom, page 196.
14. Landis, page 406.
15. A. I. Gordon, 1964, pages 100–101.
16. Kirshenbaum, pages 96–97.
17. Rubenstein, page 142.
18. Baber, 1939, pages 172–173.
19. Levinson and Levinson, page 112.
20. A. I. Gordon, 1964, page 172.
21. Lehrer, page 54.
22. Kirshenbaum, page 107.
23. Danglow, page 9.
24. Slotkin, 1942a, page 227.
25. J. E. Mayer, 1961a, pages 142–143.
26. *Ibid.*, page 173.
27. Kirshenbaum, page 164.
28. Hollingshead and Redlich, page 163.
29. Goldhurst, page 35.
30. A. I. Gordon, 1964, pages 338–342.
31. *Ibid.*, page 341.
32. Gertrude, page 46.
33. Fiedler, 1964, page 135. An American radical's self-discovery of his latent Jewish identity is the theme of Paul Jacobs' autobiography, *Is Curley Jewish?* Jacobs asked himself how much of his adult life as a radical, union organizer, and journalist was guided by the Jewish identity he thought he had discarded in adolescence. As he re-examines his life history, Jacobs has no doubt that the bald and middleaged man he is today is Jewish—albeit "a Jewish radical of a rather peculiar kind"—but he is fascinated to reflect on how much his latent Jewishness was at work during his period of "emancipation."
34. Coon, pages 33–34.
35. Kertzer, pages 60–63.
36. Bossard and Boll, page 106.
37. Mack, page 32.

38. Bloom, page 191. Rabbi Polish documents and interprets the reaction of an assimilated Jewish college student, to the death of his father. In 1940, Rabbi Polish recalls, the young stranger burst into his office at the Cornell University Hillel Foundation "asking for the rabbi on the campus. No one ever knew him to be a Jew and he knew no Jews. Ski coach, champion skier in Europe, he had lived for some time at the Sigma Chi house. But that day he came in search of a rabbi. He had received word that his father had been killed in Prague by the Nazis, and this estranged man who had long ago left Judaism now sought Jews among whom to mourn and a Jewish way in which to grieve. He wanted to come to my home where, unshod, he could sit on the floor in solitary bereavement. He wanted to join in a daily *minyan* throughout his eleven-month period of mourning. This man, who had thrown his lot unreservedly with a non-Jewish world, had come home." Rabbi Polish adds the interpetive comment: "It was not only death that recalled him. It was the covenant which death had reawakened in him." (1965, pages 65–66)

39. Bossard and Boll, pages 17–20.

40. Lewisohn, 1928, page 771.

41. Tashman, Chapter 2.

42. Baber, 1937, page 712.

43. *Ibid.*, page 714.

44. Baber, 1937, page 711. See also Baber, 1939, pages 171–172.

45. Landis, 1949, page 404.

46. Levinson and Levinson, page 130.

47. A. I. Gordon, 1964, page 289.

48. *Ibid.*, page 293.

49. J. E. Mayer, 1961a, page 122. Mayer reports that most of his 45 intermarried couples expected that their children would be socially identified as Jews regardless of what their parents' preference might be: "Others will feel that since the children have some Jewish blood, they're Jewish." "Some people say that if a person is one sixteenth Jewish—he's Jewish." (p. 121)

50. Sokolsky, 1933, page 144.

51. *Ibid.*, page 143.

52. *Ibid.*, page 144.

53. Fiedler, 1964, page 120.

54. Memmi, 1966, pages 101–104.

55. Recht, page 770.

56. Lovell, page 5.

57. Devereaux, pages 80–81.

58. Mann, pages 131–132.

59. *Ibid.*, pages 87–88.

60. *Ibid.*, page 86.

61. *Ibid.*, page 86.

62. *Ibid.*, pages 86, 88.

63. *Ibid.*, pages 93, 95, 97–98.

64. *Ibid.*, page 100.

65. *Ibid.,* pages 103–104.
66. *Ibid.,* pages 123–124.
67. *Ibid.,* pages 128, 130.
68. *Ibid.,* page 131.
69. *Ibid.,* page 88.
70. *Ibid.,* page 105.
71. Rosten, page 47. The tendency for parents to have "no Jewish friends" was of course much stronger for the Gentile controls (57 per cent) than for mischlings (2 out of 15, or 13 per cent).
72. *Ibid.,* pages 42–47.
73. *Ibid.,* page 50.
74. *Ibid.,* page 45.
75. *Ibid.,* page 50.
76. *Ibid.,* from Table IV, page 41.
77. *Ibid.,* page 48.
78. *Ibid.,* page 57.
79. *Ibid.,* page 48.
80. *Ibid.,* page 49.
81. *Ibid.,* page 49.
82. *Ibid.,* page 51.
83. *Ibid.,* page 100.
84. *Ibid.,* page 52.
85. *Ibid.,* page 104.
86. *Ibid.,* page 105.
87. *Ibid.,* page 104.
88. *Ibid.,* page 105.
89. *Ibid.,* page 61.
90. *Ibid.,* page 38.
91. *Ibid.,* page 105.
92. *Ibid.,* page 53.
93. *Ibid.,* page 52.
94. *Ibid.,* page 54. Rosten wonders whether a harmonious mixed marriage in itself gives the child "a false impression of what it means to be a Jew or a Gentile in the world beyond the home," or whether the mischling's parents deliberately repress any hint of anti-Semitism as a fact of life. In any case, "the results were the same—a severe lack of preparation which magnified the mischlings' first encounter with prejudice." (Rosten, pages 51–52.)
Rosten attaches special significance to Eric Erikson's view that a person's ego identity is "based upon two simultaneous observations: the immediate perception of one's own self-sameness and continuity in time, *and the simultaneous perception of the fact that others recognize one's sameness and continuity.*" (1959a) Elsewhere Erikson deals more specifically with the adolescent's search for identity, and alludes to the confusion suffered by the mischling child who has been raised to regard himself as no different from his elite Gentile peers, and discovers that his status group does not recognize the mischlings' definition of his identity. The result of this role confusion, says Erikson, is that the

adolescent feels impelled to choose between extremes rather than search out a workable synthesis or integration of ethnic roles:

The wholeness to be achieved [during adolescence] I have called a sense of inner identity. The young person, in order to experience wholeness, must feel a progressive continuity between that which he has come to be during the long years of childhood and that which he promises to become in the anticipated future; between that which he conceives himself to be and that which he perceives others to see in him and to expect of him. . . The adolescent search for a new and yet a reliable identity can perhaps best be seen in the persistent endeavor to define, to overdefine, and to redefine oneself and each other in often ruthless comparison; while the search for reliable alignments can be seen in the restless testing of the newest in possibilities and the oldest in values. Where the resulting self-definition, for personal or for collective reasons, becomes too difficult, a sense of role confusion results; the youth counterpoints [i.e., polarizes] rather than synthesizes his sexual, ethnic, occupational, and typological alternatives and is often driven to decide definitely and totally for one side or the other. (Erikson, 1959b, pages 91–92.)

95. *Ibid.*, page 54.
96. *Ibid.*, from Table V, page 40.
97. *Ibid.*, page 67.
98. *Ibid.*, from Table VI, page 41.
99. *Ibid.*, pages 65–66.
100. *Ibid.*, page 63.
101. *Ibid.*, page 109.
102. Rosten does report that "many mischlings had experienced a feeling of rejection from the Jewish as well as the Gentile community," and adds that four of the 15 told of rebuffs from Jewish girls:

It's strange, but the only trouble I ever had on a date was with a Jewish girl. I called her up and she said, "I'm sorry I can only go out with Jewish boys." I told her I was half-Jewish—what could I do? She said, "Well, I guess so," but she did not seem too happy about it. (page 62)

Reading Rosten's total report, rather than the above citations alone, one is led to conclude that the mischling has easier access to Jewish peer groups than to Gentile.

103. *Ibid.*, page 66.
104. *Ibid.*, page 3.
105. *Ibid.*, page 95.
106. *Ibid.*, page 45.
107. *Ibid.*, page 46.
108. *Ibid.*, page 45. Since the Harvard mischlings had not been raised as Jews and do not regard themselves as Jews, how might we interpret the personal importance they seem to attach to a knowledge and appreciation of the Jewish tradition? Erikson suggests an answer to this question, in his reflection that "in order to lose one's identity, one must

first have one; and in order to transcend, one must pass through and not bypass ethical concerns." (Erikson, 1959b, page 100.)

109. *Ibid.*, page 45.
110. *Ibid.*, page 47.
111. *Ibid.*, page 64.
112. *Ibid.*, page 47.
113. *Ibid.*, page 46.
114. *Ibid.*, page 47.
115. *Ibid.*, pages   15–16.
116. *Ibid.*, page 99.
117. *Ibid.*, page 64.
118. *Ibid.*, page 3. Rosten offers this as an autobiographical footnote, but he himself falls within the definition of his study group, being a Harvard undergraduate of Jewish-Gentile parentage.
119. *Ibid.*, page 66.
120. *Ibid.*, page 63.
121. *Ibid.*, page 96.
122. *Ibid.*, page 86.
123. *Ibid.*, page 66.
124. *Ibid.*, page 67.
125. *Ibid.*, page 108.
126. *Ibid.*, page 109.
127. *Ibid.*, page 98.
128. *Ibid.*, page 78.
129. *Ibid.*, pages 106–107.
130. *Ibid.*, page 55.
131. *Ibid.*, page 59.
132. *Ibid.*, page 40.
133. *Ibid.*, page 61.
134. *Ibid.*, page 2.
135. *Ibid.*, page 60.
136. *Ibid.*, page 56.
137. *Ibid.*, pages 55–56.
138. *Ibid.*, page 69.
139. *Ibid.*, page 69.
140. Sharaf, page 111.
141. *Ibid.*, page 49.
142. *Ibid.*, page 116.
143. Rosten, from Table VII, page 73.
144. *Ibid.*, page 74.
145. *Ibid.*, page 55.
146. *Ibid.*, page 69.
147. *Ibid.*, page 117.
148. *Ibid.*, page 103.
149. *Ibid.*, page 66.
150. *Ibid.*, page 55.
151. *Ibid.*, page 108.

152. *Ibid.*, page 77.
153. *Ibid.*, page 77.
154. *Ibid.*, page 78.
155. *Ibid.*, page 84.
156. *Ibid.*, pages 78–79.
157. *Ibid.*, page 78.
158. *Ibid.*, page 79.
159. *Ibid.*, page 80.
160. *Ibid.*, page 81.
161. *Ibid.*, page 78.
162. *Ibid.*, page 81.
163. *Ibid.*, page 85.
164. *Ibid.*, page 85.
165. *Ibid.*, page 81.
166. *Ibid.*, page 82.
167. *Ibid.*, page 82.
168. *Ibid.*, page 83.
169. *Ibid.*, page 91.
170. *Ibid.*, page 91.
171. Kertzer, page 223.
172. Baber, 1937, page 706.
173. Koenig, page 238.
174. Engelman, 1940, page 166.
175. *Ibid.*, page 166.
176. Rubenstein, page 128.
177. *Ibid.*, page 129.
178. *Ibid.*, page 129.
179. L. Freeman, pages 374–375.
180. *Ibid.*, page 375.
181. *Ibid.*, page 375.

CHAPTER 5

1. Gordon (1964), p. 200. This classic drama is characterized by Rabbi Kirshenbaum in exquisite detail:

Parents come to the rabbi wringing their hands in desperation, bewailing their bad luck. 'Who would have thought our one and only son would do this thing to us? Try talking to him—perhaps you will be able to do something. We can't bear it. He has made us so unhappy. . . . We have gone through every stage of agony. Financially things were never too well with us, but we always gave our child the best of everything. After all he is our only son, the apple of our eye—he is all our hope and all our life. How happy we were when he won a scholarship at high school and a second one at college! He was so popular for his intelligence, his good manners, his speech, and his gentlemanly behavior.

'Yesterday we were prepared for the great event—his graduation from college with top honors. He had offers from large companies offering him fine career opportunities. You can imagine how thunderstruck we were when our son came to us after the ceremony, in cap and gown, escorting a non-Jewish girl and introducing her to us: "This is June, my fiancee. I think it's time you all got acquainted." We were stunned and speechless. Suddenly all our hopes had been blotted out.

'Afterwards, whenever we started speaking to him we became hysterical and broke down. Please send for him, Rabbi; perhaps you will succeed in explaining to him the tragedy he's caused his parents. He will drive us to the grave. He is smart and understands—he will listen to you.'

'Did your beloved and only son receive a Jewish education?' asks the rabbi.

'Who had time for that?' the mother immediately changes her tone with a touch of annoyance. 'As a child he was rather delicate. When he was about to become thirteen we engaged a Hebrew teacher who prepared him for *bar mitzvah*. What more could we have done?' [Much more, by the rabbi's standard, as he proceeds to tell them, placing responsibility for their son's marriage choice squarely on the shoulders of the parents, for neglecting their son's 'Jewish education.'] pp. 18–19.

2. Pool, pages 6–7.

3. Bohannan, page 329. The importance that Jews attach to *social allegiance* compared with adherence to a religious creed, is nicely demonstrated in Sobel and Mirsky's report on the Birmingham (Michigan) congregation's "experiment in Jewish religious radicalism." Under the leadership of "atheist" Rabbi Sherwin Wine, the suburban congregation held firm against unfavorable publicity, until they were denied the use of the local Masonic Temple as a meeting hall and reluctantly accepted the offer of the Unitarian Church to use its facilities.

"Dissension within the Temple resulted from outside attack on one issue alone: the question of 'Jewishness.' Members said they were not afraid of being called atheists. They did not like the appellation, but they did not consider it a charge worth denying. . . . But the charge of assimilation or 'un-Jewishness' stung deeply. While it is true that a small percentage of Temple members manifested what might be considered a low degree of Jewish group attachment, the majority were reasonably high in their commitment to Jewish symbols and values. Reading books of Jewish interest, cooking and eating traditional Jewish food, working on behalf of the State of Israel—these were the activities which the group considered most meaningfully Jewish for them." (pages 41–42.)

4. Landis, 1960, pages 344–345.

5. Cited by A. I. Gordon, 1964, page 70, from study by Sklare and Vosk, q.v.

6. Monahan and Kephart.

7. Lenski, page 289, *see also* Winch, Greer, and Blumberg, page 269.

8. Orlansky, page 382.
9. Kramer and Leventman, page 189.
10. Hurvitz. Theodor Reik devotes the final chapter of his book *Pagan Rites in Judaism* to the topic of "Family Loyalty." The extended family is discussed in further deail in Chapter 8 of this book.
11. Bressler, page 566.
12. Hurvitz, page 218.
13. Ruppin, page 106.
14. Memmi, 1966, page 92.
15. *Ibid.*, pages 90–105. Albert Memmi is perhaps the only contemporary Jewish intellectual who has written autobiographically on the topic of mixed marriage.
16. From Teitelbaum, Table 68, page 203.
17. *Ibid.*, page 99.
18. *Ibid.*, from Table 33, page 107.
19. J. E. Mayer, 1961a, page 147.
20. *Ibid.*, page 147.
21. Slotkin, 1942a. *See* Table 3:7 of this book.
22. J. E. Mayer, 1961a, page 147.
23. Bamberger, page 10.
24. Sklare, 1964.
25. Eichorn, 1963, pages 111–112.
26. Dean, page 254.
27. Kahn, pages 25–27.
28. Kaplan, 1934. *See also* Bamberger, and Eichorn, 1963.
29. Kirshenbaum, page 19.
30. Polish, 1964, page 36.
31. Rubenstein, page 125.
32. Franzblau, pages 21–22.
33. Rubenstein, page 142.
34. *Ibid.*, page 141.
35. Kaplan, 1934, page 418.
36. Shanks, page 374.
37. Franzblau, page 22.
38. J. E. Mayer, 1961a, page 128.
39. *Ibid.*, page 128.
40. *Ibid.*, page 142.
41. A. I. Gordon, 1964, pages 339–340.
42. Drachsler, page 80.
43. Sklare and Greenblum, page 309.
44. *Ibid.*, page 306.
45. *Ibid.*, page 319.
46. *Ibid.*, page 320. Psychiatrist Franzblau noted that Jewish parents sometimes insist that their errant offspring consult with a psychiatrist before the parents will give their consent to an intermarriage. He suggests that a psychiatrist's services might be more productively engaged in helping the *parents* cope with the crisis. (He also recommends that rabbis counsel parents who are emotionally distraught over an inter-

marriage, to seek the help of a psychiatrist in easing their emotional burden.)

47. Sklare and Greenblum, page 313.
48. *Ibid.*, pages 313–314.
49. *Ibid.*, page 311.
50. *Ibid.*, page 138.
51. *Ibid.*, page 311.
52. J. E. Mayer, 1961a, page 128.
53. *Ibid.*, page 132.
54. *Ibid.*, page 129.
55. *Ibid.*, page 129.
56. *Ibid.*, page 127 fn.
57. *Ibid.*, page 142.
58. *Ibid.*, page 130.
59. *Ibid.*, page 131.
60. *Ibid.*, page 129.
61. *Ibid.*, pages 129–130.
62. Goldhurst, page 33.
63. Bondarin, page 243.
64. In the novel *Letting Go,* Paul—a young Jewish graduate student—marries a sensitive, somewhat unstable girl, Catholic in background but not in practice. She eagerly accepts the Jewish faith. Paul's father and mother are both outraged, but it is the *father* who never recovers from the crisis, who reacts as if he were engulfed in a formless, nameless tragedy. Roth describes in detail the corrosive influence of this disappointment on the father's morale and health, and one wonders if the author is describing a prototype of the Jewish parents' reaction to an intermarriage.
65. A. I. Gordon, 1964, page 288.
66. *Ibid.*, pages 170–171.
67. *Ibid.*, page 173.

CHAPTER 6

1. Murdock, pages 284–85. Klineberg offers an extensive discussion of the incest taboo and patterns of avoidance—with many anthropological, historical, and clinical citations. (pages 138–150) For his 1967 A.P.A. Presidential Address, Lindzey drew together a wide range of observations—from experimental genetics, anthropology, and psychoanalysis—on the incest taboo.
2. Murdock, page 290.
3. Cited by Freud, 1912a, page 902.
4. *Ibid.*, page 901.
5. Murdock, page 291.
6. Freud, 1912a, page 901.
7. Murdock, page 292.
8. *Ibid.*, page 260.

9. *Ibid.*, page 296.

10. Murdock, page 297. Opposing Murdock's view that the incest taboo was established primarily to stabilize social relations *within* the group, and secondarily proved adaptive in stabilizing relations between groups, is the school of thought represented by Service, who argues that the stabilization of relations *between* groups was the earlier and primary *object of* the incest taboo. The control of sexual jealousy *had already been solved* by pre-human primate groups, Service supposes, through the maintenance of a hierarchy of dominance statuses; "it was the relations between groups that were dangerous and unordered." (page 45)

Service cites Tylor's 1888 conjecture that tribes must have discovered that reciprocal outmarriage provided a unique means for keeping up a permanent alliance: "Savage tribes must have had plainly before their minds the simple practical alternative between marrying-out and being killed out." (Tylor, page 267) [Tylor recalls Hamor's offer to Jacob, in the Book of Genesis: "Intermarry with us; give your daughters to us and take our daughters for yourselves. You can thus live among us: the land shall be open to you to settle in, move about freely in it, and acquire holdings." (Genesis, page 262)]

The basis of human culture, Service aptly argues, is man's capacity for *sharing.* Sharing is based on man's capacity for symbolic language, which enables him to deal with "future times, other places, and even non-existent things and places. . . ." (page 35) (A child cannot really *share* until he can understand that his present sacrifice will be reciprocated at some later time in a yet-unknown way.) Reciprocal outmarriage is a significant kind of sharing, one which "has the same social results as other kinds of balanced reciprocal exchanges." (page 46) The early marriage rule in human society, Service conjectures, was probably an alliance with a specific other group. The incest taboo would then serve as a means of maintaining the marriage rule. "Since young females must be married out of the group, it would be disruptive of this rule to permit sex relations and the emotional ties engendered thereby, within the group." (page 46)

It would seem consistent with the Murdock view to argue that the pre-human mode of controlling sexual jealousy by maintaining a dominance hierarchy was not conducive to the development of *human* culture. The monopolization of power and privilege, the maintenance of group stability through threat and suppression, may not generate a social climate favorable for the development of man's human potential. Perhaps it was necessary to establish an atmosphere of reciprocity *within* groups before reciprocal relations between groups would be possible.

Is it not possible that the sharply hierarchical structure of the primate group was an evolutionary dead end? Perhaps the emergence of human culture required more broadly reciprocal role relations, and this state of "brotherly love" became possible only when men renounced their sisters, mothers and daughters as sex objects. Compared with the primate horde, human culture effects a more widespread distribution of sexual privilege. From this point of view, human culture becomes the liberator rather than the suppressor of the sex impulse.

11. The incestuous wish is an ambiguous concept, referring to sexual attraction toward cross-parent *or* sibling. Fluegel holds that the baby's original love object is his mother. Erotic attraction toward sister is regarded as a sign of emotional development, the arrival at "a normal transitional phase" or stepping-stone from attachment to mother, to the seeking of a sanctioned love object. (page 89)

12. Murdock, page 293.

13. Berlyne, q.v., has been a leading investigator and theorist of exploratory behavior.

14. Konorski, pages 226–227.

15. Murdock, page 294.

16. *Ibid.*, page 284.

17. Kinsey, 1948.

18. Hernton, page 18.

19. From Figure 11:9, Kimble, page 341.

20. Rosenbaum, page 39.

21. *Ibid.*, from Figure 2, page 39.

22. Freud, 1912a, page 814.

23. *Ibid.*, page 810.

24. *Ibid.*, page 807.

25. Murdock, Table 2, page 19. To Bohannan, residential classification is one of the oldest and thorniest problems in social anthropology. Bohannan objects to Murdock's classification of residence rules as too arbitrary and fixed. (pages 87–99) The evaluation of Bohannan's objections, and the scrutiny of Murdock's evidence, lies beyond the scope of this book.

26. *Ibid.*, from Table 2, page 19.

27. *Ibid.*, page 202.

28. *Ibid.*, page 18.

29. *Ibid.*, page 217.

30. *Ibid.*, pages 205–207.

31. *Ibid.*, pages 206–207.

32. Freud sensed the connection between the practice of exogamy and a culturally-patterned fear of a punishing father, a theory for which he found anthropological support, as set forth in his essay *Totem and Taboo*. In this essay Freud describes the totemic system of the Australian aborigines, their organization into hereditary clans each of which designates as its object of worship a totem animal (or more rarely a plant or force of nature) which is claimed as "the tribal ancestor of the clan, as well as its tutelary spirit and protector. . . ." The law of the totem places its members "under a sacred obligation not to kill their totem, to abstain from eating its meat or from any enjoyment of it. Any violation of these prohibitions is automatically punished."

Freud was impressed by the fact that "almost everywhere where the totem [system] prevails, there also exists the law that the members of the same totem are not allowed to enter into sexual relations with each other; that is, they cannot marry each other. This represents the exogamy which is associated with the totem."

This strong association between totemism and exogamy suggests that the incest taboo is felt as enforced by a "punishing father figure." The impulse to strike back, to destroy the oppressor, requires an elaborate system of control represented by the sacred vows and rules of the totem. The dread of endogamy as a threat to the survival of the tribe is interpreted here as a generalized avoidance habit based on the acquisition of the incest taboo under conditions of severe threat.

33. Mead, page 68. One feels impelled to ask: What is the common condition of life which led tribesmen in the mountain settlements of New Guinea and dwellers in the Eastern European *shtetl* to converge upon extended family relations as a dominant social value? The answer perhaps lies in the fact that both groups lived on the edge of poverty. Where there are few other resources by which persons can satisfy their physical and psychological needs, human relations becomes a prime and prized resource.

34. Zborowski and Herzog, page 74.

35. *Ibid.*, page 78.

36. *Ibid.*, page 73.

37. *Ibid.*, page 77.

38. *Ibid.*, page 80.

39. According to Zborowski and Herzog it was assumed that persons attracted to manual or non-verbal skills were either temperamentally or intellectually unsuited for the life of learning. On the other hand, status accrued to middle class occupations because they were more likely to afford the independence and leisure for religious study.

40. Zborowski and Herzog quote from an interview: "In our family, we girls couldn't just marry anybody. I remember there was a fellow courting my sister. He came from Odessa and was a tailor. He was rich and he was goodlooking and he wanted to marry my eldest sister. So my mother (a widow) asked her brothers, and they said 'No.' How could she even think of marrying her first daughter to a tailor from a *prosteh* family? And if she married her oldest daughter to a tailor, to whom would she already marry her youngest daughter? To a musician? And my sister didn't marry the tailor." (pages 272–73)

41. Zborowski and Herzog, page 78.

42. Zborowski and Herzog, page 273. Interestingly, Berelson and Steiner used the term "intermarriage" to describe marriage between persons of different social classes: "Marital partners are selected primarily within classes, although there is a sizeable amount of *intermarriage between neighboring ranks.*" (page 482) In a 1966 issue of *Midstream*, journal of Conservative Judaism, a passing reference is made to the "rate of *intermarriage between Oriental and European Jews.*" (vol. 12, no. 6, page 8) Italics added.

43. Zborowski and Herzog, page 272.

44. *Ibid.*, page 319.

45. *Ibid.*, page 85.
46. *Ibid.*, page 84.
47. *Ibid.*, page 86.
48. *Ibid.*, page 87.
49. *Ibid.*, page 83. Weyl quotes and comments upon the description of matchmaking contained in Miriam Zunser's memoirs of *shtetl* life at the turn of the century: "The search, as Mrs. Zunser describes it, was for families 'kneaded and soaked through' with rabbis. Despite the Jewish reputation for preoccupation with money," Weyl notes, "matchmakers would praise a prospective groom as 'a find, an ornament, a savant, a scholar who *did not know the face of a coin.*'" (Weyl, page 187, italics added)
50. *Ibid.*, page 84.
51. *Ibid.*, page 276.
52. On the custom of preparing a written marriage contract, Ausubel writes in a serio-humorous vein:

Nothing whatsover was left to fate or to the imagination. With meticulous precision, this in order to avoid vulgar squabbles and misunderstandings later on, [the future father-in-laws would] note down exactly how much dowry the bride would bring her husband. They'd render an itemized account of her trousseau down to her last underskirt and bustle, making plain of what materials this and that garment was to be made, whether of batiste, velvet, or satin. They'd make it perfectly clear whether the groom could expect a heavy gold watch and chain, or just a silver one without a chain, as a wedding gift from his future father-in-law. Black on white the bride's father would inscribe as an everlasting memorial his agreement to provide the young couple with bed and board for the first few years of wedded life, and to furnish the son-in-law with pocket money so much per month or annum. Also the groom's gifts to the bride were carefully recorded so that later on there'd be no cause for cavil or complaint. Now to the naked untrained eye all this might seem as only the mercenary transaction of small shopkeepers. But to those concerned the sentiment of the heart wasn't in the least bit compromised by calling a spade a spade and then getting a good grip on the spade in the end. (pages 100–101)

53. "Kest," Universal Jewish Encyclopedia. A disaffected son of the 18th Century *shtetl*, Solomon Maimon prefaces this *Autobiography* by describing the three classes of Polish Jews: the working people, the learned professions, and "those who merely devote themselves to learning without engaging in any remunerative occupation . . . [This] class consists of those who, by their pre-eminent abilities and learning, attract the regard of the unlearned, are taken by these into their families, married to their daughters, and maintained for some years with wife and children at their expense. Afterwards, however, the wife is obliged to take upon herself the maintenance of the saintly idler

and the children (who are usually very numerous); and for this, as is natural, she thinks a good deal of herself." (Maimon, page 4.)

Wrote Rabbi Heschel in 1950: "The ambition of every Jew [of the *shtetl*] was to have a scholar as a son-in-law, and a man versed in the Torah could easily marry a well-to-do girl and obtain *kest* for a few years or even permanently, and thus have the good fortune of being able to study in peace. Nowadays [as did Maimon in 1793!] we speak disparagingly of this custom. But few institutions have done more to promote the spiritual development of large masses of people." (Heschel, 1950, pages 48–49.)

54. "Kest," Universal Jewish Encyclopedia.
55. *Ibid.*
56. Mark, page 66.
57. The Jewish view of the ages of man, as codified by Samuel the Younger, of the first century A.D., is inscribed as Mishnah 24, Chapter 5, of Pirke Aboth:

> . . . At five years old one is fit for the study of the Scripture, at ten years for the Mishnah, at thirteen for fulfilling the commandments, at fifteen for the Talmud, *at eighteen for marriage, at twenty for seeking a livelihood,* at thirty for full strength, at forty for understanding, at fifty for counsel, at sixty a man attains old age, at seventy gray hairs, at eighty the gift of special strength, at ninety he bends beneath the weight of years, at a hundred he is like a man who has already died and passed away and ceased from the world. (pages 88–90, italics added; translator's brackets—to designate interpolations—have been eliminated for clarity.)

The Code of Jewish Law likewise designates eighteen or twenty as the proper age for a young man to marry. Interestingly, Freud likewise arrived at the age of twenty as the time limit beyond which "the benefit . . . of abstinence . . . cannot any longer be taken for granted; it may lead to other injuries even when it does not lead to neurosis," wrote Freud. (1908, page 91)

58. Abraham Cohen, page 44.
59. Zborowski and Herzog, page 84.
60. *Ibid.,* pages 271–272.
61. *Ibid.,* page 274.
62. *Ibid.,* pages 81–82.
63. *See* Rappaport.
64. Weyl, page 184.
65. *Ibid.,* page 184.
66. *Ibid.,* page 274.
67. *Ibid.,* page 283.
68. *Ibid.,* page 284.
69. Zborowski and Herzog's characterization of the *shtetl* culture, upon which much of the foregoing description is based, is undoubtedly over-idealized and nostalgic in tone, avoiding whatever observations might disturb an idyllic conception of shtetl life. It is interesting to note

that, in collaboration with Landes, Zborowski documented those aspects of the shtetl culture which might disturb the sensibilities of the Western reader, in a 1950 article for *Psychiatry*.

Eastern European immigrants did not always romanticize their shtetl background. According to Podhoretz (1953), there was a widespread feeling that "the Jewishness of the ghetto was not actually Jewishness at all, but a withered and stunted version of it. The ghetto had perverted the true spirit and character of Judaism, and thus had produced a degenerate breed of Jews with nothing of the dignity and bearing of men whose cultural heritage entitled them to walk upright with their fellows. . . ." (page 262)

The ugliness and hypocrisy of shtetl life was the subject matter of the renowned satirist and father of Yiddish literature, Solomon Abramowitsch (1836–1917), who wrote under the pen name of Mendele. A major theme of Mendele was "the outranking of learning by wealth." (Kutzik, page 32) Says Podhoretz: "The bitterness and hatred of Mendele's satire . . . [portrayed ghetto Jews as] degraded by centuries of misery and poverty, ignorant of everything but the 'useless' scholasticism of Rabbinic studies, boorish, dirty, and vile, so complacent that they were unwilling even to dream of better worlds." (page 262) A full and valid description of shtetl life would make use of the observations of Mendele, and integrate the content of the Landes and Zborowski article into the Zborowski and Hertzog study.

70. Zborowski and Herzog's omission of the topic of intermarriage cannot mean that the phenomenon was unknown to the *shtetl*. Sholom Aleichem's classic tale of family life in the *shtetl*—*Tevya the Dairyman*, which inspired the Broadway Hit musical *Fiddler on the Roof*—was written in Czarist Russia, and the intermarriage of Tevya's daughter Chava is perhaps the major tragedy recorded in this chronicle of countless hardships and uncertainties. The author gives a graphic portrayal of the family's terror and anguish over Chava's marriage to a Gentile postal clerk, and the apostasy which it required. Tevya suffers poignantly in his conflict between his tender feelings toward Chava and his moral obligation to denounce and reject her.

71. Baron, page 166.

72. Stephen Birmingham's chronicle of New York's German Jewish elite makes many references to such *mésalliances*. Even as late as 1950, this elite group "still seemed unprepared . . . for Felicia Warburg's marriage to Robert W. Sarnoff—whom one member of the crowd explained was 'the son of that Russian radio man,' Brigadier General David Sarnoff, chairman of the board of RCA." (page 23)

73. Bernard, page 270.

74. Sargent and Williamson, page 72.

75. Bohannan, page 146.

76. Reik, 1962, page 86. For an essay on "The family: conveyance of a tradition," see Schrecker.

77. *Ibid.*, page 85.

78. Murdock, page 1.

79. *Ibid.*, page 2.
80. *Ibid.*, page 2.
81. Seward, 1956, page 257.
82. Doob, page 44. Neither social psychologists, nor personality theorists, nor clinicians have adequately studied the influence of the extended family (aunts, uncles, cousins, grandparents) on the emotional security or personality development of the individual in our society. How does family experience prepare the individual for relating to persons outside his family? Is it possible that the nuclear family, with its sharp and immediate division between members of the household and others, predisposes the individual to relate to persons outside the family with a polite but distant friendliness? Is it possible that the distant and gradual boundaries of the extended family prepares the individual to establish new relationships on a basis of kinship-like intimacy?

We know much more about the damaging effects upon the individual of a broken home and a disorganized family life. Much of the theorizing about the adjustment problems of the American Negro concerns his long history of family dislocation. According to Drake and Cayton, Negroes commonly blame their troubles on the failure of their group to stick together (page 709), on the claim that Negroes stand "divided against one another more than any other race in the world." (page 723) In the words of one Negro respondent: "The one thing that holds us back more than anything else is lack of unity. It always seems that we hate to see each other get ahead, and instead of helping we always hinder." (page 725) Cothran surveyed 174 New Orleans Negroes on the prevalence of 30 conceptions of white people. The most widely shared conception of white people (shared by 89 per cent of his sample) is that whites "stick together" (page 461). Cothran's respondents showed far greater unanimity on this conception than on many other traits which Negroes are presumed to attribute to white people (e.g., whites feel superior, do not care to be among Negroes, whites are very ambitious, or whites are very shrewd).

83. Young, page 122.
84. Litwak has pointed out that Parson's argument is based on studies of the passing remnants of the extended peasant family in a working class group. The authoritarian structure of this "classic extended family" and its demands of geographical propinquity and occupational involvement did indeed conflict with the demands of a mobile, democratic industrial society. Likewise, studies of small town society point to a conflict between extended family loyalties and upward mobility.

In an urban middle class society, however, says Litwak, one may observe a "modified extended family" that facilitates rather than impedes the adjustment of the nuclear family: uniting a group of nuclear families on an equalitarian basis, "with a strong emphasis on these extended family bonds as end values," and also providing "significant and continuing aid to the nuclear family," especially in the initial stages of their career.

Contrary to the prevailing view that an upwardly mobile family must break away from their extended family, in order to associate with others of equal or greater social rank—Litwak points out that status can also be achieved by gaining deference from one's admiring family. Moreover, since "the family visit can be isolated from friends' visits, especially in large cities, there need be no conflict between association with an extended family of inferior status and association with persons of equal or greater occupational attainment." Litwak refers to a study of 97 white middle-class Protestant parents of married children in which it was demonstrated that about 70 percent contributed sufficient aid (mainly financial) to married children "to influence their status position." Litwak concludes, contrary to Parsons, that "modified extended family relations are more consonant with occupational mobility than the isolated nuclear family."

The extensive kin network of a group of predominantly native-born New York City Jews, is the topic of a 1967 publication by Leichter and Mitchell. (See closing paragraphs of Chapter 8, and accompanying *fns.*)

85. Winch, Greer, and Blumberg, page 272.
86. Berman and Seward, page 458.
87. *Ibid.,* page 460.
88. Jerome Singer, pages 485–486.
89. Buhler, page 511.
90. *Ibid.,* page 515.

CHAPTER 7

1. Lenski, page 92.
2. *Ibid.,* page 33.
3. *Ibid.,* page 33.
4. *Ibid.,* pages 33–34.
5. *Ibid.,* page 35.
6. *Ibid.,* pages 48–49.
7. *Ibid.,* page 195.
8. *Ibid.,* pages 194–195.
9. *Ibid.,* page 196.
10. *Ibid.,* page 38.
11. *Ibid.,* pages 72–73.
12. *Ibid.,* page 288.
13. Population growth provides, of course, an inverse index of community stability, and a comparison of the increase in the size of the Jewish communities of Detroit and Washington shows a most significant difference:

| | Number of Jewish residents | | Percentage |
	1932	1962	of increase
Detroit (Mich.)	75,000	89,000	18.6
Washington (D.C.)	16,000	40,000	150.0

In view of the fact that Washington more than doubled its Jewish population since 1932 (i.e., it is a city of "newcomers") , it is difficult to accept Rosenthal's statement, "My research shows in considerable detail that this community . . . is representative of communities of this size." Letter to the editor, *Commentary*, August 1964, page 16.

14. Glazer, 1955b, pages 1728, 1726.

15. Quoted by Loewenstein, page 118.

16. Sherman, 1961, page 66; quoting Glanz, q.v.

17. *Ibid.*, page 66; quoting Tcherikower, q.v.

18. *Ibid.*, page 66; quoting Stuart E. Rosenberg, q.v. Stephen Birmingham likewise documents the public disdain of the acculturated German Jews for the "uncouth, unwashed" immigrants from Eastern Europe. "The *American Hebrew* asked: 'Are we waiting for the natural process of assimilation between Orientalism and Americanism? This will perhaps never take place.' The *Hebrew Standard* stated it even more strongly: 'The thoroughly acclimated American Jew . . . has no religious, social or intellectual sympathies with them. He is closer to the Christian sentiment around him than to the Judaism of these miserable darkened Hebrews." (page 318)

In Germany and Austria the Eastern European Jewish immigrant was likewise an embarrassment to the acculturated and Westernized Jew. Sigmund Freud's son Martin recalls his paternal grandmother as a person whose Eastern European manners had not the remotest resemblance to Viennese gentility:

> Grandmother came from East Galicia. It might not be known by many people that Galician Jews were . . . absolutely different from Jews who had lived in the West for some generations. They, these Galician Jews, had little grace and no manners; and their women were certainly not what we should call 'ladies'. They were highly emotional and easily carried away by their feelings. . . . In many respects they would seem to be untamed barbarians to more civilized people. . . . (Martin Freud, page 11.)

19. Osofsky tells how the 1890–1914 Southern Negro migration to New York City influenced the life of the city's older Negro community: "Racial antagonism was rekindled in a variety of ways. White churches, for example, which had formerly allowed small numbers of Negroes to participate in regular services, now attempted to ease their Negro members out. . . . The separation that was evident in the churches was true of many other areas of racial contact in the city." (p. 41)

"Negroes who had lived in the city for generations," Osofsky continues, "especially those who gloried in the easing of racial tensions during the late nineteenth century, blamed the southern migrants for reversing this trend. . . . [The Negro aristocracy] railed against the lower-class southern Negro with the virulence of good white racists. . . . 'The middle-class old timers are thoroughly embarrassed by the raucousness, vulgarity, and violence with which they find themselves surrounded,' a Negro clergyman concluded. 'They do everything possible to disassociate themselves from it.' " (p. 43)

In 1908 a New York Negro newspaper editorialized: "We believe the South is the best place for the great masses of the Afro-American people." Osofsky comments: "This same theme was emphasized and re-emphasized in a whole spate of articles, editorials and speeches printed in Negro journals in the years preceding the First World War." (page 44)

20. Kramer and Leventman, pages 41–42.

21. Park and Miller, pages 234–235. Stephen Birmingham insists that the "massive programs of philanthropy" undertaken by the German Jews, were initiated "not out of the great religious principle of *tsedakah*, or charity on its highest plane, given out of pure loving kindness, but out of a hard, bitter sense of resentment, embarrassment, and worry over what the neighbors would think." (page 321) It is difficult to imagine that motives of embarrassment and resentment could suffice to force a group of wealthy citizens to impose upon themselves "a tithing system of raising money, something painfully like taxation. . . . Wealthy Germans, having been brusquely informed of how much they were expected to contribute, emerged from meetings of the United Hebrew Charities with red and angry faces." (page 322) On the other hand, Birmingham describes the German Jewish elite as "a citadel of privilege, power, *philanthropy*, and family pride." (page 19, italics added) Likewise, Birmingham records the Friday evening blessing that patriarch Jacob Schiff would customarily recite:

> . . . Continue to bless us with Thy mercy
> So that we may be able to share our own plenty
> With those less fortunate that ourselves,
> Blessed be Thy name forevermore. Amen.

"He always stressed 'With those less fortunate than ourselves,' " Birmingham adds (page 200) —an observation which casts some doubt on Birmingham's view that the massive programs of philanthropy maintained by the German Jews on behalf of the Eastern European immigrants had little or nothing to do with the Jewish tradition of *tsedakah*.

22. Davenport, page 371. *Also see* Sokolsky, 1935, Chapter 2, "Jews Who Pass."

23. Wise, page 24–25.

24. A. I. Gordon, 1964, pages 305–306.

25. Erich Rosenthal, 1960.

26. Glazer, 1955b, pages 1727–1728.

27. Cahnman, page 178.

28. *Ibid.,* pages 178–179.

29. Greifer, pages 269–270.

30. Wessel, page 442.

31. *Ibid.,* page 442.

32. Tumin, 1957, pages 33–34.
33. Gans, 1958, page 640.
34. Kramer and Leventman, page 212.
35. Glazer, 1957, page 122.
36. *Ibid.*, page 122.
37. Shosteck, page 35.
38. *Ibid.*, pages 35–36.
39. Sherman, 1961, page 125.
40. *Ibid.*, page 125.
41. Commentary, page 71.
42. *Ibid.*, page 77, quoting Bernard J. Bamberger.
43. *Ibid.*, pages 78–79, quoting Eliezer Berkovits.
44. *Ibid.*, page 86, quoting Ira Eisenstein.
45. *Ibid.*, page 101, quoting Arthur Hertzberg.
46. *Ibid.*, pages 115–116, quoting David Lieber.
47. *Ibid.*, page 141, quoting Harold M. Schulweis.
48. *Ibid.*, page 145, quoting Ezra Spicehandler.
49. *Ibid.*, page 158, quoting Walter S. Wurzburger.
50. *Ibid.*, page 142, quoting Schulweis.
51. Landes and Zborowski, page 447.
52. J. E. Mayer, 1961a, page 14.
53. Sklare, 1964, page 47.
54. A. I. Gordon, 1959, page 244.
55. Kennedy, 1963, page 31. In the same non-problematical spirit, Hollingshead comments upon his 1949 study on the intermarriage rate of 437 white couples in New Haven, saying, ". . . Kennedy's and our data show . . . we are going to have three [melting] pots boiling merrily side by side with little fusion between them for an indefinite period." Hollingshead, 1950, page 624.
56. Glazer and Moynihan, page 160.
57. *Ibid.*, page 16.
58. Finkelstein, page 1787.
59. A. I. Gordon, 1964, page 209; see also Shulman.
60. A classical representation of the Hebrews' disdain of mixed marriage is the refusal of the sons of Jacob to let their sister marry the prince of the Canaanites, who had fallen in love with the Hebrew maiden. "We cannot do this thing, to give our sister to one who is uncircumcised," answered the sons of Jacob, "for that would be a disgrace to us." (Genesis 34:13). In Deuteronomy, the children of Israel are commanded to defeat the inhabitants of the Promised Land, but ". . . not make marriages with them, giving your daughters to their sons or taking their daughters for your sons. For they would turn away your sons from following me, to serve other gods; then the anger of the Lord would be kindled against you, and he would destroy you quickly." (Deuteronomy 7:1-4)
61. Porush, page 19.
62. A. I. Gordon, 1964, page 198.
63. Anonymous, 1939a, page 45.

64. Seward, 1956, page 213.

65. *Ibid.*, page 257.

66. On the topic of group solidarity, Brandeis wrote: "To describe the Jew as an individualist is to state a most misleading half-truth. He has to a rare degree merged his individuality and his interests to the community of which he forms a part. This is evidenced among other things by his attitude toward immortality. Nearly every other people had reconciled this world of suffering with the idea . . . [that] those living righteously here would find individual reward hereafter. . . . The doctrine of individual immortality found relatively slight lodgment among us. As Ahad Ha'am so beautifully said: 'Judaism did not turn heavenward and create in Heaven an eternal habitation of souls. It found "eternal life" on earth, by strengthening the social feeling in the individual. . . .' " (page 65)

On group solidarity as a mental health resource, see Srole and Langner, page 306. Their viewpoint is reviewed in Chapter 11 of this book.

67. Mordecai Kaplan addressed himself to the paradox that Jews who value their sense of community should work so actively to break down residential barriers. Enforced segregation is an *injustice*, Kaplan argues, and denies the Jew of his *right* to live wherever he finds it convenient. He must oppose segregation as offensive to his sense of justice, though as a Jew he would be happier to enjoy good living conditions in a Jewish neighborhood. (1956, page 69.)

68. Shanks, pages 374–375.

69. *Ibid.*, page 375.

70. Salo Baron, whom we paraphrase in this catalog of Jewish dualisms, asks, "Did not ancient Pharisaism accept determinism and free will, and the medieval Jewish philosophers, God's transcendence and immanence as coexisting realities in defiance of all logical consistencies?" (vol. 1, page 20)

71. Glazer, 1957, pages 9–10.

72. *Ibid.*, page 54.

73. *Ibid.*, page 55.

74. *Ibid.*, page 67.

75. Heschel, 1959, page 200.

76. Malin, page 80.

77. *Ibid.*, pages 104–105.

78. *Ibid.*, page 107.

79. *Ibid.*, page 115.

80. Fiedler, 1959a, page 5.

81. Man's struggle for survival could not, in itself, have produced human civilization. Long before the dawn of civilization, primitive man must of necessity have already acquired "the skills necessary for the preservation of individual life and of the group. Culture is a uniquely human invention and must have arisen out of uniquely human characteristics," Roe argues. (page 10) In pursuing this problem, Roe draws heavily on Maslow's self actualization theory. "All that a man

can be he *must* be if he is to be happy. The more he is fitted to do, the more he must do." Finally, Roe recalls Maslow's principle that self actualization can emerge freely only after man's more primary needs—physiological, safety, love, and esteem needs—have been satisfied. (page 29) By analogy, one might argue that the goals of Jewish life are governed not so much by the Jews' struggle for survival, but by a need to utilize centuries of cultural experience in minority group living, and a need to fulfill the Jews' unique potentialities for bi-cultural living. To paraphrase Roe, "all that the Jews *can* be they *must* be if they are to be happy. The more they are fitted to do, the more they must do."

82. Kaplan, 1934, page 39.
83. Wise, pages 26–27.
84. Sherman, 1961, pages 283–284.
85. In 1905 F. H. Giddings pointed out that "if we have regard not to New England and Virginia alone, but the entire area of the United States, there has never been a time since the Constitution was adopted when our population has not been composite. In the colonial period the Dutch had settled New Amsterdam, the Swedes had come to New Jersey, Pennsylvania and Delaware, the French Huguenots to the Carolinas, the Germans to Pennsylvania and the Scotch-Irish to Pennsylvania and the valleys leading southward through Virgina to Carolina and Georgia. In the North West Territory there were many descendants of the French colonists, others were added to the American people by the Louisiana purchase, while the acquisition of Florida, Texas, New Mexico and California brought in a Spanish element, most of which, however, presently disappeared into Mexico and Cuba.

"It thus appears that the popular notion that the American people were at one time of almost purely English blood which has since 1820 been suffering dilution through foreign immigration, has never been quite true to fact." (Drachsler, page 285)
86. Kallen, 1924, page 113.
87. Kaufmann, page 90.
88. Belth, page 315.
89. Kramer and Leventman, pages 172–173.
90. *Ibid.*, page 173.
91. P. I. Rose, page 269.
92. *Ibid.*, page 269.
93. *Ibid.*, page 269.
94. Kramer and Leventman, page 208.
95. *Ibid.*, page 140.
96. Kaufmann, page 191.
97. Dean, page 258. Tumin (1957) likewise assumes that parallel practices are the direct consequence of exclusion by the elite group. Jewish country clubs, fraternities, literary societies, professional societies, and similar parallel groups can not be adequately accounted for as products of social exclusion. The *American Heritage* magazine may give rise to a *Greek Heritage*—just as *Life* gave rise to *Ebony*. One cannot say

that exclusion or discrimination was directly involved here. Nor was it because Christian Scientists excluded Jews that Rabbi Lichtenstein founded a "Jewish Science" movement. In each case a minority group borrows and adapts cultural patterns of the majority group—just as the dominant group borrows speech, culinary and other cultural patterns from various minority groups.

98. Sanua, page 45.

99. *Commentary*, page 138. A generation ago, Steinberg (1933, page 33) quoted from Israel Zangwill to characterize "the contemporary crazy-quilt of Jewish practice." Wrote Steinberg: Zangwill "puts into the mouth of an Irish maid employed in a Jewish household this sage observation: 'Tonight being yer Sabbath, you'll be blowing out yer bedroom candle, though ye won't light it; Mr. David'll light his and blow it out too; and the old misthress won't even touch the candlestick. There's three religions in this house, not wan.'"

The freedom with which individual Jews maintain their own Sabbath rules is likewise illustrated by the comment of an American Jewish informant on the practices of his friends in Israel, where he spent a year of study. Some would answer the telephone, but would not answer the doorbell. Some would not answer the telephone, but would answer the doorbell. Others maintained a prohibition against both, and nonbelievers would—of course—answer the doorbell or the phone. To avoid offending, this informant added to each entry in his telephone and address book a symbol denoting the person's Sabbath rule.

100. Kramer and Leventman, page 107. Trachtenberg agrees "that Jews who win their way into Gentile social circles are quite pleased with and proud of their accomplishment and that generally, Jews though they may openly disparage such an achievement, do so in extenuation of their own failure to gain acceptance. They too would be flattered to mix socially with Gentiles, if that were possible." (page 280)

101. Kramer and Leventman, pages 108–109.

102. *Ibid.*, page 170.

103. Sklare and Greenblum, pages 271–272.

104. *Ibid.*, page 281.

105. *Ibid.*, page 282.

106. *Ibid.*, page 282.

107. *Ibid.*, page 288.

108. *Ibid.*, pages 288–289.

109. *Ibid.*, page 107. This observation may point to the insecurity felt by lower status Jews living in a predominately middle class and upward-mobile group. The problem of the lower status Jew may be particularly acute in the smaller community.

110. Dean, page 251.

111. Kramer and Leventman, page 118.

112. Teitelbaum, page 11.

113. *Ibid.*, page 12.

114. *Ibid.*, from Table 56, page 189.

115. Rose and Rose, page 249.

116. Adapted from Dean, page 259.
117. Kramer and Leventman, page 107.
118. Rose and Rose, page 249.
119. Drachsler, page 118.
120. Dean, page 250.
121. Jacobs, page 20. Memmi (1962, pages 195–196) likewise conjectures that radicalism has a special appeal to the person who felt that his Jewishness kept him outside the national community.
122. Riesman, 1942, page 55.
123. Maslow, 1951, pages 27, 29.
124. In his essay, "A Philosophy for 'Minority' Living," Riesman deplores the "non-Protestant" businessman, a stranger to "the Protestant market ethic," who has yielded to "the special pressures of modern capitalism" to become a businessman without values, "a caricature of the American careerist." Now Riesman describes this non-Protestant stranger as a Jew whose "irreverent attitude toward power becomes contempt for what remains of Puritan ethics of business and professional enterprise. [Likewise, Jewish] irreverence toward authority degenerates into an indiscriminate disrespect for convention . . ."

Riesman contrasts this caricature of the Jew as a rootless opportunist with the following idealized portrait of Anglo-Saxon rectitude: *"Even today,* the *typical* Protestant businessman still makes money as a by-product of his devotion to his work and his organization; the money . . . serves as proof of fulfillment of ethical duty. . . . Business was . . . originally the expression of their religion. . . . The Puritan . . . strain in our culture permitted a development of a kind of ethics intertwined with business . . . [which to Riesman may represent] a crystallization of decent standards of personal intercourse." (pages 60–61, italics added.)

Compare the above eulogy, with Norman Podhoretz's characterization of old-stock Massachusetts Yankees as "privileged descendants of some of the most rapacious merchants history has ever known. . ." (1967, page 38)
125. Jewish Post and Opinion, page 3.
126. *Ibid.,* page 3.
127. Shanks, pages 374–375.
128. Weisberger, page 153.
129. Freeman and Kassebaum, page 55.
130. Kramer and Leventman, pages 180–181.
131. *Ibid.,* pages   180–181.
132. Kertzer, page 155.
133. Shosteck, page 47.
134. Weisberger, page 154.
135. Freeman and Kassebaum, page 60.
136. Shosteck, page 46.
137. Quoted by Tumin, 1961, pages 109–110.
138. Mandelbaum, page 230.
139. Barron, page 8. Barron hypothesizes that the practice of com-

munity exogamy by Derby Jews is a by-product of their economic status, which permits the luxury of frequent contact with neighboring Jewish communities. (He probably neglects the significance of community exogamy in the Jewish tradition.) In any case, Barron points out, this practice does *not* prevail in other numerically small religious groups of Derby which likewise have an endogamous tradition. The Greek Orthodox and Greek Catholics of Derby, for example, have a higher rate of intermarriage than the Jews.

140. Spiro, 1956, pages 91 fn.
141. Shosteck, page 48.

CHAPTER 8

1. Newman, page 198.
2. The themes of fickleness and faithlessness are not altogether absent from Yiddish proverbs about women:

> A young wife is like a pretty bird, which must be kept in a cage.
> Women are long of hair and short of wit.
> Crying and laughing are easy for a woman.
> Tell a woman a secret and cut out her tongue.

And there are Yiddish proverbs that eulogize women without reference to their power over the lives of men:

> A housewife is like a watchdog.
> A comely wife is half a livlihood.
> A man's first wife is a boon to the flesh.
> There's nothing so dear as one's own wife.

But the attribution of *power* to women—power for good or for evil —seems to be a special characteristic of proverbs of the Jewish culture. Proverbs cited in the text and in the above footnotes are translated by this author from Bernstein and Segel. The proverbs in their original form (given in the order of their presentation) are as follows:

> A vieb shlelt af de fiss, un varft fun de fiss.
> A veib macht fun dem man a nar on a har.
> Az dos veib geyt in de hoysen, mus der man vigen dos kind.
> Az dos veib geyt in spodek, geyt der man in pantofel.
> Az dos veib shtarbt iz zie noykem on dem man—zi macht ihm tsum nar.
> Az Got vil machen eynem tsum nar, nemt er bei ihm tzu af der elter dos veib.
> A shtum veib shelt nit mit'n moyl, nor mit di hend.
> Dos veib macht fun'm man vos zie vil.
> Vu dos veib regirt, vert men ibergefirt.
> Vi dos veib iz a malka, azoy iz der man a melech.
> Veiber fihren tsum guten oder tsum beyzen—s'sei-vi-sei ferfihren zey.

A mammeh iz a pokrishke—zie dekt tsu di kinders chissroynos un
dem mans bizoynes.
A shtib ohn a balabosteh iz vie a vugen ohn reder.
Tateh, behalt mich—ot geht de mammeh!

3. Landes and Zborowski, page 452.
4. Mark, page 65. For a positive view of the immigrant Jewish mother
in the United States, see Blau.
5. Landes and Zborowski, pages 449, 450, 452–453.
6. *Ibid.*, page 454.
7. *Ibid.*, page 450.
8. Write Zborowski and Herzog: "When a wife is angry at her husband
she may refuse to go to the mikva so that he 'can't come near her.'
The weapon is a potent one, and if it is used too long the mother-in-
law may intervene, dragging the recalcitrant wife to the rabbi and insisting that she be 'brought to reason.' " (Page 286)
9. Landes and Zborowski, page 452.
10. *Ibid.*, page 452.
11. *Ibid.*, page 454.
12. *Ibid.*, page 454.
13. *Ibid.*, page 453.
14. *Ibid.*, page 454.
15 *Ibid.*, page 455.
16. The choice of a sanctioned mate who bears certain significant similarities to one's mother is by no means peculiarly Jewish, but is defined by Fluegel as "the final stage of the whole process of development . . . the attainment of maturity as regards the direction of the
love impulse." (page 102.)
    Normally, Fluegel adds, the similarity between the lover's chosen
mate and his original love object is "not perceptible to the lover himself; the [associative] bond is an unconscious one. Nevertheless, this
bond is often sufficiently clear to any keen observer whose eyes have
once been opened to the fact of its existence." (page 104)
17. Landes and Zborowski, page 455.
18. Kazin, 1966, pages 39–40.
19. Landes and Zborowski, page 453.
20. *Ibid.*, page 455.
21. *Ibid.*, page 453.
22. *Ibid.*, page 455.
23. *Ibid.*, pages 454, and 454 fn. The *nachas* which a man seeks from
a son-in-law is expressed in a joke about a simpleminded fellow who
comes home from the market and, glowing with pride, tells his wife
that he has arranged to have a "jewel of a young man" come to live
with the family as a son-in-law on *kest*. "Are you *meshugge?*" his wife
cries. "We don't have a daughter." "Ah well," answers the simpleminded husband, "there's no harm in having a proper sort of son-in-
law around the house."
24. Gollancz, page 182.

25. Landes and Zborowski, page 456.
26. *Ibid.*, page 457.
27. Cahnman, page 183.
28. *Ibid.*, page 183.
29. *Ibid.*, page 190.
30. Kirshenbaum, pages 72–73.
31. Guttman, page 10.
32. Kahn, page 13.
33. *Ibid.*, page 13.
34. *Ibid.*, pages 16–17.
35. *Ibid.*, page 67.
36. Wessel, page 442.
37. J. E. Mayer, 1961a, page 63.
38. Teitelbaum, page 61.
39. Reported by Sanua, page 455.
40. Orlansky, page 382.
41. Burma, page 21.
42. Minnis, page 49.
43. Belth, page 313. Kramer and Leventman likewise report that upper status second generation Jews "do not feel socially accepted by their Gentile neighbors unless they have already met as members of the same organization." (pages 108–109.)
44. Kramer and Leventman, page 176.
45. *Ibid.*, page 173.
46. *Ibid.*, pages 181–182 fn.
47. *Ibid.*, page 187.
48. Packard, page 278.
49. On the neurotic origins and consequences of overprotection, Freud wrote: "The neurotic woman who is unsatisfied by her husband is over-tender and over-anxious in regard to the child, to whom she transfers her need for love, thus awakening in it sexual precocity. The bad relations between the parents then stimulate the . . . child . . . to experience intensities of love, hate and jealousy while yet in its infancy. . . [Since he cannot express] this precocious sexual state . . . the conflict at this age contains all the elements needed to cause lifelong neurosis," and thus is a neurosis transmitted from one generation to the next. (S. Freud, 1908, page 97.)
50. Lowenstein, page 134.
51. Seward, 1956, page 257.
52. Freud, 1917, page 367.
53. Sears et al., page 30.
54. *Ibid.*, page 56.
55. *Ibid.*, page 441. Mothers were rated on "emotional warmth" partly on the basis of how they answered the question: "Do you think babies are fun to take care of when they're very little, or do you think they are more intersting when they grow older?" In perusing the following sample responses, the reader will have no difficulty in distinguishing between "warm" and "cold" mothers:

(1) "I don't know. I love little babies. I love to do with little babies. I love to teach them things. . . . But at the same time, I think they are interesting when they grow up, too. I found them interesting all the way along. I just love kids."

(2) "Well, to tell the truth, I got a kick out of my children from the minute they were born until today. They do something different every day it seems."

(3) "I don't like them too little . . . I never handled a baby before I had him. Never, not that small."

(4) "They're more interesting as they get older. Up until they're up to six months old, they're just a routine to take care of them." (pages 52, 53.)

56. *Ibid.,* page 59.

57. About 250 freshmen at a Midwestern urban university answered this question in their own words. After all responses were categorized by blind analysis, a total of 90 protocols were drawn to fit the sex- and ethnic group categories listed in Table 8:2. The great majority of the students are third generation Americans. About 90 per cent of the Jewish group indicate that their grandparents were born in Eastern Europe. The "Eastern European" Gentile group consists mainly of Catholics whose grandparents were born in Poland. The "Western European" Gentile group consists of Protestants and Catholics who designate that their grandparents were born in the United States, Scandinavia, or Germany.

58. Reik, 1964, pages 168–170.

59. In *Remember Me to God,* Richard's ambition to become a Protestant Yankee seems in part to express his dissatisfaction with the role behaviors of husband, wife, and parent as he sees them enacted by his parents:

"A Jew can learn a lot from [the real Yankees]. The Yanks live below their means and they don't care if they look cheap. But they know how to enjoy life, and a father and his sons arise before daybreak together to shoot flying geese from a small rowboat in the marshes. A Jew doesn't know enough to take recreation. He just keeps working, working, working, so his wife can show their friends some new kind of a piece of furniture or rug that all the Jewish ladies have just found out about. His idea of relaxation is to take his wife to a restaurant for lobster or Chinese food and bicker with her there instead of at home. *Or if he is the easy-going type that doesn't like to bicker, his wife considers him a dope who has nothing to say* . . . Sometimes the men start a Masonic lodge to get away from their wives, but all they do there is get sore at each other in arguments over who should be the officers.

"A Jewish mother thinks she is a better housekeeper, but actually she is too good. She wants a fireplace, but she won't allow a fire in it, because it might get dirty. She keeps yelling at the kids not to play on the lawn. You hesitate to invite a friend for dinner because you know she will make a whole operation out of it, and spend two days cleaning and cooking too much stuff and worrying and making all kinds of complicated jello molds with whip cream. A Yankee mother reads intellectual books, and if the house is a little dusty she still enjoys life. . . . Yankees give their daughter horseback lessons, but Jewish mothers just yell at their daughters to practice piano. Of course not everybody can afford horseback lessons, but even if a family is poor they should make every effort to at least send their young children to a neighborhood dancing school, even if only once a month, instead of always putting piano and music lessons first, because dancing develops poise." (pages 84–85.)

60. Reik, 1962, pages 84–85.
61. *Ibid.*, page 84.
62. *Ibid.*, page 84.
63. Warner and Srole, page 113.
64. *Ibid.*, page 113.
65. *Ibid.*, pages 113–114.
66. *Ibid.*, page 116.
67. *Ibid.*, page 116.
68. *Ibid.*, page 117.
69. *Ibid.*, page 114.
70. *Ibid.*, page 103.
71. *Ibid.*, page 114.
72. *Ibid.*, page 114.
73. Adapted from Table 6, page 271, Winch, Greer, and Blumberg. Authors report obtained differences significant at 0.01 level (Gamma =0.52).
74. Kertzer, page 269.
75. Leichter and Mitchell, page 110. Study based on questionnaires received from queries mailed to 298 couples, a random sampling of intact families served by the Jewish Family Service of New York, followed up by interviews. Returns totalled 210, covering 67 per cent of families sampled. Follow-up interviews showed that non-responding families tended to harbor negative feelings toward the agency. The investigators conjecture that non-responders were also *less* acculturated than the responding majority, and might well have even greater kin involvement than those for whom data were available. (page 309)
76. Leichter and Mitchell uncovered a sharp contrast between family service agency clients and their caseworkers on "values pertaining to different areas of kinship." (page 231) A clearer understanding of existing differences between client and counselor conceptions of what is "natural and normal" would undoubtedly improve the counseling process.

CHAPTER 9

1. Kinsey, 1948, pages 486, 487.
2. *Ibid.*, page 486.
3. Gold, page 149.
4. It may be argued that citations from ancient sources fail to repre-

sent a present-day Church viewpoint on sex and the good life. It is instructive from this standpoint to read the essay on "Catholicism and Sex" prepared for the 1961 *Encyclopedia of Sexual Behavior,* by Alphonse A. Clemens, Professor of Sociology and Director of the Marriage Counseling Center, Catholic University of America. Professor Clemens avers that the Catholic view of sex has nothing in common with puritanical attitudes, and assures his reader that the Church regards the sex act as good, noble, and even dignified "when rightly used." (page 228) There is nothing wrong with experiencing pleasure in the fulfillment of the marriage contract. Clemens continues, but it is un-Christian "to strive to intensify the pleasurableness of the sex act simply for the sake of pleasure." (page 229) Clemens reminds the reader that "physiologically viewed, the sex act is exclusively designed for generative purposes." (page 233) Interestingly, an article which opens by disclaiming any connection with puritanism offers this eulogy of sexual abstinence: "In its ascetic doctrines Catholicism teaches that, exalted as is the proper use of sex, *the sacrifice of sexual love* for the purpose of a more intense dedication to God *is deemed even more desirable* . . . Furthermore, the practice of celibacy serves as a mute but effective refutation to those who think that continence is impossible." (page 231, italics added)

5. When the rabbis were asked: How can *yetser ha'ra* be called good? they responded: "Were it not for that impulse, man would not build a house, marry a wife, beget children, or conduct affairs of business." (Bokser, page 70; ascribed to *Bereshith Rabbah,* 9–10.)

6. Maimonides, page 264.

7. Gollancz, page 63.

8. *The Shulchan Aruch* was compiled by Joseph Caro, a refugee from Inquisitorial Spain, and has become the popular authority on Jewish law. It was first printed in Venice in 1564. Even today, as Blankfort notes, in the training of an Orthodox rabbi, "a complete knowledge [is] required of [this] master code of laws. . . It is in essence the index of Yea and Nay for the Orthodox Jew, the sacred and divinely inspired standard of proper and just conduct." (Blankfort, p. 16) We shall refer to this work as *The Code.*

9. Code, page 7.

10. *Ibid.,* page 6.

11. *Ibid.,* pages 6–7.

12. *Ibid.,* pages 6–7.

13. *Ibid.,* page 6.

14. *Ibid.,* page 7.

15. Song of Solomon 1:2, 4:9 and 10, 5:1.

16. B. Z. Goldberg, page 163.

17. Code, page 13.

18. *Ibid.,* page 13.

19. *Ibid.,* page 13.

20. *Ibid.,* page 13.

21. *Ibid.,* page 13.

22. B. Z. Goldberg, page 163.
23. A mystical commentary on the Bible, the *Zohar* first appeared in Spain in the thirteenth century, and "is most likely the product of many authors in many periods. . . . It has remained . . . a highly revered work among all classes of Jews, especially among the pious Hasidim." Kramer, S. G., in *Encyclopedia of Jewish Knowledge.*
24. Gollancz, page 67.
25. B. Z. Goldberg, page 164.
26. *Ibid.,* pages 173–174.
27. *Ibid.,* page 173.
28. *Ibid.,* page 174.
29. *Ibid.,* page 179.
30. *Ibid.,* page 174.
31. Glasner, page 576.
32. The most celebrated commentator on the Bible and Talmud, the writings of Rashi (1040–1105) "became the textbook for rabbis and students. It may well be said that without it the Talmud would today be a sealed book. . . . Rashi's commentary was the first Hebrew book to be printed." Reichman, in *Encyclopedia of Jewish Knowledge.*
33. B. Z. Goldberg, page 176.
34. Dunlap, page 203.
35. Code, page 15.
36. *Ibid.,* page 7.
37. B. Z. Goldberg, pages 164–165.
38. Code, page 15.
39. *Ibid.,* pages 15–16.
40. *Ibid.,* page 16.
41. *Ibid.,* pages 13–14. Henry Raphael Gold notes that the Talmud (Niddah 17) justifies the requirement of darkness for cohabitation "lest there be a sudden exposing of bodily blemishes." (Gold, page 149)
42. Code, page 14.
43. *Ibid.,* page 17.
44. *Ibid.,* page 17.
45. Leviticus 18:19.
46. Code, page 21. ". . . The primitive prohibition of coitus during menstruation is probably the most widely accepted of all restrictions upon human sexual behavior," writes Corner. "In primitive cultures the menstruating woman has always been regarded not only as dirty, but also as dangerous . . . to all other manifestations of reproductive functions. Thus her influence is especially damaging to crops, to domestic animals, and even more devastating to men." (page 737.)
47. Code, page 22.
48. *Ibid.,* page 23.
49. *Ibid.,* pages 21 and 30.
50. Maimon, page 131.
51. *Ibid.,* page 17.
52. *Ibid.,* page 18.

53. Glasner, page 579. Although psychiatrists and counselors nowadays go to great lengths to reassure adolescents (and worried parents) that masturbation is altogether normal—citing Kinsey's statistics on the general prevalence of this habit—it is interesting to note that Freud himself was quite severe in his condemnation of masturbation. He wrote:

> [As] substitutive measures of sexual satisfaction [masturbatory acts are] by no means harmless; they predispose to the numerous forms of neurosis and psychosis [since they push back] sexual life to its infantile form. [Masturbation undermines the character, Freud held, because it provides an important gratification through passive means] instead of by energetic effort. [Because it is usually accompanied by unrealistic fantasies, masturbation may also lead to passive and unrealistic attitudes toward life. Freud likewise frowned upon heavy petting, acts] in which other parts of the body assume the role of the genitalia [in order to avoid normal intercourse, as ethically reprehensible and degrading—] an otiose diversion [lacking] spiritual participation. (Freud 1908, pages 94–95)

54. Code, page 6.
55. *Ibid.*, page 9.
56. Jacob Katz, page 107. Jewish law and ethics are based on the assumption that "the intensity of the ordeal of sexual temptation [is so great] . . . that a celibate has practically no hope of withstanding the temptations of the flesh." Katz contrasts this attitude of Talmudic Judaism with "the optimism of Catholic sexual morality, which believes in man's ability to overcome his desires," and with secular tendencies to gloss over the problem and minimize the importance of the sexual impulse. Katz, Jacob, pages 138–139.
57. *Ibid.*, page 139.
58. Code, page 18.
59. *Ibid.*, page 17.
60. *Ibid.*, page 16.
61. *Ibid.*, page 18.
62. *Ibid.*, page 17.
63. *Ibid.*, page 20.
64. *Ibid.*, page 19.
65. *Ibid.*, page 19.
66. *Ibid.*, page 21.
67. *Ibid.*, page 17.
68. *Ibid.*, page 18.
69. *Ibid.*, page 17.
70. *Ibid.*, page 18.
71. *Ibid.*, pages 17, 18.
72. Freud, 1908, pages 88–90.
73. *Ibid.*, pages 90–91.
74. According to the *Encyclopedia of Jewish Knowledge*, Shekinah refers to the visible presence of God, and in the Pentatuch the term is often used as a synonym for God. The term "gradually assumed a

mystical meaning," says Bakan, who conjectures that Freud drew his concept of sexuality from "the complexity of meaning associated with the Shekina. . . ." In Kabbala the concept of God's Divine Presence "becomes highly feminized," Bakan notes; "the female counterpart of God, and part of God himself."

For the benefit of those to whom the mystical experience seems altogether alien, William James drew a parallel between the mystical experience and the less exalted glow of intoxication. To James it seemed clear enough—"public opinion and ethical philosophy" notwithstanding — that the appeal of alcohol lies in "its power to stimulate the mystical faculties of human nature. . . . Sobriety diminishes, discriminates, and says no; drunkenness expands, unites, and says yes. It is in fact the great exciter of the *Yes* function in man. It brings its votary from the chill periphery of things to the radiant core. It makes him for the moment one with truth. Not through mere perversity do men run after it. . . . The drunken consciousness is one bit of the mystical consciousness, and our total opinion of it must find its place in our opinion of that larger whole." (James, pages 377–378)

75. Goodenough, pages 18, 19.
76. *Ibid.*, page 18; cited as a digest of the Zohar, Bereshith I, 49a–50b (ET, I, 156–160; FT, I, 286–293).
77. Glasner, page 577.
78. Proverbs 30:15–16.
79. Edwardes and Masters, page 28.
80. Jacob Katz, page 144.
81. *Ibid.*, pages 144–145.
82. Glasner, page 577.
83. *Ibid.*, page 584.
84. Kinsey, 1948, page 486.
85. Code, page 14.
86. Glasner, page 582.
87. Quoted by Glasner, page 576.
88. *Ibid.*, page 576.
89. Kaplan, 1942, page 155 fn. Kaplan, Mordecai, *Haggadah,* p. 155 fn. Maurice Samuel's *Haggadah* translation renders the lines in question as follows: Nine are the months of childbirth,
Eight are the days of the *milah* . . .
One might ask whether the use of the Hebrew *milah* is not a euphemism. Not necessarily; *circumcision* describes a surgical procedure, *milah* connotes a religious ceremony which includes circumcision, benediction and bestowing a name upon the child.
90. Olsvanger traces this Yiddish proverb to a pun on Psalm 75:7, which he translates, "Nor yet from the wilderness, cometh lifting up." The Hebrew term for *wilderness* (midbor) resembles the word for *to talk*. To be *lifting up* carries the additional meaning of pregnancy. (p. 180)
91. Wilson, pages 10–11.
92. *Ibid.*, page 38.

93. *Ibid.*, page 99.
94. *Ibid.*, page 64.
95. *Ibid.*, page 64.
96. Reik, 1962, page 314.
97. *Ibid.*, page 314.
98. The term *neurotic exogamy* appears to have been used first by Abraham, 1913. Here we are concerned not with the actual rate of neurotic intermarriage, but with the tendency toward exogamy, the tension toward intermarriage, the feeling that one would be more capable sexually with a Gentile wife. As Franzblau notes, there are Jews who might intermarry but "reject the dictates of their own hearts because they know their parents would be so violently opposed."
99. Glasner, page 580. In the pages of *Kiddushin,* the rabbis defend the right of an illegitimate to move into a community where his misbegotten origins are unknown, and the rabbis counsel against exposing a person who has so rehabilitated himself.
100. Joseph Katz, page 147.
101. Gold, page 148; citing as his Talmudic reference, Nedarim 20.
102. Joseph Katz, page 147. Katz observes that the German Hasidic movement of the thirteenth century produced "a veritable catalog of penances for each separate [sexual] sin. The severity of the mortification and self-debasement that these penances involved goes beyond what people today are likely to regard as reasonable or within man's capacity to endure. The fact that the guilty parties themselves asked for severe penances to atone for their sin—and there are cases where the rabbi gave a more severe ruling in order to pacify the questioner—indicates that although sexual purity did not reign supreme, the ideal itself was firmly entrenched. . . ." (pages 147–148)
103. In that rare document on provincial Jewish life in 18th Century Poland, the *Autobiography* of Solomon Maimon, the author does not hesitate to describe—and even dramatize—the excesses and shortcomings of the Polish Jews of his time. From the standpoint of sexual conduct, however, Maimon describes the Jews as models of rectitude:

> They are not gallants, but your women are safe from any snares with them. . . .

> The sacredness of their marriages, and the ever fresh tenderness which arises from this, deserves especially to be mentioned. . . .

> Finally, what innocence rules among unmarried persons! It often happens that a young man or woman of sixteen or eighteen years is married without knowing the least about the object of marriage. Among other nations this is certainly very seldom the case. (Maimon, pages 130–131.)

We shall suppose that Maimon refers to the Jewish youth's lack of *practical* knowledge, or experience, rather than ignorance of the elementary facts of sexual intercourse *per se.*

The stories of Isaac Bashevas Singer (see his collection of stories, *Short Friday*) include tales of sexual adventure—and even orgies—in a *shtetl* setting.

104. Barron, 1946, page 8; translation rewritten by this author.

105. Ehrmann, page 89.

106. *Ibid.,* page 213.

107. *Ibid.,* page 89.

108. *Ibid.,* pages 236–237.

109. *Ibid.,* page 280.

110. *Ibid.,* page 89.

111. Kinsey, page 496.

112. *Ibid.,* pages 473, 476.

113. *Ibid.,* page 483.

114. *Ibid.,* page 486.

115. Glazer, 1955a, page 142.

116. From Table 130, Kinsey, 1948, page 482.

117. Kinsey, 1953, page 304.

118. From Table 89, Kinsey, 1953, page 342. Kinsey's table has been simplified by eliminating "devout" groups. This author has added a *median* percentage for "moderately devout" and "religiously inactive." The number of cases for each subgroup range from 59 to 1155, with a median of 305.

119. Ehrmann, page 236.

CHAPTER 10

1. Orlansky, page 387.

2. Koenig, 1948.

3. Freedman, page 313. Freedman adds, "One hardly knows whether to be saddened or heartened by this. Perhaps, to some degree, both." (page 313)

4. In this study we have referred to this author as Critic.

5. Morse and Allport quoted by Tumin, 1961, page 66.

6. Peter I. Rose, page 272.

7. James Fuchs, page 59.

8. Linton, 1951, quoted by Inkeles and Levinson, page 980.

9. Inkeles and Levinson, page 978. In 1910 Max Nordau rejected the concept of national character in a way that implies some anxiety that such a concept would convey the impression that group differences are either fixed or inherited:

> The explanation of the fact that large groups appear to possess decided characteristics, in so far as it is not due to the illusion of a prejudicial or superficial observer, lies simply and solely in the stage of civilization attained by them, and the decisive influence of example upon them. A super-psychology has no more existence than a super-soul. The collective organism is a mystical delusion. (Nordau, page 130)

10. *Ibid.,* page 978.
11. Floyd Allport's pioneer textbook, *Social Psychology,* presents the classic defense of an empirical social psychology against the "group mind" objections.
12. Linton, 1951, page 144.
13. Simon, page 290.
14. Wortis, page 144.
15. *Ibid.,* pages 144–146.
16. *Reik,* 1962, page 208.
17. *Ibid.,* page 241.
18. J. E. Mayer, 1961a, page 60 fn.
19. Browne, page 98.
20. Reik, 1962, page 209.
21. Riesman, 1942, pages 43–44.
22. Reik, 1962, page 231.
23. *Ibid.,* page 231.
24. Freud, 1915, page 321.
25. Loewenstein, page 140.
26. Quoted by Loewenstein, page 140. So sharply self-critical are the Jewish jokes Freud retells in his *Wit and its Relation to the Unconscous,* Ernst Simon was moved to comment: "I do not know whether one often finds a people that makes merry so unreservedly over its own shortcomings." (page 282)
27. "State of Jewish Belief," page 127.
28. *Ibid.,* pages 154–155.
29. Simon, page 305.
30. Reik, 1962, pages 106–107.
31. *Ibid.,* page 210.
32. *Ibid.,* pages 209–210.
33. *Ibid.,* page 40.
34. *Ibid.,* pages 64–65.
36. Riesman, 1954, page 55.
37. Loewenstein, page 179.
38. Riesman, 1954, page 61.
39. *Ibid.,* page 67.
40. Loewenthal, page 140.
41. Maslow, 1951, page 26.
42. *Ibid.,* page 28.
43. Maslow's conception of the self-actualizer is described further later in this Chapter. *See also* footnote 162.
44. Critic, page 257.
45. *Ibid.,* page 258.
46. *Ibid.,* pages 257–258 fn.
47. Steinberg, 1947, pages 75–76. Steinberg qualifies his statement by observing that the doctrine that evil should be endured "has always been honored more in the breach than in practice, even by its official proponents." He further observes that the Jewish tradition does require that a man "submit to injury . . . when the sole alternative

is . . . inflicting injury on an innocent third party . . . Jewish law ordains [that] a man shall prefer to die rather than to commit murder." (pages 76–77)

48. Critic, page 258.

49. *Ibid.*, page 257.

50. Blankfort, pages 12–13.

51. Riesman, 1954, pages 56–57.

52. Solomon Maimon rebelled against the 18th Century Polish *shtetl* in which he was born and raised, and in his *Autobiography* did not hesitate to heap ridicule on the unsavory aspects of shtetl life—its poverty, filth, ignorance, pedantry, and superstition. Maimon was careful to point out, however, that while provincial Jews were ignorant of Western rules of politeness, they adhered to their own rules of charity, honesty, and loyalty:

> . . . Their manners and way of life are still rude; but they are loyal to the religion of their fathers and the laws of their country. They do not come before you with courtesies, but their promise is sacred. They are not gallants, but your women are safe from any snares with them. . . . Their children do not learn by heart any *forms* for expressing love and respect for their parents . . . but they show that love and respect all the more heartily. (pages 130–131)

> Rabbi Heschel, who eulogizes the culture of the *shtetl* with a poetic rapture, concedes that the Jews of Eastern Europe showed a "neglect of manners." (Heschel, 1950, page 100.)

53. Spiro, 1956, page 99.

54. Kertzer, page 250.

55. Lenski, page 156 fn. Lenski's survey is reported in fuller detail later in this chapter.

56. Spiro compared results of the Moral Ideology Test of a group of Israeli *kibbutz* children, whose behavior was conspicuously audacious, with norms for a presumably non-Jewish group of Midwestern American children, and found a relative *absence* of "conflict with authority figure" themes in the imaginative productions of the Israeli group. (Only four per cent of their responses deal with obedience or disobedience of authority, compared with 20 per cent of responses of the American group.) This finding suggests that for the Israeli group at least, *chutspa* betokens a lack of awe for authority *qua* authority. "Indeed," Spiro concludes, "proper respect for authority is the *least* important of all the values mentioned in the test." (Spiro, 1958, page 323)

57. Writes Feinsilver: ". . . The colorful 'T.L.' for *tochos lecker* (backside licker), is the earthy Yiddish description of an apple-polisher or boot-licker. I recall once in my teens," she writes, "being confused when a visiting young lady remarked by way of opening conversation, 'I have a T.L. for you.' As she explained, the initials stood for 'Trade List,' which meant she had a compliment for me and in order to hear

it I had to supply one about her. Over twenty years later, I now realize she must have been the subject of a camouflage of *tochos lecker* by some ingenious grownup. . . ." (pages 486–487)

58. Kaufmann, pages 126–141.
59. Reik, 1962, pages 167–168.
60. McGill, page 267. Italics added.
61. Glazer, 1955a, pages 144–145.
62. *Ibid.*, page 145, summarizing Saenger.
63. *Ibid.*, page 142.
64. Jerome Singer, page 479.
65. Baber, 1937, page 711.
66. J. E. Mayer, 1961a, page 60 fn.
67. Zorbaugh, page 51.
68. Haveman and West, page 54.
69. *Ibid.*, pages 54–55.
70. *Ibid.*, page 56.
71. *Ibid.*, page 58.
72. Critic, page 251.
73. Reik, 1962, page 58.
74. *Ibid.*, page 190.
75. *Ibid.*, page 153.
76. Tumin, 1957, page 33.
77. Lewisohn, 1928a, page 253.
78. Hollingshead and Redlich, page 162.
79. *Ibid.*, page 160.
80. Sears, et al., page 344.
81. Park, 1921, pages 101–102.
82. Kertzer, page 204.
83. *Ibid.*, pages 4–5.
84. Kramer and Leventman, pages 460–461 fn.
85. *Ibid.*, pages 176–177. Alongside the 34 per cent who express a preference for Jewish friends, 10 per cent explicity want to have both Jewish and Gentile friends, and 56 per cent "claim to have no preference about whether or not their friends are Jewish." (page 177)
86. Critic, page 255.
87. Kutzik, page 25.
88. Loewenstein, page 129.
89. Reik, page 169.
90. Orlansky, pages 381–382.
91. Allinsmith and Allinsmith studied Gallup poll data on religious identity, political affiliation, and income level—and were led to conclude that with a rise in income level, Jews were *less* likely to shift from the Democratic to the Republican Party than any other religious denomination.
92. Lawrence Fuchs, pages 190–191. Glazer is quite skeptical over the extent to which the radicalism and liberalism of American Jews stems from the Jewish tradition; he prefers to believe that the immigrants

brought with them "the political attitudes they had adopted in Europe." (1957, page 136)

93. James Fuchs, page 60.
94. Lawrence Fuchs, page 186.
95. *Ibid.*, page 183, 184.
96. Gollancz, page 308.
97. *Ibid.*, page 340.
98. Sherman, 1963, pages 84–85, 88.
99. *Ibid.*, page 95.
100. Gans, page 430.
101. Kramer and Leventman, pages 16–17. Discussing "the principle of change" from the standpoint of the parents who initiated change in religious practice, Sklare and Greenblum's Lakeville respondents view the modernizing of religious standards *not* as a weakening of the tradition, but as a help in transmitting Jewish identity, i.e., in making Jewishness more appealing to the younger generation. (page 306)
102. Arthur A. Cohen, 1959, page 63.
103. Steinberg, 1947, page 87.
104. Wise, page 24.
105. *Ibid.*, page 25.
106. Reik, 1962, page 195.
107. Herberg, page 275.
108. Reik, 1962, page 19.
109. *Ibid.*, page 120.
110. Wouk, page 137.
111. Reik, 1962, page 140.
112. Weisberger, page 154.
113. Podhoretz, 1953, page 263.
114. Rubenstein, page 141.
115. Reik, 1962, page 133.
116. Kutzik, page 23.

In the following paragraphs Rabbi Kirshenbaum attempts to describe the loss of communal feeling and the rise of individualism even amongst observant Jews:

> For generations Jews derived not only their holiness from the synagogue but also personal pleasure. How keen was the Jew's happiness when he awoke early in the morning to pray in unison with his fellows. . . . He felt delight and ecstasy in the Sabbath and festivals. It never occurred to him that by going to the synagogue he was maintaining it, that he was supporting Judaism or that the future of Judaism depended upon him. Through all the generations he went to his synagogue, prayed collectively, followed the customs of Judaism for his own sake, for his own satisfaction.

> In recent years major changes have come about in Jewish life. Jews attend 'to maintain and help the synagogue.' Jews pray in

order to ensure a *minyan*; Jews make efforts to preserve the Sabbath and its festivals; Jews give money to support Jewishness. . . . Jews are constantly contributing for their faith, for their fellow Jews. For themselves, however, they take nothing, for seemingly they need nothing.

A feeling of superiority, that the Jew is superior to his religion, that the individual is higher in the scale of values than the community, is seen in the attitude and actions of the present generation of Jews; it exists even among those who have a closer link with the synagogue and Jewish observance.

The Jew who attends synagogue on the Sabbath and who participates in synagogue activities feels that he is working on behalf of the synagogue. . . . Modern Jews consider that they are making personal sacrifices to contribute to the maintenance of Judaism— and not that Judaism maintains and keeps *them* together. When a Jew attends the synagogue on the high holy days nowadays, he feels he has bestowed a gift. He is proud of his achievement. The synagogue should thank him. He is a philanthropist. (Kirshenbaum, pages 132–133.)

117. Kutzik, page 23.
118. *Ibid.*, pages 23–24.
119. Baron, 1936, page 21.
120. Hertz, page 397.
121. Belth, page 312.
122. Seward, 1956, pages 256–257.
123. Sargent and Williamson, page 152.
124. Wiener, pages 11–12. In the foregoing pages of his autobiography, Wiener writes:

At all times [of Jewish history], the young learned man, and especially the rabbi, whether or not he had an ounce of practical judgment and was able to make a good career for himself in life, was always a match for the daughter of a rich merchant. Biologically this led to a situation in sharp contrast to that of the Christians of earlier times. The Western Christian learned man was absorbed in the church, and whether he had children or not, he was certainly not supposed to have them, and actually tended to be less fertile than the community around him. On the other hand, the Jewish scholar was very often in a position to have a large family. Thus the biological habits of the Christian tended to breed out of the race whatever hereditary qualities make for learning, whereas the biological habits of the Jew tended to breed these qualities in. To what extent this genetic difference supplemented the cultural trend for learning among the Jews is difficult to say. But there is no reason to believe that the genetic factor was negligible. I have talked this matter over with my friend, Professor J. B. S. Haldane, and he certainly is of the same opinion. Indeed, it is quite possible that in giving this opinion I am merely presenting an idea which I have borrowed from Professor Haldane.

For an elaboration of the thesis that Jewish marriage practices give Jews a genetic advantage in intellectual creativity, *see* Weyl.

125. Loewenstein, page 135.
126. Quoted by Loewenstein, page 369 fn.
127. Quoted by Reik, 1962, page 210.
128. Reik, 1962, page 116.
129. The survival of learning as a cardinal ideal in Jewish life is the topic of Ruth Tennenbaum's article, "Jewish parents in a child guidance clinic; a study in culture and personality," and in Strodbeck's comparison of Italian and Jewish immigrant groups.
130. Edward L. Clark sampled 10 fall semester periods from 1925 to 1941, for over 6,000 liberal arts freshmen at Northwestern University. He compared first semester grades for Jewish and non-Jewish students, controlling for differences in aptitude test scores.
131. Glazer, 1955a, pages 140–141.
132. Bernard, pages 267–268.
133. Glazer, 1955a, page 142.
134. Maslow, 1954, pages 200–203. Maslow's group of self-actualizing people included a number of his personal friends and acquaintances, as well as eighteen public figures, contemporary and historical.
135. Maslow, 1954, page 218.
136. *Ibid.,* page 217.
137. *Ibid.,* page 220.
138. *Ibid.,* page 208.
139. *Ibid.,* page 207.
140. *Ibid.,* page 226.
141. *Ibid.,* page 227.
142. *Ibid.,* page 224.
143. *Ibid.,* page 214.
144. Freud, 1917, page 367.
145. Maslow, 1954, page 207.
146. *Ibid.,* page 226.
147. *Ibid.,* page 215.
148. Gollancz (pages 60–63) cites traditional Jewish prayers for the following occasions: on drinking wine, on eating food prepared from grain, on eating fruit, on eating flesh, fish, eggs or cheese, on smelling fragrant woods, on smelling odorous plants, on smelling odorous fruits, on smelling fragrant spices, on smelling fragrant oil, on seeing lightning, falling stars, mountains, or great deserts, at the sight of the sea, on seeing beautiful trees or animals, on seeing trees blossoming the first time in the year, on seeing a sage distinguished for his knowledge of the Law, and on seeing wise men distinguished for other than sacred knowledge. The benedictions are phrased as brief celebrations of the richness of human experience, e.g.—

Blessed art thou, O Lord our God, King of the universe, who givest a goodly scent to fruits.

Blessed art thou, O Lord our God, King of the universe, who hast made thy world lacking in nought, but hast produced therein goodly creatures and goodly trees wherewith to give delight unto the children of men.

149. Maslow, 1954, page 244.
150. *Ibid.*, page 215.
151. *Ibid.*, pages 242–243.
152. *Ibid.*, page 244.
153. *Ibid.*, page 245.
154. *Ibid.*, page 259.
155. *Ibid.*, page 239.
156. *Ibid.*, page 239.
157. *Ibid.*, page 238.
158. *Ibid.*, page 240.
159. *Ibid.*, page 238.
160. Maslow, 1954, pages 233–234.
161. *Ibid.*, page 227.
162. This author asked Prof. Maslow, by letter, if anyone had ever conveyed to him the impression that his "self actualizer" described a Jewish style of life. He replied: "No, but I've thought of it—not very extensively or thoroughly."
163. Srole, Langner, *et al.*, pages 319–320.
164. Moynihan and Glazer, page 175.
165. Reik quotes Freud as saying: "Because I was a Jew, I found myself free of the prejudices which restrict others in the use of the intellect; as a Jew, I was prepared to be in the opposition and to renounce agreement with the majority." (Reik, 1962, page 210) .
166. Jones, vol. 1, page 271. See also Ernst Simon.
167. Jones, vol. 2, page 412.
168. Lewin, 1946, pages 202–203.
169. *Ibid.*, page 203.
170. *Ibid.*, page 206.
171. In his critical essay on *The Web and the Rock*, Walser describes Esther Jack as "one of Wolfe's great living creations." (page 103) The characterization is based on Aline Bernstein, a married woman eighteen years older than Wolfe who met her aboard ship when Wolfe, at age 25, was returning from his trip to Europe. Aline "was to be his constant companion for the next five years. . . . Her husband's wealth did not deter her from an established career in the theatre as costumer and scene-designer. Evidently she was attracted to Wolfe partially because she understood his ambition to be a playright. But whatever the cause, Wolfe was not himself unresponsive," Walser adds in a spirit of understatement. (page 34)
172. Wolfe, page 369.

173. *Ibid.*, page 312.
174. *Ibid.*, page 313.
175. *Ibid.*, page 447.
176. *Ibid.*, page 434.
177. *Ibid.*, page 476.
178. *Ibid.*, page 476.
179. *Ibid.*, pages 547–548.
180. *Ibid.*, pages 279–289.
181. *Ibid.*, page 380.
182. *Ibid.*, page 443.
183. *Ibid.*, page 387.
184. *Ibid.*, page 390.
185. *Ibid.*, pages 450–451.
186. *Ibid.*, page 464.
187. *Ibid.*, page 486.
188. *Ibid.*, page 539.
189. *Ibid.*, page 582.
190. *Ibid.*, page 662.
191. For a literary interpretation of Thomas Wolfe's use of the city as a symbol, see Gelfant's essay.
192. Wolfe, page 377.
193. *Ibid.*, page 382.
194. *Ibid.*, page 391.
195. *Ibid.*, page 382.
196. *Ibid.*, page 379.
197. *Ibid.*, pages 596–597.
198. *Ibid.*, page 364.
199. *Ibid.*, page 374.
200. *Ibid.*, pages 403–404.
201. Boris Levinson, 1962c, page 314. For all the "99 differences," Yeshiva College freshmen deviated from the norms for men in general to an extent that is statistically significant beyond the .01 level of confidence; that is to say, the probability is less than one in one hundred that obtained difference could have occurred by chance.
202. Each item is quoted as it appears in the MMPI questionnaire. The response in parenthesis (True or False) indicates which response choice was significantly greater for Yeshiva College freshmen than for men in general.
203. Dahlstrom and Welsh, page 64.
204. *Ibid.*, pages 65–66.
205. *Ibid.*, page 64.
206. Boris Levinson, 1962a, page 27.
207. Spiro, 1958, page 10.
208. *Ibid.*, page 11.
209. *Ibid.*, page 13.
210. *Ibid.*, page 14.
211. *Ibid.*, page 14—quoting Zborowski and Herzog, page 297.
212. *Ibid.*, pages 49–50.

213. Spiro, 1956, page 106.
214. *Ibid.*, page 124.
215. Spiro, 1958, page 49.
216. *Ibid.*, page 30.
217. *Ibid.*, pages 37–38.
218. *Ibid.*, page 39.
219. *Ibid.*, page 220.
220. *Ibid.*, pages 59–60.
221. *Ibid.*, page 230.
222. *Ibid.*, page 57.
223. *Ibid.*, page 58.
224. *Ibid.*, page 58.
225. Spiro, 1956, page 124.
226. *Ibid.*, page 125.
227. Spiro, 1958, page 194.
228. *Ibid.*, page 202.
229. *Ibid.*, page 218.
230. *Ibid.*, pages 219–220.
231. *Ibid.*, pages 224–228.
232. *Ibid.*, page 277.
233. *Ibid.*, page 220.
234. *Ibid.*, page 22.
235. Of the thirteen traits which kibbutz parents ranked in order of importance for the character training of their children, the four *highest-ranking* traits were:
    1. Work
    2. Love of humanity
    3. Responsibility to kibbutz
    4. Good character
The four *lowest-ranking* traits were:
    *10. Cooperation
    11. Private initiative
    *12. Good manners
    *13. Respect for parents
From this evidence, one would conclude that traits related to decorum and obedience (asterisked above) hold a relatively low priority in the values of these kibbutz parents. (Spiro, 1958, pages 20–21.)
236. *Ibid.*, paraphrased from pages 268–270.
237. *Ibid.*, paraphrased from page 275.
238. *Ibid.*, paraphrased from pages 260–261 fn.
239. *Ibid.*, page 264.
240. *Ibid.*, page 320.
241. *Ibid.*, page 322.
242. *Ibid.*, page 322. See fn. 55, this Chapter.
243. *Ibid.*, page 322. Spiro (1958, pages 424–427) contrasts the sabra children's audacity toward fellow chaverim, with their shyness toward strangers.
244. *Ibid.*, page 324.

245. In his 1956 volume, Spiro describes chutspa-related parental behavior: gossip, petty criticism, quarreling, complaining (pages 104–105), shouting, turmoil (pages 202–203), and overt discourtesy toward guest concert performers (page 162).
246. Spiro, 1958, page 295. It should be noted that the high school children are trained for agricultural work through daily *work* experience in the kibbutz. Nevertheless, the absence of technical courses in the high school curriculum is noteworthy.
247. *Ibid.*, page 394.
248. *Ibid.*, pages 394–395.
249. *Ibid.*, page 395.
250. *Ibid.*, page 453.
251. *Ibid.*, page 397.
252. *Ibid.*, pages 276–278.
253. *Ibid.*, page 327.
254. *Ibid.*, page 333.
255. *Ibid.*, page 328.
256. *Ibid.*, pages 302–307.
257. *Ibid.*, page 307.
258. *Ibid.*, page 332.
259. *Ibid.*, page 328.
260. *Ibid.*, page 327.
261. Spiro, 1956, page 29.
262. *Ibid.*, page 32.
263. *Ibid.*, pages 42–43 fn.
264. *Ibid.*, pages 221–222.
265. *Ibid.*, pages 153–154. Perhaps a better translation of the underlying idea would be the *integrated personality.*
266. *Ibid.*, page 51 fn.
267. In the mind of one natural scientist, Jewish personality is "nothing but a bundle of mannerisms preserving the identity of a de-territorialized man." (Ardrey, page 307) According to his logic, the Jew "should cease to be a Jew when he becomes re-territorialized." When he visited Israel, Ardrey was pleased to see his theory confirmed; the Israelis are not Jews, he says flatly:

It's not just physique, it is posture, a manner of walking, a manner of speaking, a manner of thought. The "Jewish personality" has vanished, replaced by that of the Israeli. . . . You go to a party in Tel Aviv and someone asks the inevitable question, "How do you like Israel?" and you answer, "Fine, but where are the Jews?" And the party goes off into the greatest laughter, for it is the nation's joke. (Ardrey, page 309–310)

Spiro observed the Israelis' "highly negative" attitude toward their shtetl origins, and hypothesized "that their hostility is a defense mechanism . . . which serves to protect them from those feelings of shame and inferiority" elicited by their identification with Jews of the *galut.*

(1958, pages 455–456) Apparently, the Israelis' "favorite joke" is taken quite seriously by certain journalists and scholars. Georgene Seward assures her readers that the Israeli-born Jew, "independent, self-assured, and healthy . . . contrasts sharply with the self-conscious, sentimental, overambitious" personality pattern of the Jew who is warped and burdened by his "exile neurosis." (1956, page 264)

Without a doubt, adaptation to communal life and an agricultural economy will elicit habits somewhat different from what is normal for urban middle class life in Western society. Such differences may indeed obscure, but do *not* preclude, the existence of significant underlying similarities. British novelist Dan Jacobson challenges the thesis of *sabra-galut* discontinuity, as follows:

> It seems to me something of a myth that the Israelis of Eastern European descent are all that much unlike their contemporaries of the *galut*. [On the basis of his own observation, Jacobson points to significant cultural traits] the descendants of Eastern European Jews still have in common in countries as distant from one another as the United States, South Africa, England, and Israel, which can range from tastes in food and jokes to intellectual aptitudes and political inclinations. (page 83.)

268. It should be noted that our analysis of Spiro's observations focused upon traits which the chaverim seem to hold in common with Jews of Eastern Europe and America. For a well-rounded characterization of the kibbutz ethos, and the personality traits of the pioneers and sabra, the reader is referred to Spiro's two volumes, from which our special observations were drawn.

CHAPTER 11

1. Freud, 1908, page 90.
2. Loewenstein, pages 135–136.
3. Orlansky cites Brill, Meyerson, and Israel Wechsler as exponents of this view.
4. Rose and Rose, pages 251–252. Srole, Langner et al. (page 306) assert—on the contrary—that the suicide rate is *lower* for Jews than for other groups. Hurvitz (1961, page 220) cites four articles supporting the generalization that Jews are *less* prone to suicide than other groups. Hurvitz also points   to the indirect evidence supporting this generalization—the fact that Jewish mortality is lower through the suicide-prone years. Gorwitz reports a lower suicide rate for Jews than non-Jews of St. Louis. Sidney Goldstein (1966), on the other hand, reports a higher suicide rate for Jews than non-Jews of Providence (Rhode Island). (Goldstein's figures are based on records of deaths at age 45 and over, and the absolute number of reported deaths by suicide was small.)
5. Loewenstein, page 136.

6. Srole and Langner, page 306.
7. Steinberg, 1933.
8. Srole and Langner, page 306.
9. Browne, page 97.
10. Dean, page 257.
11. Loewenstein, page 144.
12. Dean, page 257.
13. Nock, 1941b, page 76.
14. Bowman, page 270.
15. Lewin, 1940, page 170.
16. Browne, pages 97–98.
17. Loewenstein, page 135.
18. *Ibid.*, page 109.
19. *Ibid.*, page 172.
20. *Ibid.*, page 115.
21. *Ibid.*, page 170.
22. Spiro, 1956, page 105.
23. Maslow, 1954, page 53.
24. *Ibid.*, page 45.
25. Reik, 1962, page 230.
26. *Ibid.*, pages 40–41.
27. Riesman, 1948, pages 64–65.
28. *Ibid.*, page 65 fn.
29. Riesman, 1942, pages 43–44.
30. Freud, 1924, page 262.
31. Fenichel, 1945, page 364.
32. Freud, 1924, page 262.
33. *Ibid.*, page 263.
34. *Ibid.*, page 259.
35. Fenichel, 1945, page 363.
36. Riesman, 1954, page 68.
37. Quoted by Orlansky, page 379, from Reik's 1929 *Imago* article.
38. "*. . . Many Negroes, consciously or unconsciously, accept in part [the white racists'] assertions of their inferiority. . . . Their lowly position and their relative lack of success lead to further self-disparagement. . . . The sweeping changes of recent years . . . [have not sufficiently healed] the old wounds of confused identity and damaged self-esteem," says Pettigrew. (page 9)
39. Loewenstein, page 174.
40. *Ibid.*, page 137.
41. Robison, page 636.
Reik, 1962, page 202.
43. *Ibid.*, page 60.
44. Loewenstein, pages 172–173.
45. *Ibid.*, page 109.
46. Sargeant and Williamson, page 152.
47. Buhler, page 524.
48. Loewenstein, page 147.

49. Since "Jewish nervousness" is a classic topic in clinical psychology, psychiatry, and social psychology, and the available data bearing on this phenomenon are fragmentary, conflicting, and therefore inconclusive—it is difficult to understand why Gurin, Veroff, and Feld chose *not* to compare Jewish and Gentile norms in their recent large-scale nationwide survey on mental health. Their sample of 2,460 American adults included 91 Jews. A comparison was made of the *two* major religious groups, Protestants and Catholics, but data on their 91 Jewish respondents were set aside along with data on persons who claimed no religious affiliation, or affiliated themselves with some group outside of the two major faiths.

50. Myers and Roberts, page 553.
51. *Ibid.*, page 556.
52. *Ibid.*, page 553.
53. *Ibid.*, adapted from Table I, page 553.
54. Srole and Langner, page 305.
55. *Ibid.*, pages 305–306.
56. *Ibid.*, page 306.
57. *Ibid.*, page 315.
58. *Ibid.*, page 306.
59. *Ibid.*, page 315.
60. In the Jewish tradition, say Srole and Langner, when some specific religious prescription is in conflict with a matter of health, there is no question but that priority goes to the person's health. (Eisenberg's anthology for Jewish Sunday School children tells of a rabbi who horrified his congregation by demanding that they break their most sacred tradition and *eat* on Yom Kippur day, to gain strength against a plague that was sweeping the countryside.) This tradition reflects "the milennial-long affinity of Jews for the field of medicine and, more recently, for its psychiatric branch, in the several roles of explorers, healers and patients. The Jewish group historically can be viewed in one perspective as a culture mobilized for the prevention and, that failing, for the healing of the ailments of body and mind." (Srole and Langner, pages 319–320.)
61. Kinsey, 1948, page 486.
62. Sanua, page 447.
63. *Ibid.*, pages 461–462. Sanua's generalization on the performance of Jewish groups on paper-and-pencil tests does *not* apply to Boris Levinson's findings on MMPI scores of Yeshiva College freshmen.
64. Sanua, pages 457–458.
65. *Ibid.*, page 458.
66. *Ibid.*, page 457.
67. Hurvitz, page 233 fn.

CHAPTER 12

1. The subject appears in some translations as "a strange woman," in others as "an adultress" (or euphemistically as "a loose woman").

The term *b'nib zarah* had this double meaning, perhaps because the Canaanites and Astartes practiced cultic prostitution, perhaps because "looser morals [were attributed to] the 'foreign' or non-Jewish members of the community," explains R. B. Y. Scott, translator of *Proverbs, The Anchor Bible*, page 43. This author has hyphenated Scott's term (changing *stranger woman* to *stranger-woman*) to eliminate the ambiguity between "there was no stranger woman in the city," and "there was no stranger-woman in the city."

2. Proverbs 5:3–20, R. B. Y. Scott translation. Intermarriage is more explicitly decried or proscribed in the following places in the Old Testament: Genesis 24 and 28; Deuteronomy 7; Joshua 23:12 and 13; Ezra 9:1 through 15, and 10:2; and Nehemiah 10:30, 13:23 through 30. It is well to point out, on the other hand, that the Old Testament does *not* advocate racial purity. Deutoronomic law sanctions and also regulates marriage with the comely heathen captive (Deuteronomy 21:10 ff.), and the book of Judges speaks with great frankness on mixed marriages (3:5–6).

As Ephraim Feldman observes, "at the very fountainhead of Jewish national life, we meet [an] infusion of foreign blood. Four out of the twelve sons of Jacob have for mothers the handmaids, that is the foreign female slaves, Bilha and Zilpa. . . . The population of the tribes Dan, Naphtali, Gad, and Asher was the offspring of Jewish fathers and non-Jewish mothers. . . . The inference is unavoidable that, according to records that we cannot possibly call into question, fully one-third of the population of Israel was of mixed descent.

"Thus, for a millenium and a half of history, [Feldman continues] and who knows for how many more during prehistoric times, the Jewish national body was being formed out of the most heterogeneous materials. Canaanite, Hittite and Edomite; Syrian and Arab; Egyptian, Greek, and his kinsmen, the Amorite, each contributed his greater or lesser quota to the making of the body of the Jewish people. Israel contributed the soul. Numerically not at all so predominant, if ethnology is to be trusted, Israel must have been psychically strong and dominant, as to mold all these multifarious ethnic elements into one distinct national individuality." (pages 13, 14)

3. Nock, 1941b, page 73.

4. Kronhausen and Kronhausen.

5. In the Cupid story, Cupid and Psyche hold their trysts in the dark of night and the spell is broken when curiosity impells Psyche to light a lamp so that she can behold her nightly visitor. In the Lohengrin legend, a mysterious young knight wins the love of Princess Elsa, and becomes her husband on the sole condition that she shall not ask his name or lineage. On the marriage night Elsa cannot resist asking the forbidden question. Lohengrin tells her but at the same time disappears. The Lohengrin legend contains, in addition, an incest theme: the powerful (and plausibly phallic) swan which draws Lohengrin's skiff is none other than Princess Elsa's brother Gottfried whose transformation into a swan is the work of the sorceress Ortrud.

6. Hernton describes the appeal of a cross-ethnic partner to Negroes

and Southern whites: "To every Negro boy who grows up in the South, the light-skinned Negro woman—the 'high yellow,' the mulatto—incites awe. The white woman incites *more* awe. As a boy I was, to say the least, confused. As I grew older, the desire to see what it was that made white women so dear and angelic became a secret, grotesque burden to my psyche. It is that to almost all Negro men, no matter how successfully they hide and deny it." (p. 64)

"Because his concept of the sex act made him think of it as something dirty, sinful and savage, the white Southerner found it difficult to relate to his own women. He was inhibited by the Calvinist interpretation of sex as befouling the dignity of man. He therefore cringed from his manly duties towards his wife, and if he did make love to her, the act was marred by his guilt and shame. . . . White women [were given] the status of sexless dolls and genteel ladies." Negro women, on the other hand, were viewed as "animals outside of the providence of God. . . . One could do anything [to a 'Negress'] without fear of reprisal from God or conscience. In order to commit an act one conceives of as degrading and sinful, one must find an object one considers degraded and iniquitous." (page 95)

As one of Hernton's white informants put it, "he enjoyed Negro women far better than he did white women, because he could 'let himself go' with Negroes. He felt no guilt for whatever he did with Negro women, but with white females he seemed to 'dam up' inside." (page 113) (Dollard describes the sexual allure of the Negro woman to the white Southerner in *Caste and Class in a Southern Town*, pages 143–144, 162, 167–168.)

Describing the neurotic white woman in search of a Negro lover, Hernton emphasizes that the forbidden lover becomes exciting in proportion to his contrast with white men—the more completely he fulfills the Negro stereotype, the more completely she feels liberated from her inhibitions toward men:

"Deep in the psyche of the young, misfit white woman there is a need *not* for a Negro but for a nigger. . . . Such women are known to pursue black men to the exclusion of white ones . . . because they, for whatever reasons, think of themselves as deformed. Therefore, in their minds, they are fit to relate only to men whom they also conceive of as deformed. . . ." (p. 46)

"Repeatedly Negro informants have reported that during the act of intercourse their white mates frequently utter the most racially vulgar and offensive epithets conceivable, such as 'Rape me, nigger, rape me!'" (p. 50)

At interracial bohemian gatherings of East Village, Negro youths learn to exaggerate, exploit and display "the *nigger* in them" to excite white women bent on "proving her liberalness or hiptitude." Hernton recalls the advice of a youth to a newcomer on how to make himself attractive to the bohemian white girl: ". . . All you have to do is walk into a party and act *black*, act mean . . ." (page 75)

7. Slotkin, 1942b, page 36.

8. *Ibid.*, page 36.
9. Child, page 138.
10. *Ibid.*, page 137.
11. *Ibid.*, page 137.
12. *Ibid.*, page 137.
13. Whyte, page 28.
14. Linton Freeman, pages 373–374.
15. Sartre, pages 105–106.
16. Kinsey, 1953, pages 323–324.
17. Park, 1934, page 81.
18. Reuter, page 75.
19. Park, 1934, page 81.
20. Reuter, page 76.
21. *Ibid.*, page 76.
22. Levinson and Levinson, page 128.
23. Franzblau, page 22. Rokeach has demonstrated that the more divergent the religious backgrounds of intermarried Protestant couples, the more likely they were to quarrel and fight both before and after marriage. Again, one might conjecture that if a man and woman who are in frequent or chronic disagreement decide to get married (whether they share the same ethnic background or not), they are using marriage to gratify a neurotic need.
24. *Ibid.*, page 21.
25. Freud, 1910, pages 193–194.
26. *Ibid.*, page 195.
27. Reik, 1962, page 194.
28. *Ibid.*, page 201.
29. Kubie, page 28.
30. Hernton, page 41.
31. Franzblau, page 24.
32. Freud, 1912b, page 209.
33. *Ibid.*, page 203.
34. *Ibid.*, page 209.
35. *Ibid.*, page 203.
36. *Ibid.*, pages 210–211. Clinical and research experience (Abraham, Fluegel, Franzblau, Kinsey, Lehrman) amply confirm Freud's judgment that preference for a cross-ethnic sex partner is an indication of sexual inhibition. Eric Fromm stands alone in claiming a special ethical value for intermarriage. Fromm eulogizes cross-ethnic marriage with rare eloquence, extolling it as a mark of humanity and liberation from racial and nationalistic prejudice:

Only if one can love 'the stranger,' only if one can recognize and relate oneself to the human core of another person can one experience oneself as a human being, and only if one can experience oneself as a human individuality can one love 'the stranger.' We have overcome incest in the narrow sense of the word, as sexual relations between members of the same family, but we still practice incest not in a sexual but in a characterological sense, inasmuch as we are not capable of loving 'the stranger,' a person with different

skin or a different social background. Race and nationalistic prejudices are the symptoms of incestuous elements in our contemporary
culture. We shall overcome incest only when we—every one of us
—are able not only to think but to feel and accept the stranger as
our brother. (Fromm, pages 306–307.)

37. Fluegel, page 51.

38. *Ibid.,* pages 52–53.

39. *Ibid.,* page 53.

40. *Ibid.,* page 112 fn.

41. *Ibid.,* page 111. This formulation would also account for the
proper young woman's attraction to the "romantic stranger." If her
upbringing makes her feel guilty about wanting to give herself to a
man of her own group, she may indulge in erotic fantasies in which
her partner is (like Lohengrin or Cupid) a mysterious stranger.
Through these fantasies, accompanied perhaps by masturbation, she
conditions herself for the "forbidden romance." Hernton expresses
the common-sense view that middle class white women who seek
Negro lovers do so because of "repeated disappointing experiences
with white men. . . ." (page 40.) This may have occurred, but it
is quite possible that both her unhappy experience with a man of her
own group, and her need for a "dark stranger" may have their source
in her intolerable guilt about sexual feelings toward a man of her
own group.

Hernton describes the Southern white woman who has been so
thoroughly indoctrinated to think of sex as shameful and vile that the
only kind of sexual fantasy she can permit herself is a fearful preoccupation with rape. (p. 19) In her fantasy life, sexual desire is
concentrated upon the Negro as a "god-phallus," an object of fear,
desire, and hate. (p. 27)

42. *Ibid.,* page 208.

43. Freud, 1912b, pages 206–207.

44. *Ibid.,* page 207.

45. *Ibid.,* page 212.

46. Landes and Zborowski, page 451.

47. *Ibid.,* pages 451, and 453 fn.

48. Murdock, page 273. The elaborate network of avoidance rules
listed in the Code of Law *(see* Chapter 9) indicates that what we call
the method of shame was extensively relied upon by the Jews to prevent sexual misconduct. A Talmud story tells of a rabbi in whose
home a group of women prisoners were quartered for a night, while
being transported from one place to another. During the night, the
rabbi was overcome by temptation, and under cover of darkness he
proceeded to carry a ladder outdoors to climb into the loft where
the women were quartered. Quite by accident, a neighbor saw the
rabbi making his way to the loft, and could not help but apologize
for causing the rabbi such shame. "Better that I be put to shame by
my neighbor," answered the rabbi, "than by the Lord of the Universe."

49. Murdock comments further: "[In] our own society . . . so thor-

oughly do we instill our sex mores in the consciences of individuals that we feel quite safe in trusting our internalized sanctions. We allow brother and sister to associate freely with one another, and even to live together and have intimate physical contacts, without fear that these conditions of sexual stimulation will produce violations of our incest taboos . . ." (page 273) To the member of a society that relies on avoidance and shaming, Western norms are difficult to understand. Lowie brought back the following recollection from his field study of the Crow Indians—"A Crow interpreter once twitted me with the indecency of Caucasians who dare reproach the Indians with looseness of morals while themselves so shameless as to speak freely with their own sisters." (page 99.)

50. The Oedipus myth is of course the classic incest story of Western literature; it is the basis of the Oedipus trilogy of Sophocles, also of tragedies by Corneille (1659) and Voltaire (1718). In more recent times, the incest theme has appeared in d'Annunzio's drama *City of the Dead* (1898), in Artzibasheff's novel *Sanine* (1907), in Thomas Mann's short story *Blood on the Wolsungs* (1905), and in Mann's novel *The Holy Sinner* (1951).

The force of the incest taboo in our culture is well illustrated by the fact that when Ezra Pound and Noel Stock translated a group of *Love Poems of Ancient Egypt,* they carefully deleted all references to "O brother beloved," and "O beautiful sister" (which one finds in the more faithful and complete translation of Sharpley), presumably because this would destroy the mood of a love poem for the Western reader. Ezra Pound could not be accused of prudery—apparently he felt, however, that it was esthetically important that the reader *not* be reminded that sibling marriage was practiced by the Pharaohs, and that the love of a prince for his sister was the Egyptian model of noble love.

52. Leviticus 18.
53. Landes and Zborowski, pages 453–454.
54. Bakan, pages 294–295.
55. *Ibid.,* pages 294, 294 fn.
56. Edwardes and Masters, page 37.
57. Landes and Zborowski, page 452.
58. Franzblau, page 23.
59. From an interpretive summary by Bronfenbrenner, pages 118–119.
60. Jerome Singer, page 481.
61. *Ibid.,* pages 484–485.
62. *Ibid.,* pages 486–487.
63. *Ibid.,* page 488.
64. *Ibid.,* page 488.
65. *Ibid.,* page 488.
66. *Ibid.,* page 489.
67. *Ibid.,* page 485.
68. *Ibid.,* page 490.
69. *Ibid.,* page 490.

70. *Ibid.*, page 491.
71. *Ibid.*, pages 492–493.
72. *Ibid.*, page 483.
73. *Ibid.*, page 496.
74. Sears et al., page 58.
75. Quoted by A. I. Gordon, page 60.
76. Freud, 1912b, page 211.
77. Landes and Zborowski, pages 453–454.

CHAPTER 13

1. A. I. Gordon, 1964, pages 53–54.
2. J. E. Mayer, 1961a, page 3.
3. Slotkin, 1942b, page 37.
4. Anna Freud, page 90.
5. *Ibid.*, pages 91–92.
6. *Ibid.*, page 86.
7. J. E. Mayer, 1961a, page 89.
8. *Ibid.*, page 89.
9. *Ibid.*, page 90.
10. *Ibid.*, page 93.
11. *Ibid.*, page 94.
12. *Ibid.*, page 99.
13. *Ibid.*, page 91 fn.
14. *Ibid.*, page 89.
15. *Ibid.*, page 91 fn.
16. *Ibid.*, page 89.
17. From cases presented by both Gordon and Mayer it is evident that alarmed parents often accepted their child's denial that "anything would come of it." Parents succumbed readily to the temptation to assuage their anxiety by accepting their child's denial or by resorting to their own denial: "It's only talk; he doesn't mean it."
18. For purposes of contrast, let us quote from respondents who *did* display a mature sense of responsibility and foresight concerning their involvement with a cross-ethnic partner:
"[Before she reluctantly dated her husband] I had avoided going out with non-Jews all the time. When I had a blind date, and the boy turned out to be non-Jewish, I didn't go out with him again, even if he was nice." (Mayer, 1961a, page 21.)
". . . I never thought of going out with Harry, as I had decided I would never marry a non-Jew. But . . . we always went home together on the subway and talked. Then we'd have lunch together sometimes too. After a few months of this I decided his not being Jewish was really no barrier, and I would just accept what came of the relationship . . ." (Mayer, page 71)
(The reader will notice that we have cited seven examples of denial—virtually all attributed to *men;* and added this footnote quoting

by contrast two statements showing mature, foresightful planning—both expressed by *women!* Though a diligent researcher could undoubtedly find examples of both foresight and denial from both sexes, it seems that vacillation and ambivalence over getting married is a more peculiarly masculine experience whether the prospective mate is cross-ethnic or not.)

19. J. E. Mayer, 1961a, page 95.

20. "The proportion of [experimental animals] approaching near enough to touch the 'food' was . . . 23 per cent in the same alley, 37 per cent in the somewhat different alley, and 70 per cent in the quite different one. This shows," the investigators conclude, "that avoidance generalized less strongly than approach to the new stimulus situations." Miller and Kaeling, pages 220–221.

21. Stonequist, 1937, pages 105–106.

22. A. I. Gordon, 1964, page 80.

23. Krech and Crutchfield, 1948, page 57.

24. *Ibid.,* page 169.

25. Alfred Adler, 1931.

26. Berman dissertation.

27. Seward, 1956, page 261.

28. See Quay, Krasner, Verplanck.

29. Edward T. Hall recalls (and paraphrases) the viewpoint of H. S. Sullivan " . . . that the unconscious is not hidden to anyone except the individual who hides from himself those parts which persons significant to him in his early life have disapproved. While they are dissociated or hidden from himself, they are there for trained observers to see . . . ." (page 64) In *The Silent Language,* Hall develops the thesis that "in addition to what we say with our verbal language we are constantly communicating our real feelings in our silent language—the language of behavior." (page 10)

30. Dealing directly with cognitive material (e.g., facts, beliefs, judgments) exposes the counselor to all the temptations and digressions of lecturing, sermonizing, advice-giving and intellectualizing. The counselor's reluctance to operate directly in this area—at least so far as his theoretical orientation is concerned—is therefore understandable. A well-developed theory of counseling, however, will allow for a more explicit formulation and management of the young person's identity problem, as described by Erikson (1959a), and by Wheelis.

31. Drake and Cayton, pages 163, 166.

32. Stonequist, 1937, pages 194–195.

33. *Ibid.,* pages 195–198.

34. The ministry is an unusual but not unheard-of vocational choice for a Jewish convert to Christianity. According to the *Encyclopedia of Jewish Knowledge,* "it was claimed, in 1925, that there were in Germany 4,500 ministers of the Evangelical Church who were born Jews . . ." (page 226)

35. Stonequist, 1937, page 197.

36. Sokolsky, 1935, page 112.

37. Stonequist, 1937, page 190.

38. Hernton describes the rare case of a white woman who becomes an ethnic convert to the Negro group: "[They] have adopted every characteristic, real as well as stereotyped, of the American Negro, from patterns of speech to the very style of walking. . . . She has that 'gyrating gait,' that bouncing of the shoulders as she talks, that slur in the voice, that earthy twirl in her pelvis as she dances, that Negro-like contempt for whites. . . . Her vocabulary is conspicuously incomprehensible to white people. . . . Unlike the liberal white woman, she does not watch her tongue among Negroes. She will call a Negro a 'nigger' with the same intimacy and warmth or self-hostility that any Negro would. In every way possible—except skin color—she has *assimilated* into the Negro world both physically and psychologically. . . . Negroes who know her, talk and act around her as they do when she is not present. She knows all secrets, she shares all guilt, she enjoys and suffers whatever Negroes enjoy and suffer. In many ways she has out-Negroed the Negro." (Hernton, pages 51–52)

39. Sklare (1964, page 21) describes the readiness of Gentile college girls to marry a Jew as "perhaps the newest factor" in the intermarriage situation, and argues that "traditional perspectives" which have guided the study of intermarriage—social mobility, personality factors, negative chauvinism—"have come to obfuscate the true nature of the problem." 52

40. A theme of Philip Roth's *Letting Go* is the embitterment of a young proselyte wife over the ostracism her in-laws have directed against both her and her husband. Libby unburdens herself to a friend:

He was an only child and very attached to his family, and now they've really been hideous. Do you know what a *mikvah* is? A ritual bath? Well, I had one. The rabbi in Ann Arbor took me to the swimming pool at the Y, and in my old blue Jantzen I had this *mikvah*. And his parents *still* won't lift the phone when he calls. We call and they hang up. I could just kill them for that. Really take a knife and drive it right in them.

[A moment later Libby adds] . . . I didn't think anybody was going to act the way they did. I thought it would be *exciting* to have Jewish in-laws. I was all ready to be—well, Christ, I had that *mikvah* in my Jantzen, and what else could I do? But not them. They don't want to be happy. They want to be miserable, *that* makes them happy. Well, it doesn't make anybody else happy. (pages 53–54)

41. Wessel, page 441.
42. J. E. Mayer, 1961b, page 190.
43. Bowman, page 271.
44. Kaufmann, page 458.
45. Stonequist, 1937, pages 126, 128–129.
46. Quoted by Stonequist, 1937, page 141.
47. See Lindzey and Rogolsky, also Allport and Kramer.
48. Child, page 81.

49. *Ibid.*, pages 111–112.
50. *Ibid.*, page 146.
51. *Ibid.*, page 111.
52. Bossard and Boll, page 66.
53. Kaufmann, pages 360–361.
54. *Ibid.*, pages 363–364.
55. Reik, 1962, pages 99–100.
56. Sumner, page 419.
57. Murdock, page 5.
58. *Ibid.*, page 6.
59. Code, page 21.
60. A. I. Gordon, 1964, page 166.
61. *Ibid.*, pages 248–249.
62. Weidman, pages 26–27. Mary's remarks bring to mind Rosten's observation that the Harvard mischlings who suffered most from social ostracism and inner conflict were those who were brought up in high-status Old Yankee neighborhoods.

Psychologists are fond of reminding their readers that one cannot deal with the question of "adjustment" without taking into account the characteristics of the psychological environment or "life space" in which the person places himself. Yet in their specific recommendations on dealing with racial prejudice, social psychologists seem to have overlooked the importance to the individual of finding a congenial social environment. For example, a Jew and his Chinese wife might find great difficulty in adjusting to life in most cities of the United States, but they might go virtually unnoticed in Honolulu, where about one-fourth of the Jewish families who hold membership in the reform temple (Emanu El) —or 37 out of 150—are intermarried. The rabbi of that congregation is quoted by Gordon to say, "As to interracial marriages, of course here in Hawaii, these present no problem. . ." (page 193)
63. Weidman, page 81.
64 *Ibid.*, pages 90–91.
65. One of Mayer's respondents observed: "A friend of mine in the neighborhood, an older girl, married a non-Jew. Her mother ran through the streets screaming and all that baloney. Then, two weeks after the wedding, they were home living with the in-laws and everything was just fine. Her father even took him into the business. So I figured no matter how much opposition my parents felt, it would be like that after the wedding, and everything would be fine."
66. Levinson and Levinson, page 112.

CHAPTER 14

1, Heiss. See Chapter 2, fn. 24, this book.
2. Teitelbaum. See Table 5:1, this book.
3. Heiss. See Chapter 2, fn. 31, this book.
4. *Ibid.*, See Chapter 2, fn. 35, this book.
5. Lehrman, Gilberstadt and Duker. See Chapter 2, fns. 42 and 94,

this book.

6. Erich Rosenthal, 1963. See Table 2:1, this book.

7. Shosteck. See Chapter 2 fn. 11, this book.

8. Louis Rosenberg, 1963, applies this principle to intermarriage rates in Canada. See Chapter 7, fn. 13, this book, for a comparison of Detroit (Mich.) and Washington (D.C.) on rate of growth.

9. Erich Rosenthal, 1963. See Table 3:3, this book.

10. *Ibid.*, See Table 3:4, this book.

11. Sklare, 1964, pages 49–50.

12. Lenski. See "The Jews of Detroit," Chapter 7, this book.

13. See "The Gentile wife," and "The Gentile husband," Chapter 3, this book.

14. See "The Harvard mischlings," Chapter 4, this book; also see John E. Mayer, 1961a, pages 60–61, and Rubenstein, page 138.

15. Merton, pages 372–373.

16. In a personal communication, an Israeli sociologist informs this author of an interesting sex-bias in "intermarriages" between Israeli Jews of Western and Oriental background. Western husband—Oriental wife partnerships seem to have a much more favorable prognosis (and are presumably more popular) than Oriental husband—Western wife partnerships. Apparently the authoritarian patriarchal norm of the Oriental Jews trains girls to be "properly subservient" to a Western husband, but trains its men to demand more subservience from a wife than a Western woman is willing to exercise. (In Israel, the term "Oriental" is applied to Jews of the Arab world.)

17. Abraham, Franzblau, Hernton, Lehrman, Levinson and Levinson.

18. See Chapter 2, "The hostile parent-child relationship" and "Interracial marriage and the feeling of rejection."

19. See "Community exogamy," Chapter 7, this book.

20. To the Gentile partner and prospective convert, the rabbi guides not only her study of the Jewish religion, but her induction into the Jewish community as well. In his article on ". . . counseling young people contemplating intermarriage," Hillel Director Alfred Jospe notes that he advises the couple *not* to marry on campus, but to celebrate the wedding in the home town of the Jewish fiancé. "I want their family and friends as well as their home-town rabbi openly involved in order to smooth the way for them." (page 40)

Involvement with the Jewish community may not be an altogether happy experience for the proselyte, who must face not only the anti-Semitism of the Gentile world, but a measure of cynicism, hostility and ignorance which is to be found inside the Jewish community. A community mobilized against intermarriage can be unkind to even the most faithful convert. The proselyte needs the rabbi's moral support, and may even need his direct intervention, if a crisis occurs. Practice of the Jewish faith without a feeling of acceptance into the Jewish community must be a sad and embittering experience. Admittedly, it calls for a high order of wisdom for a rabbi to educate his congregation in the kindly treatment of proselytes without appearing to advocate intermarriage. (The foregoing deals specifically with the problems of the proselyte wife.)

21. Typically, the distraught parents make an impossible demand upon the rabbi; he might anger or alienate the engaged couple but he cannot ordinarily force them to change their plans. It may, however, fall within the rabbi's power to comfort the parents, relieve them of some of the guilt they feel for "whatever went wrong" in the upbringing of their child, and reassure them against their feelings of ostracism for their offspring's violation of "the law of the tribe." The rabbi who uses the crisis as an occasion for sermonizing on hypocrisy and backsliding accomplishes nothing and passes up an opportunity to comfort the distressed.

One can only guess about what rabbis actually say to the distraught parents. In writing on the topic, rabbis sometimes give the impression that the only aspect of intermarriage worthy of serious concern is the *religious* aspect, and that worries about "what people will say," or how to face Gentile *machotonim,* smacks of gossip and snobbishness and tribalism.

Addressing the Jewish community of Australia and New Zealand in 1946, Rabbi Danglow warned that unless Jews restrict their objections to intermarriage to religious grounds exclusively, it may be inferred that Jews regard Gentiles as inferior people. (page 4)

[In 1934 Rabbi Mordecai Kaplan warned that America] is certain to look with disfavor upon any culture which seeks to maintain itself by decrying the intermarriage of its adherents to those of another culture. By accepting a policy which does not decry marriages of Jews with Gentiles, providing the homes they establish are Jewish and their children are given a Jewish upbringing, the charge of exclusiveness and tribalism falls to the ground. With such an attitude, there would no longer be any occasion for pointing to the racial pride of the Jews. What is valuable is the Jewish social heritage, or civilization, and not physical descent. (page 419)

To an intellectual it seems altogether reasonable to maintain a clear distinction between religious values and social considerations. An intellectual can become intrigued with the proposition that there's nothing wrong with a Jew marrying a Gentile so long as their children are brought up in a Jewish home. But the Jew who lives closer to the world of day-to-day realities knows that a Jewish home by definition requires a Jewish father, a Jewish mother, Jewish grandparents, and Jewish relatives. Likewise, as Jewishness is experienced in his day-to-day life, there is no distinction between faith and folk. An exclusive concern with the religious aspect of intermarriage certainly obscures more than it explains. There need be no conflict between religious values and feelings of group solidarity in a tradition which holds that God, Torah, and Israel are one.

22. See "The Harvard mischlings," Chapter 4, this book.

23. The following group of observers—psychiatrist, rabbi, social psychologists, and essayist—disagree widely on the intermarriage issue, but show a remarkable unanimity in assessing the problem of raising children of mixed parentage:

To Franzblau, "one of the strongest arguments . . . [against] mixed marriages is that whether or not the marriage itself is a success, invariably the children resulting from it have their problems. They are the victims in almost every case." (page 22)

Rabbi Kirshenbaum, extremist opponent of intermarriage, alludes darkly to "children who grow up to be self-haters and Jew-haters, and who despise their parents for the marriage and its consequences." (page ix) Krech and Crutchfield, whose social psychology textbook takes an explicitly assimilationist stand, concede that "children resulting from some mixed marriages in our society find themselves rejected by the very groups with which they would normally seek identification, and they are consequently faced with many difficulties of adjustment. The realization of what is in store for children of mixed marriages serves as a deterrent for such marriages," the authors conclude. (1948, page 508)

To Leslie Fiedler, the mischling's identity problem is "the most desperate of psychological games." (1964, page 120)

24. See Chapter 4, "The childless intermarriage."

25. See Chapter 1, "The assimilationist viewpoint in social psychology." Are textbook writers the opinion-*makers* of social psychology, or do they reflect the prevailing climate of opinion in their profession? This author is inclined toward the latter view.

26. For example, the researches and writings of Kramer and Leventman, Teitelbaum, Lenski, Milton Goldberg, Sarnoff.

27. Foote and Cottrell, page v.

28. *Ibid.*, page 24.

29. See "The negative incubus," Chapter 1; Chapter 7, fn. 116, Chapter 10, fn. 267; see "Neurotic aggressiveness," Chapter 11, this book. See Riesman, 1942, on "strident and greedy" Jews; Seward, 1956, Chapter 11, on warped and timid Jews; see Glazer and Moynihan, on cautious, timid, fearful, and opportunistic Jews. See Maslow, on hostile and aggressive Jews, Ch. 11, fn. 23.

Behavioral scientists are much more impressed with the discontinuities and disruptions in Jewish life than with its consistencies and continuities. Glazer, 1957, cannot believe that the liberalism of American Jews stems from the Jewish tradition; preferring to believe that the immigrants brought with them "the political attitudes they had adopted in Europe." (page 136) To Glazer and Moynihan it is but a quirk of fate that the founder of psychoanalysis was a Jew and not a German anti-Semite. (page 175). Behavioral scientists are even inclined to overlook the dominant, central, centuries old tradition of Jewish learning, in accounting for the academic achievement of American Jews; preferring to interpret it as neurotic overcompensation, and hostility toward one's Gentile classmates. Riesman, for example, describes the hard working Jewish student as a "rate buster," comparing him to "the Polish steel worker or Italian track-layer or Japanese truck farmer who had lost, under the new conditions, all conventional and group-enforced limits on hours and pace of work." (Riesman, 1951, page 524)

30. See "The doctrine of adjustment," Chapter 1, this book.

31. In a 1967 editorial in *Trans-action,* Horowitz and Rainwater discuss "the escalating interest of even the most academic of social scientists in the possibilities of their work for creating as well as describing society," and endorse the calculated risk involved in "institutionalizing social science as part of the federal government's efforts to assess the state of the nation." (page 2)

32. Tumin, 1957, expresses concern that in an affluent society with a rapidly growing intellectual elite, there is relatively little incentive for "the active pursuit of open and sharp debate . . ." "Perhaps never before has there been so much room in the well-paying portions of the occupational ladder for the skills and talents of intellectuals. . . . [As a consequence] many of the ablest [potential] critics of the social order . . . have been in a sense, bought off by the social order. . . .

"Any social order stands in danger when it becomes smug regarding its past and even smugger about its future. . . . The mobility of . . . society in general has made creative criticism highly undesired and unpopular. And the mobility of prior critics has made significant numbers of them deny their histories and the value of their prior criticism. Those denials have helped them move quickly and surely into the ranks of those who feel it important to applaud. The active pursuit of open and sharp debate—an indispensable condition for the maintenance of an open society—is thus seriously endangered." (page 35) Tumin suggests that a vicious cycle is set in motion as conformity—requiring an abandonment of one's traditional values, responsibilities and rights—increases insecurity, and insecurity increases the need to conform.

What Tumin says about "the social order" and its potential critics has much relevance, it seems, to the academic situation and the behavioral science field in particular.

33. In a 1955 comment, Srole seems to argue that his prediction of the disappearance of the Jews was upset by the rise of Nazi and domestic anti-Semitism. These forces operated "as a powerful catalyst for the reintegration of the American Jewish community . . . at a point in time when it may have been in danger of losing a considerable segment of its next generation," Srole argued. (page 277)

34. Srole, Langner, et al., page 306.

35. McClelland, 1961, page 364.

36. To Kutzik (pages 37–38), Riesman's cry for *individualism* expresses discomfort over all forms of Jewish group life. In *The Lonely Crowd* (page 336) Riesman rejects the "small-time culture dictators" who tell him what his leisure style and friendship practice should be. Jewish group life seems so alien and unlovely, it appears to Riesman

that the only plausable reason why Gentiles sometimes express a positive interest in "Jewish folksiness" is that they are "so afraid of being thought ethnocentric. . . ." (1954, page 160). The appeal of the Yankee elite culture to a Jewish intellecual is well portrayed in Riesman's eulogy of "the typical Protestant businessman" (1954, pages 60–61), and in his romantic portrait of the patrician Yankee professor (Riesman, 1951).

We are less concerned here with Riesman's individual viewpoint than with how well he articulates a prevailing viewpoint in academia, which sees virtually nothing of value in the Jewish cultural tradition or in Jewish group identification. Stuart E. Rosenberg offers some penetrating insights into the antagonism between the Jewish middle class and its intellectuals:

> Most Jewish intellectuals cannot empathize with the malaise of the middle-class American Jew because they are themselves afflicted with their own unique brand of Jewish restlessness and unsettlement. They play at the game of denying it, and thus do not understand those Jews who still hold on to their Jewishness or Judaism. In their case, the desire to avoid what they consider the Jewish community's *extreme conformism to middle-class patterns* succeeds in impelling them to adopt the *extreme conformism of the non-conforming intellectual community.* (page 252)

> Thus, the clannishness of the average American Jew continues to strike their intellectual brethren as mere tribalism. They see in the Jewish desire to marry within the group a primitive fetish still at work. They are appalled by the seeming lack of universality in the contemporary Jewish spirit in America, when they contemplate the fact that of all other religions or ethnic groups the Jews still retain the highest proportion of in-marriage. . . . (page 253)

> . . . Because they can attribute little intrinsic meaning to either Jewishness or Judaism, many Jewish intellectuals see in this situation sinister rather than benign influences. And they buttress this view by accusing the American Jew of exploiting a neurotic fear of anti-Semitism as a justification for an exclusiveness that refuses to sanction intimate contact with the world of the non-Jew . . . (pages 254–255)

> [Middle-class] American Jews may be generous for the wrong reasons; but at least they are generous! They may sometimes band together for the wrong reasons; but, at least, they stand with one another, and do not seek to run away from themselves or their responsibility to one another. (page 255)

Bibliography

Abel, T. M., and F. L. K. Hsu (1948), "Some aspects of personality of Chinese as revealed by the Rorschach test," Journal of Projective Techniques, 12, 79–93.

Abraham, Karl (1909), "The significance of intermarriage between close relatives in the psychology of the neuroses," in author's Clinical Papers and Essays on Psychoanalysis. Vol. II. New York: Basic Books, 1955, 21–36.

——— (1913), "On neurotic exogamy," in author's Clinical Papers and Essays on Psychoanalysis. Vol. II. New York: Basic Books, 1955, 48–50.

Adams, Romanzo (1937), Interracial Marriage in Hawaii. New York: Macmillan.

Adler, Alfred (1929), "Early recollections and their significance," Chapter 8 in Problems of Neurosis; a Book of Case Histories. London: Kegan Paul.

——— (1931), What Life Should Mean To You. New York: Grosset and Dunlap.

Adler, Morris (1964), "What is a Jew?" Harper's, 228, No. 1364, January, 41–45.

——— (1965), "The Jew—a profile." In Jewish Heritage Reader, q.v., 3–4. New York: Taplinger. 3–4.

Aleichem, Sholom (ca. 1913), Tevye's Daughters. New York: Crown, 1949.

Allinsmith, Wesley, and Beverly Allinsmith (1948), "Religious affiliation and politico-economic attitude," Public Opinion Quarterly, 12, 377–389.

Allport, Floyd (1924), Social Psychology. Boston: Houghton Mifflin.

Allport, G. W., and B. M. Kramer (1946), "Some roots of prejudice," Journal of Psychology, 22, 9–39.

Anonymous (1939 a), "I married a Jew," Atlantic Monthly, 136, January, 38–46. Author is referred to in text as Gertrude.

Anonymous (1939 b), *I Married a Jew*, New York: Dodd, Mead and Company. Expanded version of *Atlantic* article listed above.

Anonymous (1940), "I was a Jew," Forum, 103, January, 8–11. Author is referred to in text as *Ted*.

Anonymous (1942), "An analysis of Jewish culture," Chapter 9 in Graeber and Britt (eds.) *q.v.* Author is referred to in text as *Critic*.

Antonovsky, Aaron (1956), "Toward a refinement of the 'marginal man' concept," Social Forces, 35, No. 1, 57–62.

Ardrey, Robert (1966), The Territorial Imperative. New York: Atheneum.

Atkinson, John W. (1957), "Motivational determinants of risk-taking behavior," Psychological Review, 64, 359–372.

Ausubel, Nathan (1951), "Love-shmove." in *A Treasury of Jewish Humor*, edited by Nathan Ausubel. Garden City: Doubleday, pages 100–101.

Baber, Ray (1937), "A study of 325 mixed marriages," American Sociological Review, 2, 705–716.

────── (1939), *Marriage and the Family*. New York: McGraw-Hill.

Bakan, David (1958), *Sigmund Freud and the Jewish Mystical Tradition*. Princeton: Van Nostrand.

Baltzell, E. Digby (1964), *The Protestant Establishment; Aristocracy and Caste in America*. New York: Random House.

Bamberger, Bernard J. (1949), "Plain talk about intermarriage," Reconstructionist, 15, No. 16, Dec. 16, 10–14.

Baron, Salo W. (1937), *A Social and Religious History of the Jews*. New York: Columbia University Press.

Barron, Milton M. (1946), "Jewish intermarriage in Europe and America," American Sociological Review, 11, 7–13.

────── (1946), *People Who Intermarry; Intermarriage in a New England Industrial Community*. Syracuse: Syracuse University Press.

────── (1951), "Research on intermarriage: a survey of accomplishments and prospects," American Journal of Sociology, 57, 249–255.

Belth, Nathan C. (1962), "The Jews in Middletown," Chapter 14 in Jacob Freid (ed.), *q.v.*, Volume I, 310–315.

Berelson, Bernard, and Gary A. Steiner (1964), Human Behavior; an Inventory of Scientific Findings. New York: Harcourt, Brace.

Berlyne, D. E. (1960), *Conflict, Arousal and Curiosity*. New York: McGraw-Hill.

Berman, Isaac, and Georgene Seward (1958), "A little Jewish boy under pressure of orthodoxy," pages 455–478, in *Clinical Studies in Culture Conflict*, Georgene Seward [editor]. New York: Ronald Press.

Berman, Louis A. (1957), The Projective Interpretation of Early Recollections. Ph.D. Dissertation, University of Michigan. Ann Arbor: University Microfilms.

────── (1966), "A comparison of Jewish and non-Jewish college students' attitudes toward their parents, and intermarriage." Unpublished study.

Bernard, Jessie (1942), "Biculturality: a study in social schizophrenia," Chapter 10 in Graeber and Britt, *q.v.,* 264–293.

Bernstein, Ignaz, and B. W. Segel, editors (1908), *Jüdische Sprichwörter und Redensarten.* Warsaw: J. Kaufmann.

Bersh, P. J., W. N. Schoenfeld, and J. M. Notterman (1953), The effect upon heart rate conditioning of randomly varying the interval between conditioned and unconditioned stimuli. Proceedings of the National Academy of Science, 39, 563–570.

Bersh, P. J., W. N. Schoenfeld, and J. M. Notterman (1956), "Generalization to varying tone frequencies as a function of intensity of unconditioned stimulus," Texas Air University, School of Aviation Medicine, USAF, Randolph AFB.

Bigman, Stanley K. (1957), The Jewish Population of Greater Washington in 1956. Washington D. C.: Jewish Community Council of Greater Washington.

Birmingham, Stephen (1968), *Our Crowd.* New York: Harper and Row.

Blankfort, Michael (1956), *The Strong Hand.* Boston: Little, Brown.

Blau, Zena Smith (1967), "In defense of the Jewish mother," Midstream, 13, 42–49.

Bloom, Leonard (1942), "The Jews of Buna," Chapter 7 in Graeber and Britt (eds.), *q.v.,* 180–199.

Bohannan, Paul (1963), *Social Anthropology.* New York: Holt, Rinehart and Winston.

Bokser, Ben Zion (1963), *Judaism; Profile of a Faith.* New York: Knopf.

Bondarin, Mary Ruth (1958), "Thy people shall be my people." In David M. Eichorn (ed.), Conversion to Judaism, *q.v.,* pages 241–243. From a sermon delivered by the author at Temple Sinai, Forest Hills, L. I., N. Y., January 31, 1958.

Bossard, James H. S. (1944), "Marriage as a status-achieving device," Sociology and Social Research, 29, September–October, 1–10.

———, and Harold C. Letts (1956), "Mixed marriages involving Lutherans—a research report," Marriage and Family Living, 18, 308–310.

———, and Eleanor Stoker Boll (1957), One Marriage, Two Faiths. New York: Ronald Press.

Bowman, Henry A. (1954), Marriage for Moderns. 3rd ed. New York: McGraw-Hill.

Boyd, Ernest (1933), "As a Gentile sees it," Scribner's Magazine, 94, October, 242–243.

Brandeis, Louis D. (1915), "The Jewish problem and how to solve it," pages 12–35 in Brandeis on Zionism; a Collection of Addresses and Statements by Louis D. Brandeis. Washington, D.C., 1942: Zionist Organization of America.

Bressler, Marvin (1952), "Selected family patterns in W. I. Thomas' unfinished study of the Bintel Brief," American Sociological Review, 17, 566.

Brill, A. A. (1929). See Lovell.

———— ed. (1938), *The Basic Writings of Sigmund Freud*. New York: Modern Library.

Bronfenbrenner, Uri (1958), "The study of identification," in *Person, Perception, and Interpersonal Behavior*, Taiguiri and Petrullo (eds.), Stanford University Press.

Brossard, Chandler (1950), "Plaint of a Gentile intellectual," Commentary, 10, No. 2, 154–156.

Browne, Lewis (1929), "Why are Jews like that?" American Magazine, January, 7.

Buhler, Charlotte (1958), "A displaced European molds herself into an American," pages 509–530, in Clinical Studies in Culture Conflict, Georgene Seward, editor. New York: Ronald Press.

Burma, John H. (1946), "The measurement of Negro 'passing,'" American Journal of Sociology, 52, No. 1, 18–22.

Cahnman, Werner J., ed. (1963), Intermarriage and Jewish Life; a Symposium. New York: Herzl Press and The Jewish Reconstructionist Press.

———— (1963), "Intermarriage against the background of American democracy," in author's Intermarriage and Jewish Life, q.v., 173–208.

Campisi, P. J. (1948), "Ethnic family patterns: the Italian family in the United States," American Journal of Sociology, 53, 443–449.

Caro, Joseph (1564). *Shulchan Aruch* [Code of Jewish Law]. Venice. See Goldin; 1927.

Cavan, Ruth (1945), *The Family*. New York: Thomas Y. Crowell.

———— (1953), *The American Family*. New York: Crowell.

Child, I. L. (1943), *Italian or American: The Second Generation in Conflict*. New Haven: Yale University Press.

Christensen, Harold T., and Kenneth E. Barber (1967), "Interfaith versus intrafaith marriage in Indiana," Journal of Marriage and the Family, 29, No. 3, 461–469.

Clark, E. (1949), "Motivation of Jewish students," Journal of Social Psychology, 29, 113–117.

Code. See Goldin.

Cohen, Abraham (1911), *Ancient Jewish Proverbs*. London: John Murray.

Cohen, Arthur A. (1959), "Why I chose to be a Jew," Harper's, 218, No. 1307, 61–66.

———— (1962), *The Natural and the Supernatural Jew; an Historical and Theological Introduction*. New York: Pantheon.

Cohen, Henry (1962), "Jewish life and thought in an academic community," American Jewish Archives, 14, No. 2, 107–128.

Cooley, Charles Horton (1922), Human Nature and the Social Order. Revised ed. New York: Scribner's.

Coon, Carleton (1942), "Have the Jews a racial identity?" Chapter 1 in I. Graeber (ed.), *Jews in a Gentile World*. New York: Macmillan, 20–37.

Corner, George W. (1961), "Menstrual cycle," in Encyclopedia of Sexual Behavior. q.v.

Cothran, Tilman (1951), "Negro conceptions of white people," American Journal of Sociology, 56, No. 5, 458–476.

Critic. See Anonymous (1942).

Dahlstrom, W. Grant, and George S. Welsh (1960), *An MMPI Handbook; a Guide to Use in Clinical Practice and Research.* Minneapolis: University of Minnesota Press.

Danglow, Jacob (1946), Intermarriage; a grave danger to the survival of our community. Pamphlet published under the auspices of the Jewish Ministers' Conference of Australia and New Zealand.

Dean, John P. (1955), "Patterns of socialization and association between Jews and non-Jews," Jewish Social Studies, 17. No. 3, 247–284.

Devereaux, George (1965), "Neurotic Downward Identification." American Imago, Volume 22, No. 1–2, 77–95.

Dollard, John (1949), *Caste and Class in a Southern Town.* New York: Harper.

Doob, Leonard W. (1952), *Social Psychology.* New York: Holt.

Drachsler, Julius (1920), *Democracy and Assimilation; the Blending of Immigrant Heritages in America.* New York: Macmillan.

Drake, St. Clair, and Horace R. Cayton (1945), *Black Metropolis.* New York: Harcourt, Brace.

Dunlap, Knight (1946), *Religion, its Function in Human Life.* New York: McGraw-Hill.

Edwardes, Allen, and R. E. L. Masters (1963), *The Cradle of Erotica.* New York: Julian Press.

Ehrmann, Winston (1959), *Premarital Dating Behavior.* New York: Holt.

Eichorn, David M. (1954), "Conversion to Judaism by Reform and Conservative rabbis," Jewish Social Studies, 16, 299–318.

——— (1963), "Conversion: requirements and results," in Werner Cahnman (ed.), Intermarriage and Jewish Life, *q.v.,* 111–121.

——— (ed.), (1965), *Conversion to Judaism; a History and Analysis.* Ktav Publishing House, Inc.

Eisenberg, Azriel, ed. (1952), *Modern Jewish Life in Literature.* New York: United Synagogue of America.

Eisenstein, Victor W., ed. (1956), *Neurotic Interaction in Marriage.* New York: Basic Books.

Encyclopedia of Jewish Knowledge. (1946) Jacob de Haas, ed. New York: Behrman.

Encyclopedia of Sexual Behavior. (1961) Albert Ellis and Albert Arbanel (eds.). New York: Hawthorn.

Engelman, Uriah Zevi (1940), "Intermarriage Among Jews in Germany, U.S.S.R., and Switzerland," Jewish Social Studies, v. 2, pp. 157–178.

——— (1960), "Sources of statistics," Chapter 37 in Louis Finkelstein (ed.), The Jews . . . , *q.v.,* Vol. II, 1510–1535.

Erikson, Erik H. (1946), "Ego Development and historical change," in Anna Freud, et al., (ed.) *The Psychoanalytic Study of the Child.* Vol. II. New York: International Universities Press.

—— (1959a), "Identity and the life cycle," *Psychological Issues,* 1, No. 1.

—— (1959b), "Identity and uprootedness in our time," presented at World Federation of Mental Health, Vienna. Published in author's Insight and Responsibility, New York: Norton, 1964, pp. 83–107.

Feinsilver, Lillian Mermin (1964), "Yiddish and American English," in Azriel Eisenberg (ed.), *The Golden Land.* New York: Thomas Yoseloff.

Feldman, Ephraim (1909), "Intermarriage historically considered," CCAR Yearbook, Cincinnati, pages 271–307.

Feldman, Irving (1961), "Dawn, by Elie Wiesel," [Book review] Commentary, 32, No. 3, 262–264.

Feldman, Leon A. (1955), "The Jewish College Student," Jewish Spectator, December, 11–17.

Fenichel, Otto (1939), "The counter-phobic attitude," International Journal of Psychoanalysis, 20, 263–274.

—— (1945), *The Psychoanalytic Theory of Neuroses.* New York: Norton.

Festinger, Leon (1957), A Theory of Cognitive Dissonance. Evanston: Row, Peterson.

Fiedler, Leslie (1959), *The Jew in the American Novel.* Pamphlet No. 10, Herzl Institute. New York: Herzl Press.

—— (1959a), "Introduction," *Waiting for God* by Simone Weil. New York: Capricorn Books.

—— (1960), "On the road; or the adventures of Karl Shapiro," Poetry, 96, No. 3.

—— (1963), "The Jew as a mythic American," Ramparts, 2, Fall, 32–48.

—— (1964), *Waiting for the End.* New York: Stein and Day.

—— (1966), "Negro-Jewish relations in America" [part of a symposium], Midstream, 12, December, pages 22–29.

Finkelstein, Louis (1960), "The Jewish religion: its beliefs and practices," Chapter 42 in the author's The Jews . . . , *q.v.,* Vol. II, 1739–1802.

—— ed. (1960), The Jews; their History, Culture and Religion. 3rd Edition. New York: Harper and Row.

Fluegel, J. C. (1929), *The Psychoanalytic Study of the Family.* London: Hogarth.

Foote, Nelson N., and Leonard S. Cottrell, Jr. (1955) *Identity and Interpersonal Competence, a New Direction in Family Research.* Chicago: University of Chicago Press.

Franzblau, Abraham N. (1954), "The dynamics of a mixed marriage," CCAR Journal, October, 21–25.

Freedman, Morris (1951), "The Jewish college student: 1951 model," Commentary, 12, No. 4, 305–313.

Freeman, Howard E., and Gene Kassebaum (1956), "Exogamous dating in a Southern city," Jewish Social Studies, 18, 55–60.

Freeman, Linton (1955), "Homogamy in interethnic mate selection," Sociology and Social Research, 39, July–August. 369–377.

Freud, Anna (1946), *The Ego and the Mechanisms of Defense*. New York: International Universities Press.

Freud, Martin (1958), *Sigmund Freud: Man and Father*. New York: Vanguard.

Freud, Sigmund (1904), Psychopathology of Everyday Life. Book I in A. A. Brill (ed.), The Basic Writings of Sigmund Freud, *q.v.*, 35–178.

———— (1908), " 'Civilized' sexual morality and modern nervousness," in Sigmund Freud, Collected Papers, *q.v.* Vol. II, 76–99.

———— (1910), "Contributions to the psychology of love. A special type of choice of object made by men." In Sigmund Freud, Collected Papers, *q.v.* Vol. IV, 192–202.

———— (1912a), *Totem and Taboo*. Book V in A. A. Brill (ed.), The Basic Writings of Sigmund Freud, *q.v.*, 807–930.

———— (1912b), "Contributions to the psychology of love. The most prevalent form of degradation in erotic life." In Sigmund Freud, Collected Papers, *q.v.* Vol. IV, 203–216.

———— (1914) "On narcissism: an introduction." In Sigmund Freud, Collected Papers, *q.v.* Vol. IV, 30–59.

———— (1915), "Some character-types met with in psychoanalytic work." In Sigmund Freud, Collected Papers, *q.v.* Vol. IV, 318–344.

———— (1917), "A childhood recollection from Dichtung und Wahrheit," In Sigmund Freud, Collected Papers, *q.v.* Vol. IV, 357–367.

———— (1924), "The economic problem in masochism." In Sigmund Freud, Collected Papers, *q.v.* Vol. II, 255–268.

———— (1949) *Collected Papers*. 5 Vols. London: Hogarth Press.

Frishman, David (1938), "The three who ate," in Azriel Eisenberg (ed.), *q.v.*, 29–33.

Fromm, Eric (1955), "Sex and character: the Kinsey report viewed from the standpoint of psychoanalysis," Ch. 27 in Jerome Himelhoch and Sylvia Fleis Fava (eds.), *Sexual Behavior in American Society*. New York: Norton, 301–311.

Fuchs, James (1928), "On so-called Jewish traits," The Vanguard, Vol. 2, No. 6, 59–63.

Fuchs, Lawrence H. (1956), *The Political Behavior of American Jews*. Glencoe: The Free Press.

Gans, Herbert J. (1956), "American Jewry: present and future," Commentary, 21, No. 5, 422–430.

———— (1958), "The origin and growth of a Jewish community in the suburbs: a study of the Jews of Park Forest." In Marshall Sklare (ed.), The Jews . . . , *q.v.*, 205–248.

———— (1962), *The Urban Villagers: Group and Class in the Life of Italian-Americans*. Glencoe: The Free Press.

Gelfant, Blanche Housman (1962), "The city as symbol," in C. Hugh Holman (ed.), *The World of Thomas Wolfe*. New York: Scribner's, 153–156.

Gertrude. See Anonymous (1939a).

Gibel, Inge Lederer (1965), "The Negro-Jewish scene: a personal view," Judaism, 14, No. 1, 14–21.

Giddings, F. H. (1903), "The American people," International Quarterly, 7, June. Cited by Drachsler, *q.v.*, 47.

Gilberstadt, Harold and Jan Duker (1965), *A Handbook for Clinical and Actuarial MMPI Interpretation*. Philadelphia: Saunders.

Glanz, Rudolph (1943), ["The immigration of German Jews up to 1880"] in Elias Tcherikower (ed.), Geshikhte fun der Yidisher Arbeterbavegung in di Faraynikte Shtatn. (History of the Jewish Labor Movement in the United States.) 2 Vols. New York:————. Cited by Sherman (1961), *q.v.*

Glasner, Samuel, "Judaism and Sex," in Encyclopedia of Sexual Behavior, *q.v.*, 575–584.

Glazer, Nathan (1950), "What sociology knows about American Jews," Commentary, 9, No. 3, 275–284.

———— (1955), "Social characteristics of American Jews, 1655–1954." In Marshall Sklare (ed.), The Jews . . . , *q.v.*, pages 138–146. Originally published in 1955 American Jewish Year Book. Also excerpted in Louis Finkelstein (ed.), The Jews . . . , *q.v.*, pages 1694–1738.

———— (1957), *American Judaism*. Chicago: University of Chicago Press.

———— and Daniel P. Moynihan (1963), *Beyond the Melting Pot; the Negroes, Puerto Ricans, Jews, Italians and Irish of New York City*. Cambridge: MIT Press—Harvard.

Gold, Henry Raphael (1965), "Sex in Jewish tradition." In Jewish Heritage Reader, *q.v.*, 147–150.

Goldberg, B. Z. (1930), *The Sacred Fire; the Story of Sex in Religion*. New York: Grove Press.

Goldberg, Milton M. (1941), "A qualification of the marginal man theory," American Sociological Review, 6, 52–58.

Golden, Joseph (1953), "Characteristics of the Negro-White intermarried in Philadelphia," American Sociological Review, 177–183.

Goldhurst, Richard (pseud.) (1953), "Growing up between two worlds," Commentary, Vol. 16, No. 1, 30–35.

Goldin, Hyman E., translator (1927), *Code of Jewish Law*. Revised edition. New York: Hebrew Publishing Co. This book is numbered as if it were printed in four volumes. All references in this study are located in the final section of this book, the first page of which is labelled CXLIII.

———— translator (1962), Pirke Aboth; *Ethics of the Fathers*. New York: Hebrew Publishing Co.

Goldstein, Sidney (1966), "Jewish mortality and survival patterns: Providence, Rhode Island, 1962–1964," Eugenics Quarterly, 13, No. 1, 48–61.

———— and Calvin Goldscheider (1966), "Social and demographic aspects of Jewish intermarriages," Social Problems, 13, No. 4, 386–399.

Goldstein, Sidney I. (1964), "Mixed marriages in the Deep South," Reconstructionist, 30, No. 2, 15–18.

Gollancz, Victor (1950), *Man and God*. Boston: Houghton Mifflin, 1951.

Goodenough, Erwin R. (1958), *Jewish Symbols in The Greco-Roman Period. v. 8, Pagan Symbols in Judaism,* New York: Pantheon Books.

Gordon, Albert I. (1949), *Jews in Transition.* Minneapolis: University of Minneapolis.

———— (1959), *Jews in Suburbia.* Boston: Beacon Press.

———— (1964), *Intermarriage; Interfaith, Interracial, Interethnic.* Boston: Beacon Press.

Gordon, Milton M. (1961), "Assimilation in America: theory and reality," Daedalus, 263–285.

———— (1964), *Assimilation in American Life.* New York: Oxford.

Gordon, Noah (1965), *The Rabbi.* New York: McGraw-Hill.

Gorwitz, Kurt (1962), "Jewish mortality in St. Louis and St. Louis County, 1955–1957," Jewish Social Studies, 24, No. 4; 248–254.

Graeber, Isaque, and Steuart Henderson Britt, editors (1942), *Jews in a Gentile World.* New York: Macmillan.

Greater Washington D. C. Study. See Bigman.

Greenburg, Dan (1964), *How to Be a Jewish Mother.* Los Angeles: Price, Stern and Sloan.

Greifer, Julian L. (1955), "Relationships in a large city; comment on John P. Dean's 'Patterns of socialization and association between Jews and non-Jews,'" Jewish Social Studies, 17, No. 3, 269–273.

Gurin, Gerald, Joseph Veroff and Sheila Feld (1960), *Americans View Their Mental Health; a Nationwide Interview Survey.* New York: Basic Books.

Guttman, Judith (1964), A letter to the editor, Commentary, 38, No. 3, 10.

Hall, Edward T. (1959), *The Silent Language.* Greenwich (Conn.): Faucett, 1961.

Hamilton, Gilbert V., and Kenneth Macgowan (1929), *What Is Wrong with Marriage.* New York: Albert and Charles Boni. A popularization of Gilbert V. Hamilton, *A Research in Marriage.*

Hansen, Marcus L. (1938), *The Problem of the Third Generation Immigrant.* Rock Island, Illinois: Augustana Historical Society.

Harkavy, Alexander (1898), *Yiddish-English Dictionary.* New York: Hebrew Publishing Company.

Haveman, Ernest, and Patricia Salter West (1952), *They Went to College; the College Graduate in America Today.* New York: Harcourt, Brace.

Heiss, Jerrold S. (1960), "Premarital characteristics of religiously inter-married," American Sociological Review, 25, 47–55.

Heller, Abraham (1942), *The Vocabulary of Jewish Life.* New York: Hebrew Publishing Company.

———— (1965), "Mixed marriages and the Rabbi," [American Jewish] Congress Bi-Weekly, 32, No. 6, 7–9.

Helper, Malcolm M. (1955), Learning theory and the self-concept. Journal of abnormal and social psychology, 55, 184–194.

Herberg, Will (1955), *Protestant—Catholic—Jew.* Garden City: Doubleday.

—————— (1959), *Judaism and Modern Man*. New York: Meridian.

Hernton, Calvin C. (1965), *Sex and Racism in America*. Garden City: Doubleday.

Hertz, Joseph H. (1956), *The Pentateuch and the Haftorahs*. London: Soncino Press.

Hertzler, J. O. (1942), "The sociology of anti-Semitism through history," Chapter 3 in Graeber and Britt, *q.v.*, 62–100.

Heschel, Abraham Joshua (1950), *The Earth is the Lord's*. New York: Henry Schuman.

—————— (1959), *God in Search of Man*. New York: Meridian.

Hilgard, Ernest R. (1962), *Introduction to Psychology*. 3rd edition. New York: Harcourt, Brace and World.

Hollingshead, August B. (1950), "Cultural factors in the selection of marriage mates," American Sociological Review, 15, No. 5, 619–627.

—————— and Frederick Redlich (1958), *Social Class and Mental Health*. New York: Wiley.

Horowitz, Irving L., and Lee Rainwater (1967), "Social accounting for the nation," Trans-action, 4, No. 6, 2–3.

Hsu, Francis L. K. (1953), *Americans and Chinese*. New York: Henry Schuman.

—————— (1961), *Psychological Anthropology*. Homewood (Ill.) : Dorsey Press.

Hulse, F. S. (1958), "Exogamie et hétérosis," Archives Suisses d'Anthropologie Générale, 22, 103–125. Cited by Pettigrew, *q.v.*, 64.

Hurvitz, Nathan (1961), "Sources of motivation and achievement of American Jews," Jewish Social Studies, 23, No. 4, 217–234.

—————— (1965), "Sixteen Jews who intermarried," Yivo Annual of Jewish Social Science, 13, 153–179. A criticism of Levinson and Levinson, q.v.

Inkeles, Alex, and Daniel J. Levinson (1954), "National character: the study of modal personality and socio-cultural systems," in Gardner Lindzey (ed.), Handbook of Social Psychology, vol. 2, 977–1020. Cambridge, Mass.: Addison-Wesley.

Israel, Robert J. (1966), "A note on counseling young people contemplating intermarriage," Campus 1966: Change and Challenge; National Conference of Hillel Directors 1965. Washington, D.C.: B'nai B'rith Hillel Foundations. Pages 47–54.

Jacobs, Paul (1965), *Is Curley Jewish?* New York: Atheneum.

Jacobson, Dan (1967), "A lost world?" [Book review] Commentary, 43, No. 6, 81–83.

Jacobson, Paul H. (1959), American Marriage and Divorce. New York: Rinehart.

James, William (1902), The Varieties of Religious Experience. New York: Modern Library.

Jewish Heritage Reader (1965). Selected, with introduction by Rabbi Morris Adler. Lily Edelman, editor. New York: Taplinger Publishing Co.

Jewish Post and Opinion, Chicago Edition (1965), "Psychiatrist, Rabbi differ on interdating," 20, No. 30, April 2, page 3.

Jones, Ernest (1953–1957), *The Life and Work of Sigmund Freud*. 3 vols. New York: Basic Books.

Jospe, Alfred (1966), "Intermarriage and conversion: issues confronting the Hillel Director," Campus 1966: Change and Challenge; National Conference of Hillel Directors 1965. Washington, D.C.: B'nai B'rith Hillel Foundations. Pages 28–46.

Kahn, Lehman (1877), Série de Six Lettres sur le Mariage Mixte. Brussels.

Kallen, Horace M. (1924), *Culture and Democracy in the United States*. New York.

Kaplan, Mordecai M. (1934), *Judaism as a Civilization; Toward a Reconstruction of American-Jewish Life*. New York: Macmillan.

———, et. al., eds. (1942), *The New Haggadah for the Pesach Seder*. Revised edition. New York: Behrman's Book House.

——— (1956), *Questions Jews Ask: Reconstructionist Answers*. New York: Reconstructionist Press.

Kardiner, Abram (1939), *The Individual and his Society*. New York: Columbia University Press.

Katz, Jacob (1961), *Tradition and Crisis: Jewish Society at the End of the Middle Ages*. Glencoe: Free Press of Glencoe.

Kaufmann, Myron S. (1957), *Remember Me to God*. Philadelphia: Lippincott.

Kazin, Alfred (1956), "Introduction," *Selected Stories of Sholom Aleichem*. New York: Modern Library.

——— (1966), "The Jew as a modern writer," Commentary, 41, No. 6, 37–41.

Kennedy, Ruby Jo Reeves (1943), "Pre-marital residential propinquity and ethnic endogamy," American Journal of Sociology, 48, 580–584.

——— (1944), "Single or triple melting pot? Intermarriage trends in New Haven, 1870–1940," American Journal of Sociology, 49, 331–339.

——— (1963), "What has social science to say about intermarriage?" in Werner J. Cahnman (ed.), q.v., 19–37.

Kent, Donald P. (1951), "Subjective factors in mate selection," Sociology and Social Research, 35, No. 6, 391–398.

Kertzer, Morris N. (1967), *Today's American Jew*. New York: McGraw-Hill.

Kimble, Gregory (1961), *Hilgard and Marquis' Conditioning*. New York: Appleton-Century-Crofts.

Kinsey, Alfred C. et al. (1948), *Sexual Behavior in the Human Male*. Philadelphia: Saunders.

——— et al. (1953), *Sexual Behavior in the Human Female*. Philadelphia: Saunders.

Kirshenbaum, David (1958), *Mixed Marriage and the Jewish Future*. New York: Bloch.

Klineberg, Otto (1954), *Social Psychology*. Revised edition. New York: Holt.

Koenig, Samuel (1942), "The socioeconomic structure of an American Jewish Community," Chapter 8 in Graeber and Britt (eds.), *q.v.*, 200–242.

———— (1948), "Methods of studying Jewish life in America," Yivo Annual of Jewish Social Science, 2–3.

Konorski, J. (1948), *Conditioned Reflexes and Neuron Organization*. New York: Cambridge University Press.

Kramer, Judith R. and Seymour Leventman (1961), *Children of the Gilded Ghetto; Conflict Resolution of Three Generations of American Jews*. New Haven: Yale University Press.

Kramer, Simon Gad (1946), "Zohar," in Encyclopedia of Jewish Knowledge, *q.v.*

Krasner, L. (1958), "Studies in the conditioning of verbal behavior," Psychological Bulletin, 55, 148–170.

Krech, David, and Richard S. Crutchfield (1948), *Theory and Problems of Social Psychology*. New York: McGraw-Hill.

———— and ———— (1962), *Individual in Society: a Textbook of Social Psychology*. A major revision of Theory and Problems of Social Psychology. New York: McGraw-Hill.

Kronhauser, Eberhard, and Phyllis Kronhauser (1961), "The Psychology of Pornography," in Encyclopedia of Sexual Behavior, *q.v.*

Kubie, Lawrence S. (1956), "Psychoanalysis and marriage: practical and theoretical issues," Chapter 2 in Victor W. Eisenstein (ed.), Neurotic Interaction in Marriage, q.v., 10–43.

Kugelmass, J. Alvin (1952), "Name-changing—and what it gets you," Commentary, 14, No. 2, 145–150.

Kutzik, Alfred J. (1959), *Social Work and Jewish Values; Basic Areas of Consonance and Conflict*. Washington (D.C.): Public Affairs Press.

Landes, Ruth, and Mark Zborowski (1950), "Hypotheses concerning the Eastern European Jewish Family," Psychiatry, 13, 447–464.

Landis, Carney, et al. (1940), *Sex in Development*. New York: Paul B. Hoeber.

Landis, Judson T. (1949), "Marriages of mixed and non-mixed religious faith," American Sociological Review, 14, 401–406.

———— (1960), "Religiousness, family relationships and family values in Protestant, Catholic and Jewish families," Marriage and Family Living, 22, 341–347.

Lebensohn, Zigmond M. (1962), "American psychiatry—retrospect and prospect," Medical Annals of the District of Columbia, 31, 379–392.

Lehrer, Leibush (1958–1959), "Problems of the Jewish ethnic character," Yivo Annual of Jewish Social Science, 12, 36–69.

Lehrman, Samuel D. (1965), "Psychopathology in mixed marriages," Paper presented at the June 1 meeting of the Long Island Psychoanalytic Society. (Manuscript)

—— (1967), "Psychopathology in mixed marriages," Psychoanalytic Quarterly, 36, No. 1, 67–82.

Leichter, Hope Jensen, and William E. Mitchell (1967), *Kinship and Casework*. New York: Russell Sage Foundation.

Lenski, Gerhard (1961), *The Religious Factor; a Sociological Study of Religion's Impact on Politics*, Economics, and Family Life. New York: Doubleday.

Levinger, Lee J. (1952), "The disappearing small-town Jew," Commentary, 14, No. 2, 157–163.

Levinson, Boris M. (1962a) "The MMPI in a Jewish traditional setting," Journal of Genetic Psychology, 101, 25–42.

—— (1962b) "Yeshiva College Subculture scale: an experimental attempt at devising a scale of the internalization of Jewish traditional values," Journal of Genetic Psychology, 101, 375–399.

—— (1962c) "A preliminary study of the Yeshiva College Subcultural Scale," Journal of Clinical Psychology, 18, No. 3, 314–315.

Levinson, Maria H., and Daniel J. Levinson (1958–59) "Jews who intermarry; socio-psychological bases of ethnic identity and change," Yivo Annual of Jewish Social Science, 12, 103–130.

—— (1965) "Rejoinder [to Hurvitz's criticisms]," Yivo Annual of Jewish Social Science, 13, 179–186.

Lewin, Kurt (1939), "When Facing Danger," in author's *Resolving Social Conflicts; Selected Papers on Group Dynamics*. New York: Harper, 1949, 159–168.

—— (1940), "Bringing Up the Jewish Child," in author's Resolving Social Conflicts, *q.v.*, 169–185.

—— (1941), "Self-Hatred Among Jews," in author's Resolving Social Conflicts, *q.v.*, 186–200.

—— (1946), "Action Research and Minority Problems," in author's Resolving Social Conflicts, *q.v.*, 201–216.

Lewisohn, Ludwig (1922), *Up Stream; an American Chronicle*. New York: Boni and Liveright.

—— (1928), *The Island Within*. New York: Harper.

—— (1928), "Reply to Charles Recht's Question . . ." (Debate on Intermarriage), American Hebrew, April 6, Vo. 122, No. 22, 771+.

—— (1936), "Jews in trouble," Atlantic Monthly, 157, January, 53–60.

Lindzey, Gardner (1967), "Some remarks concerning incest, the incest taboo, and psychoanalytic theory," American Psychologist, 22, No. 12, 1051–1059.

—— and S. Rogolsky (1950) "Prejudice and identification of minority group membership," Journal of Abnormal and Social Psychology, 45, 37–53.

Linton, R. (1949) "Problems of status personality." In S.S. Sargent and Marian W. Smith (eds.), *Culture and Personality*. New York: The Viking Fund, 163–173.

—— (1951) "The concept of national character." In Alfred H.

Stanton, and Steward E. Perry (eds.), *Personality and Political Crises*. Glencoe: Free Press, 133–150.

List, Kurt (1947) "Jerome Kern and American Operetta," Commentary, 3, No. 5, 433–441.

Litwak, Eugene (1960) "Occupational mobility and extended family cohesion," American Sociological Review, 25, February, 9–21.

Locke, Harvey, George Sabagh, and Mary M. Thomes (1957) "Interfaith marriages," Social Problems, 4, April, 329–333.

Loewenstein, Rudolph M. (1951), *Christians and Jews*. New York: International Universities Press

Lovell, Mildred (1929), "Are we unduly nervous? A study in Jewish behavior." Jewish Tribune, April 5, p. 5. [An interview with A. A. Brill.]

Lowie, Robert H. (1935), *The Crow Indians*. New York: Farrar and Rinehart.

Mack, Rebecca E. (1933), "You are a Jew and a Jew you are." Pamphlet published by the author. Jersey City, N. J.

Maier, Joseph, and William Spinrad (1957), "Comparison of religious beliefs and practices of Jewish, Catholic, and Protestant students," The Phylon Quarterly, 18, No. 4, 355–360.

Maimon, Solomon (1793), Solomon Maimon: An Autobiography (translated from the German, with additions and notes, by J. Clark Murray). London: Alexander Gardner, 1888.

Maimonides, Moses (1190), *The Guide of the Perplexed*. Chicago: University of Chicago Press, 1963.

Malin, Irving (1965) *Jews and Americans*. Carbondale: Southern Illinois University.

Mandelbaum, David G. (1935) "A study of the Jews of Urbana," Jewish Social Service Quarterly, 12, 230–

Marden, Charles F. (1952), *Minorities in American Society*. New York: American Book Company.

Mark, Yudel (1965), "The shtetl." In Jewish Heritage Reader, *q.v.*, 63–70.

Maslow, Abraham (1951), "Resistance to acculturation," Journal of Social Issues, 7, No. 4, 26–29.

—— (1954), *Motivation and Personality*. New York: Harper.

Mayer, John E. (1961a) Jewish-Gentile Courtship, an Exploratory Study of a Social Process. New York: Free Press.

—— (1961b) "Intermarriage patterns: a hypothesis," Sociology and Social Research, 45, No. 2, 188–195.

Mayer, Kurt (1952) *The Population of Switzerland*. New York: Columbia University Press.

McArthur, C. (1956) "Personality of first and second children," Psychiatry, 19, 47–54.

McClelland, David C. (1958) "Risk taking in children with high and low need for achievement," In John W. Atkinson (ed.), *Motives in Fantasy, Action, and Society*. Princeton: Van Nostrand. 306–321.

——, A.L. Baldwin, U. Bronfenbrenner, and F.L. Strodtbeck (1958), *Talent and Society*. Princeton: Van Nostrand.

———— (1961), *The Achieving Society*. Princeton: Van Nostrand.

McGill, Nettie Pauline (1937), "Some characteristics of Jewish youth in New York City," Jewish Social Service Quarterly, 14, 267.

Mead, Margaret (1935), *Sex and Temperament in Three Primitive Societies*. New York: New American Library.

Memmi, Albert (1960), *Strangers*. New York: Orion Press. Originally published in French under the title *Agar*.

———— (1962), *Portrait of a Jew*. New York: Orion Press.

———— (1966), *Liberation of the Jew*. New York: Orion Press.

Merton Robert K. (1941), "Intermarriage and the social structure: fact and theory," Psychiatry, 4, 361–374.

Meyer, Hershel (1941), "Nationalism and Jewish self-hatred," Medical Leaves, 3.

Meyerson, Abraham (1920), "The 'nervousness' of the Jew," Mental Hygiene, January.

Mihaly, Eugene, *et al.* (1963) "Report of the special committee on mixed marriage," Central Conference of American Rabbis, Seventy-third Annual Convention [Yearbook]. New York: Central Conference of American Rabbis.

Miller, Neal E., and Doris Kraeling (1952) "Displacement: greater generalization of approach than avoidance in a generalized approach-avoidance conflict," Journal of Experimental Psychology, 43, 217–221.

Minnis, Mhyra (1953) "Cleavages in women's organizations," American Sociological Review, 18, 47–53.

Monahan, Thomas P., and William M. Kephart (1954) "Divorce and desertion by religious and mixed religious groups," American Journal of Sociology, 59, No. 5, 454–465.

Munroe, Ruth L. (1955), *Schools of Psychoanalytic Thought*. New York: Dryden.

Murdock, George P. (1949) *Social Structure*. New York: Macmillan.

Myers, Jerome K., and Bertram H. Roberts (1958) "Some relationships between religion, ethnic origin and mental illness," in Marshall Sklare (ed.), The Jews . . . , *q.v.*, 551–559.

Nathan, Marvin (1932), *The Attitude of the Jewish Student in Colleges and Universities Toward his Religion*. New York: Bloch.

Newcomb, Theodore M. (1950) *Social Psychology*. New York: Dryden.

————, Ralph H. Turner, and Philip E. Converse (1965) *Social Psychology; the Study of Human Interaction*. New York: Holt, Rinehart, Winston.

Newman, Louis I. (1948), "Religious aspects [of the Kinsey Report]—a Jewish viewpoint," pages 193–200 in Sex Habits of American Men; a Symposium on the Kinsey Report, edited by Albert Deutsch. New York: Grosset & Dunlap.

Nock, Albert Jay (1941a) "The Jewish Problem in America; Part I," Atlantic Monthly, 167, June, 669–706.

———— (1941b) "The Jewish Problem in America; Part II," Atlantic Monthly, 168, July, 68–76.

Nordau, Max (1910) *The Interpretation of History*. New York: Willey Book Co.

Noyes, Arthur P. (1948) *Modern Clinical Psychiatry*. Philadelphia: Saunders.

Olsvanger, Immanuel (1947) *Roeyte Pomerantsen; Jewish Folk Humor* . . . New York: Schocken.

Orlansky, Harold (1946) "Jewish personality traits: a review of studies on an elusive problem," Commentary, 2, No. 10, 377–383.

Osofsky, Gilbert (1966) *Harlem: the Making of a Ghetto*. New York: Harper and Row.

Packard, Vance (1959) *The Status Seekers*. New York: D. McKay Company.

Park, Robert E., and Herbert A. Miller (1921) *Old World Traits Transplanted*. New York: Harper.

Park, Robert E. (1934) "Race relations and certain frontiers." In E.B. Reuter (ed.), *Race and Culture Contacts*. New York: McGraw-Hill, 57–85.

Parsons, Talcott (1953) "Revised analytical approach to the theory of social stratification." In R. Bendix and S. M. Lipset (eds.), *Class, Status and Power*. Glencoe: Free Press, 92–128.

Pearl, Raymond and Celeste Franklin. (1940) "Jewish and Christian Intermarriages in Budapest: a Footnote to Recent Social History," Bulletin of The History of Medicine. March, 8, No. 3, 497–508.

Pettigrew, Thomas F. (1964) *A Profile of the Negro American*. Princeton: Van Nostrand.

Pirke Aboth. See Goldin, Hyman, 1962.

Podhoretz, Norman (1953) "Sholom Aleichem: Jewishness is Jews," Commentary, 16, No. 3, 261–263.

——— (1963) "My Jewish problem—and ours," Commentary, 35, No. 2, 93–101.

——— (1967), *Making It*. New York: Random House.

Polish, David (1960) *The Eternal Dissent; a Search for Meaning in Jewish History*. New York: Abelard-Schuman.

——— (1964) "The problem of intermarriage—will moderation help?" CCAR Journal, 11, No. 4, 33–37.

——— (1965) *The Higher Freedom; a New Turning Point in Jewish History*. Chicago: Quadrangle Books.

Pool, David De Sola (1918) *Intermarriage*. (Pamphlet), Jewish Welfare Board, New York: U. S. Army and Navy.

Porush, Israel (1946), Appendix to Danglow, *q.v.*

Potter, David (1954), *People of Plenty; Economic Abundance and the American Character*. Chicago: University of Chicago Press.

Pound, Ezra and Noel Stock, translators (1962) *Love Poems of Ancient Egypt*. Norfolk, Connecticut: New Directions. Compare with Sharpley, *q.v.*, for evidence of Pound's deletion of incest references.

Price, Frances (1958), "More than converted—convinced." In David M. Eichorn (ed.), *Conversion to Judaism* . . . , q.v., pages 261–263. First published in Women's League Outlook, publication of the National Women's League of the United Synagogue of America, and was reprinted in the Jewish Digest, April 1958.

Proverbs, Ecclesiastes; *The Anchor Bible*. Introduction, translation and notes by R. B. Y. Scott. Garden City: Doubleday, 1965.

Quay, Herbert C. (1958) The Effect of Verbal Reinforcement on the Recall of Early Memories. Dissertation Abstracts, 19, 1118–1119.

Rappaport, Samuel (1919), "Aus dem religiösen leben der Ostjuden . . . Ehe," Der Jude, Vol. 3, 79–88.

Recht, Charles (1928) "Why intermarriage?" American Hebrew, 122, No. 22, 720+.

Reichman, Solomon (1946) "Rashi," Encyclopedia of Jewish Knowledge, *q.v.*

Reik, Theodor (1929) "Zur psychoanalyse des Juedischen Witzes," Imago, 13.

———— (1962) *Jewish Wit*. New York: Gamut Press.

———— (1964) *Pagan Rites in Judaism*. New York: Farrar, Straus and Co.

Resnick, Reuben R. (1933) "Some sociological aspects of intermarriage of Jew and non-Jew," Social Forces, 12, 94–102.

Reuter, Edward B. (1931) *Race Mixture; Studies in Intermarriage and Miscegenation*. New York: McGraw-Hill.

Ribalow, Harold (1957) "From 'Hungry Hearts' to 'Marjorie Morningstar,' the progress of an American minority told in fiction," Saturday Review, Sept. 14., 46–48.

Riesman, David (1942) "The politics of persecution," Public Opinion Quarterly, 6, 41–56.

———— (1951) "[Contribution to] Seven professors look at the Jewish student; a symposium," Commentary, 12, No. 6, 524–525.

———— (1953) *The Lonely Crowd*. New York: Doubleday.

———— (1954) *Individualism Reconsidered, and Other Essays*. Free Press: New York. "A philosophy for 'minority' living," pages 55–69, first published 1948. "Some observations concerning marginality," pages 153–165, first published 1951.

Roberts, Robert (1938) "Negro-White Marriages in Chicago," Master's degree study from materials gathered in 1938 for Cayton-Warner research program. See Drake and Cayton, page 137 fn.

Robison, Sophia (1958) "A study of delinquency among Jewish children in New York City." In Marshall Sklare (ed.), The Jews. . . . , *q.v.*, 535–541.

Roe, Ann (1956) *The Psychology of Occupations*. New York: Wiley.

Rokeach, Milton (1960) *Open and Closed Mind*. New York: Basic Books.

———— (1965) "Paradoxes of religious belief," Trans-action, 2, No. 2, 9–12.

Rose, Arnold and Caroline B. Rose (1965) *Minority Problems; a textbook of readings in Intergroup Relations*. New York: Harper and Row.

Rose, Peter I. (1961) "Small-Town Jews and Their Neighbors in the

United States." Jewish Journal of Sociology, (England), 3, December, 174–191. Reprinted in Rose and Rose, pp. 265–273.

Rosen, Bernard C. (1951) *Religious Beliefs and Practices of Jewish Adolescents: a Study in Reference Group Behavior.* New York: Anti-Defamation League.

Rosenbaum, Gerald (1953) "Stimulus generalization as a function of level of experimentally induced anxiety," Journal of Experimental Psychology, 45, 34–43.

Rosenberg, Bernard, and Gilbert Shapiro (1958) "Marginality and Jewish humor." Midstream, 4, No. 2, 70–80.

Rosenberg, Louis (1939) *Canada's Jews.* Montreal: Canadian Jewish Congress.

———— (1963) "Intermarriage in Canada 1921-1960." In Werner J. Cahnman (ed.), Intermarriage . . . , *q.v.,* 57-81.

Rosenberg, Stuart E. (1954) *The Jewish Community in Rochester,* 1843–1925. New York: Columbia University Press.

Rosenthal, Chanele (1965), "Yiddish is my second love." In David M. Eichorn (ed.), Conversion to Judaism . . . , *q.v.,* pages 265–268.

Rosenthal, Erich (1960) "Acculturation without assimilation? The Jewish community of Chicago, Illinois," American Journal of Sociology, 66, No. 3, 275–288.

———— (1963) "Studies of Jewish intermarriage in the United States," American Jewish Year Book, 64, 3–53.

Rossman, Evelyn, pseudonym (1954) "The community and I," Commentary, 18, No. 5, 393–405.

Rosten, Philip M. (1960) "The mischling; child of the Jewish-Gentile marriage." Honors paper submitted to the Department of Social Relations, Harvard University.

Roth, Philip (1962) Letting Go. New York: Random House.

Rothman, Nathan (1957), "The mark of hypocrisy," Saturday Review, 40, No. 37, Sept. 14, pages 8 and 48.

Rubenstein, Richard L. (1963) "Intermarriage and conversion on the American college campus." In Werner J. Cahnman (ed.), Intermarriage . . . , *q.v.,* 122–142.

Runes, Dagobert D. (1952) *Of God, the Devil and the Jews.* New York: Philosophical Library.

———— (1966) *Concise Dictionary of Judaism.* New York: Philosophical Library.

Ruppin, Arthur (1940) *The Jewish Fate and Future.* New York: Macmillan.

Saenger, Gerhart H. (1945) "Social status and political behavior," American Journal of Sociology, 51, 103–113.

Samuel, Maurice, translator (1942) *Haggadah of Passover.* New York: Hebrew Publishing Co.

Sanua, Victor D. (1959) "Differences in personality adjustment among different generations of American Jews and non-Jews." In Marvin K. Opler (ed.), *Culture and Mental Health.* New York: Macmillan, 443–466.

Sargent, S. Stansfeld, and Robert C. Williamson (1958) *Social Psychology*. Second Edition. New York: Ronald Press.

Sarnoff, Irving (1951) "Identification with the aggressor: some personality correlates of antisemitism among Jews," Journal of Personality, 20, 199–218.

Sartre, Jean-Paul (1946) *Anti-Semite and Jew*. New York: Grove Press, 1962.

Schachter, S. (1959) *Psychology of Affiliation*. Stanford: Stanford University Press.

Schrecker, Paul (1949) "The family: conveyance of tradition." In Ruth N. Anshen (ed.), *The Family; its Function and Destiny*. New York: Harper, pp. 406–425.

Schwartz, Charlotte T. (1965) "Not all intermarriages are mixed; case history of a serious convert," National Jewish Monthly, 80, No. 1, 26+.

Scott, R. B. Y. *See* Proverbs.

Sears, Robert R., Eleanor E. Maccoby, and Harry Levin (1957) *Patterns of Child Rearing*. Evanston: Row, Peterson.

Seidler, Murray, and Mel Jerome Ravitz (1955) "A Jewish peer group," American Journal of Sociology, 61, No. 1, 11–15.

Service, Elman R. (1962) *Primitive Social Organization; an Evolutionary Perspective*. New York: Random House.

Seward, Georgene (1956) *Psychotherapy and Culture Conflict*. New York: Ronald Press.

——— (1958) *Clinical Studies in Culture Conflict*. New York: Ronald Press.

Shanks, Hershel (1953) "Jewish-Gentile intermarriage: facts and trends," Commentary, 16, No. 4, 370–375.

Sharaf, Myron R. (1959) *An approach to the theory and measurement of intraception*. Unpublished Ph.D. thesis. Harvard University.

Sharpley, C. Elissa (1923) *Anthology of Ancient Egyptian Poems*. London: John Murray.

Sherif, Muzafer (1936) *The Psychology of Social Norms*. New York: Harper.

Sherman, C. Bezalel (1961) *The Jew Within American Society; a Study in Ethnic Individuality*. Detroit: Wayne State University Press.

——— (1963) "The unaffiliated Jew." In Belden Menkus (ed.), *Meet the American Jew*. Nashville: Broadhurst Press, 84–95.

Shosteck, Robert (1953) Small-town Jewry Tell Their Story; a Survey of B'nai B'rith Membership in Small Communities in the United States and Canada. Washington, D.C.: B'nai B'rith Vocational Service Bureau.

Shulman, Charles E. (1964), "Mixed Marriage, Conversion and Reality," CCAR Journal, 11, No. 4, 27–32.

Simon, Ernst (1957) "Sigmund Freud, the Jew," Leo Baeck Institute Yearbook, 2, 207–305.

Simpson, George Eaton, and J. Milton Yinger (1965) *Racial and Cultural Minorities*. Third edition. New York: Harper and Row.

Singer, Isaac Bashevis (1964), *Short Friday*. New York: Farrar, Straus and Giroux.

Singer, Jerome (1958), "Heritage of the Ghetto in the second generation," pages 479–508, in Clinical Studies in Culture Conflict, Georgene Seward, editor. New York: Ronald Press.

Sklare, Marshall (1955) *Conservative Judaism*. Glencoe: Free Press.

———, and Marc Vosk (1957), The Riverton Study: How Jews Look at Themselves and their Neighbors. Pamphlet. New York: American Jewish Committee.

———, editor (1958), *The Jews; Social Patterns of an American Group*. Glencoe: Free Press.

——— (1964) "Intermarriage and the Jewish future," Commentary, 37. No. 4, 46–52.

———, and Joseph Greenblum (1967), *Jewish Identity on the Suburban Frontier; a Study of Group Survival in the Open Society*. (Volume I of the Lakeville Studies) New York: Basic Books.

Slotkin, J. S. (1942a) "Adjustment in Jewish-Gentile intermarriage," Social Forces, 21, 226–230.

——— (1942b) "Jewish-Gentile intermarriage in Chicago," American Sociological Review, 7, 34–39.

——— (1942c) "Social factors in amalgamation," Sociology and Social Research, 26, No. 3, 346–351.

Sobel, B. Z., and Norman Mirsky (1966) " 'Ignosticism' in Detroit; an experiment in Jewish religious radicalism," Midstream, 12, No. 5, 35–45.

Sokolsky, George (1933) "My mixed marriage," Atlantic Monthly, 152, 137–146.

——— (1935) *We Jews*. Garden City: Doubleday.

Spiro, Melford (1956), *Kibbutz; Venture in Utopia*. New York: Schocken.

——— (1958), *Children of the Kibbutz*. Cambridge: Harvard University Press.

Srole, Leo (1955), "Impact of anti-Semitism, comment on John P. Dean's 'Patterns of Socialization and association between Jews and non-Jews,' " Jewish Social Studies, 17, No. 3, 275–278.

———, Thomas S. Langner et al. (1962), Mental Health in the Metropolis; The Midtown Manhattan Study. New York: McGraw-Hill.

"State of Jewish Belief, The; a Symposium," Commentary, August, 1966, 42, No. 2, 71–160.

Steinberg, Milton (1933) "How the Jew does it," Atlantic Monthly, 152, July, 26–38.

——— (1947), *Basic Judaism*. New York: Harcourt, Brace.

Stember, Charles, and others (1966) Jews in the Mind of America. New York: Basic Books.

Stonequist, Everett V. (1937) *The Marginal Man; a Study in Personality and Culture Conflict*. New York: Scribners.

——— (1942) "The marginal character of the Jews." In Graeber and Britt (eds.), *q.v.*, Jews in a Gentile World, 269–310.

Strauss, Anslem (1954) "Strain and harmony in American-Japanese war-bride marriages," Marriage and Family Living, 16, No. 2, 99–106.

Strodtbeck, Fred L. (1958) "Family interaction, values, and achievement." In Marshall Sklare (ed.), The Jews . . . , q.v., 147–168.

Sullivan, Harry Stack (1953), The Interpersonal Theory of Psychiatry. New York: Norton.

Sumner, William Graham (1906) Folkways. Boston: Ginn and Company.

Sussman, Marvin B. (1953) "The help pattern in the middle class family," American Sociological Review, 18, 22–28.

Sward, Keith, and Meyer Friedman (1935) "Jewish temperament," Journal of Applied Psychology, 19, 70–84.

Tarde, Gabriel (1895) Laws of Imitation. New York: Holt, 1903.

Tashman, Harry F. (1959) The Marriage Bed; an Analyst's Casebook. New York: University Publishers.

Tcherikower, Elias (1943) ["How the American Jews received the Russian Jewish immigrants"], in the author's Geshikhte fun der Yidisher Arbeterbevegung in di Faraynikte Shtatn. (History of the Jewish Labor Movement in the United States.) Vol. 1. New York: Cited by Sherman (1961), q.v.

Teitelbaum, Samuel (1953), Patterns of Adjustment Among Jewish Students. Northwestern University Ph.D. dissertation.

Tennenbaum, Ruth (1939) "Jewish parents in a child guidance clinic; a study of culture and personality," Smith College Studies in Social Work, 10, No. 1, 50–76.

Terman, Louis M., and Melita H. Oden (1947), The Gifted Child Grows Up. Stanford, Calif.: Stanford U. Press.

Thomas, John L. (1951), "The factor of religion in the selection of marriage mates," American Sociological Review, 16, No. 4, 487–491.

—— (1956), The American Catholic Family. New York: Prentice-Hall.

Thomas, W. I. (1928), The Unadjusted Girl. Boston: Little, Brown.

—— (Bintel Brief study.) See Bressler.

Trachtenberg, Joseph (1955), "Religious background of anti-Semitism; comment on John P. Dean's 'Patterns of socialization and association between Jews and non-Jews,'" Jewish Social Studies, 17, No. 3, 279–281.

Trainin, Isaac N. (1963), "Remarks on intermarriage in metropolitan areas," pages 168–172 in Intermarriage and Jewish Life; a Symposium, Werner J. Cahnman, editor. New York: Herzl Press and the Jewish Reconstructionist Press.

Tumin, Melvin (1957), "Some unapplauded consequences of social mobility in a mass society," Social Forces, 36, No. 1, 32–37.

—— (1961) An Inventory and Appraisal of Research on American Anti-Semitism. New York: Freedom Books.

Universal Jewish Encyclopedia. (1962) New York. "Kest."

Veroff, Joseph, Sheila Feld, and Gerald Gurin (1960), "The use of thematic apperception to assess motivation in a nationwide interview study." *Psychological Monographs*.

Verplanck, W. S. (1955), "The control of the content of conversation: reinforcement of statements of opinion," *Journal of Abnormal and Social Psychology*, 51, 668–676.

Vorhaus, Martin G. (1959), *Adam's Rib; an Analysis of Normal Bisexuality in Each of Us*. New York: Horizon Press.

Walser, Richard (1961) *Thomas Wolfe, an Introduction and Interpretation*. New York: Barnes and Noble.

Warner, W. Lloyd, and Leo Srole (1945), *The Social Systems of American Ethnic Groups*. New Haven: Yale University Press.

Weidman, Jerome (1958) *The Enemy Camp*. New York: Random House.

Weisberger, Ralph M. (1963), "Intermarriage in the small community," pages 143–157 in *Intermarriage and Jewish Life; a Symposium*, Werner J. Cahnman, editor. New York: Herzl Press and The Jewish Reconstructionist Press.

Wessel, Bessie Bloom (1948), "Ethnic family patterns: the American Jewish family," *American Journal of Sociology*, 53, No. 6, 439–442.

Wexberg, Erwin (1929), *Individual Psychology*. New York: Cosmopolitan Book Corp.

Weyl, Nathaniel (1966), *The Creative Elite in America*. Washington, D.C.: Public Affairs Press.

Wheelis, Allen (1958), *The Quest for Identity*. New York: Norton.

Whyte, William Foote (1943a), "A slum sex code," *American Journal of Sociology*, 49, No. 1, 24–31.

———— (1943b), *Streetcorner Society: the Social Structure of an Italian Slum*. Chicago: University of Chicago Press.

Wiener, Norbert (1953) *Ex-Prodigy; My Childhood and Youth*. New York: Simon and Schuster.

Williams, Robin M., Jr. (1964) *Stranger Next Door; Ethnic Relations in American Communities*. Englewood Cliffs, N. J.: Prentice-Hall.

Wilson, S. J. (1964), *Hurray for Me; a Nostalgic Novel of Childhood*. New York: Crown Publishers.

Winch, Robert F. (1943), "The relationship between courtship behavior and attitudes toward parents among college men," *American Sociological Review*, 8, April, 164–174.

———— (1952), *The Modern Family*. New York: Holt.

————, Scott Greer, and Rae Lesser Blumberg (1967), Ethnicity and extended familism in an upper-middle-class suburb, American Sociological Review, 32, No. 2, 265–272.

Wirth, Louis (1926), "Some Jewish types of personality," *Publications of the American Sociological Society*, No. 20.

————, and H. Goldhamer (1944), "Passing." In O. Klineberg (ed.), *Characteristics of the American Negro*. New York: Harper, 301–319.

Wise, Stephen S. (1944), *As I See It*. New York: Jewish Opinion Publishing Corp.

Wolfe, Thomas (1937), *The Web and the Rock*. New York: Harper.

Wolfenstein, Martha (1958), "Two types of Jewish mothers." In Marshall Sklare (ed.), The Jews . . . , q.v., 520–534.

Wortis, Joseph (1954), *Fragments of an Analysis with Freud*. New York: Simon and Schuster.

Wouk, Herman (1959), *This Is My God*. Garden City: Doubleday.

Young, Kimball (1956), *Social Psychology*. Third edition. New York: Appleton-Century-Crofts.

Zangwill, Israel (1909), *The Melting Pot*. New York: Macmillan.

Zborowski, Mark, and Elizabeth Herzog (1952), *Life Is With People*. New York: International Universities Press.

Zorbaugh, Harvey W. (1929), *The Gold Coast and the Slum*. Chicago: University of Chicago Press.

Zunser, Miriam Shomer (1939), *Yesterday*. New York: Stackpole Sons.

Glossary

Since Yiddish is based on middle high German, in this vocabulary list a word is presumed to be derived from German unless otherwise noted. Where the original pronunciation or meaning varies considerably from Yiddish usage, this too is noted. The reader will note that words referring to ordinary mundane objects and affairs (e.g., *aydem af kest, gefillte fish, knishe, kreplach, proste yidn, shtetl*) are likely to be of German or Slavic origin—while words referring to the religious tradition, ceremony, or ethics (e.g., *emes, kovod, nachas, nogid, toiveh, yichas, yoysher*) are of Hebrew origin. Yiddish ordinarily is written in Hebrew characters; as transliterated below, *ch* is pronounced as in the German *ach*. Otherwise the reader is asked to follow English rather than German pronunciation norms (e.g., *s* as in *soup, z* as in *zoo*).

In assembling this Glossary, the author has been aided by the following works (listed in the Bibliography): I. Bernstein, whose Glossary is particularly rich and scholarly, Heller, Zborowski and Herzog, Olsvanger, Runes, Harkavy, and the Encyclopedia of Jewish Knowledge.

AGADA (Heb. To narrate)—That portion of the rabbinic literature which is non-legal (non-Halachic) in spirit; includes biblical interpretations, sayings, fables, parables, allegories, philosophy, popular science, history, legend, and mysticism.
AYDEM—Son-in-law.

AYDEM AF KEST—Young man living with his wife in the home of her parents, who are maintaining the young couple (and their offspring) for an agreed-upon period of time.

BAALSHEM (Heb. Master of the Name)—Hasidic rabbi to whom is attributed the power to work miracles in the name of God.

BAAL TSCHUVA (Heb.)—Penitent; usually refers to a person who is doing penance for a sexual transgression.

BAAL YICHAS (Heb. Master of pedigree)—One who is known to have forebears of wealth or learning.

BALABOSTEH (Heb. *baal ha'bayit,* Master of the household; final syllable, *-teh,* is a Slavic feminine ending)—Lady of the house.

BAR MITZVAH (Heb. Son of the Commandment)—Ceremony of induction into the community of adult males, observed at a boy's thirteenth birthday, which marks the age of religious duty and responsibility.

BAS MITZVAH (Heb. Daughter of the Commandment)—Ceremony of recent origin, patterned after the *bar mitzvah* and adopted by Conservative and Reform congregations, to honor a girl's attainment in religious education.

BEN TOYRAH (Heb. Son of Torah)—A scholar, a man of learning.

BERIEH (Heb. *biryah,* productivity)—A proficient housewife.

BES-MEDRESH (Heb. *bet ha'midrash,* House of learning)—Place for religious services and study; synagogue.

BINTEL-BRIEF—"A packet of letters," name of an advice column in the *Jewish Daily Forward.*

CHALLA (Heb.)—Sabbath loaf.

CHAVER (Heb., pl. *Chaverim*)—Comrade.

CHEDER (Heb. A room)—Elementary school for Hebrew language and religious instruction.

CHEYDER—see *Cheder.*

CHOSSEN (Heb.)—Bridegroom.

CHOSSEN-BOCHAR (Heb. Bridegroom-boy)—An adolescent boy, or young man, of marriageable age; an "eligible bachelor" by *shtetl* standards.

CHUTSPA (Heb.)—Audacity, shamelessness, impudence, boldness, cheek, insolence.

DAVEN—To recite a prayer or religious service.

DROSHEH (Heb.)—Discourse, sermon, or interpretation of a talmudic problem.

EBIGE KEST—Permanent maintenance of a couple and their children, by parents of the wife, as stipulated in the marriage contract.

EMES? (Heb. *Truth*)—Honestly? Is that the truth?

FARZESSENEH—A woman who has sat out too long—hence, an old maid, a spinster.

GALUT (Heb. Exile)—Diaspora; also, the hardships of life endured by Jews as a minority group in Exile.

GEFILLTE FISH—Fish slices from which most of the meat has been removed, chopped, seasoned, and refilled, to be simmered in a rich broth (also fish balls so prepared)—a Sabbath delicacy.

GER (Heb.) —Proselyte to Judaism.

GER TSEDEK—A righteous proselyte.

GEVALT!—Help!

GOY (Heb. One who belongs to another nation) —A Gentile, a non-Jew.

HADAR MITZVAH (Heb. Adornment of the Commandment) —Talmudic principle that the more beautifully a *mitzvah* is carried out, the more worthy it is.

HAGGADAH (Heb. The narrative) —A booklet containing the text recited at the festival meal (*Seder*) of Passover—stories, psalms, and prayers celebrating deliverance from bondage in Egypt.

HALACHA (Heb. Law) —Portions of the *Talmud* which deal with regulations and legal decisions, as distinguished from *Agada*.

HANUKKAH (Heb. Dedication) —Festival commemorating the rededication of the Temple by the Maccabees who in 167 B.C. were victorious over the Syrian Greeks.

HASID (Heb.) —Member of a sect of Jewish mystics that originated in 18th Century Poland.

HESED (Heb.) —Loving kindness.

ILUY (Heb. Superior) —A genius, an intellectually gifted person.

KALLEH (Heb.) —Bride.

KALLEH-MOYD—A girl of marriageable age.

KAVANAH (Heb. Devotion) —A mystical joy, an ecstatic spirit, of worship, as distinguished from a sense of duty (*mitzvah*) toward religious practice.

KASHRUT (Heb. That which is fit, proper) —Religious dietary laws.

KEST (German *Kost*—Board) —Responsibility for providing board and maintenance to a young couple and their children, assumed by the parents of the bride for an agreed-upon period of time.

KIBBUTZ (Heb. A gathering) —Communal agricultural settlement. (Modern Hebrew)

KIDDUSH (Heb. Sanctification) —Benediction for sanctification of the Sabbath or Holiday.

KNISHE (Little Russian) —Fried or baked turnover, filled with chopped meat, potatoes, or groats.

KOVOD (Heb.) —Honor, respect, deference.

KREPLACH (German *Krapfen*) —Small pockets of dough filled with chopped meat (similar to ravioli), boiled and usually served as dumplings with chicken soup.

KVETCH—A chronic complainer.

LAMDN (Heb.) —A Talmudic scholar, an erudite man.

MACHOTON (Heb.)—Kinsman through marriage. (plural *Machotonim*)

MACHOTONOSHAFT—"Kinsmanship," matters relating to *machotonim*.

MENSCH—A person, a real person, a worthy human being.

MIDRASH (Heb. Exposition) —Homiletical and poetic portions of the *Talmud* and later rabbinic literature, serving to explain and popularize the Scriptures.

MINYAN (Heb. Quorum)—A quorum of ten men, required for public worship.

MISCHLING—A person of mixed parentage. (Note: this is a German term; it is not Yiddish. In the Jewish tradition, a person is either a Jew or a Gentile—whatever his parentage may be.)

MISHPOCHO (Heb.)—Family, relatives, kinsmen.

MIKVAH (Heb.)—Ritual bath.

MISHUGGE (Heb.)—Insane, mad, frantic, irrational, cranky.

MITZVAH (Heb. Command)—A religious or moral obligation, the fulfillment of such an obligation, or the satisfaction that comes therefrom.

NACHAS (Heb.)—Spiritual joy, pleasure, or satisfaction.

NOGID (Heb.)—A man whose use of wealth has made him an important member of the community.

PESACH (Heb.)—Passover, celebration of the Exodus. See *Haggadah*.

PIDYON HA'BEN (Heb. Redemption of the son)—Ceremony honoring a first-born son.

PIRKE ABOTH (Heb. Chapters of the Fathers)—Tractate of the *Talmud* dealing with religious, moral, and ethical principles—popularly designated as *Ethics of the Fathers*.

PROSTEH YIDN—People of low status, ordinary folks without claim to refinement or education.

RESPONSA (Latin—*Responsa prudentorium*—The answers of those more knowing)—Branch of rabbinic literature comprising an interchange of rabbinic opinion on matters of Jewish law and ritual. (Yiddish—*Shales u'teshuves*.)

SABRA (Heb. Cactus)—A native-born Israeli. (Modern Hebrew)

SEDER (Heb. Order)—The Passover service.

SHADCHAN (Heb.)—Matchmaker, marriage broker.

SHEKINAH (Heb. Radiance)—The felt presence of God.

SHIDDACH (Heb.)—Match, marriage.

SHIKSA (Heb. *Shekets*—An abominable thing)—A Gentile girl. (Note: *Shiksa* does not carry the pejorative tone indicated by its etymology.)

SHIVA (Heb. Seven)—Seven days of intensive mourning after the death of a member of the nuclear family (parent, spouse, sibling, or child).

SHLEMIEL—A person for whom nothing ever turns out right.

SHTETL—A small-town Jewish community of Eastern Europe.

SHUL—Synagogue.

TALMUD (Heb. Study)—A compilation of Biblical interpretations completed around 500 A.D., including laws, rules, and regulations—as well as philosophical, allegorical, and poetic writings.

TOCHOS LECKER (Backside licker)—A lick-spittle, bootlicker, toady, an abjectly ingratiating or patronizing person.

TOIVEH (Heb. *Tovah*)—A favor, a good deed.

TORAH (Heb. Instruction)—From its most restrictive to its most general meaning: (1) Mosaic law, (2) the five books of Moses (the Pentatuch), (3) the entire Hebrew Bible, (4) both the Bible, the

Talmud, and the entire body of Jewish law, doctrine, ethics, and philosophy, (5) Instruction, knowledge, and the pursuit of knowledge. Writes Rabbi Abraham Mayer Heller, "No single definition adequately conveys the meaning of Torah." (page 197)

TSEDAKAH (Heb.) —Charity; the *mitzvah* to help the poor and needy.

VOS MACHSTU?—How are you? (familiar form)

YASHAR! (Heb. Justice, righteousness) —Let's be fair! Let's be honest! (Modern Hebrew)

YESHIVA (Heb. Academy) —School of higher Jewish learning where Talmud was the major and frequently the exclusive subject of study. (In U.S. the term has been extended to elementary parochial schools that teach secular as well as Jewish knowledge.)

YETSER HA'RA (Heb. The evil impulse) —Violent passion, temptation, the sexual impulse.

YETSER HA'TOV (Heb. The good impulse) —Altruistic motives, the impulse to do good.

YICHAS (Heb. Pedigree) —Lineage, reputation, prestige.

YICHAS ATSMO (Heb.) —Earned status, recognition as a self-made man.

YICHAS OVOS (Heb. *Yichas aboth*) —Inherited status, social prestige based on a distinguished lineage, recognition as a member of a good family.

YIDDESHE MAMMEH—A woman who embodies the virtues of Jewish motherhood.

YOYSHER!—See *Yashar!*

ZOHAR (Heb. Illumination) —A mystical commentary on the five books of Moses, probably written about 1290 A.D., fostered opposition to formal ceremonial laws of the rabbis, and promoted prayer and devotion as a way of transcending earthly existence and seeking union with God.

Index